ORGANIZING KNOWLEDGE
Second edition

Organizing Knowledge

An Introduction to Information Retrieval

Second Edition

Jennifer Rowley

Published by
Ashgate
Ashgate Publishing Limited
Gower House
Croft Road
Aldershot
Hants GU11 3HR
England

Ashgate Publishing Company
Old Post Road
Brookfield
Vermont 05036
USA

British Library Cataloguing-in-Publication Data.
A catalogue record for this book is available from the British Library.

Library of Congress Cataloguing-in-Publication Data
Rowley, J. E.
   Organizing knowledge: an introduction to information retrieval/Jennifer Rowley. — 2nd ed.
      p.   cm.
   Includes index.
   ISBN 1–85742–004–7 (hbk): — ISBN 1–85742–005–5 (pbk)
   1. Machine-readable bibliographic data.   2. Cataloging—Data processing.   3. Information retrieval.   4. Knowledge, Theory of.
5. Classification.   6. Indexing.   I. Title.
Z699.35.M28R68   1992
025.5′24—dc20   92–5186
                        CIP

ISBN 1 85742 004 7
ISBN 1 85742 005 5 (pbk)

Typeset in 10pt Times by Poole Typesetting (Wessex) Ltd, Bournemouth and printed in Great Britain by Billing & Sons Ltd, Worcester.

Contents

List of figures

Acknowledgements

It would be impossible to list all of those to whom I owe a debt of some kind in the creation of this book. The ideas gathered here have been drawn from many other writers in this field, and my first debt is to all of those who have contributed to the 'organization of knowledge'. I am grateful to all of the publishers, database producers, systems suppliers and authors who have permitted me to use extracts from their works. These are individually acknowledged as they appear. The structure of this edition still owes much to the inspiration of Christopher Needham's *Organising Knowledge in Libraries*, although it has evolved significantly from the earlier plan.

Seven years ago when I finished the manuscript of the first edition of this work, I could not envisage producing a second edition. Motivation has nevertheless come from several sources. Above all else I have been inspired and humbled by the number of people who have read and learnt from the first edition. Despite its marked United Kingdom perspective (as my American reviewers were correct to point out), I have met readers from Eastern Europe, Australia, South America and Africa who have appreciated the broad overview of this text. I hope that they find this edition at least as useful as the first.

I have tried to take account of reviewers' comments on the first edition, and am particularly indebted to the following three people who reviewed the first edition and offered advice on the second: Peter Willett, Department of Information Studies, University of Sheffield; Cheryl Schauder, Department of Information Services, Royal Melbourne Institute of Technology, and Sara Shatford Layne, Cataloging Division, University of California, Los Angeles. I have tried to take account of all of their comments, but have had to accept that there are limitations as to what can be included between the covers of one book.

I should also like to acknowledge the value of colleagues in the Department of Library and Information Studies at Manchester Polytechnic who share my enthusiasm for information retrieval: Shelagh Fisher, Frances Slack and John Farrow.

Once again I am grateful to my family, Peter, Shula and Zeta, who have had to tolerate my portable microcomputer on the dining room table and my absorption in it for too long.

Crewe and Alsager College
January 1992

List of abbreviations

Note: This is a list of the more common abbreviations used in this text. On occasions it has proved difficult to discriminate between acronyms and abbreviations but, in general, acronyms are not included. For information on acronyms the reader should consult the index. Key databases, hosts, software packages and cooperatives are included, but the coverage in these areas is not comprehensive, since to produce such a complete list would take more space than it merits.

AA Code	Anglo-American cataloguing code 1908
AACR	Anglo-American Cataloguing Rules
AACR1	Anglo-American Cataloguing Rules, first edition
AACR2	Anglo-American Cataloguing Rules, second edition
AACR2R	Anglo-American Cataloguing Rules, second edition (Revised)
ADP	Automatic Data Processing Inc.
AGRIS	Agricultural Information System
ALA	American Library Association
BC	Bibliographic Classification Scheme (Bliss)
BC2	Bibliographic Classification Scheme, second edition
BCA	Bliss Classification Association
BCM	British Catalogue of Music
BCOP	Birmingham Libraries Cooperative
BEDIS	Book Trade Electronic Data Interchange Standards Committee
BIOSIS	Biosciences Information
BL	British Library
BLAISE	British Library Automated Information Service
BLBSD	British Library Bibliographic Services Division
BLCMP	formerly Birmingham Libraries Cooperative Mechanization Project
BLDSC	British Library Document Supply Centre
BM	British Museum
BNB	British National Bibliography
BOSS	BLCMP Online Support Service

BSI	British Standards Institution
BSO	Broad System of Ordering
BT	Broader term
BTI	British Technology Index
BUCOP	British Union Catalogue of Periodicals
CAFS	Content Addressable Filestore
CAG	Cooperative Automation Group
CARL	Colorado Alliance of Research Libraries
CAS	Chemical Abstracts Services
CATSS	Cataloguing Support Service (UTLAS)
CBI	Cumulative Book Index
CC	Colon Classification Scheme
CCF	Common Communications Format
CCL	Common Command Language
CD-I	Compact Disc Interactive
CD-ROM	Compact Disc Read Only Memory
CIHM	Canadian Institute for Historical Microreproduction
CIP	Cataloguing-in-Publication
CIS	Cataloguing-in-Source
CODER	Composite Document Expert Retriever
COM	Computer Output Microform
COMARC	Cooperative Machine Readable Cataloguing
COMPASS	Computer Aided Subject System
COMPENDEX	Computerized Engineering Index
CONSER	Conversion of Serials
COPOL	Council of Polytechnic Libraries
CRC	Coordinating Revision Committees (UDC)
CRG	Classification Research Group
CTI	Current Technology Index
CURL	Consortium of University Research Libraries (UK)
DALNET	Detroit Area Library Network
DBMS	Database Management System
DC	Dewey Decimal Classification Scheme
DIANE	Direct Information Access Network for Europe
DOC	Dewey Online Catalogue
DVI	Digital Video Interactive
EARN	European Academic Research Network
ECHO	European Commission's Host Organization
ESA-IRS	European Space Agency Information Retrieval Service
ESRO	European Space Research Organization
EURONET	European Network System

FID	Fédération International de Documentation
GMD	General Materials Designation
ICCP	International Conference on Cataloguing Principles
IDF	inverse document frequency
IFLA	International Federation of Library Associations
IIB	Institut International de la Bibliographie
IO	ILLINET Online
INIS	International Nuclear Information System
INSPEC	Information Service – Physics, Electrical, Electronics and Computers and Control
IPs	Information Providers
IPSS	International Packet Switch Stream
IRRD	International Road Research Documentation System
IRS	Information Retrieval Service (of ESA)
ISBD	International Standard Bibliographic Description
ISBD(CM)	ISBD for Cartographic Materials
ISBD(CP)	ISBD for Component Parts
ISBD(G)	ISBD for General framework
ISBD(M)	ISBD for Monographs
ISBD(NBM)	ISBD for Nonbook Materials
ISBD(PM)	ISBD for Printed Music
ISBD(S)	ISBD for Serials
ISBN	International Standard Book Number
ISI	Institute for Scientific Information
ISDN	Integrated Services Data Network
ISDS	International Serials Data Systems
ISO	International Standards Organization
ISSN	International Standard Serial Number
JANET	Joint Academic Network (UK)
JSC	Joint Steering Committee (for the revision of AACR)
KWIC	Keyword in Context
KWOC	Keyword out of Context
LASER	London and South East Region
LC	Library of Congress
LCC	Library of Congress Classification Scheme
LCSH	Library of Congress Subject Headings
LOCAS	Local Catalogue Service
LSP	Linked Systems Project

MARC	Machine Readable Cataloguing
MARC(S)	Machine Readable Cataloguing (Serials)
MEDLARS	Medical Literature Analysis and Retrieval System
MEDLINE	MEDLARS On-Line
MeSH	Medical Subject Headings
MIMD	Multiple-Instruction Stream, Multiple-Data Stream
MSCDEX	MS-DOS CD-ROM Extensions
NACO	Name Authority Cooperative
NCET	National Council for Educational Technology
NEMROC	Newcastle Media Resources Organization Committee
NLM	National Library of Medicine
NPAC	National Program for Acquisitions and Cataloguing
NSDC	National Serials Data Centre
NT	Narrower term
NTIS	National Technical Information Service
NUA	Network User Address
NUC	National Union Catalog
NUI	Network User Identity
OCLC	Online Computer Library Centre
OLIS	Ohio Library and Information System
OPAC	Online Public Access Catalogue
ORACLE	Optional Reception of Announcements by Coded Line Electronics
PDN	Public Data Network
PEs	Processing Elements
PFDS	Pergamon Financial Data Services
PMEST	Personality-Matter-Energy-Space-Time
PRECIS	Preserved Context Indexing System
PSE	Packet Switching Exchange
PSS	Packet Switch Stream
PTT	Post, Telephone and Telegraph Authority
RECON	Retrospective Conversion
RLG	Research Libraries Group
RLIN	Research Libraries Information Network
RT	Related term
SCOLCAP	Scottish Libraries Cooperative Automation Project
SCONUL	Standing Conference of National and University Libraries

SCORPIO	Subject Content Oriented Retriever for Processing Information Online
SDC	Systems Development Corporation
SDI	Selective Dissemination of Information
SHE	Subject Headings for Engineering
SIMD	Single-Instruction Stream, Multiple-Data Stream
SLA	School Library Association
SLIC	Selective Listing in Combination
SNI	Standard Network Interconnection
SOC	Subject Online Catalogue
SOLINET	South Eastern Library Network (US)
STN	Scientific and Technical Information Network
SWALCAP	South West Area Libraries Cooperative Automation Project
TFPL	Task Force Pro Libra
UBC	Universal Bibliographic Control
UBCIM	Universal Bibliographic Control International MARC
UDC	Universal Decimal Classification Scheme
UKCSO	United Kingdom Central Statistical Office
UKLDS	United Kingdom Library Database System
UNESCO	United Nations Educational, Scientific and Cultural Organization
UNIBID	UNISIST International Centre for Bibliographic Description
UNIMARC	Universal MARC format
UNISIST	United Nations Information Systems in Science and Technology
UTLAS	University of Toronto Library Automation System
VDU	Visual Display Unit
VISCOUNT	Viewdata and Interlibrary Systems Communications Network
WIMP	Windows, Icons, Pop-up Menus
WLN	Western Library Network
WORM	Write Once Read Many (Discs)

Periodicals

The following periodicals are prominent in containing contributions relevant to the current debate on the organization of knowledge.

Aslib Proceedings
Byte
Catalogue and Index
Cataloguing and Classification Quarterly
CD-Rom Professional
Database
The Electronic Library
The Indexer
Information Processing and Management
Information Process Manager
Information Scientist
Information Storage and Retrieval
Information Technology and Libraries
Information World Review
International Cataloguing
International Classification
International Forum on Information and Documentation
Journal of Documentation
Journal of Information Science
Journal of the American Society for Information Science
Library Micromation News
Library Resources and Technical Services
Library Science with a Slant to Documentation
Library Technology Reports
Libri
Medical Databases
Microcomputers for Information Management
Netlink
Online
Online Review
Program

Special Libraries
Software review
Vine

Many other periodicals also include contributions on special aspects of the organization of knowledge.

Introduction

The organization of knowledge and information retrieval have a wide internatio-nal perspective. The use of networks for online information retrieval, access to library catalogues and document delivery means that systems developed in one country are increasingly being accessed by users all over the world. Computer-based databases using both magnetic and optical storage media can be created to handle documents in a wide variety of different formats. Alongside these electronic documents, libraries still hold major collections of printed and other materials. International telecommunications networks, which are increasingly offering spe-cialized wide-band data transmission facilities through optical fibre networks and satellites, potentially offer access to both electronic and print documents. A wealth of information is open to the user.

The organization of knowledge is concerned with establishing systems for orga-nizing documents and information so that they can be retrieved by the user as and when required. No longer can information professionals restrict their perspective to systems that operate within one organization or one library, although they may still have responsibility for maintaining such a system. The document or the information that the user requires may be located anywhere in the world. Today there is usually a means whereby the existence of that document or piece of information can be identified, and the document in which the information is contained be delivered to the user. The world is not yet perfect. Economic, political, social and technological factors may militate against the free flow of information, but the information professional needs to be aware of what might be possible as the barriers come down.

The objective of any catalogue, index or database is to facilitate the retrieval of documents. The indexing process creates a description of a document or piece of information; this is achieved either intellectually by a person or automatically by a computer. Successful retrieval depends on the ability of the searcher to specify a query statement which in some sense matches the document description. Thus the processes of indexing and searching – or the organization of knowledge and information retrieval – are inextricably linked. Since all information professionals are concerned either with the creation and implementation of systems for infor-mation retrieval, with the actual retrieval of information or with the teaching of information retrieval to end-users, they must thoroughly appreciate the principles involved.

The structure of this book reflects the author's approach to the subject which is that many information retrieval systems have common elements, and that they differ from one another in how they select possible formats and facilities from the range available. The structure of this book has stood the test of time well. Part I outlines the contents of databases and manual files, indexes and catalogues. It is necessary to establish what data we have in a database before we can start to search it. Part II moves on to consider two types of access points – names and titles. Part III considers subject access, in terms of both classification and alphabetical indexing languages, and indexing systems. Part IV examines the ways in which records and their search keys are incorporated into different kinds of systems. Part V gathers together some other assorted topics. There are other issues that might have been included or more fully analysed; the evaluation of information retrieval systems and records management, for instance, are only discussed briefly. When the reader can spot other omissions, this book will have succeeded in its introductory role; the reader will be ready to move on to more specialized texts.

PART I
RECORDS

1 The tools of information retrieval and the organization of knowledge

Introduction

The organization of knowledge is a process that has been recognized as necessary for thousands of years. As the quantity of knowledge expands, the need to organize it becomes more pressing. In those branches of library and information management which are concerned with knowledge or information and its use for recreation, education or commercial gain, the organization of knowledge is an essential preliminary to the effective exploitation of that information. A vast number of different means of organizing knowledge have been devised and exploited since the earliest of times, although many of the systems in use today have evolved over the past 100 or so years. During the last 20 years the variety of approaches to the organization of knowledge has proliferated with the introduction of computer-based methods.

Any attempt to organize knowledge must, in order to justify the effort involved, have an objective. Some people like order for its own sake, but it is rarely an economic proposition to engage in organizing large collections of knowledge without some more explicit purpose. In general terms, the objective of the organization of knowledge is to permit that information or knowledge to be found again on a later occasion. Thus the organization of knowledge and its later retrieval, sometimes known as information retrieval, are very much part of the same process. Poor organization makes it difficult to find something later, whereas if everything has a place and its location is known, when any item is required it can be picked out immediately. This principle applies as much to objects, such as the tools in a workshop, as to units of knowledge or information.

There is another principle which can be identified from our analogy with the organization of objects. If someone else puts your things away but is unfamiliar with your usual system, then the objects may be organized, but that does not mean that you can find things. Organization in itself has limited value. The organization must be sensible, according to some criterion, and preferably familiar to, or at least expected by, the user. Thus it becomes plainer still that it is not possible to divorce the organization of knowledge from information retrieval. This simple observation also goes some of the way towards explaining the variety of tools, methods and

3

systems which are encountered in the organization of knowledge. Each department of knowledge, with its own set of users, may require a different system, although this diversity must be tempered by the fact that, when interacting with various different collections of knowledge, any one user would obviously find it easier if each set were organized or could be accessed in a manner consistent with what had been encountered in other systems.

Before advancing to a more detailed consideration of specific tools, it will be useful to consider some definitions of the basic concepts which have already been introduced in this section. *The Oxford English Dictionary* proposes the following definitions:

- *to organise* is to (1) furnish with organs, make organic, make into living being or tissue; become organic; (2) form into an organic whole; give orderly structure to, frame and put into working order; make arrangements for.
- *knowledge* is knowing, familiarity gained by experience; person's range of information; a theoretical or practical understanding of; the sum of what is known.
- *to retrieve* is to (1) recover by investigation or effort of memory, restore to knowledge or recall to mind; regain possession of; (2) rescue from bad state, revive, repair, set right.
- *information* is (1) informing, telling; thing told, knowledge, items of knowledge, news.

Notice that the definitions of information and knowledge are both closely intertwined. The definitions of the infinitives to organize and to retrieve are both active, the element which says 'to put into working order' being particularly appropriate.

In this work we are concerned with the organization of knowledge and information retrieval in a specific context. In particular we are concerned with those techniques which are of interest to library and information managers. These will include techniques and tools found and used in libraries, as well as other approaches used in the management of information in organizations. However, one important feature to note about such systems is that some of them do not in fact organize knowledge or retrieve information. Some are actually concerned with the organization and retrieval of documents or references to documents.

What is a document? A document is a record of knowledge or information or a creative expression. A document's creator has recorded ideas, feelings, images, numbers or concepts in order to share them with others. Libraries have conventionally been concerned with books , but 'the collection' in most libraries goes beyond the book. Very few libraries would not also collect conference proceedings, reports, microfilms, serials and maps. Small collections of videos, slides, filmstrips and computer software are held by many libraries, whilst others, often described as resource centres, actually specialize in such media. Organizations also keep extensive collections of documents in the form of records or files which may contain letters, invoices, leaflets, personnel documents and a host of other items. Many people also have their own private collections of documents, both in the form of books and files. All such documents need organization so that their contents can be retrieved when required.

Three fields which have had separate lines of development are moving closer together; all can profitably make use of many of the tools of the organization of knowledge. These fields are:

- catalogues and bibliographies, which are used by librarians to list the documents in a collection or on a specified subject;
- indexing and abstracting services, which are used by information scientists to identify the documents that are required to meet a specific subject request; and
- records management systems, which are the responsibility of records managers and archivists to maintain an orderly collection of records.

These categories are intended to represent stereotypes, and as such describe extremes. Nevertheless, although the three fields share some common goals, they have followed different development paths. To take just the issue of standards. In the cataloguing world standards for the creation of records are widely applied; however, because of insufficient incentive until relatively recently, standards for record creation in both abstracting and indexing services and in the museum, archives and records management world have been widely ignored. Subject searching in both computerized catalogues and computerized abstracting and indexing services would benefit from the same range of facilities. Yet many of the search facilities that have been available for 20 years for the searching of abstracting and indexing databases are still in the process of being translated into computerized catalogues.

This book tries to offer a wide overview. Although professional specialization is inevitable, the new information professional needs wide horizons. The old divisions are being eroded, making it all the more important that a textbook of this nature offers an integrated framework.

Known–item searching and browsing

In any of the environments discussed above, the objective of the organization of knowledge is successful subsequent retrieval. Before embarking on a study of the various approaches to the organization of knowledge, it is important to grasp that different people may wish to retrieve a document or unit of information for different reasons, and therefore may approach the retrieval process in different ways. A fundamental difference in searching strategy is between known–item searching and browsing.

Known–item searching is performed by users when they know what they are

5

looking for and usually possess some characteristic of the information or clue by which they can identify the item (such as author, title, colour or correspondent).

Browsing is performed when the user has a less precise view of the information or documents that may be available and is not sure whether his requirements can be met or precisely how they can be met. Browsing may be general or purposive. Purposive browsing occurs when the user has a fairly specific requirement, whereas general browsing may be used as an opportunity to refine the user's perception of his requirements.

One user might retrieve a document as a result of known–item searching, whereas another user might retrieve that same document as the outcome of general browsing. The information retrieval system must be able to support both types of users in their searches. One of the most significant challenges in the design of information retrieval systems is the need to cater for different users with different requirements. Unfortunately, many of these requirements are difficult to predict when a database or document collection is first being organized or indexed.

Documents and document surrogates

Some systems for the organization of knowledge arrange the documents themselves so that they, or parts of them, can later be retrieved. These systems include:

- the arrangement of books and other materials on shelves in a library;
- the arrangement of files in records management systems; and
- source databases where the textual and other data in a document are held in electronic form, while indexing is based on the content of the document.

If all documents were electronic in nature and supported easy searching, all systems could deal with documents and their contents. Although the numbers of electronic documents are increasing rapidly, print on paper remains widespread; it is likely that the document surrogate will continue to find a place in the organization of documents and information.

Many information retrieval systems are thus based on document or information surrogates. A *surrogate* is a substitute for the document or information, or a representation of it, and is usually very much shorter than the original for which it substitutes.

Document surrogates may take a variety of forms. The traditional catalogue entry or bibliographic citation discussed in Chapter 2 are document surrogates. Alternatively, a surrogate may be no more than a code, such as a page number in a book index or an ISBN (International Standard Book Number). The surrogate is organized and used as the basic component in retrieval; the user retrieves the surrogate, which then leads him on to the document. The surrogate must contain, or be itself, a pointer to the whereabouts of the document or information that is sought.

1.1 Tools for the organization of knowledge

In order to organize knowledge, librarians and information workers have created a variety of tools. Traditionally the tools of information retrieval have been catalogues, bibliographies and printed indexes. Now computer-held databases and their indexes are central to the organization of knowledge. The traditional tools have not yet been made totally redundant by computer–based systems, but they have a much more limited application than previously.

This section introduces some definitions of common terms concerned with the tools for the organization of knowledge. These definitions are the first elements of a language concerning information retrieval which will be used subsequently in this work.

- A *catalogue* is a list of the materials or items in a library (or, traditionally, a list of the books in a library), with the entries representing the items arranged in some systematic order. A catalogue may be held as a card catalogue, microfilm catalogue or as a computer database.
- A *bibliography* is a list of materials or items which is restricted in its coverage by some feature other than the materials being gathered in one library collection. A bibliography may list the materials published in a certain country, on a given subject or in a given form, or its coverage may be restricted by a number of other factors. Bibliographies may be printed or computer databases.
- An *index* is a pointer or indicator or, more fully, a systematic guide to the items contained in, or concepts derived from, a collection or database. Another dictionary definition is that an index is an alphabetical list of references, usually at the end of a book.
- A *computer-held database* is a little more difficult to define both simply and effectively. A database is a collection of similar records, with relationships between the records. According to this definition, catalogues and indexes are databases, and this is indeed the case. A computer-held database is held in machine readable format. A catalogue database is one type of computer-held database. There are also other types of bibliographic databases. A bibliographic database comprises a set of records which refer to documents (such as books, films, periodical articles or reports). Other databases store actual facts and figures and text. Databases may contain references to documents or actual information on various subjects. Access to the contents of databases is via some computer-searching technique, often using a computer workstation.
- A *file* is a collection of letters or documents dealing with one organization, person, area or subject. Files may hold paper documents or be computer-based.

These types of information retrieval tools have a number of common features. To

Figure 1.1   Production of the tools for the organization of knowledge

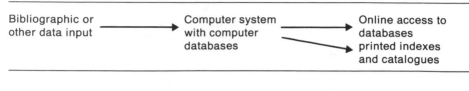

Figure 1.2   A sample catalogue entry

Judge, Arthur William

Car maintenance and repair/by Arthur W Judge.–6th edition.–London:
Chapman and Hall, 1972.–466p.:ill; 19cm.– (Motor Manuals;4).–
ISBN 0412 01050

start with, most catalogues, indexes, files, databases and bibliographies provide access to information or documents. This access is achieved by organizing the tools so that a user may search under a specific access point, heading or index term (for example, subject term, author name, title or date). Similar types of headings or access points are evident in all the above categories of tools. In addition to similar access points, all categories of tools include some description (however abbreviated) of the documents or information which they serve to organize. The remainder of this work, therefore, will be a general discussion of these access points and these descriptions. Many of the former are equally relevant to a variety of the devices used for the organization of knowledge.

The various tools are also intertwined in their production. Although some catalogues, indexes and bibliographies are generated traditionally, most are derived from a computer database. Figure 1.1 summarizes the production of many printed indexes and catalogues. Data in various forms (according to the type of product required subsequently) may be put into a computer database, reorganized by the computer system and used to produce printed products. The same database may also be examined directly by online access.

1.2   Basic characteristics of the tools of information retrieval

1.2.1   Printed catalogues

Any catalogue comprises a number of entries, each entry representing or acting as a surrogate for a document. There may be several entries per document or merely one. Figure 1.2 shows a simple entry or record in a catalogue.

The entry shown in Figure 1.2, like all other catalogue entries, comprises two sections: the heading (which is the author's name in this example) and the description (starting with the title 'Car maintenance...'). Variations in the extent of the description between a set of entries account to a large extent for the distinction between main, added and unit entries. These ideas are explored more fully in Chapter 2.

Headings determine the order of the catalogue sequence. The entries in an author catalogue will have authors' names as headings, and the catalogue will be organized alphabetically according to the authors' names. Similarly a subject catalogue will have headings which represent the subject content of the documents. The entry in Figure 1.2, then, could be filed in an author catalogue. The types of catalogue commonly found in libraries are:

1. *Author catalogues* which contain entries with authors' names as access points. Authors may be persons or corporate bodies; the term author is normally extended to include writers, illustrators, performers, producers, translators or others with some intellectual or artistic responsibility for a work.
2. *Title catalogues* contain entries with titles as access points. Some libraries and information units make title entries for all items being indexed, but in other situations title entries are made selectively.
3. *Author/title catalogues* contain both title and author entries. Since both titles and authors' names are alphabetical, it is easy to interfile authors' names and titles in a single filing sequence.
4. *Subject catalogues* have an indication of the subject of the documents being indexed as their access points. The entries are arranged in an appropriate systematic order. There are two significantly different types of subject catalogue:
   (a) *Alphabetical subject catalogues* have access points which are words or index terms designed to summarize the subject content of the document, such as Cars, Lawyers, etc. In a non-computerized catalogue, these entries are arranged alphabetically according to the subject heading.
   (b) *Classified subject catalogues* have access points which are classification symbols (for example 682.9 or QC275) which have been drawn from a classification scheme (see Chapter 14). In a classification scheme, each subject is allocated a piece of notation, which is used to represent the subject. Where appropriate, the headings will be arranged according to the filing sequence of the notation (for example, alphabetically for letters or numerically for numbers).

The catalogues that have been identified above have one type of access point. To catalogue a complete library collection, however, a number of these single access point catalogues will normally be required.

A classified catalogue is traditionally a catalogue with three or four separate

Figure 1.3   Entries in classified and dictionary catalogues

Classified catalogues	Dictionary catalogues
1. Brown, R.	Brown, R.
How to play chess/R. Brown.	How to play chess/R Brown.
Macmillan, 1983.–66p.	Macmillan, 1983.–66p.
794.1	794.1
2. How to play chess/R Brown.	How to play chess/R Brown.
Macmillan, 1983.–66p.	Macmillan, 1983.–66p.
794.1	794.1
3. 794.1	Chess
How to play chess/R Brown.	How to play chess/R Brown.
Macmillan, 1983.–66p.	Macmillan, 1983.–66p.
794.1	794.1
4. Chess 794.1	

sequences: an author/title catalogue or index (or separate author and title catalogues), a classified subject catalogue, and a subject index to the classified catalogue. Figure 1.3 shows the entries in a classified catalogue for a book which presents relatively few cataloguing problems.

A dictionary catalogue is a catalogue with only one sequence which contains author, title and alphabetical subject entries interfiled. Since all of the headings are alphabetical words, it is possible to interfile entries regardless of the nature of their headings.

Figure 1.3 shows the different entries to be included in the *classified* and the *dictionary* catalogues. The distinction between these two types of catalogues represents two opposing avenues to the subject approach to information: classified and alphabetical headings. Both the classified (or ordered) approach and the alphabetical (or direct) approach to subjects are important in any situation where consideration is being given to the organization of knowledge. For instance, even a dictionary catalogue uses the symbols of a classification scheme to indicate the shelf location of documents. The documents themselves, especially if they are non-fiction, are likely to have been arranged in accordance with a classification scheme. A classified catalogue, on the other hand, must be supported by an alphabetical subject index which serves to translate the user's normal language into the notation of the classification scheme. The dictionary and classified catalogues do not represent attempts to avoid the alternative device, be it classified or alphabetical subject headings, but rather show different emphases.

The purpose of a subject catalogue can be seen to have two elements:

1.   To obtain documents on a specific subject, and
2.   To note documents on related subjects.

Both components are important, but whereas the dictionary catalogue is designed

Figure 1.4   Relative merits of classified and dictionary catalogues

Classified catalogue

1. Provides collocation of related subjects.
2. The subject Index collocates distributed relatives; that is, draws together related subjects which are otherwise scattered by the classified order.
3. Shelf order is reproduced.
4. Subject index-to-shelf enquiries are rapid and can bypass the more complex classified subject catalogue.
5. Convenient for the generation of lists of documents in given subject areas, such as reading lists and simple bibliographies.
6. The notation avoids language problems. Whatever a user's native language, the same notation can be used to represent a subject.
7. It is easy to make use of effective guiding which groups entries into broad subject categories.

Dictionary catalogue

1. The single alphabetical sequence is easy to understand.
2. The sequence, headings and references are independent of a classification scheme and may thus avoid the pitfalls of any specific scheme.
3. Leads direct to a given subject (which has a known name) at one referral.
4. Some collocation of related subjects occurs by accident (if subjects have names which are alphabetically close to one another).
5. There is no organized structure of relationships.
6. References help to indicate relationships and are more explicit statements of such relationships than are found in a classified catalogue.
7. The alphabetical approach is widely used in printed indexes and databases.

to give priority to the first objective, the classified catalogue recognizes the importance of the second. Figure 1.4 tabulates a comparison of the classified and dictionary catalogues.

With computerization the distinction between types of catalogues has become less significant. For very little additional cost it is possible to print (on paper or microfilm) or display on screen as many catalogue sequences as are deemed appropriate for a given application.

1.2.2   Printed indexes

It is perhaps fortunate that the array of terms used to describe indexes is a little more restricted than those used in respect of catalogues.

Two basic types of indexes are common: author indexes and subject indexes. A subject index has alphabetical terms or words as headings; these terms represent concepts or subjects. Entries are arranged in alphabetical order according to the letters in the heading. Where the works of a number of authors are listed in one index, an author index will provide access via authors' names. The index is

Figure 1.5   An extract from a book index

Cabbage	60
Cabbage, red	63
Carrot	64
Cauliflower	65
Caustic lime	17
Celery	68
Celery, self-blanching	68
Celery, non self-blanching	69
Circular greenhouses	29
Cloches	37
Cropping table	14
Cucumber	72

arranged alphabetically according to the authors' names. The 'descriptive part' of the entry in an index will vary considerably depending upon the information or document collection being indexed. Indeed, in order to discuss indexes any further, it is necessary to introduce some of the contexts in which indexes are to be found.

A *book index* is an alphabetically arranged list of words or terms leading the reader to the numbers of pages on which specific topics are considered or on which specific names appear. Many non-fiction books and directories include an index. Many book indexes are predominantly lists of subject terms. Some also include the names of bodies or persons in the same sequence. Occasionally a separate author index might be created, for instance, in an extensive bibliography or reading list. Many of the principles which apply to the construction of alphabetical subject descriptors in catalogues are also relevant to the construction of book indexes. Generally, the terms used in a book index will be more specific than those encountered in an alphabetical subject catalogue. An extract from a book index is shown in Figure 1.5.

A *periodical index* is an index to a specific periodical title (for example, *Proceedings of the London Mathematical Society* or *Library Association Record*). Usually indexes are generated at intervals to cover several issues. For instance, an annual index, covering all issues within one year, is quite common. Annual indexes may later be consolidated into five- or ten-yearly cumulations. Periodical indexes are very similar to book indexes. The major difference is that a periodical index relates to a number of issues and to contributions from a number of different authors. This means that the location of information on a subject needs to be indicated by giving a volume or date of issue, in addition to page numbers. More significantly, an author index may be useful. Periodicals may, then, have either subject, author or even title indexes, or any combination of these three.

Indexing journals (and the indexes to printed abstracting journals) are alphabetical indexes to the literature of a subject area. Usually, many of the entries relate to periodical literature, but monographs, conference proceedings, reports and other literature may also be covered. The key component in an indexing journal is an alphabetical subject index, in which the headings are terms representing the subject concepts covered in the documents listed in the indexing journal. The 'description' is the bibliographical citation which gives details of the document. Many indexing journals also include an author index, which permits the literature of a subject area to be approached via authors' names.

1.2.3 Current awareness services

Current awareness services are not necessarily to be regarded as tools for the organization of knowledge, but since they are important in the dissemination of information and since many of the techniques discussed in other sections of this work are of relevance in their production, some simple definitions are introduced here.

A *current awareness service* is a service designed to alert information users to new information in a specific field which they have previously decided is of interest to them. Current awareness services can be derived from large external databases such as are discussed in Chapter 19, or they may be one product of an in-house information retrieval system of the type considered in Chapter 21.Thus some current awareness services can be purchased from external vendors, whilst others may be offered by a library or information unit to particular groups of users. Current awareness services are not specifically intended to have archival value, although any database from which they are generated can have a valuable archival function.

There are a number of formats in which current awareness services can be encountered. Two basic forms are possible: *bulletins* and *selective dissemination of information* (or SDI). A bulletin will be a printed list or set list for consultation on a VDU, which is published and distributed to a number of users on a specific subject area such as building products or cancer research. Most such bulletins list titles or abstracts, together with citations of relevant new documents in the subject area. Some bulletins offer a digest of the information, and others actually include extracts from the documents announced (particularly if these are newspaper articles). New bulletins will usually be issued at monthly, weekly or daily intervals.

The other form of current awareness service is that of SDI. In an SDI service the user specifies his own individual interests in detail, and these are then expressed in terms of a user-interest profile. The user then receives, on a regular basis, notifications of new documents or information which fall within the topic specified in his profile. Most SDI systems use the computer to perform the selection of announcements and are thus able to offer this individualized service to many users. SDI can be printed or can be made available for online viewing, in which case the user goes to the terminal to study the new notifications at regular intervals. Other options are Standard and Group SDI. These services are not individualized, but rather are based either on a set of standard profiles (Standard SDI) from which the user can choose, or on a group profile which bridges the interests of a group of people.

1.2.4 Bibliographies

Bibliographies are lists of books and other materials, restricted by some feature other than their physical presence in a library. Such a list can be limited by geography (for example, the *British National Bibliography* covers books with a British imprint) by language (the *Cumulative Book Index* covers books in the English language) or by subject (as is evident in the *London Bibliography of the Social Sciences*). Lastly a bibliography may concentrate on a specific physical form, such as the *British National Film and Video Catalogue* which seeks to cover films and videos. In the sense that both bibliographies and catalogues are lists of bibliographic records, all of the arrangements that have been discussed for catalogues may be equally applicable in a bibliography; in general, there is no reason why the same principles should not be used in bibliography as in catalogue compilation. To go further, the catalogues of major libraries, or the union catalogues of a large cooperative can be important bibliographical tools in their own right. Thus the British Library's *General Catalogue of Printed Books* is both a catalogue and a bibliographical tool, while the *National Union Catalog* (US) is a major catalogue with much wider functions.

1.2.5 Computer databases

The records in computer databases are structured in order to suit the information that is being stored for various applications. Bibliographic databases provide references to documents in a similar way to printed abstracting or indexing journals or catalogues. Typical records in an abstracts-based bibliographic database are shown in Figure 6.3.

Such databases may be stored on magnetic media such as disks and accessed either locally or remotely. This may include access to catalogue databases either within one library system or over a network which links databases associated with the holdings of a number of libraries. Equally, other databases may be accessed on the computers of the online hosts, so that users from all over the world can extract data from the available databases via appropriate telecommunications networks. An alternative method of storing databases is to record the data on optical disks, the most prevalent form at present being CD–ROM. These options for accessing data stored in a database are explored more fully later. We shall start by reviewing a few basics about databases in general.

Databases can be described as either reference or source databases. *Reference databases* refer or point the user to another source (such as a document, an organization or an individual) for additional information or the full text of the document. Reference databases can be further subdivided into:

- Bibliographic databases which include citations and often abstracts of the printed literature, and
- Referral databases which offer references to information or data such as the names and addresses of organizations and other directory type data.

Source databases contain the original source data. Again, source databases can be subdivided into:

- Numeric databases which contain numerical data of various kinds, including statistics and survey data;
- Full-text databases of newspaper items, technical specifications and software, and
- Text-numeric databases which contain a mixture of textual and numeric data (such as company annual reports) and handbook data.

A computer database is structured within the computer, but this structure is not particularly important to the user. Records can be retrieved by character strings (that is, sequences of letters and numerals). What is retrieved and how it may be retrieved are more important to the user. Obviously, what can be retrieved depends upon what is in the database in the first place and the way in which the information has been structured. Typically some parts of records can be searched and their elements used as search keys. Retrieval facilities will vary between systems, but it is usual to be able to search bibliographic databases by authors' names, subject words in titles, classification numbers, assigned subject terms, as well as combinations of these. Retrieval from a computer database offers more options than retrieval from a printed index. The search keys and the possible combinations of search keys are more numerous in a computer database. Also, several options normally exist with respect to the proportion of the record which is displayed or printed on any particular occasion.

Whilst the nature and application of databases are considered in various other places in this work, it is perhaps important to establish that the database can be the source of many other printed products, since the data input into a computer database can be rearranged into a variety of different formats and selections to meet different requirements. Figure 1.6 shows the products and services available from BIOSIS as an example of the range of products that may be available from the creation of a database. Note that the database producer develops more than one database, in addition to current awareness services, CD–ROM products and printed abstracts journals.

15

Figure 1.6   Products and services available from BIOSIS

Printed Reference Publications
   Biological Abstracts
   Biological Abstracts (Reports, Reviews, Meetings)
   Zoological Record
   Abstracts of Entomology
   Abstracts of Mycology

Current Awareness Services
   BioResearch Today
   BIOSIS Standard Profiles
   BIOSIS Information Transfer System
   BITS Software
   Current Literature Alerting Service
   BIOSIS Perspectives Series

Online Products and Services
   BIOSIS PREVIEWS
   Biological Abstracts on tape
   BIOSIS PREVIEWS authority file tapes
   TOXLINE
   BIOBUSINESS
   BIOSIS register of Bacterial Nomenclature
   Zoological Record online
   BIOSIS Connection

Compact Disc Products
   Biological Abstracts on compact disc
   Biological Abstracts (Reports, Reviews, Meetings) on compact disc

Microform Services
   Biological Abstracts and Biological Abstracts (RRM) in microform
   Zoological Record in microform

1.3   Functions of document and information organization tools

The description of the tools for the organization of knowledge in the earlier sections of this chapter goes some way towards identifying the purposes of these tools.

As early as 1876, Charles Ammi Cutter defined the purposes of a catalogue; if broadly interpreted, these purposes apply to any tool for the organization of knowledge. Cutter defined the range of functions of a catalogue thus:

1.   To enable a person to find a document of which
    the author, or
    the title, or
    the subject is known.
2.   To show what the library has

by a given author
on a given subject (and related subjects)
in a given kind (or form) of literature.
3. To assist in the choice of a document
    as to its edition (bibliographically)
    as to its character (literary or topical).

Of course, not all catalogues or other tools for the organization of knowledge aim to fulfil all these functions.

The first function concentrates on the identification and location of documents from the various pieces of information that a user might bring to the catalogue or index. In a printed catalogue or index, a user is constrained to look under the headings provided. It is important that the user should be supplied with enough detail regarding the catalogued or indexed documents to be able to decide whether it matches the information they have brought to the retrieval device. Having been alerted to the existence of a document, the user needs information concerning its actual location in order that it may be examined. In a library catalogue, the classification number, which indicates the position of a document on the library shelves, makes it possible to locate the document. In a bibliographic database there may be no direct information as to the whereabouts of the document, or the user may be referred to a document delivery service or a major library. Increasingly online ordering is possible via document delivery services.

The second function of the catalogue is concerned with keeping a record of the library stock as well as helping library users to find documents of whose existence they are unaware. A catalogue must show the extent of a collection and facilitate an assessment of its quality with respect to its authors, subjects and forms.

The third function is achieved primarily by the description in an index, catalogue or database. By giving details such as the title, edition, publisher and pagination, the description should help the user decide how relevant and helpful the document will be by distinguishing it from others and by indicating its nature (for example, subject or quality).

1.4 Catalogues, indexes, databases and document arrangement

The tools of the organization of knowledge have not been exhaustively listed until document arrangement has been considered. All of the devices considered so far arrange and provide access to surrogates or representations of documents. As identified in the previous section, an important component of the retrieval process is the location of the document itself. Document arrangement aids direct retrieval. In some systems and libraries, documents have been arranged in a serial number order or some other simple order. However, normally documents will be arranged in some systematic order which facilitates the examination of the documents, either with or without the intercession of an index or catalogue.

Although important, document arrangement has two fundamental limitations:

1. Documents (in any printed form) can be arranged in only one order (perhaps by name, title or subject). For example, if a set of documents has been arranged according to subject, then the reader who wishes to identify all the books by a given author will need to sift the entire collection.
2. Each document can be put in only one place in any given sequence. For example, a document with several authors or many subjects cannot be arranged in accordance with more than one author's name or subject label unless there are multiple copies of the work in the collection or filing system.

Catalogues, indexes and databases help to overcome these two limitations.

Recommended reading

Note: There are very few texts with broad scope in this field. Other texts are listed in later chapters of this book as appropriate.

Booth, P F and South, M L (1982), *Information filing and finding*, Buckden: Elm.

Chapman, L (1990), How to catalogue 2nd edition, London: Library Association.

Hunter, E (1991), *Cataloguing*, 3rd edition, London: Library Association.

Lancaster, F W (1991), Indexing and abstracting in theory and practice, London: Library Association.

Saye, J. D (1991), *Manhiemer's cataloguing and classification: a workbook*, Basel: Dekker.

2 Records in printed indexes and catalogues

Chapter 1 reviewed the basic tools for the organization of knowledge. It is evident that in a printed index there may be different types of records or entries. The headings of entries may vary, as may the nature and quantity of the description provided. This chapter reviews the different types of entries to be found in indexes and catalogues. The basic terminology introduced here may be encountered both in printed and card indexes and catalogues, and also in records management systems and computer–based versions of indexes and catalogues.

2.1 Entries

In catalogues there are two possible approaches to the provision of multiple entries for one work. One of these is the use of main and added entries. The main entry is the complete catalogue record of the document; this may be made under a classification number, an author's name or under a title. In a classified catalogue the main entry will be one of those in the classified sequence (see Figure 2.1). In a dictionary catalogue, the main entry will be an author entry (see Figure 2.2).

In a catalogue using main and added entries, any entries in addition to the one main entry are added entries which thus provide a range of access points. Figure 2.1, an extract from the *British National Bibliography*, shows added entries in the Author/Title Catalogue. Added entries may have subject labels, authors' names or titles as headings.

In an author catalogue as part of a classified catalogue, added entries may be expected either under

1. Personal names of collaborating authors, writers, editors and compilers, translators, illustrators and other persons involved in the creation of a work, or
2. Corporate body names, where such a body is prominently named within the work.

In other sequences added entries may be made under titles if the title has not been used as the main entry heading. Added entries under series titles are to be expected.

Figure 2.1 British National Bibliography extracts: a classified arrangement
(a) Classified sequence

---

332 — FINANCE

332.0941 *(DC20)*
Dunkley, P. (Peter)
The monetary and financial system / Peter Dunkley, Peter Gutmann. — Worcester : Osborne, c1990. — 104p ; 22cm
Includes index
ISBN 0–9510650–9–2 (pbk) : £4.95 : CIP rev.
1.Ti 2.Gutmann, P. T. G. (Peter T G) 3.*Finance* 4.*Great Britain*   B90–35493

332.4 — MONEY

332.45605 *(DC20)*
Currencies and interest rates. — 1989–. — Cheltenham (Belgrave House, Imperial Square, Cheltenham, GL50 1QB) : Corporate Treasury Consultants. — v. ; 30cm
Each issue has a distinctive title
ISSN 0957–6584 = Currencies and interest rates : No price
1.Corporate Treasury Consultants 2.*Foreign exchange. Rates (Taxation)*   B91–17363

332.8 — INTEREST AND DISCOUNT

332.82 *(DC20)*
Interest rate spreads analysis : managing and reducing rate exposure / Citicorp. — London : McGraw-Hill, 1990. — xiii, 190p : ill ; 26cm
ISBN 0–07–707362–2 : £45.00 : CIP rev.
1.Citicorp 2.*Interest (Finance)*   B90–19438

333.7 — NATURAL RESOURCES AND ENERGY

333.72 *(DC20)*
Wilkinson, James, *1941–*
Green or bust / James Wilkinson. — London : BBC Books, 1990. — 202p ; 20cm
ISBN 0–563–36032–1 (pbk) : £4.99 : CIP rev.
1.Ti 2.*Environment. Conservation*   B90–40480

333.79240973 *(DC20)*
Cohen, Bernard L. (Bernard Leonard), *1924–*
The nuclear energy option : an alternative for the 90s / Bernard L. Cohen., — New York ; London : Plenum Press, c1990. — x, 338 p. : ill. ; 22 cm.
Includes index
ISBN 0–306–43567–5 : No price
1.Ti 2.*Nuclear energy. Policies* 3.*United States*   B91–18813

336.2 — PUBLIC FINANCE. TAXATION

336.2070941 *(DC20)*
Pritchard, W. E. (William Edward), *1936–*
Tolley's tax planning for new businesses : a practical guide to the opportunities and pitfalls / by W. E. Pritchard. — 3rd ed. — Croydon : Tolley, c1990. – xiv,130p ; 23cm
Previous ed.: 1987. — Includes index
ISBN 0–85459–463–9 (pbk) : No price
1.Ti 2.*Business enterprise. Taxation* 3.*Great Britain*   B91–16445

337 — INTERNATIONAL ECONOMICS

337.142 *(DC20)*
Featherstone, Kevin
The successful manager's guide to 1992 : working in the new Europe / Kevin Featherstone. — London : Fontana, 1990. – xii,242p : 1 map ; 20cm. — (The Successful manager)
Includes bibliographies and index
ISBN 0–00–637520–0 (pbk) : £4.99 : CIP rev.
1.Ti 2.Sr: The Successful manager 3.*Economic integration* 4.*European Community*   B90–43123

The **Regions** and European integration: the case of Emilia–Romagna / edited by Robert Leonardi and Raffaella Y. Nanetti. — London : Pinter, 1990. – 205p : ill ; 23cm. — (A Publication of the European University Institute)
Includes bibliographies and index. – Includes index
ISBN 0–86187–149–9 : £25.00 : CIP rev.
1.Leonardi, Robert 2.Nanetti, Raffaella Y., 1943– 3.European Economic Community 4.Sr: A Publication of the European University Institute 5.*Economic conditions* 6.*Italy*
B90–44078

Figure 2.1 Cont.
(b) Subject index (using COMPASS)

Effectiveness	
Personnel. Training. Effectiveness	658.312404
Egypt	
Egypt, *History*	932
Elections	
Elections	324.70973
Electoral systems	
Electoral systems	324.630941
Electrical engineering	
Electrical engineering	621.3
Electrical engineering	621.3092
Electricity	
Electricity	537
Electrocardiography	
Humans, Heart, Electrocardiography	616.1207547
Electrochemistry	
Electrochemistry	530.417
Electrochemistry	660.297
Electromagnetic compatibility	
Electromagnetic compatibility	621.384
Electromagnetism	
Electromagnetism	537
Electronic equipment	
Electronic equipment	621.381505
Electronic games	
Electronic games	794.8
Electronic games	794.805
Electronic games	794.82
Electronic mail	
Electronic mail	384.34
Electronics	
Electronics	338.47621381094
Electronics	621.38101105
Electronics. Industries	338.47621381
Elephants	
Elephants. Conservation	639.97961
Elites	
Elites	305.5520954
Embroidery	
Embroidery	746.44
Embroidery	746.442
Embroidery. Patterns	746.443

(c) Author / title catalogue

Tracing your Scottish ancestry / Kathleen B. Cory. — *Polygon (pbk). £5.95 : CIP rev.*
929.10720411   Issue 2128   ISBN 0–7486–6054–2
Tracking dinosaurs / Martin Lockley. — *Cambridge University Press. No price : CIP entry (Oct.)*
567.91   Issue 2129   ISBN 0–521–39463–5
Tracks
Bridges / Kate Petty and Terry Cash. — *A & C Black. £5.95 : CIP rev.*
624.2   Issue 2130   ISBN 0–7136–3315–8
Tunnels / Kate Petty and Terry Cash. — *A & C Black. £5.95 : CIP rev.*
624.193   Issue 2130   ISBN 0–7136–3313–1
Tractors of Thomson's Yard
Rufus to the rescue [Maisner, Heather]. — *Walker (pbk). £1.99*
823.914[J]   Issue 2128   ISBN 0–7445–1714–1
Tracy, James D., *1938–*
The Political economy of merchant empires / James D. Tracy, editor. – *Cambridge University Press. No price : CIP entry (Dec.)*
382.09   Issue 2130   ISBN 0–521–41046–0
Tracy, Robert
Stone / Osip Mandelstam ; translated from the Russian with an introduction and notes by Robert Tracy. — *Collins Harvill (pbk). £6.95 : CIP rev.*
891.713   Issue 2128   ISBN 0–00–272145–7
Trade finance : payments and services / D.B. Cox. — 4th ed. — *Northwick (pbk). £13.00 CIP rev.*
332.042   Issue 2130   ISBN 0–907135–65–x
Trade negotiations in the OECD : structures, institutions and states / David J. Blair. — *Kegan Paul International. £40.00 : CIP entry (Sept.)*
382.9   Issue 2131   ISBN 0–7103–0432–3

Figure 2.2 Cumulative Book Index extract: a dictionary arrangement

Mann, Judith
A guide to great inexpensive Asian restaurants in Seattle & Puget Sound. 166p il $8.95
1989 Pacific Rim Press
ISBN 0–9619290–2–2   LC 88–61584
Mann, Nancy
Instant access guide to Lotus 1–2–3; [il. by Bob Brunsdon] 248p il $14.95 1988 Price/
Stern/Sloan
ISBN 0–89586–735–4   LC 88–207390
Mann, Richard A.
Essentials of business law. See Smith, L. Y.
Mann, Sally, 1951–
At twelve; portraits of young women; introduction by Ann Beattie. Q 53p il $25 1988
Aperture
ISBN 0–89381–296–X; 0–89381–330–3 (pa)
LC 87–71950
Mann, Stephan C., 1948–
The neuroleptic malignant syndrome and related conditions. See Lazarus, A.
Mann, Vivian B.
(ed) See Gardens and ghettos
Manned space flight

History
Juvenile literature

Dolan, E. F. Famous firsts in space. $13.95 1989 Cobblehill Bks.
Manners and customs

Juvenile literature

Langley, A. People. 1989 Gareth Stevens Children's Bks.
Manning, Gary L.
(ed) See Whole language
Manning, Maryann Murphy
(ed) See Whole language
Manors

England
Themes, motives

Cornforth, J. The search for a style. $39.95 1989 Norton
Manpower policy

United States

Seitchik, A. From one job to the next. 1989 Upjohn Inst. for Employment Res.
Man's social nature. 2nd ed Waszek, N. 1988 Lang, P. (Frankfurt am Main)

Additional subject headings or classification numbers may also be used as headings for added entries.

The second approach to the provision of multiple entries is the unit entry approach. This uses the same unit or entry wherever a given work is listed. The same entry appears in all sequences, with only different headings superimposed in order to distinguish one entry from another. Thus, in a unit entry catalogue all entries contain the same quantity of detail. The unit entry approach was popular in card and sheaf catalogues and indexes, because the physical reproduction of entries to be inserted in different sequences was simpler if the same basic record could be used. With the fading significance of these physical forms, some of the rationale for unit entries has disappeared. Others might argue that the unit entry approach is similar to that in a computer database where the same record may be accessed by means of a number of different search keys.

2.2   References

A reference is not generally as helpful to the user of a catalogue or index as an entry might be. This is because a reference provides little direct information about a document, but rather refers the user to another location or entry where this information can be found. Nevertheless, references are common in indexes and catalogues. References represent economy of cataloguing effort when compared with an added entry.

There are two types of reference: 'see' and 'see also'. These operate in a similar fashion whether they are used to link authors' names or subject headings.

A 'see' reference directs the user from a name, title, subject or other term which has not been used as an entry heading to an alternative term which does occur as a heading or descriptor. 'See' references may link two subject terms with similar meanings (for example, Currency see Money) or variant author names (for example, Council for the Education and Training of Health Visitors, see United Kingdom. Council for the Education and Training of Health Visitors), or different titles (for example, Cookery course see *Delia Smith's Cookery Course*).

A 'see also' reference connects headings or index terms which are in some way related, where both are regarded as acceptable for use as headings for entries. For example, the following 'see also' reference

Monasteries see also Abbeys

links two headings under which entries may be found. The searcher is recommended to examine entries under both index terms if it is likely that documents might prove to be relevant. A 'see also' reference may be used between different headings for the same person, when some of that person's works have been entered under each of the headings linked by 'see also' references. 'See also' references can be used between the names of related but independently entered corporate bodies, and also to connect the titles of related works.

Explanatory references may be either 'see' or 'see also' references which give a little more detail than merely the direction to look elsewhere. An example might be:

Devon, Sarah
    For works of this author published under other names see

Murray, Jill   Treves, Kathleen.

Some libraries make more extensive use of references, in preference to added entries, than others. A reference is always shorter than an added entry, and in some circumstances the economies which accrue mean that it is normal practice to employ a reference. In these instances a reference is not only shorter than an added entry, but removes the need to make multiple added entries. For example, added entries could be made under both NCET and the National Council for Educational Technology. If this practice is adopted then two new entries will be necessary for every new document to be entered under the name of this corporate body. A reference such as

N.C.E.T. see National Council for Educational Technology

once inserted in an index or catalogue will suffice for any subsequent documents to be entered under the name of this corporate body; only one added entry with respect to this name need be made for each new document added to the index. Although author names have been used to illustrate this point, it is important to recognize that the same arguments are equally applicable to references under subject terms.

3 Description of documents: principles and monographs

The description of a document as part of a catalogue entry acts as a document surrogate. A description represents the document in various catalogues, indexes and databases. Access points serve to determine where the record will be filed or how it may be found, but the description is necessary in order for the document itself to be located and retrieved.

Document descriptions may be drafted for a wide variety of different kinds of library material, but some common principles can be established. This chapter identifies some central principles and practices appertaining to description, and goes on to exemplify these principles and practices with reference to descriptive cataloguing practices for monographs.

Documents need to be described wherever they are represented by a surrogate for the purposes of the organization or retrieval of information. Descriptions may be included in catalogues, bibliographies and other listings of documents. Since different applications may place different demands upon the description to be included, the practices pertaining to the description of documents may vary.

3.1 Purpose of the description

Note: Throughout this chapter the term 'document' is used to refer to any item which might be found in a library or information centre, records collection, archive or database, including books, periodicals, magnetic tapes, video cassettes, microforms, artefacts, manuscripts, letters, samples and so on.

The description may have three possible purposes:

1. to *identify* or individualize the document being catalogued or indexed, or to give sufficient information for the reader to be able uniquely to identify the work;
2. to *characterize* the document or to give information to assist in the choice of a document by indicating aspects of its character such as its subject, authorship, style, physical format, level and date; and
3. to act as a subsidiary component in determining filing order.

All the elements in any bibliographic description are intended to contribute to one or more of these purposes. Any framework for description must determine:

1. what information should be given in the description, including the extent of detail required;
2. in what order the information should be given; and, preferably,
3. the punctuation needed to divide and distinguish between the elements of the description.

3.2 Standards and bibliographic description

There are a number of standards for bibliographic description, some of which are more widely applied than others. Also a greater degree of standardization can be expected in some types of application than in others. The area in which standards for bibliographic description have had the most impact is in catalogues and catalogue record databases. Catalogues, then, are easy to examine as a group because there has been a good deal of standardization with respect to the document records they contain. We will therefore consider the standards used in catalogues at some length.

Exchange of machine-readable records in an attempt to economize on and streamline the cataloguing process has made the use of standard records highly desirable. The programme of International Standard Bibliographic Descriptions (ISBDs), which was developed during the 1970s, has been an important component of successful standardization. The International Standard Bibliographic Descripton for Monographs (ISBD(M)) was adopted by the International Federation of Library Associations (IFLA) Committee on Cataloguing in 1971, and was followed by International Standard Bibliographic Descriptions for other categories of materials including the ISBD(S) for serials, the ISBD(PM) for printed music, the ISBD(CM) for cartographic materials and the ISBD(NBM) for nonbook materials.

Since different committees were responsible for evolving these standards which were proliferating to cover different types of materials, it was becoming increasingly difficult to ensure that no inconsistencies arose between the standards. Hence in 1976 the general framework ISBD(G) was agreed. The International Standard Bibliographic Descriptions offer a framework for bibliographic description and satisfy the three points listed at the end of section 3.1. Although they thus identify the components of the description, their preferred order and the necessary punctuation, they offer no assistance on how to choose and present each of the components to be included. To provide this type of guidance is the function of a cataloguing code. However, in order for a cataloguing code to be helpful in this respect, its recommendations clearly must not conflict with the framework for bibliographic description specified by the ISBDs. The Anglo-American Cataloguing Rules 1988 Revision (AACR2R) (see Chapters 8 and 9 for fuller details) does indeed follow the recommendations of the ISBD programme. In fact, one reason for the first edition being supplanted by a second was the adjustments necessary to make AACR consistent with the ISBDs. AACR2R therefore also shows the components to be included in a bibliographic description, their order and punctuation. In addition, AACR2R provides guidelines on how to handle more intractable situations such as in deciding on which of six authors' names to record in a description, or which date to give when there are a variety of copyright and reprint dates but no imprint date.

In 1981 the ISBD Review Committee was formed by IFLA with the objective of performing five-yearly reviews of the ISBDs for monographs, serials, cartographic and nonbook materials. Revised editions of the ISBD(M), the ISBD(CM) and the ISBD(NBM) were all published in 1987, and the revised edition of the ISBD(S) in 1988. The ISBD(CF) for computer files has been developed over recent years and was published in 1990. Work continues on the ISBD(A) for rare and antiquarian books, a draft of which was circulated in 1988. The revised ISBD(PM) was published in 1990, and work continues on a revised version of the ISBD(G). Also in 1988 a publication that offered guidelines for the application of the ISBDs to the description of component parts was published.

Bibliographic descriptions in lists and databases other than library catalogues (such as in printed abstracting and indexing journals or the databases which relate to them) are less likely to be entirely consistent with any one standard, although users might view standardization as desirable. Most database producers have in-house guidelines for bibliographic description and aim to achieve consistency of citation within their products. There is a good deal of common ground between the bibliographic descriptions used in these various lists, but practices vary in specific details, such as the extent of description given and the order in which elements are cited.

However, although database producers choose to adhere to in-house rules, there are international standards which can be applied and, indeed, do influence practice. First, the ISBDs and cataloguing codes such as AACR2R can be applied to some documents such as monographs, conference proceedings, reports and other complete works. However these guides fail to provide a satisfactory solution for the description of parts of documents. In particular, a database may be concerned to list separately individual periodical articles and single papers in conference proceedings. (More discussion on this topic will be found in Chapter 4.)

3.3 Principles of description

In preparing the description of a document it is necessary to make certain preliminary decisions if different cataloguers are to produce the same record from one

Figure 3.1 Chief sources of information according to AACR2R

Type of Material	Source
Books, pamphlets and printed sheets	Title page
Cartographic materials	Cartographic item itself
	Container or case, the cradle and stand of a globe, etc.
Manuscripts	Title page
	Colophon
Music	Title page
Sound recordings	
Disc	Disc and label
Tape (open reel-to-reel)	Reel and label
Tape cassette	Cassette and label
Tape cartridge	Cartridge and label
Roll	Label
Sound recording on film	Container and label
Motion pictures and video recordings	Film itself and its container (if integral part of item)
Graphic materials	Item itself including any labels and the container
Computer files	Title screen
Three-dimensional artefacts and realia	Object itself with any accompanying textual material and container
Microforms	Title frame
Serials (printed)	Title page

document, even if it is agreed that the description should perform a recognized function. These general considerations include:

1. *The source of the information* for the description. In order that all cataloguers use the same basis of information for the description, it is necessary to designate a chief source of information. Preference is normally given to information within the document itself in order to facilitate matching the record and its document on subsequent occasions. When the information available in the document is not sufficient to form a helpful record, supplementary information from other sources may be required. For books the chief source of information for some elements of the description is the title page. Thus, for instance, a title statement will be extracted from a title page, and not from the cover or the spine. Plainly some elements of the description cannot be found on the title page, and must be taken from elsewhere in the document. Pagination, for instance, can only be discovered by examining the work. Figure 3.1 gives the chief sources of information according to AACR2R.

2. *Organization of the description.* Having decided upon the essential elements for

a catalogue record (as discussed in 3.4 below), it is important to adopt a consistent order for citing them. This order is demonstrated by Figure 3.2.

3. *Punctuation* must be established and adopted consistently. Punctuation is essential to partition the components of the description. An international standard which makes recommendations for punctuation, such as the ISBDs, is important for the international exchange of records.

4. *Levels of detail in the description.* Different applications demand different degrees of detail in the description. In a small general library simple records are adequate, whereas a large special collection will require that works with similar titles or different editions of the same work be distinguished from one another. AACR2R identifies three distinct levels of detail. If libraries and other cataloguing or indexing agencies adopt one of these specific levels, the interchange of bibliographic records may be facilitated. It is important to recognize that although these three levels cater for the majority of applications, some libraries will opt for rather less detail than specified even in level 1 (maybe just title, publisher and date), while others may opt for full descriptive cataloguing which extends beyond that specified in level 3. Figure 3.3 shows the components to be included in the three levels of description. (The main components are discussed more fully in the next section.) Figure 3.4 gives an example of how these levels may be applied.

3.4 Components of the description

The ISBD(G) identifies eight main areas within a bibliographic description. This section explores the reasons for the inclusion of each of these areas and discusses some of the common problems that pertain to each.

1. *Title and statement of responsibility area*
The title of a work is well established as the first component of the description. This is because the title of a work is the primary individualizing element for a given document, and distinguishes one work from another by the same author. The purpose of the title, in bibliographic description, is then:

(a) to indicate the nature and content of the document. For example, with non-fiction the title summarizes the subjects covered by the document and may indicate the level or approach to the subject.

(b) to identify the document uniquely. The title, taken together with the author's name, is sufficient to identify a work uniquely (although not to distinguish between editions of the same work).

(c) to determine the position of the description amongst other descriptions with the same heading (for example, to distinguish works by the same author and entered under the same author heading).

Figure 3.2 The ISBD(G)

Area	Prescribed preceding (or enclosing) punctuation for elements	Element	
Note: Each area, other than the first, is preceded by a point, space, dash, space (.–).			
1. Title and statement of responsibility area		1.1	Title proper
	( )	1.2	General material designation
	=	1.3	Parallel title
	:	1.4	Other title information
		1.5	Statements of responsibility
	/		First statement
	;		Subsequent statement
2. Edition area		2.1	Edition statement
	=	2.2	Parallel edition statement
		2.3	Statements of responsibility relating to the edition
	/		First statement
	;		Subsequent statement
	,	2.4	Additional edition statement
		2.5	Statements of responsibility following an additional edition statement
	/		First statement
	;		Subsequent statement
3. Material (or type of publication) specific details area			
4. Publication, distribution (etc.) area		4.1	Place of publication, distribution, etc.
			First place
	;		Subsequent place
	:	4.2	Name of publisher, distributor, etc.
	( )	4.3	Statement of function of publisher, distributor, etc.
	,	4.4	Date of publication, distribution, etc.
	(	4.5	Place of manufacture
	:	4.6	Name of manufacturer
	,)	4.7	Date of manufacture
5. Physical description area		5.1	Specific material designation and extent of item
	:	5.2	Other physical details
	;	5.3	Dimensions of item
	+	5.4	Accompanying material statement

(Continued)

(Figure 3.2   Continued)

Area	Prescribed preceding (or enclosing) punctuation for elements		Element
6. Series area		6.1	Title proper of series
	=	6.2	Parallel title of series
Note: A series statement is	:	6.3	Other title information of series
enclosed by parentheses.		6.4	Statements of responsibility relating to
When there are two or more			the series
series statements, each is	/		First statement
enclosed by parentheses.	;		Subsequent statement
	,	6.5	International Standard Serial Number
			of series
	;	6.6	Numbering within series
	.	6.7	Enumeration and/or title of subseries
	=	6.8	Parallel title of subseries
	:	6.9	Other title information of subseries
		6.10	Statements of responsibility relating to
			the subseries
	/		First statement
	;		Subsequent statement
		6.11	International Standard Serial Number
			of subseries
	;	6.12	Numbering within subseries
7. Note area			
8. Standard number (or		8.1	Standard number (or alternative)
alternative) and terms of	=	8.2	Key title
availability area	:	8.3	Terms of availability and/or price
	( )	8.4	Qualification (in varying positions)

Source: International Federation of Library Associations. Working Group or the General International Bibliographic Description. *ISBD(G): General International Standard Bibliographic Description: Annotated Text.* London IFLA International Office for UBC, 1977.-

31

Figure 3.3   The three levels of description as in AACR2R

1.0D1. First level of description. For the first level of description, include at least the elements set out in this schematic illustration:

Title proper/first statement of responsibility, if different from main entry heading in form or number or if there is no main entry heading. — Edition statement. — Material (or type of publication) specific details. — First publisher, etc., date of publication, etc. — Extent of item. — Note(s). — Standard number.

1.0D2. Second level of description. For the second level of description, include at least the elements set out in this schematic illustration:

Title proper (general material designation) = parallel title: other title information/first statement of responsibility; each subsequent statement of responsibility. — Edition statement/first statement of responsibility/relating to the edition. — Material (or type of publication) specific details. — First place of publication, etc.: first publisher, etc., date of publication, etc. — Extent of item: other physical details; dimensions. — (Title proper of series/statement of responsibility relating to series, ISSN of series; numbering within the series. Title of subseries, ISSN of subseries; numbering within subseries). — Note(s). — Standard number.

1.0D3. Third level of description. For the third level of description, include all elements set out in the section 3.4 that are applicable to the item being described.

Figure 3.4   An example of the application of different levels of description

First level of description
Gypsy ballads/Federico García Lorca — Warminster: Aris & Phillips. c1990. — viii, 161p. — ISBN 0–85668–490–2.

Second level of description
Gypsy ballads = Romancero gitano translated and with an introduction and commentary/Federico García Lorca; translated by R. Harvard; illustrated by M. Gollanz. — Warminster: Aris & Phillips, c1990. — viii, 161p: ill; 22cm. — (Hispanic classics). — ISBN 0–85668–490–2.

Third level of description
Gypsy ballads = Romancero gitano translated and with an introduction and commentary / Federico García Lorca; translated by R. Harvard; illustrated by M. Gollanz. — Warminster, New York: Aris & Phillips, c1990. — viii, 161p: ill; 22cm. — (Hispanic classics). — ISBN 0–85668–490–2.

Where there are a number of titles associated with different editions or versions of a work, it may be necessary to identify a uniform title where the title is used as a heading. (This topic is explored more fully in Chapter 11.)

With a limited number of exceptions (see AACR2R 1.1B) the 'title proper is transcribed exactly as to order, wording and spelling'. This practice ensures that a later match can be achieved between the document and its description.

The statement of authorship is also transcribed as it appears in the work. The function of the author statement is to:

(a) indicate the relationship between authors and their work;
(b) further uniquely identify the work; and
(c) indicate, particularly with well-known authors, the likely quality or style of a work. This function is particularly significant with fiction.

2. *Edition area*

The edition statement is included if stated in the document, in the form that it is given in the document. It is normally taken to indicate that the document has been revised if a work has progressed to a second or subsequent edition. A work which has gone into a number of editions is likely to have proved its worth and may be a standard text. It is useful to note that first editions are rarely specified as such and that edition statements are normally only to be found in second and subsequent editions. For a user it is often important to be able to identify the current edition of a work, especially if the text has been revised significantly between editions.

Editors and compilers of editions of works are recorded together with the edition statement (for example, third edition or second revised edition) in the edition area. Responsibility for the edition must be distinguished from responsibility for the work.

3. *Material (or type of publication) specific details area*

This is a special area that has been reserved for items of important information which are necessary for certain categories of material. The content will vary according to the type of material being considered. It is especially useful for serials and maps. For serials, the volume and part numbers and the dates of issue are included; for maps, the scale and other mathematical data. For many other categories of material nothing will be recorded in this area.

4. *Publication, distribution (etc.) area*

The primary components in this area are place of publication, publisher's name and date of publication (that is, the date of the edition). For some categories of materials it can be difficult to distinguish publishers from distributors and/or producers. AACR2R allows for the inclusion of the place of distribution and the distributor's name, if this is required. For example, in various graphic materials, such as slide sets, film strips and motion pictures, the roles of publishers and distributors may not be as well defined as in traditional monograph publishing.

The imprint is given in the language of the document. The place of publication usually indicates the location of the main offices of the publishers and is intended to help in identifying the publisher. The place of publication may also warn of biases in approach or differences in terminology that arise in the text. For example, a work on law by a Canadian publisher is likely to emphasize Canadian law and legal practice and therefore may have little value for a student of American law. However, works from international publishing houses may be more difficult to characterize in this way.

The name of the publisher obviously aids in the identification of the origins of a document and indicates the agents who have prepared a work for the marketplace. The publisher's name may also be some indication of the quality of a document. Various publishers have reputations for specific styles, subject areas or material for specific audiences. The publisher's name is given in the briefest form in which it can be understood.

The date of the edition is arguably the most important part of the imprint or distribution/publication area. The date may serve to distinghish distinct editions of the same work which are not otherwise labelled. The date of the edition is generally taken to indicate the approximate date of the information contained in the work and is thus important in indicating the currency of the document. Currency is more important in subjects where developments are rapid than in more stable areas. If no edition or imprint date can be ascertained, then an attempt is made to determine a date from amongst any other dates given within the work, such as copyright dates and reprint dates. In the absence of any date the cataloguer is required to estimate a date and give this, indicating that it is an estimate.

5. *Physical description area*

Physical description is the area that varies most with the particular type of material. Nevertheless, four fundamental aspects are similar for all types of material.

The first component of the physical description for all items except one–volume monographs is an indication of the specific *medium designation* which states the nature of the item; for example, 1 map, 1 jigsaw puzzle, 4v. The next component indicates the *extent* of the item or its size. For monographs this statement gives the number of pages and, if appropriate, the number of plates. The number of slides in the set would be the equivalent. The extent of an item is important in selection. Obviously a book on the chemistry of mercury which runs to 200 pages will give less detail than one which runs to 600 pages.

The other physical details to be given will depend upon the features that are important for the type of material under consideration. These points will be discussed further in Chapter 4 on the cataloguing of nonbook materials. In the case of monographs these other physical details include the *illustration statement*. This indicates whether a work is illustrated, whether the illustrations are coloured or black and white, and the type of illustrations to be found, for example maps. Books on some subjects need illustrations; for example, art books will be expected to have pictures and geography books maps. The *dimensions* of the item may also be important. For a monograph the height of the book is normally given in centimetres. If the book has an unusual shape then both the height and the width will be included. The height of a book is of minor importance, except as an indication of the overall size of the text. For other materials size may be more significant since it may determine the nature of the equipment to be used in association with the item.

6. *Series area*

The series area includes the series title, an indication of the responsiblity for the series (often series editors) and, if the work is one of a numbered series, the number of the individual work within the series. To the user who recognizes or is familiar with other works in the same series, the series statement may provide a useful indication of the style and level of a document. In general, the series statement is a source of information about the authority, approach and intention of the content of a document. In certain special cases, as with report series, government publications and standards, the series statement is important in placing the individual document in the context of other works in the series.

7. *Note area*

If the recommendations of AACR2R are followed, the elements included in the previous areas of the description are carefully controlled. In the note area, however, any additional information which the cataloguer feels could be of value to the user may be included. The items that are recorded in the note area and the style in which they are recorded are at the discretion of the cataloguer.

Notes may perform one of the following two functions:

(a) elucidate or develop the existing description, such as information relating to earlier editions, the nature of illustrations and performers of musical works; and

(b) characterize the document more fully by adding information on the subject matter (content or level) and possibly the document's relationship to other documents.

Notes should be made in the most succinct form possible without loss of clarity. Notes may relate to any of the previous elements of the description (title, authorship, edition, editorship, publisher area, physical description area or series area). In addition notes may be made on the relationship between the document and other publications, as well as on the nature, scope, language or literary form of the work's contents or partial contents (that is, highlighting significant sections). AACR2R recommends that notes be given in the order reflected in the preceding description.

8. *Standard number and terms of availability area*

In this section standard numbers, such as International Standard Book Numbers (ISBNs) or International Standard Serial Numbers (ISSNs) are the first elements to be recorded. These form a brief and unique identification of a specific title and are important in control. Price and other terms of availability are also given. These details are primarily useful as a record of expenditure or to organizations or individuals contemplating the purchase of a work. (Examples of descriptions of monographs can be found in Figures in Chapters 1 and 2.)

Recommended readings

Note: Many of the items listed at the end of Chapters 8 and 9 also comment on bibliographic description.

Gorman, M (1987), 'Bibliographic description: past, present and future', *International Cataloguing*, **16** (4), 43.

ISBD(CM) (1987), *International Standard Bibliographic Description for cartographic materials*, Federation of Library Associations and Institutions, rev edition, London: IFLA UBCIM.

ISBD(M) (1987), *International Standard Bibliographic Description for monographic publications*, Federation of Library Associations and Institutions, rev edition, London: IFLA UBCIM.

ISBD(NBM) (1987), *International Standard Bibliographic Description for non-book materials*, Federation of Library Associations and Institutions, rev edition, London: IFLA UBCIM.

ISBD(S) (1988), *International Standard Bibliographic Description for serials*, Federation of Library Associations and Institutions, rev edition, London: IFLA UBCIM.

Maltese, D (1982), 'A standard for bibliographic citations: proposal for the use of ISBD', *International cataloguing*, **11** (2), 19–21.

4 More on bibliographic description: nonbook media, periodicals and analytical cataloguing

The preceding chapter has introduced the essential characteristics of bibliographic descriptions. General points have been illustrated with reference to the cataloguing of books. This chapter takes the opportunity to look at an assortment of other aspects of bibliographic description. First, the cataloguing of nonbook media is considered, and later special attention is focused on periodicals and analytical cataloguing.

4.1 The cataloguing and bibliographic description of nonbook media

Much attention in the early 1970s was focused specifically on the cataloguing and organization of nonbook media. It is a matter of opinion whether nonbook media merit separate discussion in respect of cataloguing practices, or whether it is sufficient to establish general principles for description which can then be applied across the spectrum of many different materials. With an increasing array of different media, general-purpose cataloguing practices would seem to offer a framework for the future. This section aims to summarize some of the special problems of nonbook media and to indicate how cataloguing principles can be interpreted in this area.

The term 'nonbook media' reflects the context in which the consideration of these types of materials in libraries arose. When the term was coined the predominant information and text-carrying medium in libraries was the book. Thus any new media could be grouped into a contrasting category of nonbook. Increasingly a significant proportion of the stock of libraries, resource and information centres are nonbooks. Collections are increasingly likely to embrace a number of different media; eventually, in a true multi-media environment, the distinction between books and nonbooks will become of historical interest only.

Nonbook media, then, may include any library information or resource centre materials other than books or monographs. Some of these items will be audiovisual, such as sound recordings, filmstrips, motion pictures and video-recordings.

Others will be printed including maps, charts and posters. The term nonbook may extend to pamphlets, microforms and serials, although these items may still be classified as books. In the last analysis the definition of nonbook is best made pragmatically in relation to the specific organizational problem under examination.

4.1.1 General problems of nonbook media cataloguing

Outlining some of the general problems concerning the cataloguing of nonbook media can provide a context for considering descriptive cataloguing problems. Nonbook media differ from books and from each other chiefly in their physical format and in the means by which they are created and marketed. The range of subjects that may be represented in nonbook materials, and the range of categories of people that can be associated with their creation, are not very different from their equivalents for books. Both the author and the subject approach for nonbook media can be regarded as broadly similar to that for all media. Many of the particular problems in cataloguing nonbook media arise in the preparation of their bibliographic descriptions.

The subject approach to all types of nonbook materials can in principle, be very similar. General classification schemes (such as the Dewey Decimal Classification) can be and are applied where appropriate, and standard lists of subject headings (such as the Library of Congress List of Subject Headings or Sears' List of Subject Headings) may be used in a catalogue or bibliography listing nonbook media. In addition there are also special classification schemes and subject headings lists which have been designed for special categories of material (for example, the British Classification of Music) or for special collections (such as pictures, local history materials or photographs). Further comments on various of these topics are to be found in the chapters on the subject approach. The subject approach required for different collections and categories of nonbook media will vary with the nature of the collection and its users. It is frequently the case, for example, that the subject categories needed to organize a collection of materials in a school resource centre will be relatively broad. Topics for portfolios might be no more specific than the motor industry, the Brontës, computers or the environment. Although these topics are covered in general classification schemes and lists of subject headings, they may not represent the most appropriate form for a collection of nonbook media.

Equally, author access has features which are more or less common to all types of materials. The question of authorship or intellectual responsibility can be more difficult to identify neatly than with books, and intellectual responsibility may need to be established for each medium. For example, the composer is normally regarded as the author of musical works, but if there is both a composer and a lyricist (writer of the words of a song), then which is to be given priority? In the creation of a motion picture there is a team of people, any of whom may be regarded as intellectually responsible for the content. These could include the author of the script, producer, director, actors, musical arrangers and so on. Undoubtedly, then, the assignment of intellectual responsibility may present fresh considerations for each new kind of medium. However, once responsibility has been allocated, the types of names that can arise will be the same for all types of materials. They will either be the names of corporate bodies or persons, and will represent the same range of problems with regard to form of names as in any other medium.

4.1.2 Basic decisions for nonbook media cataloguing

Certain fundamental decisions concerning the strategy for nonbook media cataloguing need to precede detailed consideration of cataloguing practices. The first decision centres on the extent of integration of entries for different materials into one sequence. A number of choices exist, including the following:

1. to produce a catalogue which integrates entries for all library or resource centre media;
2. to produce two catalogues, one of which contains all the entries pertaining to books, and the other all the entries concerning nonbook media; and
3. to produce as many different catalogues as there are types of media represented in any library or resource centre collection.

The integration of catalogue entries for different types of media into one catalogue sequence facilitates common access to information, regardless of the physical form in which it is recorded. A common catalogue encourages users to regard the different information-carrying media as part of a range. For example, in a school resource centre an integrated catalogue brings a variety of media to the attention of the teacher or the pupil at one consultation. Equally, integration removes the need to decide how to categorize media in determining the different catalogue sequences. For example, can one catalogue cover all graphic materials, or would it be advisable to opt for one catalogue for filmstrips, another for posters and a third for slides?

The chief limitation of integrated cataloguing of different media is the constraint that this approach places upon cataloguing practices. For an integrated catalogue to be successful, access points, including classification numbers, should be compatible for all types of material. In addition, compatible practices for the description of library materials are desirable for both staff and users. Practice as regards integration varies considerably. In reality the extent of integration of catalogue entries for different media often depends on administrative considerations, such as which section of the library is responsible for the compilation of catalogues for the various media.

The second major decision in respect of nonbook cataloguing is the selection of a cataloguing code. Some codes have been specifically designed to cater for one type of material whereas other codes attempt to offer an integrated or consistent approach across all or many nonbook media.

There is only space to review briefly the special problems associated with the descriptive cataloguing of nonbook media. The general ISBD(G) framework certainly provides an outline, and the components which constitute a bibliographic description have been introduced in Chapter 3. Nevertheless, since each group of materials presents unique problems in the way in which the general framework is to be interpreted, AACR2R allots a separate chapter for each category of material. In order to demonstrate some of the problems which arise from the variety of formats, some key features of the descriptive cataloguing of various media are identified below. First, however, it is necessary to establish the source of the information to be used in the description, or at least to identify the chief source of information. In Figure 3.1 the chief sources of information for a number of different categories of material have already been listed.

4.2 Cartographic materials

According to AACR2R, cartographic materials are all those which represent, in whole or in part, the earth or any celestial body. This will incude two- and three-dimensional maps and plans; aeronautical, navigational and celestial charts; atlases; globes; block diagrams; sections, aerial photographs with a cartographic purpose and bird's eye views, and so on.

One of the main problems with descriptive cataloguing of maps is the fact that maps are often sold as part of a series. For instance, the Ordnance Survey 1:25,000 map constitutes a number of maps covering separate areas, such as Congleton and Sheffield. These maps can be bought as a series or individually. The map cataloguer has to decide whether to treat these maps as separate works or as parts of a series. This dilemma is illustrated more fully in section 4.7 which considers the concept of a distinct work and explores the styles of analytical cataloguing.

Another important component to be included is the mathematical data area; this is inserted in the materials specific area after the statement of responsibility. The mathematical data area includes a statement of scale and a statement of projection if given. Scales are normally presented as a representative fraction expressed as a ratio, but provision is made for other statement of scale where there is uncertainty or variation. Some examples are:

Scale: 1:50,000
Scale ca 1:500,000
Scale 1:10,000 – 1:20,000
Scale varies

The physical description of maps also merits special attention. This will include:

1. the number of physical units of a cartographic item, for example:

   1 globe
   3 maps
   10 plans;

2. other physical details such as the number of maps in an atlas together with their material, colour and mounting, for example:

   3 maps: col
   1 globe: col, wood
   1 map: col., mounted on cloth;

3. dimensions, that is, height × width in centimetres, for example:

   1 map: col.; 35 × 50 cm.
   1 map: col., on sheet 55 × 63 cm.
   1 plan; 25 × 60 cm on sheet 31 × 130 cm.
   1 map; 80 × 57 cm folded to 21 × 10 cm.

In the note area, contents notes can be particularly appropriate. Parts, insets and maps on the verso of other maps need to be specifically indicated. For example:

Insets: social and political conditions. —Air distances from New York.—
Includes 7 insets
Includes key to 250 place names.

In addition, where two or more significant maps are on the same sheet or in the same volume, 'with' notes may be used to link separate entries for the individual maps on the same sheet.

4.3 Music

Music can include a variety of forms, such as works about musicians and music, music scores and recordings. The cataloguing of music involves many special problems, both in description and headings. An effective music cataloguer needs to understand the various formats in which music can be published and also needs to have an appreciation of the various contexts in which music is used.

One of the most daunting aspects of music cataloguing arises from the fact that music and music recordings have international value. The user is not concerned whether the text on a music score or a record sleeve is in a foreign language; thus the music cataloguer is very likely to be handling a disproportionate number of foreign-language documents.

A further problem which is particularly apparent in music cataloguing is the definition of a 'work'. One musical theme can be rewritten for different instruments, or different parts can be written for different instruments in an ensemble or orchestra. The same theme may be used by a single instrument, accompanied by a voice or several voices or used to accompany a film, to name but a few of the options. It is a considerable problem to relate all these interconnected pieces of music to one another in a faithful and helpful manner.

When the cataloguer turns to the description of a piece of music, a common problem is the absence of a title page as the chief source of information. Figure 3.1 has shown some of the solutions to this problem for a few of the formats in which music is encountered.

Provided that these considerable problems with music cataloguing can be negotiated, the description of books about music and musicians and music scores has much in common with the cataloguing of monographs. The description of books about musicians and music can be approached with the aid of Chapters 1 and 2 of AACR2R, whilst special attention is focused on music scores in Chapter 5. Careful treatment of the presentation of uniform and conventional titles is necessary however.

Sound recordings are dealt with in Chapter 6 of AACR2R. A few comments on the cataloguing of sound recordings might be helpful. Chapter 6 covers discs, tapes, piano rolls and sound recordings on film. The first stage is the definition of the chief source of information for each separate medium. Another special feature is that the trade name or brand name may be used as the name of the publisher, if this is provided.

The physical description of sound recordings must include as many of the following elements as are appropriate:

1. extent or number of physical units, for example:

    1 sound cassette
    2 sound cartridges.

2. total playing time, for example:

    on 1 side of 1 sound disc (13 min).

3. other physical details including, as appropriate, type of recording, playing speed, groove characteristics, track configuration, number of tracks, number of sound channels and recording and reproduction characteristics. For example:

    1 sound cassette (60 min): 17/8 ips, stereo, Dolby processed.
    1 sound disc (7 min): 78 rpm, microgroove.

4. dimensions, according to medium. For example:

    sound discs: diameter in inches, such as 1 sound disc: 12 in.

sound cassettes: height × width and width of tape if other than standard, such as
1 sound cassette (65 min); 7¼ × 3½ in, ¼ in tape.

Moving on from the physical description of sound recordings, there are elements
of the notes which are especially important. Notes arc common for names of
performers and the medium in which they perform (if this information has not
already been given elsewhere in the entry). Contents notes are expected particularly
in respect of collections of well-known works. A list of the titles of the individual
works, possibly accompanied by statements of responsibility, is useful.

4.4 Computer files

The cataloguing rules for the description of computer files were significantly
revised in Chapter 9 of AACR2R. This chapter covers the description of files that
are encoded for manipulation by computer. These files comprise data and programs which may be accessed directly or remotely. In the cataloguing of these
items it has been important to make a distinction between the intellectual product,
such as the data or the programs, and the storage medium in which these are held.
   The chief source of information for computer files is the title screen. The basic
components of the description are those common to all materials that are catalogued in accordance with AACR2R. Four areas that might deserve special attention are the edition arca, the file characteristics area, the physical description area
and the notes area.

1. The edition statement is often represented by a statement of version or release.
    The file characteristics area includes:

    (a) a statement of designation, indicating the type of file, such as computer
         data, computer program(s) or computer data and program(s); and
    (b) number of records statements etc., such as
             for data: computer data (eg 1 file: 250 records)
             for programs: Computer program (eg 1 file: 200 statements).

3. The physical description area includes statements (with examples) of:

    (a) the extent of item (eg 1 computer disk; 3 computer laser optical disks);
    (b) other physical details (eg 1 computer disk: sd., col.);
    (c) dimensions (eg 1 computer disk: col., 51/4in.); and
    (d) accompanying material (eg 1 computer disk; 31/2 in. + 1 demonstration
         disk + 1 user manual).

4. The notes area provides an opportunity to record further details concerning
    the nature and scope of the computer file as well as systems requirements. The

nature may be further clarified, for example, by including the words 'word processor'. A range of systems requirements can be recorded covering aspects of the computer configuration on which the file can be accessed. For example: IBM PC; 64K; colour card; 2 disk drives.

4.5 Periodical article citation

Periodical article citation could be regarded as one type of analytical entry. With periodical article citation, details and access are given in respect of only part of a serial or periodical, that is, in respect of the individual article. The components of a full citation for a periodical article are typically:

- document identification number,
- author(s) names'
- title and
- source reference.

Sometimes the following additional data or a subset of these elements are also given:

- sponsoring agency and its report reference number,
- contract number,
- original language and/or source of a translation and
- any other additional descriptive notes.

Different agencies engaged in preparing citations to periodical articles have different standards. Typically such citations are to be found in current awareness services, computer databases and indexing and abstracting services. There are standards which can be referred to in citing periodical articles, but these are not always applied in practice. Each agency must establish its own practices in accordance with its own specific requirements.

For articles in periodicals there are a number of International Standards Organization standards. ISO 690-1987: 'Documentation — Bibliographical References' gives suggestions concerning the structure of a bibliographic reference for periodical articles. BS5605:1978 also gives recommendations for citing publications by bibliographical references.

Some comments on each of the four primary components of the periodical article citation are in order. The document identification number is the number which provides the unique identification of the document in the database or publication where the document is cited. The number will not usually be standard for the work, but will be assigned to the periodical article when its record is added to the database. Author(s) name(s) provide rapid identification of an article. The

Figure 4.1 Some examples of nonbook media catalogue records

Maps

Deutschland (cartographic material).—
  Scale 1:800,000.—Stuttgart:
  R.V. 1967
  1 map: col.; 98 × 76cm.

  Road map route numbers, distances
  and showing places of tourist interest.

Ordnance Survey one-inch tourist map
  (cartographic material)
  Scale 1:63,360.—Southampton:
  Ordnance Survey

  The Peak District. 90 × 75cm.
  folded to 23 × 12cm. 1963.

Music score

  Dvorak, Antonin
  (Concertos, cello, orchestra, op. 104, B minor)
  Konzert h-moll für Violincello und Orchester, Opus 104/
  Antonin Dvorak; herausgegeben von Max Pommer.—Leipzig;
  London: Peters, 1976.—1 miniature score (86p.); 15cm.

Sound recording

  Bruch, Max
  (Concertos, violin, orchestra, no. 1, op. 26, G minor)
  Violin concerto no. 1 in G minor, op. 26.—London:
  Ace of Clubs, 1953.—on 1 side of 1 sound disc (20 min.):
  33⅓ rpm, mono.; 12 in.—ACL 64
  Violin: Campoli. London Symphony Orchestra, Anatole Fistoulari,
  conductor.
  With: Havanaise; Introduction and rondo capriccioso, op. 28/
  Saint-Saëns.

Computer Files

XTREE(TM): the new standard for file and directory management/ Executive Systems,
  Inc.—2nd ed.—Computer program.—Sherman Oaks, Ca: Executive Systems, 1985.
1 computer disk: col; 5¼in + 1 user guide (50p.; 13 × 14cm) in case 16 × 17 × 2cm.
System requirements: IBM PC XT/AT or IBM PC XT/AT compatible; ms-dos or PC-DOS
2.0 or greater; 192 K RAM.

Facts on file/Facts on File
  Computer data.—New York: Facts on File, (1990).
  A weekly record of contemporary history compiled from world-wide news sources;
    coverage 1982 to date.
  Online access via Dialog Information Services.
  Corresponds to the printed Facts on File world news digest.
  File size: 31692 records in January 1990, updated weekly.

name(s) may be entered in an author index or merely given as part of the description. Despite the advantages to be gained by standardization, various practices regarding the form of the author(s) name(s) persist. There will be increasing numbers of instances in which it would be desirable to match the entries on different databases. Author(s) name(s) must be an important element in the matching process and common practices between different databases would make matching simpler. Cataloguing codes such as AACR2R provide systematic guidelines on the citation of author(s) name(s), but these are not always heeded.

The title of an article is another important identifier and also indicates the subject content. In the interests of document identification, the title is normally quoted verbatim in order that the document record can be successfully and confidently matched with the document at a later stage. Uninformative or unclear titles may be augmented by additional words which are usually enclosed in square brackets in order to distinguish them from the authentic title. Titles of foreign language publications are generally cited in both the original language and the translation language.

The description of the source of a periodical article comprises: periodical title, date of issue, volume number, issue number and pagination. The first element, the periodical title, will often appear in an abbreviated form. ISO 4–1972: 'Documentation – International Code for the Abbreviation of Titles of Periodicals' and ISO 833: 'Documentation – International List of Periodical Titles Word Abbreviations' provided early guidelines for title abbreviations. ISO 833 was replaced by the 'International List of Title Word Abbreviations', published by the ISDS International Centre and jointly maintained by it and the national ISDS centres. This list has since been replaced by the 'List of Serial Title Abbreviations' which is published jointly by the ISDS and the ISO. ISO 4 – 1972 has been extensively revised as ISO4–1984: 'Documentation – Rules for the Abbreviation of Title Words and Titles of Publications'.

Many organizations work from their own standard list of abbreviations. Journal titles will normally be accompanied by an indication of the issue in which a specific article is contained. Volume and issue and part numbers will serve this purpose. These may be presented in a variety of ways, for examle, volume 6, number 8, or 6(8). In addition it is common to give the date of an issue, for example, March 1992. The date of the issue is cited as fully as is necessary to identify the issue and usually in the form given in the publication, for example, Spring 1992 or 3 May 1992. Page numbers are also necessary and may be inserted in one of many positions. Page numbers should be cited in accordance with the exact pages on which the text of an article appears, for example, 56–58, 61, 68–73. Pagination should be inclusive and should show full page numbers (that is 234–246, not 234–46).

Punctuation will be present in the citation and should serve to distinguish one component from its neighbour. Figure 4.2 shows some examples of periodical article citations from printed sources.

46

Figure 4.2   Some periodical article citations: examples from printed sources

Art Bibliographies Modern

08351 Tory Hughes: 'art is a conversation, not a conversation piece'. Barbara Hamaker. *Ornament* (U.S.A.), vol. 13, pt. 2 (Winter 1989), p. 60–3, 6. 3 illus. (2 col.)
Focuses on Tory Hughes's assemblage and collage necklaces, whose inspiration stems from her nomadic childhood, when she travelled around the world absorbing many different cultures. Although many possessions were lost during these travels, she always kept her personal treasures close to her; these necklaces are a way of uniting these miscellaneous elements into a coherent whole.

08347 Wie das Kapital in Seife umgeschmolzen wird (How capital will be recast in soap). Thomas Huber. *Kunstforum International* (G.F.R.), no. 104 (Nov.–Dec. 1989), p. 192–203. 11 col. illus.
The artist presents a series of assemblages he made for the Hypobank in Augsburg, G.F.R. He explains how being commissioned by a bank affected his approach and choice of subject-matter and describes his place of work in the bank building.

09202 Blitz bits. Gaynor Williams. *Design* (U.K.), no. 488 (Aug. 1989), p. 28–9. 16 illus. (13 col.)
Examines the recent design of the Imperial War Museum in London. The author notes some of the problems facing designers and emphasizes the complete integration of approach between graphics and interiors.

Biological Abstracts

66007. VAN DER KAMP, B. J.* and D. E. N. TAIT. (Dep. Forest Sci., Univ. British Columbia, Vancouver, B.C., Can. V6T 1W5.) PHYTOPATHOLOGY 80(12): 1269–1277. 1990. **Variation in disease severity in the lodgepole pine-western gall rust pathosystem.**
The number of western gall rust (*Endocronartium harknessii*) infections per tree was measured in a lodgepole pine (*Pinus contorta*) population consisting of 3,215 trees in 20 blocks, established from a single, large seed lot collected and planted near Prince George, B.C. Canada. Average disease incidence in these blocks varied from 0.58 to 6.07 infections per tree. A method is presented that allows the prediction of tree frequencies by disease severity classes for each block from a single distribution of relative susceptibility. Resistance genes appear to interact multiplicatively. The most susceptible 10% of the population was estimated to have an infection rate about 800 × as high as the least susceptible 10%. The implications of this wide range in susceptibility for stability of the pathosystem are discussed.

66012. MAIERO, MARISA*, TIMOTHY J. NG and THOMAS H. BARKSDALE. (Dep. Agron. and Horticulture, Box 30003, New Mexico State Univ., Las Cruces, N.M. 80003.) PHYTO-PATHOLOGY 80(12): 1365–1368. 1990. **Inheritance of collar rot resistance in the tomato breeding lines C1943 and NC EBR–2.**
Collar rot is a tomato seedling disease caused by the fungus *Alternaria solani*. Reistance and susceptible parents, F_1, F_2, and backcross generations were evaluated for collar rot resistance in a greenhouse. Genetic analyses included midparent-hybrid comparisons, diallel analysis, and generation mean analysis. The genotypes C1943 and NC EB–2 were most resistant to collar rot. Additive and dominant effects were important in controlling the trait, and collar rot resistance was incompletely recessive to susceptibility.

Current Technology Index

Contribution of n.m.r. spectroscopy to the study of catalyst functionality: structural investigation on hydrotreated petroleum fractions. C. Vecchi & S. Marengo. *Fuel*. 69 (Jun 90) p. 706–9

Advanced control aids management, B. Tinham. *Control and Instrumentation*, 21 (Nov 89) p. 62–6

Continued

Figure 4.2   Continued

Intelligent electronics clamp down at Coryton refinery. [Mobil Oil Corporation] [Foxboro]
S. Ford. *Process Engineering*, 71 (Aug 90) p.28–9

Physics Abstracts

**50806 Detrital remanence, inclination errors, and anhysteretic remanence anisotropy:
quantitative model and experimental results.** M. J. Jackson, S. K. Banerjee, J. A.
Marvin, R. Lu, W. Gruber (Dept. of Geol. & Geophys., Minnesota Univ., Minneapolis, MN,
USA).
Geophys. J. Int. (UK), vol. 104, no. 1, p. 95–103 (Jan. 1991).
It is suggested that inclination errors in detrital remanent magnetization (DRM) may be recognized and corrected
by measurement of the anisotropy of anhysteretic remanent magnetization (ARM). ARM anisotropy reflects
directional variations in the remanence capacity of relatively fine-grained magnetic particles in rocks or sedi-
ments, generally the same particles that carry the stable component of DRM. Relative vertical and horizontal DRM
magnitudes are controlled by this directional remanence capacity, as well as by the alignment efficiency of the
particle magnetic moments, which in turn is governed by the relative intensities of the vertical and horizontal
components of the ambient magnetic field. Thus the respective vertical and horizontal components of palaeoin-
tensity, and therefore palaeofield inclination, may be obtained by normalizing the measured DRM components by
parallel ARM intensities. (39 refs.)

50808 A kinetic model of crack fusion. Z Czechowski (Inst. of Geophys., Polish Acad. of
Sci., Warsaw, Poland).
Geophys. J. Int. (UK), vol. 104, no. 2, p. 419–22 (Feb. 1991).
The paper presents a kinetic approach to the problem of fusion of cracks. A kinetic equation for the size
distribution function of cracks is derived. By division of all cracks into three groups a set of three simple equations
is obtained. From a numerical analysis of the simple model implies that periodic solutions appears if the intensity
of nucleation of little cracks is big enough and a stress release mechanism at the crack source is included. The
periodic solutions can be interpreted as repetitive episodes of seismicity. (5 refs.)

50809 Field-impressed magnetic anisotropy in rocks. D. K. Potter, A. Stephenson (Dept.
of Phys., Newcastle upon Tyne Univ., UK).
Geophys. Res. Lett. (USA), vol. 17, no. 13, p. 2437–40 (Dec. 1990).
The application of alternating (AF) or direct (DF) magnetic fields to two weakly anisotropic rock specimens which
remain static, significantly alters their measured low-field anisotropy of magnetic susceptibility (AMS) by superimposing an anisotropy which has the form of an ellipsoid of revolution with its unique axis aligned along the field
axis. Previous AF history is also shown to significantly influence the acquisition of isothermal remanent magnetization (IRM). Thus it is essential that rocks should not be used for low-field AMS analysis or for IRM anisotropy
studies if they have previously been subjected to static AF demagnetization. AMS studies should also not be
carried out on rocks which carry a significant remanence. The field-impressed effects were also strongly
dependent upon whether the ferrimagnetic particles in the rocks were predominantly multidomain or uniaxial
single-domain. The results add support to the authors' suggestion that these effects could provide a rapid,
nondestructive, means of determining the predominant domain state of ferrimagnetic particles in rocks. (14 refs.)

4.6   Serials and their records

Serials cataloguing and the maintenance of adequate records of serials stock
present two distinct categories of problems. One area has already been tackled in
the last section, namely, the citation of individual parts of serials. The other area is
the maintenance of appropriate records of serials collections and the bibliographic
control of serials titles which we shall consider below.

The cataloguing of serials is an area which has presented many problems, too many of which remain only partially resolved. With improved bibliographic control over serial titles the situation has been eased, but the cataloguing of serials has not advanced to the same extent as that of monographs.

The first problem which faces the serials cataloguer is the definition of a serial. The International Serials Data System (ISDS), based in Paris, defines a serial as 'a publication issued in successive parts and intended to be continued indefinitely'. The definition continues: 'serials include periodicals, newspapers, annuals, journals, memoirs, proceedings, transactions etc. of societies, and monographic series. A serial can be in print or near print form and its parts usually have numerical or chronological designations.' In practice, this definition coincides reasonably well, but certainly not completely or precisely, with that assigned by many individual libraries to the term 'serial'.

Serials, then, are distinguished from monographs by their ongoing nature. Any serials control system will have fewer titles to handle, but must record more detail for each title and can expect a greater number of transactions per title. Usually, serials control systems operate separately from monograph systems, but still need to cover the three functions of ordering and acquisitions, cataloguing and circulation control. For serials, however, much of the record keeping may centre upon the acquisitions subsystem, as opposed to, say, the circulation control subsystem which may be viewed as more central for books. Obviously, some type of record is required to represent each serial title. Before proceeding to consider this aspect, however, it is worth first considering some underlying features of serials control, and then reviewing some of the organizational factors which to some extent determine the nature of records for serials.

Five key issues which are unique to serials present problems with regard to cataloguing and other serials control subsystems. These are:

1. Successive issues are received at regular or irregular intervals, and it is important to note and respond to the arrival or non-arrival of individual issues.
2. Subscriptions must be renewed at regular intervals.
3. Catalogue records must describe both the serial and the library's holdings of the serial.
4. Serials change their titles, are published under variant titles (for example, translated titles) and may change their frequency of publication, editor, format and other features.
5. Serials need to be cumulated and bound.

In general, a large amount of data needs to be recorded for each serial title, and amendments to individual records will be common.

Various standards have emerged in recent years for the bibliographic recording of serials. One agency responsible for such a standard is the International Serials Data System (ISDS) whose International Centre is in Paris. This is an international registry of serial publications and serves to contribute to the standardization of serial citations, partly by the maintenance of common principles, cataloguing rules and a machine–readable format. There are 46 centres in 25 countries participating in the scheme including the British Library which is responsible for serials published in the UK. Its National Serials Data Centre (NSDC) acquires information about changes in serial publication patterns from publishers, organizations, existing catalogues and legal deposit. Its functions, together with other centres, are to:

1. provide identification and bibliographic control of the entire serials population;
2. assign ISSNs;
3. register serials published within respective countries and send records to Paris, and amend and update records;
4. build and maintain files, and
5. take part in standardization programmes and activities in relation to serials and their bibliographic control.

All serials entered in the ISDS are assigned a key title and an ISSN.

The three main objectives of the ISDS, as listed below, centre on the provision of bibliographic control:

1. to build and maintain an international register of serials from all countries and all disciplines, with sufficient information for the unambiguous identification of serials;
2. to make this information available to all countries, organizations and individuals; and
3. to establish a network of communications among libraries, secondary information services, publishers of serial literature and international organizations.

The ISDS has been in operation since 1971.

Another trend in the movement towards bibliographical control of serials was the formulation of the International Standard Bibliographic Description for Serials, ISBD(S), which was issued in 1974 and revised in 1988. This was developed separately from the ISDS outlines for identification and differs from it in several respects, mainly due to differing objectives. The ISDS record was developed independently of cataloguing rules, but the ISBD(S) was developed with cataloguing in mind and is thus rather fuller than the ISDS format. This latter does not, for example, have a title proper or edition area. The particular area of conflict is the title area. For the ISDS the key title is constructed according to the rules in the 'Guidelines for ISDS', but the ISBD(S) dictates that the title proper must be transcribed. This has caused particular problems with generic titles (such as Annual Report or Bulletin) because the rules used to form the ISDS key title and those used to form the title in the ISBD(S) are slightly different. A major problem is that the ISBD(S) does not provide precise advice on what constitutes a major or minor title change and may disregard the latter, whilst under the provisions of the ISDS minor title changes would require a new record, including a new ISSN and a new key title. This, in turn, leads to the situation where several ISSNs and key titles can apply to one ISBD(S). Conversely, the ISDS rule that a publication in several formats (for example, microfilm and paper) can keep the same ISSN leads to one ISDS record having several ISBD(G) records.

Obviously, ISBD(S) has been incorporated into AACR2R. However, the latter has created additional problems with choice of entry or access points for serials. Serials with generic or non-distinctive titles were entered under the corporate body issuing them according to AACR1. This led to inconsistencies with ISDS practice and resulted in changes in the recommendations for entry of serials for AACR2R. Now almost all serials are entered under title. These changes have meant modifications, some very time-consuming, to serials catalogues in libraries. One of the predictable outcomes of entry under title has been the proliferation of serials titles. For example, one record in *Serials in the British Library* may include four titles: a uniform title as heading, a title proper at the beginning of the descriptive part of the record, a key title and an abbreviated key title both in the notes.

A further contribution to the international bibliographic control of serials was the CONSER Project (Conversion of Serials). Begun in 1973, CONSER was conceived by an *ad hoc* discussion group of American and Canadian librarians on serials databases. They aimed to create a consolidated database, with OCLC as host. The 12 original participants began to convert their records into machine-readable form, using the Minnesota Union List of Serials (MULS) and the Library of Congress MARC(S) file as a base. CONSER's guidelines on standards – the 'Agreed-upon-Practices' – stated that the requirements of ISSN, ISBD(S), AACR, US MARC, Canadian MARC and the ALA catalog code should all be met. This inevitably created some problems, and one serial may be represented by more than one record. These records are now available through the Library of Congress MARC(S) records. From 1982, CONSER also took over responsibility for producing *New Serial Titles*. CONSER is the American ISDS centre as well as the US national serials database. British libraries can access the CONSER database either directly through OCLC or via BLAISE.

Other cooperatives and libraries also have serials records. Those of BLCMP union serials list have been used as part of the basis of a national database. Newcastle University Library uses a record for serials which includes elements which pertain to both catalogue or holdings records and ordering data.

4.7 Analytical cataloguing

Most of the cataloguing conducted by libraries and other cataloguing agencies is concerned to produce records pertaining to individual works. This emphasis upon 'the work' reflects the packaging of text, information, music, graphics and so on,

Figure 4.3   Some serials records

(a) Serials in the British Library

PC leisure. — Winter 1989–. — London: EMAP Business and Computer, 1989–. — v.: col.ill; 30cm
ISSN 0959–1567 = PC leisure: No price

Paul Sacher Stiftung
Veröffentlichungen der Paul Sacher Stiftung. — Bd. 1.–. — Winterthur: Amadeus, 1990–. — ill, music.

Payline. — No. 1 (Feb. 1990)–. — Glasgow (24 Sandyford Place, Glasgow G3 7NG): Scottish Low Pay Unit, 1990–. — v.: ill, ports; 30cm. — Quarterly
ISSN 0959–602x = Payline (Glasgow): £10.00 per year

The PC buyers guide. — Issue 1 (Dec. 1988)–. — London: Dennis, 1988–. — v.: ill (some col.); 30cm. — Six issues yearly. — Continues: The Buyer's guide to the Amstrad PC. — Description based on: Issue 3 (Apr 1989)
ISSN 0956–8697 = PC buyers guide: £2.95 per issue

(b) Ulrich's international Periodicals Directory

613   US   ISSN 0279–3547   RA773
HEALTH; the magazine for total well-being. 1969. m. $22. Family Media, Inc., Women's and Fashion Group, 3 Park Ave., New York, NY 10016. TEL. 212–340–9200. Ed. Hank Herman. adv. bk. rev. charts. illus. stat. circ. 1,000,000. (also avail. in microform from UMI; reprint service avail. from UMI) Indexed: Biol. Abstr. R.G. Acad.Ind. Biol.Dig. Can.Per. Ind. C.I.N.I. CHNI. Curr.Lit.Fam.Plan. Gen.Sci.Ind. Mag.Ind. PMR. Phys.Ed. Ind. Sportsearch. TOM.
Formerly: Family Health (ISSN 0014–7249);
Incorporating: Today's Health (ISSN 0040–8514)
Description: Edited for active, health-conscious women with information on the world of health-nutrition and related fields. Departments include health, beauty, food, nutrition and others.

613.194   UK   ISSN 0017–8888
HEALTH AND EFFICIENCY. (Text in English, French, German) 1899. 16/yr. $48. Peenhill Ltd., 2nd floor, 67–73 Worship St., London EC24 2DU, England. Ed. Kate Sturdy. adv. bk. rev. illus. circ. 130,000.
Description: News, views and reflections on the nudist and naturist scene, including areas where nudity and naked living are accepted.

613.7   US   ISSN 0893–6242   RA565.A1
HEALTH & ENVIRONMENT DIGEST. 1987. m. $75 (foreign $90) Freshwater Foundation, 2500 Shadywood Rd, Box 90, Naverro, MN 55392. TEL 612–471–9292. Ed. Barbara Scott Murdock. index. circ. 1,500. (looseleaf format; back issues avail.)

and indicates to the subsequent user what packages are available for use or consultation. In the sense that libraries lend works as units, and publishers and distributors also make works available as entire units, this approach is understandable. Nevertheless, the conventional bibliographic approach of listing individual works has limitations, one of the most obvious being that it is sometimes difficult to decide what constitutes a separate work. Is the individual monograph in a monograph series the work, or should the whole series be seen as the work? With a set of Ordnance Survey maps, should the entire set be treated as one map, or should the individual components covering the various areas of the country be regarded as distinct works? The definition of a 'work' has eluded cataloguers for many years, and AACR2R has not found a solution. In fact, AACR2R has been criticized on the grounds that it does not identify the cataloguing unit to which its rules refer. The need to identify the cataloguing unit is becoming more pressing as the variety of available media expands and as computerized cataloguing systems offer new opportunities. Unfortunately, these factors simultaneously make the resolution of the situation more intractable.

Analytical cataloguing aims to emphasize the content of documents, rather than relying entirely upon cataloguing whole works. Obviously with the definition of what constitutes an entire work still pending, it is not easy to define analytical cataloguing precisely. Perhaps it is sufficient to say that analytical cataloguing identifies the components of works to a greater extent than in normal cataloguing practice. The intention is to provide access to specific parts of works. Analytical cataloguing is valuable in respect of any type of media, but many of its ideas have been tested most thoroughly in the context of monographs and serials. To take a simple example, analytical cataloguing would aim to make the text of *Hamlet* equally accessible whether it had been published as a separate volume or whether it was only part of a volume containing a collection of Shakespeare's plays. Similarly, there is no reason why a substantial chapter on China in a book considering the whole of Asia should not be as valuable as a separate leaflet on China. Analytical cataloguing thus seeks to overcome physical packaging.

Analytical cataloguing is practised to varying extents in libraries. Abstracting and indexing services and associated databases are often relied upon to provide access to the contents of works, but some libraries also feel that it is appropriate to undertake some local analytical cataloguing. The constraint which prevents extensive analytical cataloguing, despite its attraction to users, is that it represents an extra burden on the processing facilities of a library. Any analytical entries which are made must be in addition to the standard catalogue entries for complete works. Each library must make policy decisions concerning whether it will indulge in analytical cataloguing and if so, to which categories of works it will apply.

Recommendations relating to analytical cataloguing practices are primarily concerned with the way in which the part of a document or work to be accessed is described. Obviously the access points for analytical entries are also important, but there is little need for separate comment upon these since they must be consistent with the access points used for the catalogue entries for complete works. In other words, in a catalogue with author and subject access, analytical entries will have either author's names or subject terms or notation as headings. No special provision need be made for analytical entries.

The format of the description in an analytical entry requires careful consideration. The style of description may depend on the nature of the relationship between the part and the whole. The parts to be described may be individual volumes in a series or parts of individual volumes. This distinction is not necessarily relevant to the literary or information content of the document, but will influence the appropriate form for the analytical entry.

There are two tools which discuss the compilation of analytical entries: AACR2R and ISBD(CP), where CP stands for component parts.

4.8   AACR2R and analytical cataloguing

In Chapter 13, AACR2R identifies the following categories of analytical entry:

1.   *Analytics of monographic series and multipart monographs*
If an item is part of a monographic series or a multipart monograph and has a title not dependent on that of the whole item, an analytical entry may be prepared in terms of a complete description of the part by using the series area. For example:

> English costume 1890–1910/R M Small.-
> Oxford: Heather Press, 1984. xx, 325p.:ill.;23cm-
> (A History of English costume; v.8).-

2.   *Note area*
If a comprehensive entry for a larger work is made, this entry may contain a display of parts in the note area (normally in a contents note). For example:

> The Wimsey family/edited by C W Scott-Giles.-
> London: Victor Gollancz, 1977.-87.:ill.;23 cm-
> Contents: The Search for Wimseys/by C W Scott-Giles.-The Early
> Wimseys/by R M Brown.-The Barons/by C R Overton.-The Earls of Denver/by N M
> Howe.-The Dukes of Denver/by R S Teem.

3.   *Analytical added entries*
If a comprehensive entry for a larger work is made that shows the part in either the title and statement of responsibility area or the note area, an added entry may be made for the heading appropriate to the part. This can give direct access to a part of a document without resorting to an additional bibliographic record for the part. For example, an added author/title entry could be made for the work, starting Overton, C R, The Barons. . .

4.   *In analytics*
If more bibliographic description is needed for the part than can be obtained by displaying it in the note area, an 'in' analytic entry may be considered. This consists of two parts: the description of the part and a short citation of the whole item in which the part is to be found. For example:

> The discovery of New Zealand/M R Costa.-

p. 210–306; 23 cm.
In: Rom, R S Australasia; discovery and early history.-Sydney:
Downunder Press, 1984.

5. *Multi-level description*

Multi-level description is normally used by national bibliographies and cataloguing agencies that prepare entries needing complete identification of both parts and comprehensive whole in a single record that shows as its primary element the description of the whole. The descriptive information is divided into two or more levels: first level for the multi-part item as a whole, and second level for information relating to a group of parts or to the individual part. For example:

Sources for a history of the Sparry family/extracted by Stella & Erle Sparry.-Trowbridge (Victoria Rd., Trowbridge,Wilts [BA14 7LD]): R E Sparry
Vol. 1: Sparry wills 1600–1699–[1982].-94 leaves in various foliations; 20 cm.

4.9 ISBD(CP)

The International Standard Bibliographic Description for Component Parts was published in its fifth draft in 1981. In the draft, a 'component part' is defined as:

Any document that for the purposes of bibliographic identification or access requires reference to a host document of which it forms a part. Component parts include articles in journals, illustrations and maps in printed text, an aria in a music score, or a music score issued with a sound recording.

There was substantial criticism of this draft, but no further revision emerged. Instead the problem has been tackled from a different angle by the publication in 1988 of 'Guidelines for the Application of ISBDs to the Description of Component Parts'. These Guidelines must be used in conjunction with the ISBDs for the host item in which the component part is located. The description of the component part comprises four segments:

1. the description of the component part;
2. a linking element relating the description of the component part to the identification of the host item;
3. the identification of the host item, and
4. details on the location of the part within the host item.

The Guidelines lead to records that are similar to those obtained through the application of AACR2R, but there are some minor differences: the location of the part within the host item – the relevant pagination – is given after the identification of the host item instead of with the description of the component part. This is illustrated by the following examples:

55

1. ISBD(CP) Version
   Music cataloguing and classification: towards 2001/Kylie Brown and Charles Forester.
   In: Journal of music – Los Angeles: Music Association. – ISSN 0018–6534.–Vol.6, no.5
   (May 1991), p. 45–56.

2. AACR2R Version
   Music cataloguing and classification: towards 2001/ Kylie Brown and Charles Forester. -
   p. 45–56; 25 cm.
   In JOURNAL OF MUSIC. -vol. 6, no.5 (May 1991)

Recommended reading

A. Nonbook materials

American Library Association, Description and Access Task Force on the Application of AACR2 (Chapter 9) to the description of microcomputer software (1983),
'A report on the problems already encountered in applying AACR2 to micro software',
Washington DC: ALA.
Betz (comp.) (1982), *Graphic materials: rules for describing items and historical collections*, Washington, DC: Library of Congress.
Descriptive terms for graphic materials: genre and physical characteristics, Washington, DC: Library of Congress, 1987.
Fothergill, R and Butchart, I (1990), *Non-book materials in libraries: a practical guide*, 3rd edition, London: Library Association.
Frost, C O (1983), *Cataloguing non-book materials: problems in theory and practice*, Littleton, Colo: Libraries Unlimited.
Gorman, M and Winkler, P W (1984), 'Guidelines for using AACR2 Chapter 9 for cataloging microcomputer software', ALA Committee on Cataloguing: Description and Access, Cataloguing and Classification Section, Chicago: ALA.
Horner, J (1976), *Special cataloguing*, London: Bingley.
Intner, S and Smiraglia, R (eds) (1987), *Policy and practice in bibliographic control of nonbook media*, Chicago: American Library Association.
LC Thesaurus for graphic materials: topical terms for subject access, Washington, DC: Library of Congress, 1987.
Richmond, S (1982), 'Problems in applying AACR2 to music materials', *Library Resources and Technical Services*, **26** (2), 204–11.
Rogers, J V (1987), *Nonprint cataloging for multimedia collections: a guide based on AACR2*, Littleton, Colo: Libraries Unlimited.
Soergel, D (1988), *Organising information: principles of database and retrieval systems*, Orlando, Flo.: Academic Press.
Stibbs, H L P (ed) (1982), 'Cartographic materials: a manual of interpretation for AACR2', prepared by the Anglo-American Cataloging Committee for Cartographic Materials, Chicago, Ottawa and London: ALA, CLA and LA.

Templeton, R and Witten, A (1984), *Study of cataloguing computer software: applying AACR2 to microcomputer programs*, London: British Library.

B. Periodicals

Note: For further readings on automation of serials management, consult some of the readings listed at the end of Chapter 21.

Anderson, D (1983), 'Compatibility of ISDS and ISBD(S) records in international exchange: the background', *International Cataloguing*, **12** (2), 14–17.

Bourne, R (1980), *Serials librarianship*, London: Library Association.

Bryant, P (1988), 'Bibliographic access to serials: a study for the British Library', *Serials*, **1** (3), 41–46.

Franzmeier, G (1983), 'Can ISDS replace ISBD(S)?' *International Cataloguing*, **12** (4), 41–44.

International Organization for Standardization Documentation (1986), 'International standard serial numbering (ISSN), Geneva: ISO.

Library of Congress, *LC rule interpretations*, edited by R M Hiatt, 1st edition, (1988), 2nd edition (1989), Washington DC: Library of Congress Cataloging Distribution Service (looseleaf cumulative edition, quarterly updates).

McQueen, J and Boss, R W (1984), 'Serials control in libraries: automated options', *Library Technology Reports*, March–April, 89–282.

Mullis, A A (ed) (1983), *ISDS Manual*, prepared by the ISDS International Centre, Paris: ISDS International Centre.

Osborn, A (1980), *Serial publications: their place and treatment in libraries*, 3rd edition, Chicago: ALA.

Paul, H (1985), 'Serials automation: yesterday, today and tomorrow', *Serials Librarian*, **10** (1/2), 91–95.

Rush, J E (ed) (1983), *Library systems evaluation guide*, vol 1: Serials Control, James E Rush Associates.

Szilvassy, J (1983), 'ISDS and ISBD(S) records in international exchange: compatibility issues', *International Cataloguing*, **12** (4), 38–41.

Unesco (1982), *Guidelines for the compilation of union catalogues of serials*, Paris: Unesco.

Woodward, H and Hobbs, S (1990), 'UKSG serials automation survey 1989', *Serials*, **3** (1), 18–22.

5 Summaries, manual files and full-text databases

5.1 Introduction

The previous chapters have considered in some detail both the statement of the source of a document and the description of documents by bibliographic records. Libraries and information centres are indeed primarily concerned with bibliographic databases, but many databases contain more than the type of bibliographic description outlined in the previous chapters. Bibliographic databases which refer to documents may include document summaries for some or all of their records. Cataloguing databases may thus include brief annotations, whereas the databases associated with abstracting and indexing tools commonly used for information retrieval will often contain abstracts or other document summaries.

The past few years have witnessed a substantial growth in the number of documents available in electronic form, coupled with the emergence of electronic publishing. Many electronic documents have a print-based equivalent or are a by-product of the creation of a printed document; some documents, such as electronic journals, exist only in electronic form. Some of the earlier applications of electronic documents were full-text databases containing extracts from legal texts or directories and statistical and chemical data. These have now been joined by a large and increasing number of other electronic documents in the form of journals, directories, encyclopedias, dictionaries and newspapers. Whilst some of these databases are available online via the online hosts, many of them are available on CD-ROM. CD-ROM and other optical storage media have fuelled the escalating number of full-text databases. Optical discs have a large capacity and cannot only store large quantities of text, but can also handle graphics and images.

5.2 Document summaries in bibliographic databases

There are a number of different kinds of document summaries. We will now consider some of the more common options:

1. An *abstract* is a concise and accurate representation of the contents of a

document, in a style similar to that of the original. An abstract covers all of the main points made in the original document, and usually follows its style and arrangement. Unless specified otherwise, abstracts are non-critical. Criticism is not appropriate in a style which aims to report, but not comment upon, the content of the original document. Abstracts are self-contained and complete, although they do assume some subject knowledge. No reference to the original should be necessary in order to understand the abstract.

2. An *annotation* is a note added to the title and/or other bibliographic information concerning a document by way of comment or explanation. In cataloguing, the term annotation is often used to refer to the notes section of a standard bibliographic description, as discussed in Chapter 3. Annotations encountered in bibliographies may be less stylized and more likely to concentrate on conveying more of the subject content of a document. Although there are some similarities between annotations and abstracts, the objectives of an annotation are generally more limited than those of an abstract, and hence the annotation will tend to be briefer.

3. An *extract* comprises one or more portions of a document selected to represent the whole. Such representative sections may not often be present in documents, but sometimes an extract from the results, conclusions or recommendations may serve to identify the key issues covered. Extracts are unlikely to offer a balanced account of the content of a document, but may be valuable to a reader particularly interested in the outcome of a study.

4. A *summary* is a restatement, within the document, of its salient findings and conclusions. A summary at the end of a document is intended to complete the orientation of the reader and to highlight the significant ideas to remember. A summary at the beginning of a document serves to prepare the reader before proceeding to the remainder of the text. A summary differs from an abstract in that it assumes that the reader will have the opportunity to peruse the accompanying text. Hence, certain elements essential to a complete understanding of the text, such as sections on background, purpose and methodology, tend to be absent from a summary.

5. Many other terms are used to denote a regurgitation or abbreviation of a document's content. An *abridgement* is usually taken to be a condensation that necessarily omits a number of secondary points. Abridgement is a relatively general term. A *précis* is an account which restricts itself to the essential points in an argument. A *paraphrase* is an interpretation of the concepts featured in a document; the writer refashions the argument in his own words. A *digest* should be a methodically arranged presentation of the main arguments in a document. A *synopsis* is one type of résumé prepared by the author of a work.

The definitions given above are intended to help in recognizing different types of document summaries. The wide array of such terms serves to demonstrate the range of perspectives on document summaries and emphasizes that any one document can be summarized in a number of different styles. Whilst one writer may look for a balanced account of the key points, another may almost exclusively emphasize conclusions; a third may deal only with a specific element of the methodology (for example, the catalyst used in a chemical process or the questionnaire used in a survey), while a fourth may be more concerned with the impact that a given document may have in the subject field than on the details of its contents. It is also important to recognize, that whilst the definitions given above represent common usage of the terms, different groups may well define the terms differently. In practice the distinction between one term and the next is not very precise.

5.3 More on abstracts

Probably the most important of the document summaries identified above is the abstract. Abstracts are widely used as an aid to the reader in assessing the contents of a document; that is, as an aid in the selection of documents for further consultation. Abstracts are found in primary publications generally accompanying reports of research and other developments in both the published and unpublished report literature, in journal articles, in reports of professional, scientific and technical meetings and conferences, theses, books and patent applications and specifications. In a journal most formal items (including articles, essays, discussions and reviews) can be expected to be accompanied by an abstract.

Abstracts have for some years been a major component in published abstracting services, literature reviews and bibliographies. Large bibliographic databases also use abstracts as the primary means of document representation. It naturally follows that many retrospective search services and current awareness services derived from or associated with these databases also feature abstracts. Wherever abstracts are found they are included to save the user's time in information-gathering and selection.

A number of types of abstracts or labels exist. The most appropriate type of abstract must be chosen in accordance with the requirements of each individual application. This will be a function of the nature of the original document (for example, language, length, audience level), the intended audience of the abstract and the resources of the abstracting agency. Some of the different types are worth examining since they demonstrate in more detail the various functions of abstracts.

Informative abstracts present as much of the quantitative or qualitative information contained in a document as possible. The objective is to aid the assessment of document relevance and, at the same time, to offer a substitute for the document when only a superficial knowledge of content is required. Thus an informative abstract actually conveys some of the information in the original, rather than restricting itself to reporting what information is available in the original. Informative abstracts tend to be relatively lengthy. Abstracts of journal articles merit 100 to 250 words, whilst those of lengthy theses or reports may extend to 500 words. Informative abstracts are appropriate for texts describing experimental work and documents with a central theme. A fully informative abstract may often be impossible to write for a wide-ranging discussion paper or review, since these documents are likely to cover a large number of separate concepts. To cover each of these concepts informatively would lead to an excessively long abstract. A working guide is to seek to make any abstract as informative as possible within the constraints of time, length and audience.

Indicative abstracts are suitable for discussions and review articles of books and, in some circumstances, conference proceedings, reports without conclusions, essays and bibliographies. An indicative abstract restricts itself to indicating the content of an item and makes general statements about the document. Indicative abstracts abound in phrases such as 'is discussed' or 'has been surveyed', but do not record the outcome of the discussion or survey. An indicative abstract is merely a sophisticated selection aid. It can be written more quickly than an informative abstract, and requires less perception and subject expertise on the part of the abstractor.

Indicative-informative abstracts are more common than either the purely indicative or the purely informative abstract. Parts of the abstract are written in the informative style, whilst those points which are of less significance are treated indicatively. When used by skilled abstractors, this mixture of styles can achieve the maximum transmission of information within a minimum length.

Although *critical abstracts* are unusual, they are often favoured by users (until they discover the cost!). A critical abstract evaluates a document and the work that it records. Typically a critical abstract will note the depth and extent of the work, commenting upon the experimentation and methodology, the assumed background of the intended audience and the significance of its contribution to the development of knowledge. A critical approach permits the abstractor to highlight particularly worthwhile documents and to dismiss those that have little new to say. In practice critical abstracts are rare and certainly do not usually feature in published secondary services. In order to prepare effective critical abstracts, the abstractor needs a sound knowledge of the subject field and of its literature in addition to abstracting skills. Such abstractors are expensive to employ.

There are a number of types of abstract which can be grouped under the term *'mini-abstracts'*. Since a title is a fair indication of document content, many indexes and current awareness services rely almost entirely upon titles. Short abstracts comprising only one or two sentences may be valuable in current awareness services where speed is essential, such as newsletters for local government officers and commercial current awareness services. Telegraphic abstracts are written in a note form or in a telegram style. Keywords or indexing terms may serve as a crude indicator of the subject scope of a document.

Statistical, tabular and numerical abstracts are a means of summarizing numerical data, which may be presented in its original tabular format. Normally, the most

Figure 5.1 Examples of five different types of abstracts

Below are five different types of abstracts relating to the same document:
J E Rowley (1990), 'Guidelines on the evaluation and selection of library software packages', *Aslib Proceedings*, **42** (9), September, 225–35.

Informative abstract
The evaluation and selection of a library software package (whether it be for library housekeeping, text retrieval or the creation of some other database) should be approached as a project. Strategies for the selection and evaluation of software packages can be based on systems analysis and design methodologies. Stages in the project should include: definition of objectives, evaluation of options, definition, selection and design, implementation, and evaluation and maintenance. The features to seek in text retrieval systems can be grouped into data entry, indexing, interactive information retrieval, output, current awareness, security, contract and other general issues. A checklist for library management systems also needs to encompass security, contract and similar general issues, but in addition needs to specify the features of the acquisitions, cataloguing and circulation control modules. Recent developments in database structures, retrieval facilities, the screen interface and integration with other systems must be noted.

Indicative abstract
The evaluation and selection of a library software package (whether it be for library housekeeping, text retrieval or the creation of some other database) should be approached as a project. Strategies for the selection and evaluation of software packages are considered. The following stages in the project are reviewed: definition of objectives, evaluation of options, definition, selection and design, implementation, and evaluation and maintenance. Some checklists of features to seek in text retrieval and library management systems are included. These are discussed in the context of new developments in software.

Extract
This article proposes a strategy for the selection and evaluation of library software packages. Two checklists review the key features of text retrieval software and library management systems.

Short abstract
Strategies for the selection and evaluation of software packages are outlined. Two checklists summarize the features to seek in text retrieval and library management software.

Keywords
Library management systems; text retrieval systems; systems analysis and design.

effective way of summarizing a table is to produce a simplified table. Such abstracts can be useful for various types of economic, social and business information.

There are other kinds of abstracts, but this introduction should demonstrate a large number of the possibilities. The examples in Figure 5.1 provide some useful comparisons between different types of abstracts.

5.4 Manual files and records management

Manual files and filing systems are still used widely for the storage, organization and retrieval of documents. Most organizations store a significant proportion of their records in manual files which may hold correspondence, sales documentation, financial documents, leaflets, official documents, contracts – indeed, any kind of document that an organization needs to retain for information or as a record of transactions or communication. Such files may be shared, restricted to one department or personal. Manual files thus form the core of the records management systems of many organizations. Libraries also use manual files for small and ephemeral items that will not stand alone on shelves. This section is a brief introduction to manual files in the wider context of full-text databases.

Physical form of files

Since accessibility to the documents stored in files is an important factor, the type of physical storage used is vital. A number of relatively straightforward possibilities exist:

1. Drawers of standard filing cabinets, with folders or pockets or both. Folders allow a set of papers on a given topic to be kept together when removed from the file. Pockets maintain a space for each category.
2. File boxes can be used and, if appropriate, interfiled with books on shelves. This arrangement may facilitate browsing across different kinds of materials.
3. Upright divider filing is a variation on filing cabinets.
4. Guard book or scrapbook-type arrangement, possibly with a loose-leaf format, is suitable for organizing and keeping cuttings, letters and other small items. The drawbacks of this form are its limited flexibility and the time taken in maintenance.
5. Small documents, such as cuttings, can alternatively be mounted on catalogue cards.
6. Aperture cards, where the full text of the document is kept in a special index card in the form of a microfiche, have been used for various collections, for instance, of patents and technical drawings.

Headings

Each file will be labelled with a heading which corresponds with the material to be organized. The possible types of headings are various, but in many files these will be subject headings of some kind, possibly drawn from an alphabetical list of subject headings or from a classification scheme. Apart from the names of subjects, the names of corporate bodies, persons, chemicals, trade products and trade names are some other possibilities. For example, a set of slides for use by teachers may be indexed according to alphabetical subject headings. A set of government publications could be filed alphabetically by the issuing bureau and then by title of the particular series in numerical order.

The principles for the construction of headings for use in files are the same as those for the construction of similar types of headings in other indexes, except that the limitations listed below may pose some problems.

Limitations of files

Leaving aperture cards aside, all files have some common limitations:

1. Files only work effectively for a limited number of documents. If the number of categories becomes large, cross-reference between individual files will be necessary. If the number of items in one category becomes large, then the user must scan a larger number of documents in order to identify relevant items.
2. Items in a file can only be stored in one place and in one sequence. It follows that only a limited number of relationships can be displayed, and retrieval tends to be inflexible.
3. Files are difficult to publish or disseminate in any form.

Against these limitations, it must be remembered that files are quick to compile and give direct retrieval (no index is necessary as an intermediate guide). The approach or basic arrangement of the file can be supplemented by additional approaches in supplementary indexes.

5.5 Source databases

Source databases contain the original source data; they are documents stored in electronic form, although some have printed equivalents. The contents of such databases may be as varied as the contents of the printed book, including numbers, tables, figures, graphics and text. Indeed such databases may go beyond the constraints of print and be truly multi-media embracing, in addition to full text and numeric data, computer software, images, sound, maps and charts. These databases can be accessed online through the online hosts or on CD-ROM or via videotext and teletext. Chapters 19 and 20 deal with these topics in greater detail, including how to search the various different databases. This chapter merely demonstrates the range and nature of the databases available.

Since a wide variety of types of source databases exists, it is difficult to make generalizations. In Chapter 1 source databases were divided into the following categories: numeric, full-text, text-numeric and referral, the last type being categorized with bibliographic databases. However, these are also source databases and so may be considered further in this section. Source databases may include the full

Figure 5.2 Some source databases available on Dialog

Full-Text Databases	Harvard Business Review (journal)
	McGraw-Hill Publications Online (journal)
	Computer News Fulltext (journal)
	Washington Post Online (newspaper)
	Los Angeles Times (newspaper)
	The Agrochemicals Handbook (handbook)
	Financial Times Fulltext (newspaper)
	IIC International Annual Reports (reports)
Directories	Ulrich's International Periodical Directory
	Moody's Corporate Profiles (also numeric)
	Kompass Europe
	ICC British Company Directory
	Extel International Financial Cards (also numeric)
	Merck Index Online
	Encyclopaedia of Associations
	Drug Information Fulltext
	D + B Canadian Dun's Market identifiers
	Disclosure Database (also numeric)
Numeric Databases	D + B – Dun's Financial Records Plus
	Econbase: Time Series and Forecasts
	ICC International Annual Reports (also full-text)
	PTS Promt (also full-text)
	Cendata (also full-text)

texts of journal articles, newsletters, newswires, dictionaries, directories and many other source materials. Some source databases do not contain the complete contents of a printed equivalent, but offer only selective coverage. Figure 5.2 lists some of the source databases available on Dialog and indicates their nature. Figure 5.3 shows typical records from several source databases.

In order to convey their contents more fully, the next section describes four source databases. These examples are taken from databases that can be accessed through the online hosts, though further examples could be drawn from those available on CD–ROM.

1. *The McGraw-Hill Publications Online database* provides the complete text of many major McGraw-Hill publications including, for example, *Byte, Chemical Engineering, Coal Week, Integrated Waste Management, LAN Times* and *Securities Week*. The database covers both general business as well as specific industries, including aerospace, chemical processing, electronics and construction.

2. *The Washington Post database* provides national political coverage and in–depth investigative reporting of government policies and operations in Washington DC and around the world.

65

Figure 5.3   Some records from source databases
(a)Disclosure on Data-Star

Sample Document

AN F181970000 8800.
CO FEDERAL EXPRESS CORP.
AD 2005 CORPORATE AVENUE
    MEMPHIS, TN 38132
    Telephone: 901-369-3600.
LE This document has footnotes (approximately 24 PC screens).
HI Ticker symbol: FDX
    Exchange: NYS
    Incorporation: DE
    Fortune number: T015
    Forbes number: SA210 AS472 PR249 MV231
    Cusip number: 0003133090
    Duns number: 05-807-0459
    Number of employees: 35,500 (SOURCE: 10-K)
    Fiscal year end: 05/31
    Latest annual financial date: 05/31/87
    Latest quarterly financial date: 02/28/88
    Auditor change: NA
    Auditor: ARTHUR ANDERSEN & CO. (SOURCE: 10-K)
    Auditor's report: UNQUALIFIED
    Legal counsel: WARING COX
    Stock transfer agent: FIRST NATIONAL BANK OF CHICAGO.
PN Primary SIC code: 4511
    SIC codes: 4511 7513
    Description of business:
    ENGAGED IN PROVIDING AN OVERNIGHT, DOOR-TO-DOOR DELIVERY
    SERVICE FOR SMALL PACKAGES AND DOCUMENTS EACH BUSINESS
    DAY BETWEEN AIRPORTS IN THE U.S.A. AND CERTAIN POINTS IN
    CANADA.
SH 52,581,975 Current Outstanding shares (SOURCE: 10-Q 03/31/88)
    4,718,110 Shares held by Officers and Directors (SOURCE: PROXY)
    6,902 Shareholders (SOURCE: 10-K).
SU Five-Year Summary

YEAR	SALES (000'S)	NET INCOME (000'S)	EPS
1987	3,178,308	-65,571	-1.27
1986	2,573,229	131,839	2.64
1985	2,015,920	76,077	1.61
1984	1,436,305	115,430	2.52
1983	1,008,087	88,933	2.03
GROWTH RATE:	53.8	-43.4	-40.6.

BA ANNUAL BALANCE SHEET ASSETS

(IN 000'S)	05/31/87	05/31/86
Cash	6,685	7,536
Marketable Securities	15,000	177,500
Receivables	399,333	347,010
Inventories	39,933	49,342
Raw Materials	NA	NA
Work in Progress	NA	NA
Finished Goods	NA	NA
Notes Receivable	NA	NA
Other Current Assets	46,529	31,902
Total Current Assets	507,480	613,290
Property, Plant/Equip.	2,712,052	2,202,601
Accumulated Depreciation	850,620	650,756
Net Property/Plant/Equip.	1,861,432	1,551,845
Investment and Advances	NA	NA
Other non-current Assets	NA	NA
Deferred Charges	NA	NA
Intangibles	NA	NA
Deposits & Other Assets	130,599	111,227
Total Assets	2,499,511	2,276,362.

LA ANNUAL BALANCE SHEET LIABILITIES

(IN 000'S)	05/31/87	05/31/86
Notes Payable	NA	NA
Accounts Payable	192,877	184,534
Current Long Term Debt	60,393	72,979
Cur Port. Capti Leases	NA	NA
Accrued Expenses	250,455	174,397
Income Taxes	NA	NA
Other Current Liabi.	NA	NA
Total Current Liabl.	503,725	431,910
Mortgages	NA	NA
Deferred Charges/Income	171,952	189,513
Convertible Debt	NA	NA
Long Term Debt	744,914	561,716
Non-Cur Capital Leases	NA	NA

Capital Surplus	571,071	530,618
Retained Earnings	536,386	598,215
Treasury Stock	NA	NA
Other Liabilities	-33,700	-42,200
Shareholder's Equity	1,078,920	1,093,223
Total Liab. and Net Worth	2,499,511	2,276,362.

IA ANNUAL INCOME STATEMENT

(IN 000'S)	05/31/87	05/31/86	05/31/85
Net Sales	3,178,308	2,606,210	2,030,661
Cost of Goods	1,986,365	489,147	370,854
Gross Profit	1,191,943	2,117,063	1,659,807
R & D Expenditures	NA	NA	NA
Sell, General & Admin Exp	587,909	1,692,518	1,350,751
Income before Depr/Amort	604,034	424,545	309,056
Deprec & Amortization	239,291	212,404	172,333
Non-operating Income	-6,166	17,569	27,444
Interest Expense	46,692	65,505	80,789
Income before Tax	311,885	164,205	83,378
Provision for Income Taxe	144,933	32,366	7,301
Minority Interest	NA	NA	NA
Investment Gains/Losses	NA	NA	NA
Other Income	NA	NA	NA
Net Inc before Extr Items	166,952	131,839	76,077
Extrao. Items & Discontin	NA	NA	NA
Net Income	166,952	131,839	76,077
Outstanding Shares	51,630	50,808	48,060.

CD ANNUAL FUNDS FLOW

(IN 000'S)	05/31/87	05/31/85
SOURCE OF FUNDS		
Income before Extr Items	166,952	76,077
Depreciation & Depletion	239,291	172,333
Deferred Income Taxes	69,018	54,393
Min Int/Equit in Sub/Aff.	NA	NA
Other Funds fm Operations	NA	NA
Total Funds by Operations	475,261	302,803
Funds used for Extr Items	NA	NA
Sales of Prop Plant&Equip	6,751	149,503
Issuance of Longterm Debt	299,911	610,807
Sale of Stock	39,521	19,049
Other Sources of Funds	NA	15,834
Total Sources of Funds	821,444	1,097,996
USES OF FUNDS		
Dividends	NA	NA
Capital Expenditures	NA	571,054
Increase in Invest	NA	NA
Decrease in Longterm Dept	116,713	438,457
Purchase of Stock	NA	2,114
Acquisitions	722,369	NA
Other Uses of Funds	159,987	52,331
Total Uses of Funds	999,069	1,063,956
Incr/Decr in Working Cap.	-177,625	34,040.

BQ QUARTERLY BALANCE SHEET ASSETS

(IN 000'S)	08/31/87	11/30/87	02/28/88
Cash	48,003	66,631	24,586
Marketable Securities	NA	NA	NA
Receivables	430,612	465,575	510,274
Inventories	41,795	43,991	47,197
Raw Materials	NA	NA	NA
Work in Progress	NA	NA	NA
Finished Goods	NA	NA	NA
Notes Receivable	NA	NA	NA
Other Current Assets	26,613	40,654	38,937
Current Assets	547,023	616,851	620,994
Property, Plant/Equip.	2,822,731	3,001,000	3,125,357
Accumulated Depreciation	908,595	968,092	1,040,541
Net Property/Plant/Equip.	1,914,136	2,032,908	2,084,816
Investment and Advances	NA	NA	NA
Other non-current Assets	NA	NA	NA
Deferred Charges	NA	NA	NA
Intangibles	NA	NA	NA
Deposits & Other Assets	140,488	138,382	167,403
Total Assets	2,601,647	2,788,141	2,873,213.

LQ QUARTERLY BALANCE SHEET LIABILITIES

(IN 000'S)	08/31/87	11/30/87	02/28/88
Notes Payable	NA	NA	NA
Accounts Payable	159,609	201,214	190,800
Current Long Term Dept	63,221	64,227	63,679
Cur Port. Capti Leases	NA	NA	NA
Accrued Expenses	266,577	309,442	273,941
Income Taxes	NA	NA	NA
Other Current Liabi.	NA	NA	NA

Figure 5.3   Continued
(b) Data monitor market reports on Data-Star

Sample document

AN	Q000202 900800
TI	BAKERY AND CEREAL: BREAD.
SO	DATAMONITOR
	106 BAKER STREET
	LONDON W1M 1LA
	TEL: 07 l–625 8548
	FAX: 071–625 5080
	TELEX: 291126 OPUS G.
DT	900301.
CN	GBR (UNITED KINGDOM).
LE	62049 Characters, approximately 37 PC screens.

TC			
	INTRODUCTION/KEY ISSUES	TX	(1)
	MARKET SIZE	TX	(2)
	MARKET SEGMENTS	TX	(3)
	COMPETITION	TX	(4)
	ADVERTISING	TX	(5)
	RETAILING	TX	(6)
	CONSUMER ANALYSIS	TX	(7)
	FORECAST	TX	(8)

TX   1 OF 8.
INTRODUCTION
This sector covers all bread sales both in the wrapped and unwrapped sector. Morning goods such as baps and rolls are covered separately.
KEY ISSUES
The key issues covered in this sector are:
– The market for bread is the dominant bakery and cereal sector, twice the size of the cakes market.
– The market has struggled to add real value while volume has increased only marginally.
– The wrapped market is dominated by two manufacturers which ... etc

Figure 5.3   Continued
(c) Reuter on Textline

Headlines display

This screen displays the headlines of the articles retrieved – with the most recent appearing first:

REUTER TEXTLINE   HEADLINES DISPLAY   85 : COMPLETE

1. 16OCT90.USA: UNILEVER UNIT AWARDS ACCOUNT TO INTERPUBLIC'S LINTAS.
    [DJNR.WSJ] (3)
2. 15OCT90.USA: LEVER BROTHERS BEGINS REGIONAL ROLLOUT FOR DETERGENT.
    [DJNR.WSJ] (6)
3. 13OCT90.GERMANY: UNILEVER BEGINS PRODUCTION OF MARGERINE IN CHEMNITZ.
    [DW.SZ] (8)
4. 12OCT90.UK: ELIDA GIBBS AWARDED LICENCE FROM DEPARTMENT OF HEALTH FOR GUM
    HEALTH TOOTHPASTE.
    [CBNB.MCHMDI] (9)
5. 12OCT90.UK: SENSIQ LAUNCHES NEW CLASSIC COLLECTION MAKE-UP RANGE.
    [MKTW] (8)
6. 12OCT90.UK: CAMPAIGN POSTER ADVERTISING AWARDS 1990 – BEST USE OF
    ILLUSTRATION.
    [CMPN] (36)
7. 12OCT90.UK: OGILVY AND MATHER LAUNCHES NEW ADVERTISING CAMPAIGN FOR
    UNILEVER'S RADION.
    [CMPN] (13)

:

U/D to view more headlines   FL/UF/SF to flag, unflag, show flagged
Article no. to view full article   \ to return to search entry
Article no. and C for context (eg 4C)   ? for help
F1–Help F2–Top F3–Back F4–Paus F5–Prt F6–PvPg F7–NxPg F8–Capt F9–Macro F10–OFF!

Article Display

This displays the complete text of any article selected:

REUTER TEXTLINE   ARTICLE DISPLAY   85: COMPLETE   Page 1/1
3. 13OCT90.GERMANY: UNILEVER BEGINS PRODUCTION OF MARGERINE IN CHEMNITZ.
    [DW.SZ] (8)

Union Deutsche Lebensmittelwerke GmbH. part of the Unilever group, has begun production of the margerine brand Rama in Chemnitz. Up until now, Rama has been manufactured in Kleve, Hamburg and Mannheim. Chemnitzer Margarine Werk GmbH is still part of the combine Planzenoel und Lebensmittelwerke Magdeburg AG. By 1991, it is expected to supply 25 to 30% of the margerine requirement of the five new federal states. The Unilever subsidiary hopes to eventually acquire the Chemnitz plant with its 128 employees, subject to the approval of the Federal Cartels Office and Treuhandanstalt.

DIE WELT   13/10/90 P10
SUEDDEUTSCHE ZEITUNG   13/10/90 P35

:

U/D to view more text/articles   FL (to flag) or UF (to unflag)
Article no. to view another article   this article
\ to return to headline display

F1–Help F2–Top F3–Back F4–Paus F5–Prt F6–PvPg F7–NxPg F8–Capt F9–Macro F10–OFF!

3. *PTS Promt* is one of the family of databases from Predicasts. This multi–industry database provides international coverage of companies, products, markets and applied technologies. Abstracts and full–text records from more than 1000 of the world's business publications are included, offering information on markets, capital expenditures, mergers and acquisitions, research and development, new products and technologies, new and expanded facilities, product sales and consumption, financial reporting, market plans and strategies, management procedures, industry and business issues and related topics.

4. *The Merck Index Online database* is the online version of the tenth edition of *The Merck Index*, an internationally recognized encyclopaedia of chemicals, drugs and biochemicals. Records contain molecular formulae and weights, systematic chemical names, generic and trivial names, trademarks and their owners, company codes, CAS Registry numbers, physical and toxicity data, therapeutic and commercial uses, and bibliographic citations to the chemical, biomedical and patent literature.

Figure 5.4   A comparison of online full-text databases against print-on-paper databases

Online full-text database	Print-on-paper database
1. Pay-as-you-go costs, therefore cheap for occasional use.	Pay once only and make investment. Cheaper for extensive multiple use by an unsupervised public.
2. Updated regularly, sometimes continuously or every day or week.	Updated less frequently, for example, monthly, annually or even five-yearly.
3. Even where the frequency of updating is the same, the time lag in availability of information will usually be less for the electronic version.	
4. Users may be able to edit, modify and otherwise contribute to the database.	Publication and printing fixes the information. Note that sometimes this stability is welcome.
5. Greater range of retrieval facilities are possible, for example free-text searching.	Retrieval is limited by the printed indexes on offer.
6. More options for formatting output –any printed copy is controlled by the user.	Format of output is determined.
7. Portability and convenience limited.	Very portable, depending on whether it belongs to the user only.
8. Workstations must be available.	No terminals, networks or other technology is necessary.

5.6   Some comparisons

It will be a long time before all documents are available in machine–readable form, and even then they will probably still be available in more than one form. Improvements in document delivery services, via the further application of techniques such as facsimile transmission, will also have an important role to play. Figure 5.4 attempts to summarize some of the strengths of online full–text databases when compared with print on paper. A further comparison could be drawn between online databses and CD–ROM–based databases.

Recommended reading

A.   Summaries

American National Standards Institute (1979), 'American national standard for writing abstracts', New York: ANSI (Z39.14–1979).

Ashworth, W (1973), 'Abstracting as a fine art', *Information Scientist*, **7**, 43–53.

Ashworth, W (1975), 'Abstracts' in *Handbook of special librarianship and information work*, 3rd edition, London: Aslib, 124–52.

Borko H and Bernier, C L (1975), *Abstracting concepts and methods*, New York: Academic Press.

Cremmins, E T (1982), *The art of abstracting*, Philadelphia: ISI Press.

Fidel, R (1986), 'The possible effect of abstracting guidelines on retrieval performances of free-text searching', *Information Process Manager*, **22**, 309–16.

Fidel, R (1986), 'Writing abstracts for free-text searching', *Journal of Documentation*, **42** (2), 11–21.

International Organization for Standardization (1976), *Documentation: abstracts for publication and documentation*, Geneva: ISO.

Lancaster, F W (1991), *Indexing and abstracting in theory and practice*, London: Library Association.

Mathis, B A and Rush, J E (1985), 'Abstracting' in *Subject information analysis*, New York: Marcel Dekker, 245–484.

Rowley, J E (1988), *Abstracting and indexing*, 2nd edition, London: Library Association.

Thompson, C W N (1973), 'The functions of abstracts in the initial screening of technical documents by the user', *Journal of the American Society for Information Science*, **24**, 270–76.

B.   Other topics

Note: Additional readings on full-text databases and searching full-text databases using natural language indexing are listed at the end of Chapters 16 and 18.

Cook, M (1986), *Management of information from archives*, Aldershot: Gower.

Cook, M and Grant, K (1986), *A manual of archive description*, London: Society of Archivists.

Meunier, J G S *et al.* (1987), 'A call for enhanced representation of content as a means of improving online full-text retrieval'. *International Classification*, **14**, 2–8.

Schellenberg, T R (1956), *Modern archives, principles and techniques*, Melbourne: Chesire. Reprinted Chicago: Midway, 1975.

Tenopir, C (1985), 'Full-text database retrieval performance', *Online Review*, **9**, 149–64.

Tenopir, C (1985), 'Searching Harvard Business Review', *Online*, **9** (2), 71–78.

Tenopir, C (1988), 'Search strategies for full-text databases', Proceedings of the ASIS Annual Meeting, **25**, 80–86.

6 Computerized record formats and database structures

6.1 Record formats

The information which is stored in databases and data banks must be organized in a way that makes it easy to retrieve. A database is comprised of a series of records. A *record* is the information contained in a database relating to one document; for example, all the cataloguing information pertaining to a specific document. Records are composed of a number of fields. The types of fields used, their length and the number of fields in a record must be chosen in accordance with a specific application. For a bibliographic database, a field will generally be provided for each important element of the bibliographic record, including classification number, author, title, edition and indexing terms.

There are two types of fields. A *fixed-length field* is one which has the same length; that is, it contains the same number of characters in each record. With this degree of consistency, it is not necessary to signal to the computer the beginning and end of any given field. The lengths of the fields are determined when the database is designed and notified to the computer just once. Fixed-length fields are thus economical on storage space, and records using fixed-length fields are quick and easy to code. The drawback of fixed–length fields is their rigidity. They are entirely satisfactory when the length of the unit of information to be inserted is predictable, so that the field length can be set to coincide with the length of the data. Fixed–length fields are therefore particularly acceptable for codes, including ISBNs, dates, language codes, journal codes, identity numbers and membership numbers. For many other types of information fixed-length fields can be inconvenient. For example, if a title field is defined to be 60 characters in length, any title exceeding 60 characters will be truncated after the sixtieth character, and the end of the title will not be stored or displayed.

With variable-length data a *variable-length field* is more appropriate. A variable-length field takes different lengths in different records. Thus a name field might contain 30 characters in one record and 45 in the next. Obviously the computer cannot recognize when one field ends and the next starts – it merely sees the whole record as a series of characters. Since the fields are of different lengths in different records, it is necessary that the beginning and end of fields be flagged in some way.

Bibliographic databases often use a variety of fixed- and variable-length fields. The formats discussed below demonstrate the use of a mixture of field types.

Within fields, individual data elements or units of information may be designated as *subfields*. Subfields can only be identified if similar data elements can be expected within a given field across a number of records. Thus, in a name field it is easy to recognize that the data elements – family name and forename – will occur in many records, so that these two data elements can be identified as possible subfields of the same field. Subfields are also usually flagged in some way.

In order to pursue this discussion further, it is necessary to consider some specific examples of record formats. The next sections therefore undertake to describe a variety of record formats.

6.2   The MARC record format

The large cataloguing record databases are structured according to a format known as the MARC format. MARC stands for *MA*chine *R*eadable *C*ataloguing. The Library of Congress, the British Library and national cataloguing agencies in countries such as Canada, Australia, West Germany and France all produce catalogue records in the MARC format. These national catalogue record databases are used by libraries in catalogue creation. Records for the stock of a specific library are downloaded from the national databases and added to the database of catalogue records for the individual library. Thus, libraries using the national catalogue record databases will either use the MARC format for their catalogue records or 'stripped down' versions of MARC or other modifications to it. Thus, with respect to catalogue records the MARC format is important.

The MARC record format was designed by the Library of Congress and the British Library with the aim of constructing bibliographic records in a machine-readable form which facilitated re-formatting for a wide variety of purposes. Early trials around 1966, conducted by the Library of Congress, used the MARC I format, but this was superseded by MARC II or MARC in 1967. As the number of countries using the MARC format expanded, variations on the basic MARC format proliferated.

These variations led to a need for the UNIMARC format in order that catalogue records could be exchanged on an international basis. National agencies creating MARC records use national standards within their own countries, but re-format records to UNIMARC for international exchange. Exchange records in UNIMARC format are offered by the national bibliographic agencies of a number of countries, including Germany, France, Portugal and South Africa. The IFLA UBCIM (Universal Bibliographic Control International MARC) Programme supports UNIMARC in order that national agencies may take advantage of cataloguing work conducted in an item's country of origin.

The comments that follow relate to UK MARC. Both UK MARC and

UNIMARC comply with ISO 2709, the international standard for bibliographic record interchange on magnetic tape.

The MARC format includes up to 61 data elements, of which 25 are directly searchable. The format is compatible with the second edition of AACR and the twentieth edition of the Dewey Decimal Classification Scheme (DDC) and can be modified to accommodate new editions of these standard cataloguing tools.

The MARC format comprises two sections: section 1 which gives information describing the bibliographic data and section 2 which holds the bibliographic data itself. Thus a segment of magnetic tape for three records could be imagined as:

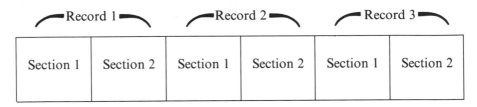

Section 1	Section 2	Section 1	Section 2	Section 1	Section 2

Section 2 is comprised entirely of variable-length fields. In order to signal where it begins, each field is identified by a three character *tag* followed by two numeric indicators. Each field also ends with a special delimiter. Tags consist of three numerals within the range 000–945. The tags have a mnemonic structure; the numerical value of the tags is consistent with the order of the components of a catalogue record, while the tags for added entry headings follow those for main entry headings. Some of the chief tags are:

    100 Personal author main entry heading
    110 Corporate name main entry heading
    240 Uniform title
    245 Title and statement of responsibility
    250 Edition and statement of edition author, editor and so on
    260 Imprint
    300 Collation
    440 Series statement
    5–– Notes.

Consistency is exhibited between tags in that, for instance, '00' will always appear in the second and third positions in a tag if the field contains a personal name. Thus

    100 is used for a main entry personal author heading
    600 is used for a subject entry personal name heading
    700 is used for an added entry personal author heading.

In addition to a tag, each of the main fields also has two field *indicators*; these are used to distinguish between the different types of information that can be entered in the same field. Indicators might variously suggest the need for title added entries, show the number of characters to be dropped in filing titles, and signal whether information such as edition and imprint statements relate to a part or the whole of a multi-part work. To take an example, in the field for main entry under a corporate author heading, the following indicators would be used in conjunction with the tag 110:

110.10   Name of government.
110.20   Corporate name excluding name of government.

Many fields in a catalogue record contain smaller distinct units, known as sub-fields. For example the imprint field includes subfields for the place of publication, the publisher and the date of publication. All subfields are preceded by a subfield code, which consists of a single symbol such as $ followed by a single letter such as b. Thus an imprint field might be coded as:

260.00 $a London $b Mitchell Beazley $c 1991

with tag, indicators and subfield codes. Subfield codes are redefined for each field. For example the subfield code b will signal different subfields within different fields. Nevertheless, where consistent subfield codes are appropriate, the same codes will be used in different fields. Thus, for instance, the subfield code used to designate the forename part of a personal name heading is always the same whether the heading is in respect of a main entry, an added subject or author entry.

Section 1 includes the record label, the directory and the control fields. Only the control fields are input by the cataloguer; the other two components are supplied by the computer. The control fields contain coded data such as the record control number (for example ISBN), language of the text, an intellectual level code or a country of publication code. These fields control access to the main record and are all fixed-length fields. Each record commences with a label and a directory. The label contains information about the record indicating, for instance, its length, status (for example, new or amended), type and class. The directory is a finding list which lists for every field its tag, the number of characters in the field and the starting character position of the field within the record.

Figure 6.1 shows screen formats and records for one catalogue database (see also Figure 10.3).

6.3   Bibliographic record formats in non-cataloguing applications

Most of the centralized and shared cataloguing projects take account of and probably use the MARC record format. This degree of standardization is not usual outside of this specific area of application. Essentially there are two different categories of systems which may be encountered: external databases such as those

Figure 6.1 An online record from BLCMP online cataloguing, including general and local records

General record

```
LEADER        1 am 2200325  B     g
001           013550855 × +
008 0         800829s1979  uk ak  00011   eng +
100 0 10      *aYourdon*hEdward +
245 0 00      *aManaging the structured techniques*d(by) Edward Yourdon +
250 0 00      *2nd ed +
260 0 00      *aEnglewood Cliffs*aLondon (etc.)*bPrentice-Hall*c1979 +
300 0 00      *avi,266p*bill, form*c24 cm +
350 0 00      *a£16.20 +
440 0 00      *aPrentice-Hall software series +


General record from UNION        Local record from UNION
LIBCODES SH  MP  KP    PP
```

Local record

```
001     001    (013550855x)    Local Monograph Format

Leader  Lea    Status (r)    Title a/e (1)    CA Exclu ( )    Sp Coll ( )
               Retro ( )     No of copies (01)

008 008        WIP ( ) Loan ( ) Wants ( ) Sp class ( ) How obt ( )
               Dept sugg ( ) Phys form ( ) Bind Code ( ) Sp coll ( )
               UC Code ( ) Bib int ( ) Stat Anal ( )

009 1 00       *a0123456 0123457 +
009 2 00       *a0123458 +
030 1 00       *aJD +
030 2 00       *aBB +
060 0 00       *a658.91 +
065 0 00       *aYOU +
```

discussed in Chapter 19 and local systems supported by software packages, such as those discussed in Chapter 21.

For the large abstracting and indexing databases, there has been little pressure to accept a standard format, and each database producer has in general chosen a record format to suit his particular database. A review of the variety of citation practices which may be encountered in abstracting and indexing services for referring to periodical articles should be sufficient to demonstrate the differences between the elements included in a record between different agencies (see Chapter 4). As demonstrated by Figure 6.2, which shows records from different databases on different hosts, databases may emerge in different record formats. In Dialog, one of the international online hosts offering access to a wide variety of databases, a very large number of different searchable fields may be identified across a number of databases. Figure 6.3 shows an extract from the alphabetical list of searchable fields for Dialog. Yet another variable factor is the growing presence of full-text databases. They demand a somewhat different record format from bibliographic records if the information is to be appropriately displayed. However, although separate formats have been created for different systems, some standards exist. Various large abstracting and indexing cooperative ventures or networks have developed their own formats. Thus there are groups of organizations with common subject interests which exchange data and cooperate in the creation of international databases. Amongst these can be numbered INIS (International Nuclear Information System), IRRD (International Road Research Documentation System), CAS (Chemical Abstracts Services), BIOSIS (BioSciences Information Services Inc.) and AGRIS (Agricultural Information System). All these networks have standard record formats, although it is regrettable that they all operate to different standards.

The record formats to be encountered in local systems (which are supported by the type of software package discussed in Chapter 20) are many and various. Some of these software packages offer cataloguing systems which will work in a MARC record format or which produce records which are compatible with it. Others do not offer such an option. Virtually all software packages offer the purchaser the opportunity to evolve a record format which suits a specific application. Frequently it is necessary for the librarian or information worker to make choices concerning record size and field size since the smaller microcomputer-based systems may impose limits on either or both. If the library or information worker is offered a choice in the design of record format, it will be necessary to decide upon the types of records to be maintained, as well as to settle which fields are to be included in each record and the length of each field. Sometimes there will also be options concerning the use of fixed- and variable-length fields. Thus, in local systems there may well be great variability in record format, as designs are implemented within the parameters set by the various software packages.

6.4 The common communication format

At present many national standard exchange formats exist. Although a number of these formats resemble one another, others differ significantly. Rarely are two national formats so similar that they can be handled by the same computer programs. The bibliographic descriptions carried by these formats differ widely according to their source. Abstracting and indexing services use different rules of bibliographic description to those widely followed in libraries. In order to tackle the lack of uniformity among national standard formats, international exchange formats have been developed. The UNIMARC format, which is used by major

Figure 6.2   Some examples of record formats in bibliographic databases (a) ORBIT search service sample record

```
AN   – 9639759
ABN  – 03–90–04949
IS   – 9012
TI   – CONVERTING AND PHARMACEUTICAL PACKAGING
AU   – Anon
LA   – English; (EN)
SO   – Converter vol. 27, no. 9, Sept. 1990, pp 8, 10, 12
NU   – ISSN 0010–8189
FS   – PK (03)
DT   – J
CO   – BOSCH R. GMBH; HASSIA
LO   – EUROPE; UNITED KINGDOM; EU; EZUKM
TN   – COLLAMAT; COMPACKER
IT   – ALUMINIUM; AMPOULE; BAR CODE; BLISTER PACK; BLISTER; CAPSULE;
       CARTONING; CARTON; COLLAPSIBLE; CONTINUOUS; CONVERT;
       DISPENSING; PHARMACEUTICAL; ENVIRONMENT; GLASS; INFUSION;
       INJECTABLE; LABELLING; LABEL; LINES; LIQUID; MACHINE; MARKETING;
       OINTMENT; ORALLY; OUTER; PACK; PACKAGED; PACKAGING; PACKED;
       PARENTERAL; PLASTIC BOTTLE; POLYPROPYLENE; POUCH; PRESSURE;
       POLYVINYL CHLORIDE; SEAL; SOLID; SOLUTION; STRIP; SURFACE;
       TABLET; THERMOFORM-FILL-SEAL; TREATMENTS; TUBE; VIAL
MH   – Pharmaceuticals and medical products (3625)
AB   – Orally administered solids (tablets and capsules) are often marketed in
       blister packs of polypropylene (substituted for PVC following environmental
       pressures) using machines like the Hassia THL 24/28 thermoform-fill-seal.
       Aluminium blisters are packed using the Klockner-Wolkogan Compacker 2.
       The printed cartons, bar coding, and cartoning operation are reviewed. UK
       packaging may change with the advent of Original Pack Dispensing. Some
       capsules are packed on continuous strip sealing machines. Orally
       administered liquids are packaged in glass or plastic bottles. Convertors
       provide printed labels, cartons and down-line outer packaging. The Collamat
       5010 and 5020 labelling machines are described. Injectable drugs
       (parenterals) are packed in ampoules and glass vials, with complete ampoule
       lines provided by Robert Bosch Packaging Ltd. Infusion solution pouches are
       described and reviewed. Surface treatment creams and ointments are
       marketed in collapsible tubes. Transdermal drug packaging is assessed.
```

Continued

Figure 6.2 Continued
(b) Some field labels for the ORBIT database

ORBIT FILE/NAME : PIRA

ELEMENT NAME	QUALIFIER	EXAMPLE
BASIC INDEX	–	BLISTER (W) PACKS
ACCESSION NUMBER	/AN	9639759/AN
ISSUE NUMBER	/IS	9012/IS
TITLE	/TI	PHARMACEUTICAL/TI
AUTHOR	/AU	/AU COOK AJ
LANGUAGE	/LA	ENGLISH/LA
SOURCE	/SO	CONVERTER/SO
JOURNAL NAME	/JN	CONVERTER/JN
LOCATION	/LO	EUROPE/LO
DOCUMENT TYPE	/DT	J/DT
INDEX TERMS	/IT	CARTON/IT
MAIN HEADING	/MH	PHARMACEUTICALS/MH
TRADE NAME	/TN	COLLAMAT/TN
COMPANY NAME	/CO	HASSIA/CO
ABSTRACT	/AB	MACHINE:/AB
PUBLICATION YEAR	/PY	1990/PY

(c) Dialog sample record

JC =			MANAGEMENT
DIALOG			CONTENTS
ACCESSION	252973	IRL8320283	DOCUMENT CODE
NUMBER	OSHA'S GENERAL DUTY CLAUSE: AN ANALYSIS OF ITS		
	USE AND ABUSE.		TI = or/TI
AU =	MORGAN, D.L.: DUVALL, M.N.		
JN =	INDUSTRIAL RELATIONS LAW JOURNAL. VOL. 5, No. 2,		
	1983.		PY =
	P. 283–321., JOURNAL. BIBLIOG. 25		SF =
	SECTION 5(A) (1) OF THE OCCUPATIONAL SAFETY AND		
	HEALTH ACT (OSHA) KNOWN AS THE GENERAL DUTY		
	CLAUSE, REQUIRES EMPLOYERS TO FURNISH		
	EMPLOYMENT AND AN EMPLOYMENT PLACE FREE		
	FROM RECOGNIZED HAZARDS. AN OVERVIEW OF THE		
	ACT AND THE LEGISLATIVE HISTORY OF THE		
DT =	GENERAL DUTY CLAUSE INDICATES THAT THE INTENT		/AB
	OF CONGRESS IN ITS ENACTMENT WAS TO		
	SUBORDINATE THE CLAUSE TO SPECIFIC STANDARDS		
	PROMULGATED AND ENFORCED BY OSHA. IT IS		
	CONTENDED THAT INSTEAD OSHA HAS OVERUSED		
	THE CLAUSE BECAUSE OF ITS OWN INEFFICIENCIES.		
	TO CURE THIS ABUSE, OSHA IS URGED TO		
	PROMULGATE PERFORMANCE STANDARDS AND		
	ADVISORY GUIDELINES.		

Continued

Figure 6.2 Continued

JU =	JURISDICTION: UNITED STATES	
CN =	INDUSTRIAL UNION DEPT., AFL–CIO V. AMERICAN	
	PETROLEUM INST., 448 U.S. 607 (1980)	CC =
SN =	OCCUPATIONAL SAFETY AND HEALTH ACT OF 1971	
	(OSHA) PUB.L.NO.	SO =
	91–596, 84 STAT. 1590.29 U.S.C. SECS. 651–678 (1976)	
	DESCRIPTORS: OCCUPATIONAL SAFETY AND HEALTH	
	ADMIN.:	/DE or /DF
	WORKING CONDITIONS; PERFORMANCE; STANDARDS;	
	SAFETY; GUIDELINES; OSHA; 0042; 0420; 0249; 2205;	
	0042; 1593; 0042	DC =

(d) Some field labels for the Dialog database

FIELD NAME	SUFFIX PREFIX	EXAMPLE
Abstract	/AB	S OCCUPATIONAL/AB
Author	AU =	S AU = MORGAN, D.L.
Case Citation	CC	S CC 448 U.S. 607?
Case Name	CN	S CN INDUSTRIAL?
Descriptor	/DE or /DF	S STANDARDS/DF
Descriptor Code	DC	S DC 2205
Document Type	DT =	S DT = JOURNAL
Journal Code	JC =	S JC = IRL
Journal Name	JN =	S JN = INDUSTRIAL RELATIONS?
Jurisdiction	JU =	S JU = UNITED STATES
Publication Year	PY =	S PY = 1983
Special Feature	SF =	S SF = BIBLIOG.
Statute Citation	SO =	S SO = PUB. L. NO. 91–596?
Statute Name	SN =	S SN = OCCUPATIONAL?
Title	/TI	S GENERAL (1W) CLAUSE/TI
Update	UD =	S UD = 8308

libraries, assumes the ISBD to be standard for the form of those data elements that describe the item. On the other hand, the abstracting and indexing services have the UNISIST Reference Manual which prescribes its own content designators to the bibliographic descriptions of various types of materials. These major formats define, organize and identify data elements in different ways and rely upon different sets of codes. Thus it has been difficult or virtually impossible to mix in a single file bibliographic records from different types of sources. This situation perpetuates the fragmentation of the information community into different groups. The Common Communications Format was thus designed with the aim of facilitating the communication of bibliographic information among sectors of the information community.

Figure 6.3   Some of the searchable fields available on a Dialog database

Abbreviations for searchable fields

AA   Asset amount, author affiliation
AB   Abstract, note
AC   Legislative authority code, country of patent application, area code, activity code, assignee code
AG   Asset greater than, grant greater than
AI   Alloys index
AL   Asset less than, grant less than
AM   Grant amount, contract amount
AN   Assignee name, accession number, agency name, abstract number
AP   Approach
AR   Authority record
AS   Agency state, agency state code, agency/service abbreviation
AT   Asset type, article type
AU   Personal author, inventor
AV   Availability on microfiche, availability
BC   Biosystematic code, branch city
BN   Biosystematic name, branch name, bureau number, book number, ISBN
BS   Branch state
BZ   Branch zip code
CA   Card alert, cited author, call number
CC   Concept code, corporate source, category code, country code, contractor company code, class code, geographic code
CF   Cosati field
CG   Contributions greater than, corporate source location
CH   Clearinghouse code
CL   Patent classification number, classification code, contributions less than, classification group, conference location
CM   Community code

In common with UNIMARC, the Common Communication Format constitutes a specific implementation of ISO 2709. The CCF supports its objectives by:

1. specifying a small number of mandatory data elements which are recognized to be essential in order to identify an item;
2. providing mandatory elements that are sufficiently flexible to accommodate varying descriptive practices;
3. providing a number of optional elements;
4. permitting the originating agency to include non–standard elements which are considered useful within its system, and
5. providing a mechanism for linking records and segments of records without imposing on the originating agency any uniform practice regarding the treatment of related groups of records or data elements.

Each record comprises four parts: record label, directory, datafields and record

81

separator. Figure 6.4 demonstrates the record structure and its application to one type of material.

6.5   Database structures and access to data

The simplest way to search a file is to go through it record by record to find the required information. For large files this is slow, so alternative approaches to locating records have been developed. (Chapter 23 describes research which revisits the scanning of complete files to retrieve information, but for the present most systems still use the approaches described below.) The database structure allows searches to be performed quickly and effectively.

6.5.1   One-way linked lists

A simple way to locate a specific record is to use a key field which might be the author field. Records are sometimes arranged in order according to the key field, but this can be inconvenient when adding, deleting and changing records. It is more usual to store records in a different order and to use a system of pointers to represent the arrangement. This is known as a one–way linked list; processing is performed by following the links. The links establish the order, so that it is not necessary continually to move data; only the pointers need be amended as data is added or deleted.

A single key approach is not satisfactory if the search needs to be done on some other record element. If, for example, the keyfield is the author field, then the pointers do not support searching for a title or subject term. To cater for this requirement, multi–indexed systems have been developed which use a number of indexes to point to records in the main file. Many of these systems are based on inverted files.

6.5.2   Inverted files

The inverted file is similar to an index. In the inverted file approach there are three separate files: the text or print file, the term file and the inverse or index file.

The *text file* contains the actual records, the other two files providing access to these records. The *index file* contains all of the indexed terms from all of the records in the database, arranged in alphabetical order. When a new record is added to the database, it is necessary to update the index file; this is achieved automatically by the search system. This location acts as the link between the index file and the term file. The *term file* location points to the place in the term file where more information is stored about each term listed in the index file.

The term file has a location number for every term in the index file. Linked to this number are the record numbers of all the records in the database that include

Figure 6.4   CCF record structure
(a) Diagrammatic representation of the CCF record structure

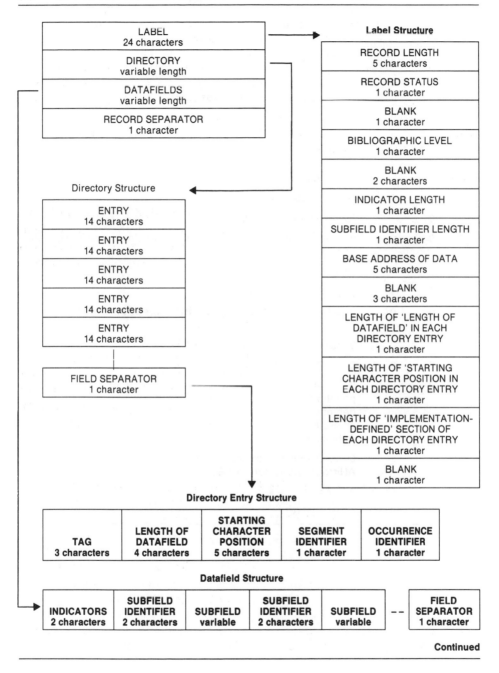

Continued

83

Figure 6.4 Continued
(b) Application of CCF record structure to a component part in a serial

Bibliographic level: a (shown in character position 7 in the record lavel).

Tag	Seg Iden	Occur Iden	Data Fields
001	0	0	011760K
020	0	0	00@AUSCA@BChemical Abstracts
021	0	0	00@AC
022	0	0	00@A19870713
040	0	0	00@Aeng
060	0	0	00@A100
086	0	0	00@A30000@BAA@C33000
086	0	1	00@A30001@BAA@C33000
200	0	0	00@AThe influence of man on the ozone layer; readjusting the estimates
300	0	0	00@AIsaksen@BIvar S.
300	0	1	00@AStordal@BFrode
330	0	0	00@AInstitute of Geophysics@BUniversity of Oslo@DBlinden, Oslo, Norway 3
490	0	0	00@Av. 10, no. 1, 1981@B9–17
610	0	0	00@ACA059001@BCA Subject Sections
620	0	0	00@AAtmosphere, Ozonosphere: (Air pollution effect on)@AAir pollution: (by chlorofluoromethane, Stratosphere ozone depletion of)@AAtmosphere, Stratosphere: (Ozone in, Effect of chlorofluoromethane and other air pollutants on)@BCA General Subject Index
620	0	1	00@AOzone@AAtmosphere@AChlorofluoromethane@ANitrogen@AChlorine@BCA keywords
015	1	0	00@As
083	1	0	00@A02@B0

Figure 6.5   One-way linked list

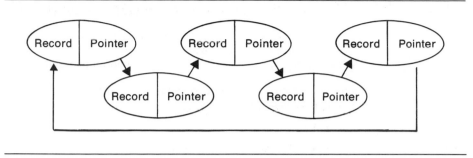

that term. The term file then links the index file with the text file. Some words are indicated as stop words. No further details of the location of stop words are stored, and searches cannot be performed on them. The database producer needs to indicate which words will be used as stopwords. The use of stopwords reduces the size of the index file.

These three files are used together in the search of a database. If a user is interested in performing a search on the word 'preservation', for instance, he enters that term at the keyboard which is then sought in the term file. If it is not present, the system responds by indicating that there are no postings for that term. If the term is found, the user will be told how many postings are available. To display the records, the index file location in the term file leads to the index file where a list of the relevant record numbers are stored. These in turn lead to the actual records in the text file, which may be displayed as required.

The posting file is particularly valuable when the search is a little more complex. If, for example, the user wants to find records about Cataloguing Networks, the index file would first be consulted for both terms 'cataloguing' and 'networks'. The computer will then examine the posting file for the two terms and compare the record numbers at each postings file location for common record numbers. The user is told how many matching records (hits) have been found. Using the same principles, much more complex searches containing several search terms and other kinds of search logic can be performed.

The reader should be warned that different authors use different terms in describing inverted files. Further, it is possible to operate with just a text file and an index file. In this configuration, the files would contain information as shown in Figure 6.6. It is generally quicker to have an intermediate file which allows the terms (input as search terms) to be checked quickly and the number of postings for each term to be displayed on the screen. The term file is a small file which can be checked quickly.

This simple description should provide some insight into how inverted file systems work. The actual file structures are often a little more complicated. For

Figure 6.6   Inverted file structures
(a) Using three files

Text file

Record 631: Library buildings: preparations for planning
Record 632: Education and training programmes for library, information and archival
personnel.
Record 633: Education and training for conservation and preservation
Record 634: Newspaper preservation and access

Term File

Term	Frequency	Location in index file
Access	1	234
Archival	1	653
Buildings	1	221
Conservation	1	121
Education	2	789
Information	1	788
Library	2	657
Newspaper	1	134
Personnel	1	799
Planning	1	671
Preservation	2	743
Training	2	157

Index file

Location	File	Document	Paragraph	Word
121	1	633	1	3
134	1	634	1	6
157	1	632	1	2
	1	633	1	2
221	1	631	1	2
234	1	634	1	3
653	1	632	1	6
657	1	631	1	1
	1	632	1	4
671	1	631	1	4
743	1	633	1	4
	1	634	1	2
788	1	632	1	5
789	1	632	1	1
	1	633	1	1
799	1	632	1	7

Continued

Figure 6.6 Continued
(b) Using two files

Text file (as previously)

Index file

Term	Frequency	File	Document	Paragraph	Word
Access	1	1	634	1	3
Archival	1	1	632	1	6
Buildings	1	1	631	1	2
Conservation	1	1	633	1	3
Education	2	1	632	1	1
		1	633	1	1
Information	1	1	632	1	5
Library	2	1	631	1	1
		1	632	1	4
Newspaper	1	1	634	1	1
Personnel	1	1	632	1	7
Planning	1	1	631	1	4
Preservation	2	1	633	1	4
		1	634	1	2
Training	2	1	632	1	2
		1	633	1	2

example, if searches can be made for terms in specific fields, then the index file must contain data on the field in which the terms are to be located. If it is possible to search terms in relation to other terms (for example, two terms next to one another), the index file must contain information about word positions within a field for each term.

The depth to which indexing is carried out – whether it be sentence, paragraph or word level – varies. For example, BASIS and DOCUMASTER gain speed on simple retrievals by indexing only to the whole document or to paragraph level, and resort to slower sequential searching for the final stages of phrase or word-related searches.

Inverted files can be created for a number of fields in a record. Figure 6.7 shows a record with its indexed fields. Note that not all fields are indexed. Inverted files can be created for author names, title words, subject terms and author–title acronyms.

Clearly the retrieval strategy described above rests upon being able to retrieve specific records, and subsequently identify fields within those records. This approach can be slow for long full-text records. The process of indexing a full-text file with long or non-existent records begins with processing the file itself. Paragraphs have to be assigned identifiers; alternatively, the position of individual words in the file must be used as identifiers.

Authority lists (in the form of lists of author headings or subject headings) and

Figure 6.7   A record showing indexed fields from Courier Plus on Dialog

Sample record

DIALOG Accession Number

```
        →  00002042              89002042
AU= ————→   Talking Deals: Dillard's Desire For Vendex Stake ←————————— /TI
JC= ————→   Barmash, Isadore                                              PD=
JN= ————→   New York Times (NY)   Sec D, p 2, col 1  Feb 2, 1989   ISSN: 0362-4331 ←——— SN=
AT= ————→   ARTICLE TYPE:   News                                          PY=
LE= ————→   ARTICLE LENGTH: Medium  (6-18 col inches)
            AVAILABILITY:   UMIACH  CATALOG NO.: 60001.01

            William Dillard Sr. plans a buyback of shares for his Dillard Department
            Stores  from Vendex International N.V. of the Netherlands, which has helped
            boost  Dillard with its  substantial investments now totalling about $570  ←——— /AB
            million  or 41%. The move reflects the fear among U.S. companies of buyouts
            by their foreign investors.

            DESCRIPTORS:    Securities buybacks; Foreign investments in the US; Retail  ←——— /DE
                            stores
/NA,NA= ——→ NAMED PERSON:   Dillard, William Sr
/CO,CO= ——→ COMPANY NAME:   Dillard Department Stores Inc; Vendex International NV
SF= ————→   SPECIAL FEATURE: Illustration
```

Search options

BASIC INDEX

SEARCH SUFFIX +	DISPLAY CODE	FIELD NAME	INDEXING	SELECT EXAMPLES
/AB	AB	Abstract	Word	S FOREIGN(W)INVESTOR?/AB
/CO	CO	Company Name[1]	Word	S VENDEX(W)INTERNATIONAL/CO
/DE	DE	Descriptor[2]	Word & Phrase	S FOREIGN(W)INVESTMENTS/DE S SECURITIES BUYBACKS/DE
/GN	GN	Geographic Name[1]	Word	S HONG(W)KONG/GN
/NA	NA	Named Person[1]	Word	S DILLARD(1N)WILLIAM/NA
/PN	PN	Product Name[1]	Word	S YOPLAIT(W)LIGHT/PN
/TI	TI	Title	Word	S DILLARD(F)VENDEX/TI

+If no suffix is specified all Basic Index fields are searched.
[1]Also searchable in the Additional Indexes.
[2]Also /DF.

ADDITIONAL INDEXES

SEARCH PREFIX	DISPLAY CODE	FIELD NAME	INDEXING	SELECT EXAMPLES
—	AN	DIALOG Accession Number		
AT=	AT	Article Type	Phrase	S AT=NEWS
AU=	AU	Author/Byline	Phrase	S AU=BARMASH, ISADORE
—	AV	Availability		
CO=	CO	Company Name[3]	Phrase	S CO=DILLARD DEPARTMENT STORE?
—	FN	File Name		
GN=	GN	Geographic Name[3]	Word & Phrase	S GN=(HONG(W)KONG) S GN=MARIETTA GEORGIA
JC=	JC	Journal/Newspaper Code	Phrase	S JC=NY
JN=	JN	Journal/Newspaper Name	Phrase	S JN=NEW YORK TIMES
LE=	LE	Article Length	Phrase	S LE=MEDIUM
NA=	NA	Named Person[3]	Phrase	S NA=DILLARD, WILLIAM SR
PD=	PD	Publication Date	Phrase	S PD=890202
PN=	PN	Product Name[3]	Phrase	S PN=MAZDA MPV
PY=	PY	Publication Year	Phrase	S PY=1989
SF=	SF	Special Feature[4]	Phrase	S SF=ILLUSTRATION
SN=	SN	International Standard Serial Number (ISSN)	Phrase	S SN=0362-4331
—	SO	Source[5]		
—	SU	Supplier Number		
UD=	—	Update	Phrase	S UD=9999

[3]Also searchable in the Basic Index.
[4]Special Feature includes GRAPH, ILLUSTRATION, MAP, PHOTOGRAPH, TABLE, REFERENCES.
[5]Includes Journal Name, Volume, Issue, Pagination, and Date, or Newspaper Name, Section, Page, Column, and Date.

thesauri will be used in conjunction with some databases, both in indexing and searching. Here there must be a link between the term file and the authority lists for specific terms, so that approved terms and their relationships can be displayed. An alternative to a separate authority list is the use of the index file.

The creation of inverted files is expensive and time–consuming. The index file may occupy as much storage as the text file. In addition, the inversion process must be undertaken whenever new batches of records are added to the file. These limitations have led to continuing research into optimum file structures.

6.5.3   Relational database structures

Text retrieval systems are often concerned with access to the contents of just one file. Other applications may be concerned to use a number of databases in conjunction with one another. The software that is used to support these kinds of applications is known as *database management systems* or DBMSs (further described in Chapter 21). Database management systems use various strategies for organizing information into a number of different files in such a way that it can be extracted efficiently to meet the requirements of a specific application. *Relational databases* are one type of structure widely used in many database applications including in the design of library management systems. Some text retrieval systems also use relational database structures, integrating text retrieval facilities into the relational environment.

In relational database systems information is held in a set of relations or tables, where rows in the tables are equivalent to records, and columns in the tables are equivalent to fields. The data in the various relations are linked through a series of keys. Figure 6.8(a) shows a simple example of a relation known as Catalogued-book. In this relation the ISBN is the primary key and may be used in other relations within a system to identify the book. If we maintain a relation called Order-book, as shown in Figure 6.8(b) for example, the ISBN acts as a link to the Catalogued-book relation. If we wished to insert titles and authors of books into an order form, these could be drawn from the Catalogued-book relation. In practice, in order to support all facets of a library management system, a relational database system must contain a number of interlinked relations.

Recommended reading

A.   MARC record format

Anderson, D (1989), 'Standard practices in the preparation of bibliographic records', London: IFLA UBCIM (UBCIM Occasional Paper 13).

Figure 6.8   Some relations from a relational library management system
(a) Catalogued–book relation occurrences

ISBN	Title	Author	Year
0–82112–462–3	Organic chemistry	A. J. Brown	1989
0–84131–460–7	Alchemy	R. M. Major	1987
0–69213–517–8	Expert systems	S. Estelle	1988
0–93112–462–1	Computer science	S. Estelle	1989
0–71143–526–6	Bibliography	J. Johns	1991

(b) Order–book relation occurrences

Order no	ISBN	Quantity ordered
678	0–82112–462–3	1
678	0–84131–460–7	4
678	0–69213–517–8	20
679	0–93112–462–1	2
680	0–82112–462–3	3
681	0–71143–526–6	2

Avram, H D and McCallum, S H (1982), 'UNIMARC', *IFLA Journal*, **8** (1), 50–54.

Bierbaum, E G (1990), 'MARC in museums: applicability of the revised visual materials format', *Information Technology and Libraries*, December, 295–99.

BLAISE (1983–), 'Cataloguing practice notes for UK MARC records', London: British Library.

Clement, H E A (1989), 'The International MARC network and national libraries', *Alexandria*, **1** (1), 25.

Crawford, W (1989), 'Understanding integrated USMARC', in *MARC for library use*, 2nd edition, Boston: Hall.

Gredley, E and Hopkinson, A (1990), *Exchanging bibliographic data: MARC and other international formats*, Ottawa and London: Canadian Library Association and Library Association.

Holt, B P *et al.* (ed) (1987), *UNIMARC manual*, London: IFLA UBCIM.

International guide to MARC databases and services, 2nd edition, London: IFLA International MARC Project, 1986.

McCallum, S H and Roberts, W D (ed) (1989), 'UNIMARC in theory and practice', Papers from the UNIMARC Workshop, Sydney (Australia), August 1988, London: IFLA UBCIM.

Plessard, M–F (1990), 'The Universal Bibliographic Control and International MARC Programme', *International Cataloguing and Bibliographic Control*, July/September, 35–37.

UKMARC Manual, 2nd edition, London: British Library, Bibliographic Services Division, 1990.

Wolf, D and Conrad, F (ed) (1986), *International guide to MARC databases and services*, Frankfurt am Main: Deutsche Bibliothek.

B. Other record formats and database structures

Davis, C H and Rush, J F (1979), *Guide to information science*, London: Library Association.

Dierick, H and Hopkinson, A (1981), *Reference manual for machine-readable bibliographic descriptions*, 2nd rev edition, Paris: Unesco/General Information Programme and UNISIST (PG1/81/WS/22).

Dierick, H (1983), 'The UNISIST reference manuals and UNIBID standardisation for development', *Program*, **17** (2), 68–85.

Flynn, R (1987), *An introduction to information science*, New York: Dekker.

Harter, S P (1986), *Online information retrieval: concepts, principles and techniques*, Orlando, Flo: Academic Press.

PART II
AUTHORS AND TITLES

7 Problems in author cataloguing and in name indexing

7.1 The purpose of the author approach

Chapter 1 describes author catalogues and indexes and cites authors' names as one access point in a computer database. Obviously the author's name has for many years provided an important access key to documents in both computer databases and, earlier, in card, microfiche and printed indexes. The author of a document is the person or organization responsible for its creation; that is, the writer of the text, the illustrator in respect of illustrations and/or others responsible for the intellectual content of a work. Generating author indexes or catalogues involves creating access points from authors' names – that is, the names of persons or organizations.

Listings other than author indexes or catalogues also involve the arranging of entries according to the names of persons or organizations, so that some of the problems that author cataloguing codes and practices attempt to resolve are also evident in other environments. A significant example is a telephone directory containing an alphabetical arrangement of the names of persons and organizations. Equally, various trade directories and similar publications need to list and organize names in a form that will enable a searcher to find information about an organization or person. The use of individual and corporate names as headings has been explored thoroughly by cataloguers. Cataloguing practices will therefore be considered in detail in this section, hopefully forming a basis for practice in other listings of names of persons and organizations.

Author catalogues have always been important in libraries. Indeed, in the past many libraries kept author catalogues to the exclusion of any other sequence. The author catalogue can be regarded as a basic record of stock. Authors' names are important search keys in trying to retrieve documents. In particular, they have been accepted as one of the more specific and memorable search keys for the retrieval of specific known documents. In contrast, the choice of a subject heading or notation presents many varied problems of interpretation. Although, as will be demonstrated below, there may be differences of opinion as to the most appropriate author heading for a work, it is considerably more difficult to achieve consistency in selection of subject labels between the indexer and searcher. The International Standard Book Number (ISBN) has provided a more specific search key than the author's name and this is used for retrieval in many computerized library management systems. However, in general, it is unreasonable to expect a user to know the ISBN of a book (except where the number is available to him through other bibliographical listings, such as might be the case in book selection). The author approach thus remains an important means of tracing a specific document, especially for fiction which tends to be known by its author. (The subject approach is useful for non-fiction, but has little value for fiction.) In the author approach there is a clear emphasis on document retrieval as distinct from information retrieval.

To be a little more precise, there are two basic reasons why users make an approach to documents through authors' names. These remain the same as in the days of Charles Ammi Cutter (see 1.3):

1. To enable a person to find a document of which the author is known.
2. To show what the library has by a given author.

Unfortunately, these two objectives are not necessarily fulfilled by any one set of solutions to the creation of author headings. Problems arise when an author uses different names in different documents. An author may change his name or use different pseudonyms for different works. There are two basic policies open to the cataloguer:

1. Enter or label all of the works of one author under or by one standard name; this could be the earliest name used by the author, the best-known name used by the author, the briefest name of the author or the most formal name used by the author.
2. Enter or label each work under or by the name on the title page of that work.

The adoption of the first of these policies will lead to all the author's works being collocated or grouped together in the catalogue. This will satisfy the second objective of an author catalogue, in that it becomes easy to review the extent of a library's collection of works by a specific author. The first objective, however, is best satisfied by the second policy. This would result in the different works of one author being entered under different headings or labels, thus making it difficult to assess the extent of the collection in respect of the works of any given author. Thus, it can be seen that the cataloguer is presented with two options; whichever is selected can only fully satisfy either objective 1 or 2, but not both. Naturally, references would be made to allow for the objective which was not primarily fulfilled, but nevertheless the basic conflict remains.

To take an example, John Creasey used his real name in some works but also a variety of pseudonyms including Gordon Asshe, Michael Halliday, J J Marric, Anthony Morton and Jeremy York. If each work were entered under the name on the title page, this author's works would be scattered under a plethora of different names. Any searcher wishing to assemble all books by John Creasey would need to be aware of all the pseudonyms under which he wrote, or be offered this information through references. On the other hand, if all John Creasey's works were entered under Creasey, John, a searcher who had been recommended a book by, say, Anthony Morton, would find no entry for the book under Morton, Anthony. Of course, in a good catalogue or index, a reference in the form of

Morton, Anthony see Creasey, John.

would assist the reader.

Objective 1 results in what is known as a *direct catalogue* because it gives direct access to a specific document. Its prime purpose is the finding of specific documents; consequently, this type of catalogue has been labelled a *finding list catalogue* or an *inventory catalogue*.

Objective 2 results in what could be described as a *collocative catalogue*, because a catalogue based on this principle collocates the writings of a particular author. Because this style of catalogue attempts to group documents which are related to each other by authorship, it is sometimes referred to as a *bibliographic catalogue*.

In practice, many cataloguers favour the direct catalogue partly because it is simpler to compile. The cataloguer merely accepts the name on the title page as the heading. If new information about the author's identity or the use of alternate names later comes to light, then new names can be covered by references linking works entered under different headings. In a collocative catalogue, new information about an author might require tedious revision of headings and entries. Nevertheless, modern cataloguing practices often represent some amalgam of the collocative and the direct approaches.

Although most of the foregoing comments apply equally well to OPACs as to more traditional card and microform catalogues, the former merit specific attention. Clearly author access remains important in OPACs, especially for known-item searching. The issues of direct access versus collocation are still pertinent, but the role is not so evident. This is partly because OPACs are implemented differently in different libraries and with different library management systems, but also because the greater flexibility of access to records offered by OPAC allows for the display of a series of listings incorporating entries under several different names which have all been generated from one basic catalogue record. Added entries and references may still be used in the display of catalogue records or headings. On the other hand, by appropriate searching of the data in fields in the catalogue record, the user may be able to retrieve records directly on the basis of additional authors or additional names. This facility is more likely to be available in access to online hosts, on CD-DOM and in other applications supported by text retrieval software than in the average OPAC.

Most OPACs are influenced by the record format of the underlying database. Since in very many cases this is the MARC record format, distinctions are evident between main and added entries and references. Direct access through additional access keys may be available through added entry and reference fields in the record format, but in listings of records, main entries, added entries and references are also evident. It is important to understand that many OPACs have been heavily influenced by cataloguing practices that evolved during the card catalogue era.

This section has begun to demonstrate some of the problems associated with the author approach. Author catalogues and indexes can be designed to meet different objectives. No one catalogue can satisfy all the requirements of all users simultaneously. The user may come to the catalogue relatively ignorant of the heading under which a work is to be found. The cataloguer must take account of this situation. Good author cataloguing depends not only upon a knowledge of established codes and rules, but also on an appreciation of the bibliographic history and context of the works being catalogued. Even within rules, a cataloguer is frequently required to exercise judgement.

7.2   The concept of authorship

What is an author? Can the British Broadcasting Corporation or the Library of Congress be an author? Who is to be regarded as the author of a motion picture? Can an illustrator be regarded as the author of a book which has little text and is comprised primarily of pictures? These questions and the many others posed in later sections of this chapter serve to demonstrate that the concept of authorship and the definition of the term 'author' need to be carefully considered. If sought headings are to be established, it is important to evolve a clear and workable definition of the concept of authorship.

However, the definition of an 'author' has taxed cataloguers for many years. Figure 7.1 shows some of the definitions of cataloguing codes of recent years. AACR2R defines authorship in terms of the intellectual responsibility for a work. An illustrator, composer, adapter, editor and/or others may be regarded as the author of a work in appropriate circumstances.

Personal authorship has been accepted for some time and indeed reflects the scholarly practice of the Western world. Personal authors are important as identifying elements of works.

The concept of corporate authorship has had a more chequered history. Until the mid-nineteenth century the concept of authorship was confined to personal authors. Even today a recent study (by Verona, listed in Chapter 10) of corporate headings in catalogues, national bibliographies and cataloguing codes revealed a chaotic state. 'Among the great number of cataloguing codes recognising corporate authorship, it is scarcely possible to find even two which interpret the concept in the same way.' Efforts are being made in the direction of an international consensus on the definition and treatment of corporate authorship. Uncertainty over this concept is amply illustrated by the change in the application of corporate

Figure 7.1   Some definitions of 'author'

Cutter:
Author, in the narrower sense, is the person who writes a book; in a wider sense it may be applied to him who is the cause of the book's existence by putting together the writings of several authors (usually called *the editor*, more properly to be called *the collector*). Bodies of men (societies, cities, legislative bodies, countries) are to be considered the authors of their memoirs, transactions, journals, debates, reports, etc.

ALA 1908:
1. The writer of a book, as distinguished from translator, editor, etc.
2. In a broader sense, the maker of the book or the person or body immediately responsible for its existence. Thus, a person who collects and puts together the writings of several authors (compiler or editor) may be said to be the author of a collection. Corporate bodies may be considered the authors of publications issued in their name or by their authority.

ALA 1949:
1. The writer of a work, as distinguished from the translator, editor, etc. By extension, an artist, composer, photographer, cartographer, etc.
2. In the broader sense, the maker of the work or the person or body immediately responsible for its existence. Thus, a person who collects and puts together the writings of several authors (compiler or editor) may be said to be the author of a collection. A corporate body may be considered the author of publications issued in its name or by its authority.

AACR1:
The person or corporate body chiefly responsible for the creation of the intellectual or artistic content of a work, e.g., the writer of a book, the compiler of a bibliography, the composer of a musical work, the artist who paints a picture, the photographer who takes a photograph.

ACCR2:
A personal author is the person chiefly responsible for the creation of the intellectual or artistic content of a work.

Source: Chan, L.M. (1981), *Cataloguing and Classification*, McGraw-Hill.

headings between the first and second editions of AACR. The rules in AACR2 point to fewer works being entered under corporate bodies as main entries than the equivalent rules in AACR1. AACR2 defines a corporate body thus: 'A corporate body is an organisation or group of persons that is identified by a particular name and that acts, or may act, as an entity'.

Corporate authors present difficulties essentially because a corporate body cannot think or write. Therefore, in the traditional sense, a corporate body cannot be an author. Nevertheless, a corporate body (or the group of individuals that comprise that body) can be intellectually responsible for the creation of a work; in addition, the name of that body may be the information that users bring to a catalogue or index. There is no ready solution to the problems associated with the 'concept of corporate bodies as authors', but current cataloguing practices are obliged to offer some pragmatic solutions. These issues are reviewed more thoroughly in Chapter 10.

7.3 Problems of author cataloguing

The compilation of an author catalogue or index presents four basic questions which need to be answered:

1. How many entries should be made?
2. Which of these entries should be regarded as the main entry?
3. What form should the headings take?
4. Which references should be made from other possible headings which have not been used as headings to entries?

For some documents these four questions are relatively easy to answer. For example, on the basis of common sense and without any external guidelines, the answers to the four questions for the following work might be:

The Odessa File/Frederick Forsyth
1. One
2. Frederick Forsyth
3. Forsyth, Frederick
4. None.

However, a glance at the title page in Figure 7.2 should be sufficient to convince the reader that the selection of author headings is not always this straightforward. Unfortunately, documents which present dilemmas in the selection of author headings are present in even the smallest library collections.

Figure 7.3 shows short extracts from the texts of a variety of documents revealing a number of authorship situations. Answers to the four basic questions could be established on the basis of common sense in each individual instance. This might produce reasonably sought headings for each individual document and would certainly facilitate fast cataloguing, but would probably lead to inconsistencies. For example, a user might reasonably expect two documents both produced by the Communications Research Centre of the University of London to be found under the same heading (for instance, University of London. Communications Research Centre), and not one under that heading and the other under Communications Research Centre. It is important that cataloguing codes establish some consistency in cataloguing practices between:

- different catalogues,

Figure 7.2   Example of a title page

INTERNATIONAL COMMITTEE OF HISTORICAL SCIENCES
COMITE INTERNATIONAL DES SCIENCES HISTORIQUES
LAUSANNE—PARIS

INTERNATIONAL BIBLIOGRAPHY
OF HISTORICAL SCIENCES

INTERNATIONALE BIBLIOGRAPHIE DER GESCHICHTSWISSENSCHAFTEN
BIBLIOGRAFIA INTERNACIONAL DE CIENCIAS HISTORICAS
BIBLIOGRAPHIE INTERNATIONALE DES SCIENCES HISTORIQUES
BIBLIOGRAFIA INTERNAZIONALE DELLE SCIENZE STORICHE

VOLUME XLVII—XLVIII
1978—1979

Edited with the Contribution of the National Committees
by Michel François† and Michael Keul

Published with the assistance of Unesco
and under the patronage of the
International Council for Philosophy and Humanistic Studies

K·G· SAUR MÜNCHEN · NEW YORK · LONDON · PARIS

101

- different cataloguers,
- different documents and between
- the cataloguers' and users' approaches.

Codes are sets of rules which indicate how different types of documents are best catalogued if sensible and consistent headings are to be established in author catalogues and indexes. Some of the major codes are considered in more detail in Chapter 8.

7.4 Conditions and cases

AACR and other recent cataloguing codes have been drafted upon the 'condition' approach to formulating cataloguing rules. A 'condition' is a relevant code problem, such as 'change of author's name' or 'dependent documents'. A 'case' is a class of documents or organizations in which that problem is found. The condition approach to drafting catalogue rules has led to attempts to treat similar problems in a similar way, regardless of the type of document (serial or dictionary) or organization (government department or conference) in which they arise. The alternative approach evident in earlier codes was to enumerate all cases (that is, all classes of documents, organizations and so on) which gave rise to problems and to make a rule for each.

The condition approach is more satisfactory in that:

1. It tends to lead to a more detailed and thorough analysis of problems, providing a framework within which otherwise hidden problems might be revealed.
2. By establishing principles, it helps to create consistency between related cases and removes the need for separate rules for different types of material. One general rule with dependent special rules is more likely to lead to a consistent approach than a number of individual and unrelated rules covering a series of separately treated cases.
3. The condition approach should require less enumeration of rules for different types of materials and therefore should require fewer rules.
4. New cases will not require new rules with a condition approach, allowing the rules to remain relatively stable. Occasionally a new authorship condition will arise which will need to be recognized by the code, but a new condition is not as frequent an occurrence as a new case.

In general, then, the analytical approach is to be preferred but it does have two limitations:

1. The practice that should be adopted for individual cases may not be clearly identified. There may also be scope for variation in the interpretation of rules

Figure 7.3   Some extracts from the text of title pages illustrating a variety of authorship conditions

1. *Outlines of a critique of technology* / Ink Kinks Ltd.
2. *The micro revoluton* / by Peter Large.
3. *Sweden in world society* / Swedish Secretariat for Future Studies.
4. *Dubrovnik, Italy and the Balkans in the late Middle Ages.* Facsimile reprints of 21 articles, originally published between 1952 and 1979. Various authors.
5. *Ethics and problems of the 21st century* / edited by K E Goodposter and K M Sayre.
6. *Millennium and charisma among Pathans* / by Akbar Salahudin Ahmed.
7. *Some personal views* / by Margaret Mead; edited by Phoda Metraux.
8. *The organisation* / by M J Newell, I A Todd, M G Woodley.
9. *To be human* / by Alexander Alland Jr.
10. *The analysis of social skill* / edited by W T Singleton, P Spurgeon and R B Stammers.—Proceedings of the analysis of social skill (conference), London, 1991.
11. *Social theories of the press* / by Hanno Hardt; foreword by James W Carey.
12. Report of the Social Sciences Research Council.
13. *The Freud-Jung letters: the correspondence between Sigmund Freud and C G Jung* / edited by William McGuire; translated by Ralph Manheim and R F C Hull; Abridged edition / abridged by Alan McGlasham.
14. *Animal models in alcohol research;* proceedings of the international conference on animal models in alcohol research, Helsinki, 1991.
15. *Medicine in the tropics* / edited by A W Woodruff.
16. Department of Health and Social Security; *Notes on the diagnosis of occupational diseases: prescribed under the industrial injuries provisions of the Social Security Act.*
17. *Progress in allergy* Volume 27 / editors Kimishige Ishizaka ... et al.; and various other contributors.
18. *Essential malariology* / Leonard Jan Bruce-Chwatt.
19. *Imperial eggs* / by Hermione Waterfield and Christopher Forbes; illustrated with works from the Forbes Magazine Collection, New York.
20. *The plan for restoration and adaptive use of the Frank Lloyd Wright home and studio* / The Restoration Committee of the Frank Lloyd Wright Home and Studio Foundation.
21. *Eva Hesse 1936–1970: sculpture* / edited by Nicholas Serote; catalogue of an exhibition held at the Whitechapel Art Gallery, London, 4 May–17 June 1991, Rijks Museum Kröller-Müller, Otterlo, 30 June–5 August 1991.
22. *Oxford and Cambridge;* photographs by Richard Gloucester, Duke of Gloucester; text by Hermione Hobhouse.
23. *Architecture: form, space and order* / by Francis Fai-Kam Ching.
24. *English heritage monitor* / Planning and Research Services, English Tourist Board.
25. *Religious buildings* / by the editors of *Architectural Record*.
26. *The natural superiority of the left hander* / by James T de Kay; second edition / edited by N M Close.
27. *Red dagger.*—London: D C Thompson.—No. 1—
28. *Olympaidd / testun gan Goscinny;* illuniau gan Uderzo; troswyd o'r Ffrangeg gan Alun Jones.

which, in the absence of any clearer advice, will lead the cataloguer to catalogue in accordance with one or two examples rather than by rules.
2. As with any categorization, the categories are likely to be imperfectly defined. Some documents will be difficult to fit into any specific condition.

These limitations are partially tackled by AACR2R by resorting to rules for special cases; details of these instances are considered in Chapters 9 and 10.

Recommended readings

Note: Many of the concepts that are introduced in this chapter are revisited in Chapters 8, 9 and 10 where appropriate readings are listed.

8 Cataloguing codes: purpose and development

8.1 Purpose of cataloguing codes

Chapter 7 has demonstrated the need for catalogue codes. As soon as we accept the need for consistency in dealing with documents which are the same or similar in some sense, it becomes evident that some guidelines or rules must be drafted in order to indicate how such consistency is to be achieved. Without such guidelines each document would need to be assessed individually, and inconsistencies would be inevitable. So, to a definition:

> A catalogue code is a systematic arrangement of laws and statutes so as to avoid inconsistency and duplication in catalogues.

A number of features of a catalogue or index can benefit from some standardization. Part I had occasion to refer to the use of catalogue codes in compiling descriptions for documents. A more complete list of the possible areas of application for catalogue codes would include:

- author main entries,
- number and type of added entries for authors,
- number and type of references for authors' names,
- title entries,
- description,
- subject headings,
- filing and
- abbreviations, glossary and punctuation.

Such a list might well lead one to wonder why we are dealing with catalogue codes here, since codes would seem to impinge on many aspects of catalogues. In practice, modern-day catalogue codes are concerned primarily with description and author headings. Since the recommendations in cataloguing codes concerning description need to be considered alongside other standards for description, it makes sense to consider this topic in its totality in Part I. Some early codes included recommendations for filing practices and subject headings, but these are usually now dealt with in a separate list or set of rules. Thus, the scope of a catalogue code is potentially wide, but in practice most codes are restricted to 1, 2, 3, 4, 5 and 8 above.

In this chapter a review of the development of cataloguing codes is given in order to explain and place in context the nature of modern cataloguing codes. This review also illustrates some of the issues which cataloguers have discussed over the years, demonstrating solutions to standards in cataloguing other than those embodied in modern cataloguing codes. An appreciation of alternative approaches is particularly important in this field where trends towards standardization are the norm.

8.2 Early cataloguing codes

Three early codes which had an important influence upon subsequent cataloguing practices deserve mention:

1. *British Museum Rules*, first published in 1841. Also known as Panizzi's 91 rules, this code covered author and title headings and description. Its influence is evident in the British Museum Catalogue and in the codes of other national and academic libraries including, for example, the Bodleian Library (University of Oxford).
2. *Cutter's Rules for a Dictionary Catalog*, first published in 1876. The code embraced author, title, subject and form entry, description and the filing of entries. *Cutter's Rules* had a significant influence upon all aspects of the dictionary catalogue, forming the point of departure for both author and subject cataloguing in the US. Cutter's contribution to subject headings is developed further in Chapters 16 and 17.
3. *Prussian Instructions*, published in 1898 and revised in 1908, were used as the basis for the German Union Catalogue. They were widely adopted in Germany, Austria, Hungary, Sweden and Switzerland, and less widely in Denmark, Holland and Norway.

8.3 The Anglo-American or Joint Code (1908)

Variously known as the Anglo-American Code, the AA Code, the Joint Code and the 1908 Code, this had an important impact upon cataloguing practices in the United States and the United Kingdom, and endured for over half a century. Certainly in the UK, and to a lesser extent in the US, there was no serious rival to the 1908 Code until the publication of the first edition of the *Anglo-American Cataloguing Rules* in 1967. Despite some well-recognized weaknesses, the code remained unchallenged and was widely used in producing bibliographic records in catalogues and bibliographies.

The 1908 Code was the result of the combined efforts of the Library Association (UK) and the American Library Association, its objective being to establish a unity of practice throughout the English-speaking world.

There are 174 rules covering author and title headings and description. Arrangement is in two broad sections: Entry and heading (1–135) and Description (136–174). Rules for author headings are in two subsections: personal authors and corporate authors. Differences emerged between the approaches adopted by the American and UK Committees, but these only pertained to eight rules. More general problems could be listed as:

1. *The analysis into conditions and cases is not complete.* There is frequent enumeration of types of documents (libretti, concordances and so on) and types of organizations (alumni, associations, churches). Enumeration can lead to inconsistencies between separate rules for different but related types of materials, excessive numbers of rules and omissions in both types of organizations and types of documents covered.
2. *Inadequate definitions.* Some of the terms are vague. For example, although the distinction between 'societies' and 'institutions' lies at the heart of the code, these terms are only defined by example.
3. *Examples* are generally poor or obscure (often in Latin or German). Many of the rules for government publications have only American examples.
4. *Tendency to ignore the author's identity as found in the document* and to prefer a real name to a pseudonym.
5. *Form headings* are sometimes suggested, such as in the case of laws and treaties.
6. *Corporate authors* present many problems. The code makes a primary division into governments, societies and institutions with the result that problems which arise in these categories, such as changes of name and subordinate bodies, are overlooked.

Eventually, in the 1930s, the Committees of the American Library Association and the Library Association began to discuss revision of the 1908 Code. On the outbreak of war in 1939, the Library Association was forced to withdraw from deliberations, leaving the American Library Association to continue alone. The ALA produced a draft code in 1941 and the final code in 1949.

8.4 The American Library Association or ALA Code (1949)

Although the 1949 Code was much longer than its 1908 predecessor, it only contained rules pertaining to headings. Any revision of the descriptive part of catalogue entries had to wait until 1967 and the *Anglo-American Cataloguing Rules*, when a new code was drafted to cover this area.

The 1949 Code was essentially an elaboration of the 1908 Code in its effort to rectify omissions. In its attempt to codify 'experience', it rejected any reliance on principles alone. In the sense that the 1949 Code did not try to identify or incorporate principles, it was only a limited improvement on the 1908 Code.

8.5 Lubetzky and catalogue code revision 1949–1967

As early as 1951, the American Library Association invited Seymour Lubetzky, consultant on bibliography and cataloguing policy to the Library of Congress, to 'prepare a general analysis of the 1949 Code. . .with special consideration of the rules for corporate authors and a discussion of the objectives and principles which should underlie a revision of the rules'. Lubetzky's report was published in 1953 and formed the basis of the analytical approach to catalogue code construction which has since been accepted and expected. The report introduced a range of ideas which have influenced subsequent code construction. In particular, Lubetzky proposed that a direct catalogue was to be preferred, with any necessary collocation achieved by references. He also proposed a set of authorship conditions which could form the basis for a code. These conditions are reflected in subsequent codes.

The ALA accepted Lubetzky's report and began work on a new code. Meanwhile in 1951, the Library Association reconstituted its Catalogue Code Revision Committee and started discussions. By 1960 a draft code had been produced and, from this date, British and American Committees cooperated closely. In 1961 an International Conference on Cataloguing Principles was held in Paris, and a statement of principles emerged which became known as the Paris Principles. After much subsequent discussion and the publication of a series of interim reports, a new code was published in 1967 as the *Anglo-American Cataloguing Rules*.

8.6 Anglo-American Cataloguing Rules or AACR (1967)

The first edition of the *Anglo-American Cataloguing Rules* (AACR1) was published in 1967 in two texts: the British text published by the Library Association, and the North American text published by the American Library Association. Complete agreement had not been possible, although the numbers of rules containing divergent practices were limited. The need for two separate texts arose largely from the reluctance of large libraries, in particular the Library of Congress, to accept new principles and rules when these might require extensive re-cataloguing.

This chapter does not consider the principles underlying AACR, nor does it review the structure of the code to any significant extent. (Aspects of these topics are developed elsewhere in this work.) Instead, we will only examine here the place of AACR in the historical development of cataloguing codes.

AACR represented a significant step towards rational and standard cataloguing practices. Timing was important. An agreed standard towards which cataloguing practice could begin to adhere was important with the first trials of the MARC (Machine Readable Cataloguing) format in 1966. Both the Library of Congress and the British National Bibliography were aiming to produce machine-readable cataloguing records which would be acceptable in a large number of libraries. A standard for cataloguing practice was a necessary prerequisite. Without AACR it is doubtful whether computerized cataloguing would have been implemented so relatively painlessly and successfully. Libraries have sufficiently different requirements of catalogues to make standardization of practice difficult enough without being hampered by the absence of a code from which they can select their own practice and make their own deviations. On the other hand, it can easily be argued that the success of AACR1 owed less to its carefully identified principles than to the obvious economic benefits to libraries adopting a standard code. Whatever viewpoint is taken, it is difficult to dispute the significance of AACR1. The code was widely accepted by libraries of all types and sizes in the English-speaking world and beyond.

AACR1 is a weighty code, not because it contains extensive enumeration, but rather because of its comprehensive coverage. The code has three main parts:

Part I: Entry and heading
Part II: Description
Part III: Nonbook materials.

Throughout, the code is based upon clearly stated principles. In particular, the intention is to produce a more direct form of entry based on information found in the document, together with a consistent attempt to distinguish between conditions and cases (see Chapter 7).

As part of the revision and review of AACR1, three amendment bulletins were published in 1970, 1971 and 1975. All three bulletins proposed modifications, but most of these were minor, with the exception of the amalgamation of the rules for collections and works produced under editorial direction (see section 9.2 for further details). In 1974 a revision of Chapter 6: Separately published monographs and other non-serial publications' concerned with the description of these materials was published. This revised chapter modified the code, in keeping with the recently agreed ISBD(M) (see Chapter 3), and proposed a slightly different description for monographs. Specifically, an internationally agreed set of punctuation was established for use in description. Other revisions followed. Chapter 12, covering audio-visual media and special instructional material, was revised in 1975, and Chapter 14 for sound recordings in 1976.

Two criticisms were quickly formulated in respect of AACR1. Its very success gave code compilers and cataloguers the confidence to criticize the new code with the object of further refining it. Two early criticisms were:

1. a lack of adequate definition of the nature of authorship and responsibility, both personal and corporate.
2. an occasional unwillingness to accept the consequences of its decisions on principles. For example in rule 43 the cataloguer is strongly advised to give full forenames, even though this might not always result in a sought heading for authors who habitually use initials (for example, C S Lewis).

A code such as AACR could only be tested thoroughly by extensive application in different types of libraries with different requirements and different materials. Other criticisms emerged, mainly centred upon the treatment of nonbook materials. The rules for nonbook materials cataloguing had not been as carefully considered by the Revision Committee since it was monograph cataloguing which needed and was given priority. Nevertheless the early 1970s saw an escalation in the variety of nonbook media in libraries and resource centres, making the need for a satisfactory cataloguing code for these materials more pressing. Part III of AACR1 enjoyed little popularity, and during the early 1970s several possible alternative codes were drafted and some were published (see Chapter 4). Typically these referred to AACR1 Parts I and II where appropriate, thus acknowledging their value. It was expected that most of these codes would be superseded by AACR's second edition.

Thus there was a need to opt for revision. A revised text could make full allowance for the expansion in the range of media in today's libraries, whilst at the same time taking into account various effects of computerization in library management systems. Equally important was the desire to achieve a single text. The Council on Library Resources agreed to fund the revision; a Joint Steering Committee for Revision of AACR met in 1974 and agreed the five authors: the American Library Association, The British Library, The Canadian Committee on Cataloguing, The Library Association and the Library of Congress. National committees were established to consider issues and proposals for revision.

8.7 Anglo-American Cataloguing Rules or AACR2 (1978)

The second edition of AACR was published in 1978, amidst some dispute as to whether it was either necessary or desirable. Many librarians viewed AACR1 as such a significant improvement upon its predecessors that they were content. Besides, any second edition threatened to require some re-cataloguing. Nevertheless, AACR2 is now widely accepted, though the second edition does differ from the first in various important aspects. AACR2 was adopted by the Library of Congress, the British Library, the National Library of Australia and the National

Library of Canada in January 1981. At an earlier stage, the Library of Congress had decided to retain certain pre-AACR headings in order to avoid the expense of extensive re-cataloguing. However, it soon reconsidered this position and abandoned what was known as its compatible headings policy from September 1982.

The most obvious changes between the first and second editions of AACR are:

1. It was finally possible to agree upon one code (there are no longer two texts).
2. The second edition has a completely different organization and structure.

AACR2 recognized that a cataloguing code of the 1980s must treat all media as equal. Thus AACR2 has two parts: Part I – Description and Part II – Entry and Heading. Part II deals with entry and heading for all types of materials. Where possible, general rules which can be applied to all media are proposed. In addition some special rules are included for special types of materials such as sound recordings. Chapter 1 of Part I establishes general rules, and each subsequent chapter deals with a specific part of the media in more detail. For example, Chapter 2 tackles books, pamphlets and printed sheets, while Chapter 3 is dedicated to cartographic materials. The intention is to establish a general framework and then to give exceptions or further explanation and examples for each area in turn. Although generally successful, this approach does necessitate the consultation of two chapters when considering the cataloguing of any given medium.

Figure 8.1 gives an outline of the main chapters and rules of AACR2R. AACR2 incorporates rather more options in terms of alternative rules than AACR1, and also allows for and identifies three levels of detail which might be adopted in descriptive cataloguing (see Chapter 3). This flexibility represents an attempt to make the code amenable to use in a variety of different library environments, rather than (as in AACR1) emphasizing the needs of major research libraries.

For some while there were calls for an abbreviated version of AACR for small libraries and for non-cataloguers. It is entirely unreasonable to expect some groups to grapple with the full length of AACR2. Plans had been made to issue a concise version of AACR1, but these never came to fruition. The cataloguing code issued by the School Library Association: *Cataloguing rules for books and other media in primary and secondary schools* (Norman Furlong and Peter Platt, 1976) represents one attempt to provide a distillation of AACR for a specific group of libraries.

The Concise AACR2 by Michael Gorman is not a true abridgement of the full edition, but rather a rewritten distillation of the essential rules and principles. Inevitably any abridgement poses the dilemma of what to leave out and what to include. This must to some extent be determined by the audience. *The Concise AACR2* is intended for cataloguers in small general libraries, especially one-person libraries, students who may want to learn about cataloguing without necessarily becoming cataloguers, and librarians who must use catalogues and need to understand the principles on which they are based. *The Concise AACR2* has 59 rules, arranged like AACR2 in two Parts as described above.

Figure 8.1 The Anglo-American Cataloguing Rules Second Edition (1988 Revision)

An outline of the main chapters and rules

Contents

Part 1 – Description

1 General rules for description
2 Books, pamphlets, and printed sheets
3 Cartographic materials
4 Manuscripts (including manuscript collections)
5 Music
6 Sound recordings
7 Motion pictures and videorecordings
8 Graphic materials
9 Computer files
10 Three-dimensional artefacts and realia
11 Microforms
12 Serials
13 Analysis

Part II – Headings, uniform titles and references

21 Choice of access points
22 Headings for persons
23 Geographic names
24 Headings for corporate bodies
25 Uniform titles
26 References

Appendices cover capitalization, abbreviations, numerals, glossary

8.8   Anglo-American Cataloguing Rules or AACR2 1988 revision

Revision of the code was entrusted to the Joint Steering Committee for Revision of AACR (JSC) whose members comprised representatives from LA, ALA, LC, the British Library, the Canadian Committee on Cataloguing and, since 1981, the Australian Committee on Cataloguing. The revision process was undertaken in liaison with the committees of IFLA working on the ISBDs and with the International Serials Data System. Three sets of revisions were published in 1982, 1984 and 1986 respectively. In 1985 a decision was taken to publish a consolidated revision which appeared as the Anglo-American Cataloguing Rules, Second edition, 1988 Revision.

A major area for revision was Chapter 9 on Computer Files which was rewritten with new examples provided. Other changes required by new technological developments were additional rules throughout the code for items for the visually impaired (such as maps containing tactile data) and rules requiring more detail in the physical description of sound recordings.

Other rules were changed in order to achieve a higher level of consistency in establishing headings. Minor amendments were made to the rules for the title proper, pseudonyms and the differentiation of persons with identical names. The rules for geographic names were altered considerably so as to eliminate previously offered options (which had led to considerable variations in the headings established by different cataloguing agencies). Other minor amendments concerned the definition of subordinate body names, uniform titles for music, headings for cartographic materials and the description of celestial charts.

A new version, The Concise AACR2, has also been published.

8.9 Authority control

Authority control can be defined as the creation of authority records for established headings, the linking of authority and bibliographic records, and the maintenance and evaluation of an authority system.

In a manual or computer-based system, authority control can be exercised by creating an authority file. This file contains all of the headings or access points – either names or subjects – that have been used previously. When cataloguers are seeking appropriate access points for a new item, they will consult the authority file in order to ascertain the form in which a name or subject has been entered previously and adopt the same form. For names, the authority file will be based on a cataloguing code, usually AACR2R. For subjects, the authority file may be based on a list of subject headings such as the Library of Congress List of Subject Headings or on other subject indexing terms.

Historically, authority control was exercised by means of manual lists and indexes. National authority control was strengthened in many countries by shared and centralized cataloguing services. Substantial further progress has been made in authority control with the advent of computer-based services. The widespread use of UK and US MARC records has led to considerable standardization in the actual headings applied. Cooperative networks with shared databases (such as WLN, BLCMP and ILLINET) have also needed to address the issue of authority control. Henigman describes work for the ILLINET Online database which reflects the holdings of approximately 800 libraries from many different sectors. The maintenance of a shared authority file for the ILLINET Online database required the development of authority control procedures that could be implemented statewide to achieve consistency in work flow, staff training and cataloguing policy. The now rather dated *International Guide to MARC Databases and Services* includes details of subject and name authority control applied by national MARC record services; a new edition is planned.

Library management systems suppliers are also recognizing the need to incor-

113

porate facilities for authority control into their systems. A useful survey of current offerings is provided by Johnston; he notes that suppliers offer a wide range of capabilities and services. The format usually preferred by librarians and used widely is the MARC format for authorities. The UNIMARC format for authorities, which should support the exchange of authorities files, was published in 1989.

The Library of Congress Cataloguing Distribution Service has both Name and Subject authority files. The Name file includes names as used by the Library of Congress which are compatible with AACR2R. The Subject file lists Library of Congress Subject Headings. Both files are available on CD–ROM as CDMARC Subjects and CDMARC Names.

8.10   The Future for Cataloguing and Cataloguing Codes

AACR2 and its embodiment in the MARC record format have facilitated the developments in networking that have taken place over the past 20 years. These developments are detailed more fully in Chapters 6 and 22. Here it is sufficient to identify some of the basic tensions which will shape the future of cataloguing and catalogue codes. In achieving a great deal of international standardization amongst libraries in the English-speaking world, significant progress has been made but more remains to be done.

Starting at the more parochial level of AACR2 itself (but not forgetting the implications for MARC of any major changes to AACR2), its editor, M. Gorman, recognized that the latest edition had not been able to take library automation fully into account. He felt that this was related to the fact that the effects of library automation have yet to be completely assessed and understood. There is no doubt that the advent of the OPAC poses a whole series of questions concerning some of the principles that underlie AACR2. Standardization remains necessary, and for the user searching more than one OPAC – possibly across networks from the work-station in his office – standardization in the contents of records will be even more desirable than previously. However, the principle of main entry is essentially redundant in the context of an OPAC; indeed, depending upon the software under which the OPAC is running, the concept of a heading (or a heading field) could be dispensed with altogether. On the other hand, some cataloguers argue that it is necessary to retain the main entry principle for the following reasons:

1. single entry listings (as in accession lists, citations and various other bibliographical listings) still require the identification of a main entry;
2. many catalogue records have not yet been computerized, and the main entry is still essential in these catalogues; and
3. the benefits to be gained from the grouping together under a single heading of all works by an author or all versions of a publication (that is, the use of the main entry as a device for collocating various versions of possible headings).

These issues concerning headings and access points are only just starting to be debated. Further progress is likely to be influenced by other factors identified below.

The extent of the description recommended by AACR2 has been a further issue for debate. Essentially, a longer record means greater intellectual effort must be applied in generating it. The time that it takes to create the record will be longer, making delays in the availability of records more likely. What optimum data to include in the description has long been the subject of research and discussion and is of central concern to both the individual library and to networks and national cataloguing agencies. An important experiment was carried out by the Bath Centre for Catalogue Research (from November 1987, the Centre for Bibliographic Management). The Centre's findings suggest that 97% of users' needs, both staff and readers, would be satisfied by a reduced description that comprised the name heading, the title and subtitle, volume or part number with volume or part title, edition statement, date of publication, a note of the publication's relationship with another work and of its bibliographical history, and the ISBN or other control number. The elements of the recommended entry were almost identical with those of the CIP entry at the time that the comparison was made. Apart from one or two omissions, this entry is similar to that for the first level of entry for description recommended by AACR2.

The debate concerning the extent of the description has been fuelled by the decreasing ability of BNB to keep its MARC file up-to-date. Various steps have been taken to improve the currency of BNB, including a great reliance on Cataloguing in Publication (CIP) records. Nevertheless the lateness of BNBMARC reduces its value as a selection tool for librarians and indirectly affects the sales of British publications. This has led publishers, bibliographic agencies, booksellers, library suppliers and librarians to enter into discussions concerning the role and content of the bibliographic record. The MARC Users' Group set up a committee, Book Trade Electronic Data Interchange Standards Committee (BEDIS), which produced a discussion paper on standards for the formatting of various kinds of data transmitted electronically in the book world.

Other challenges also face AACR2. Wider adoption in the non-English speaking world may be possible. The development of AACR2 to cater for the requirements of cataloguing archival collections and museum objects is another area for consideration.

The future for catalogues involves users having access to numerous OPACs from their own home or workplace. Bibliographic records for those OPACs may be created centrally by cataloguing agencies or by publishers; alternatively, some may be generated or enhanced by the individual library or archive. All of these developments are likely to have implications for cataloguing and catalogue codes but, because of the huge inertia associated with the existing large databases, progress will be evolutionary rather than revolutionary.

Recommended reading

AACR2 decisions and rule interpretations: a consolidation of the decisions and rule interpretations for the Anglo-American cataloguing rules, 2nd edition, made by the Library of Congress, National Library of Canada, the British Library and the National Library of Australia. Compiled by C D Cook, Ottawa: Canadian Library Association, 1981.

American Library Association (1949), *ALA Cataloging rules for title entries*, 2nd edition, Chicago: American Library Association.

Anderson, D (1989), *Standard practices in the preparation of bibliographic records*, rev. edition, IFLA UBCIM Programme.

British Museum (1936), *Rules for compiling the catalogues of printed books, maps and music in the British Museum*, rev. edition, London: British Museum.

Cutter, C A (1904), *Rules for a dictionary catalog*, 4th edition, Washington DC: Government Printing Office. Republished London: Library Association, 1953.

Gorman, M (1978), 'The Anglo-American Cataloguing Rules, 2nd edition', *Library Resources and Technical Services*, **22** (3), 209–26.

Gorman, M (1981), *The concise AACR2: being a rewritten and simplified version of Anglo-American Cataloguing Rules*, 2nd edition, Chicago: American Library Association.

Gorman, M (1989), *The concise AACR2 1988 revision*, Chicago: Ottawa, London: American Library Association, Canadian Library Association, Library Association.

Gorman, M and Winkler, P W (eds) (1978), *Anglo-American cataloguing rules*, 2nd edition prepared under the auspices of the American Library Association, the British Library, the Canadian Committee on Cataloguing, the Library Association and the Library of Congress. Chicago: American Library Association.

Gorman, M and Winkler, P W (eds) (1988), *Anglo-American cataloguing rules*, 2nd edition, revised and prepared under the direction of the Joint Steering Committee for Revision of AACR. Ottawa, London, Chicago: Canadian Library Association, Library Association, American Library Association.

Henigman, B (19xx), 'Networking and authority control: on-line catalog authority control in Illinois', *Information Technology and Libraries*, **10**(1), 47–54.

Hunter, E J (1986), 'AACR2: revision mechanisms and procedures', *Catalogue and Index*, **82**, 4–7.

Hunter, E J (1989), 'Examples illustrating AACR2 1988 revision', London: Library Association.

Hunter, E J (1989), *Introduction to AACR2*, London: Bingley.

International Conference on Cataloguing Principles (Paris, 1961), 'Statement of principles', Report of International Conference on Cataloguing Principles', London: National Central Library, 1963.

Johnston, S H (1990), 'Current offerings in automated control: a survey of vendors', *Information Technology and Libraries*, **8** (3), 236–64.

Library Association and American Library Association Cataloguing Rules: author and title entries, London: Library Association, 1908.

Lubetzky, S (1953), *Cataloguing rules and principles: a critique of the ALA rules for entry and a proposed design for their revision*, Washington DC: Library of Congress.

Maxwell, M (1989), *Handbook for AACR2 1988 revision*, Chicago: American Library Association.

Piggott, M (1988), A topography of cataloguing, London: Library Association.

Piggott, M (1990), *The cataloguer's way through AACR2: from document receipt to document retrieval*, London: Library Association.

Richmond, P A (1980), 'AACR2: a review article', *Journal of Academic Librarianship*, **6** (1), 30–37.

Shinebourne, J A (1979), 'A critique of AACR', *Libri*, **29** (3), 231–59.

Shinebourne, J A (1980), 'Fundamental considerations concerning author-title catalogues and cataloguing codes', *Catalogue and Index*, **58**, 3–5.

Simonton, W (1979), 'An introduction to AACR2', *Library Resources and Technical Services*, **23** (3), 321–39.

Templeton, R and Witten, A (c. 1984), *Study of cataloguing computer software: Applying AACR2 to microcomputer programs*, London: British Library.

Weihs, J and Howarth, L (1988), *A brief guide to AACR2, 1988 revision and implications for automated systems*, Ottawa: Canadian Library Association.

9 The Anglo-American Cataloguing Rules and author access

This chapter focuses on the way in which AACR2R tackles the problems associated with author cataloguing. This will not only serve as a fuller basis for understanding AACR2R, but also provide an opportunity to study in detail the range of problems and solutions associated with the formulation of author headings.

In this chapter we shall take a condition approach to catalogue headings (see Chapter 7), and make reference to principles, rules and practices as they are indicated in AACR2R. In many respects, principles and practices outlined in this chapter apply equally to AACR1, AACR2, AACR2 (1988 Revision) and the Concise AACR2. However, for ease of reference the rules numbers cited here apply to AACR2 (1988 Revision).

Part II of AACR2R deals with headings, uniform titles and references. Figure 8.1 (above) listed the main chapters in this part of AACR2R. The road to satisfactory author headings starts in Chapter 21 with the choice of access points.

9.1 Choice of access points

The first stage in the choice of access points must be the definition of an author. Most catalogue codes then proceed to recommend the use of this author's name as a heading in the author catalogue or index. For works written by one person or created by one person, this presents few problems. However, when more than one person is responsible for a work, particularly if they perform different functions with respect to it (such as illustrator and editor, or performer and composer) the situation is more complicated. First, several access points are often required in order that access can be achieved via the names of several different authors. Then, since most catalogues currently function on a main and added entry system, it is necessary to select the author whose name will be used as the main entry heading. AACR2R assigns this main entry status to the person who is 'chiefly responsible for the creation of the intellectual or artistic content of a work'. The selection of a corporate body's name as a heading is more complex, the problems and solutions involved being explicitly examined in Chapter 10. The remaining rules for choice of access points (such as in Chapter 21 of AACR2R) are really just qualifications of this basic statement. In AACR2R the choice of main entry is described in relation to the conditions of authorship in each work.

9.2 Conditions of authorship

The main conditions of authorship are categorized below. These conditions can (usually) be applied to both persons and corporate bodies, but in this section, examples will be given only in respect of personal authorship. For examples of corporate bodies as authors, the reader is referred to Chapter 10.

9.2.1 Works for which a single person or corporate body is responsible (21.4)

For works of single personal authorship or emanating from one corporate body, entry is made under the author. For example,

Project financing/by Christopher Emerson.
Entry under the heading for Emerson.

Collected writings/Francis Wormald.
Entry under the heading for Wormald.

Single personal authorship includes writers of books, composers of music, compilers of bibliographies, cartographers, artists, photographers and, in certain cases, performers of sound recordings, films and video-recordings. (*Note*: All rules in Chapter 21 speak in terms of 'entry under the heading for'. The form and style of headings will only be established in later chapters.)

Even in this apparently straightforward situation, complications can arise. For instance, subrules of 21.4 deal with works erroneously or fictitiously attributed to a person or corporate body, and with official communications.

9.2.2 Works of unknown or uncertain authorship or by unnamed groups (21.5)

Works with unknown or uncertain personal authorship or works emanating from a body that lacks a name are to be entered under title. This category includes anonymous works. For example,

The Birthday present.
No author given. Entry under title.

9.2.3   Works of shared responsibility (21.6)

A work of shared responsibility is one where the work has arisen from collaboration between two or more persons or corporate bodies performing the same kind of activity in the creation of the content of a work. In the interests of keeping numbers of entries to a manageable level, works of shared responsibility are divided into two main categories:

1.   Those works where a principal author is indicated, in which case entry is under the heading for that principal author (21.6B). For example,

> Animals by air/Neville Whittaker assisted by Jack Waterman.
> Entry under heading for Whittaker.

2.   Those works where no principal author is indicated, in which case entry is under the heading for the author named first if responsibility is shared between two or three persons or corporate bodies. For example,

> Instructor's manual to accompany Principles of accounting / John G. Helmkamp, Leroy F. Imdieke, Ralph E. Smith.
> Entry under the heading for Helmkamp.

If responsibility is shared between more than three persons or corporate bodies (and no principal author is indicated), then entry is made under the title. For example,

> Parental involvement in Anson House / S. Beveridge, R. Holmes, J. Houseman, J. Smith.

> Entry under title.

> Drawing for pleasure / Norman Battershill, R. Brown, S. Imdiehn, R. Look.

> Entry under title.

These guidelines are reasonably satisfactory, but do involve establishing criteria to identify whether or not one author should be regarded as having principal responsibility. These include the layout of the title page and the typeface and type sizes used for authors' names.

9.2.4   Collections and works produced under editorial direction (21.7)

Collections of independent works or extracts from independent works by different persons or bodies, and works produced under editorial direction are to be entered under title if the work has a collective title. A collection without a collective title is to be entered under the heading appropriate to the first contribution named in the chief source of information. For example,

The pleasures of murder / edited by Jonathan Goodman.

Entry under title.

Focus on teaching: readings from The elementary school journal / edited by Walter Doyle and Thomas L. Good.

Entry under title.

Inside classrooms: a collection of case studies by teachers / [edited by Mick Wilson].

Entry under title.

Note that AACR1 distinguished between collections and works produced under editorial direction, entering the first under title and the second under editor. It was latterly agreed that whilst this distinction led to sensible entries in some instances, it was difficult to maintain and often led to works being arbitrarily allocated to one or other of the categories.

9.2.5   Works of mixed responsibility (21.8)

A work of mixed responsibility is one in which collaboration between two or more persons or corporate bodies performing different kinds of activities (such as the translator or reviser of a work written by another person) has occurred. The problem is to decide who to select as being mainly responsible. Rules in AACR2R give guidance on how to make this choice; in other words, how to identify who is chiefly responsible.

AACR2R divides works of mixed responsibility into two groups:

(a)   *Works that are modifications of other works*, such as:
   (i)   adaptations of texts (21.10). Here entry is under adapter for a paraphrase, rewriting, adaptation for children or version in a different literary form (e.g. novelization or dramatization). For example,

   Naval wings/Adrian Vicary; rewritten for children by Steven Zaloga.

   Entry under heading for Zaloga.

   (ii)   illustrated texts (21.11) where an artist has provided illustrations for an already established text. Here entry is under the heading appropriate for the text (that is, normally the writer of the text). For example,

> Fanny and the monsters/Penelope Lively; illustrated by John Lawrence.

Entry under heading for Lively.

(iii) revisions of texts (21.12). When an edition has been revised, enlarged, updated, condensed, etc. by another person, entry is made under the original author if the original author is named in the statement of responsibility or when the person is named in the title proper and no other person is named in the statement of responsibility or other title information. Otherwise entry is made under the reviser. For example,

> Zen doctrine of no-mind: the significance of the Sutra of Hui-neng (Wei-Lang)/Daisetz Teitaro Suzuki—2nd ed./edited by Christmas Humphreys.

Entry under heading for Suzuki.

(iv) texts published with commentary (21.13) are entered under the commentator if the commentary is emphasized. But if the edition of the work is emphasized, then the work is entered accordingly as an edition of the original work.

> Mother Courage and her children/Bertolt Brecht; translated from the German by John Willett; with commentary and notes by Hugh Rorrison.

Entry under heading for Brecht.

(v) translations (21.14) are entered under the heading appropriate to the original. For example,

> Action and existence: anarchism for business administration/Pierre Guillet de Monthoux; translated by D E Weston.

Entry under heading for de Monthoux.

(vi) texts published with biographical/critical material (21.15) are entered under the biographer/critic if the work is presented as a biographical/ critical work; if the biographer/critic is represented only as editor or compiler, entry is under the heading appropriate to the work.

Special rules also follow which deal with mixed responsibility in respect of adaptations of art works (21.16), reproduction of two or more art works (21.17), musical works (21.18), musical works that include words (21.19), other musical situations (21.20–21.22) and sound recordings (21.23), but sufficient has been said to illustrate the nature of mixed responsibility in works that are modifications of other works.

(b) *Mixed responsibility in new works*

    (i) collaboration between artist and writer (21.24). Works that involve collaboration between an artist and a writer are to be entered under the heading for the one who is named first in the chief source of information, unless the other's name is given greater prominence. For example,

> How to make and use your own visual delights / Richard Romo and Boone Brinson; edited by Nancy Stanley; illustrations by Boone Brinson.

> Entry under heading for Romo.

> My truck / Margaret Wolff; illustrated by Val Hunt.

> Entry under heading for Wolff.

> Colin and Maggie's odd little book—of ends/illustrated by Maggie Guillon; poems by Colin Stanley.

> Entry under headings for Guillon.

    (ii) reports of interviews or exchanges (21.25) are to be entered under the participant if the report is essentially confined to the words of the person(s) interviewed. If the report is largely in the words of the reporter, then entry will be made under the heading for the reporter.

    (iii) Spirit communications (21.26) are to be entered under the heading for the spirit!

    (iv) academic disputations (21.27) are generally entered under the heading for the faculty moderator.

9.2.6 Related works (21.28)

We now come to the sixth and last condition of authorship. Related works are separately catalogued works that have a relationship to another work. These include continuations and sequels; supplements; indexes; concordances; incidental music to dramatic works; cadenzas; scenarios; screenplays and so on; choreographies; librettos and other texts set to music.

A related work is entered under its own heading according to the earlier rules above. An added entry is made for the work to which it is related. For example,

> Cumulative book index: a world list of books in the English language . . . supplementing the United States catalog.

Main entry under title of the work.
Added entry under the heading for the United States catalog.

9.3 Special rules

It is worth noting that AACR2R does not succeed in giving explicit instructions for the cataloguing of all categories of material within the framework of a conditions approach. Some categories of material defy helpful categorization and need to be treated as special cases. Thus Chapter 21 concludes with a number of special rules. These are:

21.31 Laws etc.
21.32 Administrative regulations etc.
21.33 Constitutions, charters and other fundamental laws
21.34 Court rules
21.35 Treaties, intergovernmental agreements, etc.
21.36 Court decisions, cases, etc.
21.37 Sacred scriptures
21.38 Theological creeds, confessions of faith etc.
21.39 Liturgical works.

9.4 Added entries

Added entries are made under any headings that 'some catalogue users might suppose that the description of an item would be found under. . .rather than under the heading or title chosen for the main entry'. In various of the rules concerning the choice of heading in AACR2R, recommendations are made concerning appropriate added entries. In the interests of clarity an integrated account of the appropriate added entry headings is to be found in 21.29 and 21.30. In the interests of economy and in order to avoid an over–complex catalogue, these rules recommend selective use of added entries; that is, added entries are only made under important subsidiary headings and not under every possible alternative heading. For example, in a work of shared authorship, if only two or three persons are involved, main entry will be made for the first named and added entries under the subsequent authors' names. If, however, four or more persons are involved, added entry is only made under the heading for the first named, with main entry under title.

Added entries appear in the form of personal name headings, corporate name headings, titles, series and name-title headings. These are discussed in more detail below.

Added entries under personal names are made in respect of:

1. Collaborators, if there are up to three. If there are four or more collaborators, entry is made under the first named
2. Writers
3. Editors and compilers (for monographic works)

4. Translators (in certain cases)
5. Illustrators (in certain cases)
6. Persons with other relationships with the work, for example addressees of a collection of letters or a person honoured by a Festschrift.

Added entries under corporate names are made for a prominently named corporate body unless it functions solely as distributor or manufacturer. The same rules apply for collaborating corporate bodies as for collaborating personal authors.

Added entries under title. An added entry is made under the title proper of every work in which the title proper has not already been used as the main entry heading, unless:

1. the title proper is essentially the same as a uniform title used as a main entry heading or as a subject heading (in a dictionary catalogue), or
2. the title has been composed by the cataloguer.

Added entries are also made for any other title (for example, cover title or caption title) which is significantly different from the title proper.

Added entries under series titles are made for each separately catalogued work in a series if the heading provides a useful collocation. Instances in which series added entries are not made include:

1. series where the items are related to one another only by common physical characteristics;
2. series where the parts have been numbered primarily for the purposes of stock control, and
3. series where all items in the series have been entered under the heading for one person.

Added entries under name-title headings may be made in respect of related works. If both the heading and the title of the related work differ from those of the work to which it is related, then an added entry should include the heading and title of the related work, followed by the description of the work to which it is related. For example:

> Muirhead, L. Russell. Southern Italy with Sicily and Sardinia.
> Southern Italy.—4th ed. / Paul Blanchard.—Ernest Benn. £14.95.
> ISBN 0–85334–246–6

9.5 Forms of headings

Once the name of the person or corporate body to be used in the heading (either main or added entry) is known, the nature of the heading must be decided. There are three components to consider:

125

1. choice of name (if an author has or uses more than one name);
2. choice of form of name (particularly if a name may be cited in various forms), and
3. choice of entry element (particularly where the name is in an unconventional form).

The problems pertaining to the form of headings are tackled in Chapters 22,23, 24 and 25 of AACR2R. Chapters 23 and 24 are concerned primarily with corporate bodies which will be considered in more detail in Chapter 10 below. Chapter 25 deals with uniform titles; its implications are considered in Chapter 11 below. This section, then, will review the basic problems surrounding the choice of form of heading, illustrating them with reference to headings for persons. This involves consideration of the provisions of Chapter 22 of AACR2R.

In Chapter 7 we have already discussed the relative merits of a uniform heading for all works of one author, and the alternative approach of using various headings according to the form of heading given in the work being catalogued. In respect of personal name headings, AACR2R in general seeks to achieve a uniform heading for any given author, irrespective of the number of names or forms of name that an author has used.

All the rules in AACR2R on the form of heading give guidance on the choice and form of the uniform heading. A number of different names or forms might be selected as the uniform heading. In order that the choice might be reasonably consistent, AACR2 recommends (22.1A) the cataloguer to 'choose as the basis of the heading for a person, the name by which he or she is commonly known'. Now, discovering the name by which an author is commonly known may well present problems, and certainly involves knowledge and judgement. A decision may be relatively easy for well-known authors, but can be difficult for more obscure ones.

As an aid to selection, the name by which a person is commonly known is determined from the chief source of information of works by that person in his or her language. If a library does not have all or most of the works of the person under consideration (and even establishing the extent of a library's collection of the works of any given author can take time), then the cataloguer will consult reference sources (both biographical and bibliographical) in an attempt to identify the best-known name. If the person works in a nonverbal context (for example, a painter or sculptor) or is not known primarily as an author, headings will again be determined from usage in reference sources. Apart from the fact that librarians may consult a variety of reference sources, there are other factors which may lead different cataloguers to different decisions. In addition, there is an element of perpetuation about the establishment of headings on the basis of reference sources: compilers of reference sources may be consulting each other in establishing their headings!

9.6 Headings for persons

Continuing from 9.5, this section picks up the three problems in respect of persons' names as headings enumerated at the beginning of 9.5.

9.6.1 Choice of name (22.2)

Many people use more than one name. An author may use a pseudonym (or assumed name) or even several different pseudonyms in his or her writings. Other authors may change their names, for instance by marriage or elevation to the nobility. Generally, AACR2R recommends that the predominant name be used, even if that name is a pseudonym. For example, where there is a predominant pseudonym, entry would be made under that pseudonym e.g. under Lewis Carroll and not Charles Lutridge Dodgson.

9.6.2 Choice of form of name (22.3)

For names which appear in more than one form, it is necessary to determine which form to use in the heading. This involves the consideration of:

1. Fullness. Names commonly vary in fullness, especially in terms of the extent of abbreviations and initials used. The predominant form is recommended, for example:

    use Murray, Reginald N *not* Murray R N
    but Hall, J L *not* Hall, James Logan.

2. Language. Particularly for well-known persons, names are likely to appear in different language forms. The choice depends upon the languages involved, the types of names and the periods. Some examples are:

    Charles V, *not* Karl V or Carlos V
    Homer, *not* Homeros or Homerus
    Oma Khayyam *not* 'Umar Khayyām.

3. Spelling. If variations in spelling of a person's name are encountered, then the form to be chosen is the official or predominant form. For example:

    Nyanaponika, Thera *not* Nanaponika, Thera.

9.6.3 Choice of entry element (22.4)

Once the name to be used in a heading and its form have been settled, it is time to decide upon the entry element or, in more general terms, to examine the preferred order of the components of a name as it is to appear in the heading. The names of the majority of persons are entered with the surname as the entry element. Thus we expect to find James Brown entered as Brown, James. However certain special types of surnames present particular problems. Compound surnames, such as Henderson-Smythe, and surnames with separately written prefixes, such as Van Gogh, present a dilemma as to which part of the surname should be represented as the entry element. For example, is Henderson-Smythe to be entered under Henderson or Smythe? And does the same practice apply if the name is originally written as Henderson Smythe (without the hyphen)?

Some people, particularly of earlier times and royalty, are not usually known by a surname. Headings for these people are normally in terms of the given name, for example, Anne Finch, Countess of Winchelsea; John, the Baptist; Thomas Aquinas. The general principle for the choice of entry element of a personal name is the person's preference (if known) or, if this cannot be determined, the way in which the name would normally appear in authoritative lists in his or her language or country.

In some instances it may be necessary to make additions to names in order to clarify to whom the name pertains or to distinguish the name from other similar names. AACR2R indicates how dates and other distinguishing terms may be used in this context. Examples of such headings might be:

Smith, John, 1924—
Smith, John, ca 1837–1896
Smith, John, Captain
Smith, John, Rev.

AACR2R also contains some special rules which offer much-needed guidance on names in more unusual languages. The rules (22.21–22.28) cover personal names not written in the Roman alphabet as well as names in a non–European language written in the Roman alphabet. Examples of languages covered are Burmese, Indic, Indonesian, Malay and Thai.

9.7 References

Once the uniform heading has been established for all main and added entries associated with a work, the cataloguer can proceed to consider the references to be included from alternative forms of heading. The different types of references have been introduced in Chapter 2. Although some guidance on appropriate references is given elsewhere in AACR2R, Chapter 26 summarizes the types of situations in which references might be appropriate in author cataloguing. One particularly helpful feature of Chapter 26 is its extensive array of examples.

'See' references (26.2A) are made from:

1. different names (not used as headings in entries), such as pseudonyms, real names, secular names, earlier names and later names;
2. different forms of the name, such as different fullness, different language form and different spelling, and
3. different entry elements, such as different elements of a compound name, part of a surname following a prefix or the family name of a saint.

A few examples of 'see' references covering all of these categories follow.

Moxham, Bernard *See* Moxham, B.J.
Nanaponika Thera *See* Nyanaponika Thera
Hammond-Innes, Ralph *See* Innes, Hammond
Hadithi, Nazar Al- *See* Al Hadithi, Nazar
Gunden, Heidi Von *See* Von Gunden, Heidi

'*See also' references* (26.2C) are made between different headings for the same person, if a person's works have been entered under more than one heading. For example:

Hall, Trevor see also Hancock, James

Explanatory references give a little more explanation as to why the link between two names is being made in the catalogue or index. The following examples serve to demonstrate how they might function:

Hammond, Ralph *For this author under other names see* Innes, Hammond
Hamilton, Charles, *1875–1961 For this author under other names see* Richards, Frank, 1875–1961

Recommended reading

Various of the readings cited at the end of Chapter 8 are useful and appropriate.

10 Catalogue and index access points for the works of corporate bodies

10.1 Introduction

Increasing numbers of documents and information-carrying media are the product not of one individual, but of a group of individuals which might be described as a corporate body. Early cataloguing codes also concerned themselves with works which were the responsibility of corporate bodies (see Chapter 8), but it was not until the Paris Principles and AACR1 that a systematic attempt was made to examine all facets of the creation of access points for such works. The rationale for a separate chapter devoted to the cataloguing of the works of corporate bodies is thus threefold:

1. The number of documents which could potentially be treated as the work of a corporate body is increasing, and the number and variety of bodies responsible for publishing and compiling information has expanded.
2. The principles detailed below for the creation of catalogue headings for the works of corporate bodies are appropriate to a wide range of indexes, directories, databases and other reference materials.
3. Users and novice cataloguers will encounter considerable difficulty in identifying appropriate headings for many works which are the responsibility of corporate bodies.

This opportunity is taken to develop one important aspect of author cataloguing in some detail.

The problems that can arise where no codes have been acknowledged to guide the indexer in the compilation of headings for corporate bodies can be seen in too many circumstances. A good example is British Telecom's telephone directories. Take Section 266 for South Manchester. To locate the telephone number for the Manchester Weather Centre, you need to know that it is listed under Meteorological Forecast Office; that G E Middleton & Co., Electrical Engineers are listed under Middleton, G E & Co, Auto Elec Engrs; and that the Excelsior Hotel is listed under Manchester Airport Hotel. Schools are listed under Manchester City Council, Education, yet Stockport schools in the same directory are listed under

Stockport Metropolitan Borough Council. Divisions and Departments. Education Division. Primary Schools (or Secondary Schools). These examples indicate the inherent complexity of the labels used to describe corporate bodies, and thus the difficulties associated with establishing labels that are predictable to the user.

In identifying the main stages in creating headings for the works of corporate bodies, the process is the same as that for personal authors. In order to settle the choice of access points, here again reference is made to Chapter 21 of AACR2R, with subsequent consultation of Chapter 23 for the form of geographic names and Chapter 24 for the form of headings for corporate bodies. Although this chapter will primarily consider the recommendations of AACR2R it is important to recognize other factors in the choice of headings to be found in catalogues and indexes in respect of the works of corporate bodies. Perhaps the most important function of a study of AACR2R in this area is to alert the student to the general problems of headings for corporate bodies, rather than to inculcate the solutions of one particular cataloguing code. In addition to AACR2R, many existing catalogues will have used AACR1 for establishing some or all of its headings for works of corporate bodies. Smaller libraries may increasingly use the Concise AACR2; here again the recommendations are not always precisely consistent with AACR2R. Other indexes or directories may use in-house codes or no code at all.

Equally important in maintaining consistency in the catalogues or indexes of one collection are in-house authority lists. These lists record the headings that have been established for a given body or person in the past by that cataloguing or indexing agency. Cataloguing codes give general guidance, which must be interpreted in specific instances. This authority list shows how the rules have been interpreted in the past by a given agency. Not all libraries maintain a separate authority list, but those that do not will often consult the catalogue in order to establish the heading that has been used for a corporate body in the past.

10.2 Choice of access points

The first decision in establishing headings for the works of corporate bodies is the very one over which code-makers have wavered. Why should one work be regarded as the cooperative intellectual creation of a corporate body and another as a collection of separate contributions from a group of individuals? The pressure to recognize corporate authorship often arises from the fact that the name of a corporate body may be the sought heading for a particular work. This assignment of intellectual responsibility is important, as we have seen earlier, since it determines the heading for the main entry.

The first step in assigning intellectual responsibility to a corporate body must be a definition of a corporate body such as offered by AACR2R:

A corporate body is an organisation or group of persons that is identified by a particular

131

name and that acts, or may act, as an entity. . ... Typical examples of corporate bodies are associations, institutions, business firms, nonprofit enterprises, governments, government agencies, projects and programmes, religious bodies, local churches and conferences.

Note also that some corporate bodies are subordinate to other bodies. . .(21.1B1). This is a wide-ranging definition which permits a cataloguer to regard any group which works together and has a name (the name is the key) as a corporate body.

If a corporate body is deemed to have some intellectual responsibility for the content of a work, then the name of that body will usually feature as a heading on either a main or added entry. AACR2R identifies the following categories of works for which the main entry may be under the name of a corporate body (21.1B2):

> **21.1B2. General rule.** Enter a work emanating from one or more corporate bodies under the heading for the appropriate corporate body if it falls into one or more of the following categories:
> a) those of an administrative nature dealing with the corporate body itself
> _or_ its internal policies, procedures, and/or operations
> _or_ its finances
> _or_ its officers and/or staff
> _or_ its resources (e.g., catalogues, inventories, membership directories)
> b) some legal and governmental works of the following types:
> laws (see 21.31)
> decrees of the chief executive that have the force of law (see 21.31)
> administrative regulations (see 21.32)
> constitutions (21.33)
> court rules (21.34)
> treaties, etc. (see 21.35)
> court decisions (see 21.36)
> legislative hearings
> religious laws (e.g., canon law)
> liturgical works (see 21.39)
> c) those that record the collective thought of the body (e.g., reports of commissions, committees, etc.,; official statements of position on external policies)
> d) those that report the collective activity of a conference (proceedings, collected papers, etc.), of an expedition (results of exploration, investigation, etc.), or of an event (an exhibition, fair festival, etc.) falling within the definition of a corporate body (see 21.1B1), provided that the conference, expedition, or event is prominently named in the item being catalogued
> e) those that result from the collective activity of a performing group as a whole where the responsibility of the group goes beyond that of mere performance, execution, etc. Publications resulting from such activity include sound recordings, films, videorecordings and written records of performances. (For corporate bodies that function solely as performers on sound recordings, see 21.23).
> f) Cartographic materials emanating from a corporate body other than a body which is merely responsibile for their publication or distribution.

The categories identified above are more limited than those recommended for use as main entry headings in AACR1.

Rule 21.1B2 identifies those cases in which corporate bodies may be used as the heading for the main entry. Other authorship conditions may also apply. For example, it is possible to encounter shared responsibility between two or more corporate bodies, or mixed responsibility where two or more corporate bodies share different functions in respect of the work.

Even in instances where the name of a corporate body is not required as the heading to the main entry, it may be used as a heading for an added entry. Chapter 9 considered the provisions for selecting headings for added entries. Figure 10.1 shows some examples of brief catalogue records for corporate bodies.

10.3 Headings for corporate bodies

10.3.1 Choice of form of headings (24.1)

Once a decision has been made with regard to the number and choice of main and added entries for any work, attention must be focused on the form of the heading to be adopted for the corporate body. Here Chapter 24 of AACR2R, supplemented by Chapters 23 and 26, is important.

The basic rules of Chapter 24, 24.1 establish the principle for selecting names, on the basis of the name by which the body is predominantly identified:

> Enter a corporate body directly under the name by which it is predominantly identified, except when the rules that follow provide for entering it under the name of a higher or related body or under the name of a government.
>
> Determine the form of a corporate body from items issued by that body in its language or, when this condition does not apply, from reference sources.

Thus an attempt is made to establish a uniform heading for all works issued by a corporate body. The exception to this general principle is when the name of a corporate body has changed. Each time a corporate body changes its name, a new heading is established and appropriate references made to link the two headings. In other words, a corporate body that has changed its name is treated as a separate entity.

10.3.2 Choice of form of heading (24.2–24.11)

Once a name has been selected, the form in which it is to be presented must be considered. Here an attempt is made to choose one form and supply references from alternate forms. This involves consideration of:

- fullness of name to be adopted,
- language of name to be adopted and
- spelling of name to be adopted.

In some cases modifications are made to the form chosen. These might involve

Figure 10.1 Headings and entries for corporate bodies

(a) Some examples of works entered under corporate body as main entry

British Sociological Association
Annual report and accounts. — The
Association, 1991

British Museum
Italian renaissance pottery in the Museum/
edited by Timothy Wilson. — British
Museum Publications, 1990

British Computer Society
Membership list. The Society, 1991

Wellcome Institute for the History of Medicine
The iconographic collections of the
Wellcome Institute for the history of
medicine / William Schupbach. — The
Institute, 1989. — 71p : ill(some col.),
1col.port; 25 cm
ISBN 0–85484–080–x (pbk): No price
1.Ti 2.Schupbach, William   B90–45713

Note: The above are drafted in accordance with AACR2R's first level of description.

(b) Some examples of works not entered under corporate body as main entry

Alderson, Ann
Architecture and building technology. —
CIRIA, 1989. — 23p
ISBN 0–86017–306–2:
1.Ti 2.Construction Industry Research and
Information Association 3.Royal Institute of
British Architects 4.Sr: Special publication
(Construction Industry Research and
Information Association), ISSN 0268–229x;
70

Directory of planning and development
consultants. — 2nd ed. —:
Surveyors on behalf of the Royal Institution
of Chartered Surveyors, c1989. — iii,88p;
21cm
Previous ed.: 1988. — Includes index
ISBN 0–85406–424–9
1.Royal Institution of Chartered Surveyors.
Planning and Development Divison

Fearnley-Whittingstall, Jane
Historic gardens: a guide to 160 British
gardens of interest / Jane Fearnley-
Whittingstall. — Webb & Bower in
association with the Historic Houses
Association and Christie's, 1990. — 160p:
col.ill; 26cm
Includes index
ISBN 0–86350–332–2
1.Ti 2.Historic Houses Association 3.Christie,
Manson & Woods Ltd   B90–00285

A Guide to engineering control. — Scottish
Development Agency, Electronics Division,
c1989. — 28p
1.Scottish Development Agency. Electronics
Division

Killen, Vincent
UK jewellery retailing. — Centre for
Business Research in association with
Manchester Business School, University of
Manchester, 1985. — i,310p
ISBN 0–903808–49–8
1.Ti 2.Pattison, Bridget 3.McCarthy, Melanie
4.Manchester Business School. Centre for
Business Research 5.Sr: Research report
(Manchester Business School. Centre for
Business Research). Retail strategy
analysis series, ISSN 0264–2026

Pilkington, N. J.
Experimental measurements of the
solubilities of selected long-lived fission
products, activation products and actinide
daughters under high pH conditions / N. J.
Pilkington, P. J. Shadbolt and J. D. Wilkins.
— Chemistry Division, Harwell Laboratory,
1988. — ii,21p

*Richmond in old photographs / [compiled by]
members of the Richmond Local History
Society; editor John Cloake. — Sutton, 1990.
— [160]p: ill; 22cm
ISBN 0–86299–855–7 (pbk):
1.Cloake, John 2.Richmond Local History
Society

Note: The corporate body headings under
which added entries would be made are
included as tracings at the bottom of each
entry.

Continued

Figure 10.1   Continued

(c) Added entries under corporate bodies

Manchester Business School. *Centre for Business Research* UK jewellery retailing [Killen, Vincent]. — Centre for Business Research in association with Manchester Business School, University of Manchester
739.270688   ISBN 0–903808–49–8

Richmond Local History Society
Richmond in old photographs / [compiled by] members of the Richmond Local History Society: editor John Cloake. — Sutton
942.195   ISBN 0–86299–855–7

Royal Institution of Chartered Surveyors. *Planning and Development Division* Directory of planning and development consultants. — 2nd ed. — *Surveyors on behalf of the Royal Institution of Chartered Surveyors*
721   ISBN 0–85406–424–9

Scottish Development Agency. *Electronics Division* A Guide to engineering control. — *Scottish Development Agency, Electronics Division*
658.5

---

additions (for example, the name of the place in which the corporate body is located, in order to distinguish two or more bodies having the same name), such as:

Twentieth Century Club (Kincaid Kan.)
Twentieth Century Club (Hartford, Conn.)

or omissions (for example, initial articles), such as Library Association and not The Library Association, or other special modifications. Special rules are included for specific types of corporate bodies such as exhibitions, conferences, subordinate and related bodies, governments, government bodies and officials, and radio and television stations. The use of these rules is illustrated in two specific categories in the next two sections.

10.4   Conferences and conference proceedings

21.1B1 confirms that AACR2R considers a conference as a corporate body, and therefore conference proceedings as the work of a corporate body. Note also from the definition of a corporate body in 21.1B1 that it must have a name in order to be regarded as a corporate entity.

21.1B1 goes on to establish that conference proceedings may be entered under the 'heading for the appropriate corporate body' provided that the proceedings fit into category (d) of 21.1B2 and also report the collective activity of a conference.

Where the conference cannot be seen to have a name, then the work will normally be treated as a collection of individual contributions by a variety of persons. In this case, the application of 21.7 will normally lead to entry under title of the conference proceedings. Figure 10.2 gives examples of brief entries for conference proceedings.

Figure 10.2   Headings for conference proceedings

(a) Conference proceedings entered under title

Images and understanding: thoughts about images, ideas about understanding /
edited by Horace Barlow, Colin Blakemore, Miranda Weston-Smith. — Cambridge:
Cambridge University Press, 1990. — xiii,401p: ill(some col.),facsims,music; 26cm
Subtitle: A collection of essays based on a Rank Prize Funds' International
Symposium organized with the help of Jonathan Miller, held at the Royal Society in
October 1986.
1.Barlow, H. B. 2.Blakemore, Colin, 1944– 3.Weston-Smith, Miranda 4.Rank Prize
Funds

*****Italian** Renaissance pottery: papers written in association with a colloquium at the
British Museum in 1987 / edited by Timothy Wilson. — London: British Museum
Publications, 1990. — [256]p: ill; 28cm
1.Wilson, Timothy, 1950– 2.British Museum

United States-East European relations in the 1990s / edited by Richard F. Staar⁻ —
New York; London: Crane Russak, 1989. — iv,328p; 24cm
Conference proceedings. —
1.Staar, Richard F. (Richard Felix), 1923–

(b) Conference proceedings entered under name of conference

COMADEM 90 *(Conference: Brunel University)*
Condition monitoring and diagnostic engineering management / proceedings
editors Raj B. K. N. Rao, Joe Au, Brian Griffiths. — Chapman and Hall, 1990. — 490p
1.Ti 2.Rao, Raj B. K. N. 3.Au, Joe 4.Griffiths, Brian

IFIP TC 5/WG 5.3/IFORS Working Conference on Software for Factory Automation
(1987: Tokyo, Japan)
Software for factory automation / edited by Tashio Sata, Gustav Olling. — North-
Holland, c1989. — x,363p
1.Ti 2.Sata, Toshio, 1926– 3.Olling, G.

International AIChE Meeting *(1988: Washington, D.C.)*
Hydrotreating catalysts / editors M. L. Occelli and R. G. Anthony. — Elsevier, 1989.
— x,295p
1.Ti 2.Occelli, M. L. (Mario Lorenzo), 1942– 3.Anthony, Rayford G. (Rayford Gaines)
4. American Institute of Chemical Engineers 5.Sr: Studies in surface science and
catalysis; v.50

International Symposium on Industrial Robots *(21st: 1990)*
21st International Symposium on Industrial Robots / edited by Thomas Lund. — IFS,
1990. — [400]p
1.Ti 2.Lund, T. (Thomas)

Northwest European Irrigation Conference *(2nd: 1987: Silsoe, England)*
Advances in irrigation / editor, E. K. Weatherhead. — UK Irrigation Association,
1989. — 214p
1.Ti 2.Weatherhead, E. K. (E Keith) 3.U.K. Irrigation Association

Note: The main entries shown in this figure are drafted in accordance with AACR2R's
first level of description.

Thus the name of a conference may be used either as a main or an added entry when cataloguing conference proceedings. In both cases it will be necessary to establish an acceptable form for the heading. 24.7A demonstrates that the components to be included in the heading for a conference are name, number, year and place. Further details are given as to the form of each of these components.

Added entries may also be necessary to cover other access points to the conference proceedings. It is normal to make added entries in respect of both important editors and significant organizations associated with the conduct or content of the conference. References will also be necessary in respect of any variant forms of headings relating to both main and added entries.

10.5   Governments and government bodies

Figure 10.3 includes some examples of headings and entries for governments and government bodies. 21.1B1 defines governments and government agencies as corporate bodies. 21.1B2 goes on to identify various categories of work which may be generated by government bodies. Amongst these are numbered certain specific legal and governmental works, such as laws, decrees and treaties; works that record the collective thought of a body, such as reports of commissions and committees; and various cartographic materials. Note that these provisions do not include research reports which have been prepared within a government agency but specifically authored by an individual. These would normally be entered under the heading appropriate to the personal author as main entry (with the corporate body probably meriting an added entry).

In considering the headings to be chosen for government agencies, it is as well to start by considering the headings for governments, since some of the former follow from the latter. 24.3E instructs (for governments): 'Use the conventional name of a government unless the official name is in common use. The conventional name of a government is the geographic name of the area. . . over which the government has jurisdiction.' Chapter 23 on Geographic Names helps in establishing the form of name of various areas. Application of Chapter 23 and 24.3E will lead to headings for governments of the type: Austria, Florence, Sweden, United Kingdom or Newcastle (N.S.W.). These headings for governments will be used in respect of works produced by governments. Some of these works are treated in the special rules at the end of Chapter 21 and include laws, administrative regulations and treaties.

Returning to government agencies, some agencies are treated as subordinate to a government, whilst others are entered independently. 24.17 declares: 'Enter a body created or controlled by a government under its own name unless it belongs to one or more of the types listed in 24.18.'

24.18 proceeds to identify and illustrate ten types of government agencies to be entered subordinately. Even when a body has been identified as subordinate, in

Figure 10.3   Headings for governments and government bodies: some records from the LCMARC database, showing
(a) MARC record format and tags
(b) At tag 110 – Government body main access point
   At tags 600 and 610 – Added access points

001	91–600880 #
008	910626$as1991$busdae1$f0$g0$h0$il$leng$oab$pW #
024.00:0/0	$a31536839$c + LCX #
040.00:0/0	$aDLC$cDLC$dDLC #
043.00:0/0	$an–us–––#
043.00:0/1	$an–us–ca #
050.00:0/0	$aKF26.5 #
086.00:0/0	$aY 4.Et 3/4:S.hrg.101–1213/pt.1–#
110.10:0/0	$aUnited States$cCongress$cSenate$cSelect Committee on Ethics #
245.10:0/0	$aPreliminary inquiry into allegations regarding Senators Cranston DeConcini, Glenn, McCain and Riegle, and Lincoln Savings and Loan$bopen session hearings before the Select Committee on Ethics, United States Senate, One Hundred First Congress, second session, November 15, 1990, through January 16, 1991$exhibits of special counsel #
260.00:0/0	$aWashington$bU.S. G.P.O.$bFor sale by the Supt. of Docs., Congressional Sales Office, U.S. G.P.O$c1991–#
300.00:0/0	$av. < 1–4 > $bill., maps$c24 cm. #
440.00:0/0	$aS. hrg.$v101–1213–#
500.00:0/0	$aDistributed to some depository libraries in microfiche #
500.00:0/1	$aShipping list no.: 91–355–P (pts. 1–2), 91–342–P (pt. 3), 91–348–P (pt. 4). #
500.00:0/2	$aItem 1009–B–4, 1009–C–4 (MF) #
504.00:0/0	$aIncludes bibliographical references #
600.10:0/0	$aCranston$hAlan Macgregor #
600.10:0/1	$aDeConcini$hDennis #
600.10:0/2	$aGlenn$hJohn$c1921–#
600.10:0/3	$aMcCain$hJohn$c1936–#
600.10:0/4	$aRiegle$hDonald W$c1938–#
600.10:0/5	$aKeating$hCharles H #
610.10:0/0	$aUnited States$cSenate$xEthics #
610.20:0/2	$aLincoln Savings & Loan Association #
650.00:0/0	$aMisconduct in office$zUnited States #
650.00:0/1	$aConflict of interests$zUnited States #
650.00:0/2	$aBank failures$zCalifornia #
810.10:0/0	$aUnited States$cCongress$cSenate$tS. hrg.$v101, etc #
001	91–600875 #
008	910522$as1991$busdae1$f0$g0$h0$i1$leng$oa$pW #
024.00:0/0	$a31536838$c + LCX #
040.00:0/0	$aDLC$cDLC #
043.00:0/0	$an–us–––#
050.00:0/0	$aKF26 #
086.00:0/0	$aY 4.G 74/9:S.hrg.101–1224 #
110.10:0/0	$aUnited States$cCongress$cSenate$cCommittee on Governmental Affairs #

Continued

Figure 10.3   Continued

245.10:0/0	$aHealth and nutrition claims in food advertising and labeling$bhearing before the Committee on Governmental Affairs, United States Senate, One Hundred First Congress, second session, June 25, 1990 #
260.00:0/0	$aWashington$bU.S. G.P.O.$bFor sale by the Supt. of Docs., Congressional Sales Office, U.S. G.P.O$c1991. #
300.00:0/0	$aiv, 383 p.$bill.$c24 cm. #
490.10:0/0	$aS. hrg.$v101–1224 #
500.00:0/0	$aDistributed to some depository libraries in microfiche #
500.00:0/1	$aShipping list no.: 91–337–P. #
500.00:0/2	$aItem 1037-B, 1037-C (MF) #
504.00:0/0	$aIncludes bibliographical references #
650.00:0/0	$aFood$xLabeling$xGovernment policy$zUnited States #
650.00:0/1	$aAdvertising$xFood$zUnited States$xCorrupt practices #
650.00:0/2	$aAdvertising, Fraudulent$zUnited States #
650.00:0/3	$aPublic health$zUnited States #
810.10:0/0	$aUnited States$cCongress$cSenate$tS. hrg.$v101–1224 #
001	91–600865 #
008	910521$as1991$bus$e1$f0$g0$h0$i1$leng$pW #
024.00:0/0	$a31536836$c + LCX #
040.00:0/0	$aDLC$cDLC #
043.00:0/0	$anwpr–––#
043.00:0/1	$an–us–––#
050.00:0/0	$aKF27 #
086.00:0/0	$aY 4.In 8/14:101–81/pt.1–#
110.10:0/0	$aUnited States$cCongress$cHouse$cCommittee on Interior and Insular Affairs$cSubcommittee on Insular and International Affairs #
245.10:0/0	$aProposed legislation to authorize a political status referendum in Puerto Rico$boversight hearing before the Subcommittee on Insular and International Affairs of the Committee on Interior and Insular Affairs, House of Representatives, One Hundred First Congress, second session . . . hearing held in Washington, DC, March 2, 1990. #
260.00:0/0	$aWashington$bU.S. G.P.O.$bFor sale by the Supt. of Docs., Congressional Sales Office, U.S. G.P.O$c1991. #
300.00:0/0	$av. <1 > $c24 cm. #
500.00:0/0	$a"Hearing held in Washington, DC, March 2, 1990"––Pt. 1. #
500.00:0/1	$aDistributed to some depository libraries in microfiche #
500.00:0/2	$aShipping list no.: 91–328–P (pt. 1). #
500.00:0/3	$a"Serial no. 101–81"––Pt. 1. #
500.00:0/4	$aItem 1023-A, 1023-B (MF) #
650.00:0/0	$aReferendum$zPuerto Rico #
650.00:0/1	$aStatehood (American politics) #
650.00:0/2	$aSelf-determination, National #
651.00:0/0	$aPuerto Rico$xPolitics and government$y1952–#
001	91–600851 #
008	910510$as1991$busdae1$f0$g0$h0$i1$leng$pW #
021.10:0/0	$a0160311926$d:26.00 #

Continued

Figure 10.3   Continued

024.00:0/0	$a31536835$c + LCX #
040.00:0/0	$aDLC$cDLC #
043.00:0/0	$an–us–––#
050.00:0/0	$aKF6654 #
086.00:0/0	$aY 4.W 36:WMCP 102–5 #
110.10:0/0	$aUnited States #
245.10:0/0	$aOverview and compilation of U.S. trade statutes$bincluding economic data$eCommittee on Ways and Means, U.S. House of Representatives. #
250.00:0/0	$a1991 ed #
260.00:0/0	$aWashington$bU.S. G.P.O.$bFor sale by the Supt. of Docs., U.S. G.P.O$c1991. #
300.00:0/0	$axii, 956 p.$c24 cm. #
500.00:0/0	$aAt head of title: 102d Congress, 1st session. Committee print. #
500.00:0/1	$aDistributed to some depository libraries in microfiche #
500.00:0/2	$aShipping list no.: 91–328–P. #
500.00:0/3	$a"March 25, 1991." #
500.00:0/4	$a"WMCP: 102–5." #
500.00:0/5	$aS/N 052–070–06729–2 #
500.00:0/6	$aItem 1028–A, 1028–B (MF) #
504.00:0/0	$aIncludes bibliographical references #
650.00:0/0	$aTariff$xLaw and legislation$zUnited States #
650.00:0/1	$aCustoms administration$xLaw and legislation$zUnited States #
650.00:0/2	$aForeign trade regulation$zUnited States #
710.10:0/0	$aUnited States$cCongress$cHouse$cCommittee on Ways and Means #
745.10:0/0	$aOverview and compilation of US trade statutes #
001	91–600850 #
008	910520$as1991$bus$e1$f0$g0$h0$i1$lengobpW #
024.00:0/0	$a31536834$c + LCX #
040.00:0/0	$aDLC$cDLC #
043.00:0/0	$af–sj–––#
043.00:0/1	$an–us–––#
050.00:0/0	$aK27 #
086.00:0/0	$aY 4.F 76/1:Su 2/4 #
110.10:0/0	$aUnited States$cCongress$cHouse$cCommittee on Foreign Affairs$cSubcommittee on Africa #
245.10:0/0	$aImpending famine and recent political developments in the Sudan$bhearing before the Subcommittee on Africa of the Committee on Foreign Affairs, House of Representatives, One Hundred First Congress, second session, October 25, 1990 #
260.00:0/0	$aWashington$bU.S. G.P.O.$bFor sale by the Supt. of Docs., Congressional Sales Office, U.S. G.P.O$c1991. #
300.00:0/0	$aiii, 66 p.$bmap$c24 cm. #
500.00:0/0	$aDistributed to some depository libraries in microfiche #
500.00:0/1	$aShipping list no.: 91–298–P. #
500.00:0/2	$aItem 1017–A, 1017–B (MF) #
650.00:0/0	$aFamines$zSudan #
650.00:0/1	$aFood relief$zSudan #

Continued

Figure 10.3   Continued

651.00:0/0	$aSudan$xPolitics and government$y1956–#
001	91–600798#
008	910510$as1991$bus$e1$f0$g0$h0$i1$lengoapW#
024.00:0/0	$a31536828$c+LCX#
040.00:0/0	$aDLC$cDLC#
043.00:0/0	$an–us–––#
050.00:0/0	$aKF27#
082.00:0/0	$a353.6$c20#
086.00:0/0	$aY 4.Ar 5/2 a:989–90/50#
110.10:0/0	$aUnited States$cCongress$cHouse$cCommittee on Armed Services$cMilitary Personnel and Compensation Subcommittee#
245.10:0/0	$aHearing on National Defence Authorization Act for fiscal year 1991–– H.R. 4739 and oversight of previously authorized programs before the Committee on Armed Services, House of Representatives, One Hundred First Congress, second session $bMilitary Personnel and Compensation Subcommittee hearings on personnel authorizations$bhearings held February 27, March 6, 15, 22, 29 and June 26, 1990.#
260.00:0/0	$aWashington$bU.S. G.P.O.$bFor sale by the Supt. of Docs., Congressional Sales Offices, U.S. G.P.O$c1991.#
300.00:0/0	$ax, 825 p.$bill.$c24 cm.#
500.00:0/0	$aDistributed to some depository libraries in microfiche#
500.00:0/1	$aShipping list no.: 91–323–P.#
500.00:0/2	$a"H.A.S.C. no. 101–50"#
500.00:0/3	$aItem 1012–A., 1012–B (MF)#
610.10:0/0	$aUnited States$cDepartment of Defense$xAppropriations and expenditures#
651.00:0/0	$aUnited States$xArmed Forces$xAppropriations and expenditures#
745.10:0/0	$aPersonnel authorizations#
001	91–600723#
008	910503$as1990$busdae1$f0$g0$h0$i1$leng$oa$pW#
024.00.0/0	$a31536826$c+LCX#
040.00:0/0	$aDLC$cDLC#
043.00:0/0	$an–us–––#
050.00:0/0	$aKF27#
070.00:0/0	$aKF27.E553 1990a#
086.00:0/0	$aY 4.En 2/3:101–134#
110.10:0/0	$aUnited States$cCongress$cHouse$cCommittee on Energy and Commerce$cSubcommittee on Health and the Environment#
245.10:0/0	$aPublic health programs$bhearing before the Subcommittee on Health and the Environment of the Committee on Energy and Commerce, House of Representatives, One Hundred First Congress, second session, February 26, 1990––Tuberculosis Control Program reauthorization––H.R. 4097, March 7, 1990––Childhood Immunization Program reauthorization.#
260.00:0/0	$aWashington [D.C.]$bU.S. G.P.O.$bFor sale by the Supt. of Docs., Congressional Sales Office, U.S. G.P.O$c1990.#
300.00:0/0	$aiii, 152 p.$bill.$c24 cm.#

Continued

Figure 10.3 Continued

500.00:0/0	$aDistributed to some depository libraries in microfiche #
500.00:0/1	$aShipping list no.: 90–466–P. #
500.00:0/2	$a"Serial no. 101–134." #
500.00:0/3	$aItem 1019–A, 1019–B (MF) #
504.00:0/0	$aIncludes bibliographical references #
650.00:0/0	$aTuberculosis$xLaw and legislation$zUnited States #
650.00:0/1	$aPublic health laws$zUnited States #
650.00:0/2	$aImmunization of children$zUnited States #
650.00:0/3	$aPreventive health services$zUnited States #
001	91–600451 #
008	910417$as1990$busdae1$f0$g0$h0$i0$leng$oa$pW #
024.00:0/0	$a31536820$c + LCX #
040.00:0/0	$aDLC$cDLC #
043.00:0/0	$an–us–––#
050.00:0/0	$aKF27 #
082.00:0/0	$a353.86$c20 #
086.00:0/0	$aY 4.AP 6/1:T 68/4/991/pt.1–#
110.10:0/0	$aUnited States$cCongress$cHouse$cCommittee on Appropriations$cSubcommittee on Department of Transportation and Related Agencies Appropriations #
245.10:0/0	$aDepartment of Transportation and related agencies appropriations for 1991$bhearings before a subcommittee of the Committee on Appropriations, House of Representatives, One Hundred First Congress, second session$eSubcommittee on the Department of Transportation and Related Agencies Appropriations #
260.00:0/0	$aWashington$bU.S. G.P.O.$bFor sale by the Supt. of Docs., Congressional Sales Office, U.S. G.P.O$c1990. #
300.00:0/0	$a7 v.$bill.$c24 cm. #
500.00:0/0	$aDistributed to some depository libraries in microfiche #
500.00:0/1	$aShipping list no.: 90–179–P (pt. 1). #
500.00:0/2	$aShipping list no.: 90–229–P (pt. 2). #
500.00:0/3	$aShipping list no.: 90–410–P (pts. 3, 5). #
500.00:0/4	$aShipping list no.: 90–406–P (pt. 4). #
500.00:0/5	$aShipping list no.: 90–422–P (pt. 6). #
500.00:0/6	$aShipping list no.: 90–445–P (pt. 7). #
500.00:0/7	$aItem 1011, 1011–A (MF) #
504.00:0/0	$aIncludes bibliographical references and indexes #
505.00:0/0	$aContents: Pts. 1–2, 191 budget justifications, Department of Transportation . . . –– pt. 3. Department of Transportation: Coast Guard . . . –– pt. 4. Department of Transportation: Federal Highway Administration . . . –– pt. 5. Department of Transportation: Federal Railroad Administration . . . –– pt. 6. Department of Transportation: Federal Aviation Administration . . . –– pt. 7. Testimony of members of Congress and other interested individuals and organizations. #
610.10:0/0	$aUnited States$cDepartment of Transportation $xApproximations and expenditures #
651.00:0/0	$aUnited States$xAppropriations and expenditure, 1991 #

Continued

Figure 10.3 Continued

745.10:0/0	$aTransportation and related agencies appropriations for 1991 #
001	91–600442 #
008	910626$as1991$bus$e1$f0$g0$h0$i1$leng$pW #
024.00:0/0	$a31536818$c + LCX #
040.00:0/0	$aDLC$cDLC$dDLC #
043.00:0/0	$an–us––– #
043.00:0/1	$an–us–ca #
050.00:0/0	$aKF26.5 #
086.00:0/0	$aY 4.Et 3/4:S.hrg.101–1190/pt. 1– #
086.00:0/1	$aY 4.Et 3/4:S.hrg.102–2/pts.7–8 #
110.10:0/0	$aUnited States$cCongress$cSenate$cSelect Committee on Ethics #
245.10:0/0	$aPreliminary inquiry into allegations regarding Senators Cranstons, DeConcini, Glenn, McCain, and Riegle, and Lincoln Savings and Loan$bopen session hearings before the Select Committee on Ethics, United States Senate, One Hundred First Congress, second session, November 15, 1990, through January 16, 1991 #
260.00:0/0	$aWashington$bU.S. G.P.O.$bFor sale by the Supt. of Docs., Congressional Sales Office, U.S. G.P.O$c1991– #
300.00:0/0	$av. < 1–4,7–8 > $c24 cm. #
490.10:0/0	$aS. hrg.$v101–1190, < 102–2 e#
500.00:0/0	$aDistributed to some depository libraries in microfiche #
500.00:0/1	$aShipping list no.: 91–219–P (pt. 1), 91–216–P (pt. 2), 91–224–P (pt. 3), 91–230–P (pt. 4), 91–224–P (pt. 7), 91–219–P (pt. 8). #
500.00:0/2	$aItem 1009–B–4, 1009–C–4 (MF) #
600.10:0/0	$aCranston$hAlan MacGregor #
600.10:0/1	$aDeConcini$hDennis #
600.10:0/2	$aGlenn$hJohn$c1921– #
600.10:0/3	$aMcCain$hJohn$c1936– #
600.10:0/4	$aRiegle$hDonald W$c1938– #
600.10:0/5	$aKeating$hCharles H #
610.10:0/0	$aUnited States$cSenate$xEthics #
610.10:0/1	$aUnited States$cSenate$xRules and practice #
610.20:0/2	$aLincoln Savings & Loan Association #
650.00.0/0	$aMisconduct in office$zUnited States #
650.00:0/1	$aConflict of interests$zUnited States #
650.00:0/2	$aBank failures$zCalifornia #
810.10:0/0	$aUnited States$cCongress$cSenate$tS. hrg.$v101–1190, etc #

many cases it will still be necessary to decide whether to make a direct or indirect subheading. For example, should the heading be: United Kingdom. Manpower Services Commission. Training Division or United Kingdom. Training Division? 24.19 directs:

> Enter an agency. . .as a direct subheading of the heading for the government unless the name of the agency has been or is likely to be used by another agency entered under the name of the same government.

Again, for the works of governments and government bodies it is necessary to

143

consider added entries and references. These will be established in keeping with the principles enumerated earlier.

Examples are given in order to illustrate the points made above.

References will also be necessary and will comprise the same types as those identified for personal authors; that is, 'see', 'see also' and explanatory references.

Recommended reading

Corporate bodies

Carpenter, M (1981), *Corporate authorship, its role in library cataloguing*, Westport, Conn. and London: Greenwood Press.

Hinton, F (1983), 'AACR2 and IFLA recommendations on corporate headings', *International Cataloguing*, **12** (1), 9–10.

IFLA Working Group on Corporate Headings (1980), 'Form and structure of corporate headings: recommendations of the Working Group on Corporate Headings', London: IFLA International Office for UBC.

Spalding, C S (1980), 'The life and death of corporate authorship', *Library Resources and Technical Services*, **24** (3), 195–208.

Verona, E (1975), 'Corporate headings: their use in library catalogues and national bibliographies: a comparative and critical study', London: IFLA Committee on Cataloguing.

Authority Control

Baer, N L and Johnson, K E (1988), 'The state of authority', *Information Technology and Libraries*, **7**, 139–53.

Dickson, J and Zadner, P (1989), 'Authority control in the online environment', *Cataloguing and Classification Quarterly*, **9** (3), 57–71.

Grady, A M (1988), 'Online maintenance features of authority files: survey of vendors and in-house systems', *Information Technology and Libraries*, **7**, 51–55.

'Guidelines for authority and reference entries' (1984), London: IFLA International Programme for UBC.

Taylor, A G, Maxwell, M F and Frost, C O (1985), 'Network and vendor authority systems', *Library Resources and Technical Services*, **29**, 195–203.

11 Titles

11.1 Types of title index

The title approach to documents and the information that they contain arises in a variety of different contexts. The title of a work is defined as

a word, phrase, character, or group of characters, normally appearing in an item, naming the item or the work contained in it.

Thus the title is a label associated with a work which both identifies the document and describes its content in broad terms. Title indexes are indexes in which the title is used as the heading or access point in entries. In a straightforward title index, the first word of the title is likely to be the filing word, and thus the most important element of the access point. Other indexes based on titles, both printed and computer-held, may provide access to words other than the first in a title.

There are in fact two distinct types of title index:

- those indexes where entry is made under title so that a user can retrieve a known item according to its title, and
- those where the title is intended to function as a crude subject index.

Both of these types of indexes will be considered in this chapter.

11.2 Titles as indexes to titles

In any context where documents are listed, such as catalogues and bibliographies, indexers will often provide some type of title index, or make some title entries in a sequence containing both title and author entries. A conventional title index is merely one in which titles in direct order are used as the headings. Since titles are essentially alphabetical characters, the sequence will normally be arranged in alphabetical order. The titles will usually be accompanied by other bibliographic details, such as author's name(s), edition statement and imprint.

Access by title, whether via an author/title index or separately via a title index, is provided basically because the title of a work is one piece of information that a user may bring to a catalogue or index in searching for a specific document. Some evidence suggests that users are equally likely to remember a title as an author. Nevertheless current cataloguing practice tends to prefer the author's name as the main access point. In general title access is regarded as secondary to author access, used when the latter is not possible or suitable for some reason. Some cataloguers and bibliographers make added title entries under the title of most works in accordance with AACR2R. Other catalogues and bibliographies only feature added entries under title where it is deemed that the author main entry heading is not likely to be obvious to users.

Titles are thus viewed as subsidiary access points when compared with authors' names. There are various reasons why author entries are preferred:

1. Entry under title has little collocative value in the sense that since titles are unique, two titles which file adjacent to one another are not particularly likely to be interrelated. Author entry gives direct access to particular documents whilst at the same time collocating documents by the same author. Thus in an author sequence, the totality of works by one author can easily be viewed.

2. Titles can easily be misquoted. In general the very uniqueness of titles makes it less likely that they will be remembered. For example, a user seeking a novel by Agatha Christie is much less likely to forget the author's name than the title of individual works. The fact that one author's name may be associated with several works means that the greater familiarity with the author's name increases the possibility of its being remembered.

3. An author's name is usually shorter than a title, and thus is arguably easier to handle and remember.

4. Titles present filing problems (particularly in the minds of users). Many titles begin with common phrases such as 'an introduction to', 'proceedings of', 'a history of' or 'simple', the common occurrence of such words leading to long filing sequences. Further, titles like *101 ways to cook beans* and *1984* do not have an obvious place in an alphabetical sequence.

In addition to main or added entries under titles, added entries are often also made in respect of distinctive series titles. AACR2R instructs: 'Make an added entry under the heading for a series for each separately catalogued work in the series if it provides a useful collocation' (21.30L). In particular, series entries are useful where the series title indicates a particular subject scope, style of approach, level or audience.

11.3   Title main entry

Title main entries are normally made in instances where there is difficulty in identifying a suitable author's name. If the recommendations of AACR2R are followed, this includes the following conditions:

1. The personal authorship is unknown or uncertain, or a work emanates from a body that lacks a name (21.5). For example,

    Successful retailing through advertising.
    Housing and supplementary benefits.

2. The personal authorship is diffuse (that is, shared between four or more persons without principal responsibility being indicated (21.6). For example,

    Baedeker's AA Scandinavia: Denmark, Norway, Sweden, Finland/ [text Waltraud Andersen et al.].—
    Classroom provision and organisation for integrated preschool children / C. Gunstone [et al.].

3. The work is a collection or work produced under editorial direction (21.7). For example,

    Electrochemical, electrical, and magnetic storage of energy / edited by W. V. Hassenzahl.
    Steroids in asthma: a reappraisal in the light of inhalation therapy / guest editor T. J. H. Clark.—

4. The work emanates from a corporate body and has no identifiable personal authorship, yet does not fall into one of the categories for which the main entry is to be made under a corporate body.

    Centrifugal pumps—hydraulic designs: sponsored by the Power Industries Division of the Institution of Mechanical Engineers: 16 November 1982. The Institution of Mechanical Engineers, London—London: Mechanical Engineering Publications for the Institution of Mechanical Engineers, 1982.—
    Denial of parents' rights in maternity.—London (163 Liverpool Rd, N1 0RF): Association for Improvements in the Maternity Services, [1983].
    Divorce and your child: a guide for separated parents / edited by Jim and Pat Wheeler.—London (37 Carden Rd., SE15): Families Need Fathers, [1982].

5. The work is accepted as a sacred scripture by a religious group (21.37). For example,

    Bible. English. Authorized.

If a work has one clearly stated title on its chief source of information (for example, title page or label), then the instruction to make an entry under the title presents few difficulties. If this is not the case, then the title to be used as a heading for the work is less obvious.

11.4 Problems with title access

When a document is required to be accessed via its title, a variety of problems can arise needing careful consideration. This could occur when:

1. the title given in the chief source of information differs from one volume to another in a multi-volume or multi-part work;
2. the title of the same document differs from one edition to another;
3. the document is known in different countries under different titles, and has titles in various languages, and
4. the document has no title of its own.

These situations require some guidelines indicating which of the variant titles to choose in any particular circumstances, and what to invent as a substitute for a title if no title is available. Taking the second situation (different editions having different titles) as an example, there are four options for the choice of title:

1. entry of each document under its respective title;
2. entry of all works under a uniform title, chosen as the earliest title;
3. entry of all works under a uniform title, chosen as the latest title, or
4. entry of all works under a uniform title, chosen as the predominant title.

In choosing the most appropriate title for use as a heading, the following two questions need to be considered:

- Which title is the sought title?
- Which title will collocate the various editions, translations, adaptations and so on of this document?

If these two questions are considered in establishing the preferred title for use in headings and as an access point, the choice of titles will be consistent with the choice of author headings, as outlined in Chapters 7, 9 and 19. As with author headings, sometimes one heading or title will be both sought and provide collocation, but on other occasions there will be a conflict between these two aims.

Plainly the choice of an appropriate title for headings in main and added entries poses problems where there are a number of titles from which to choose. Titles are also an important secondary filing element in entries which are arranged primarily by author. In large catalogues covering extensive collections of works by major authors (such as Shakespeare or Dickens), many works will be entered under the one author's name. Within the works of one author the entries will be arranged by title. The question arises as to whether to use the title page title of each work for the filing arrangement, or whether to seek to establish some uniform titles that can be applied to related works (for example, different editions, translations and adaptations of *Macbeth*) so that they file together, or whether to accept an arbitrary sequence under the author's name.

AACR2R generally recommends collocation, although it is suggested that the extent of collocation and the need for uniform titles are matters for local decision. Works which are particularly likely to merit the establishment of uniform titles are those which are either well known and/or available in a variety of adaptations, translations and editions. The local cataloguer must also take account of the purpose and nature of the collection and its catalogue.

11.5 Uniform titles

A uniform title is the title by which a work that has appeared under varying titles is to be identified for cataloguing purposes. 25.2A instructs:

When the manifestations (other than revised editions, see 25.2B) of a work appear under various titles, select one title as the uniform title as instructed in 25.3–25.4.

Use a uniform title for an entry for a particular item if:
1) the work has appeared (in other than revised editions) under different titles proper, and the item being catalogued bears a title proper that differs from the uniform title
or 2) the title proper needs the addition of other element(s) (see 25.5) to organize the file
or 3) the title used as the main or added entry heading for a work needs to be distinguished from the title used as the main or added entry heading for a different work (see also 25.5B)
or 4) the title of the work is obscured by the wording of the title proper (e.g., because of introductory words or statements of responsibility present in the title; see also 25.3B).

A number of instances in which uniform titles are useful are considered below:

1. Individual titles
   (a)   Works created after 1500. The uniform title is the title in the original language by which the work has become known through use in manifestations of the work or in reference sources. For example,

   > Dickens, Charles
   > [The Pickwick Papers]
   > The posthumous papers of the Pickwick Club

   (b)   Works created before 1501. The title chosen as the uniform title is that which is used in modern reference sources. If these are inconclusive, the title used is that most frequently found in the following order of preference: (1) modern editions, (2) early editions, (3) manuscript copies.
   The title in the original language is used except for a work originally written in, for instance, classical Greek, when a well-established English language title is preferred. For example:

   > Homer
   > [Odyssey]
   > not Odyssea or Odysseia

Provision is made for additions to uniform titles to aid clarity. Instructions are also included for parts of works and for two works issued together (25.6–25.7).

2.   Collective titles
Various standard uniform titles can be used to cover collective titles including all or some of the works of a given author. These are best demonstrated by example:

> Maugham, W Somerset
> [Selections]
> The Somerset Maugham pocket book

> Shakespeare, William
> [Poems]
> The Complete poems of William Shakespeare

> Tolkien, J R R
> [Short stories. Selections]
> Best short stories of J R R Tolkien

3.   The Bible (25.17–25.18)
Sacred scriptures are entered under uniform title as main entry. Many of these works have numerous editions, translations, selections and so on, making it necessary to control the components to be used in a uniform title. The general form of heading for the Bible is (in order of appearance):Bible. O.T. or N.T. Individual book or group of books. Language. Version. Year. For example:

> Bible N.T. Corinthians. English. Authorized.
> Bible. English. Revised Standard. 1959.

4.   Music (25.25–25.36)
Music, especially classical works, often requires the establishment of a uniform title. The general form of uniform title for music is: initial title element followed by medium of performance. For example:

> nocturne, piano; ballads; woodwind quartet; string orchestra.

Some works require additional elements. In particular, a title that consists solely of the name(s) of type(s) of composition requires the following elements in addition to the statement of the medium of performance: serial number, opus number or thematic index number and key. For example:

> trios, piano, strings, no. 1, op. 1, no. 1
> scherzo, piano, op. 20, A major

5.   Laws, etc. (25.15)
It is common to establish a uniform title for important laws. For single laws, the title is chosen from (in this order of preference): (a) the official short title or citation

title; (b) an unofficial short title or citation title as used in legal literature; (c) the official title of the enactment, and (d) any other official designation. For example:

New Zealand   Copyright Act 1962

Collections of laws are entered under Laws, etc. For example:

United Kingdom
Laws, etc.
Halsbury's Statutes of England.

11.6   Title indexes as surrogate subject indexes

Printed title indexes which could be used as elementary subject indexes were one of the first products of computerized information retrieval systems. Such indexes are a simple example of natural language indexing. These indexes are based on the premise that titles, or more specifically the words in titles, convey the subject content of the document to which the title pertains.

Each title is arranged in an alphabetical sequence according to each of its keywords in turn. Thus a title such as *Grow and freeze your own vegetables* might be entered in three places in the alphabetical sequence: under 'grow', 'vegetables' and 'freeze'. The other words in the title ('and', 'your', 'own') would clearly not merit index entries, and the compiler would have been instructed not to make entries for these words. The exact format of the index and its entries will vary from one method to another, as discussed below. Title indexes of this type could be generated manually, but they are particularly easy to produce with the aid of standard program computer packages.

Subject-type title indexes thus have two important attractions. They are both cheap and quick to produce by computer and do not necessarily require human intervention. Obviously if such indexes did not have severe limitations, there would be little need to produce any other type of subject index. These limitations are considered in the following sections. Title-based subject indexes have nonetheless been used as indexes to local abstracting and indexing publications, published abstracting and indexing services, reports collections, bibliographies, as well as subject indexes to classified catalogues.

11.7   KWIC and KWOC indexes

There are a number of variations on the basic subject-type title index. A KWIC or *Key*word *In* *C*ontext index is the most readily produced type. A KWIC index is based upon the 'keywords' in the titles of the batch of documents to be indexed. All words in the titles of the documents will be compared by a computer with a pre-

Figure 11.1   A KWIC index: extract from Biological Abstracts

N HYPOTONIA PSYCHIATRIC	**INSTITUTIONALIZATION** /OBSERVATION	66383
POTENTIAL FARM MANAGER	/PROSPECTS FO	67583
DS A FIRST STEP TOWARDS	**INSTITUTIONALIZATION?**	
	PHYSICAL DIS	67011
OLOGY/ HBV-INFECTION IN	**INSTITUTIONALIZED** PATIENTS HEPATITIS	66824
OUTSIDE OF HEALTH CARE	**INSTITUTIONS** HUMAN WASTE DISPOSAL!	66664
OF PEOPLE IN AGED CARE	IN AUCKLAND NEW ZEALAN	66822
EMPERATURE WATER DEPTH	**INSTREAM** FLOW DELPHI METHOD BEAVER	59811
ISHERY/ INTEGRATING THE	FLOW INCREMENTAL METHODOL	59580
F THE PHYSICAL ACTIVITY	**INSTRUMENT** FOR THE LIFE IN NEW ZEALA	66501
R DEVELOPMENT OF A NEW	HUMAN PHEOPHORBIDE SPE	63354
TIONAL SLEEP ASSESSMENT	SLEEP PATHOLOGY BREATHI	66379
N DICKINSON DIAGNOSTIC	SYSTEMS DATABASE BIOCHE	62517
PRECISION OF A PORTABLE	TO ASSESS VIBROTACTILE PE	67962
NT-1'-ENYLGLUTARIC ACID	**INSTRUMENTAL** ANALYSIS CHEMICAL DEG	66078
TICS OPERATIVE DELIVERY	DELIVERY/ LABOR WITH	65511
HUMAN BILE BY MEANS OF	NEUTRON ACTIVATION AN	67994
NANCE IMAGING/ MODERN	TECHNIQUE IN THE DIAG	58569
/ MICROPROCESSOR-BASED	**INSTRUMENTATION** FOR AMBULATORY BE	66988
TICS CEREBRAL PALSY/ AN	**INSTRUMENTED** CHAIR FOR ASSESSING SE	66991
HY SURGICAL TREATMENT/	GAIT ANALYSIS AFTER SE	64085
LAGELLAR ROOTS AS VITAL	**INSTRUMENTS** IN CELLULAR MORPHOGENE	59124
IMARY METHOD HUMAN AIR	**INSUFFLATION** TUBAL DYSFUNCTION SOUN	67510
AL CARE NESTING THERMAL	**INSULATION** FORAGING KOWHAI BUSH KAI	59635
INTAKE GROWTH HORMONE	**INSULIN** /ENDOCRINE AND METABOLIC REG	67952
WITH ANOREXIA NERVOSA	/RESPONSES OF GROWTH HORMON	64741
TIONS FOR PREGNANCY RAT	/ROLE OF PROLACTIN VERSUS GR	60098

selected stop list or stopword list. This stop list is input to the computer before indexing commences and contains all those words which appear in the text but have no value as access words in an index. Typically, connectives and qualifiers (such as 'than', 'a', 'where', 'he', 'she', 'it') will feature in the stop list. Any words which are present in the titles being indexed but are not in the stop list will be treated as 'keywords'. An entry will be produced in respect of every keyword, with these entries arranged in alphabetical order. The keyword is printed 'in context' or, in other words, together with the remainder of the title in which the keyword originally featured. Entry words may be aligned in a centre or in a left-hand column. The rest of the space on the line is occupied by the remainder of the title and some brief source reference which leads the user to the document or to another listing, perhaps including abstracts. Figure 11.1 shows the format of a typical KWIC index.

Clearly a KWIC index format is very restrictive. Since each title can occupy only one line, longer titles are truncated and only brief source references are included. Some users find the format of KWIC indexes unacceptably awkward, particularly the alphabetical arrangement by keywords down the centre of a page and the wrapped-round titles.

KWOC or *Keyword Out of Context* indexes are intended as an improvement upon KWIC indexes with regards to layout and presentation. A KWOC index is still a title index and is constructed in exactly the same way as a KWIC index. However, the display of the index entries differs. The keywords are extracted from the titles and displayed as headings. Under each keyword the complete title and source reference are given. There are no inherent limitations on the space available for each entry. There is a distinct superficial similarity between a KWOC index and an index arranged under assigned or controlled subject headings. A KWOC index can be identified by the following features however:

- all of the words that appear as headings have been extracted from titles;
- some of the headings are unqualified adjectives, for example, circular, handicapped or young, and
- in an unmodified KWOC index, all the headings will be one-word terms.

11.8   Advantages of title-based subject indexes

The advantages of title-based subject indexes include such facts as:

1. a large number of documents can be indexed quickly and cheaply.
2. the absence of human interpretation of content leads to perfect predictability and consistency in the generation of index entries. If a word appears in the title of a document then, unless that word features in the stop list, an entry will be generated in association with it.
3. the final index will mirror current terminology. The words provided as access points in the index are those used by the authors of the documents being indexed. The language of the index thus automatically evolves with the language of the subject as used by authors in the titles of their works. Anyone familiar with the terminology of the subject that the index covers will find the index easy to use.
4. the cumulation of separate index sequences into one integrated index is straightforward.

11.9   Limitations of title indexes as subject indexes

Looked at critically, title indexes are seen as only crude subject indexes which, to be effective, demand imagination and searching skills on the part of the user. Obvious limitations include the following:

1. Titles do not always constitute an accurate summary of the contents of a document. The informativeness of the index depends upon the information

153

contents of the titles that comprise it. Even a descriptive title is by nature succinct and therefore severely limited in the quantity of information it conveys. Equally important is the fact that a title only reflects the main theme of a document; subsidiary themes are not represented. Some titles are not intended to be informative, but rather to attract attention; for example, 'Piggy in the middle'.

2. Long sequences of entries under certain keywords will almost be inevitable if they are central to the literature of any subject area. Several pages of entries under one keyword are discouraging to say the least. Subarrangement at entry terms can break up long sequences of entries listed under the same keyword. Double KWIC and Permuterm indexes arrange pairs of keywords, so that the entries under one keyword are organized according to the second keyword. Thus entries with any given pair of keywords will file next to one another. Unfortunately, in allowing for collocation by pairs of words, Double KWIC and Permuterm indexes require two entries for each pair of words, rather than one entry per keyword in a normal KWIC index. Thus these indexes contain more entries than a straight KWIC index and are inclined to be relatively bulky.

3. Title indexes suffer from an absence of tight control over terminology. With machine indexing, some irrelevant and redundant entries are inevitable. Entries are dictated according to the arbitrary appearance of words in titles. Different words may also be used to represent the same concept by different authors: what to one is a 'strike' to another is an 'industrial dispute'. Similar and closely related subjects are likely to be scattered under different keywords. Further, no guidance can be expected on alternative terms that might prove fruitful or that are related to the seacher's initial search term.

Some of the above limitations of title indexes can be overcome by exercising a measure of control over the index terminology and by inputting and instructing the computer to print a number of predetermined links or references between key-words. However, any refinement involves greater human intervention which can easily overturn the arguments in favour of subject indexes based upon titles. Some of these issues are considered further in 16.8 in the wider context of natural language indexing.

Recommended reading

Ayres, F H et al. (1968), 'Author versus title: a comparative survey of the accuracy of the information which the user brings to the library catalogue', *Journal of Documentation*, **24** (4), 266–72.

Elvin, P J (1986), 'Making better KWOC indexes even better', *Electronic Library*, **4**, 282–89.

Feinberg, H (1975), *Title derivative indexing techniques: a comparative study*, Los Angeles: Scarecrow Press.

Hodges, P R (1983), 'Keyword in title indexes: effectiveness of retrieval in computer searches', *Special Libraries*, **74**, 56–60.

Matthews, F W and Shillingford, Λ D (1973), 'Variations on KWIC', *Aslib Proceedings*, **25** (4), 140–52.

Petrarca, A E and Lay, W M (1969), 'The double-KWIC coordinate index: a new approach for preparation of high quality printed indexes by automatic indexing techniques', *Journal of Chemical Documentation*, **9**, 256–61.

PART III
SUBJECTS

12 The subject approach: introduction, processes, tools and simple evaluation

12.1 Subjects

Users often approach information sources not with names (as have been considered in Part II), but with a question that requires an answer or a topic for study. Users seek documents or information concerned with a particular subject. In order to make some provision for this common approach to information sources, it is necessary to arrange documents – and document surrogates in catalogues, indexes, bibliographies, computer databases and so on – in such a way that items on specific subjects can be retrieved. Thus, the subject approach is extremely important in the access to and the exploitation of information, documents and data.

Before we discuss the provision that libraries and information workers make for the subject approach, it may be useful to consider the preliminary question: What is a subject? In talking about a subject we generally refer to a given area of knowledge or to the contents of an information source of a given scope. A subject might be considered to be defined by:

- an area of interest,
- an area in which an individual researcher or professional works,
- an area in which an individual writes or
- an area of knowledge which is studied.

Consider a well-known subject area such as geography. Ask your friends what they think geography is. Study the definitions of geography in a number of dictionaries and encyclopaedias. Examine a few syllabuses for basic courses in geography. Note the different definitions and the different boundaries for this one subject area. It is easy to see that users and separate pieces of literature may hold different perspectives on one subject. The points of divergence in perspective can broadly be summarized by the facts that:

- different labels are used, and
- different concepts of scope and associations with other subjects are evident.

These factors help to explain the basic problems in identifying a satisfactory subject approach as well as the vast array of different tools required in the subject approach to knowledge.

It is possible and convenient to select a perspective on the scope, associations and labels for subjects which coincides with the way in which those subjects are handled in the literature. In libraries, most devices for the organization of knowledge concern themselves primarily with organizing literature. This policy of reflecting the subject labels and relationships present in the literature of a subject is known as being consistent with *literary warrant*. On the basis of literary warrant, any classification scheme or indexing language will reflect the subjects (and the relationships between subjects) present in the literature that the scheme or language has been designed to organize. This could be regarded as a pragmatic approach to the design of devices for the organization of knowledge by subject. The main limitation of this pragmatic approach lies in the time – and collection–dependency of the resulting tool. All collections alter over time; in order to remain effective, the classification device must evolve in keeping with the development of the collection.

There is an alternative method for the design of subject retrieval devices, and that is to build languages or schemes which depend upon some theoretical views about the nature and structure of knowledge. As will become apparent later, this theoretical approach is also important in determining the nature of subject devices for the organization of knowledge.

12.2   Indexing languages

The term indexing language can seem rather daunting and has certainly had different meanings in its different incarnations. Here an indexing language is simply defined as:

> a list of terms or notations that might be used as access points in an index.

This definition does not exclude the names of persons, bodies, chemicals, trade names and so on, but since we are concerned primarily with the subject approach, this list as discussed in the next few sections will concentrate on terms which describe subjects. An alternative definition of an indexing language is:

> the set of terms (the vocabulary) and the devices for handling the relationship between them in a system for providing index descriptions.

An indexing language may also be referred to as a retrieval language.

Indexing languages may be of three distinct types:

1.   *Controlled indexing languages* or *assigned-term systems* are indexing languages

in which a person both controls the terms that are used to represent subjects and executes the process whereby terms are assigned to a particular document. Normally an authority list identifies the terms that may be assigned. Indexing involves a person assigning terms from this list to specific documents on the basis of subjective interpretations of the concepts implied; in so doing, the indexer exercises some intellectual discrimination.

There are two types of controlled indexing languages: *alphabetical indexing languages* and *classification schemes*. In alphabetical indexing languages, such as are embodied in thesauri and subject headings lists, subject terms are the alphabetical names of the subjects. Control is exercised over which terms are used, but otherwise the terms are ordinary words. In classification schemes each subject is assigned a piece of notation, the usual objective being to place a subject within a context with respect to other subjects. Both classification schemes and alphabetical indexing languages are used in a variety of contexts, and most of the remainder of Part II will concentrate on controlled language indexing. Both types of devices are commonly applied in catalogues, indexes to books and periodicals, bibliographies, current awareness bulletins, selective dissemination of information, computerized databases and data banks, abstracting and indexing services, encyclopaedias, dictionaries and directories. Classification is also prominent in the physical arrangement of documents.

2. *Natural indexing languages* or *derived-term systems* are not really a separate language at all, but the 'natural' or ordinary language of the document being indexed. Any terms that appear in the document are candidates for index terms. In practice, natural language indexing tends to rely upon the terms present in an abstract or the title of a document, although sometimes the full text of a document is used. Depending on how it is achieved, natural language indexing based upon the full text of a document may be very detailed; alternatively, it may establish some mechanism for deciding which terms are the most important in relation to a particular document. In computer indexing, this will involve statistical analysis of the relative frequency of occurrence of terms. In human indexing, some judgement would be required in selecting terms. Many of these problems can be minimized by restricting indexing to titles and abstracts. Either a computer or a person can execute natural language indexing. The computer may well use a list of terms deemed to be useful in indexing (that is, a type of thesaurus) to identify appropriate terms.

Strictly natural language systems are only one type of derived-term system. A derived–term system is one where all descriptors are taken from the item itself. Thus author indexes, title indexes and citation indexes, as well as natural language subject indexes, are derived-term systems.

3. *Free indexing languages* do not consist of a list of terms distinct from those used to describe concepts in a subject area. Indexing is 'free' in the sense that there are no constraints on the terms that can be used in the indexing process. Free language indexing is distinct from natural language indexing in that the

161

latter is constrained by the language of the document being indexed; the former is not. Free language indexing may be conducted by humans or computer. When executed by humans with a sound knowledge of a subject and its terminology, free language indexing can result in an index which is both consistent in the assignment of index terms and which matches the perspective of index users. However successful, human free language indexing is very dependent upon the skills of the individual indexer. Computerized free language indexing is, for all practical purposes, the same as natural language indexing. The computer must have some basis for assigning indexing terms; if a pre-assigned list of terms is not supplied, the computer itself must assign terms on the basis of those present in the document being indexed.

Both natural language indexing, and, to a lesser extent, free language indexing are used extensively in producing both printed indexes and in gaining access to computerized databases and data banks. Some applications of natural language indexing based upon titles of documents have already been considered in Chapter 11. Natural language indexing will be used throughout Part III for purposes of comparison with controlled language indexing. It will also be considered in some detail in parts of succeeding chapters on alphabetical indexing languages and alphabetical indexing systems.

Controlled term indexing languages are claimed to be more consistent and therefore more efficient, but the many tests on indexing languages have failed to prove this convincingly. Many databases include terms from controlled indexing languages and also support searching on the text of the record, thus offering what might be regarded as the best of both worlds.

12.3   Functions of subject access

Subject access normally seeks to fulfil both of the following functions:

- to show what a library, information source or database includes on a particular subject, and
- to show what a library, information source or database includes on related subjects.

Different approaches to the organization of knowledge may emphasize the relative importance of either the first or second objective, but it is difficult to neglect one without impairing the effectiveness of the other. That the two objectives are interdependent can be demonstrated by examining the first objective.

Specific subject

A book on vegetable gardening may contain equally valuable information on growing tomatoes as a book devoted entirely to growing tomatoes. Thus a book on a related subject can, to varying extents, substitute for a book on the specific subject being sought. Even a user who starts a search with a specific subject in mind may find that it does not quite match his requirements after all. A user might start by looking for a map of London, when he really wants a map of Camden; he might believe that the more specific subject (Camden) will not be covered independently. Later, after examining maps of the area, he may discover that what he is really interested in is Parliament Hill. The inclusion of related subjects can thus often help the user with a specific search, particularly where he is not adequately familiar with the subject being sought or the way in which the subject is likely to be handled or packaged in the literature.

Relationships

Figure 12.1 shows a small hierarchy or group of ranked subjects which makes some statement concerning the relationships between those subjects. This hierarchy shows the general subject area of building and its *subordinate* subject areas: building materials, auxiliary construction practices, construction in specific materials, wood construction, roofing and so on. Subordinate to each of these subject areas are other topics. For example, plumbing and pipe fitting are subordinate to utilities. The converse of a subordinate subject is a *superordinate* subject. Again, then, building is superordinate to building materials, auxiliary construction practices and so on. Two subjects at the same level in the hierarchy (for example, both subdivisions of the same parent or superordinate subject) are said to be *coordinate*. Thus, utilities and heating are coordinate to one another, as also are wood and slate.

Relationships such as those shown in the hierarchy in Figure 12.1 are known as *semantic* relationships, representing connections between associated subjects. Although we may disagree about detail, semantic relationships between subjects are reasonably stable and reflect the consensus of opinion concerning their connections. Thus, we all agree that one component of a building is a roof (and not vice versa!), that chemistry is a branch of science, or that an Alsatian is a dog. There is some agreement as to the permanence of these relationships; they can be expected to alter only as knowledge advances.

There are other relationships between subjects known as *syntactic* relationships which arise from the context of subjects in specific documents – from the syntax. Thus a document such as

A farm spelling pictures teaching jigsaw

brings the concepts farming and spelling into a related context. Plainly, there is not

163

Figure 12.1 The subdivisions of building in the Dewey Decimal Classification Scheme

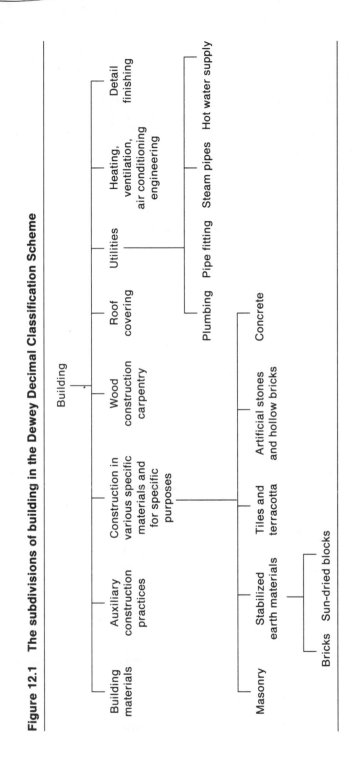

always a connection between farming and spelling; indeed, many other documents can be identified where these subjects are not connected. Syntactic relationships thus occur in documents, but are less permanent than semantic relationships. In any subject device, it is necessary to distinguish between syntactic and semantic relationships and to make a different kind of provision for each.

Both classification schemes and alphabetical indexing languages fulfil both of the basic objectives of a subject device. The distinction arises from different emphases. Classification schemes specialize in showing networks of subjects and displaying the relationships between subjects, and thus are particularly suited to achieving the second objective. Alphabetical indexing languages specialize in establishing specific labels for subjects and providing direct access to individual subjects. Nevertheless, as will be amply demonstrated throughout the remaining chapters in Part II, all subject devices must attempt to fulfil both objectives.

12.4 The subject indexing process

Indexing is the process whereby indexes and associated tools for the organization of knowledge are created. Indexing may be conducted manually or may rely to varying extents upon the facilities for the manipulation and ordering of data offered by the computer.

If the resulting index is to be effective and efficient, the assignment of notation from a classification scheme or the application of subject headings from a recognized list involves skill and judgement. Clearly, the only totally adequate indication of the content of a document is the text of the document in its entirety. Any other indication of document content, such as classification notation or alphabetical subject headings, are partial representations of content. Three stages are necessary in assigning terms from indexing languages when intellectual indexing is performed:

Familiarization→Analysis→Translation

The objective in executing these three stages is to construct a document profile which reflects its subject. Most documents have many characteristics that might be identified by a searcher as the criterion by which the document would be selected as relevant. Any set of search keys for a document can be described as a *document profile*. Different types of indexes and different user groups may require different sets of search keys (or different document profiles) to be developed in respect of one document. Some of the available search keys have already been considered in Part II; that is, personal and corporate names. The other important class of search keys are the subject labels which will be discussed below. Let us now consider the various stages in framing a document profile.

Step 1: Familiarization This first step involves the indexer becoming conversant

165

with the subject content of the document to be indexed. Documents are comprised of words, and searchers and indexers use words to represent or convey concepts; at this stage however, it is important for the indexer to attempt to identify the concepts that are represented by the words. In order to achieve good consistent indexing, the indexer must have a thorough appreciation of the structure of the subject and the nature of the contribution that the document is making to the advancement of knowledge. From time to time the indexer may need to consult external reference sources in order to achieve a sufficient understanding of the document content for effective indexing. Certainly it will always be necessary to examine the document content, concentrating particularly on the clues offered by the title, the contents page, chapter headings and any abstracts, introduction, prefaces or other preliminary matter.

Step 2:   Analysis   The second step towards constructing an index involves the identification of the concepts within a document which are worthy of indexing. Any one document covers a number of different topics. Take, for example, a book entitled *Wills and Probate*. This book contains sections on making a will, executors, administration of an estate, pensions, tax, house ownership, grants and intestacy, to name but a few. Usually it is possible to identify a central theme in a document and to produce a summary of document content based upon this central theme. Frequently, but not always, this same process will have been attempted by the author when inventing the title, which explains why the title is often a useful aid to indexing. Clearly an index must permit access to a document by its central theme, but to what extent should access be provided to secondary or subsidiary topics considered within a document? This question can only be answered with reference to specific indexing environments. In catalogues, for instance, it is common to index no more than three separate subjects for any one document. Indexers for *Chemical Abstracts* are instructed as follows:

> index every measurement, observation, method, apparatus, suggestion and theory that is presented as new and of value in itself; [also] all new chemical compounds and all elements, compounds and other substances for which new data are given (American Chemical Society, *Chemical Abstracts Service Directions for Abstractors*; Columbus, Ohio: ACS, 1971).

It is helpful to have such guidelines concerning the types, range and number of concepts to be indexed in any indexing situation, although precise guidelines are not always drafted and the choice of concepts to include may be left to the discretion of the indexer. More consideration will be given to this topic in section 12.5.

Many traditional indexing approaches have sought to find a label or indexing term which is *co-extensive* with the content of the document being indexed; that is, the scope of the indexing term and the document are similar. For example, for the book on *Wills and Probate*, it would not be sufficient to index this book under the term 'Wills' alone, since this heading would not reveal the section of the book on 'Probate'.

(*Note*: The term 'analysis' has been used here in its restrictive meaning. Some authors use 'analysis' to apply to all processes associated with the construction of a document profile of any kind. In this definition 'analysis' subsumes cataloguing, indexing, classification and abstracting.)

Step 3: Translation Having identified the central theme of a document, this theme must be described in terms which are present in the indexing language. In controlled language indexing, this will involve describing the concepts in terms of the classification scheme, thesaurus or list of subject headings which is being used. For example, a free interpretation of the subject of a document might be:

Social conflict and educational change in England and France between 1789 and 1848.

The concepts represented in this summary might be translated into an alphabetical description of the form:

Education—History—England—Social Conflict—France

or into a classification notation such as 942.073.

To take another example:

Radioactivity in the surface and coastal waters of the British Isles, 1977

might be converted to an alphabetical description such as:

Water pollutants—Radioactive materials—Great Britain

or into a classification notation such as 628.16850941.

This translation will involve not only labelling the subject, but possibly also indicating related subjects, as has been discussed earlier. The guiding principle in translating concepts into the indexing language of any given system must be that the terms selected and the relationships indicated are consistent with the 'normal' user's perspective on the subject. This coincidence between indexing and user approach is known as *user warrant*. In other words the indexing system must be tailored to the needs of the users of the index. Given that different users may have different perspectives on the same subject, it is clear that different indexing languages and systems may be appropriate for different subjects and environments, and even for the same subject in a different environment.

Consider, for example, medicine. The approach suitable in specialized indexing tools for medical research will need to be very specific in order to differentiate between closely related subjects. A collection of general medical books in a public library may deal with the same range of topics, but the indexing can be broader than in a specialist context, and the terms used for the same thing may

167

be different. What a doctor might refer to as 'rubella' will probably be called 'German measles' by the mother of the child with the complaint.

Apart from differing needs of users, indexing approaches may differ on policy grounds. Some types of indexing are appropriate where it is desired to concentrate on generating excellent indexes. Others are less concerned with perfect indexing, but rather demand that the searcher exercise his skills thoroughly, offering him the appropriate facilities to do so. It is important to recognize, then, that a variety of different indexing approaches are inevitable, not only for reasons of history and indexer preference, but because different situations demand different approaches.

12.5 The searching process

Information retrieval follows from the generation of an index. Although this work concerns itself primarily with the organization of knowledge and the production of indexes, catalogues and databases, it is imperative that the indexer should have an appreciation of how the index is to be used. Indeed, the selection of an indexing approach is crucially dependent upon user requirements. Equally, it is important that a searcher should have a clear understanding of indexing methods. Indexing and searching, then, are integral one to another, making a few comments on searching in order here. These are also intended to demonstrate the similarity between indexing and searching, and to show how indexing tools feature in the searching process. These comments are as true for author searching (Part II) as subject searching, and they are introduced here only for convenience.

Searching an index, a catalogue or a database can be viewed as involving the same three stages as indexing:

Step 1: Familiarization A searcher must be adequately familiar with what he wishes to retrieve. Although this may seem an obvious statement, there are many instances when the searcher is not fully aware of what can or might be retrieved. Two common circumstances may arise:

(a) the searcher is an information worker trying to extract documents or information on behalf of someone else. Here familiarization can be partially achieved by conducting a reference interview with the end user. The reference interview should ascertain both a clear subject profile and also other characteristics of the required documents or information, such as any constraints on date, language, source or level. The intermediary (information worker) also needs to be conversant with the sources to be searched.

(b) the searcher may be the end user, possibly approaching the search in some ignorance of his real requirements or of the literature that might be available to meet those requirements. Some degree of ignorance of this kind is not unusual since the usual objective in consulting an information source is to become better informed. If the search is to be successful, the user will learn about the subject and its literature during the searching process.

(Of course, an even more unfortunate situation would be where the end user, poorly informed about the information or documents required, charges the information worker to conduct a search on the basis of incomplete or inaccurate information.)

Step 2: *Analysis* When the objective is clear, the next step is to analyse the concepts present in a search. Sometimes, particularly for a straightforward search in a printed index, it will be sufficient to establish these concepts in the searcher's mind. On other occasions, where the search must be specified with a number of interacting concepts and other parameters, it will be necessary to write the concepts down. For example, if information is required on 'primary education' and this is a heading in the appropriate printed index, then the search profile merely involves the term 'primary education'. If, however, the searcher seeks information on 'Recovering hydrogen from coal tar in a continuous electrofluid reactor' and is interested only in reports, books or periodical articles which review the subject after 1980, then there is clearly scope for a more complex search profile. Aspects of this will be considered in Chapter 17. Building a search profile has much in common with building a document profile during indexing. The *search profile* will comprise a series of search keys representing subjects and other characteristics of the search requirements which together indicate the scope and nature of the search.

Step 3: *Translation* of the concepts in a search profile will involve consultation of the thesaurus, classification scheme (or its index) or list of subject headings that has been used in constructing the index to be searched. Often the quality of the translation may be tested by examining the items indexed under a number of possible terms that might have been used to describe a subject in an index. Thus a searcher might consider perusing entries under sweets, chocolates and confectionery. Once a satisfactory entry point has been identified in an index, the instructions or guidelines in the index may help the searcher in improving retrieval. Such experimental retrieval may be more necessary for searches using the natural language of the document. Here consultation of an inverted file which has been constructed in the indexing of the text may aid in identifying word forms and search terms. An online thesaurus is useful if available. If not, other sources of subject terminology, such as thesauri and dictionaries, may be consulted.

Although there are parallels between searching and indexing, it is important to remember that successful information retrieval does not depend only upon effective exploitation of indexing. It is no good searching an information source (printed or computer-held) efficiently and with a sound understanding of its construction if that source does not provide access to the information or documents that are being sought. Many searches involve the use of more than one source, and all searches require that the most appropriate source be chosen. There is more to effective information retrieval than indexing, though this is certainly an essential component of the process.

12.6   Measures of index effectiveness

Some simple measures of index effectiveness are introduced at this point in order to approach different indexing methods critically. Extensive theory exists on the evaluation of indexes and indexing, but regrettably there is not space to treat this topic at any length here. Some authoritative texts on the subject are listed at the end of this chapter.

For any user approaching an index or a computerized information retrieval system, there will be a number of records in the system relevant to the topic of his search, while the remainder will be of no interest on that occasion. Even for those items that are designated relevant, some may be judged to be highly relevant, whilst others may be regarded as partially or only marginally relevant. Various scales of relevance ratings may be established. For example, if a user desires information on asbestos roofing, there may be records for documents in the index that deal specifically with this topic which would be selected as highly relevant. However, although subject may be the primary consideration in the assessment of relevance, it is not the only factor that determines whether a user wishes to be alerted to the existence of a document. A user may reject a document because it is in a language that he cannot read or because it is dated. Relevance is a subjective measure. Documents rarely exactly match a user's requirements because information can be packaged in almost as many different ways as there are participants in a subject area. Inevitably an author writes from his understanding and perspective; a user probably has a different background, level of understanding and experience of the same subject.

Consider again those documents indexed by the system that may be partially relevant to a given user's search. Suppose that, although our reader is primarily interested in asbestos roofing, only a limited quantity of material directly concerned with this topic is represented in a collection. It is, however, possible to broaden the search and find additional information on asbestos roofing by retrieving general documents on roofing and extracting pertinent sections. The end result will be more information on asbestos roofing traced, but only by considering all of the documents listed under the much broader category of roofing. Thus many non-relevant documents will have been retrieved and examined in the process of sifting relevant from non-relevant. These non-relevant documents are frequently referred to as '*noise*'. Notice that it would be possible to improve recall until every relevant document is retrieved by scanning the entire document collection, but such perfect recall (that is, retrieving every relevant document) would be accompanied by a drop in the proportion of relevant documents found.

We have begun to identify, then, two conflicting objectives which are present in any search. Ideally we would like both to maximize recall – the number of relevant documents retrieved – at the same time as ensuring that all the documents retrieved were relevant. In practice, it is not possible to achieve these twin objectives simultaneously.

The concepts introduced above have been more precisely defined, leading to a consensus regarding their meaning and to experimental measurements. The following definitions are important in the evaluation of indexes:

$$\text{Recall ratio} = \frac{\text{Number of relevant documents retrieved}}{\text{Total number of relevant documents in the system}} \times 100\%$$

$$\text{Precision ratio} = \frac{\text{Number of relevant documents retrieved}}{\text{Total number of documents retrieved}} \times 100\%$$

One easy observation from these definitions is that indexes are measured in terms of their effectiveness in retrieval. This serves to support some of the statements made in Section 12.5 and again emphasizes that a good index is one which permits effective retrieval.

As discussed above, precision (or the proportion of relevant documents retrieved) is related to recall (the extent of retrieval of relevant documents). More specifically, recall is inversely proportional to precision, and vice versa; in other words, as one increases, the other must decrease. In practice the application of recall and precision in the evaluation of indexes is hindered by the difficulty of evaluating some of the components in the definition. For example, without scanning the entire index, it is impossible to estimate the total number of relevant documents in the system, a figure that is required in the calculation of recall. Clearly it is easier to measure precision than recall. A useful application of recall in practice is not to seek a measure of absolute recall (as defined above), but rather to use recall to compare two different indexing systems, by defining what is known as *relative recall*.

$$\text{Relative recall} = \frac{\text{Number of documents retrieved in system 1}}{\text{Number of documents retrieved in system 2}} \times 100\%$$

Clearly this definition can be generalized in order to compare a number of different systems and thus provide a useful comparative measure.

Since recall goes up as precision goes down, it is clearly not possible to achieve a system which gives full recall at the same time as full precision. Thus in index, catalogue or database design, the indexer must choose an appropriate blend of recall and precision for each individual application. Quite frequently a user will be satisfied with a few items on a topic as long as they are relevant and meet other criteria such as language, date and level. Here, high precision but low recall is satisfactory. On other occasions a user may want every document or piece of information on a topic traced, and then high recall must be sought to the detriment of precision.

Recall and precision are measures of index effectiveness, indicating the extent to which relevant documents are retrieved. But a good information retrieval system must also be efficient and cost-effective. Other measures used to evaluate the efficiency of the system might include the following:

- The *time* that it takes to perform a search. This is an important parameter for the individual user, but unfortunately general measures are likely to prove elusive. The time that it takes to perform a search in a system is a function of a number of factors, including the user's previous experience with the system, aspects of system design and the nature of the search. In an experimental situation some of these variables could be controlled, and average search times could be computed for different systems. The time taken to perform a search is not only influenced by the indexing language and system, however, but also by system response times, search strategies that are available and the style of the dialogue in a computer-based system.

- *Cost* is a further measure of system effectiveness. Clearly, it is desirable to minimize search costs which include any expense associated with the acquisition of the source or access to it, as well as the searcher's time. Information retrieval systems embrace online access to external databases, searching of OPACs and CD–ROM, but the economics of making use of these different media varies dramatically. External database costs are cumulated on a pay–as–you–go basis; CD–ROM are acquired on subscription, so the more searches performed, the lower the per search cost. With an in-house database, the cost to the organization can be assessed as capital and ongoing, a major component being that of creating and maintaining the database. Intellectual indexing using a controlled language may incur a significant initial expense, but may assist users with quick and effective retrieval and thus reduce the amount of user education and other support facilities. Natural language indexing tends to shift the intellectual effort necessary for effective retrieval to the end-user. Again, it is difficult to calculate the cost of a search, but the searcher will always consider this factor and seek a cost-effective means of information retrieval.

- *User-friendliness* is another criterion that might be used to evaluate a system since it will affect the cost of searching and the speed with which retrieval can be achieved. It will also have some impact on training commitments required of users, and whether end-users can be expected to use the system independently or whether they will need the assistance of an intermediary. Interface design and the nature of the indexing language are two of the factors that will

172

influence the user-friendliness of a system. These are discussed further in subsequent chapters in this section.

12.7 Other features of indexes

Recall and precision interact with other characteristics of indexes. Some of these are briefly introduced here.

- *Specificity*, or the degree of specificity of indexing, must be established during planning for the index and reviewed from time to time thereafter. Specificity of a system is the extent to which it permits the indexer to be precise about the subject of a document. A completely specific statement of document content would have to be the text of the document itself. Obviously a more formal and more summarized profile is required in most indexing systems. In any index the level of specificity is normally determined by the extent and type of subjects listed in the system. For instance, it is desirable that a scannable number of documents be listed under each heading in a catalogue. With a given size of collection, say 20,000 documents, the appropriate number of headings can be identified on the basis of seeking to create scannable categories. A set number of categories will largely determine the specificity of the headings to be included in the index. A fundamental theoretical rule of subject indexing is that each heading should be *co-extensive* with the subject of the document; that is, the label and the information or documents found under that label should match. In practice this can only be achieved within the constraints of any given indexing language and system.

  The relationship between precision and recall and specificity is interesting. The higher the specificity of indexing, the more likely that search outputs will show high precision. Lower specificity will be associated with lower precision but high recall. Continuing our previous search, if the term 'asbestos roofing' does not exist in the system, then we must search under the broad term 'roofing'. Documents can only be identified as relevant by scanning the rather larger numbers of documents listed under the broader heading.
- *Exhaustivity* of indexing has some impact on recall and precision. As has already been discussed, most documents have more than one theme. The indexer is required to consider which topics within a document to represent in an index. In many traditional catalogues, access will only be provided to two or three main themes. A more specialized collection may be indexed in greater depth or with greater exhaustivity; up to 20 or 30 separate themes may be identified and indexed in one document. The indexer can either be constrained as to the number of themes to index per document, or be given the option of indexing as many themes as possible. Exhaustivity is repre-

sented by the number of themes that are indexed in a document. This is approximately measured by the number of index terms assigned to a document (although it is possible that more than one index term may be necessary to represent some themes). High exhaustivity tends to be a feature of databases indexed automatically on the basis of the text of the document.

In contrast to higher specificity, higher exhaustivity increases recall at the cost of impaired precision. The more secondary themes that are indexed in a document, the more documents that will be retrieved, but in many instances these will treat the topic being sought only as a subsidary subject and so be judged as only marginally relevant. A high exhaustivity of indexing, then, is beneficial where a thorough search is required, but may be a handicap when only a few highly relevant documents are sought.

• *Error* will be present in any system which involves human intervention. Computers are reliable and less prone to error provided they are instructed or programmed appropriately and correctly. Errors, such as indexers assigning unsuitable terms to concepts or omitting relationships, will affect precision by producing unsuitable documents in response to a search; on the other hand, the same documents will fail to be identified when a search is conducted under the terms which should have been assigned to the document, thus reducing recall. Documents and information can be lost forever by faults in inputting. Thus care in indexing is essential and systems should be designed in such a way as to minimize the possibility of error. Clear instructions are essential in indexing tools such as thesauri, subject headings lists and classification schemes.

Recommended reading

Austin, D (1986), 'Vocabulary control and IT', *Aslib Proceedings*, **38** (1), 1–15.

Bakewell, K G B (1978), *Classification and indexing practice*, London: Bingley.

Beghtol, C (1986), 'Bibliographic classification theory and text linguistics, aboutness analysis intertextuality and the cognitive act of classifying documents', *Journal of Documentation*, **42** (2), 84–113.

Buchanan, B (1979), *Theory of library classification*, London: Bingley.

Eisenberg, M and Schamber, L (1988), 'Relevance: the search for a definition' in C L Borgman and E Y H Pai (eds), *Proceedings* of the American Society for Information Science, 51st Annual Meeting, **25**, Medford: Learned Information for ASIS, 164–68.

Foskett, A C (1982), *The subject approach to information*, 4th edition, London: Bingley.

Foskett, D J (1974), *Classification and indexing in the social sciences*, 2nd edition, London: Butterworth.

Harrod, L (ed) (1978), *Indexers on indexing*, New York: Bowker.

International Standards Organisation (1985), 'Documentation – methods for examining documents, determining their subjects and selecting index terms', Geneva: ISO, (ISO 5963–1985(E)).

Lancaster, F W (1986), *Vocabulary control for information retrieval*, 2nd edition, Arlington, Va: Information Resources Press.

Lancaster, F W (1991), *Indexing and abstracting in theory and practice*, London: Library Association.

Lancaster, F W et al (1989), 'Subject analysis', in M Williams (ed), *Annual Review of Information Science and Technology*, **24**, Amsterdam: Elsevier.

Langridge, D W (1973), *Approach to classification*, London: Bingley.

Langridge, D W (1976), *Classification and indexing in the humanities*, London: Butterworth.

Langridge, D W (1989), *Subject analysis: principles and practice*, London: Library Association.

Maltby, A (1975), *Sayer's manual of classification for libraries*, 5th edition, London: Deutsch.

Maltby, A (1976), *Classification in the 70's: a second look*, London: Bingley.

Regazzi, J J (1988), 'Performance measures for information retrieval systems – an experimental approach', *Journal of the American Society for Information Science*, **39** (4), 235–51.

Rowley, J E (1988), *Abstracting and indexing*, 2nd edition, London: Library Association.

Saracevic, T et al (1988), 'A study of information seeking and retrieval', *Journal of the American Society for Information Science*, **39** (3), 161–216.

Vickery, B C (1975), *Classification and indexing in science and technology*, 3rd edition, London: Butterworth.

Note: Other works which provide a general introduction to the subject approach are listed at the end of the introduction.

13 The theory of bibliographic classification

13.1 Why theory?

A study of bibliographic classification could concentrate solely upon the major and some of the more minor bibliographic classification schemes used today. However, although such a study might permit some comparison of different schemes, this pragmatic approach would not provide the parameters for comparison; nor, indeed, would it identify any criteria that classification schemes should meet. A study of the underlying features of the classification process and the components of a classification scheme is thus a preparation for the more critical and informed application of classification schemes. Further, classification and the network of relationships between subjects can be a fascinating study in itself, even devoid of application.

This chapter is relatively succinct and goes little further than identifying the major ideas concerning classification theory that have emerged during the twentieth century and before, and indicating their applications. There are, in summary, two important applications for classification theory:

1. New theories can be applied in the development and revision of existing schemes. These are often large general schemes.
2. New theories can be used as the basis for new schemes. Most such new schemes will not be general, but rather special classification schemes designed for a particular application or subject.

Before proceeding it may be wise to offer some definitions. The *Shorter Oxford English Dictionary* defines a class as

> a number of individuals (persons or things) possessing a common attribute and grouped together under a general or 'class' name; a kind, sort, division.

To continue, a classification scheme is defined as 'an orderly arrangement of terms or classes'. The application of such a scheme to a set of documents should result in the ordering or arranging of that set of documents into groups or classes according to their subject content. In so doing the classifier should group docu-

ments on the same subject together into one class, and arrange classes of documents in a useful order with respect to one another.

Classification, then, is the grouping of like objects. It is not self-evident. If a
small child is asked to group a set of objects he may gather together items
according to their colour (for example, all brown objects) or according to their
normal use (for example, all cutlery). Similarly with classification, the grouping is
not self-evident. The classification scheme is intended to act as an authority in
selecting the relationships to be shown.

A classification scheme comprises three components:

- the *schedules*, in which subjects are listed systematically showing their relationships;
- the *notation* which is the code for use in the index or catalogue and has a self–
  evident order which helps in signalling the arrangement; and
- the alphabetical *index* which provides an entry vocabulary or a list of terms
  for first consultation, as well as identification of the place of a subject within
  the scheme.

In order to support these three elements and to ensure that schemes are updated, it
is important to have some organization which takes responsibility for revision and
publication.

This chapter considers each of these components of a classification scheme in
turn. The ideas introduced in this chapter form the basis for the comparison and
evaluation of some of the major schemes in Chapter 14.

13.2   Schedules

The schedules – the list of subjects – are the heart of the classification scheme. The
schedules determine which subjects can be effectively represented by the scheme,
and which relationships are most effectively reflected by it. What must be recognized is that in approaching different collections, different users at different periods
in time will place varying requirements on a scheme, both in terms of the subjects
that should be included and also in terms of the relationships that need to be
shown. Any scheme which attempts to remain stable over an extended time period
will in some sense be a compromise.

13.2.1   The requirements of an effective schedule

Before examining the two main means of constructing classification schedules, it is
as well to consider what the objectives of the designer of a classification scheme
should be. Although some of the criteria listed below may appear obvious, it is
necessary to state them because, sadly, some of the major schemes do not meet

these standards. It is easiest to discuss the criteria for effective schedules on two levels: first, in terms of the main classes or groups in the scheme, and second, in relation to the treatment of specific subjects.

In a general classification scheme, a main class is one of the broad classes into which knowledge is divided before further analysis begins and for which there is no broader containing class. In respect of the main classes, the following requirements can be specified:

1. All major disciplines should be represented. Any major omission will lead to a group of documents which cannot be classified under the scheme. In a general scheme, all disciplines in human knowledge must obviously be represented. In a special scheme it is sufficient to identify the main subjects of the application to be covered.
2. The space in the scheme for a discipline should be approximately proportional to the size of the literature of that discipline. If not, subjects with limited literature may be subdivided too extensively, producing unused or little used subdivisions, whereas 'large' subjects, if allocated only the same number of subdivisions, will have some trying to accommodate unmanageable quantities of literature. If main classes are unbalanced in size and more subdivisions are made in some classes than others (to cater for the extensive literature of a larger subject), then long notations may result in the 'larger' areas. Measuring the size of the literature of a discipline may present problems, however.
3. The order of classes should bring related subjects into proximity. The object of classification is to group related subjects and, at the same time, to separate them from other subjects in other groups. With a large stock the order of main classes may not be particularly important, although most users would appreciate disciplines placed adjacent to related disciplines. Thus, language and literature, medicine and physiology, and botany and agriculture could conveniently be placed close to each other. Although recognizing some such affinities between subjects, it is more difficult to find an overall order of main classes which suits everybody.
4. 1, 2 and 3 have assumed a stable body of knowledge. This is not the case, so the fourth criterion must require that there be provision for major change in the main classes in order to reflect:

    (a) the extension of developing disciplines, as measured by the relative size of the literature, and as has been evident recently in various areas of the social sciences and in computer science;
    (b) the reduction of contracting disciplines, as measured by the relative size of the literature, and as has been evident for some time in religion and philosophy; and
    (c) the changing relationships between disciplines and the growth of interdisciplinary topics, such as energy and industrial safety.

Within main classes, the schedules must meet requirements in respect of their ability to cover all subjects and all the relationships that might be encountered in the literature to which the scheme will be applied. It is important that:

1. There be a clear place for each simple subject, which is regarded as falling within one of the major disciplines in the scheme. Thus there must be a clear place for poetry, probably in the discipline of literature, and a clear place for lasers, probably in the discipline of physics.
2. There must be a clear place for every complex subject likely to be encountered in the literature. Thus, within the discipline of literature, there must be a place not only for poetry, but also for nineteenth-century German poetry, and a place somewhere for the use of fibre optics in cable television.
3. The order of subjects must be systematic and generally acceptable to the anticipated users of index or collection; it should also facilitate effective browsing between related subjects. Thus, for example, various books on growing different flowers (such as roses, chrysanthemums, dahlias and sweet peas) should be close to one another when arranged on shelves in accordance with the classification scheme.
4. There must be provision for changes necessary to keep the coverage of subjects adequate for new literature. In other words, there must be scope for:

    (a) new simple and complex subjects. Although provision must be made for new simple subjects, new complex subjects are much more likely to occur. Knowledge generally evolves from an identifiable base, and often new subjects arise from the coming together of two previously separate subjects.
    (b) topics which have ceased to be the subject of new literature to be deleted from the scheme at an appropriate moment.
    (c) a recognition of changes in the relationships between subjects.

5. Schedules must be published (either internally or externally), so that the scheme can be applied by those who might find it useful.

In the attempt to match the above criteria, there are two fundamentally distinct avenues leading to the construction of the schedules of a classification scheme. These two methods, *faceted classification* and *enumerative classification*, are introduced in the next two sections. Faceted classification is now accepted as the more systematic way of constructing a classification scheme in today's environment of rapid development of knowledge and of the literature in which that knowledge is recorded. However, many of the major bibliographic classification schemes in use in libraries today were constructed according to the principles of enumerative classification. Thus an appreciation of both methods is necessary to an understanding of classification schemes.

13.2.2 Enumerative classification

Enumerative classification schemes aim to enumerate or list all subjects present in the literature which the scheme is intended to classify. Thus all simple and all compound or complex subjects are listed. Since to present all subjects in the literature would generate very lengthy schedules, the listing of subjects must be selective. The enumeration is normally achieved, first, by identifying the main disciplines to be covered by the scheme, either on a philosophical or pragmatic basis, and allocating each a main class status. Second, each discipline is divided into subclasses. This process of subdivision is continued until an appropriate level of specificity has been achieved, and all subjects that are required to be represented have been listed in their appropriate places. The object is to provide one place, and one place only, for each subject. Figure 13.1 shows how this process can be executed.

The Library of Congress Classification Scheme is very evidently enumerative, but then all the major classification schemes are. The enumeration in such schemes reflects an analytical approach to knowledge, with subjects subdivided into their component subfields. The subdivision of a subject defines the categories in that area of the scheme. Such schemes are essentially analytical in nature, but do not permit any synthesis or joining together of concepts that have been divided from one another.

Enumerative classification can be reasonably effective if subjects are divided by applying a consistent 'characteristic of subdivision'. In other words, it is important that all subclasses of a more general class are types of the same thing. One major criticism of many of the major schemes is that they do not subdivide subjects according to consistent characteristics. For instance, a quick examination of the subclasses of the architecture schedules in Dewey shows that the subdivisions are not all of the same type. Instead, they include classes covering architectural periods (for example, Ancient Architecture from the earliest times to ca. 300, and Architecture from 300–1399), the purpose of buildings (e.g. public structure, buildings for religious purposes) and method (architectural structure) (see Figure 13.1).

To consider effective division by a 'principle' or 'characteristic', consider the garments in a clothes shop. They can first be divided by the principle or characteristic of function (into, for example, overcoats, underwear, dresses) and then further subdivided within these functional groups by other principles or characteristics such as size, price range, material or colour. It is important to recognize that division must be by one principle at a time. In other words, all the classes for functions of clothes must be first enumerated before we proceed to consider subdivision by other principles, such as price. This consistency in subdivision is important in improving the predictability of the classification and minimizing the opportunities for cross-classification (see below). For example, if we seek a document on the economic history of Germany and we know that works on history are

Figure 13.1 The subdivisions of architecture in the Dewey Decimal Classification Scheme

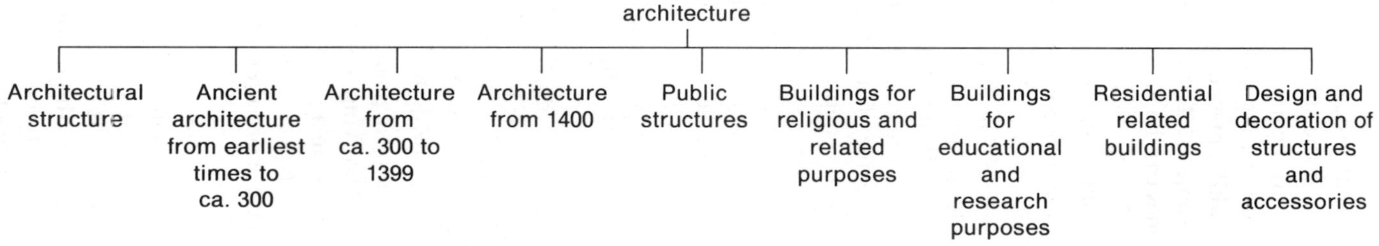

architecture

| Architectural structure | Ancient architecture from earliest times to ca. 300 | Architecture from ca. 300 to 1399 | Architecture from 1400 | Public structures | Buildings for religious and related purposes | Buildings for educational and research purposes | Residential related buildings | Design and decoration of structures and accessories |

arranged first by country, then by social process and then by period, it will be easier for us to find this document than if the subdivision was less systematic.

Although the enumerative approach to the design of a classification scheme can be traced to the Greeks, long experience has shown that enumerative classification schemes are relatively inflexible and, whilst providing a working subject order, do not always adequately allow for all subjects. The problems that are encountered with enumerative classification schemes can be identified as follows:

1. If all subjects, simple or compound, are listed in schedules, then the list becomes very long. The alternative – faceted classification – requires only the listing of simple one-concept subjects (from which notation for compound subjects can be constructed as necessary) and permits much more succinct schedules. Excessive schedule length has been one reason for the use of the faceted approach in updating major schemes. For instance, in a fully enumerative scheme it would be necessary to list a category for 'flavourings used in the cooking of foods in hotels' if this degree of specificity were required.

2. Since the enumeration of all subjects generates excessively long schedules, in practice the listing of subjects must be selective (even if relatively long schedules are acceptable). Any complex subjects which are not present in the scheme must be placed in a more general category where they cannot be distinguished from other subjects. The selection of certain subjects to be specified and the omission of other subjects is rather dependent upon the collection to be classified; thus, especially with regard to the selection process, it is difficult to design a scheme which is suitable for a number of different libraries.

3. Cross-classification, or the availability of more than one place for a subject, is quite common in a discipline-oriented scheme – that is, a scheme which starts by choosing main classes to coincide with major disciplines. Pottery, for example, may be treated as art, science or technology, and within a discipline-oriented scheme the opportunity will probably exist to classify pottery in at least any one of these three disciplines. In general, schemes with disciplines as main classes present problems in classifying 'concretes'. In such schemes it is often difficult to identify all literature on a given concrete at one location. For example, railways, children, substances (such as gold), ethnic groups, computers or rabbits may all have more than one place in an enumerative discipline-based classification scheme.

4. Enumerative schemes can be difficult to revise to take account of new developments. Every new subject which emerges in the literature and has a reasonable number of documents associated with it must be added to the list in the enumerative scheme. Further, because it is difficult to overhaul the basic structure of an enumerative scheme without complete revision of certain sections, it is necessary to add new subjects into the existing framework of relationships. Especially if the new subject is one which upsets the previous

structure of relationships, it will be difficult to fit into the existing order. Even when drastic revision is seen to be necessary and accepted, the point in time at which to conduct this extensive review can be difficult to select. The emergence of new complex subjects presents no cause for revision in a faceted scheme, provided that the simple subjects from which the complex subject can be constructed are already present. Of course, in both enumerative and faceted schemes, it is necessary to take cognizance of new simple subjects.

This list of problems with enumerative schemes is not intended to demonstrate that enumerative schemes are not effective in the organization of knowledge. Most major libraries use them in order to organize the stock on their shelves, and many use these schemes in the catalogues that provide access to that stock. However, it is necessary to recognize these limitations of enumeration so that they can be over-come in practice. Further, these less than satisfactory aspects of enumerative classification help to explain the rationale for the search for more effective methods of designing classification schemes.

13.2.3   Faceted classification

Faceted classification is accepted as providing a sound theoretical basis for the construction of classification schemes. In various guises, the basic concepts have found application in the design of a number of special classification schemes and have influenced the revision of major bibliographic schemes. Although some years ago it seemed that a new general classification scheme based upon the theory of faceted classification might emerge and be widely adopted, organizational factors have militated against this.

Faceted classification rests upon the definition of the concept of a facet. First, however, some preliminary ideas. Faceted classification arises particularly from the need for classification schemes to accommodate complex or multi-concept subjects. Any area of knowledge embraces a number of complex subjects and some single-concept subjects. For systematic treatment, the former must be divided into their component, single-concept subjects. Thus, the list in Figure 13.2 (below) shows some title-like statements of complex subjects within which more than one simple concept can in general be identified. These single-concept subjects are referred to as *isolates*. Faceted classification starts by examining the literature of an area of knowledge and identifying its isolates. In taking isolates from the literature, faceted classification rests firmly on literary warrant.

A *facet*, then, is the sum total of isolates formed by the division of a subject by one characteristic of division.

In other words, in the literature of a given subject area, it is normally possible to identify a number of facets and, by applying several characteristics of subdivision, to divide isolates into facets. A characteristic of subdivision is an attribute or property which all concepts in a given facet have in common and by which isolates can be grouped. Some examples of facets for the subject of office management would be kinds of office, services and procedures, accommodation, equipment and supplies, personnel, organization, and control and finance. In music literature the main facets are composer, executant (for example, instrument or voice), form of composition, elements of music, character of composition, technique, common subdivisions (for example, periodicals, encyclopaedias).

This process of analysis into facets is called *facet analysis*, and the resultant classification is termed a faceted classification. Using this type of analysis as a basis, it is possible to produce a schedule of standard terms to be used in the subject classification of documents. It should be plain that the making of a classification scheme by this process involves *analysis*, as single concepts must be identified and distinguished one from another. Once constructed, the application of the classification schemes involves *synthesis* or the drawing together of the single concepts which are listed in the scheme from their different facets in order to specify compound subjects. Thus, these schemes are sometimes known as *analytico-synthetic*.

Making a faceted classification scheme

In order to demonstrate further how a faceted classification scheme is constructed, it is necessary to identify the various stages in building such a scheme and then to illustrate these points by application to a specific subject area. This we shall now proceed to do. The making of a faceted classification scheme is a six-stage process:

1. *Identify facets and group isolates into them.* It is important that the characteristics of division used in this process should be mutually exclusive in order to avoid cross-classification (documents on one and the same subject being classified at different places in the scheme). The enumeration of isolates should be exhaustive or complete for the subject area. This can only be achieved by examining the literature of the subject area thoroughly for any isolates that might possibly have been overlooked. Once organized into facets, the single concepts that have previously been referred to as isolates become known as 'foci' (singular–focus). Ranganathan proposed five basic types of facets which may occur in many subject fields; these form a useful checklist in many subjects and include:

    - Personality, for example, types of libraries, crops, languages
    - Matter – constituent materials, for example, metals, plastics, components.
    - Energy – problem, method, process, operation, technique
    - Space – place, location
    - Time – period

    Vickery has postulated that the following series of facets (or a subset of them) may be expected:

Thing – part, constituent – property – measure – patient – process/action operation – agent – (space – time).

2. *Order foci within facets*   A helpful order of foci within facets must be sought. Standard reference works and experts may be consulted, but their appropriate order will depend upon the nature of the subject and the perspectives of its users. First, a facet may be divided into subfacets or subclasses by the application of an additional single characteristic of subdivision. For example a health and safety engineering facet would have subfacets such as fire protection, explosive prevention, radiation and electrical protection and others. The process of identification of subfacets within facets will depend very much upon the nature of the latter. One facet within a subject area may have several subfacets, whilst others may have none. Once subclasses or subfacets have been identified and the foci grouped into these, then foci can be arranged or ordered within the facet or subfacets, as appropriate. There are many potential ways of ordering or arranging foci, but some common ones are:

- simple to complex (that is, simplest aspects of a subject first, followed by more complex aspects, methods or equipment);
- spatial or geographical or geometric (for example, the arrangement of geographical areas according to their spatial location);
- chronological, historical or evolutionary;
- canonical, according to the established order, or
- alphabetical (a useful choice when there is a list of similar types of properties or objects and no other obvious order is preferred).

3. *Decide combination order of facets*   The combination order of facets (or their citation order when the scheme is used to classify documents) has to be settled next. The scheme lists simple or single concepts which have to be combined in order to accommodate complex subjects as they are encountered in documents. This citation order must be selected in accordance with the user's requirements and perspective; it may follow the educational and scientific consensus of opinion as to which are the more important groupings. It is vital to recognize that citation order determines the main categories for shelf arrangement and thus the nature of collocation. Classification scatters as it collocates, since it groups primarily by the features listed in only one of the facets applied in classifying a document. For example, a document on mathematics in primary schools could be classified first either by the grade facet or by the subject facet. Although the classification notation will subsequently incorporate the notation of the second facet, the document will be placed physically according to the first facet; that is, this document will either be placed with other documents on mathematics or with other documents on primary schools. It is necessary to decide upon a citation order so that such documents are classified in a consistent manner.

Various standard citation orders have been proposed. Ranganathan's fun-

185

damental facets have been important in this area. The five facets identified above have been used as the basis for a standard citation order, that is PMEST. A number of variations on this basic order was also proposed by Ranganathan.

4. *Decide schedule order of facets* Before the schedules can be finalized, the order of the facets in the schedules must be determined. In the interests of ease of application, the schedule order of facets is usually the combination order of the facets defined in stage 3 above, or in some cases the reverse of the combination order. Deviations from this basic order may be useful, particularly with regard to what are known as differential facets and common facets.

    Differential facets are subfacets which are placed adjacent to specific facets to which they apply; they are not generally used with all of the facets in the scheme.

    Common facets may occur anywhere in the schedule order; although listed only once, they can be applied anywhere in the citation order as required to qualify appropriate concepts.

5. *Append notation* Naturally a classification scheme is not complete until the notation has been added. However, notation is never added to the schedules until the basic order of subjects has been determined. Notation for classification schemes will be considered at greater length in section 13.3.

6. *Compile and index* The compiler of the classification scheme will no doubt be all too familiar with the order of subjects within the scheme, but in the interests of other users, an index will be a necessary guide to the concepts used and their location within the scheme. Indexes are considered further in section 13.4.

    The scheme may well now be complete, but revision is recommended from time to time and thought must be given as to how this might be achieved. Revision is considered in section 13.5.

An example of a simple faceted classification for literature

This section examines the application of the principles of facet analysis to the design of a simple classification scheme for documents on literature. This scheme can also be used to classify the literature to which these labels apply; if so, this ceases to be a strict subject classification and becomes to some extent a classification by the form in which the literature is written; for example, its language and literary form. We follow through the six steps enumerated above.

1. The titles shown in Figure 13.2 can be used as a basis for the types of subjects available in the literature to be classified. From these subject statements, it is possible to gather isolates. Note that isolates can be divided into the following facets:

Figure 13.2   Some titles in literature for the identification of isolates

Note: These title-like statements are used to show statements of complex subjects in literature

1. A Collection of nineteenth-century French literature
2. Golden age Spanish poetry
3. Italian fiction
4. A Collection of eighteenth-century literature
5. A Collection of essays on nature
6. English medieval fiction
7. Russian drama
8. Tibetan epic poetry
9. Early Hebrew literature
10. Twentieth-century Bulgarian literature
11. A Collection of poetry
12. A Collection of English poetry
13. American satire
14. German speeches of the 1600s
15. A Collection of humour about cricket
16. Dutch Renaissance literature
17. Afrikaans literature
18. Danish letters about politics
19. Scottish literature.

- period; for example, medieval period, twentieth century
- form; for example, essays, poetry
- theme; for example, about cricket, about politics
- language; for example, English, Italian.

Obviously once these facets have been identified, it is a relatively simple matter to group the isolates into the appropriate facet.

2. Once foci have been grouped into facets, they must be ordered. For this scheme it would seem sensible to order the foci within each facet differently according to the nature of the facet. Thus we might propose the following broad arrangements within facets:

- period facet; ordered chronologically
- form facet; related forms grouped together
- theme facet; related themes grouped together
- language facet; precedence given to major languages and their literatures.

At this stage it becomes possible to start to draft the types of lists that are shown in Figure 13.3. This is not an exhaustive listing of all foci, but merely identifies and organizes those that can be derived from Figure 13.2 and its subject statements.

187

Figure 13.3   A draft of a faceted classification scheme for literature

Notation for Facet	A	C	E	G
Notation for Foci	**Language**	**Form**	**Period**	**Theme**
1	American	Poetry	Pre-Medieval	Nature
2	English	Epic poetry	Medieval	Cricket
3	German	Drama	15th C	Politics
4	Dutch	Fiction	16th C	
5	Afrikaans	Essays	17th C	
6	Danish	Speeches	18th C	
7	French	Letters	19th C	
8	Spanish	Humour	20th C	
9	Italian	Satire		
10	Russian			
11	Tibetan			
12	Hebrew			
13	Bulgarian			

3. Next the combination order of facets must be settled. We could accept language, form, period, theme. Since materials are classified and grouped first by language, all literary forms such as poetry are scattered according to language.
4. The schedule order of facets must next be decided. Here we have adopted a schedule order which follows the citation order.
5. Once all other preliminary decisions have been made, notations can be assigned to the scheme. Figure 13.3 shows a simple but effective notation. For example, 'A collection of nineteenth century French literature' would be A7E7; 'English medieval fiction' would attract the notation A2C4E2.
6. No index is shown here, but this would be the last stage in the compilation of the scheme; besides attempting to classify some items by the scheme, the index serves to check the scheme's likely effectiveness.

13.2.4   Developments in classification theory and the Classification Research Group

The concepts associated with the application of facets in the theory of library classification and associated citation orders were first tested extensively by Ranganathan in the Colon Classification (see 14.5). Other ideas on the theory of classification were enumerated by Bliss and embodied in the Bliss Bibliographic Classification Scheme, First Edition. Work on the theory of classification has extended far beyond that which is evident from a study of existing classification schemes and the practice of library classification.

The Classification Research Group (CRG) has been a major force in the development of classification theory, contributing significantly towards work on a new general bibliographic classification scheme. The CRG was formed in 1948 after a Royal Society Scientific Information Conference. Early work led to the production of over 20 special schemes in various areas of knowledge. The experience thus gained provided a grounding for work on the development of a new general scheme, the first step in this regard being to identify main classes. It was felt to be important that these main classes should be selected on the basis of a theory or set of principles. This theory would ensure that the need for new main classes was minimized and that the basic framework of the scheme would appropriately admit every subject. The search for main classes was first concentrated upon 'entities' or things. The theory of *integrative levels* emerged, the essence being that the world of entities evolves from the simple towards the complex by an accumulation of properties or influences from the environment. Thus an early draft of some of the major integrative levels was of the following form:

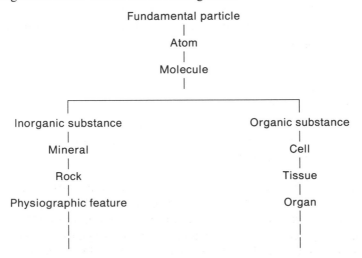

The CRG set about trying to define a series of integrative levels upon which it would be possible to base the main classes and their order for a new general classification scheme. Work was centred upon the tabulation of entities. Simultaneously with the work on integrative levels was consideration of citation order. Five fundamental relationships were noted between concepts, and these relationships were expressed in terms of a series of relational operators. Eventually this work on citation orders came to fruition in the rather unlikely context of a new indexing system, PRECIS.

Although the work of the CRG makes fascinating reading and has contributed magnificently in clarifying the principles of classification, much work remains to be done. The original impetus of the CRG has been diverted into specific applications. These include the development of the PRECIS indexing system (see 17.4), and the preparation of the second edition of the Bliss Bibliographic Classification Scheme (see 14.5).

In parallel with the work of the classification theorists, general systems theory has evolved to consider similar problems. General systems theory is the product of various philosophers of science, such as Bertalanffy and Laszlo, and is an important area of study for the intending classification theorist.

Other work relating to the development of classification has been conducted under the auspices of UNISIST. In 1971 plans were established to provide an international switching language which could indicate the subject fields of all publications. Although the original intention was that this would be an intermediate language between two established languages (for example, German natural language – switching language – French natural language), the product of the work has been a new general classification scheme known as the Standard Reference Code or the Broad System of Ordering (BSO). The final draft of the BSO was published in 1978. More details are given in section 14.6.

Work on automatic classification should not be overlooked, although a brief mention only is permitted. Various studies have been conducted in order to assess the extent to which computer analysis of text can contribute to the generation of a practical classification scheme. This is a fresh avenue of approach and shows some promise.

13.3   Notation or codes

Notation or codes are appended to a sequence of topics in order to arrange them in some clearly defined order. Thus notation or code may be used in organizing books on shelves or files in a filing cabinet.

Notation has an important impact on the effectiveness of a classification scheme. Poor notation can impair the ability of a scheme to accommodate new subjects and can hinder effective retrieval. Nevertheless, it is worth reiterating that notation is added to the list of subjects that comprise the schedules of a classification scheme *after* the subjects to be included and their order have been settled. A unique notational symbol should be provided for each individual subject, whether it be simple or complex. The purpose of notation is to impose a self-evident ordering on the subjects listed in the scheme. As we have aready seen, whilst the systematic ordering of subjects might adhere to some consensus, it will not be obvious to all users of a scheme; it is the purpose of notation to permit ease of filing or ordering.

13.3.1   Types of notation

If notation is to offer a self-evident ordering, then it is important that the symbols used for the notation have a self-evident order in themselves. There are only two sets of symbols whose orders are reasonably universally recognized: the letters of the Roman alphabet (either small or capitals) and Arabic numerals. Other symbols are encountered in the notation of classification schemes, and although on occasions it may be an advantage to include symbols whose filing position is not predefined, these symbols always detract from automatic ordering. Any symbols other than letters and numbers need to have their filing value defined. Consider, does a ':' file before or after a '?'? Some schemes use punctuation marks in their notation; others use letters from the Greek alphabet.

Apart from the different character sets that can be used for notation, there are two different types of notation – pure and mixed. *Pure notation* uses only one kind of symbol; for example, letters or numbers. The Dewey Decimal Classification Scheme is one such pure notation, using numbers only in most instances; for example 714.67, 456.7. A *mixed notation* uses more than one kind of symbol such as a mixture of letters and numbers or a mixture of lower case and upper case letters in specifying subjects. Mixed notations are relatively common; the Library of Congress Classification Scheme uses a mixture of letters (upper case) and numbers; for example, DA783.

Notation is used in two contexts: in catalogues and indexes, and in arrangement of documents. Not only is notation important in providing an ordering in both of these contexts, but it also frequently acts as the vital link between any of the following: the schedules in a classification scheme, the printed and published index to the schedules of the classification scheme, the classified sequence in a catalogue or index, and the classified order adopted for document arrangement. Since notation has this function of linking various sequences, an acceptable notational system must fulfil certain basic requirements. It is easiest to discuss these in terms of the human requirements upon notation; indeed, even with computer-based catalogues and indexes, people will be required to use and write or remember notation (at least until the day when document arrangement is no longer relevant, or when machines are widely available to re-file information, regardless of size or form). Obviously, computers and the use of notation in computerized systems may place additional constraints upon the nature of notation or, conversely, may eliminate the need to consider some of the characteristics listed below. For instance, whilst a person may be concerned about the length of notation, this is not usually important to a computer; moreover, a computer has little use for mnemonics (it does not forget!). Expressiveness, on the other hand, can be extremely useful in building search strategies in computer-based systems.

13.3.2   Ease of use

The notation or code must be easy for users to remember, write, type and match. Factors which influence the use of notation include the following:

1. *Simplicity*, or the ease with which notation can be remembered. It is, for example, generally easier to remember 681.945.6 than 6819456, and easier still to remember a mixed notation such as 532CRM721.
2. *Brevity* can make an obvious contribution to ease of use. The shorter the

notation, the easier it is to remember. A number of factors determine the length of the notation in a classification scheme. These include:

(a)   The *base* of the notation, or the number of characters in the character set. Obviously, using A to Z as the basic character set, 26 subjects can be represented by single character notation. Using 1 to 9 as the base, to cover 26 subjects some would have to be allocated a two-character notation.

(b)   The *allocation* of the notation will also affect its length. Uneven allocation of notation to subjects with the same size of literature, (or the same number of subdivisions being allocated different notational space) will cause notation for some subjects to be exceptionally long. For example, suppose French literature is denoted by 56 and Bulgarian literature by 768, then the notation of all subdivisions of Bulgarian literature will be one character longer than their equivalents in French literature. Uneven allocation will thus lead to some subjects having relatively short notation at the expense of others with relatively long notation. In practice, uneven allocation often arises with the development of subjects; the original allocation of the scheme becomes less balanced with time and the emergence of new subdivisions. Provision for *synthesis* often leads to long notation, for two reasons. First, synthetic schemes tend to facilitate detailed specification, and thus inclusion of a larger number of subjects. In order to distinguish between all these subjects, it is inevitable that longer notations are used. In addition, synthesis often requires the use of a facet indicator, to mark the beginning of a new facet; for example, ',',':'.

(c)   *Expressiveness* can be another feature which contributes to a lengthier notation. Each step of subdivision involves an extra character (see below).

3.   Deliberate *mnemonics* are devices which help the user to remember and recall the notation for given subjects. In addition to ease of use and brevity, either systematic and/or lateral mnemonics may be exploited. *Systematic mnemonics* is the use of the same notation for a given topic wherever that topic occurs. Synthetic devices often lead to this type of mnemonics. For example, in the tables in the Dewey Decimal Classification Scheme, 42 is always used for England and Wales, and 03 for Dictionaries and Encyclopaedias. Further, 9 is used to represent history and geography in a number of different contexts.

Literal mnemonics are abbreviations or letters which are easily associated with the name of a subject. Thus we might use 'C' for Chemistry or 'M' for Music. Unfortunately, literal mnemonics can only be applied to a very limited number of subjects in a scheme or the order of subjects will be distorted.

Figure 13.4   Allocation of notation showing gaps for insertion of new subjects
(An extract from Library of Congress Classification Scheme)

	Invention
	Invention
1517	General (II)
1519	Special products and processes, A–Z (III)
	.A8 Atomic power
	.C45 Chemicals
1521	Employees' inventions
1525	Designs and models (II)
	Licenses
	Including compulsory licenses
1528	General (II)
1530	Foreign licensing agreements (II)
1532	Assignments (II)
1536	Infringement. Patent litigation and procedure (II)
1544	Patent attorneys. Patent practice (II. modified)

Thus 'M' for Music will mean that an adjacent class, such as Fine Arts, must be denoted 'N'.

13.3.3   Hospitality

It is necessary that any notation be hospitable to the insertion of new subjects. It is fruitless trying to revise subjects already represented in a scheme unless a notation can be appended to accommodate any new or modified subjects. Generally, updating calls for the insertion of new topics within existing classes, but it should also be possible to insert a new main class if the need arises. There are two means whereby notation can accommodate, or be hospitable to, new subjects:

1. *Unassigned notation* within the sequence or gaps into which subjects can be inserted. For example, examine Figure 13.4. Plainly, any new subjects can be offered notations which have not previously been used. This approach is not always satisfactory because gaps may not be left in the notation at the appropriate place where a new subject belongs. Further, it is necessary to predict in advance the areas in which new subjects are likely to arise and to leave gaps accordingly; this forecasting is obviously difficult.
2. *Decimal notation* can be used. A new subject can be inserted almost anywhere in a sequence by the use of decimal subdivision. Thus, if 51, 52 and 53 are all allocated, and a new subject needs to be inserted between the subject at 51 and that at 52, its notation can be provided by decimal subdivision. This will be given the notation 515 (or any notation from 511 to 519). Note that decimal notation is also possible with letters. Thus, ABN can be inserted between AB and AC.

Figure 13.5   Extract from the British Catalogue of Music Classification Scheme

Actual notation	Subject	Hypothetical expressive notation
RW	String instruments	RW
RX	Bowed string instruments	RWA
S	Violin	RWAA
SQ	Viola	RWAB
SQQ	Viola d'amore	RWABA
SR	Cello	RWAC

13.3.4   Expressiveness

An expressive notation expresses or displays the relationship structure of subjects within the scheme. In this it helps the user to recognize the structure of the scheme and to identify general subjects and their associated subdivisions. Expressiveness often relies upon decimal subdivision which may become less systematic with the addition of new subjects. Thus, in the Dewey Decimal Classification we find:

620 Applied Physics
621 Mechanical Engineering
621.3 Electrical Engineering
621.48 Nuclear Engineering
624 Civil Engineering.

The need to insert Electrical Engineering and Nuclear Engineering subsequent to the drafting of the scheme has detracted from the expressiveness of the original version. A truly expressive notation would show all the different branches of Engineering as equivalent. For instance:

620   Applied Physics
621   Mechanical Engineering
623   Electrical Engineering
625   Nuclear Engineering
627   Civil Engineering.

In order to achieve the above expressiveness, major reallocation of notation would have been required; this is not deemed desirable.

Some schemes deliberately opt for a non-expressive notation. A good example is the British Catalogue of Music Classification which abandons expressiveness in favour of allocating brief notation to the most common concepts. Figure 13.5 shows a small extract. The third column, which gives a hypothetical expressive notation, demonstrates that it is longer in most instances than the actual notation allocated in column one. A compromise between expressive and non-expressive notation is to be found in the Second Edition of the Bliss Bibliographic Classification Scheme.

13.3.5   Synthesis

There must be the possibility of achieving synthesis within the notation if any synthetic elements are present in the scheme. In major enumerative schemes, synthesis is often controlled by careful instructions regarding citation order and the way in which the notation for complex subjects is to be built up from its components. In faceted schemes, synthesis is often achieved with the intercession of a facet indicator which makes it possible to identify which parts of the notation have been drawn from any distinct facet. Capital letters and various punctuation symbols such as:,∅,', may be enlisted as facet indicators. Thus in the notation FcdEdm, it is possible to observe that the notation Fcd comes from one facet and Edm from a second. Without the use of the capital and small letters in combination, it would not have been possible to identify how this piece of notation had been synthesized.

Some schemes use *retroactive notation* in order to signal new facets. Retroactive notation makes it possible to indicate distinct facets without recourse to mixed notation. Thus, the self-evident order of a single character set is maintained. Retroactive notation is achieved by subdividing a letter by letters which follow it in the alphabet (since retroactive notation based upon numbers would be rather restrictive in the number of classes or facets that could be indicated, letters are normally used). Take, for example, BMNFRSMXZWY as a synthesized piece of notation. In the synthesized notation, an earlier letter than the letters prior to it in the notation signals a new facet; for example, B, F, M and W in the above signal new facets.

13.3.6   Flexibility

Some users and classifiers find it beneficial to have a notation which is sufficiently flexible to permit a variety of citation orders to be adopted as appropriate to the document and the user's perspective. Thus, for instance, the Universal Decimal Classification would permit notation to be combined in different orders. 766 for commercial graphic art and 659.3 for mass communication may be combined as 766:659.3 or 659.3:766.

13.3.7   Shelf notation

Notation which is to be inscribed on the spine of books may need to be shorter than that used in catalogues, indexes, databases and bibliographies. It is helpful if an abbreviated notation (which merely shows the broad subject category to which the document belongs) can be readily derived from the full notation. Expressive notation is generally easier to truncate – by deleting final characters to create the notation for a more general subject. For example, in Figure 14.3, the notation

641.493 could be assigned for the Preservation of Poultry and used in the catalogue, but the truncated notation 641.4 could be used for shelf arrangement.

13.4   Index

The index to the classification scheme, which is published as part of the scheme, serves two purposes:

1.   to locate topics within the systematically arranged classification, and
2.   to display related aspects of a subject which have been scattered by the order of subjects chosen in the main classified order.

The index should complement the classification scheme, and the relationships shown in the index should supplement those in the main classified sequence. There are two types of indexes to be found in classification schemes: a relative index and a specific index. The relative index is the more common.

A *relative index*, as originally proposed by Melville Dewey, contains at least one entry for each subject in the scheme. By use of the alphabetical sequence, it gathers together all aspects of a concrete subject which are likely to have been scattered by a discipline-orientated approach in the basic order of the scheme. Figure 14.4 shows a number of entries concerned with 'land' and its variants and located at a variety of places in the main sequence.

A *specific index* can be devised if the classification scheme is such that there is only one location for each subject. Thus one specific entry can be made for each subject in the index. This will be appropriate for simple subjects in a faceted classification scheme.

Many of the points which are made concerning alphabetical indexes in Chapters 15, 16 and 17 may also be applied to the construction of indexes to classification schemes.

13.5   Organization and revision

For a scheme to be successful in the long term it is vital that there should be an organizational structure to support it. Initially, it is necessary that the scheme be published and available for purchase, and that its use be generally promoted. But the most important function of the organization is to provide a mechanism for the revision of the scheme. The use of a scheme in centrally or cooperatively produced catalogue records can also be important in establishing its future.

Revision is necessary to make provision for emerging subjects. In order that the scheme remains popular, it is vital that revision is conducted with regard to users' needs. To this end some consultative procedure is to be recommended. However, lengthy and complex consultative committees can hinder revision and make for a slowly changing scheme. A number of publication strategies are possible for announcing the modifications to classification schemes:

1. publish a new edition at appropriate intervals, for example every few years.
2. publish new editions of parts of the schedules at intervals, for example, new editions of specific subject areas.
3. publish changes as they are accepted in a periodical publication, cumulating these in a new edition of all or parts of the schedules, as suitable.

These new schedules will reflect the following means of revision of the new subject structure and listing:

- expansion, to permit the addition of new subjects or more specific subdivision of existing subjects;
- reduction, to take out subjects and their subdivisions which are no longer used;
- relocation, in order to rectify an inappropriate placement, to eliminate dual provision (more than one place for one subject) and to make room for new subjects;
- changes in terminology, to allow for new subject descriptions to be incorporated into the scheme as subjects change their names.

Although revision is necessary so that the schedules remain suitable for classifying new literature, it must be remembered that there is a gulf between publishing the schedules in an updated form and applying them. When new schedules are made available to an organization using a classification scheme, it has three options:

1. ignore the new schedules;
2. use the new schedules to classify new stock, but leave the old stock classified according to earlier editions of the schedules; or
3. use the new schedules to classify new stock, and also reclassify the old stock, which has usually been classified according to an earlier edition of the scheme.

Option 3 clearly requires the most work, but equally clearly is the most satisfactory. However, as Figure 13.6 demonstrates, reclassification can be a major exercise involving much relocation of stock, and this is clearly a serious disincentive.

Particularly in a large organization, reclassification can be a major exercise, although it can be facilitated by the support given by computer-based catalogue records. Thus Dewey's policy of *integrity of numbers* has found great favour: an undertaking has been made that a piece of notation will not be revised and given another meaning. This limits the need for libraries to reclassify, but also restricts the revision process of the Dewey Decimal Classification Scheme.

Figure 13.6   The elements of a reclassification exercise

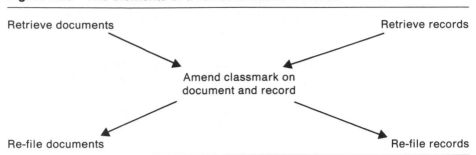

Retrieve documents   Retrieve records

Amend classmark on
document and record

Re-file documents   Re-file records

Recommended reading

Austin, D (1969), 'Prospects for a new general classification', *Journal of Librarianship*, **1** (3), 149–69.

Austin, D (1976), 'The CRG research into a freely faceted scheme', in Maltby, A., *Classification in the 1970s: a second look*, London: Bingley, 158–94.

Beghtol, C (1986), 'Bibliographic classification theory and text linguistics: aboutness analysis, intertextuality and the cognitive act of classifying documents', *Journal of Documentation*, **42**, 84–113.

'Classification Research Group and information control', London: Library Association, 1970 (LA Research Pamphlet No 1). The work of the Classification Research Group (CRG) is reported in its bulletins. The first three of these were published as separates and are now out of print. Since No 4, the bulletins have appeared in the *Journal of Documentation* in the following issues:

12 (4), 1956, 227–30 (Bibliography of publications by members)

14 (3), 1958, 136–43 (Bulletin 4: BCM Classification)

15 (1), 1959, 39–57 (Bulletin 5: Cranfield)

17 (3), 1961, 156–68 (Bulletin 6: New general classification)

17 (3), 1961, 169–72 (Bulletin 7: Special classifications)

20 (3), 1964, 146–69 (Bulletin 8: Integrative levels; bibliography)

24 (4), 1968, 273–91 (Bulletin 9: New general classification)

29 (1), 1973, 51–71 (Bulletin 10: General classification; PRECIS)

34 (1), 1978, 21–50 (Bulletin 11: New general classification; PRECIS; BSO; bibliography of publications)

Farradane, J E L (1961), 'Fundamental fallacies and new needs in library classification', Chapter 9 of *Sayers memorial volume*, London: Library Association.

Farradane, J E L (1970), 'Analysis and organization of knowledge for retrieval', *Aslib Proceedings*, **22** (12), 607–16.

Foskett, D J (1970), *Classification for a general index language*, London: Library Association (Research Publication No 2).

Hunter, E (1988), *Classification made simple*, Aldershot: Gower.

Jeffreys, A (1980), 'Classification in British university library practice', *Catalogue and Index*, **57**, 6–8.

Leo Jolley Memorial seminar, delivered on 20 June 1977. 'The theory of integrative levels and its application to classification and indexing systems', *Aslib Proceedings*, **30** (6), 1978, 192–237.

14 Bibliographic classification schemes

14.1 Introduction

There are a number of important general classification schemes. Each of these is sufficiently significant to repay study in its own right, and some are an essential preliminary to understanding catalogues, indexes and shelf arrangement of stock in libraries. In addition, an appreciation of the distinction between such general schemes and special classification schemes is a component of the complete appreciation of classification practice.

A study of the major general schemes reveals a wide gulf between theory (as outlined in the previous chapter) and practice (as reflected in the major schemes). The existing major general classification schemes observe few of the theoretical bases for sound classification. In particular, most were constructed before the ideas of facet analysis were developed. Thus these major schemes are essentially enumerative and suffer from the limitations of enumerative classification outlined in the last chapter. Clearly, the originators of the major schemes cannot be criticized for being ignorant of principles which were not recognized when their schemes were initiated. Indeed, knowledge was more limited and collections generally smaller when the schemes were devised, and so an analytic approach to classification would have been less appropriate than it is today.

Nevertheless, whatever the basis for the major enumerative schemes, they must be judged for their suitability for application in current libraries and information centres. It is therefore reasonable to apply the principles of facet analysis in order to evaluate the schemes and to identify any limitations. Also, within the constraints imposed by the basically enumerative framework, the revisers of the major schemes do attempt to take account of a more systematic approach to classification in any proposed revisions of these schemes.

The three major schemes – the Library of Congress Classification Scheme, the Universal Decimal Classification Scheme and the Dewey Decimal Classification Scheme – are treated in most detail, since they account for a good proportion of classification practice. Other general schemes that demonstrate specific features of classification theory or practice are mentioned briefly, and the rationale for special schemes is explored.

14.2   The Dewey Decimal Classification (DC)

The Dewey Decimal Classification (abbreviated to either DC or DDC) is arguably the most important bibliographic classification scheme. It boasts a strong organizational basis, being published and revised regularly by the Forest Press and edited by part of the Processing Department of the Library of Congress on the advice of the Decimal Classification Editorial Policy Committee. It features elements of many of the trends in classification theory and practice over the past 100 years. Perhaps most important of all, it is used in libraries of all types throughout the English-speaking world and has been translated into many languages. It has found particular favour in public libraries in the UK and the US and is also used extensively in school and college libraries. It is difficult to ascribe the popularity of the DC to any particular feature, and its continuing use is probably related to the combination of desirable or acceptable features. DC has also been used in the British National Bibliography (BNB) and is used in both BNB MARC and LC MARC records.

Despite its pre-eminence, or possibly because of it, DC has its critics. DC is certainly not regarded as the perfect classification scheme even in sectors where there is no serious alternative. It is considered rather as a pragmatic solution to the classification of library and information materials; however its contribution in this context should not be underrated.

The scheme has passed through 20 editions. The twentieth edition is published in four volumes: volume 1, introduction and tables; volume 2: schedules, 000–599; volume 3: schedules 600–99; volume 4: index, manual. The scheme has been praised for its clear and well-presented schedules, and this is definitely one of its strengths even if the schedules may seem a little daunting on first acquaintance.

14.2.1   Main classes

The scheme is divided into ten main discipline-oriented classes as shown in Figure 14.1. The scheme is basically enumerative with simple and composite or compound subjects listed within each class. Each main class can be subdivided into ten major subclasses, and then each of these subclasses into ten more specific classes and so on, until all subjects that need to be specified have been enumerated. There are exactly ten subclasses available at each step of division, a restriction which has sometimes hindered any systematic development (where, for instance, a subject needs to be subdivided into 12 main subclasses or branches). Obviously sometimes not all ten of the possible subclasses are necessary, so that subdivision of a subject may be into less than ten subclasses. This limit of ten has been a particular handicap in respect of the main classes.

The limited notational base provided by numbers (instead of, say, letters) has required that all subjects be fitted into ten main classes. This has led to some unlikely liaisons. For instance, Music and Sports both find themselves in the Arts.

Figure 14.1   Dewey Decimal Classification Scheme: main classes

000 Generalities
100 Philosophy and psychology
200 Religion
300 Social sciences
400 Language
500 Natural sciences and mathematics
600 Technology (Applied sciences)
700 The arts
800 Literature and rhetoric
900 Geography and history

Agriculture and Medicine are both treated in the Applied Sciences, and the Social Sciences class, 300, subsumes Economics, Politics, Law and Education. Some would argue that many of these areas are disciplines in their own right and merit their own main class.

Other critics have turned their attention to the order of the main classes in DC. This order is consistent with the established relationships between subjects at the time that the scheme was first published (1876), but produces some strange collocations for today's literature. In particular:

- Language 400 is divided from Literature 800
- Technologies are separated from their underlying class; for example, Chemistry 540 but Chemical technology 660.
- Buildings at 690 is separated from Architecture at 720.

Also within main classes there are occasional unlikely collocations. One of the most obvious of these is Psychology at 150, within the Philosophy class, 100.

Another problem with the main classes is that they are unbalanced. Today, the quantity of literature in the class 100 Philosophy is small compared with that in, say, the 500 Science, or 600 Technology classes. The apportionment of subjects to main classes reflects the state of knowledge when the scheme was designed.

14.2.2   Synthesis

Elementary synthesis was introduced to the scheme as early as the second edition. By the twentieth edition synthesis had become a well-established mechanism for allowing detailed specification without resorting to exceedingly lengthy schedules. Synthesis operates in two ways: through the tables and through the 'add to' instructions.

The twentieth edition has seven tables, as listed in Figure 14.2. These tables may be applied, in carefully selected subject areas and under the guidance of explicit instructions, in order to subdivide a subject found in the main schedules. Thus

Figure 14.2   Dewey Decimal Classification Scheme: tables

Table 1 Standard Subdivisions
Table 2 Geographic Areas, Historical Periods, Persons
Table 3 Subdivisions of Individual Literatures
Table 4 Subdivisions of Individual Languages
Table 5 Racial, Ethnic, National Groups
Table 6 Languages
Table 7 Groups of Persons

whilst the main schedules may give a number for 'Cats', by the application of Table 1 it is possible to distinguish between a document which is an encyclopaedia concerned with cats, and a document on societies concerned with cats. The Tables remove the need to list 'common subdivisions' in each of the many places where they might be applied; indeed, one list suffices for applications with respect to many different subjects.

The content of the Tables is reminiscent of the Tables in the Universal Decimal Classification, and, indeed, they were to some extent inspired by the latter. However, the use of the Tables in DC is much more closely monitored than it is in UDC. Table 1 may be used anywhere in the schedules, entirely at the discretion of the classifier. Tables 2, 5, 6 and 7, however, may only be applied by the classifier where instructed. Sometimes such instructions are in the main schedules, but on other occasions they may be found in one of the other Tables, for example Table 1 or Table 4. Table 3 is intended solely for use in the 800 literature main class, and Table 4 for use in the 400 language main class.

Generally, notation from the Tables is added to notation in the schedules to make a more specific number. A few examples are useful. In the first example below, 743 for Drawing is taken from the main schedules, and 03 for Dictionaries is added from Table 1 to make the notation 743.03 for a dictionary of drawing.

	Main schedule	Table		Final notation
1.	Drawing	Dictionaries		A Dictionary of Drawing
	743	03		743.03
		Table 1		
2.	Farmhouses	Delaware		Farmhouses in Delaware
	631.21	09	751	631.2109751
		Table 1	Table 2	
3.	Psychology	Cherokees		Psychology of Cherokees
	155.84	975		155.84975
		Table 5		
4.	French language	Dictionary/English language		English/French bilingual dictionary
	44	3	21	443.21
		Table 4	Table 6	

Instructions for the use of Tables is always given either in the Tables or in the main schedules where the Tables are to be applied. These instructions determine the citation order of the various concepts represented by the Schedules and the Tables and remove the need for facet indicators such as would be required were more flexibility of citation order permitted.

The other synthetic device in DC is the 'add to' instructions. This permits subdivisions which are enumerated under one subject in the schedules to be used in other specified parts of the schedules, as instructed. For example, the extract in Figure 14.3 instructs the user to apply various preservation techniques (in 641.41–641.47) to various meats and allied foods (in 641.49). Thus 'freezing poultry' is 641.49353, taking '53' from 641.453.

Like tables the 'add to' instructions remove the need to repeat subdivisions under several different subjects.

14.2.3 Notation

The notation used in DC is pure and consists solely of numbers. The numbers are used decimally. The simplicity and flexibility of the notation of DC are recognized to be two of its strengths.

A particularly attractive feature of the notation is its expressiveness. Although expressiveness is maintained as far as possible, it has to be sacrificed on occasions in order to insert new subjects. So, for example, we find:

551.577 Precipitation
551.578 Specific forms of precipitation
551.579 Snow surveys

where the latter two numbers are, strictly, subdivisions of the first. Generally, the notation is hospitable to new subjects, since they can be inserted by decimal subdivision. For example 611.5 can be used to represent a new subject which has links with the subjects at both 611 and 612; however, unless the new subject is a subdivision of 611, to place it at 611.5 will impair the expressiveness of the notation.

The notation is reasonably simple. It is made easier to remember by inserting a decimal point after the first three numbers, and by grouping subsequent digits into threes, for example 641.738 423. The notation from the Tables provides systematic mnemonics to a limited extent, since the same notation is used for a concept whichever main class number it qualifies. Thus 03 (from Table 1) becomes identified with a dictionary or encyclopaedia and recurs in the notation for the Generalia class 030 for general dictionaries and encyclopaedias. Similarly 09 from Table 1

**Figure 14.3   Dewey Decimal Classification Scheme: extract showing 'add to'
instructions**

> **641.4–641.8 Food preservation, storage, cooking**
> Class comprehensive works in 641.3
> .4   **Food preservation and storage**
> Class comprehensive works on food preservation in 664.028

> 641.41–641.47 Preservation techniques for fruit and vegetables, for food
> as a whole
> Class comprehensive works in 641.4, preservation techniques for meat and
> allied foods in 641.49
>
> .41   Preliminary treatment
> .42   Canning
> .44   Drying and dehydrating
>   Including freeze-drying
> .45   Low-temperature techniques
> .452   Cold storage
> .453   Deep freezing
>   *For freeze-drying, see 641.44*
> .46   Brining, pickling, smoking
> .47   Use of additives
> .48   Storage
> .49   Meat and allied food
>   Class storage of meat and allied food in 641.48
> .492   Red meat
>   Add to base number 641.492 the numbers following 641.4 in 641.41–641.
>   47, e.g., canning red meat 641.4922
> .493   Poultry
>   Add to base number 641.493 the numbers following 641.4 in 641.41–
>   641.47, e.g., freezing poultry 641.49353
> .494   Seafood
>   Add to base number 641.494 the numbers following 641.4 in 641.42–
>   641.47, e.g., brining seafood 641.4946
> .495   Other animal flesh
>   Examples: frogs, turtles, snails, insects

represents geographical and historical treatment while 900 is the main class for
Geography and History.

The concept of a three-figure minimum for all notation was introduced in the
second edition. Thus main classes are denoted by 300, 600, 800 and so on, and not
just 3 or 6.

The expressive notation facilitates abridgement in order to specify broader
categories. Thus long notation with exact specification may be used in catalogues
or national bibliographies; the class number appropriate to shelf arrangement for a
small collection may be derived from the full notation merely by deleting final
digit(s).

14.2.4   Index

An important feature of the scheme in its creator's eyes was the relative index. The rather more detailed enumeration (1000 classes listed) than in previous schemes necessitated an alphabetical index to the classes. Note how related subjects are drawn together in the extract from the index in Figure 14.4. The relative index has been influential in indexing practice, and many of its principles are incorporated into indexing methods, such as chain indexing.

14.2.5   History and organization

In 1876, Melville Dewey published *A Classification and subject index for cataloguing and arranging the books and pamphlets of a library*. This first edition consisted of 12 pages of introduction, 12 pages of tables and 18 pages of index. It had three novel features:

1. relative location, instead of the more usual fixed location. In fixed location, notation was physically attached to certain places on the shelves and books were always filed in the same place. Fixed location is difficult to maintain with a fast-growing collection;
2. relatively detailed specification, which was made possible because of the change from fixed to relative location, and
3. the relative index, which became necessary once a reasonable number of subjects had been enumerated.

With the second edition a further important principle was established. This was the concept of 'integrity of numbers'. Dewey recognized that extensive reclassification was unpopular and that a classification scheme needed to remain relatively stable from one edition to the next. In the second edition Dewey announced that henceforth the structure of the scheme would not be fundamentally changed.

Up to and including the fourteenth edition, progress seemed synonymous with ever–increasing detail. However, much of the detail in the fourteenth edition was a product of haphazard revision. For example, medicine ran to 80 pages, whereas the schedule for chemical technology had hardly been modified since the second edition. The fifteenth edition, published in 1951, represented a determined effort to update and unify the schedules. More balanced schedules were achieved by pruning the 31 000 subjects enumerated in the fourteenth edition to 4700. Also, many subjects were relocated and the index was drastically pruned. Although the fifteenth edition met with some success, it was not generally popular.

A period of seven years was set as the publication cycle for new editions; the sixteenth edition thus appeared on time in 1958. In respect of the extent of enumeration and location of some topics, the sixteenth edition reverted to the fourteenth. A detailed index was published in a separate volume. The sixteenth

Figure 14.4   Dewey Decimal Classification Scheme: extract from the Relative Index

Land transfer	
economics	333.33
law	346.043 6
Land transportation	388
engineering	629.049
military engineering	623.61
see also Ground transportation	
Land trusts	
law	346.068
Land use	333.73
agricultural surveys	631.47
community sociology	307.33
economics	333.73
law	346.045
public administration	350.823 26
central governments	351.823 26
local governments	352.96
Land valuation	333.332
Land vehicles	388
engineering	629.049
transportation services	388
see also Automotive vehicles	
Landed gentry	305.523 2
	T1—086 21
Lander County (Nev.)	T2—793 33
Landes (France: Dept.)	T2—447 72
Landing	
aeronautics	629.132 521 3
manned space flight	629.458 8
Landing (Military tactics)	355.422
Landing accidents	363.124 92
see also Transportation safety	
Landing craft	359.835 6
design	623.812 56
engineering	623.825 6
naval equipment	359.835 6
naval units	359.325 6
Landing fields	387.736
see also Airports	

edition contained the first of the Pheonix schedules. Thus completely new – or Pheonix – schedules were included for Inorganic and Organic Chemistry. The sixteenth edition was probably the first of the more recent editions to be widely accepted.

The seventeenth edition met with mixed reactions. It introduced greater facilities for synthesis, and the Areas Table appeared for the first time. A more careful distinction was made between common and subject subdivisions. Pheonix schedules for General and Special Psychology were included, and examples of Western bias were less evident. For example, non–Christian religions were developed in more detail, and in many places a user was able to treat his own country or religion as the preferred category.

The eighteenth edition, published in 1971, is significant in having been adopted by the Library of Congress and BNB for their MARC records. This move has probably affirmed the future of DC. The eighteenth edition continued changes made in the sixteenth and seventeenth editions. In the interests of clarity, the 'divide like' instructions of earlier editions were modified to 'add to' instructions. The last five tables listed in Figure 14.2 were first introduced in the eighteenth edition. Pheonix schedules for Law and Mathematics were included.

The nineteenth edition, published in 1979, included Pheonix schedules which merged 329 and 324 to give a new schedule for the Political Process, and provided a completely new schedule for Sociology. The schedule for energy and energy resources was one of a range of expansions. Transfer of Civilization from 910–919 to 930–990 and new area divisions for 41–42 were also incorporated.

In 1983, Forest Press decided to opt for the concept of continuous revision which means that Pheonixes and major revisions will be released as separates between editions. The changes will be included on MARC copy as soon as they are published. This method should make it easier for libraries to absorb the changes. The ramifications of this policy are:

1. New editions will essentially be cumulations and therefore a longer gap will exist between editions. A gap of 10 to 12 years is to be expected.
2. More than the normal two Pheonixes will be published between editions. This policy has allowed the preparation of the Pheonix on data processing and computer science, for instance, which was published without waiting for the twentieth edition.

The twentieth edition was published in 1989 in four volumes. The most striking change was the presence of a manual which describes policies and practices of the Decimal Classification Division of the Library of Congress, offers advice on classing difficult areas and explains how to choose between related numbers. The general format has also been improved, with an increase in the number of notes in the schedules and tables. The 'see also' note which informs the user about related subjects is new. The only completely revised schedule is 780 Music, although there are a number of other revisions and expansions. Amongst these are revisions of the numbers, of sanitary and environmental engineering, and of pottery and porcelain. Various sections of the Tables have also been revised. The Relative Index has been pruned to eliminate many unlikely entries.

Although libraries may classify new stock by the latest edition of DC, earlier editions remain important because many libraries are reluctant to reclassify, and thus leave stock classified according to earlier editions long after they have been superseded.

The main method of revision has been by the publication of new editions. However, 'DC&: Decimal classification: additions, notes and decisions' is a useful means by which modifications can be announced in advance of a new edition so that reactions can be assessed before a revision is finally settled. As mentioned above, Forest Press decided on a policy of continuous revision in 1983.

Abridged editions of DC, giving less detail than the full edition, have been available since 1894. The latest abridged edition, the twelfth, was published in 1989, shortly after DC20 on which it is based. The abridged edition is widely used in smaller general libraries, specifically school libraries and small public libraries. There is also an *Introduction to Dewey Decimal Classification for British schools*, third edition, compiled by B A J Winslade and published in 1977. This is a further abridged version.

Dewey established the Lake Placid Club Education Foundation which has provided funds for the continuation of the scheme. In 1923 the Editorial Office was moved to the Library of Congress. Thus the scheme has a sound organizational backing. Consultation with users is achieved via the Decimal Classification Editorial Policy Committee, the British Liaison Committee and the Australian Liaison Committee. Forest Press, publisher of the scheme, has been acquired by OCLC.

The use of DC in BNB has also been important in establishing DC in British libraries. When BNB began publication in 1950 it relied upon the fourteenth edition of DC. This edition was found to be inadequate in several respects, and the same could be said of all editions until the eighteenth. By 1971, BNB was using a mixture of DC15, 16 and 17 grafted on to a DC 14 base and modified according to BNB's own scheme. The emergence of the MARC Project led BNB to opt for standard DC18 and confirmed the inclusion of DC numbers in both LC and BNB MARC records.

14.2.6 The future

The future of DC is assured. The scheme is extensively used in many libraries and in national bibliographies such as the British National Bibliography. Cooperation between the British Library Bibliographic Services Division, publishers of BNB, and the Decimal Classification Division has become more fruitful in recent years, and this is likely to further confirm the future of DC. Many changes in cataloguing and classification can be expected in the next ten years and these must impinge upon DC, influencing its future function and the way in which the scheme will evolve. But with the continuing need for shelf arrangement, DC will remain necessary.

Regular updating and revision must continue in order to provide for better balance of detail throughout the scheme, for new topics and complex subjects, and to make the scheme more attractive to users outside the English-speaking world.

Appropriate revision should ensure that the scheme keeps up to date, but large-scale reclassifying remains unpopular and an uneasy balance between updating and stability must be maintained; this balance is becoming increasingly difficult to sustain as knowledge changes rapidly.

14.3   Library of Congress Classification Scheme

The detailed classification scheme of the Library of Congress was evolved between 1899 and 1920, and was largely the responsibility of Herbert Putnam, Librarian of Congress, 1899–1939. The scheme consists of 21 classes set out in 47 separately published schedules. Some schedules for some subject areas have now gone through several editions. Science, for instance, is in its seventh edition. Other schedules, notably those for Law, have yet to be published in a complete form. (Law of Europe is now completed, but African, Asian and Soviet Law are still in progress.) The scheme was designed for the Library of Congress and many of its features derive from this fact. Nevertheless, other libraries do use the scheme. In particular LCC has been regarded as suitable for the classification of large general libraries, specifically those that have been established for research purposes. Included amongst these are university and large research libraries in the US and the UK.

Although LCC is used by other libraries, in order to understand the format of the scheme it is necessary to recognize that it was intended to fit the LC collections and services as closely as possible, without reference to outside needs and influences. In this sense, although general in scope, in its purpose it is a special scheme.

14.3.1   Principles

The following five principles underlie the construction of LCC and are important in determining its character:

1. LC is based on literary warrant, as is evident in the collections of the Library of Congress. In other words, it is based on library collection, not theory.
2. The emphasis in the scheme is to some extent on the social sciences, as this reflects the interest of the Congress. Political science and Education are well represented.
3. The minutely detailed classification is of the type appropriate to an extensive collection.
4. The scheme is intended to provide a systematic approach to the arrangement of books on shelves.

5. The scheme covers all knowledge, despite being special in purpose.

14.3.2 Main classes

The basic outline of main classes is based upon Charles Ammi Cutter's Expansive Classification which is essentially by discipline. The alphabetical notation used to designate main classes permits many of these to be included, as shown in Figure 14.5.

Main classes are divided into subclasses which are further subdivided into form, place, time and subject aspects. The scheme is largely enumerative. Like all enumerative schedules, those of LC are bulky, extending to some 10 000 pages. The scheme is essentially intended for one library – the home of the scheme's compiler and classifier. This is given as one reason why the need for synthesis is limited. Individual classes were originally developed by different specialists and are now kept up to date by individual cataloguers as new topics are added to the collections. There is not necessarily any overall plan for the development and maintenance of the schedules. Parts of the schedules differ in various respects from other parts. It thus becomes difficult to talk in general terms about the scheme, although there are a number of features which appear reasonably consistently between different parts of the schedules.

14.3.3 Synthesis

The scheme boasts very little synthesis. Nevertheless, some classes contain tables which may be used to extend the classes shown in the main schedules. Types of tables can be divided into three groups:

1. Form divisions exist in some classes, sometimes listed as a separate table. For instance the History schedules show period divisions as part of the schedules.
2. Subject subdivisions are gathered together into tables in some schedules, such as Language and Literature. See Figure 14.6(a).
3. Geographical divisions are sometimes given in full in the main schedule, and sometimes elsewhere as tables in classes. The notation for any given geographical division varies between classes and between different parts of the same class. See Figure 14.6(b).

14.3.4 *Notation*

The notation of LCC is mixed, including both letters and numbers. Main classes are denoted by a capital letter, and in most classes a second capital letter is used to signal major sections or subclasses. For example, Q stands for Science and QA for Mathematics, a subclass of Science. Arabic numerals are used to denote further divisions, in an integral manner, running from 1 to 9999, as necessary. Gaps are

Figure 14.5 Library of Congress Classification Schedules

A	General Works. 4th ed. (1973) ....
B–BJ	Philosophy. Psychology. 4th ed. (1989) ....
BL,BM,BP,BQ	Religion: Religions. Hinduism, Judaism, Islam, Buddhism. 3rd ed. (1984) ....
BR–BV	Religion: Christianity, Bible (1987) ....
BX	Religion: Christian Denominations (1985) ....
C	Auxiliary Sciences of History. 3rd ed. (1975) ....
D–DJ	History (General) History of Europe, Part 1, 3rd ed. (1990) ....
DJK–DK	History of Eastern Europe: General, Soviet Union, Poland (1987) ....
Soon!	
DL–DR	History of Europe, Part 2, 3rd ed ....
DS	History of Asia (1987) ....
DT–DX	History of Africa, Australia, New Zealand, etc. (1988) ....
E–F	History: America. 3rd ed. (1958) Reissue with supplementary pages, 1965 ....
G	Geography. Maps. Anthropology. Recreation. 4th ed. (1976) ....
H–HJ	Social Sciences: Economics. 4th ed. (1981) ....
HM–HX	Social Sciences: Sociology. 4th ed. (1980) ....
J	Political Science. 2nd ed. (1924). Reissue with supplementary pages, 1966 ....
J	Political Science, 3rd ed. (Unindexed cumulation through 1989) ....
K	Law (General) (1977) ....
KD	Law of the United Kingdom and Ireland (1973) ....
KDZ,KG–KH	Law of the Americas, Latin America, and the West Indies (1984) ....
KE	Law of Canada (1976) ....
KF	Law of the United States. Prelim ed. (1969) ....
KJ–KKZ	Law of Europe (1989) ....
KJV–KJW	Law of France (1985) ....
KK–KKC	Law of Germany (1982) ....
L	Education. 4th ed. (1984) ....
M	Music and Books on Music. 3rd ed. (1978) ....
N	Fine Arts. 4th ed. (1970) ....
P–PZ	Language and Literature Tables. Supersedes the tables in the P Schedules. (1982) ....
P–PA	Philology, Linguistics, Classical Philology, Classical-Literature (1928) Reissue with supplementary pages, 1968 ....
PA	Supplement: Byzantine and Modern Greek Literature. Medieval and Modern Latin Literature (1942). Reissue with supplementary pages, 1968 ....
PB–PH	Modern European Languages (1933). Reissue with supplementary pages, 1966.
PG	Russian Literature (1948). Reissue with supplementary pages, 1965 ....
PJ–PK	Oriental Philology and Literature, Indo–Iranian Philology and Literature. 2nd ed. (1988) ....
PL–PM	Languages of Eastern Asia, Africa, Oceania; Hyperborean, Indian, and Artificial Languages. 2nd ed. (1988) ....
P–PM	Supplement: Index to Languages and Dialects. 4th ed. ....
P–PM	Supplement: Index to Languages and Dialects. 3rd ed. (1983) ....
PN,PR,PS,PZ	General Literature, English and American Literature, Fiction in English, Juvenile Belles Letters. 3rd ed. (1988) ....
PQ	Part 1: French Literature (1936). Reissue with supplementary pages, 1966 ....
PQ	Part 2: Italian, Spanish, and Portuguese Literatures (1937). Reissue with supplementary pages, 1965 ....
PT	Part 1: German Literature (1989) ....
PT	Part 2: Dutch and Scandinavian Literatures (1942). Reissue with supplementary pages, 1965 ....
Q	Science. 7th ed. (1989) ....
R	Medicine. 5th ed. (1987) ....
S	Agriculture. 4th ed. (1982) ....
T	Technology. 5th ed. (1971) ....
U	Military Science. 4th ed. (1974) ....
V	Naval Science. 3rd ed. (1974) ....
Z	Bibliography and Library Science. 5th ed. (1980) ....

Figure 14.6(a)   LC Subject subdivisions – an extract from the Literature schedules

Tables of subdivisions under individual authors

I (98 nos.)	II (49 nos.)		Authors with ninety-eight or forty-nine numbers—Continued
	23	73	Doubtful, spurious works Cf. 70 (Table 1); 36, 86 (Table II)
42	.A2+	.A2+	Collections
43	.A5-Z	.A5-Z	Special, A–Z
44			Works edited by the author under consideration
45	24	74	Imitations. Adaptations
46			Parodies
47	25	75	Relation to the drama and the stage. Dramatization.
48	26	76	Translations (Comparative studies, etc.) Illustrations (Portfolios, etc. without text, illustrations with quotations) Prefer N8215, or the special artists in NC–NE as the case may be Classification of illustrations in P may be preferred in the case of a few authors of the first rank whose works have inspired many artists Illustrated editions with other editions Portraits, etc., of the author with his biography

Biography, criticism, etc.

			Bibliography, see Z8001+
51	29	79	Periodicals. Societies. Collections
52	30	80	Dictionaries, indexes, etc. Class here general encyclopaedic dictionaries only For special dictionaries, **see** the subject, e.g. characters, **see** 78 (Table 1); 39, 89 (Table II); concordances and dictionaries, **see** 91–92 (Table 1); 45, 95 (Table II)
.5	.5	.5	Historical sources and documents of the biography of authors For sources of literary works, **see** 71 (Table 1); 36, 86 (Table II) Autobiographical works
53	31.A2	81.A2	Autobiography
54	.A3–39	A3.–39	Journals. Memoirs
.3	.A4	.A4	Letters (Collections). By imprint date
.4	A41–49	.A41–49	Letters to and from particular individuals. By correspondent (alphabetically)
55	.A5–Z	.A5–Z	General works
56			Early life. Education
57	32	82	Love and marriage. Relation to women
58			Later life
59	33	83	Relations to contemporaries. Times, etc. Cf. 73 (Table 1); 36, 86 (Table II)
60	34	84	Homes and haunts. Local associations. Landmarks Cf. DA

left in the apportionment of notation in order to permit new subjects to be inserted. Alternatively this can be done by decimal subdivision. Figure 14.6(b) shows extracts from the tables where decimal subdivision has been necessary. Cutter numbers are used to further subdivide subjects. These consist of a capital letter followed by numbers. For example at HD 8039 for Labour, .B3 may be added (that is, HD8039.B3) to represent bakers, or .E5 (ie HD8039.E5) to represent Engineers. There is little mnemonic value to the notation, but some literal mnemonics have been attempted, for example, G for Geography, T for Technology.

14.3.5   Index

Each class has its own index. There is no official index to the whole scheme, although an index has been published. In the absence of a full index, users must be sure of selecting the appropriate main class before consulting the index of a specific class. The Library of Congress Subject Headings can be exploited as a general index, since it shows LCC numbers for many of the headings listed. This is published annually. Approximately 36–40 per cent of headings show LC class numbers.

14.3.6   Organization and revision

Each main class is revised individually without reference to any other class. Occasionally cross-references are included between classes. Revision, which is done by subject cataloguers at the LC, is continuous. As new books are received, new places are found to accommodate them.

New editions of schedules are published as staff and time permit. All changes are published as soon as they occur in *LC Classification – Additions and Changes*, a quarterly publication which, unfortunately, is not cumulative. Periodically, however, Gale Research Company publishes *Library of Congress Classification Schedules – A Cumulation of Additions and Changes*.

Both LC and BNB MARC records contain LCC class numbers. These reflect revisions in practices concerning the application of LCC class numbers as they occur. Equally the class numbers used on LC cards perform the same function.

14.3.7   The future

It is difficult to predict what the future holds for LCC. The scheme is primarily used by LC itself and by other extensive research collections such as large academic libraries. In such contexts, computerization of cataloguing and diversification of media will undoubtedly affect the application of LCC, but changes are likely to be slow because of the size of the libraries involved and because computerization of large numbers of cataloguing records is a huge task. The size of the collections which currently use LCC is likely to be a significant factor in its perpetuation.

214

Figure 14.6(b)   LC Geographical subdivisions – an extract from the Fine Arts schedules

Tables of subdivisions				
I		II	III	III-A
	South America-Continued			
35	Colombia	69	104	104
36	Ecuador	71	107	107
37	Guyana (British Guiana)	73	110	110
.2	Surinam (Dutch Guiana)	.2	.2	.2
.4	French Guiana	.4	.4	.4
38	Paraguay	75	113	113
39	Peru	77	116	116
40	Uruguay	79	119	119
41	Venezuela	81	122	122
42	Europe	83	125	125
43	Great Britain. England	85	128	128
44	England— local	87	131	131
45	Scotland	89	134	134
46	Ireland	91	137	137
47	Wales	93	140	140
	Special artists, A—Z		142	142
48	Austria	95	143	143
49	France	97	146	147
50	Germany	99	149	151
.6	Germany (Democratic Republic, 1949–)	100.6	151.6	154.6
51	Greece	101	152	155
52	Italy	103	155	159
53	Netherlands	105	158	163
54	Holland	107	161	167
55	Belgium. Flanders	109	164	171
56	Russia in Europe	111	167	175
	For Caucasian republics, **see** Russia in Asia			
57	Scandinavia	113	170	179
58	Denmark	115	173	183
59	Iceland	117	176	187
60	Norway	119	179	191
61	Sweden	121	182	195
62	Spain. Spain and Portugal	123	185	199
63	Portugal	125	188	203
64	Switzerland	127	191	207
65	Turkey	129	194	211
66	Other Balkan states	131	197	215
67	Bulgaria	133	200	219
(68)	Montenegro, **see** 71, 141, 212, 235 (.Y8)	(135)	(203)	(233)
69	Rumania	137	206	227

The improvement and refinement of classification at the Library of Congress are undertaken with the recognition that any change will affect the location of previously classified books.

14.4 The Universal Decimal Classification Scheme (UDC)

The Universal Decimal Classification Scheme (UDC) emerged from an attempt by two Belgians, Paul Otlet and Henri LaFontaine, to commence the compilation of the 'universal index to recorded knowledge' in 1894. Contributors to the scheme would be drawn from all over the world, and the index would be international in scope. Had this venture succeeded, the face of bibliographical control today would have been completely different. However, the most valuable long-term effect of the plans for this index was the classification scheme which was devised in order to arrange it. A classified rather than an alphabetical approach was necessary in the index because an internationally acceptable notation was important. DC was already in existence, and since its notation comprised numbers only was reasonably universal. With Dewey's permission, UDC was developed from the fifth edition of DC. A conference in 1895 established the Institut International de la Bibliographie (IIB) to be responsible for the index. The first edition of UDC was published in 1905. We return to the history of the scheme later.

As its origins suggest, UDC was designed for detailed indexing of documents and not for shelf arrangement. Thus, over the years it has been used to index reports, trade literature, periodical articles and other similar documents. The features which contribute to UDC's suitability for detailed indexing are particularly valued in special libraries. Thus, UDC has been extensively employed in special libraries and information centres in locations all over the world since the early 1900s. It is also the most widely used general classification scheme on the Continent of Europe, and this in an environment where libraries have not generally seen the virtue of published classification schemes, preferring to use their own private schemes. Since there is a preponderance of special libraries and information units in the science and technology subject areas and, in the light of UDC's consultative revision policies, UDC has been developed most fully in the areas of science and technology.

Prior to the 1970s UDC was frequently to be found in large card indexes in special libraries and sometimes in abstracting and indexing tools. Since the introduction of computer-based indexing systems, alphabetical indexing languages have become more prevalent and UDC has suffered a reduction in use. Ironically, this has left shelf arrangement of stock in special libraries as one of the main domains of application of UDC.

The features which characterize UDC and which make it appropriate for the applications discussed above are:

- its extensive synthetic devices,
- its cooperative revision procedures and
- its detailed specification.

14.4.1 Main classes

The overall outline of the schedules follows DC, but there are some differences in notation, and the two schemes have diverged at various points since the original adoption of the structure of DC5 for UDC. The main classes are listed in Figure 14.7. This outline shows class 4 to be vacant, linguistics having been moved from 4 to 8 in 1963 to make room for future developments. Otherwise the general structure is readily seen to be reminiscent of DC. With this structure, UDC inherited various of the weaknesses of DC. Both are essentially enumerative (although extensive provision for synthesis is made). In both, the main class order can be criticized on the grounds of the separation of Sciences from their respective Technologies. Some of the problems in main class order and allocation are alleviated by careful definition of any overlapping classes in order to clarify where any given document should be classified.

14.4.2 Synthesis and auxiliaries

The auxiliaries, a central feature of UDC, permit much more scope for flexible synthesis than can be achieved with DC or LCC. The auxiliaries may be divided into two groups according to whether they can be used anywhere in the scheme (common auxiliaries) or are only appropriate to specific parts of it (special auxiliaries). The auxiliaries offer a series of facets and facet indicators which permit flexible synthesis. These auxiliaries may be used when required at the discretion of the individual cataloguer (unlike DC where specific instructions are given for most applications of the Tables or the 'add to' device). Also, any number of auxiliaries may be included in one class number provided they are all required in order to label the document adequately. The auxiliaries can be divided into signs and subdivisions and are listed in Figure 14.8.

The first auxiliaries are essentially signs which permit the combination of two or more numbers from the main schedules. These are the plus, the stroke, the colon, the square brackets and the double colon. The first three of these can be illustrated further:

- $+$ is used to join the notation of two subjects which are commonly associated with one another, but which are separated by the normal sequence in UDC. For example, 539.1 + 621.039 Nuclear science and technology. In essence the '+' defines a new broader discipline by creating a piece of notation which represents the merging of two separate subjects.
- / is used to indicate a broader heading in the same way as +, the only

217

Figure 14.7   Main classes of Universal Decimal Classification (UDC)

0 Generalities. Science and knowledge. Organization. Information etc.	5 Mathematics and natural sciences.
1 Philosophy. Psychology.	6 Applied sciences. Medicine. Technology.
2 Religion. Theology.	7 Arts. Recreation. Entertainment. Sport.
3 Social sciences. Law. Government.	8 Language. Linguistics. Literature.
4 (Vacant)	9 Geography. Biography. History.

difference being that the component subjects are normally found adjacent to one another in the basic sequence. For example, 23/28 Christianity. Thus 23/28 represents the amalgamation of all of the subjects with notations between 23 and 28 into a new broader subject. Thus 23/28 is equivalent to $23 + 24 + 25 + 26 + 27 + 28$, provided that all of these notations have been assigned to subjects. Both $+$ and $/$ are extending devices, and compounds formed with them file before the simple number.

- : is used to combine two or more numbers from the main schedules in order to represent the separate concepts present in a multi-concept subject. For example, 331.2:687.9 Wages in the brush industry. The relation sign,:, is the most commonly used of these three devices and is characteristic of UDC numbers.

It should be noted that the relation sign does not indicate anything about the nature of the relationship between two subjects, but merely states that two or more concepts are treated in relation to one another in a document. Some theorists feel that the : is too imprecise and there is a need to state the nature of a

Figure 14.8 Universal Decimal Classification – auxiliary tables and filing order for devices

Common auxiliary tables

+ (plus) Addition, e.g. 59 + 636 Zoology and animal breeding

/ (stroke) Extension , e.g. 592/599 Systematic zoology (everything from 592 to 599 inclusive)

: (colon) Relation, e.g. 17:7 Relation of ethics to art

[ ] (square brackets) Algebraic subgrouping, e.g. 31:(622 + 669) (485) Statistics of mining and metallurgy in Sweden (the auxiliary qualifies 622 + 669 considered as a unit)

:: (double colon) Order-fixing or irreversible relation, especially in computerized systems, e.g. 061.2 (100)::002FID International Federation for Documentation (if no entry is required under 002)

= (equals) Language, e.g. = 20 in English; 59 = 20 Zoology, in English

(0...) (brackets-nought) Form, e.g. (051) Periodicals; 59 (051) Zoology periodicals

(1/9) (brackets-one-to-nine) Place, e.g. (4) Europe; 59 (4) Zoology of Europe

(= ...) (brackets-equals) Race and nationality, e.g. (=3) Germanic races; 17 (=3) Ethics in Germanic races

"..." (quotation marks) Time, e.g. "19" the 1900s (loosely, 20th century); 17"19" Ethics in 20th century

* (asterisk) Codes and notations (non-UDC), e.g. atomic mass number, 546–42*90 Strontium 90

A/Z (alphabetic extension) Names etc., e.g. REM (or Rembrandt); 75REM Paintings of Rembrandt

.00 (point-nought-nought) Point of view, e.g. .002.5 Tools, machinery, equipment aspect; 622.002.5 Mining: tools, machinery, equipment

-0 (hyphen-nought) To be developed. So far, there are two sections: -03 Materials, e.g. -033.5 Glass etc.; 683.512-003.5 Glass bottles

-05 Persons, e.g. -053.2 Children (in general); 17-053.2 Ethics in children

Special auxiliary tables

The meaning of these varies according to where in the main table they are listed; the notation used is:

-0/-9 (hyphen-nought-to-nine), e.g. 62-1 General characteristics of machines etc. (in engineering)

.0 (point-nought), e.g. 624.01 Structures according to material and material method of construction (in civil engineering)

'(apostrophe), e.g. 547.1'13 Organometallic compounds (in organic chemistry) relationship, not just to signal its existence. Others would argue that flexibility is useful.

It is evident that when two or more pieces of notation are combined with, for instance, the colon, the order in which they are combined – their citation order – needs to be considered. For example, should the final class number be 331.2:687.9 or 687.9:331.2? Criteria must be established for the preferred citation order in any given library. Further comments on citation order are included later.

In addition, a mechanism for generating added entries under second and subsequent numbers in a combined number must be invented and adopted. A process known as 'cycling' – where each number is in turn brought into the first position in the combined number – can be employed in order to generate headings for added entries. Plainly if only two numbers have been put together for the main number, added entry headings can be generated merely by reversing the component number (e.g. main entry under 331.2:687.9 and added entry under 687.9:331.2). The alternative to extensive added entries in a classified sequence, which can lead to extremely complex sequences, is to rely upon thorough subject indexing.

The other common auxiliaries have more in common with the Tables in DC:

- Language ($=$...) symbolizes the language in which a document is written. For example, 657$=$20 a work on accountancy written in English.
- Form of presentation (0...) lists bibliographical forms. For example, 623.821 (042) lectures on battleships.
- Place (1/9) lists places both in the usual specific geographical divisions and also other aspects of place. For example, 656.1(85) transport in Peru.
- Race and nationality ($=$...) are based on the common auxiliaries of language and may be developed from the main linguistics schedule. For example, 394.25($=$951) Chinese carnivals.
- Time '...' permits date to be specified in detail or other features of time to be reflected. For example, 551.509 '405' long-term weather forecasting.
- Alphabetical and non-decimal numerical division are merely indications of how to list individuals or items which can be symbolized by a number or alphabetical abbreviation. For example,

  929 Schil   Biography of Schiller
  820 Shak   The Works of Shakespeare

- Point of view (00...) may either be added to the main number or used in conjunction with the colon to given an extended facet indicator. In either application, the device is intended to provide a means of systematically ordering the subdivisions of a given number.

Other auxiliary devices are indicated in Figure 14.8. Special auxiliaries are signalled by $-0/-9$, $\cdot 0$, or '. These are listed in the area of the schedule to which they may be applied. An auxiliary listed under a given number may be applied to any subdivision of that number. For example in 534-6, the -6 may be applied to all subdivisions of 534, such as 534.63. Thus, 534-6 (Subsonic vibrations) provides -6 which can be applied with 534.63 (Measurement of frequency) to give 534.63-6 (Measurement of the frequency of subsonic vibrations).

Given this array of auxiliaries and the possibility of applying any number of them simultaneously, it is plain that a citation order for the inclusion of auxiliaries in a number must be settled. The recommended citation order is the reverse of the filing order.

Not only is a citation order necessary for individual numbers, but a filing order for arranging numbers for different subjects with respect to one another must be determined. None of the notational devices used in synthesis has any inherent filing order with respect to any other, so any proposed order will be artificial and must be learnt by classifiers and users. The recommended order is shown in Figure 14.8, except that the simple number is inserted after ' + ' and '/', and direct divisions added after special auxiliaries.

Libraries may settle their own filing and citation orders. The extent of application of the synthetic devices will vary from one library to another. There are no particular benefits to be gained from identical application of UDC in different libraries, even though standard schedules from which local variations may depart have some value.

14.4.3   Notation

The notation is similar to that of DC. The three figure minimum is not required for main classes and their subclasses. Consequently notations such as the following are to be found:

6   Technology. Applied Sciences.
63   Agriculture. Forestry. Stock breeding. Animal produce. Hunting. Fisheries.
633   Field crops. Industrial crops

Note also the notation for each of the main classes, as shown in Figure 14.7. The decimal point is introduced after *every* three digits; for example, 631.589.2 Hydroponics. Each of the auxiliaries has a unique piece of notation, as shown in the previous section. The main criticism of the notation is that for more specific subjects it can be extremely long.

14.4.4   Index

The UDC has no overall index. Only certain editions have an index, their nature being determined by the editing organization for that language.

14.4.5   History and organization

After the publication of the first edition of UDC in 1905, the 1914–1918 War and the unfavourable climate after that war led to the demise of the index, but UDC continued. The second edition of UDC was published between 1927 and 1933, while the third edition spanned the years 1934–52. The first and second full editions were in French and the third in German.

The IIB became the Fédération International de Documentation (FID) in 1937 and continued to support UDC. Eventually the British Standards Institution became the official English editorial body; the publication of the full English edition, which was long overdue, began with the fourth edition in 1943. This full English edition is still incomplete. Work has now commenced on the second and third full English editions. The full edition is published in a number of separate volumes, each pertaining to a specific subject area. There is no general distinction between successive full English editions.

In addition to the full edition, there exist abridged and medium editions of the scheme. The first British abridged edition was published in 1948, the second in 1957, and the third, and last to date, in 1961. The medium edition, which is available in various languages, contains about 30 per cent of the total tables. In actual application special libraries will often use the abridged edition as a general scheme to cover all subjects in their collection, together with the full edition for their particular subject speciality. Alternatively, they may opt to use just the medium edition.

14.4.5   Revision

UDC's revision structure has always been essentially consultative. One of the problems with consultation over several different language versions and many subject areas is that revision becomes slow and difficult to coordinate. In 1984, the FID Council established a limited life UDC Management Group to implement change. A new management structure, which came into effect at the end of 1986, has a UDC Management Board, supported by a small number of specialist committees and a two-tier revision structure. Revision is the responsibility of five Coordinating Revision Committees (CRCs), each covering a broad subject area. CRCs will identify priorities and seek out people to help in the revision of those priority areas. FID continues to rely on its national members and UDC bodies for support.

14.5   Other general classification schemes

There have been a number of other general classification schemes devised over the past 100 years. As indicated above, DC, LC and UDC are the classification schemes most widely used in libraries today, though special schemes may be important in other contexts. Two general schemes that have represented important milestones in the evolution of classification are briefly mentioned here: Ranganathan's Colon Classification and Bliss' Bibliographic Classification.

The Colon Classification, devised by S R Ranganathan and first published in 1933, is chiefly of interest for its development of facet analysis. Each edition since the fifth in 1957 has, theoretically, been published in two stages: Stage 1, the basic classification which gives sufficient detail for most books; and Stage 2, 'microthought' to cover periodical articles, patents and related materials. The first edition comprised basic classes analysed into facets, using the colon as the notational device for synthesis; the colon was therefore an integral feature of the scheme to which it gave its name. The Colon Classification is widely used in the Indian subcontinent, but the style of enumeration of subjects is not regarded as appropriate for Western libraries.

The overall pattern of the main classes is Science and Technology, then Humanities, and lastly the Social Sciences. Because all classes comprise simple isolates, grouped as foci within facets and subfacets, the schedules themselves are relatively succinct. Specialized subjects are catered for by the combination of foci.

Initially, Ranganathan used an *ad hoc* approach to analysis and citation order, but by the fourth edition he had started to establish the different kinds of facets to be found in each class. Facets, he observed, could be accommodated in five groups identified by Personality, Matter, Energy, Space and Time (as introduced above in 13.2.3). The citation order PMEST and various other facet formulae can be ascribed to Ranganathan.

The Bibliographic Classification was the work of Henry Evelyn Bliss. In addition to BC, he also published two other major works on classification: *The organisation of knowledge and the system of the sciences* (in 1929) and *The organisation of knowledge in libraries and the subject approach to books* (first edition 1933, second edition 1939). These works, together with BC, represent a significant contribution to classification theory. However, despite some very sound features, the scheme foundered due to lack of organizational backing for its revision. The full schedules of the first edition appeared between 1940 and 1953, and the second edition started to emerge in 1976. These two editions of the scheme are quite distinct.

Bliss believed that the most important aspect of a classification scheme was the order of its main classes. In BC all of the main classes can be grouped into four main areas: Philosophy, Science, History and Technologies and Arts. Within main classes facets are carefully identified and many foci are listed. However, Bliss was hostile to complete analysis, preferring to opt for a more detailed enumeration of subjects. Specification of compound subjects is largely achieved through the use of the Systematic Schedules; these schedules are extensions of the common subdivisions of other schemes.

BC had a long gestation period, with the first outline being published in 1910, and the full schedules in three volumes between 1940 and 1953. The first edition was essentially the work of one man and was published by the H W Wilson Company. In 1967, the British Bliss Classification Association (BCA) was formed to take over responsibility for BC; work began on its revision in 1969 under the editorial direction of Jack Mills. In 1975, the BCA decided to publish the second edition of the scheme in parts, commencing in 1977 with the Introductory volume and Classes J (Education), P (Religion) and Q (Social Welfare). Classes H (Anthropology, Human Biology, Health Sciences), K (Society), T (Economics, Management of Economic Enterprises) and J (Education) have also been published, while classes A/AL (Philosophy and Logic), AM/AW (Mathematics, Probability and Statistics) and R (Politics and Public Administration) are expected soon.

The overall order of main classes in the second edition remains essentially the same as in the first edition. The details in each class are developed with strict application of analytico-synthetic principles. Volume 1, the Introductory volume, contains the common facets as well as a lengthy introduction which represents a very authoritative account of various aspects of classification theory.

14.6 The Broad System of Ordering

The Broad System of Ordering (BSO) is a general classification scheme which was designed primarily for information exchange and switching. Together with BC2 it represents one of the major new general classification schemes of recent years. BSO was prepared by the International Federation for Documentation with the support of Unesco, and was published in 1978–79. The scheme was initiated under the auspices of UNISIST with the intention of providing a switching language. A true switching language would permit the translation of natural language concepts expressed in, say, German, into a classification notation; from that notation it would provide a natural language expression of those same concepts in, say, French. One essential feature of a switching language is that it be at least as specific as the languages to and from which it supports switching. The BSO is not likely to support this function very successfully because it is a relatively broad and unspecific classification scheme, with only sufficient specification for the classification of organizations concerned with the control of information (for example, libraries, clearing houses, abstracting and indexing agencies) and not to support the indexing of, say, individual periodical articles.

The scheme was essentially devised by a team of three: Coates, Lloyd and Simandl, and has a number of interesting features. The system has fairly low specificity; topics are not included on the usual basis of literary warrant, but rather on the basis of organizational warrant. In other words, a topic is included if there is an information centre, source or service covering it. Not surprisingly this can lead to gaps and uneven coverage of subjects. The BSO includes 3500 concepts. Within each class the concepts are analysed, using gradation by speciality and facet techniques. Facet analysis underlies the structure, but is not emphasized by facet indicators as in a more conventional faceted classification scheme. Extensive provision for synthesis is made including auxiliary schedules, 'expand like' instructions and synthetic features in the notation. However, the rules for synthesis are fairly complex and may be difficult to operate. The basic order of main classes resembles fairly closely that of BC, identifying the following main areas (into which main classes can be categorized);

Knowledge generally
Science and technology
Education
Human needs
Humanities, cultural and social sciences
Technology
Language, linguistics and literature
Arts
Religion and atheism

There is an index to the schedules, but this has been criticized in connection with the inadequate size of its entry vocabulary, the number of entries in the index only exceeding those subjects listed in the schedules by about 25 per cent. Further work on the index would make the scheme more effective. The notation is basically numerical and non-expressive, the latter aspect being felt to limit the scheme's usefulness in computerized databases. Probably the major factor which must be addressed before the scheme can be moved out of the realm of an interesting example of developments of classification theory into a practical classification scheme is its organizational backing. As already noted, development and revision of classification schemes are essential to their continued usefulness. Being designed by a small three-man team, financial and organizational support needs to be forthcoming if BSO is to have an assured future.

Plans are underway for a revised edition, which should be published in the near future as a self-financing project. The FID relinquished responsibility for the scheme in 1990, and copyright is in the hands of the BSO Panel.

14.7 Special classification schemes

The classification schemes that have been considered so far are general bibliographic classification schemes in that they attempt to encompass all of knowledge. Special classification schemes exist with more limited aims of covering just one main subject area, or are compiled in accordance with the interests of one user group. Apart from the separately published special classification schemes, there are also many local variations of general classification schemes in use for special applications. In some senses these could also be regarded as special classification schemes.

225

Special classification schemes are generally devised for a particular purpose and are to be found in the following environments:

1. Indexing and abstracting services and their databases; for example, Library and Information Science Abstracts, the British Catalogue of Music, INSPEC database.
2. Catalogues and shelf arrangements of special collections, especially industrial and research establishment libraries; for example, London School of Business Classification.
3. Catalogues and shelf arrangements of special collections, especially those of public libraries; such as children's collections, local studies collections and map collections.
4. Records management systems where files are stored in a topic-related order.

14.7.1 Different types of special classification schemes

A list of the different types of special classification schemes may help to indicate how these schemes may be designed for a variety of different purposes:

1. schemes restricted to a conventional subject area or discipline; for example, music, insurance, chemistry.
2. schemes restricted to an association of topics such as might be encountered in local collections in an industrial library or an archive.
3. schemes restricted to a certain type of reader; for example, children; university students, general browsers.
4. schemes restricted to a certain physical form; for example, pictures, records.
5. schemes restricted to a certain form of publication; for example, patents, trade catalogues, unpublished archives.
6. schemes restricted to bibliographies, indexing and abstracting services, and associated databases.
7. schemes restricted to a certain form of presentation of ideas; for example, fiction, plays.

14.7.2 Rationale for special classification schemes

Special classification schemes are generally devised for an application for which no major general scheme is suitable. Typical problems which arise with major schemes are that:

1. they often do not give sufficient detail for accurate specification of highly complex subjects;
2. they do not cater for the specialist viewpoints of any given application, since alternative approaches are not normally provided;

3. they do not provide for flexible combination as is demanded by highly specific subjects;
4. any flexibility or detailed specification which is possible is too often achieved by unnecessarily lengthy notation, and
5. the filing order is not always helpful.

Most current special classification schemes have been devised with the aid of facet analysis and are thus faceted classification schemes.

Whilst it may seem attractive to design a classification scheme for each different set of circumstances, it is important to remember the drawbacks of special classification schemes and to assess thoroughly whether a published general scheme will not, after all, be acceptable. Amongst the disincentives to compiling and maintaining a special classification scheme can be numbered the following:

1. the work involved in compiling the scheme;
2. the work involved in revision, especially if it seems advisable to publish the scheme, or if the scheme needs drastic revision to adapt to the changing remit of a special library or information service;
3. limited opportunity is usually available for cooperation in application of classification or in its compilation and revision; and
4. users need to learn a scheme which may be unusual or unique and which they might find difficult.

Despite the problems of special classification schemes, they do represent an opportunity to match users' perspectives and the organization of literature to an extent not often possible in a general classification scheme; as a result, such schemes will always have a place in the organization of knowledge.

Perhaps the major problem in devising a special classification scheme is the definition of the subject area to be covered. First, it is necessary to define 'core' topics which form a homogeneous subject field, and then to assess whether users' needs can be matched by one field or whether two are necessary. Having identified core topics, marginal or fringe topics must be listed, and the type of treatment that they are to receive settled. It is important to realize that the scope of a scheme which apparently focuses on a relatively narrow area may be quite wide by the time all fringe topics (which are relevant to or have some impact upon the core area) have been noted.

14.7.3 Some examples of special classification schemes

The easiest means of illustrating some of the foregoing points is to introduce in outline some special classification schemes.

1. *Cheltenham Classification.* The Cheltenham Classification is a scheme for a

227

specific user group. Although it covers all knowledge, it has been designed to apply specifically to collections in school libraries. It aims for a more helpful order than the major schemes by following the groupings of subjects as they are taught in schools. For example, each language is followed by its literature, and material on jobs and careers is given a significant place.

2. *Bogg's and Lewis Map Classification.* This is an example of a classification which is restricted to a specific physical form – maps and atlases. Main classes are based upon a division of localities into continents. One particular strength is that it is possible to specify both the area and the subject of the map. Detailed specification is achieved with a relatively limited length of notation.

3. *Fiction Classifications.* Fiction classifications are used extensively in public libraries. Categorizing fiction according to a subject classification is widely recognized as difficult and unhelpful. Many public libraries follow a scheme similar to Corbett. In 1978, McClellan proposed a scheme based on main categories where subdivision is by readability ratings. Thus, the symbol for easy-reading historical and period novels would be F8a.

4. *The London Classification of Business Studies.* The London Classification of Business Studies is a classification and a thesaurus for business libraries, the second edition having been published in 1979. The first edition had met a growing need for a special classification scheme in this area, since it was published in 1970 during a period of rapid growth for business schools and business libraries. By the publication of the second edition the scheme had been adopted by 75 libraries, many outside the UK. The schedules are divided into three main areas. The notation is primarily letters, but it also uses numbers to denote concepts in the auxiliary schedules. Thus, *China's industrial revolution: politics, planning and management, 1949 to the present* is classified at JKD 552/61T while *Interview skills training: role play exercises* is classified at FBGD/NFJ.

5. *Classification of Library and Information Science.* This scheme was developed by the Classification Research Group. The final version was published in 1975, but possibly the earlier version – which is used in *Library and Information Science Abstracts* – is better known. The citation order was at first unsatisfactory and modifications were made in order to better reflect the needs of users. The citation order now gives precedence to processes, such as circulation control and cataloguing, rather than to types of libraries.

6. *British Catalogue of Music Classification.* The British Catalogue of Music Classification was developed by Coates for the British Catalogue of Music in 1960. It is also used in various music libraries and has influenced the development of music schedules in BC2 and DC. The schedules are divided into two parts, one covering music scores and parts, and the other concerned with music literature. The facets for music scores and parts are: Executant (for example, trumpet), Form of Composition (for example, march) and Character of Composition (for example, military). The facets for music literature need to

Figure 14.9 Outline of the classification scheme used in Library and Information Science Abstracts (LISA)

CORE SUBJECTS (A/Z)

A	LIBRARIANSHIP
Ab/z	Common Subdivisions (Form)
B	Common Subdivisions (Subject)
Bge/i	Research
Bji	Biographies
Bk	Profession
Bki/o	Library Associations
Bm/z	Professional Education
Buf	Library Schools
C	Common subdivisions (Time-History)
D	Common Subdivisions (Place). By Dewey DC with minor modifications
E/H	Libraries and Special Categories of Users
Ea	Libraries in General
F	Public, Official and Government Libraries
Fs	National Libraries
Fv/z	Public Libraries
Gc/m	Academic Libraries
Gd/Gg	University Libraries
Hb/s	Special Libraries
Ht/Hyh	Institutional Libraries. Services to the Physically Isolated and Handicapped
Hu	Hospital Libraries
Hyj/k	Youth and Children's Libraries
HykGp/z	School Libraries
Hym/Hzy	Users by Special Characteristics
Hz (0–9)	Users by Special Occupations. By UDC
J	Use of Libraries and Library Materials
K/M	Library Stock and Materials
Lvx	Archives
Mg/x	Audio-Visual Materials
M (0–9)	Library Materials by Subject Interest. By UDC
N/Q	Organisation and Administration
Oq/y	Computers
P	Staff
Q/Qu	Buildings and Equipment
R/S	Reader Services
Rm	Information Work
Rmi	Instructions in Use of Libraries and Library Materials

Rn/t	Information Services (Published and Distributed Services)
Ru/v	Reference Work
Ry	Cultural Activities (Extension Work)
S/Z	Technical Processes and Services
Sb/c	Acquisitions
Scm	Interloans
Se/f	Preservation of Material
Shc/jn	Circulation
Sk/x	Copying Services
T/Z	Information Storage and Retrieval
Th/Uzh	Cataloguing
V	Subject Indexing
X	Classification
Zj	Computerised information storage and retrieval
Zjj	Optical discs
Zm	On-line information retrieval
ZmNxa	Videotex
Zp	Automatic indexing

FRINGE SUBJECTS (1/9)

154	Communication
16	Computers
169	Word Processing
181	Telecommunications
182/188	Organisation and Administration
21	Knowledge and Learning
23/25	Education
28	Museums
3	Authorship
4/45	Reading
46/48	Writing
5/54	Bibliography
61/65	Printing
66/68	Copying
69	Bookbinding
7/77	Publishing
752	Copyright
773	Published Materials
78	Bookselling
7883	Public Lending Right
8	Audio-Visual Materials
87	Microforms
9 .	Other Subjects. By UDC

be more numerous and include Composer, Executant, Form, Elements of music, Character, Technique and Common subdivision. For instrumental music, for example, subjects in the Executant facet would include type of executant, size or complexity of executant body, accompanying executant and original executant (for arrangements). The notation is also interesting, being entirely comprised of letters. More details of this notation were given above in 13.3.4.

14.8   Classification in online searching

Classification can be used in all types of online retrieval systems as an aid in subject searching. There are three main ways in which classification can be used in online searching:

1. *Direct classification search*, where the user enters a classification code and the system responds with records of items classified at or near the entered code. Most online catalogues and some online hosts provide this facility. The most usual approach is to lead users to a display of brief bibliographic records in class number order, so that they can browse further.
2. *Classification as a linking device or pivot.* Many UK libraries provide a subject index linking alphabetically arranged descriptive headings to classification codes. A similar arrangement in an OPAC may allow the user to enter the system with alphabetical search terms and translate them into classification codes, and then identify the records associated with those codes. There is no reason why the intermediate stage should not be eliminated or why a search that starts with alphabetical index terms cannot be directly translated into records at appropriate class numbers.

    Such a linking system may be particularly useful in multilingual databases, with subject access through UDC. One development of the link is the pivot. This is based on the very obvious observation that, if a record has been identified as being relevant, other records at adjacent class numbers may also be of interest; thus the search can be developed by looking at the records associated with nearby class numbers. BLCMP is one of the few OPACs to offer a classmark pivot.

    A classmark pivot feature, using DC, was also incorporated in OKAPI. OKAPI experience with pivots suggests some guidelines for the design of pivot-based systems:

    - where there is a screenful of records at a specific classification code, there should be a means of skipping to the next or previous codes;
    - where adjacent codes are likely to denote related subjects, some account should be taken of the nearness of adjacent codes;

- the system should not encourage users to look at books classified nearby unless they are closely related;
- with an enumerative classification such as LC, it may be impossible to generalize about when it is worth offering adjacent codes, and
- even if the possibility exists that other books with the same class number are relevant, the system should not offer these without establishing that this is so.

3. *Direct or indirect searching of classification schedules.* The indexer has access to schedules that the searcher in general does not have available online or even in printed form; thus there is likely to be a mismatch between the indexers' and searchers' perspectives. One way to enhance the searchers' understanding of the indexing is to make the schedules available online. The schedules of DC, at least, are available in machine-readable form.

The Dewey Decimal Classification Online Project is the most substantial piece of research available on the use of classification in online catalogues. The project was carried out in 1984–85, with the following objectives:

- determining strategies for searching and displaying DC in an online catalogue,
- demonstrating DC as a searchers' tool for subject access, browsing and display, and
- testing DC's effectiveness as a searchers' tool.

The team designed two experimental catalogues known as DOC (Dewey Online Catalogue) and SOC (Subject Online Catalogue). SOC and DOC were similar except that the latter's records were enhanced with text from Dewey schedule captions, notes and relative index. DOC allowed hierarchical browsing of the schedule captions, as well as direct subject searching. In DOC the words of Dewey captions, notes and relative index entries were used to index class numbers and their captions. Thus when the user input a search term, a class number would be retrieved. Nevertheless, various problems were identified including the terminology of some of the captions and the fact that class numbers tended to be too general and have too many postings.

Above all, searchers wanted to go straight to records and were irritated by having to pass through the display of the classification schedules. Although it is sometimes useful to engage in hierarchical browsing, this is essentially subsidiary to the direct keyword approach. On the other hand, the use of keywords from Dewey as a means of generating additional keywords for records was extremely fruitful and allowed better retrieval even if, on occasions, there was some loss of precision due to the granularity of the classification.

There has also been some significant research into the use of UDC in online searching systems. Buxton reports a project that examined the potential for the use of UDC in a number of online catalogues, databases and information retrieval packages in terms of their ability to allow searching on UDC numbers. He concludes that these systems show a number of deficiencies in dealing with UDC numbers unless written with UDC in mind. A first problem is the punctuation. It is suggested that spaces be used to split up UDC numbers so that the various parts of the numbers can be used as separate search terms; also that punctuation marks be replaced with letters. An alternative might be to use separate subfields for different parts of the number. Clearly, then, some problems with UDC may need to be investigated, including the following:

1. the fact that the notation is not always expressive of the hierarchy;
2. the use of ranges – each level in the hierarchy needs its own number;
3. the precoordination of main numbers;
4. the existence of various notational inconsistencies, especially in the use of notation for auxiliaries, and
5. the fact that areas of knowledge, rather than concepts, are classified.

There are a number of projects to put UDC schedules into machine-readable form. The prospect for holding UDC schedules as a thesaurus is promising, but the schedules will need some adjustment before they can be adopted in an operational system.

Recommended reading

Dewey Decimal Classification Scheme

Batty, C D (1981), *An introduction to the nineteenth edition of the Dewey Decimal Classification*, London: Bingley.

Berman, S (1980), 'DDC 19: an indictment', *Library Journal*, **105** (5).

Bull, G and Roberts, N (1980), 'Dewey Decimal Classification, 19th edition (Review)', *Journal of Librarianship*, **12** (2), 139–42.

Butcher, P (1979), 'Dewey? we sure do! a review of DDC19', *Catalogue and Index*, **55**, 1, 7–8.

Comaromi, J P (1976), 'Conception and development of the Dewey Decimal Classification', *International Classification*, **3** (1), 11–15.

Comaromi, J P (1976), *The eighteen editions of the Dewey Decimal Classification*, Albany, New York: Forest Press.

Comaromi, J P (1978), 'Use of the Dewey Decimal Classification in the United States and Canada', *Library Resources and Technical Services*, **22** (4), 402–408.

Comaromi, J P (1991), *Dewey Decimal Classification, twentieth edition: a study manual*, Libraries Unlimited.

Custer, B A (1978), 'The responsiveness of recent editions of the Dewey Decimal

Classification to the needs of its users', in *General classification systems in a changing world*, The Hague: FID, 81–84.

Custer, B A (1979), 'Dewey 19', *Catalogue and Index*, **53**, 1–2.

Dewey, M (1979), *Abridged Dewey Decimal Classification and relative index*, 11th edition, edited under the direction of B A Custer, Albany, New York: Forest Press.

Dewey, M (1979), *Dewey Decimal Classification and relative index*, 19th edition, edited under the direction of B A Custer, Albany, New York: Forest Press.

Jelinek, M (1980), 'Twentieth Dewey: an exercise in prophecy', *Catalogue and Index*, **58**, 1–2.

Koster, C (1981), 'Dewey in the UK: a British viewpoint', *Catalogue and Index*, **62**, 5–7.

Sifton, P (1989), 'Workbook for DDC 20: practical introduction to Dewey Decimal Classification, edition 20', Canadian Library Association.

Vann, S K (1976), 'Dewey Decimal Classification', in Maltby, *A Classification in the 1970s: a second look*, London: Bingley, 226–55.

Library of Congress Classification Scheme

Canadian Library Association (1974), *An index to the Library of Congress Classification* by M Elrod *et al.*, Ottawa: Canadian Library Association.

Immroth, J P (1976), 'Library of Congress Classification', in Maltby, A, *Classification in the 1970s: a second look*, London: Bingley, 81–98.

Library of Congress, *Subject Cataloging Division Classification*, 34 vols, Washington: Library of Congress, 1901-

Library of Congress, *Subject Cataloging Division LC Classification – additions and changes*, Washington DC: Library of Congress, List 1-, March/May 1928-

Markham, J W (1990), 'LCC, DDC, and algae', *Library Resources and Technical Services*, **34** (1), 54–61.

Olsen, N B (1974), *Combined indexes to the Library of Congress Classification schedules*, Washington: US Historical Documents Institute.

Universal Decimal Classification

British Standards Institution, *British Standard full English edition of the Universal Decimal Classification*, London: BSI, 1943-

British Standards Institution (1961), *British Standard 1000A:1961 Abridged English Edition of the Universal Decimal Classification*, 3rd edition, London: BSI (FID no 289).

Foskett, A C (1973), *The Universal Decimal Classification: the history, present status and future prospects of a large general classification scheme*, London: Bingley.

Hindson, R (1981), 'UDC in the UK: a report on the 1979/80 survey', *Aslib Proceedings*, **33** (3), 93–101.

Lloyd, G A (1976), 'Universal Decimal Classification', in Maltby, A, *Classification in the 1970s: a second look*, London: Bingley, 99–118.

Perreault, J M (1969), *Towards a theory for UDC*, London: Bingley.

Robinson, G (1979), *UDC: a brief introduction*, The Hague: FID, (FID no 574).

Other schemes

Abridged Bliss Classification (1967), London: School Library Association.

Baker, S L (1988), 'Will fiction classification schemes increase use?' *Reference Quarterly*, **27**, 366–76.

Baker, S L and Shepherd, G (1987), 'Fiction classification schemes: the principles behind them and their success', *Reference Quarterly*, **27**, 245–51.

Batty, C D (1966), *Introduction to the Colon Classification*, London: Bingley.

Bliss, H E (1939), *The organization of knowledge in libraries*, 2nd edition, New York: H W Wilson.

Bliss, H E (1940–53), *A bibliographic classification*, New York: H W Wilson, vol. 1, 1940, vol. 2, 1947, vols 3 and 4, 1953.

'The Broad System of Ordering' (1979), *International Forum on Information and Documentation*, **4** (3), 3–27.

'BSO: Broad System of Ordering; schedule and index', (1978), 3rd revision prepared by the FID/BSO Panel, The Hague and Paris: FID/Unesco (FID no 564).

'The BSO manual: the development, rationale and use of the Broad System of Ordering' (1979), prepared by the FID/BSO Panel, The Hague: FID (FID no 580).

Coates, E J (1960), *The British catalogue of music classification*, London: Council of the British National Bibliography.

Dahlberg, I (1980), 'The Broad System of Ordering (BSO) as a basis for an integrated social sciences thesaurus?' *International Classification*, **7** (2), 66–72.

Foskett, D J and Foskett, J (1974), *The London education classification: a thesaurus/classification of British educational terms*, 2nd edition, London: University of London Institute of Education Library.

Gopinath, M A (1976), 'Colon Classification', in Maltby, A, *Classification in the 1970s: a second look*, London: Bingley, 51–80.

Maltby, A and Gill, L (1979), *The case for Bliss*, London: Bingley.

Mills, J (1976), 'Bibliographic classification', in Maltby, A, *Classification in the 1970s: a second look*, London: Bingley, 25–50.

Mills, J and Broughton, V (1977–), *Bliss Bibliographic Classification, Vol. 1: Introduction and auxiliary schedules; Other classes*, London: Butterworth.

National Library of Medicine (1969–), *The National Library of Medicine Classification: a scheme for the arrangement of books in the field of medicine and its related sciences*, 3rd edition, Bethesda, Maryland: NLM.

Neelameghan, A *et al.* (1973), 'Colon Classification, Edition 7, Schedules of basic subjects', *Library science with a slant to documentation*, **10** (2), 222–60.

Ranganthan, S R (1965), 'Colon Classification, edition 7(1971): a preview', *Library science with a slant to documentation*, **6** (3), 123–42.

Ranganathan, S R (1965), *The Colon Classification*, Rutgers: The State University Graduate School of Library Science. (Rutgers series on systems for the intellectual organisation of information, Vol. 4.)

Ranganathan, S R (1990), *Elements of library classification*, New York: Advent (reprint).

Ranganathan, S R (1990), *Philosophy of library classification*, New York: Advent (reprint).

Satija, M P (1990), 'A critical introduction to the 7th edition (1987) of the Colon Classification', *Cataloging and Classification Quarterly*, **12** (2), 125–38.

Soergel, D (1979), 'The Broad System of Ordering – a critique', *International Forum on Information and Documentation*, **4** (3), 21–24.

Vernon, K D C and Lang, V (1979), *The London Classification of business studies: a classification and thesaurus for business libraries*, 2nd edition, revised by K G B Bakewell and D A Cotton, London: Aslib.

Vickery, B C (1960), *Faceted classification: a guide to construction and use of special schemes*, London: Aslib.

Classification in online retrieval

Buxton, A B (1990), 'Computer searching of UDC numbers', *Journal of Documentation*, **46** (3), 193–217.

Chan, L M (1990), 'The Library of Congress Classification System in an online environment', *Cataloging and Classification Quarterly*, **11** (1), 7–25.

Cochrane, P A and Markey, K (1985), 'Preparing for the use of classification in online cataloging systems and online catalogs', *Information Technology and Libraries*, **4**, 91–111.

Foskett, D J (1991), 'Concerning general and special classifications', *International Classification*, **18** (2), 87–91.

Freeman, R R and Atherton, P (1968), 'Final report of the research project for the evaluation of the UDC as the indexing language for a mechanized reference retrieval system', New York: American Institute of Physics.

Gilchrist, A and Stachan, D (eds) (1990), *The UDC: essays for a new decade*, London: Aslib.

Godart, W (1991), 'Facet classification in online retrieval', *International Classification*, **18** (2), 98–109.

High, W H (1990), 'Library of Congress Classification numbers as subject access points in computer-based retrieval', *Cataloging and Classification Quarterly*, **11** (1), 37–43.

Hill, J S (1984), 'Online classification number access: some practical considerations', *Journal of Academic Librarianship*, **10** (1), 17–22.

Hill, J S (1990), 'Things are taking a little longer than that: a response to Dewey Decimal Classification in the online environment', *Cataloging and Classification Quarterly*, **11** (1), 59–69.

Johansen, T (1987), 'Elements of the non-linguistic approach to subject relationships', *International Classification*, **14**, 11–18.

Karhula, P (1990), 'The use and usability of the UDC in classification practice and online retrieval' in A Gilchrist and D Strachan (eds), *The UDC: essays for a new decade*, London: Aslib, 47–53.

Loth, K and Funk, H (1990), 'Subject search in ETHICS on the basis of the UDC', in A Gilchrist and D Strachan (eds), *The UDC: essays for a new decade*, London: Aslib, 35–46.

Markey, K and Demeyer, A N (1986), 'Dewey Decimal Classification Online Project: evaluation of a library schedule and index integrated into the subject searching capabilities of an online catalog', Final report to the Council on Library Resources, Chicago: OCLC (OCLC/OPR/RR-86/).

Morris, L R (1990), 'The frequency of the use of Library of Congress Classification numbers and Dewey Decimal Classification numbers in the MARC file in the field of library science', *Technical Services Quarterly*, **8** (1), 37–49.

Pepler, J (1990), 'The impact of computers on classification theory', *Journal of the Society of Archivists*, **11** (1/2), 27–31.

Siegel, E R *et al.* (1984), 'A comparative evaluation of the technical performance and user acceptance of two prototype online catalog systems', *Information Technology and Libraries*, **3** (1), 35–46.

Subject access. 'Report of a meeting sponsored by the Council on Library Resources', edited by K W Russell, Dublin (Ohio), 7–9 June 1982, Washington DC: Council on Library Resources, 1982.

Svenonius, E (1983), 'Use of classification in online retrieval', *Library Resources and Technical Services*, **27** (1), 76–80.

Wajenberg, A S (1983), 'MARC coding of DDC for subject retrieval', *Information Technology and Libraries*, **2** (3), 246–51.

Walker, S (1991), Views on classification as a search tool on a computer. In: Computers for Libraries International 91: proceedings of the fifth annual conference on Computers in Libraries, held in London in February 1991; conference chairman J. Eyre, London: Meckler.

15 The alphabetical subject approach

15.1 Introduction

Although there are a number of different means of facilitating the alphabetical subject approach to documents and information, all these different approaches share common problems. Some aspects of the creation of a good alphabetical subject index, whether it be printed or computer-based, recur in any subject approach to information. The underlying problems of the subject approach, the components of the indexing process and some concepts which facilitate its discussion have already been introduced in Chapter 12. It is important that Chapter 12 should be familiar to the reader before any attempt is made to consider the alphabetical subject approach further. This brief chapter merely serves to draw together some common problems in alphabetical indexing (which feature in a different way in classification schemes). Perhaps predictably, many of these problems are concerned with the label that is given to a subject in an alphabetical index.

15.2 Naming a subject

On first inspection it might appear that the words used in indexes to represent concepts could be determined by reference to normal usage, but to be effective, even in an alphabetical index, such labels need more careful consideration. Many different words may be used to represent the same concept. In order to achieve some helpful grouping of, and clear labels for, those concepts, it is necessary to recognize closely related variants. Natural language indexing has its own solutions, but even in this context, the same problems are encountered; this aspect is discussed further in Chapter 16. It is simpler to think about the problems outlined below in the context of controlled language indexing.

Labelling of subjects presents problems mainly because, in order to achieve a user-orientated system, the various potential approaches of different users must be catered for. If a subject has more than one name, a library catalogue or index must bring all material on that subject together (within the limitations of the scope of the collection or index) under one of those names, and also cater for users who use different names. Specific problems include the following:

1. *Synonyms,* or terms with the same or similar meanings, are present in every subject area. Near synonyms are most common, with true synonyms (which mean exactly the same thing and which are used in precisely the same context) being more unusual. However, even near synonyms may be regarded as equivalent for some purposes, but not others. For example, in a general index it might be adequate to regard Prisons and Dungeons as one and the same, but in a specialist index devoted to Criminology, this would probably not be acceptable. Some common situations in which synonyms arise are listed below:

    (a) Some subjects have one stem, for example, sterilizer, sterilizing, sterilized; or computing, computers, microcomputers, computed, computation. Sometimes it is acceptable to treat such words or concepts as equivalent to one another, but on other occasions it is important to differentiate between them.
    (b) Some subjects have both common and technical names; these different names must be recognized and reflected in the index in accordance with the audience for whom the index is intended. Examples of such terms are salt and sodium chloride, radish and raphanus sativus.
    (c) Changes in usage of terms over time can also present problems. The Library of Congress, for instance, started with the term 'Electronic calculating machines' but had to modify this, in keeping with later normal usage, to 'Computers'.
    (d) Some concepts are described differently in different versions of one language. American and English English are two good examples of differences in usage. For example, the following terms may all be used for the same object: Eyeglasses, Spectacles, Glasses.

    The merging of synonyms carries implications for the effectiveness of the index in terms of precision and recall. If two terms are merged, precision is impaired but recall may be improved.

    All unused terms must be included in the entry vocabulary of an index; that is, they must be present as access points in some form if it is considered at all likely that a user might seek information under the unused term. These unused terms will normally be present in an index only in order to direct the user to the used or preferred terms.
2. *Homographs,* or words which have the same spelling but very diverse meanings, must be identified. In normal usage (as opposed to index usage) the meaning of a homograph is established by its context. If one word is used out of context as an index heading, plainly it will be difficult to establish the interpretation to be placed on the homograph. Examples of homographs are: Duty (obligation), Duty (taxation); Ring (to ring, as in telephone, or to draw a

238

circle around), or Ring (as in a mathematical concept, a finger ring, a ring of toadstools). In a special index the meaning of a homograph may be obvious by its location within a given subject. Thus the term Ring in an index to mathematics is well defined. In a general index it may only be possible to distinguish between different meanings of the one homograph by using scope notes or qualifying terms wherever the term arises, and thus in some way replace the context that is normally absent in respect of index terms.

3. *Plurals and singulars* All nouns have a plural and a singular form. It may seem petty to distinguish between the plural and singular form, and therefore unnecessary to include both in the index. If both are nouns is there any difference between Farms and Farm? Generally the plural and singular of the same noun are regarded as equivalent, but there are a number of instances when it is necessary to treat the plural and the singular forms as distinct. Consider the different meanings, for example, of Exercise and Exercises, Church and Churches. If one form only is permitted, it is common practice to adopt the plural.

4. *Multi-word concepts* Some subjects cannot be described satisfactorily with one word, but require two or more words for their specification. Examples might be: Origin of Species, Information retrieval, Country walks or Extra-terrestrial beings. Whichever word in the term is used as the main entry point in an index, the user might first seek the subject under the other word in the term. Once an entry has been identified, the user will expect to find the complete term in order to distinguish it from others containing the same words. Access must be provided via all significant words in the multi-word term. Thus if Exceptional children is the preferred term, when the user looks under Children he must also be able to trace a route to the document. Usually references can serve to direct users from words not used as the primary entry word to the word that does have this status. Sometimes terms are presented in direct order, for example, Military Hospitals, but on other occasions the terms may be inverted, for example, Hospitals, Military. Inversion may offer the advantage of grouping like subjects. For example, inversion to Hospitals, Military will cause this heading to file alongside other headings commencing with the word Hospitals. The disadvantage of inversion is a reduction in predictability. How is a user to know which multi-word terms in a system have been inverted and which have not; or, with three-word terms or more, which option for rearrangement of the words has been chosen?

5. *Complex subjects,* like multi-word terms, may require labels which contain many words. The distinction between complex subjects and multi-word terms is that the former contain more than one unit concept. However, each of these concepts may be potential search keys and as such may be described by terms which exhibit any one of the problems listed in 1 to 4 above. With complex subjects, citation order becomes even more vital. For example, it is evident that 'a bibliography of history' is not the same thing as 'a history of bibli-

ography'. The same two terms, 'bibliography' and 'history' serve to describe both subjects, and it is only the order in which they are cited and, in natural language, the connecting words that distinguish the statements of the two subjects.

The presence of a variety of concepts in the statement of one subject area has been referred to in Chapter 12 as a means of defining syntactic relationships. It is these syntactic relationships and the ways in which they can be handled which are primarily responsible for the distinction between pre-coordinate and post–coordinate indexing systems – approaches which will be considered in Chapter 17.

15.3   Indicating relationships

Although the predominant problem of the alphabetical subject approach concerns the naming of subjects, as has already been demonstrated in Chapter 12, any tool for the organization of knowledge must also take into account the relationships between subjects. To reiterate, there are two main categories of relationship: the syntactic relationships mentioned above are, for example, evident in a topic such as Sugar and health where the concepts 'Sugar' and 'Health' are drawn together in this particular context. Obviously either of these concepts may also be present in other circumstances, where the existence of the relationship defined in this document is largely irrelevant.

Semantic relationships show aspects of the genus-species relationships and are expected to reflect assumed and widely accepted subject relationships. For example, 'Terrier' will always be a type of 'Dog'. Provision must be made for linking related subjects. This is normally effected by references and other devices indicating relationships in thesauri and subject heading lists, as well as alternative entries.

This then is a brief résumé of the problems which must be recognized by any indexer and for which the index must allow.

15.4   Why Controlled Vocabularies?

A natural language system takes index terms directly from titles, abstracts, citations or full text. There is no scope for distortion from indexer interpretation; indexing error is minimized and new terms can be added directly to the vocabulary as needed. Nevertheless, the preceding sections have identified the problems, mostly associated with language, that need to be tackled in order to overcome the imperfections of natural language as a basis for search keys in an information retrieval system. In an ideal system the user would be able to pose a question in natural language, and the computer would search the texts and provide a sufficient group of relevant documents. Research and some operational systems, such as

LIBERTAS and STATUS IQ, are moving in this direction, but most systems still offer the following two options:

- using natural language indexing and allowing the user to deal with the vagaries of that language, or
- using a controlled language and asking the user to adhere to an artificially imposed vocabulary.

Controlled indexing languages are widely used in many systems because of their versatility in:

1. indicating the general concept and its structure in the subject area;
2. establishing a language that mirrors as closely as possible the language found in the literature and the language used by potential users;
3. employing pre-coordinated phrases as appropriate to reduce false drops to a minimum;
4. supplying a standard vocabulary by controlling synonyms and ensuring that only one term of a potential list of similar terms will be used in indexing a given concept;
5. defining ambiguous terms and distinguishing homographs, and
6. showing semantic relationships amongst terms.

Recommended reading

General works on this subject are listed at the end of Chapter 12, whilst more specific readings can be found at the end of Chapters 16, 17 and 18.

16   Alphabetical indexing languages

16.1   Introduction

Control is exercised in respect of the terms used in an index because of the variety of natural language. Such control may involve the barring of certain terms from use as index headings or access points. The terms which are to be used are likely to be specified, and synonyms recognized and probably eliminated (for example, Packaging may be indicated as preferable to Wrapping). Preferred word forms will also be noted; for instance, Heat may be preferred to Hot. The easiest way to exercise this type of control over index terms is to list or store the acceptable terms in a vocabulary. Such lists will embody both specific decisions concerning preferred words and also, by example, decisions relating to the form of words to be used (for example, singular or plural, nouns or adjectives). There are two types of controlled indexing language – thesauri and subject headings lists. These two tools have the same two basic functions:

- to control terminology used in indexes, and
- to control the display of relationships between concepts in indexes.

On the other hand, they differ in their area of application and to some extent in the way in which they seek to fulfil these two basic functions.

16.2   Subject headings lists

Subject headings lists are lists of index terms, normally arranged in alphabetical order, which have been given authority for use in an index, catalogue or database for describing subjects. Such a list seeks to negotiate the problems of the alphabetical subject approach as outlined in the previous chapter. Section 16.6 (below) makes a more direct comparison between subject headings lists and thesauri, while Section 16.7 considers the compilation of such lists.

The basic functions of a subject headings list (as identified in section 16.1 above) may be focused more precisely in the following terms:

1.   the list records terms which shall be used in a catalogue, index or database and

indicates the form in which they shall be shown; it thus acts as an authority list for index terms and their form;

2. the list makes recommendations about the use of references for the display of relationships in a catalogue, index or database in order to guide users between connected or associated terms.

Thus a subject headings list is primarily a guide to the indexer or cataloguer in the creation of index records. Most information about terms and their relationships that could be of assistance to the user of the index will be transferred from the list to the index or catalogue itself.

Subject headings lists are normally generated for a particular purpose. As in any alphabetical indexing language, it is important that the language reflects the current requirements of the user and the literature; thus it is fairly common to have to modify a standard list or compile a fresh list when a new application is envisaged. It is therefore more important to understand the principles on which such lists are based than to be able to negotiate all the niceties of any particular list.

There are some published lists of subject headings which are plainly intended for a special purpose. Amongst these might be numbered the School Library Association's *List of Subject Headings, Medical Subject Headings* (or MeSH) from the National Library of Medicine (US), and *Subject Headings for Engineering* (or SHE) used in the Engineering Index. The most effective means of reviewing the structure of such specialized lists is to consider two of the traditional subject headings lists which cover all subjects: *Sears' List of Subject Headings* and the *Library of Congress List of Subject Headings*. These two lists have formed the basis of indexing practice, theory and discussion in respect of alphabetical subject catalogues for some years.

16.3   Sears' List of Subject Headings

Now in its twelfth edition (1982), *Sears' List of Subject Headings* was first written by Minnie Sears and published in 1923. It was designed as a list of subject headings for use in the dictionary catalogues of medium-sized libraries and is still widely used by school and small public libraries, particularly in the United States. Its overall structure and principles are similar to those of the *Library of Congress List of Subject Headings*, though differences arise from Sears' being designed for smaller libraries. The headings, for instance, are less complex (Sears' would include city planning, rather than LC's Cities and towns – planning); less numerous (e.g. Sears' includes only Art, French instead of LC's Art–France and Art, French), and less specific.

Apart from its undoubted value in its own right, Sears' provides a valuable model or point of departure for others wishing to devise alphabetical subject headings lists for applications in which Sears' itself would not be appropriate.

Both functions of subject headings lists are fulfilled by Sears'. Terminology is controlled by establishing the terms that are to be used in an index or catalogue. These are indicated in bold type. Other terms which are useful access points but which will not be used as index terms are listed in light type. The form or style is also controlled by indicating, for each term, the extent of abbreviation or the order of the words. In general, the following word forms are included; where it is possible to describe a subject with a single noun, this is preferred.

1. single nouns; for example, Diseases.
2. compound headings; for example, Disinfection and disinfectants.
3. adjective with noun; for example, Cultural relations; Art, French.
4. phrases; for example, Discrimination in housing.

Some headings may be subdivided. In each instance guidance is given on how subdivision is to be made and on the form of headings. Types of subdivisions include:

1. subdivisions by physical form of the document; for example, Diseases – Dictionaries.
2. subdivisions that show non-comprehensive treatment; for example, Chemistry – Societies.
3. subdivisions that show special aspects; for example, Education – History.
4. subdivisions that show chronology; for example, US – History – 1783–1809.

Some headings may also be subdivided by place, or alternatively, some places may be subdivided by subject; for example, Agriculture – France or Paris – Population. Sometimes geographical subdivision is in terms of the adjectival form; for example, Music, German.

The display of these subdivisions in the list varies. Some are listed adjacent to the term to which they are to be applied and in the form in which they are to be applied in the main list. Other, generally applicable subdivisions, are shown in a separate list for easy reference. Subdivisions that might be applied to certain types of headings (such as places, literatures, and so on) are shown under key headings in the main list. Key headings exist for persons (for example, Presidents – United States); places (for example, United States, Ohio, Chicago); languages and literatures (for example, English languge, English literature) and wars (for example, World War, 1939–1945).

The three following principles are employed in Sears' for the selection and assignment of subject headings:

1. Specific entry is generally recommended. The level of specificity that is desirable in any index is a function of the collection being indexed, its use and its patrons. The principle of specific entry as applied in Sears' recommends that as

specific a heading as is available in the list should be assigned. For example, a book on Bridges should be entered under Bridges and not under a broader heading such as Engineering, nor doubly under both headings.

2. Headings are selected for inclusion in Sears' on the basis of common usage. Thus popular or common names of subjects are included in preference to technical or specialist jargon. Unfortunately for the non–American user, the headings consequently correspond to current American usage in both use of terms and spelling, and often need amendment to make them consistent with usage elsewhere.

3. Uniformity and consistency in application of subject headings is important. An attempt is made to offer one heading for each concept, a principle which the indexer should try to adhere to consistently.

In acknowledging these principles, Sears' is consistent with traditional ideas on the construction of alphabetical subject catalogues; these are also followed in the *Library of Congress List of Subject Headings.*

Some categories of headings are deliberately omitted from Sears'. These include:

- proper names; for example, names of persons, names of families, names of places;
- corporate names; for example, names of associations, names of institutions, names of government bodies;
- common names; for example, names of animals, tools, diseases, and chemicals.

Plainly, to list a reasonable number of terms in each of these categories would expand the list considerably. The indexer is expected to insert headings into the index or catalogue in these categories as and when they are required. Such headings should be constructed in accordance with the principles underlying Sears'.

Sears' gives instructions for creating references for insertion in an index or catalogue to show relationships between subjects. Any terms in light type which are not to be used as headings in the catalogue direct the cataloguer to a 'used' heading covering the same or a similar concept. See, for example, Country churches in Figure 16.1(a).

Most used headings, such as Country life in Figure 16.1(a), will be accompanied by some indication of their relationship to other terms. A fairly full entry is displayed in the example below. This extract from Sears' includes two types of guidance to the cataloguer:

1. assistance in considering alternative headings, (for example, see also Agriculture – Societies; Farm Life; and so on);
2. suggested headings from which references might be constructed and inserted in the catalogue (for example, Rural life).

245

Figure 16.1(a)   A small extract from Sears' List of Subject Headings

Country churches. **See Rural churches**
Country houses. **See Architecture, Domestic**
Country life (May subdiv. geog.) 307.7; 630.1
    Use for descriptive, popular and literary works on living in the country. Materials
        dealing with social organization and conditions in rural communities are
        entered under **Sociology, Rural**
    See also Agriculture – Societies; Farm life; Farmers; Outdoor life; Sociology, Rural
    x Rural life
    xx **Farm life; Outdoor life; Sociology, Rural**

(b) References generated by the instructions under a main subject entry

Main subject entry

Country life
Cottage life today/ M N Rimmer 2nd. edition. – London: Granada Publishing,
1991.—301p.—(Lifestyles).

References

Rural life see **Country Life**
Farm life see also Country Life
Outdoor life see also Country Life
Sociology, Rural see also Country Life

References to be inserted in the catalogue may be either 'see' or 'see also'. Figure
16.1(b) shows how the instructions in the extract from Sears' can be converted into
entries and references in a catalogue. The references which are suggested are not
obligatory and should only be made as appropriate with regards to the item being
indexed.

'See' references are generally used to link two terms which represent similar
concepts, but which are presented in a different form. These might include references from:

1. synonyms; for example, Gaels see Celts.
2. the second part of a compound heading; for example, Dusting and spraying
    see Spraying and dusting.
3. the second part of an adjectival heading; for example, Furniture, Built-in see
    Built-in Furniture.
4. an inverted heading to the normal order; for example Natural Gas see Gas,
    Natural.
5. variant spellings; for example, Color see Colour.
6. opposites; for example, Intemperance see Temperance.
7. singular to plural forms; for example, Mouse see Mice.

'See also' references link two headings, both of which will be accepted for indexing.

Such references permit users to extend their search to related subjects. 'See also' references link connected subjects which may be coordinate, for example, Vases see also Glassware. Alternatively, the subjects linked by 'see also' references may be a general subject and its more specific subdivision, for example: Crime see also Crimes without victims.

General references, in the form of either 'see' or 'see also', may also be employed on occasions. Such references will be used where the entry term is a relatively common term, and where the use of specific entries instead of the one general reference could lead to extensive (undesirable) lists of specific references. Typically general references may be used in respect of a common subdivision.

16.4 Library of Congress Subject Headings

The Library of Congress subject headings is the pre-eminent authority list for subject headings. First published in 1909, it is used not only by the Library of Congress but widely across the United States; since the headings are included in USMARC tapes, the list can be consulted wherever in the world MARC tapes are used. The 13th edition (1990) contains subject headings employed in cataloguing at the Library of Congress since 1898. Information about new and changed headings is contained in MARC tapes, in LC Subject Headings weekly lists, in the quarterly *LCSH* in microfiche and in the Cataloging service bulletin. The entire subject authority file is also available on CD–ROM.

16.4.1 Types of Headings

The list contains both approved and non-approved headings. Approved headings are listed in bold type, such as **Art, Children as artists**. A heading may take one of the following forms:

1. single nouns, for example,

    Cats; Poetry.

    Homographs may need a modifier in parenthesis to clarify the meaning that is associated with them, for example

    Cold (Disease)

2. adjectival headings, which comprise either a noun or noun phrase with adjectival modifier, for example,

    Agricultural credit
    English Literature,

247

or inverted adjectival headings, where the inversion is used to bring the noun into the position of the entry element, for example,

Geography, Historical
Maps. Statistical.

3. Conjunctive phrase headings, with two or more nouns, noun phrases or both, with or without modifiers connected by 'and' or ending with 'etc', for example,

Literature and science
Debtor and creditor
Bolts and nuts

4. Prepositional phrase headings, with nouns, noun phrases or both, with or without modifiers connected by a preposition, for example,

Children in motion pictures
Federal aid to youth
Cataloging of art

Some headings combine these varous forms, for instance,

Harp and percussion with string orchestra.

Headings may also be subdivided as indicated below.
The heading may have a scope note to indicate the application or meaning of the heading, for example,

Irreligion
Here are entered works dealing with a condition of complete absence of religion.

Library of Congress class numbers are also attached to some headings.
Terms that are related to the preferred heading are shown. Since the 11th edition, these relationships have been indicated with the use of the abbreviations UF, NT, RT and BT. (see p. 251). For example:

Gravity waves
[QA 927 (Mathematical)]
UF Waves, Gravity
BT Gravity
Hydrodynamics
Waves

UF is applied to those terms which are included in order to expand the entry vocabulary. These terms will be included in the list, but are shown in light face type and the indexer is directed towards the preferred heading. For example,

Grease
    USE Lubrication and lubricants
       Oils and fats

Associate relationships are expressed by RT, for example,

Squirrels,
    RT Rodentia

General SA (see also) references may also be made to an entire group of headings as an economy measure, for instance,

Cranberries
    – Diseases and Pests
    SA names of pests eg Cranberry root-worm

The Library of Congress subject headings make extensive use of subject subdivisions as a means of combining a number of different concepts in a single heading. Composite topics may therefore be represented by subject headings followed by a series of subdivisions. For example,

Art – Study and teaching – Italy – Naples

16.4.2 Subdivisions

Subject headings may be further subdivided by form, topical, period and geography. Some of the form and topical subdivisions are for general application and are known as free-floating. Subdivisions usually represent a form or aspect of the main subject and not a subordinate subject. To elaborate a little further, it is useful to examine each of the main types of subdivisions, as follows.

1. Form subdivisions reflect the form or arrangement of the subject matter, for example,

    Engineering – Dictionaries

2. Topic subdivisions are subject subdivisions, for example,

    Engineering – Research

3. Free-floating form and topic subdivisions may be used with headings within a given category. Normally, in order to maintain control over the use of subdivisions, each combination of main heading and subdivision must be approved. Exceptions are common or free-floating subdivisions. These are listed at one chosen or model heading and may also be used elsewhere within a category.

4. Period subdivisions are used to indicate the history of a place or subject, such as,

    English fiction – 19th Century
    English language – Grammar – 1950–

    Period subdivisions appear in various forms and, apart from a small list of exceptions, are not free-floating.
5. Geographic subdivisions indicate geographical treatment. Headings may be subdivided by the name of a country or other political entity, a region or a geographic feature. For instance,

    Sports – England
    Banks and banking – France

16.4.3   References

There are instructions in the list for the creation of appropriate see and see also references. The new symbols NT, USE need not necessarily be transferred to library catalogues where traditional entries can still be made. For example, if we chose to make see and see also references for a work on Gravity waves, the following entries could result:

Subject heading: Gravity waves
References:
Waves, gravity
  see Gravity waves

Gravity
  see also Gravity waves

Hydrodynamics
  see also Gravity waves

Waves
  see also Gravity waves

16.4.4   Other points

Personal and corporate names may be used as headings, and geographic names may be used as main headings and also as subdivisions. Apart from a few model entries, these are not included in the list but must be established by the cataloguer. A form that conforms with the recommendations of AACR2R and is consistent with use elsewhere in the catalogue should be sought. Cataloguers are assisted by the *Name authorities* (cumulative microfiche edition) which lists the forms of names and corporate headings that might be used in subject cataloguing but which are not shown in the list. An important auxiliary aid is the *Subject cataloging manual: subject headings*, a third edition of which was published in 1989 and updated in 1990.

Despite the appearance of the LC list in recent years, it is important to recognize that the list is not a thesaurus. A thesaurus offers terms for individual concepts and shows the relationships between those terms. The Library of Congress list includes many terms which encompass more than one concept. It offers guidance on the establishment of subject headings which have several layers of subdivisions and which, as such, can only be described as pre-coordinate headings. In other words, the list operates at a much higher level of pre–coordination of concepts than one would expect a thesaurus to support. Some examples of headings should illustrate this point:

Knowledge, Sociology of
Automobile driving on mountain roads
Cooperative marketing of farm produce
Mites as carriers of disease

The reader is invited to analyse these headings into their component concepts.

16.4.5 Limitations of subject lists

Although traditional subject headings lists are important, they do have limitations. Both Sears' and the Library of Congress List of Subject Headings have been criticized on the following counts:

1. Headings tend to be broad and cannot represent complex or specific subjects accurately.
2. Headings are not constructed and selected systematically. Scan, for example, the headings listed under 'Libraries'. When terms such as 'Libraries, Children's' are found alongside 'Business libraries', it is far from obvious whether terms are being inverted or put in direct order. Such variations not only confuse users about the forms of headings, but also make it difficult for a cataloguer inserting a new heading for local use to discern the principles which should be heeded to retain consistency of approach.
3. References are not always constructed systematically. References may not be recommended where they could be appropriate or useful; in other places, too many references can make for a very tedious search.
4. Subarrangement under headings is not purely alphabetical. For instance 'Sculpture – Technique' precedes 'Sculpture in motion'.

These limitations of traditional lists of subject headings should not necessarily be taken as faults in their construction. Some of the criticisms arise from conflicting opinions as to the basic purpose of a list of subject headings. Nevertheless, the fact that these general lists cannot serve for every application has triggered a search for more consistent approaches to constructing headings, together with the development of special lists of subject headings and thesauri.

16.5   Thesauri

A thesaurus could be defined as 'a compilation of words and phrases showing synonyms, hierarchical and other relationships and dependencies, the function of which is to provide a standardized vocabulary for information storage and retrieval systems'. The thesaurus is an authority list showing terms which may, and sometimes may not, be used in an index to describe concepts. Each term is usually given together with terms which are related to it in one of a number of ways. The aims of the thesaurus are, first, to exert terminology control in indexing and, second, to aid in searching by alerting the searcher to the index terms that have been applied.

Although there are standards which provide guidance on the construction of thesauri, until recently there has not been a 'standard' thesaurus, or even a thesaurus which is widely used as a norm. In 1981, the British Standards Institution published its *Roots Thesaurus*, which is intended to be a model thesaurus from which terms may be drawn. This is discussed in more detail later in this section. Thus there are many different thesauri, some published and others strictly in-house. A thesaurus is normally tailored to meet the specifications of a particular application. Very often thesauri will be limited in subject scope, for example, to music, education or agriculture. Thesauri have been used extensively since around the 1950s to index special collections of documents, abstracts, bulletins, current awareness tools, Selective Dissemination of Information Systems, online databases, encyclopaedias and a variety of other bibliographical tools. Since there is no typical thesaurus, we may examine some of the more common features of existing published thesauri.

16.5.1   Key features of thesauri

The main list of index terms is the core of the thesaurus and defines the index language. This listing must be present in any thesaurus and normally features, in a single alphabetical sequence,

1. *descriptors*,   or terms which are acceptable for use in indexes to describe concepts, and
2. *non-descriptors*,   or terms which are not to be used in the index but which appear in the thesaurus in order to expand the entry vocabulary (terms through which the user can enter the thesaurus and be directed to the appropriate term) of the indexing language.

Descriptors are normally accompanied by some display of relationships between them and other words in the indexing language.

Most indexing terms in a thesaurus are 'uniterms' or single-concept terms, although in some instances a deliberate decision may be made to include some multi-concept terms. The form of terms, whether they be descriptors or non-descriptors, may be one of:

1. single words; for example, Horror, Hosiery, Journalism, Counting.
2. phrases of two or three words, often comprising a noun and an adjective; for example, Country life, Electric meters, Electric power plants.
3. two words linked by 'and' or '&'; for example, Joy and sorrow, Boats & boating.
4. compound phrases; for example, Employees' representation in management, Victim offender relationships.
5. names of persons, bodies, places; for example, Smith, John, BLCMP, Paris. (Note: names of persons, bodies and places may be included in the main thesaurus, or they may be the subject of a distinct authority list.)

Concepts are represented by these words or terms. Concepts should, in general, be described as simply as possible, whilst retaining sought and well–known terminology. Thus, single-word terms or (failing an appropriate single–word term) two-word terms are preferred to longer terms in describing concepts. Shorter terms are more likely to be present in the same form in both the indexer's and the searcher's normal vocabulary for the subject.

Generally the singular form of words is used for processes and properties (e.g. Liquidation, Classification), and the plural for classes of people who perform such processes (e.g. Liquidators, Classifiers). Multi-word terms should be entered in their preferred form in their natural order. Abbreviations should only be used if their meanings are known to users.

Index terms do not always stand alone, but are sometimes defined more precisely by the use of both qualifiers and scope notes. *Qualifiers* function as an integral part of the index term, so that terms of the form:

Moving (House)
Mergers (Industrial)

are created and used. *Scope notes*, on the other hand, may be present in a thesaurus but are unlikely to be transferred to an index. Scope notes define the scope of the index term by indicating its meaning and clarifying the use of the term in the thesaurus. Scope notes are sometimes designated by the abbreviation SN (for Scope Note). So we might have:

Remedial education
(Instructing individuals to overcome educational deficiencies or handicaps in content previously taught but not learnt).

253

Industrial management
SN – Application of the principles of management to industries.

Relationships between the terms in an indexing language are also indicated in most published thesauri. These relationships can be viewed as belonging to one of three main categories: preferential, hierarchical or affinitive:

1. *Preferential* relationships generally indicate preferred terms or descriptors and distinguish such terms from non-descriptors or non–preferred terms. These relationships thus perform the vital function of identifying index terms. Statements conveying preferential relationships between terms indicate which terms are to be treated as equivalent to one another, or which concepts are to be grouped together under one index term. Preferential relationships are indicated by statements of the form:

    A is not authorized, see B instead

    where A and B are taken to be two index terms, with A a non-descriptor and B a descriptor. Examples might be:

    Temperance see Intemperance
    Disabilities USE Handicaps
    Urban Life USE Urban culture.

    There are variations on the basic statement of a preferential relationship. The following statement, for instance, suggests that in indexing or searching for Folk drama, both of the terms Drama and Folk Culture should be used:

    Folk Drama
    USE Drama and Folk Culture.

    The following statement represents another variation on the basic preferential relationship:

    Programming languages USE Fortran, Algol, Cobol, Basic.

    This statement directs the user to adopt a number of more specific terms in preference to the general term.

    All statements indicating preferential relationships will usually appear in both direct and inverted forms. Thus the thesaurus user may approach a term from 'either direction'. It would be normal, for instance, for the statement:

    Games USE Sports

    to be complemented, at the appropriate point in the alphabetical sequence, by

Sports UF Games

where 'UF' is a common abbreviation for 'use for'.

2. *Hierarchical* relationships are represented in the thesaurus by statements of the form:

A is permitted, but consider using B or C or,. . ., N instead

where, as above, A, B, C, . . ., N are index terms (that is, descriptors) and B and C and so on are related to A via some hierarchy of relationships. Hierarchical relationships must be indicated in order that users may transfer from a first access term to related terms, and to broaden or narrow the search parameters. The indication of such relationships helps the searcher and the indexer to select the most specific term available as a label for any given concept in the thesaurus. The searcher is kept better informed as to related terms under which additional information or documents have been indexed. Hierarchical relationships take one of two forms, depending upon whether A is subordinate to B, C, . . ., N, or whether B, C,. . ., N are subordinate to A. Broader terms are generally indicated by the abbreviation 'BT'. For example:

Remedial reading
BT Reading

suggests that Remedial reading is a subordinate topic to Reading. Narrower terms are signalled by the abbreviation 'NT'. Thus,

Libraries
NT Public libraries

notes that Public libraries are a type of Library. In most instances it is to be expected that 'NT' and 'BT' statements should be accompanied by their inverse. Thus the above example would normally be complemented by:

Public libraries
BT Libraries.

Hierarchical relationships may also take the form of coordinate relationships, in which case they may be represented by 'RT' or related term in a similar manner to affinitive relationships below.

3. *Affinitive* relationships are a further type of connection between index terms, and thus may be codified by a similar statement to that encountered in respect of hierarchical relationships:

A is permitted, but consider using B or C or,. . ., N as well or instead.

Although the statements of affinitive and hierarchical relationships are similar, they differ in the nature of the relationships that they signal. Affinitive relationships that exist between terms are not necessarily connected to one another in any fixed hierarchical manner. Affinitive relationships are often indicated by the code 'RT'. An example might be:

Food
RT Vegetarianism
Dinners
Cookery.

It is usual for 'RT' to be reflexitive, the above example concerning Food would be accompanied by a series of inversions of the statement of the form:

Vegetarianism
RT Food
Cookery
RT Food.

It is important to remember that such relationships as are displayed in the thesaurus may not be transferred to the index. This is an important reason why the searcher should consult the thesaurus prior to the start of a search.

Other abbreviations are encountered in some thesauri. Amongst them can be listed: 'GT' Generic to; 'SA' See also; 'TT' Top term in a hierarchy; 'XT' Overlapping term; 'AT' Associated term; 'CT' Coordinate term; 'ST' Synonymous term; and 'SU' See Under.

Figure 16.2 shows some extracts from thesauri.

In addition to the relationship display which is incorporated into the alphabetical list of subject terms, thesauri often incorporate other lists which help to show the relationships between terms. Published thesauri, in particular, are likely to include one or more of the following types of lists:

1. *Hierarchical displays.* Various of the key terms in the thesaurus may be drawn in an alphabetical sequence, with a more complete hierarchical display of the connected terms having more specific meanings.
2. *Categorized displays.* Thesaurus terms are grouped under a series of category headings which correspond to the main subfields within the area covered by the thesaurus.
3. *Permuted lists of terms.* These lists arrange terms under each of the words in a term; thus Industrial management would appear in two places in the alphabetical sequence: under industrial and under management. Such lists aid access to second and subsequent words in terms.
4. *Graphic displays.* Various imaginative graphic displays have been proposed. Numbered amongst these are Euler circles, arrowgraphs and the circular thesaurus. The attraction of such displays is that multi–dimensional relationships between subjects may be shown since any one subject can be displayed in juxtaposition with several others.

Figure 16.2   Some Thesaurus Extracts from ERIC and INSPEC
The ERIC Thesaurus (12th edition, 1990)

(a) Main alphabetical list

DOGMATISM   *Jul. 1966*
   CIJE: 203   RIE: 99   GC: 120
RT Authoritarianism
    Beliefs
    Ideology
    Opinions
    Personality Traits
    Totalitarianism

Domestics (1970 1980)
use HOUSEHOLD WORKERS

DOORS   *Jul. 1969*
   CIJE: 12   RIE: 8   GC: 920
BT Structural Elements (Construction)
RT Construction Materials

DORMITORIES   *Jul. 1966*
   CIJE: 397   RIE: 262   GC: 920
UF Dormitory Living #
    Residence Halls
BT Housing
RT College Buildings
    College Housing
    Educational Facilities
    House Plan
    Living Learning Centers
    On Campus Students
    Resident Advisers
    Resident Assistants
    Residential Colleges

Double Employment
use MULTIPLE EMPLOYMENT

DOUBLE SESSIONS   *Dec. 1969*
   CIJE: 7   RIE: 11   GC: 350
SN School days consisting of separate
    sessions for two groups of students
    in the same instructional space, e.g.,
    one room used by one fourth-grade
    class in the morning and by another
    fourth-grade class in the afternoon
UF Split Sessions
BT School Schedules
RT School Organization
    Space Utilization

Continued

Figure 16.2   Continued

(b) Rotated display of descriptors

```
                                EXERCISE
                    MUSCULAR    EXERCISE    Use EXERCISE
                    PHYSICAL    EXERCISE    Use EXERCISE
                                EXERCISE PHYSIOLOGY
                                EXERCISE (PHYSIOLOGY) (1969 1980)
                     WRITING    EXERCISES
                                EXHAUST STACKS    Use CHIMNEYS
                                EXHAUSTING (1969 1980)    Use VENTILATION
                                EXHAUSTION    Use FATIGUE (BIOLOGY)
                                EXHIBITS
                                EXILES    Use REFUGEES
                                EXISTENTIALISM
                                EXOGAMOUS MARRIAGE    Use INTERMARRIAGE
                    FACILITY    EXPANSION
                     SCHOOL     EXPANSION
                                EXPECTANCY    Use EXPECTATION
                                EXPECTANCY TABLES
                   WORK LIFE    EXPECTANCY
                                EXPECTATION
                                EXPENDITURE PER STUDENT
                                EXPENDITURES
                   CONSUMER     EXPENDITURES    Use CONSUMER ECONOMICS
                    LIBRARY     EXPENDITURES
                                EXPENSES    Use EXPENDITURES
                     INITIAL    EXPENSES (1966 1980)    Use EXPENDITURES
             MINIMUM INITIAL    EXPENSES    Use EXPENDITURES
           MINIMUM OPERATING    EXPENSES    Use OPERATING EXPENSES
                   OPERATING    EXPENSES
                                EXPERIENCE
    SUPERVISED OCCUPATIONAL     EXPERIENCE (AGRICULTURE)    Use SUPERVISED
                                    FARM PRACTICE
                    LANGUAGE    EXPERIENCE APPROACH
                                EXPERIENCE BASED EDUCATION    Use
                                    EXPERIENTIAL LEARNING
```

Continued

Figure 16.2   Continued

(c) Subject categories

Groups Related to PHYSICAL AND MENTAL CONDITIONS

HEALTH AND SAFETY   210

Medicine and health, health conditions and services, and diseases; health occupations; health facilities; professional and paraprofessional health education; parts of the body; and accidents and safety. *See also* DISABILITIES.

DISABILITIES   220

Physical and mental disabilities; special education; communication disorders, processes, and therapies; and equipment and personnel serving the disabled. *See also* LEARNING AND PERCEPTION and INDIVIDUAL DEVELOPMENT AND CHARAC-TERISTICS. For emotional and psychiatric conditions see MENTAL HEALTH.

MENTAL HEALTH   230

Mental illness and mentally ill persons; therapies promoting mental welfare; mental health facilities personnel; and psychology. *See also* COUNSELING.

COUNSELING   240

Guidance and counseling; guidance personnel; counseling techniques; and rehabilitation. *See also* MENTAL HEALTH.

(d) Two-way hierarchical term display from the ERIC Thesaurus.

:: INSTITUTIONS
: SCHOOLS
FREEDOM SCHOOLS

: EDUCATION
FREE EDUCATION

:::: LIBERAL ARTS
::: HUMANITIES
:: FINE ARTS
: VISUAL ARTS
FREEHAND DRAWING

:: INSTITUTIONS
: SCHOOLS
FREE SCHOOLS

::: LANGUAGES
:: INDO EUROPEAN LANGUAGES
: ROMANCE LANGUAGES
FRENCH

:::: LIBERAL ARTS
::: HUMANITIES
: LITERATURE
FRENCH LITERATURE

:: INSTRUCTION
:WRITING INSTRUCTION
:: LITERACY
::LANGUAGE ARTS
: WRITING (COMPOSITION)
:: CURRICULUM
: COLLEGE CURRICULUM
FRESHMAN COMPOSITION

:: RELATIONSHIP
: INTERPERSONAL RELATIONSHIP
FRIENDSHIP

FRINGE BENEFITS

FUEL CONSUMPTION

FUELS
. COAL

:: LANGUAGES
: AFRICAN LANGUAGES
FULANI

Continued

Figure 16.2　Continued

(e) Main alphabetical list from the INSPEC Thesaurus (1991)

television rediffusion
   USE rediffusion

television signals
   USE video signals

television standards
   UF HD-MAC
         MAC system
         multiplexed analogue component system
   BT standards
   TT standards
   RT television
         video signals
   CC B6420; B6430
   DI January 1969

television stations
   UF stations, television
   RT television antennas
         television broadcasting
         television equipment
         television systems
         television transmitters
   CC B6420
   DI January 1969

television studios
   BT studios
   TT studios
   RT television broadcasting
         television cameras
   CC B6430
   DI January 1969

television systems
   NT cable television
         closed circuit television
         community antenna television
         high definition television
   BT telecommunication systems
   TT telecommunication systems
   RT audio-visual systems
         bandwidth compression
         television broadcasting
         television equipment
         television reception
         television stations
   CC B6430
   DI January 1969

Continued

Figure 16.2   Continued

(f) Hierarchical list from the INSPEC Thesaurus

cybernetics
. artificial intelligence
. . knowledge engineering
. . . explanation
. . . inference mechanisms
. . . knowledge acquisition
. . . knowledge representation
. . planning (artificial intelligence)
. . spatial reasoning
. biocybernetics
. . brain models
. economic cybernetics

data acquisition
. SCADA systems

data conversion
. analogue-digital conversion
. digital-analogue conversion

data handling
. data analysis
. data reduction
. electronic data interchange
. . EFTS
. . . automatic teller machines
. error handling
. list processing
. merging
. sorting
. symbol manipulation
. table lookup
. text editing

decomposition
. spinodal decomposition

deformation
. bending
. creep
. . diffusion creep
. . irradiation induced creep
. . recovery-creep
. elastic deformation

5. *A classification scheme.* Thesauro Facet, compiled by English Electric, is a notable example of a thesaurus supported by a full faceted classification scheme. This format is becoming common in new thesauri, partly because of the recognition of the importance of viewing both relationships and subject terms in one tool. With such an arrangement, the thesaurus provides direct alphabetical access to a subject and class notation. The classification scheme shows relationships and facilitates browsing between subjects. The *Root Thesaurus* described in the next section also incorporates this arrangement.

16.5.2 The Root Thesaurus

The British Standards Institution *Root Thesaurus* is an important attempt to provide a standard list of terms from which terms for thesauri and indexing languages can be selected and more application-oriented lists derived. It is potentially important both with regard to making the compilation of thesauri for specific applications easier, and also with regard to enhancing the similarities between lists for different applications. Since the *Root Thesaurus* did not emerge until 1981, it has not had a great impact on existing thesauri to date, but it could well be important in the future.

The thesaurus is available in a printed version or on magnetic tape. Not all topics are covered, but a broad group of industrial topics are represented, including measurement, environmental and safety engineering, energy technology and communication. Figure 16.3 shows that there are two lists – classified and alphabetical – and demonstrates the relationships between them. Note that the alphabetical list shows synonyms, broader terms, narrower terms and related terms, but these are signalled by an innovative notation. The *Root Thesaurus* designations are also independent of specific language (that is, French, German, Italian). Thus,

$$=$$ is equivalent to UF
$$-$$ is equivalent to Use
$$<$$ is equivalent to BT
$$>$$ is equivalent to NT
$$—$$ is equivalent to RT

Other refinements are also available which permit the part of the hierarchy from which a term is drawn to be specified.

16.5.3 Multilingual thesauri

A multilingual thesaurus is one which can be used to support indexing and searching in several languages. There is growing interest in multilingual thesauri for application in international information retrieval networks. Multilingual thesauri present a special set of problems. Several parallel editions in the different languages are to be recommended. Difficulties may arise where equivalent terms do not exist in all of the languages of the thesaurus. A switching language, in the form of a notation, may be used to translate terms from all natural languages and as an intermediate between the various languages.

16.5.4 Software for Thesaurus Maintenance

Only a limited amount of software is available for developing and maintaining thesauri. Milstead reviews some packages for personal computers, while Rowley provides an analysis of packages that are available as integral modules in text information management systems (see Reading list). Special thesaurus software has a number of advantages over the alternative, which is usually the use of a database package or a word processing package to store terms. A key feature of the thesaurus database is that it requires specialized management; not only must relationships be recorded and updated, but certain constraints on relationships must be imposed.

A thesaurus module that is integrated into the software used for database creation, maintenance and searching is particularly valuable. A thesaurus developed with such a module can support the following functions:

1. validation of indexer input; it controls indexing by rejecting unauthorized or misspelt terms;
2. addition of candidate terms to the thesaurus during the indexing process;
3. automatic switching, preferably with notification, from non-preferred terms to preferred terms during both indexing and searching;
4. review of a term's relationships, so that other terms can be considered either during indexing or searching, and
5. automatic explosion of searches when requested, to include specified types of related terms.

Software to support thesaurus maintenance should offer certain facilities. These could briefly be listed as:

1. *Format in which the thesaurus is to be made available.* Thesauri may be printed or available on screen. Software that supports the creation of printed thesauri needs to cater for layout, typesetting and formatting of the printed page, or else interface with a word processing or desk–top publishing package.
2. *Relationships that can be stored.* Typically 'broader term', 'narrower term', 'related term', 'use' and 'use for' are a basic set. It should also be possible to indicate scope notes and to store other relationships.
3. *Thesaurus maintenance during indexing.* There needs to be a link between the thesaurus and the data input screens for the database so that new terms can

SUBJECT DISPLAY SCHEDULE

Notation		Sample first page

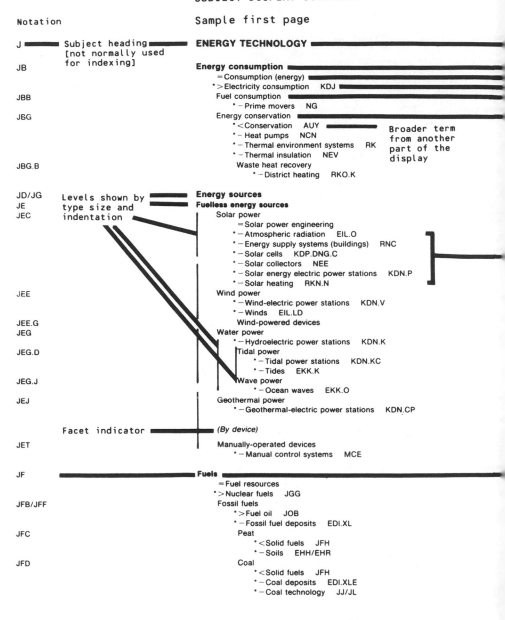

Notation		
J	Subject heading [not normally used for indexing]	**ENERGY TECHNOLOGY**
JB		**Energy consumption**
		=Consumption (energy)
		*>Electricity consumption KDJ
JBB		Fuel consumption
		* – Prime movers NG
JBG		Energy conservation
		*<Conservation AUY
		* – Heat pumps NCN
		* – Thermal environment systems RK
		* – Thermal insulation NEV
JBG.B		Waste heat recovery
		* – District heating RKO.K
JD/JG	Levels shown by	**Energy sources**
JE	type size and	**Fuelless energy sources**
JEC	indentation	Solar power
		=Solar power engineering
		* – Atmospheric radiation EIL.O
		* – Energy supply systems (buildings) RNC
		* – Solar cells KDP.DNG.C
		* – Solar collectors NEE
		* – Solar energy electric power stations KDN.P
		* – Solar heating RKN.N
JEE		Wind power
		* – Wind-electric power stations KDN.V
		* – Winds EIL.LD
JEE.G		Wind-powered devices
JEG		Water power
		* – Hydroelectric power stations KDN.K
JEG.D		Tidal power
		* – Tidal power stations KDN.KC
		* – Tides EKK.K
JEG.J		Wave power
		* – Ocean waves EKK.O
JEJ		Geothermal power
		* – Geothermal-electric power stations KDN.CP
	Facet indicator	(By device)
JET		Manually-operated devices
		* – Manual control systems MCE
JF		**Fuels**
		=Fuel resources
		*>Nuclear fuels JGG
JFB/JFF		Fossil fuels
		*>Fuel oil JOB
		* – Fossil fuel deposits EDI.XL
JFC		Peat
		*<Solid fuels JFH
		* – Soils EHH/EHR
JFD		Coal
		*<Solid fuels JFH
		* – Coal deposits EDI.XLE
		* – Coal technology JJ/JL

Broader term from another part of the display

CORRESPONDING ENTRIES FROM ALPHABETICAL LIST

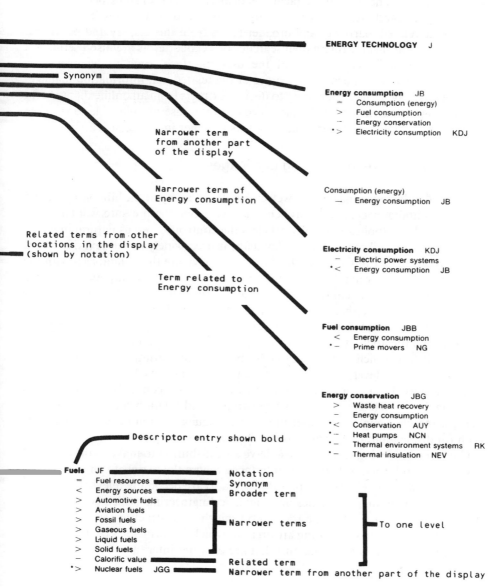

Figure 16.3   Extract from the BSI Root Thesaurus showing subject display schedule and alphabetical list

optionally be included in the thesaurus during indexing, and also reviewed later for completion of relationship indication.

4. *Searching.* The most basic facility is display of relationships between terms during a search session. This facility is enhanced if it is possible to select specific related, narrower and broader terms from this display and perform a search upon them. More global searches on related terms are also useful.

5. *User interface.* The quality of the user interface, such as whether it is windows based, is normally a feature of the related text information management package. The opportunity to display extracts from an online thesaurus in windows is particularly valuable, since it is often useful to be able to view the thesaurus alongside other screen displays in either indexing or searching.

16.5.5   The Future for Indexing Languages

Controlled indexing languages are well embedded in many of the bibliographic and catalogue databases created today. Only severe economic pressure will eliminate them from these applications. Nevertheless the controlled versus natural indexing language debate still rages. Natural language is used widely in full-text databases, as discussed further in Chapter 19. Many users navigate these databases with the assistance of any available controlled indexing terms; they may even search a related database with controlled index terms first, in order to identify some documents and refine their search strategy before moving on to the natural language of the full-text databases. The extensive availability of natural language indexing and the ability to search the full texts of documents mean that facilities in search software which support searching based upon natural language indexing must be further developed. A central feature in improved access via natural language may be a computer–based thesaurus or lexicon that is not used in indexing, but which shows all the word variants and relationships between terms that the searcher might encounter in natural language searching, and is available both for display and to expand and develop search strategies.

Controlled indexing languages also have a contribution to make in the design of systems that offer natural language interfaces, where the searcher can input terms in natural language. Principles applied in thesauri are becoming relevant in solving problems in computer linguistics or Linguistic Engineering, which is a branch of Artificial Intelligence. Machine translation, machine abstracting, speech recognition and language understanding are areas in which the principles of thesauri may be useful. Characteristics of thesauri that are of wider interest are:

*   mapping of a term's meaning,
*   mapping and selective definition of semantic and other relations between different terms in a natural language, and
*   establishment of preferential terms.

16.6 Thesauri and subject headings lists – a quick comparison

The previous two sections have introduced thesauri and subject headings lists. Clearly both tools record controlled indexing languages, but they are utilized in different environments. A clearer demarcation might be drawn between the traditional subject headings lists and thesauri by the following summary of differences:

1. Thesauri are likely to contain terms that are more specific than those found in subject headings lists.
2. Thesauri tend to avoid inverted terms (such as Sculpture, German).
3. Headings in thesauri are not subdivided. For instance Education – Bibliographies would not normally be featured in a thesaurus, whereas headings of this type are common in traditional subject headings lists. Situations where subdivisions might have had some utility are served by the coordination of index terms at the search stage (see 17.2).
4. The relationship display in a thesaurus is often more extensive than that in a subject headings list.
5. Different types of relationships are noted in a thesaurus by the use of 'RT', 'NT' and 'BT', instead of 'see also' which is frequently used to indicate all relationships, whatever their nature, in a subject headings list.
6. The relationships between the terms listed in a thesaurus will often not be transferred to the index. Dictionary catalogues usually contain 'see' and 'see also' instructions linking related headings.
7. Thesauri often boast an additional explicit statement of the structure of the relationships between terms in the form of categorized lists or displays.

16.7 Compiling a thesaurus or list of subject headings

All alphabetical indexing languages must be tailored to the application for which they are intended. Whilst standard published lists of terms provide useful models and certainly aid the searcher of a large publicly available database, any information worker needing to establish an in-house database, catalogue or index will need to consider devising a local list of indexing terms. Even in situations where there is a published list covering the requirements of the type of library or the subject area to be indexed, this list is likely to require adjustment in order to make it compatible with local requirements. A good thesaurus or list of subject headings is not necessarily one that has been carefully presented, printed and published, with a plethora of effective relationship displays, but rather a list that has been compiled to serve in the retrieval environment in which it is called upon to operate. This section, then, identifies a three-step process for the compilation of a thesaurus or a subject headings list.

Step 1: Establish the purpose of the indexing language

Preliminary decisions concerning the anticipated use of the thesaurus must be made before any work is undertaken. This planning phase involves moving from a vague impression that a thesaurus might be useful to a fairly precise profile in terms of the following parameters:

1. *Subject field*   to be covered must be determined by making explicit statements concerning the limits of topic coverage and the depth to which various aspects of the subject are to be examined. Subject field definition arises from the scope of the information service or system that the indexing language is expected to serve. This, in turn, depends upon users and user interests; it may be necessary to conduct a survey to discover or update the profile of user interests.
2. *Type of literature*   to be covered may determine, amongst other features, the amount of detail required. Books, for example, are normally indexed in less detail than periodical articles.
3. *Quantity of literature*.   The sophistication of a thesaurus and the specificity of its index terms are usually related to the number of documents to be covered by the indexing system for which the indexing language is being planned. In simple terms, the essence of subject organization is the division of literature (or references to literature) into manageable or scannable categories, with each category being associated with an index term. Thus, the more documents that an indexing system is likely to embrace, the greater the number of index terms that are likely to be necessary for convenient retrieval (given that the number of documents which constitute a scannable category does not vary).
4. *Type of information storage system*   in which the list is to be used may carry implications for the nature of the terms to be chosen. The system may be essentially pre- or post-coordinate or neither, and may be either manual or computerized.
5. *Resources of the information system*   will impose constraints upon the nature of the indexing language. There are two types of resources: those available and necessary for initial design, and those required for the development and application of the indexing language. Probably one of the most essential resources is sufficient time for initial thesaurus construction to ensure that the compilation is of a high quality. A good list will save time in later indexing and searching.
6. *Users*   of the information system may influence the explicitness of detail in a list. The nature of the users, their background, their work, the frequency with which they use the system and their mode of access to it (that is, through an intermediary information officer or directly) are all factors to be considered.
7. *Use*   to which the information system will be put impinges upon most of the earlier issues, but there are elements of the nature of use which can be considered in their own right. The number and types of questions likely to be posed to the system have implications for the amount of effort directed into thesaurus construction that can be justified.

Full consideration of the above factors should form a firm basis for the design of an effective thesaurus or list of subject headings.

Step 2: Establish the characteristics of the indexing language and the way in which they are to be embodied in the thesaurus or list of subject headings

The purpose of the list will colour decisions concerning the indexing language. A number of the factors to be considered in this stage include:

1. *The nature of the language.* The relative merits of free, natural and controlled language need to be evaluated. The comments in this section most readily pertain to controlled indexing languages but, by extension, some of them are equally relevant to natural or free indexing languages.
2. *Specificity* of the language must be settled at a level suitable for application.
3. *Exhaustivity.*
4. *Level of pre-coordination* (see Chapter 17). In planning the nature of the indexing language, the basic language evaluation devices must be taken into account (see Chapter 12).
5. *Thesaurus or list of subject headings and its structure.* Once the characteristics of the retrieval language have been agreed, the way in which the language will be recorded or printed must be determined. A straightforward alphabetical list must form the core of the language list. Some type of graphic or other relationship display may also be helpful, as may separate lists of subheadings, instructions for use, and so on. The thesaurus may be kept in machine-readable form and sections printed only as required.

Step 3: Start to compile the language

Now the compilation of index terms can begin. This involves:

1. *Identification of the main subject areas* in a more explicit manner than was required in the planning stage. A description of the main subject areas forms the skeleton of the main list of terms. Such deliberations on subject scope will normally lead to a preliminary list of significant (especially the more general) terms, with these terms collected into groups that reflect the relationships between them.
2. *Selection* of terms to be included in the thesaurus. Once terms have been accepted for inclusion they must obviously be recorded, so that this stage and the next one must proceed simultaneously. The preliminary list which was compiled at the last sub-stage must be developed. Synonyms, related terms and other variants must now be collected, either by human selection or with the aid of the computer. Humanly selected terms may be derived from a number of sources, in particular other lists of words used in the subject area, including:

(a)   other thesauri, classification schemes and information retrieval tools;

(b)   documents in the subject area, such as periodical articles, databases, indexing and abstracting journals, encyclopaedias and dictionaries; and

(c)   previous knowledge and experience of indexers, index language compilers and users.

The more structured the source of words, the more likely it is that the terms in the source will already be in a standard form ready for lifting wholesale and little modified into a thesaurus. These sources, which form the basis of the intellectual selection of terms, may be augmented or ousted by the machine selection of terms. Some or all of the terms in an index language may be derived automatically from the text of the documents to be indexed. Here again the documents of the subject area, such as periodical articles and research reports, will provide the terms to be included in the language.

3.   *Recording of terms.* In a totally machine-selected thesaurus, the listing of terms will be printed or displayed by the computer, and often no further effort is necessary. If the thesaurus includes humanly selected terms, it is necessary to record the chosen terms. The most convenient manual format for recording terms is to write each term on a card, and to note underneath any comments about the term that are to feature in the thesaurus or list of subject headings. Each card will show a term and any necessary scope notes, related terms and synonyms. For ease of consultation, cards should be kept in alphabetical order in accordance with the main term on the card. Alternatively, terms may be recorded with the aid of thesaurus software as described in 16.5.

4.   *Checking of relationships* which are to be indicaed under each of the terms. Most relationships should be shown in both their direct and inverse forms. Checks on relationships that must be represented can be executed by examining each card in turn and seeking cards which show related terms. A more systematic approach involves assessing terms and their relationships in subject-related groups. These subject groups may be refined by constructing facets and hierarchies relevant to the subject being investigated. Any new concepts or terms that emerge during this examination of relationships must also be inserted in the deck of cards. The checking of relationships is very much easier with thesaurus software. Inverse relationships may even be generated automatically. However, it is still necessary to examine each term and its relationships.

5.   *Finalization of the thesaurus.* Now is the time to conduct the final check on each of the features of the list. Terms should be reviewed for consistency and appropriate level of pre-coordination, word form and level of specificity. Classificatory or other indicators of relationships should be checked and recorded in their final form. If any links are necessary between displays and listings, some notation must be introduced. All listings for the final thesaurus must be converted to the format appropriate for typing, printing or input to a computer database, and each feature checked, edited and tested on some

examples. An introduction explaining the nature and scope of the indexing language will enhance its value.

6. *Revision of the list.* The list or thesaurus cannot be static. It must be updated. New terms and relationships may be added as they arise, or in batches at pre-determined intervals. Updating an in-house thesaurus is relatively easy. A published thesaurus or a thesaurus or list which is involved in an international indexing effort may need a more clearly established revision programme. Each amendment may need to be agreed by users, and equivalent terms in various languages may need to be added to a multilingual list. Lists of amendments or new editions are possible mechanisms for announcing changes.

16.8   Natural indexing languages

It is difficult to discuss natural indexing languages in general terms. This is partly because, with natural language indexing, the indexing language is that of the relevant input documents. In its pure form a listing of all the terms in such a language will only remain current until the next batch of documents is added to the system. Furthermore, since each system indexes a separate set of documents, each system will have a different natural indexing language. Thus, the language is derived from the documents input to the system, whether they be abstracts, full text, citations (including titles, periodical titles and so on) or lists of controlled or uncontrolled index terms. Obviously one of the unique features of natural language indexing is the lack of control of vocabulary. This permits the entire variety of natural language to be reflected in the indexing, the strengths and weaknesses of natural language indexing deriving from this basic characteristic.

This work tackles two other areas which are relevant to natural language indexing: Chapter 11 discusses the generation of printed indexes based upon the words in titles; it also reviews some of the basic strengths and limitations of natural language indexing in the context of printed indexes based entirely upon titles alone; Chapter 17 considers post-coordinate indexing and online searching of databases. Natural language indexing is important in searching online databases, especially full-text databases.

16.8.1   Stoplists and golists

In its pure form natural language indexing has some obvious limitations. Plainly, indexing on the text of a document involves indexing every word, some of which do not convey any subject concepts. Thus we can easily start to compile a list of irrelevant prepositions, conjunctions and articles such as an, a, the, and, for, to, his, these. Most natural language indexing operates with the aid of a stoplist which lists all such redundant terms and rejects their inclusion as index entries. Of course some terms may be difficult to categorize as stop or non-stop. Think, for instance of machine, lines, plunge. In some systems these might be useful in indexing, in others they might not. Thus although it is possible to establish a stoplist covering a number of standard terms not suitable for indexing, this normally needs to be modified to reflect the circumstances of each system. The use of a stoplist in title indexing is discussed in Chapter 11.

In natural language indexing which uses a stoplist only, the indexing language is open; there is no record other than the index itself of the indexing terms that have been assigned. The indexing changes gradually with time as the natural language of the documents covered by the index evolves.

The other approach to natural language indexing is to index on both a stoplist and a golist. A golist includes all of those terms that would create useful entries in the subject area being indexed. Thus the golist must be machine-stored and is used by the computer in the assignment of index terms. Like the stoplist, the golist can also be displayed or printed out for consideration prior to updating or other modification. The golist is sometimes known as a thesaurus and, indeed, is a form of natural language thesaurus. In the process of indexing each new batch of documents, new words will from time to time appear in the text. Being new, they will not appear in the golist and the computer will not know whether or not to treat them as indexing terms. In this case, the human indexer will be provided with the terms not recognized by the computer, and must decide whether to list them in the golist or the stoplist, or perhaps to leave them unlisted so that they will be output for human indexer consideration on each occurrence. Obviously this last option permits the human indexer some control over the allocation of index terms. Perhaps it is useful to observe that to the extent that the human indexer selects the terms for inclusion in the golist, the indexing language is controlled. However, the allocation of index terms and the variety of forms in which concepts or names might appear are not controlled.

16.8.2   Attractions of natural language indexing

The attractions of natural language indexing may be divided into two categories:

1. *Economic factors.* The intellectual input at the indexing stage is minimal even in systems where, in the interests of enhanced consistency, there is some intervention at the indexing stage. Indexing can thus be achieved at a detailed level, often including many terms per document, with almost no indexing effort. The effort must be input in another way – in retrieval. Effective retrieval from natural language indexed databases requires sophisticated search software. The user must become familiar with the facilities of this search software and therefore may need more training than for the retrieval of information from a database which has been indexed with a controlled indexing language. For example, search software offers the types of facilities discussed in Chapter 17, including the ability to search on words in pre-determined fields, the ability

to search on word stems and to search on words with variant spellings, and then the ability to rank the retrieved material according to its relative significance.

2. *Language factors.* In some circumstances natural language indexing may reflect more closely the terms used by the searcher. For instance, if the searcher seeks documents on 'Greenhouses' and this is not an index term in the appropriate controlled indexing language, then documents on this topic will be difficult to retrieve directly. Also, in controlled indexing language databases, there is often an assumption that a user will be prepared to chase strings of references or to consult a sometimes complex thesaurus. This may not always be the case. The other problems that sometimes occur in controlled language indexing (but are avoided by natural language indexing) arise from human error. Human indexers sometimes make inappropriate judgements, misinterpret ideas, have lapses of memory or concentration, and generate omissions and inconsistencies in their indexing.

Although printed indexes tend to be either controlled or natural language, many large databases can now be searched in both ways. Often, controlled index terms are used to identify a relatively large set of potentially relevant references, and then string searching (or natural language searching) used to identify specific documents from within that set. To pursue our simple example above: if Greenhouses is not a term in our controlled language, we might search under Glasshouses instead and retrieve a set of documents which had the controlled index language term Glasshouses assigned. We might then perform a string search on the term 'Greenhouses' to discover whether this term appeared in the text of any of the documents retrieved by the original search. This mixture of approaches is designed to yield maximum retrieval for as many users as possible by combining the different strengths of controlled and natural language indexing.

16.8.3 Circumstances in which natural language indexing is particularly appropriate

1. Searches that predominantly involve specific words or phrases known to have been used in the source material. Obvious examples are unique proper nouns, such as brand names and company names, although there can be problems with:

    - company names that may be either in full or abbreviated; for example, DEC, Digital Equipment
    - company names that may appear with or without a hyphen; for example Perkin Elmer, Perkin-Elmer
    - brand names that consist of common words; for example Crest, Tube Investments, and companies known by two or more names; for example GPO, British Telecom.

Most of these problems can be overcome with the use of Boolean and contextual logic.

2. Slogans, quotations and catch-phrases, which may or may not be indexed under a controlled indexing language; for example interracial adoption.
3. Geographic names can be very direct labels, but can also cause a number of well-known problems. These include:

- place names which recur in different states and countries; for example Berlin in New Hampshire and Germany;
- vague place names; for example Tyneside, the Peak District, and
- different levels of specificity; for example West Midlands, Birmingham, Midlands.

To overcome these problems users must think of all the various names that might have been applied, and must understand something of the geography and administration of the locality concerned. A further problem is the fact that place names may appear in a trivial context. For example, a headline announcing 'President Bush at Oxford hears of Second Falkland Crisis' does not merit retrieval under Oxford but does require to be retrieved under Falkland.

16.8.4 Circumstances in which natural language indexing meets with many problems

Indexers have used controlled language indexing and authority lists of standard forms of terms and names for many years. These practices have emerged from the fact that natural language indexing is often not adequate, as discussed in Chapter 12. However, it seems worth rehearsing some of the arguments in this particular context again, identifying specifically how these problems can be negotiated in a database using natural language indexing.

1. Semantics, including synonyms, variant word forms, autonyms and so on. The user must consider all the possibilities. In this he may be assisted by the opportunity to use truncation, alphabetical lists of terms showing word variants, and so on.
2. Homographs and words where the meaning is context-dependent. Terms with dual meanings, for example, intelligence (either an individual's analytical and reasoning abilities or information on an adversary) must be recognized as such by the searcher. Contextual logic may help to eliminate unwanted uses of homographs.

3.   Hierarchical and other relations. No cross-references can be expected. Retrieval of documents on a search topic, by using terms for a broader or narrower concept, relies heavily both on the searcher's ingenuity and on any additional relationships that the database indexer might have added to link the natural language index terms.

Figure 16.4 offers a quick comparison of controlled and natural language indexing.

Recommended reading

Aitchison, J (1986), 'A Classification as a source for a thesaurus: the Bibliographic Classification of H E Bliss as a source of thesaurus terms and structure', *Journal of Documentation*, **42**, 160–81.

Aitchison, J and Gilchrist, A (1987), *Thesaurus construction*, 2nd edition, London: Aslib.

Aitchison J *et al.* (1979), *Thesaurofacet: a thesaurus and faceted classification for engineering and related subjects*, Whetstone: English Electric Company.

American National Standards Institute (1974), 'American national standard guidelines for thesaurus structure, construction and use', ANSI Z39.19.

Barnett, L (1987), 'Indexing and retrieval in ERIC: the 20th year', in *Thesaurus of ERIC Descriptors*, 11th edition, Washington DC: Educational Research Information Center, Bureau of Research, x–11.

Batty, D (1989), 'Thesaurus construction and maintenance: a survival kit', *Database*, February, 13–20.

Berstein, L M and Williamson, R E (1984), 'Testing of a natural language retrieval system for a full text knowledge base', *Journal of the American Society for Information Science*, **35**, 235–47.

Blair, D C and Maron, M E (1985), 'An evaluation of retrieval effectiveness for a full-text document retrieval system', *Communications of the Association for Computing Machinery*, **28**, 289–99.

British Standards Institution (1979), 'Guidelines for the establishment and development of monolingual thesaursi', London: BS 5723.

British Standards Institution (1985), *Root Thesaurus*, 2nd edition, Hemel Hempstead.

Calkins, M L (1980), 'Free text or controlled vocabulary? a case history, step-by-step analysis. . .plus other aspects of search strategy', *Database*, **3**, June, 53–67.

CDMARC Subjects, Washington: Library of Congress, Cataloging Distribution Service; cumulates every three months.

Chan, L M and Pollard, R (1988), *Thesauri used in online databases: an analytical guide*, New York: Greenwood Press.

Clemencin, G (1988), 'Querying the French Yellow Pages: natural language access to the directory', *Information Processing and Management*, **24**, 633–49.

Figure 16.4 Controlled and natural indexing languages: some simple comparisons

Controlled indexing language

1. Assigned by indexer
2. Records will be grouped under a more limited number of descriptions
3. Descriptions under which records are grouped will be predictable and defined
4. Records may not always be assigned to the description that the user expects, and human error can mislead
5. Relationships between terms are indicated and can be exploited
6. Language can only be changed by modifications to the thesaurus or other authority list; this process may be slow, leading to a relatively static language
7. Common in traditional bibliographic databases and catalogues
8. Intellectual effort is primarily in indexing
9. Each record is likely to be retrievable by a limited number of search terms
10. Retrieval is likely to offer high precision and low noise; it may be necessary to broaden a search strategy
11. There is no need to type in all synonyms
12. False drops are minimized
13. Pre-coordinated terms may be used to control linkage of words such as Age Factors, Attitude to Death (MeSH)

Natural indexing language

1. Assigned by computer
2. Records will be scattered under a greater number of descriptions
3. Descriptions are drawn from the natural language of the documents being indexed
4. The computer assigns terms consistently, so that if a term appears in an indexed field of a record, it will certainly be possible to retrieve the record via that term
5. Relationships will not be indicated unless some intellectual effort has been directed towards including them
6. Language can change with the age of the documents as a subject field develops. The language is therefore dynamic and is likely to reflect current usage
7. Frequently encountered in full-text databases
8. Intellectual effort is primarily in searching
9. Each record is retrievable by a relatively large number of search keys
10. A relatively high number of irrelevant documents will be retrieved
11. It is necessary to type in all of the synonyms and word variants to complete an exhaustive search
12. False drops are likely to be encountered, due to words having more than one meaning
13. There is no control of the linkage between words so that there is no differentiation, for example, between computers for design and design for computers

276

Cleverdon, C W (1977), 'A Comparative evaluation of searching by controlled language and natural language in an experimental NASA database', Frascati: European Space Agency, Space Documentation Service.

Dubois, C P R (1984), 'The use of thesauri in online retrieval', *Journal of Information Science*, **2** (1), 63–66.

Dubois, C P R (1987), 'Free text vs controlled vocabulary: a reassessment', *Online Review*, **11**, 243–53.

Dykstra, M (1988), 'LC subject headings disguised as a thesaurus', *Library Journal*, **113** (4).

Engineers Joint Council (1967), *Thesaurus of engineering and scientific terms*, New York: Engineers Joint Council.

Frohmann, B (1990), 'Rules of indexing: a critique of mentalisms in information retrieval theory', *Journal of Documentation*, **46**, 81–101.

Fugmann, R (1985), 'The five-axiom theory of indexing and information supply', *Journal of the American Society for Information Science*, **22**, 116–29.

Fugmann, R, 'An interactive classaurus on the PC', *International Classification*, **17** (3/4), 133–37.

Ganzmann, J (1990), 'Criteria for the evaluation of thesaurus software', *International Classification*, **17** (3/4), 148–57.

Gilchrist, A (1971), *The thesaurus in retrieval*, Aslib: London.

Haykin, D J (1951), *Subject headings: a practical guide*, Washington, DC: Government Publishing Office.

International Standards Organisation (1974), *Guidelines for the establishment and development of monolingual thesauri*, Geneva.

Kleinbart, P (1985), 'Prolegomenon to intelligent thesaurus software', *Journal of Information Science*, **11**, 45–55.

Kristensen, J and Jarvelin, K (1990), 'The effectiveness of a searching thesaurus in free-text searching in a full-text database', *International Classification*, **17** (2), 77–84.

Lancaster, F W (1986), *Vocabulary control for information retrieval*, 2nd edition, Arlington, Virginia: Information Resources Press.

Library of Congress Subject Headings (1991), prepared by the Subject Cataloging Division Processing Services, 14th edition, Washington: Library of Congress, Cataloguing Distribution Service. Also available as a cumulative microform edition; updated every three months.

Mandel, C A (1987), 'Multiple thesauri in online library bibliographic systems: a report prepared for the Library of Congress Processing Services', Washington DC: Library of Congress Cataloging Distribution Service.

Mandelstam, M (1988), 'Thesaurus on equipment for disabled people', *Journal of Documentation*, **44** (2), 144–57.

Maniez, J (1988), 'Relationships in thesauri: some critical remarks', *International Classification*, **15** (15), 133–38.

Markey, K *et al.* (1980), 'An analysis of controlled vocabulary and free text search statements in online searches', *Online Review*, **4**, 225–36.

Medical Subject Headings (MeSH), Bethesada: National Library of Medicine; annual update.

277

Milstead, J L (1990), 'Thesaurus software packages for personal computers', *Database*, December, 61–65.

Perez, E (1982), 'Text enhancement: controlled vocabulary vs free text', *Special Libraries*, **73**, July, 183–92.

Piternick, A B (1984), 'Searching vocabularies: a developing category of online search tools', *Online Review*, **8**, 441–49.

Rada, R (1981), 'Connecting and evaluating thesauri: issues and cases', *International Classification*, **14**, 63–68.

Rada, R et al. (1988), 'Creating and evaluating entry terms', *Journal of Documentation*, **44** (1), March, 19–41.

Rowley, J (1991), 'Thesaurus modules in text management software' in Peter Gillman (ed), *Text retrieval: information first*, London: Taylor Graham.

Schmitz-Esser, W (1990), 'Thesauri facing new challenges', *International Classification*, **17** (3/4), 129–32.

Sears' List of Subject Headings, 13th ed, edited by B M Westby, New York: H W Wilson.

Sievert, M E (1983), 'Hedge trimming and the resurrection of the controlled vocabulary in online searching', *Online Review*, **7**, 489–94.

Subject cataloging manual: subject headings, 3rd edition, Washington: Library of Congress Cataloging Distribution Service, 1989, updated.

Svenonius, E (1986), 'Unanswered questions in the design of controlled vocabularies', *Journal of the American Society for Information Science*, **37**, 330–40.

Tenopir, C (1987), 'Searching by controlled vocabulary or free text', *Library Journal*, 15 November, 58–59.

Townley, H M and Gee, R D (1980), *Thesaurus making: grow your own wordstock*, London: Deutsch.

Wheeler, G (1991), 'Maintaining a controlled vocabulary for a large online database', in *Computers in Libraries International '91*: Proceedings of the fifth Annual Conference on Computers in Libraries, February 1991, London: Meckler, 115–19.

17 Indexing systems: principles and printed indexes

17.1 Introduction

This chapter starts by identifying the concepts associated with indexing systems. Since the concept of an indexing system had its origins in a print-based environment, it is appropriate first to examine how these concepts are applied in printed indexes. Chapter 18 continues the examination of indexing systems, but with an emphasis on computer-based systems.

The following two definitions of an indexing system are offered:

1. An indexing system is the means whereby an indexing language can be applied to make an index.
2. An indexing system is a set of prescribed procedures for organizing the contents of records of knowledge or documents for the purposes of retrieval and dissemination.

Both definitions have common roots, but their perspectives differ somewhat, the second definition being slightly broader in scope.

The creation of a series of entries for inclusion in a catalogue or printed index is an indexing process which must involve some system, which we might call an indexing system. Most of the work on indexing systems stems from the need to devise index headings or search keys in such a way that it is possible to retrieve compound or multi-concept subjects. Although elementary one–concept subjects are also represented in indexes constructed according to these methods, the problems that such subjects present are limited. Much of this chapter therefore is concerned with the specification or retrieval of multi–concept subjects.

Although compound subjects have been introduced in Chapters 12 and 15, it is useful to review the nature of such subjects with the aid of an example. Take the subject: 'Torsion in the reinforced concrete in service cores in tall buildings'. If we were to seek to index or retrieve documents on this subject, we could start by recognizing that it contains four separate elementary or unit concepts: torsion, reinforced concrete, service cores, tall buildings.

In indexing or retrieving such a subject it is not only necessary to recognize the presence of the various unit concepts, but also to cater for each concept. One user might use the term torsion, another reinforced concrete, and yet another tall buildings, each user possibly seeking the document for different purposes. It is in order to tackle this type of problem that indexing systems have evolved.

Allowing for some polarization for effective analysis, indexing systems can be divided into two basic categories: pre-coordinate and post-coordinate. Not every index necessarily exhibits all the features of one or other of these systems; indeed, some will possess elements of both. Nevertheless, this basic divide remains a useful distinction. A brief introduction to specific kinds of indexing systems will be given here, with more details developed in subsequent sections.

17.1.1   Pre-coordinate indexing systems

Pre-coordinate indexing is conventional indexing of the type commonly found in printed indexes, where a document is represented in the index by a heading or headings consisting of a chain of terms. The lead term determines the position of the entry, and the qualifying terms are subordinate to it. Thus for the previously cited example, a heading of the form:

Buildings, Tall: Service cores; Concrete, Reinforced:Torsion

might be established. A second example, 'The use of computers in the cutting of shoes', might be shown by a heading such as:

Shoes: Manufactures: Computers: Cutting

Because the coordination of index terms in the index description is decided before any particular search is made, the index is termed a pre-coordinate index. Note that the headings in such an index are relatively specific compared, for example, with one-concept headings such as Shoes or Cutting.

Pre-coordinate indexes are particularly prevalent as printed indexes. Often the computer is used to aid in the processing of such indexes, and sometimes computer processing is responsible for the creation of multiple entries from one string of index terms. Printed indexes which incorporate the principles of pre-coordinate indexing are to be found to varying extents in abstracting and indexing journals, national bibliographies, indexes to journals and, to some extent, in subject indexes to library catalogues. Pre-coordinate index terms also emerge in the assigned index terms in computer databases.

Two issues recur in all pre-coordinate indexes. The first issue concerns the consistent description of subjects. With many concept headings, consistency must be instilled both into the terms used to describe the individual concepts that comprise the multiple concept heading and also into the order in which those individual concept terms are cited or listed. Before a consistent citation order can be achieved, some principles must be established and agreed concerning an acceptable citation order. At the two extremes, the order may simply be decided for each topic as and when it arises, and followed thereafter, or some theoretical basis or rules for the ordering of terms or concepts may be derived. A theoretical basis to citation order should produce a more highly structured system whose objective is to achieve consistent citation orders between similar yet distinct subjects. However many indexing systems evolved over the last century when detailed specification of subjects was unnecessary. Indexes based on such traditional subject headings lists tend to use very little structuring of citation order. Citation orders need not be comparable between subjects, nor is there any comprehensive set of principles that determines the citation order selected. Yet even these indexes recognize some rules concerning the structure of headings.

The second issue that all indexers must consider is the need to provide access for those users who approach the subject being indexed from one of the 'secondary' concepts. Only one term can appear in the primary position in the prescribed citation order. The preferred citation order should be that which is believed to match the majority approach of the many users who can be expected to retrieve information on the topic. However, no citation order, no matter how well-founded, will prove suitable for every searcher. References or added entries must supplement the first or main entry and cater for access from other angles. At least one reference or added entry is usually deemed to be necessary from each of the 'secondary' concepts in the preferred order. In the same way that citation orders may have more or less theoretical foundation, equally reference generation may either follow a pre–determined pattern or the reference or added entries to be included may be designed on an *ad hoc* basis. Usually there is some pattern to the generation of additional references in order to keep the number of auxiliary references to an acceptable level. Also, if a simple algorithm for the generation of index entries can be stated, then additional entries and references can be printed by computer, using the primary index string as input data.

Both the above issues arise because pre-coordinate systems are fundamentally one-place systems. One-place systems are convenient under circumstances where it is desirable to have only one main entry for each document, as in many bibliographies and catalogues. Such systems may also have advantages for the searcher. A number of searches can be conducted simultaneously by tracing entries under similar headings. Also search strategy can be modified relatively easily where only refinements or slight modifications in index terms are appropriate.

17.1.2   Post-coordinate indexing systems

Post-coordinate indexing systems (sometimes known as coordinate indexing systems) start from the same identification of multi-concept subjects and their component unit concepts as do pre-coordinate indexing systems. However, once the multi-concept subject has been analysed into its component concepts, the two systems diverge. Entries in a post-coordinate index are made under terms which represent the unit or elementary concepts. No attempt is made to establish index headings or search keys which reflect all the component elementary concepts at any one time. Thus a post-coordinate index for the examples considered previously might have entries under the following headings:

Buildings, Tall	[and]	Shoes
Service cores		Manufacturers
Concrete, Reinforced		Computers
Torsion		Cutting.

Thus for each of these two examples there will be four entries under relatively broad headings. This approach eliminates, at one stroke, the two problems which exercise the designer of a pre-coordinate index – citation order and reference structure.

However, new problems are introduced. If the collection could equally well have been indexed pre-coordinately, then it is likely that, with time, some of these relatively broad headings which avoid coordination will have a large number of entries associated with them. Thus, the searcher will seek some type of assistance in sorting through the large numbers of index entries which are likely to be found under various headings. Therefore, in order to specify the search topic more closely, coordination will be sought at the search stage. Coordination is effected after a request for a search has been initiated; hence, these systems are referred to as post-coordinate. Search aids are available in the form of logical statements which combine terms in order to be able to trace subjects according to a more specific document profile.

In general, then, a post-coordinate index is simpler to produce than a pre-coordinate index because it shifts the responsibility for coordination of index terms to the searcher. Post-coordinate systems, which rely upon either controlled indexing languages (particularly those which comprise mainly one-concept terms) and/or natural language indexing, are common in online searching of computer databases. They are also evident in SDI profiles and other applications which involve retrieving a set of documents from a more comprehensive computer database.

The indexing language used in either a post-coordinate or a pre-coordinate indexing system might be very similar. There is no reason why, for example, the terms representing unit concepts in each system should not be the same or not be drawn from the same thesaurus listing.

17.2 Principles of pre-coordinate indexing systems

17.2.1 Citation orders

Very early in the history of alphabetical subject headings it was recognized that headings should be formulated in accordance with some principles. The forerunner of many recent ideas and the force behind some of the remaining traditional systems was Charles Ammi Cutter. Cutter started to identify principles which were further developed by Kaiser, and much later Coates and others. Coates identified a preferred citation order for concepts in subject headings which caters well for specific subjects.

1. *Cutter's Rules for a Dictionary Catalogue* were published in 1876 and form one of the earlier codifications of the problems and some solutions concerning the alphabetical subject approach. The issue of citation orders for composite subjects was not considered systematically, and Cutter's recommendations serve more to illustrate problems than to demonstrate solutions. Cutter selected catalogue headings on the basis that they should be terms in general usage and accepted by educated people. In addition to problems with new subjects which lacked 'accepted' or established names, this guiding principle engendered inconsistency in the form of headings. Equally, Cutter's devotion to natural language posed problems with multi-word terms. Sometimes the natural language ordering of words in a term would cause it to be filed under the first and possibly lesser significant term. To avoid unhelpful sequences, Cutter argued that when it could be established that the second term was definitely more significant, then inversion of headings was acceptable. This was all very tidy, but who was to judge significance?

   Despite the inconsistencies inherent in Cutter's fundamental premises, he did give some guidance on citation order under certain specialized conditions. For example, he believed that where subject and place are both elements of a topic, subject should precede place in scientific and related areas, but that place should take precedence in such areas as history, government and commerce. For the humanities, including literature and art, the adjectival form of the country or language was recommended (for example, German Poetry). Cutter's practices and policies were a starting point and remain important today because they are embodied in the *Library of Congress List of Subject Headings* and Sears' *List of Subject Headings*.

   Composite subjects were clearly less prevalent in Cutter's day and principles in subject heading formulation less vital. The information that most modern indexes must organize exists in greater quantities and concerns much more complex subjects than Cutter could have anticipated. The sheer bulk of the headings and the complexity of reference structures in a dictionary catalogue based on the Library of Congress Subject Headings is sufficient to confirm that a more systematic approach might prove fruitful.

2. *Kaiser's Systematic Indexing* embodied the first consistent approach to the problems of significance order. The treatise arose from Kaiser's work in indexing information relating to business and industry. Kaiser's starting point was the observation that many composite subjects can be analysed into a combination of a 'concrete' and a 'process'. He suggested that if subjects with these two components were cited in the order Concrete, then Process, that the headings thus produced would usually coincide to some extent with natural language usage. Thus a document on the 'Servicing of ships' could be indexed under: 'Ships; Servicing'. Where place was one of the concepts present in a subject, Kaiser made a double entry, once under the Concrete and once under Place. Thus a document on 'Shipbuilding in Japan' would be entered under each of the two headings: Shipbuilding – Japan and Japan – Shipbuilding. One problem on which Kaiser alighted was that many processes can be further analysed into a concrete and a second process; for example, 'Steelmaking' can become 'Steel-Production'. This feature hindered consistency because some subjects had potential for being analysed in different ways. Kaiser also investigated the effect of grouping subheadings of a subject. Instead of a straight alphabetical arrangement, subheadings were grouped according to their subject. For example, all subheadings representing processes were grouped together ahead of those referring to places. This may help in subject organization, but one of the main advantages of an alphabetical sequence, its self-evident order, is sacrificed in the process.

3. *Coates and the British Technology Index.* E J Coates made one of the most significant contributions to the formulation of subject headings. His ideas are embodied in the then *British Technology Index* (now *Current Technology Index*), of which he was the editor for many years. Coates started his study of citation order by noting and reaffirming Kaiser's theories of Concrete-Process. He then went on to evolve rules to cater for the citation orders appropriate to a wide range of composite subjects. Kaiser's Concrete-Process was relabelled Thing–Action. Coates believed that in order to conceptualize an action, it was necessary to visualize the thing on which the action was being performed. This principle was used to establish an extended citation order:

Thing – Part – Material – Action

According to Coates, this resulted in headings whose first component was the most likely to come into the mind of the searcher. The following headings show the citation order advanced by Coates:

1. Steel, Low alloy: Welding, Electron beam
2. Steel: Production: Coking: Coal: Blending: Plant
3. Sugar Cane: Harvesters

4. Piles; Concrete, Bored: Testing: Ultrasonics
5. Television: Transmission: Computers

Note that when headings are read backwards with appropriate prepositions inserted, they make a title-like phrase describing the subject. Thus index headings often derive easily from natural language order by straight inversion and the omission of prepositions.

4. *Articulated subject indexes* are based on title-like phrases that have some conventions concerning citation order. However, these conventions do not require any theoretical structure which recognizes concept categories.

The title-like phrase combines concepts in the order in which they would be listed in an ordinary sentence or phrase. For example, an indexing string for an articulated subject index might take the form:

< Soil-resistant < Finishing > > of < Carpets > and < Wall-Coverings >

where the brackets are used to designate terms that are to appear as index headings. The indexer then expresses the subject using a stylized English sentence and the computer generates a series of entries with a complete subject statement at every entry point. The computer is programmed to recognize cues such as prepositions and punctuation; it thus generates a series of entries each comprising an entry term and a qualifying phrase.

17.2.2 Reference structure

In order to permit the index user to approach a composite heading via one of the concepts that does not take first position in the citation order, it is necessary to consider how access may be provided to secondary concepts. Remember that a user may also approach the concepts in index headings via a synonym or related term. Links between related terms and synonymous terms must also be a feature of the index. At present, however, we will concentrate on how to gain access to secondary concepts in the primary citation order. Each type of pre-coordinate indexing system must incorporate some rules for the generation of references or added entries. Many systems rely upon moving the index terms in the heading through the various positions in the heading. Particularly if a computer is to be responsible for creating a series of headings from one index string, it is desirable that there be some algorithm for the generation of references and added entries. Also, economy dictates that every possible entry cannot be printed. Consider a complex heading with six individual concepts. Obviously, for each term to appear in the lead position, at least six entries are necessary. If it is intended that each term should occupy each position in a heading, the largest number of possible distinct headings or arrangements of index terms is 720. Obviously this is far too many references or added entries. Some means must be found of selecting from the

720 possible entries those which are the most helpful. Several different solutions to this problem have been put forward.

Cutter recommended a network of references, recognizing that a systematic approach to reference structure was necessary in order to produce an effective index. However, in the interests of economy, Cutter restricted links to downward references leading from broader to narrower subjects, and largely ignored upwards and sideways links. This practice is continued in dictionary catalogues but is of limited success and makes little contribution to the structure of references necessary to cater for a composite subject.

Chain indexing creates a number of index entries, as shown in the next section. The second and subsequent entries cater for the terms hidden in the first entry. Each heading becomes at the same time simpler and less specific. *Current Technology Index* also bases its reference structure on chain procedure. The first reference comprises all the components in the heading, but in inverted order. The second reference retains the inverted order but removes the first element of the preferred citation. Other references follow, with the progressive removal of terms. If A, B, C and D are index terms, chain procedure would create the following four entries:

```
A   B   C   D
B   C   D
C   D
D
```

Entries for a document on 'the law concerning Sunday performances in the theatre in France' would be as follows:

```
Law: Sunday performance: Theatre: France
Sunday performances: Theatre: France
Theatre: France
France
```

The reference structure used in PRECIS indexing will be developed in 17.4. Known as shunting, this procedure would create the following entries with A, B, C and D as index terms:

```
1.  A
       B   C   D
2.  B   A
       C   D
3.  C   B   A
       D
4.  D   C   B   A
```

which, using the same example as above, would cause the following entries:

```
1.  Law
```

286

Sunday performances   Theatre   France
2. Sunday performances   Law
Theatre   France
3. Theatre   Sunday performances   Law
France
4. France   Theatre   Sunday performances   Law

Other approaches to the movement of the components of index headings in order to generate additional entries are also possible. Three techniques are *cycled or cyclic indexing, rotated indexing* and *SLIC indexing.* Cycled indexing involves the movement of the first lead term to the last position in the subsequent entry. This process is repeated until each concept has occupied the lead position. Rotated indexing involves each element in turn becoming the heading under which an entry is filed, but no change in citation order takes place. SLIC indexing, or Selective Listing in Combination, involves the combination of elements, but in one direction only. These techniques are demonstrated below:

Cyclic indexing

A	B	C	D		Law: Sunday performances: Theatre: France
B	C	D	A		Sunday performances: Theatre: France: Law
C	D	A	B		Theatre: France: Law: Sunday performances
D	A	B	C		France: Law: Sunday Performances: Theatre

Rotated indexing

A	B	C	D		*Law*: Sunday performances: Theatre: France
A	*B*	C	D		Law: *Sunday performances*: Theatre: France
A	B	*C*	D		Law: Sunday performances: *Theatre*: France
A	B	C	*D*		Law: Sunday performances: Theatre: *France*

SLIC indexing

A	B	C	D		Law: Sunday performances: Theatre: France
A		C	D		Law: Theatre: France
A			D		Law: France
B		C	D		Sunday performances: Theatre: France
C			D		Theatre: France
D					France

17.3   Chain Indexing

Chain indexing is a system which was devised in order to generate subject indexes to a classified sequence in a catalogue or on shelves, or to a classification scheme. Thus chain indexing has been widely used in generating subject indexes to classified catalogues. Similar systems are used to produce the relative indexes which form part of the published editions of many classification schemes. In principle, chain indexing is a manual means of generating index entries, although some aspects of the system may be seen in computer-generated printed indexes such as

Current Technology Index. It is also possible to use a computer to produce a subject index to a classified sequence using the basic structure of chain indexing.

A subject index to a classified sequence in a catalogue, index or bibliography has essentially the same functions as the subject index to the published schedules of a classification scheme. These are

- to translate a natural language term into a class number and
- to collocate distributed relatives.

These functions have already been considered in 13.4 when discussing relative indexes to classification schemes. Chain indexing is closely connected with relative indexes. For example, index entries of the form

Nervous system:Surgery 617.48

are generated. Plainly such an entry permits the location of an appropriate classification number. 'Nervous system' is the entry term under which the user would search. 'Surgery' helps to distinguish between the type of documents that have been classified at 617.48 from those classified at other numbers related to the Nervous system. In this sense it provides a context for the entry term.

17.3.1 *Chain indexing procedure*

Chain indexing is a procedure which is supposed to lead to the inclusion of entries in an alphabetical index for every helpful entry point, without excessive use of index entries. In that it suggests a method for establishing the citation order of subjects within a heading for an index entry, it is an indexing system. As a system in application, chain indexing relies upon the existence and structure of subjects in a classification scheme. With a fully faceted classification scheme (see 13.2.4), chain indexing is purely mechanical and straight-forward. In less well structured schemes, the application of chain indexing is more of an art.

The steps in producing index entries according to chain indexing are:

1. Assign the appropriate class number from the schedules of the classification scheme in use to the document being indexed. Indexing is dependent upon the specific classification scheme in use.
2. Examine the hierarchical or other subject structure of the area of the schedules from which a class number has been drawn. Specifically, locate the appropriate class number and note the more general topics under which it has been placed.
3. Construct the first index entry by taking a natural language description of the most specific concept in 'the chain', as revealed in step 2 above, and qualify it with terms which represent other concepts in the chain. These qualifying terms should be included in the order that they appear in the chain, moving from specific to more general subjects. Only such qualifying terms as are necessary

to give the context of the entry term within the classification scheme need be included.

4. Make the second entry by choosing a term to represent the second most specific concept in the 'chain' and then qualify this term with more general concept terms, in the same way as in the first index entry.

5. Construct the remainder of the index entries in a manner consistent with the previous index entries, as above.

Example: Suppose that we have a document to index which is an item of Classical Period German Poetry.

1. First the class number is assigned. In DC19 this would be 831.6
2. The hierarchical chain may be recorded, thus:

8 Literature
  3 German
    1 Poetry
    .6 Classical Period

In this case, since DC has largely expressive notation, each notational digit stands for an additional step in the relationship structure.

3. The first index entry is under the most specific concept 'Classical Period', thus:

Classical Period: Poetry: German: Literature   831.6

4. The second index entry, under the next more general subject is:

Poetry: German: Literature   831

5. The remaining index entries are:

German: Literature   830
Literature   800.

17.3.2   Characteristics of chain indexing

1. Chain indexing is a simple mechanical routine for generating a limited number of index entries for a subject.

2. Chain indexing is closely tied to the structure (but not necessarily the terminology) of the classification scheme. A poorly structured scheme requires the exercise of a good deal of initiative on the part of the indexer in order to overcome or avoid the poor structure.

3. The procedure generates a number of index entries for each subject, but only one of these entries is specific. The other index entries are more general. This means:

(a)   a searcher finding a more general entry is expected to scan the subdivisions of the number to which he has been directed. This may be an unrealistic expectation.

(b)   economies are made in the total number of index entries required for a collection of documents because frequently many of the more general index entries will apply to more than one specific subject. Literature 800, for example, will be included in the entries for every class number in the Literature schedules or 800s. Once this entry has been included in the index, it will not be necessary to add it again.

4.   The effect of the procedure is to invert the structure of the classification scheme. Thus, subjects which are divided by the classification scheme will be drawn together by the index. For example, under Poetry one might find:

Poetry: German Literature	831
Poetry: Latin Literature	871
Poetry: Russian Literature	891.71

Thus various types of poetry are shown in juxtaposition in the index despite having widely differing class numbers.

5.   Although chain indexing developed in the context of a formal classification scheme, its principles can be adopted elsewhere where information is structured, such as in a book index. The specific entry term followed by a context (or more general) term is an approach that has wide applicability.

17.4   PRECIS indexing

The PRECIS indexing system (Preserved Context Indexing System) is a set of procedures for producing index entries which is important for both its practical and theoretical contributions to the field of indexing. PRECIS indexing takes a very systematic approach to citation order and demonstrates the effective application of computers in the production of printed indexes. PRECIS indexing is also important in that, until 1991, it was the method used to produce the subject indexes to the British National Bibliography and is still used in various other indexes to catalogues and library materials.

In keeping with its acronym, PRECIS is an alphabetical subject indexing system that both presents a 'precis' of the subject content of a document at each entry point in the printed index, and also displays index terms in context. The index user can enter the index via any of the concepts present in the complex subject, and locate at that entry point the full description of the subject. Each index entry has both a lead term and terms conveying the context, which are displayed in such a way that the entry is as explicit as possible. However, in any given application, there must also be a controlled vocabulary to which the PRECIS routines can be applied. Thus PRECIS is an indexing system which, like any such system, must be supported by an indexing language. Some of the features of index entries generated according to PRECIS indexing are:

1. All entries contain all of the index terms used in the description of the topic.
2. Access is possible via each and any of the index terms.
3. All terms in the line following the lead term appear in an order that ensures that specific terms are listed first, followed by more general terms.
4. The subject description is clearly stated in each entry.
5. Index entries usually occupy two lines.

All index entries and references in a PRECIS index derive from index strings, one string for each multi-concept subject indexed. This string codifies syntactic relationships, establishes a citation order, and triggers the generation of references for semantic relationships. The role of the string in establishing a citation order for the component parts of each index entry is probably the most important feature of PRECIS indexing. Citation order must be related to the syntactic relationships inherent in the subject to be indexed. Syntactic relations, which arise from the syntax, are document-dependent and need not be constant. For example, both the following two topics are composed of the same component concepts, but the relationships between the concepts are different:

'The indexing of computer software'
'The use of computer software in indexing'

It is the distinct syntactical relationships of these subjects which are responsible for their separate identities as subjects. PRECIS relies upon citation order (with some support from prepositions and so on) to record syntactical relationships; role operators, which are a central feature of the system, are assigned to concepts in such a way that this is achieved. Role operators are listed in Figure 17.1.

17.4.1 Steps in PRECIS indexing

1. Identify the elements or concepts of the compound subject that are to be reflected in the index entries. A concept is defined as a topic matching a PRECIS operator (see below) and may on occasions be a composite subject.
2. Express the concepts to be indexed in terms acceptable to the vocabulary used in the index. The vocabulary used in conjunction with PRECIS by the British National Bibliography was split into two sections, one part for Entities (or things) and the other for Attributes (properties of things, such as colour, weight; activities of things, such as flow, machining; and properties of activities, such as slow, turbulent). The terms present in these vocabularies were hierarchically arranged in order to indicate any fundamental generic relationships and to suggest references that might be made as links between terms.
3. Assign a role operator to each term identified in 2 above. Role operators

Figure 17.1 PRECIS role operators

Role operators

Main line operators

Environment of observed system	0	Location
Observed system (Core operators)	1	Key system: object of transitive action; agent of intransitive action
	2	Action/Effect
	3	Agent of transitive action; Aspects; Factors

A _____

Data relating to observer	4	Viewpoint-as-form
Selected instance	5	Sample population/Study region
Presentation of data	6	Target/Form

Interposed operators

Dependent elements	p	Part/Property
	q	Member of quasi-generic group
	r	Aggregate
Concept interlinks	s	Role definer
	t	Author attributed association
Co-ordinate concepts	g	Co-ordinate concept

B _____

Differencing operators (prefixed by $)	h	Non-lead direct difference
	i	Lead direct difference
	j	Salient difference
	k	Non-lead indirect difference
	m	Lead indirect difference
	n	Non-lead parenthetical difference
	o	Lead parenthetical difference
	d	Date as a difference

Connectives (Components of linking phrases; prefixed by $)	v	Downward reading component
	w	Upward reading component

C _____

Theme interlink	x	First element in co-ordinate theme
	y	Subsequent element in co-ordinate theme
	z	Element of common theme

Source: Austin, D (1974), *PRECIS: a manual of concept analysis and subject indexing*, London: Council of the British National Bibliography.

reflect the role that each concept plays in the context of this particular subject. A role operator may designate a term (for example as a location or as a statement of viewpoint). Each operator has a filing value which has been designated in order to ensure that terms appear in the index string in an order that will produce a meaningful set of index entries. The order thus determined embodies 'context dependency'; each term in the string sets each successive term in context.

4. Arrange the index terms in accordance with the filing values of the role operators that the terms have been allocated. The end product of this stage will be an index string which encompasses both terms and operators.
5. Anticipate the index entries that the index string will cause to be generated and make any necessary adjustments to indexing. In particular note (for example by ticking) those terms that merit a turn in the lead position and those that do not.
6. Insert computer instruction codes in the positions of the operators in the string. These instruction codes convert the role operators into machine–readable manipulation codes and show which terms are to be used as entry terms. The order of terms in the string is retained. This stage marks the end of the indexer's task. The computer has now been provided with the wherewithal to complete the generation of index entries.
7. The computer takes the index string with its machine-readable manipulation codes and creates a series of entries by rotating the component terms with which it has been provided. Each entry has three fundamental positions:

    LEAD   Qualifier
    Display

This layout shows the lead term in the context of wider terms on the same line (the Qualifier) and narrower terms (the Display) on the second line. The first entry takes the first component of the string as the index term, leaving the remainder of the string in the Display position. In successive index entries the previous lead term is shunted into the Qualifier position, and the first term in the Display moves into the lead position. This procedure will generate entries according to the standard pattern. Sometimes, in the interests of comprehension or helpfulness, modifications to the standard pattern are desirable.

The computer will also examine individual terms in the string in order to assess whether any references are necessary in order to show semantic relationships between terms and other related terms. These relationships will be indicated automatically by the printing of 'see' and 'see also' references for terms which the computer has encountered previously and for which instructions for the generation of such references already exist in its store. For new terms, instructions must be given to the computer concerning the generation of 'see' and 'see also' references.

Each of the above steps will now be applied to a specific example. The topic for

293

which index entries are to be generated is: 'The Measurement of the diameter of bearings in a dynamo'.

The first two steps require that the individual concepts present in the topic be recognized and expressed in the terms available in the controlled vocabulary. These terms might be:

Dynamos
Bearings
Diameter
Measurement

The third step involves the assignment of role operators. First, an action term is located. Here 'Measurement' is an action term; thus the operator for an action term is assigned to 'Measurement', namely: *(2) Measurement.* The object of the action is next identified and coded (1). Hence: *(1) Dynamos.* 'Bearings' are part of the Key system 'Dynamos' and thus may be denoted by (p), thus: *(p) Bearings,* and likewise: *(p) Diameter.*

Next, the organization of terms according to the filing value of their operators gives an indexing string:

(1) Dynamos
(p) Bearings
(p) Diameter
(2) Measurement

Step 5 involves the designation of lead terms. If all terms merit a lead term except 'Measurement', then

✓
(1) Dynamos

✓
(p) Diameter

✓
(p) Bearings

(2) Measurement

Once the computer instruction codes have been inserted in step 6, the computer will generate the following index entries:

1. Dynamos
   Bearings. Diameter. Measurement
2. Bearings. Dynamos
   Diameter. Measurement
3. Diameter. Bearings. Dynamos
   Measurement

and other references, such as:

Size see Diameter
Dimensions see also Diameter

Ball bearings see Bearings
Lubrication see also Bearings.

17.5 COMPASS (Computer Aided Subject System)

Whatever its future application, PRECIS indexing represents a significant contribution to the theory of subject indexing. PRECIS was replaced by COMPASS in the British National Bibliography (BNB) in January 1991. COMPASS is based on PRECIS, but reduces the latter to its basic components as a subject authority system. COMPASS is more cost effective and focuses on those elements of PRECIS that are valuable in the online mode. The two-line index entry, with its concepts of lead and non-lead terms, is redundant in the online context. This allows COMPASS to dispense with most of the complex coding of PRECIS, thus making indexing easier.

COMPASS continues the following principles that are inherent in PRECIS:

- an open-ended, controlled and structured vocabulary,
- the arrangement of terms into subject strings, organized by principles of context dependency, and
- the reuse of records for subsequent titles on the same subject.

On a more practical level, then, COMPASS takes from PRECIS:

- an authority file of controlled terms and subject statements.
- a network of related terms, including broader, narrower and used and non-used terms.

A core file of authority records is being created from the old PRECIS subject authority file using WLN software. This file will contain two main types of records: term records and string records.

Term records are expressions of simple concepts; they are divided into topical terms and geographical concepts. These records control the vocabulary, provide a thesaural framework and can be linked to other terms as well as to bibliographic records.

String authority records are combinations of two or more terms expressing complex subject concepts. These records are composed of single concept expressions which must be present in the term authority records. Typical string authority records also have a third subfield for connecting words which show relationships between the terms in the string but are not required in their own right.

These subject records form part of a larger file of authority records which also includes personal and corporate names. These names no longer form part of the subject record.

When a BNBMARC record is created, data from the subject authority file is added to bibliographic data in fields 660 (topical descriptors) and 661 (geographical descriptors). Names as subjects, topical terms and strings are held separately in the record. The appropriate fields may look like:

```
660.0$aPolitics
661.0$bGreatBritain
600.1$aThatcher$hMargaret
```

Since the components are held separately, the subject authority records 'Politics' and 'Great Britain' can be reused.

The introduction of COMPASS has affected the subject index to BNB. References are no longer used, but the British Library plans to publish a thesaurus listing authority terms and showing relationships between them. In the classified section of BNB, subject data appears as a numbered tracing. Extracts from the new BNB are shown in Figure 2.1.

17.6   Citation indexing

Almost all papers, notes, reviews, corrections and correspondence published in many scientific and other journals contain citations to associated works, usually listed in reading lists or bibliographies at the end of the work. Such citations are intended to place the document in the context of related literature which contributes to a similar subject area. The documents cited may support and provide precedent for, illustrate or elaborate on what the author has to say. Citations, then, are explicit author–designated links between various items in the literature. For each document that is cited, a reference is given to identify its source; each reference normally includes title, author, and when and where the cited document was published. A citation index seeks to exploit these in-built links between documents and to facilitate the identification of networks of cited, and thus associated, documents.

17.6.1   What is a citation index?

Undoubtedly the most important citation indexes are the products of the Institute for Scientific Information (ISI): Science Citation Index, Social Sciences Citation Index and Arts and Humanities Citation Index, together with their machine-readable and searchable databases: SCISEARCH, SOCIAL SCISEARCH and ARTS and HUMANITIES SEARCH. ISI's products are also available on CD–ROM. Other citation indexes have been produced, such as a Citation Index for Statistics and Probability in 1973. Citation indexes have always been important in law literature; Shephard's Law Review Citations has been published since 1968 as a continuing index to more than 100 law reviews and journals.

ISI's citation indexes comprise two central components: the Citation index and the Source index. Although other indexes are available, these two are essential to a citation index and can be held in printed or machine-readable form. The Source index lists all documents included in the journals covered by the index, and issues published in the time span of the particular cumulation. The Citation index lists, in alphabetical order by author's name, the citations made in any of the source documents and indicates for each cited document, its source document. Thus, under a cited document, every source that cites the document is represented. More complete details of source documents can be located in the Source index.

17.6.2 Advantages of citation indexes

Citation indexes represent a very different approach to the indexing, organization and retrieval of documents than that offered by the conventional subject index. Nevertheless, citation indexes do seek to link documents according to their content (or at least the perception of their content held by the author of the source work). Although there are limitations to the value of citation indexes, they do have some very distinct advantages over more usual indexing techniques; these are likely to assure citation indexes a continuing place in the information market. The advantages of citation indexes can be enumerated as follows:

1. There is no need to assign subject terms and thus there is no intellectual effort required during indexing. The computer merely needs to be fed with the source documents and their citations; with the appropriate software, it will generate the indexes (in printed or machine-readable form). This obviously facilitates the rapid processing of large quantities of documents.
2. A fairly extensive coverage of the literature can be achieved by including only a limited number of source documents. If the key journals in a field are identified, then via the bibliographies of the contributions to these journals, a much wider coverage of the literature can be achieved.
3. There are no artificial limits on the length of bibliographies, so no limits are imposed on the depth or exhaustivity of indexing in a citation index.
4. No problems arise in association with word usage. Citation indexes circumvent many of the problems that must be tackled in subject indexing (such as finding the appropriate label for a concept, the emergence of new terms, new meanings for old words, technical and common names and other variations in terminology).
5. Citations can be used across documents irrespective of the language of the source or cited document.
6. Searching can be more precise and direct.
7. A search can be extended over time by cycling; that is, starting with a source document, identifying those documents which it cites, and then identifying those documents which the original cited document cites, and so on. Cycling makes it possible to build up an historical perspective of the development of a

subject together with the key documents which record those major developments.

8. When compared with KWIC-type title indexes, citation indexing is often more
extensive and of a greater depth. With title indexes the number of index entries
is limited by the number of significant terms in the title. With citation indexes
the number of index entries is limited by the number of citations given in a
document.

9. Interesting perspectives of cross-disciplinary developments can be gathered
from citation indexes in a way that would be difficult with traditional indexes
which tend to concentrate on a specific discipline such as physics, chemistry or
education.

10. A number of ancillary factors relating to the development of knowledge can be
examined such as the extent of self-citation, the evolution of concepts, the
extent of citation between documents in different languages and co–authorship
patterns.

11. The scope of a citation index, especially those published by ISI, is interdisciplinary and also crosses time barriers in a way that a normal index would not
do. For example, in a normal indexing service all the documents listed in the
issue for a specific month will have been published in the last year or so. A
citation index may include documents covering several years.

17.6.3   Disadvantages of citation indexes

Given such an impressive array of advantages, it may seem surprising that conventional subject indexes to the literature continue to be produced. There are some
features of citation indexes which prevent them from completely ousting other
indexes. These are:

1. Inconsistency and inaccuracies in citation practices between different documents. Inconsistencies are mostly merely annoying, although it can be difficult
to be sure whether a group of citations which look similar all relate to the same
document. Inaccuracies can mean that it is impossible to identify the documents to which citations relate. The citation index will reflect any inaccuracies
in the citations which are present in the original bibliography.

2. Citation indexes rest upon the assumption that citations represent a link
between documents. No distinction is drawn between the citation of a document for serious academic purposes and a citation for frivolous reasons.
Authors can cite another article because it is related in making a contribution
in the same area or because the two pieces use the same methodology. Sometimes authors cite another document to lend authority to their own work or
because they wish to demonstrate that they are aware of a document, rather
than because they have used the ideas contained in it.

3. Different types of documents provide citations to varying extents. Trade

literature, popular magazines and newspapers do not abound with citations. Even within the professional journal, different types of essays may by their nature incorporate varying levels of citation. For example, review articles are expected to be supported by extensive bibliographies, whilst it is unusual for a letter to carry more than the odd citation.
4. The source literature for citation must be defined, often as a set of periodicals. This will mean that monographs may be less well covered by a citation index than might be desired (although they will still feature as cited documents).

The future of citation indexing promises to be interesting. It is important to recognize that citation indexing hinges upon the continuation of documents as separate units and the perpetuation of the practice of citing other works. Citation indexing would need to be carefully rethought in order to cater for the electronic journal, especially if it becomes necessary to cover both the printed and computer-based journal literature simultaneously.

17.7 Book Indexing

Book indexes are one type of printed index. Having few special features, they deserve little direct attention. The information manager is likely to make use of book indexes in searching for information and may possibly have to compile a book index. Since book indexes are compiled either by specialist indexers or by authors themselves, their quality can vary considerably. Nevertheless, the entries in a book index may in future be used as a source of additional search keys to enhance records in bibliographic databases. Together with contents pages, they have been muted as possible sources of data to help extend the contents of bibliographic records in order to improve subject searching.

The book index offers ready access to items of information in a book. Figure 1.5 shows a small extract from an index to a book. Entries may be the names of persons, corporate bodies or places, or alphabetical index terms to represent subjects, followed by the page numbers on which information is to be found. The same principles can be used in establishing headings as are outlined elsewhere in this text. Headings for persons, places and corporate bodies can follow the model offered by AACR2R which can also identify principles, as appropriate, regarding best known names and the use of abbreviations of names.

Subject entries can also be established with reference to the principles outlined elsewhere in this book. The problems of the variability of language and the indication of relationships between subjects still need to be addressed. One major difference is that, whilst working with a controlled indexing language and trying to instil consistency in the terms used to describe subjects, the indexer will not normally have a separate subject headings list or thesaurus. The terms must reflect the content of the book and will vary from one book to another. Nevertheless the format of subject entries can follow the forms of words in a thesaurus and adhere to generally accepted principles (concerning, for example, the use of singulars and plurals). The principles of chain indexing may also be applied. For example, if pages 47–61 of a book deal with Security, if pages 47–49 focus on door locks and pages 56–61 on window locks, the following entries are appropriate:

Security	47–61
Door locks	47–49
Window locks	56–61

There is no need to subdivide the entry under Security to show the different aspects that are considered. The reader will discover this when he consults the pages indicated. On the other hand, to cater for the reader who might search under the term Locks, it may be useful to include the additional entry

Locks	
doors	47–49
windows	56–61.

Both 'see' and 'see also' references should be used to link related subjects in the same way as in other catalogues and indexes. For example:

Chimneys see Flues
Carports see also Garages

See references should be replaced by additional entries where the latter offer quick and economical access to information. For example from the users' viewpoint it is more helpful to make the two entries:

United States of America 234
USA 234

than to use one entry and a cross reference, USA see United States of America.

Indexes should subdivide entries rather than offer long lists of page numbers. Subdivision should be considered when there are six page references or less, as appropriate. In the example below a number of subdivisions are shown under the topic Joints. Note also that the grouping of subdivisions under one heading will tend to 'collocate distributed relatives' as in any chain or relative index.

Joints	
brickwork	170
concrete	164
jigs for	126
metal	252
pipes	265, 275, 281
welded	258

Exhaustivity of indexing and specificity are other concerns. The index is not a concordance of every word, concept or name that appears in the book. The indexer needs to exercise judgement as to the depth of indexing required. An over-long index will be confusing and unhelpful, whereas a long text with only a scant index will make it difficult to pinpoint and consult specific subjects. Depth of indexing will be affected by the nature and length of the book. It is perhaps useful to view the chapter structure of the book, as reflected in the contents page, as equivalent to the classified arrangement. Most authors attempt to provide a framework in which related topics are considered in juxtaposition with one another. A well structured book should be easier to index, and may need a less detailed index, than a poorly structured book. Specificity of index headings can be guided by the content of the book.

In compiling a book index, the indexer will make various decisions about the types of names and concepts to include and their filing order. It is helpful, although not very common, if such key decisions are briefly described at the beginning of the index in an introductory note.

There are now a number of software packages which can be used to assist in the compilation of indexes to books and periodicals. The indexer still needs to work through the book, selecting appropriate terms for inclusion, but instead of record-ing these terms on cards or slips, they can be entered directly into the computer. The computer then automatically manipulates, merges and sorts the entries to produce the final index.

Words in entries can be manipulated in a number of different ways including the following:

1. *Flipping*, where the entry 'stainless steel sinks' can be flipped to 'sinks, stainless steel';
2. *Half-flipping*, where the entry 'panel – pins' can be half–flipped to 'pins';
3. *Yanking*, where any heading or subheading can be yanked to another entry; for example, the subheading 'installing' may be yanked from 'showers – installing' to 'sockets – installing'; and
4. *Rotating* which allows headings and subheadings within an entry to be rotated to generate additional entries. For example, 'Horticulture, glasshouses, con-struction' might be rotated to produced the additional entries:
   Glasshouses, construction, horticulture
   and Construction, glasshouses, horticulture.

Other facilities that might be offered include producing see and see also references, disregarding articles or other character strings when sorting, and distinguishing between subheadings and inversions. Entries can sometimes be created initially in a word processing package and then transferred to the indexing software for format-ting, editing and sorting. Some word processing software, such as Wordstar, offers automatic index generators. These depend on the indexer indicating which words or phrases in a document to use as index entries.

The British Standards Institution has prepared BS3700, 'Recommendations for preparing indexes to books, periodicals and other documents'. The United States standard is ANSI Z39.4–1974, 'Basic criteria for indexes'. In the UK, the Society of Indexers, and in the US, the American Society of Indexers, together with the Australian Society of Indexers and the Indexing and Abstracting Society of Canada act as a focus for standards and professional activities for indexers.

Recommended reading

American National Standards Institute (1984), 'American standard for library and information sciences and related publishing practices – basic criteria for indexes', New York: ANSI (Z39.4–1984).

Anderson, J D and Radford, G (1988), 'Back of the book indexing with the nested phrase indexing system (NEPHIS)', *Indexer*, **16** (2), 79–84.

Anderson, M D (1971), *Book indexing*, Cambridge: Cambridge University Press (reprinted 1979).

Armitage, J E and Lynch, M F (1967), 'Articulation in the generation of subject indexes by computer', *Journal of Chemical Documentation*, **7** (3), 170–78.

Armitage, J E and Lynch, M F (1968), 'Some structural characteristics of articulated subject indexes', *Information Storage and Retrieval*, **4**, 101–11.

Austin, D (1974), 'The development of PRECIS: a theoretical and technical history', *Journal of Documentation*, **30** (2), 47–102.

Austin, D and Digger, J A (1977), 'PRECIS: The PREserved Context Index System', *Library Resources and Technical Services*, 13–30.

Austin, D and Dykstra, M (1984), *PRECIS: a manual of concept analysis and subject indexing*, 2nd edition, London: British Library.

Bakewell, K G B (1975), 'The PRECIS indexing system', *The Indexer*, **9** (4), 160–66.

Bawden, D (1988), 'Citation indexing', in *Manual of online search strategies*, Boston, Mass: G K Hall, 44–83.

Coates, E J (1960), *Subject catalogues: headings and structure*, London: Library Association. Reprinted with new preface in 1988.

Costello, J C (1966), 'Coordinate indexing', in S Artandi (ed), *Rutgers series on systems for the intellectual organization of information*, Rutgers: State University, Graduate School of Library Science.

Craven, T C (1986), *String indexing*, Orlando: Academic Press.

Cross, R C (1980), *Indexing books*, Cambridge, Mass: World Guild.

Cutter, C A (1904), *Rules for a dictionary catalogue*, 4th edition, Washington, DC: Government Printing Office.

Dykstra, M (1985), *PRECIS: a primer*, London: British Library.

Farradane, J (1980), 'Relational indexing', *Journal of Information Science*, **1**, 267–76, 313–24.

Foskett, A C (1968), 'SLIC indexing', *Library World*, **70** (817), 17–19.

Garfield, E (1964), 'Science Citation Index: a new dimension in indexing', *Science*, **144** (3619), 649–54.

Garfield, E (1979), *Citation indexing, its theory and application in science, technology and humanities*, New York: Wiley.

Jolley, J L (1975), 'Punched feature cards', *Journal of Documentation*, **31** (3), 199–215.

Kaiser, J (1911), *Systematic indexing*, London: Pitman.

Keen, E M (1964), 'Citation indexes', *Aslib Proceedings*, **16** (8), 246.

Keen, E M (1977), 'On the generation and searching of entries in printed subject indexes', *Journal of Documentation*, **33**, 15–45.

Langridge, D (1976), 'Review of PRECIS', *Journal of Librarianship*, **8** (3), 210–12.

Martyn, J (1975), 'Citation analysis', *Journal of Documentation*, **31** (4), 290–97.

Mills, J (1955), 'Chain indexing and the classified catalogue', *Library Association Record*, **57** (4), 141–48.

Pao, M L (1988), 'Term and citation searching: a preliminary report', Proceedings of the American Society for Information Science, **25**, 177–80.

Pao, M L and Worthen, D B (1989), 'Retrieval effectiveness by semantic and citation searching', *Journal of the American Society for Information Science*, **40**, 226–35.

Salton, G (1989), *A syntactic approach to book indexing*, Ithaca, New York: Cornell University (Technical report TR 89–979).

Richmond, P A (1981), *Introduction to PRECIS for North American Usage*, Littleton, Colorado: Libraries Unlimited.

Verdier, V (1981), 'Final report of the PRECIS/translingual project', London: British Library Research and Development Department.

Weintraub, D K (1979), 'An extended review of PRECIS', *Library Resources and Technical Services*, **23** (2), 101–15.

Wheatley, A (1978), 'A manual of printed subject indexes: report to the British Library Research and Development Department', Aberystwyth: College of Librarianship.

Wilson, T D (1971), *An introduction to chain indexing*, London: Bingley.

18 Indexing systems: computer-based systems

18.1 Introduction

This chapter continues the theme of the previous chapter in considering indexing systems. Post-coordinate indexing systems are virtually all computer-based; even those computer-based systems that rely upon pre-coordinated subject headings (of the type discussed in Chapter 17) offer facilities for the further coordination of terms at the search stage. Many of the facilities that characterize text-based retrieval systems are designed to allow the user to coordinate concepts during a search.

Early post-coordinate indexing systems were, however, distinctly card-based, and the literature abounds in pictorial terminology. Marginal storage cards or *edge notch cards* allowed index terms to be represented by codes of holes punched around the edge of a card on which was recorded a document reference. *Aperture cards* were a form of edge notch card that permitted the storage of the document details on the card in microform format. *Dual dictionaries* were printed computer-produced indexes; two lists were produced, and the user was invited to coordinate terms by comparing the document numbers listed under two terms. *Optical coincidence cards*, peek-a-boo or Batten cards were one of the more popular formats for a post–coordinate card index. Each card represented one index term and had a grid which provided for the coding of document numbers. Coordination was achieved by superimposing cards on one another and seeking coincident holes. Any number of imaginative enhancements of these systems were to be found in indexes of special collections and special libraries. However, these card indexes have been superceded by computer-based systems which have incorporated the most valuable principles established earlier.

Both card-based systems and computer-based systems share the fundamental features of a post-coordinate index, as follows:

1. None of the entries in the system is specific. Relatively large numbers of documents are associated with each index term, so that if searchers approach the index as if it were a printed index, they will need to undertake extensive scanning of the entries associated with a given term.

2. There will be more entries in a post–coordinate indexing system than in one based on pre–coordinate indexing principles (although the number of entries in the latter will depend upon the incidence of references and multiple entries).

3. There will be fewer different index terms in the index than in an equivalent pre–coordinated system. In full-text systems, however, the number of entries is likely to escalate.

Post-coordinate indexing systems are characterized by search logics – such as Boolean search logic – which are central to searching in computer-based systems. It is therefore appropriate to view computer-based systems as largely post-coordinate, although they may include some facilities for pre-coordinated terms, such as searching on phrases. In general it is useful to think in terms of the level of coordination of a system, rather than to attempt to categorize it as pre– or post–coordinate.

Computer-based information retrieval systems include the services of the online search service suppliers, CD–ROM products, Inhouse text information management systems and Online public access catalogues. The data to be searched may include terms from controlled indexing languages as well as terms from the natural language of the documents or records. Search facilities are intended to cater for searching based both on controlled and natural languages. Special sections later in the chapter consider the use of thesauri in searching, classification in online searching and the searching of full-text databases where natural language indexing may feature. More details of CD–ROM, external online search services, text information management systems and online public access catalogues are to be found in later chapters in this book. This chapter attempts to identify the common retrieval facilities that are featured in most of these environments.

There are two major components of the search interface: the search facilities which support the development of search strategies, and the interface through which such facilities can be accessed. We first review briefly the options for interface or dialogue design, before proceeding to examine the search facilities themselves.

18.2 Dialogue styles

Until a few years ago virtually all of the information retrieval systems within the ambit of this book used commands as their sole dialogue style. Recent significant advances in the design of dialogues have impinged upon online hosts, CD–ROM search software and OPACs. From their inception CD–ROM and OPACs have been designed for the end-user. To compete effectively, online hosts have also had to introduce end-user services. The average end-user cannot be expected to learn and remember command languages, so other dialogue styles have been adopted. A number of different styles may be used at different places in the same interface. There are five basic options for dialogue style, as outlined below.

1. Menu selection

The user is presented with a menu offering a number of different options on the screen. The options are displayed either as commands (for the more experienced user) or as short explanatory pieces of text. One option is selected by keying in a code for that option or by pointing to it with a mouse or pointing device. Menus are generally recognized to be helpful to the novice and occasional user, but they can be tedious for the more experienced; moreover, the user is constrained to select only one of the menu options. A further disadvantage of early systems was that the menu occupied significant parts of the screen. Many menus are now pop–up or pull–down or appear in windows which can be switched on and off.

Some obvious limitations of menus are:

- a lot of information is displayed on the screen which takes time to read;
- only a limited number of options may be displayed on one screen;
- most systems have a menu hierarchy which users need assistance to navigate through, and
- they are not suitable for the inputting of large quantities of data such as numbers or text.

In search interfaces, provision is often made for the specification of search terms which must be entered. Except in systems with natural language interfaces, Boolean operators must still be used. Help systems are also necessary, but further work needs to be done in order to achieve an optimum help system for different applications. It is rare for help to be offered on how to select terms or how to combine them into an effective search strategy. Nor is help usually available on how to modify a search strategy if it does not produce the desired results.

Menu-based systems may be less successful for online searching than in OPACs, CD–ROM and in-house text retrieval applications. Costing strategies and the slow speed of a menu-based search are likely to be more significant for online searching on external hosts. For online searching, menu systems may work best for the experienced online searcher who knows how to search in general, but is not familiar with the command language of a particular host.

2. Command languages

In dialogues based on commands, the user enters his instructions as pre-set commands; the computer recognizes these and takes appropriate action. The command language for a given system is a feature of the software and must include commands for all of the functions that the user might wish to perform. Since different hosts, database producers and software suppliers will wish to differentiate their product from that of their competitors, standardization in command languages will inevitably remain problematic. Command languages are potentially the most powerful interface, but carry the overhead of learning. The main advantages of command languages are economy of screen space, the direct addressing of objects and functions by name, and the flexibility of system functions.

All command languages have a word set, described as a *lexicon*, and rules that state how the words may be combined, which is known as a *grammar*. The words identify objects and operations. Objects will be described by nouns and operations by verbs. Usually commands can be truncated, often to three characters (such as DIR for DIRECTORY, PRT for PRINT). Abbreviations must be unique within a given command language.

3. WIMP interfaces (windows, icons, pop-up menus)
Windows subdivide the screen space so that different operations can be taking place on the screen at the same time. Windows have a number of uses. Screen areas can be separated for error messages, control menus, working area and help. Two or more processes can be run in different windows or two files can be viewed simultaneously. The use of window-based environments is likely to increase, especially in application to CD–ROM.

Menus have been discussed earlier in this section. Pop-up menus are menus which occupy only part of the screen and can be displayed on request and then switched off again.

Icons, or pictorial representations of objects in the system, were pioneered by Xerox in the Star System and by Apple in the Lisa and Macintosh interfaces. The system operates by selecting objects and moving them with the cursor. For example, to delete a file you move a folder into the waste paper bin. In direct manipulation interfaces, icons can be addressed by pointing at them with a mouse or another similar cursor–control device. Pointing allows objects to be selected. Direct manipulation allows objects to be moved around the screen in a dragging operation. Although these interfaces have limitations (such as potential ambiguity of the icons and difficulty in representing functional operations), they are easy to use. To some extent windows and icons are likely to remain a feature of future information retrieval systems.

4. Form filling
In a form-filling dialogue, the user works with a screen–based image of a form. The screen form will have labels and spaces into which data can be entered. It should be possible to move a cursor to any appropriate position on the form for the entering of data. In searching, form filling usually requires the user to enter one or possibly more search words to identify the field whose values are to be scanned for the presence of the search term.

5. Question and answer
Users of a question and answer dialogue are guided through their interaction by questions or prompts on the screen. They respond by entering data at the keyboard. On receiving the user's response, the computer will evaluate it and act accordingly. This may involve the display of data, additional questions or the execution of a task, such as the saving of a file. This dialogue style is well-suited to

occasional and novice users, but can be slow since each question requires a response which must be evaluated before the user can proceed to input more data.

18.3 Retrieval facilities

Standard retrieval facilities are available in most text retrieval systems, including access to an external online host, in-house text retrieval systems, CD–ROM and OPACs. These facilities have traditionally been offered via a command-based interface and are largely developed in the software used by online hosts and in text information management software used for in-house text databases. Similar facilities are increasingly being incorporated into the interfaces used in CD–ROM and OPAC applications, but these are more frequently embodied in a menu-based environment and sometimes the facilities are not used explicitly. For example, in an OPAC search for documents on Chemistry for Biologists, the user may input the phrase 'Chemistry for Biologists', but the system will perform the search 'Chemistry AND Biologists'. The retrieval facilities that are used in these applications are appropriate in a text-based environment where the user does not know what documents are available and/or does not know the terms by which they can be retrieved. In many database applications, records can be retrieved by using pre-assigned codes, in which case many of the facilities described below become redundant. In this environment searching can be evaluated with the application of concepts such as precision and recall, though there is often some doubt as to whether the search has retrieved all relevant items.

The retrieval facilities described below can, then, be used for retrieval on all kinds of databases (including bibliographic and source databases) and may be applied with terms either from controlled indexing languages or from the natural language of the record.

18.3.1 Basic facilities

Basic facilities are determined by the nature of the application, but they also help to set the environment in which the search will proceed. Help and news can be useful. In online searching of external hosts, further aids include log-on and log-off facilities, together with the opportunity to change default values (such as screen width and length). These facilities are not usually necessary when using a local OPAC, but probably will be necessary in access to an external OPAC. Choice of the database may be a further preliminary.

18.3.2 Entering and selecting search terms

The user must be able to identify an appropriate search term and then enter it as such. Identification of search terms can be assisted by the display of search term listings. In the systems of online hosts, this is achieved by a command, such as

Dialog's EXPAND (E). The display will normally show a section of the inverted file, listing index terms and their number of postings. A reference may also be given for each term so that it can easily be selected; in CD–ROM systems it is more common to select a term by positioning the cursor.

A command must be available for entering a search term. This may merely be the term itself, such as Market (as in BRS/SEARCH) or S Market (as in Dialog).

18.3.3   Combining terms and Boolean search logic

Search logic is the means of specifying combinations of terms which must be matched in retrieval. Boolean logic is employed in searching most systems in order to link terms from both natural and controlled indexing languages. The logic is used to link the terms which describe the concepts present in the statement of the search. As many as 20, 30 or more index terms may be linked together by means of search logic in order to frame the search statement. Search logic permits the inclusion of all synonyms and related terms, and also specifies acceptable and unacceptable term combinations. The Boolean logic operators are AND, OR and NOT. Figure 18.1 uses Venn diagrams to help explain how each of these operators may be used. The sets of documents indexed-under the two index terms A and B are each represented by a circle.

In an online search, the profile is evolved or modified as the search progresses. The statements are framed one at a time, and feedback is available at each stage. For instance, a request posed to the computer to search for the occurrence of an individual term usually results in a statement which gives the number of documents whose records are stored in association with that term, such as

1   616   CARNATIONS

At any stage in the search the result of linking terms by the search logic of the system can be viewed. A request to the computer such as

COMBINE 1 AND 2

where 1 and 2 are sets of documents that have previously been noted, leads to something of the form:

4   8   COMBINE 1 AND 2

Here the number of documents satisfying the previous logic statement (that is, 8 documents) is indicated. With this type of facility search strategy can be refined to give the most profitable output. Further complex search strategies are possible with the intercession of other kinds of logic (see below) and the use of brackets. Figure 18.2 shows how the statements in an online search make use of Boolean logic operators.

Figure 18.1 Boolean logic operators

Operator	Search type	Venn diagrams	Meaning
AND	Conjunctive		Logic product, symbolized by A AND B, A,B, A × B or (A) (B). Both index terms A and B must be assigned to a document for a match. For example, Optic × Fibre × Cable × Television implies that all of the above four terms must have been assigned to a document for a match.
OR	Additive		Logical sum, symbolized by A or B, or A + B. Only one of the two index terms A or B needs to be associated with a document for a match. This operator is usually introduced when A and B can be regarded as equivalent for the purposes of the search. For example, TV + Television would serve to retrieve all documents with either the term TV or the term Television assigned.
NOT	Subtractive		Logical difference, symbolized by A NOT B or A-B. The index term must be assigned, and assigned in the absence of the term B for a match. For example, Fibre Optics – British Telecom requires all documents on Fibre Optics except those indexed also under British Telecom.

310

Figure 18.2 A basic online search on Dialog
(a) The basic search process

Retrieving information on DIALOG involves a conversation between you and the computer. In response to the system prompt (a question mark), you enter a command telling the computer what to do and then press the ENTER key to send the command to DIALOG. The system responds to the command, and sends you a prompt for the next instruction.

Once you are connected to DIALOG, your online search usually will follow a sequence similar to that shown below and in the sample search on the next page. The commands that you would enter are shown in bold face type in the sample search. The basic search process, the commands used, and their abbreviations are described below.

Search Process	Command Examples
(1)* Connect to a specific database with BEGIN n (where n is the File number). Also use BEGIN n to change databases; the sets in your previous search will be erased. (Refer to the Database Catalog for file numbers.)	BEGIN 48 B48
(2) Search for records by SELECTing search terms and combining them (or the sets that contain them) with logical or proximity operators (see p. 8).	SELECT AEROBIC? S SHOE? OR FOOTWEAR S S1 AND S2
(3) Look at some or all of your results at your terminal with TYPE. Enter the set number, the format number, and the records you wish to view (see page 10).	TYPE S3/6/1-2 T S3/5/1 T S3/3/1,6–8,12
(4) Request that the results be PRINTed offline and mailed to you. Enter set/format/records after the command (see page 10).	PRINT S3/5/ALL PR S3/7/1–10
(5) Change databases with BEGIN, or disconnect your equipment from DIALOG with LOGOFF. You will receive an estimated cost for your search session.	LOGOFF.

*A special DIALOG feature called OneSearch℠ allows you to conduct your search in more than one database at a time by entering more than one file number after BEGIN, e.g., BEGIN 50,53.

(b) The display of the search

TOPIC: Find information on aerobics shoes. (The SPORT (File 48) database is used in this example; you might also look at the business databases for information about the sales and marketing of aerobic shoes, the medical files for more information on injury prevention, or at the patent files to identify patents for athletic footwear.)

(1) **? begin 48**
       08sep88 12:26:27 User053951
              $0.12   0.004 Hrs File1
       $0.12   Estimated cost File1
       $0.12   Estimated cost this search
       $0.12   Estimated total session cost   0.004 Hrs.
File 48:SPORT DATABASE 1977– Aug 88
       (COPR. SIRC 1988)

Continued

Figure 18.2   Continued

Set Items   Description

(2) **? select aerobic(w)exercise? or aerobic(w)dance or aerobics**

	4263	AEROBIC
	20369	EXERCISE?
	185	AEROBIC(W)EXERCISE?
	4263	AEROBIC
	2694	DANCE
	378	AEROBIC(W)DANCE
	170	AEROBICS
S1	664	AEROBIC(W)EXERCISE? OR AEROBIC(W)DANCE OR AERO-BICS

See page 8 for information on using the ? to specify truncation and the (w) to specify that terms be adjacent.

? select shoe? or footwear

	1827	SHOE?
	92	FOOTWEAR

? select s1 and s2

	664	S1
	1849	S2
S3	26	S1 and S2

(3) **? type s3/6/1–2**

3/6/1
0219460
Choosing the right shoe for you. What you need to know when buying shoes for running, walking, court sports, aerobics and fitness.

3/6/2
0219446
On your feet: aerobic shoes.

? type s3/5/1
3/5/1
0219460
Choosing the right shoe for you. What you need to know when buying shoes for running, walking, court sports, aerobics and fitness.
Australian fitness & training annual (Sydney, Aust.), 1988, 64–76
LANGUAGE(S): English DOCUMENT TYPE: Journal article
COUNTRY OF PUBL.: Australia
LEVEL: Basic
SECTION HEADING: 905340 Clothing – Shoes
KEYWORDS: shoes; selection; evaluation

(4) **? print s3/5/all**
P087: PRINT S3/5/ALL (items 1–26) est. cost of $7.80

(5) **? logoff**

	08sep88 12:27:43 User053951	
	$1.47	0.021 Hrs File48
	$0.25	1 Types in Format 5
	$0.00	2 Types in Format 6
	$0.25	3 Types
	$7.80	26 Prints in Format 5
	$7.80	1 Print transaction(s)
$9.52	Estimated cost File 48	
$9.52	Estimated cost this search	
$9.64	Estimated total session cost	0.024 Hrs.

Logoff: level 17.8.10 C   12:27:46

The Boolean operators AND, OR and NOT are subject to a few variations. BASIS uses AND NOT and allows abbreviations; Dialog uses * for AND and + for OR. More than one operator may be used in a search strategy (for instance, Software AND Industry OR Industries), but care needs to be taken with the priority of execution. For example, with the sequence given above Dialog would process the AND search before the OR search. Problems of priority can be overcome by heeding the priority rules of a given system or by using parentheses; for instance, Software AND (Industry OR Industries).

18.3.4 Weighted term searching and relevance ranking

In most search statements or document profiles it is possible to designate certain concepts as being more significant than others. Weights are a quantitative measure of the prominence of various index terms in the description of a subject and may form the basis of an alternative search logic. This section discusses the use of weights in search profiles, although it is also possible to assign weights to concepts in document profiles – that is, to indicate the primary concepts in a document and discriminate between these and subsidiary concepts.

Weights as originally used were assigned by the searcher or indexer intellectually on the basis of the significance of a concept. Most current systems assign weights on the basis of some statisitcal analysis of term frequency.

In its role in formulating search profiles, weighted term logic may be introduced either as a search logic in its own right, or as a means of reducing the search output of a search whose basic logic is Boolean. Whichever application is encountered, weighted term search logic is most commonly associated with computer-based systems.

In an application where weighted term logic is the primary search logic, search profiles are framed by combining index terms in a simple logical sum. Each term is assigned a weight which reflects its significance in determining the relevance of a document to the search question, and document references worthy of printing are selected on the basis of a threshold weight.

A simple SDI-type profile using weighted term search logic is displayed below. The *search description* given is 'the effect of alcohol on the performance of drivers of motor vehicles'. A simple *search profile* (which does not explore all possible synonyms, but does serve to illustrate weighted term logic) might include:

7 Motor vehicles	6 Alcohol
7 Cars	5 Blood alcohol
7 Vehicles	4 Drivers
7 Motor cars	3 Performance
7 Motor vehicles	2 Drowsiness
7 Buses	1 Ergonomics

A threshold weight appropriate to the specificity of the searcher's enquiry must be established. For instance, a threshold weight of 13 would retrieve all documents with the following combinations of terms assigned:

Motor vehicles and Alcohol (7 + 6)
Cars and Alcohol (7 + 6)
Cars, Drivers and Performance (7 + 4 + 3)
Motor vehicles, Blood alcohol and Drowsiness (7 + 5 + 2)

Documents with the following terms assigned would be rejected on the grounds that their combined weights did not exceed the pre-selected threshold:

Alcohol and Drivers (6 + 4)
Performance and Drowsiness (3 + 2)
Ergonomics and Motor vehicles (1 + 7)

A different threshold weight would cause either a larger or smaller set of documents to be selected as relevant. By modifying the threshold weight, the search specification can be broadened or narrowed.

Weighted term search logic may also be used to supplement Boolean logic. Here weighted term logic is a means of limiting or ranking the output from a search that has been conducted in response to a search profile which was framed in terms of Boolean logic operators. In the process of the search, prior to display or printing, the computer ranks references according to their weighting; those documents with sufficiently high rankings will be deemed relevant and eventually retrieved.

Weights are used in systems that offer relevance ranking. For example, in STAUS IQ, once the user has posed a question, the system will identify relevant documents and rank them according to their weights. The system will thus respond with something like:

- 102 articles have been retrieved and ranked
- 6 articles contain all significant concepts
- Articles 1–6 have a score equal to or exceeding 75%
- Articles 7–17 have scores of between 50–75%
- Articles 18–102 have scores between 25–50%.

The user can then browse through the articles, starting with the most relevant.

BRS has an option called 'occurrence' that lists the part of the document in which terms appear. ORBIT's GET command lets the user rank and analyse search results in terms of the field values present. ESA–IRS offers the ZOOM command that analyses how frequently terms occur in a set of items in order to select the best terms to enter subsequently.

18.3.5   Specifying fields to be searched

The ability to search for the occurrence of terms in specific fields within the record makes it possible to be more precise in searching. For example, in BRS/SEARCH, MATTHEW.AU would find any document where MAKEPEACE appeared in the

314

author (AU) paragraph. In Dialog AU = MAKEPEACE would have a similar effect.

To achieve correct field matches, it is important to know which fields are indexed, and whether they are word or phrase indexed. Fields, their codes and whether they are indexed are specific to databases and hosts. In some systems there is only one single inverted file, and fields cannot be specified. Figure 18.3 shows the indexed fields for one Dialog database.

Combinations of field codes may be needed and can be stated together with operators. For example: SS (SOFTWARE OR PROGRAM)/TI,AB will search for SOFTWARE and PROGRAM in both the title and abstract fields.

18.3.6 Truncation and search term strings

Truncation is another search device which can be particularly useful in natural language information retrieval systems, although it can also be applied with controlled languages. In any given system, certain characters will be selected to designate truncation. When the computer recognizes one of these characters, it will search for a specified word stem, regardless of whether it is found in the text as a complete word, or whether other characters are necessary at the beginning or end of the stem in order to construct a true word. The effect of truncation in searching is that all words with common stems are treated as equivalent, and thus the need to make an exhaustive list of word variants is eliminated. This is likely to lead to shorter and less complex profiles for searches, the gains being most obvious in a natural language system. Here, for example, it is possible that all the following words might be relevant to a search on the applications of computing in a specific sector (say, accountancy): Computer, Computers, Computing.

If the computer were instructed to search on the stem 'Comput*' all of these words would be acceptable, and documents indexed under any of them would be retrieved as relevant. It should be noted, however, that truncation can be the cause of 'False Drops'. For example, the stem 'Comput*' might retrieve documents indexed under Computation and Computed, in addition to those documents indexed previously under other words with this same stem. Over-severe truncation must be carefully avoided. For example, Cat* could retrieve documents on both Catalogues and Cats!

Truncation may be more restrictive. The number of characters required to appear either before or after the stem may be specified. For example, Comput $2 could select all words with the stem Comput followed by precisely two characters, and would thus retrieve documents indexed under Computed but not those under Computers, and so on.

The examples cited above have used right-hand truncation, which results in the amalgamation of words with different suffixes. Left-hand truncation, which disregards prefixes, is also possible in many systems. Left-hand truncation is especially useful in chemical databases where, for example, *phosphate can be used to match

Figure 18.3   A menu-based search on BRS

ENTER DATABASE NAME_: **menu**

MENU
WELCOME TO BRS/MENUS
MAIN MENU

SERVICE	NUMBER
Search Service	1
BRS/MENUS Update (11/1/91)	11
How To Use BRS/MENUS	12
Customer Services	13
Return to Command/driven BRS	99

ENTER SERVICE NUMBER OR H FOR HELP--> **1**

BRS/MENUS SEARCH SERVICE LIBRARIES

LIBRARY NAME	LABEL
Business and Finance	BUSI
Medicine and Pharmacology	MDPH
Physical and Applied Sciences	PHAS
Life Sciences	LFSC
Education	EDUC
Social Sciences and Humanities	SOCS
Reference and Multidisciplinary	REFE
Practice Databases	PRAC

ENTER LIBRARY OR DATABASE LABEL, OR M TO RETURN TO MAIN MENU--> **Efsc**
[CHOOSING A SECTION → CAN BYPASS + CHOOSE A DATABASE HERE]

LIFE SCIENCES   SCREEN 1 OF 2

DATABASE	LABEL
AIDS Abstracts from the Bureau of Hygiene & Tropical Diseases	AIDD
AGRICOLA (1980 to Date)	CAIN
(1970 to 1979)	CAIB
BioBusiness	BBUS
BIOSIS Previews (1978 to date)	BIOL
(1970 to 1977)	BIOB
(1970 to date)	BIOZ
CAB Abstracts	CABA
Cambridge Scientific Abstracts Life Sciences	CSAL

ENTER LABEL, L TO RETURN TO LIBRARY MENU, OR PRESS ENTER FOR MORE -->
caba

CABA 1972–SEP 1991 (9109)

Continued

Figure 18.3   Continued

ENTER Y TO DISPLAY DATABASE DESCRIPTION OR PRESS ENTER TO BEGIN SEARCHING--> **y**

CAB Abstracts is a comprehensive flle of worldwide agricultural information produced by CAB International (formerly the Commonwealth Agricultural Bureaux). Every branch of agricultural science is covered including crop science and production, animal science and production, forestry, crop protection (pest control), machinery and buildings, biotechnology, economics and sociology. Of particular note is the comprehensive and unique coverage of veterinary medicine, human nutrition, developing countries, and leisure, recreation and tourism. Over ten thousand primary journals in over 50 languages are scanned by CAB International, as well as books, reports, and other publications. Over 85% of the literature is abstracted (all abstracts are in English), while less important works are reported with bibliographic details only. Indexing is detailed and comprehensive using a controlled vocabulary (CAB Thesaurus). DISPLAY OPTIONS:

SHORT: AN,HC,TI,TT,AU,CA,IN,SO,PB,LG,LS,YR
MEDIUM: AN,HC,TI,TT,AU,CA,IN,SO,PB,LG,LS,YR,DE,GL
LONG: ALL FIELDS
ENTER SEARCH TERMS, COMMAND, OR H FOR HELP
SEARCH 1--> **h**

BRS/MENUS SEARCH HELP

FOR HELP WITH:	HELP [SCREENS] ENTER:
Basic Commands (H, S, D, PC, R, C, M, L, O)	1
Search Terms	2
Connectors (OR, AND, SAME, WITH, NOT)	3
Truncation ($)	4
Searching Specific Fields (e.g. YEAR, AUTHOR, TITLE)	5
Advanced Commands	6

FOR MORE HELP ENTER: A NUMBER, ANY COMMAND, ANY CONNECTOR, OR ENTER X TO EXIT HELP--> **1**

BRS/MENUS BASIC COMMANDS

FOR HELP WITH:	Enter:
Help	H
Search	S
Display Documents	D
Print Documents Continuously	PC
Review Search	R
Change Databases	C
Return to Main Menu	M
Change Libraries	L
Sign Off	O

Continued

Figure 18.3 Continued

FOR MORE HELP ENTER ANY COMMAND, PRESS ENTER TO CONTINUE, ENTER G TO GO BACK OR X TO EXIT HELP--> **s**

HELP   S: RESUME SEARCH   SCREEN 1 OF 1

Enter the command S to RESUME SEARCHING when you find yourself at a prompt that is not a search prompt. You can return to your search by entering an S at this prompt:

PRESS ENTER TO CONTINUE OR ENTER COMMAND--> s

and you will return to a search prompt:

ENTER SEARCH TERMS, COMMAND, OR H FOR HELP
SEARCH 4-->

PRESS ENTER TO CONTINUE, ENTER A CONNECTOR, G TO GO BACK OR X TO EXIT HELP-->x [EXIT HELP SCREENS]

ENTER SEARCH TERMS, COMMAND, OR H FOR HELP   [SEARCHING]
SEARCH 1--> **intermediate technology**

 ANSWER 1 472 DOCUMENTS FOUND

ENTER SEARCH TERMS, COMMAND, OR H FOR HELP
SEARCH 2--> **1.de.**

 ANSWER 2 50 DOCUMENTS FOUND

ENTER SEARCH TERMS, COMMAND, OR H FOR HELP
SEARCH 3--> **h**

| BRS/MENUS SEARCH HELP | [HELP SCREENS] |
FOR HELP WITH:	ENTER:
Basic Commands (H, S, D, PC, R, C, M, L, O)	1
Search Terms	2
Connectors (OR, AND, SAME, WITH, NOT)	3
Truncation ($)	4
Searching Specific Fields (e.g. YEAR, AUTHOR, TITLE)	5
Advanced Commands	6

FOR MORE HELP ENTER: A NUMBER, ANY COMMAND,
ANY CONNECTOR, OR ENTER X TO EXIT HELP--> **1**

                    BRS/MENUS BASIC COMMANDS

FOR HELP WITH:	Enter:
Help	H
Search	S
Display Documents	D

Continued

Figure 18.3   Continued

Print Documents Continuously	PC
Review Search	R
Change Databases	C
Return to Main Menu	M
Change Libraries	L
Sign Off	O

FOR MORE HELP ENTER ANY COMMAND, PRESS ENTER TO CONTINUE, ENTER G TO GO BACK OR X TO EXIT HELP--> **d**

HELP   D:DISPLAY DOCUMENTS   SCREEN 1 OF 4

To display documents, enter the command, D at a search prompt:

SEARCH 3--> d

BRS/MENUS will then prompt you for the number of the search answer containing the documents you wish to see:

ENTER ANSWER NUMBER-->

Next, you will be asked for the format in which you want the documents displayed:

TI (title only)
S (short format)
M (medium format)
L (long format)
TD (tailored display)

PRESS ENTER TO CONTINUE, ENTER G TO GO BACK OR X TO EXIT
HELP--> **x** [EXIT HELP SCREENS]

ENTER SEARCH TERMS, COMMAND, OR H FOR HELP
[ONLINE PRINTING – SCREEN BY SCREEN]
SEARCH 3--> **d**

ENTER ANSWER NUMBER--> **2**

ENTER TI (TITLE ONLY), S (SHORT FORMAT), M (MEDIUM FORMAT), L (LONG FORMAT) TD (TAILORED DISPLAY)--> **ti**

ENTER DOCUMENT NUMBERS--> **1–10**

ANSWER 2   CABA   SCREEN 1 OF 3

1
TI TITLE: Intensification of smallholdings in Africa by appropriate mechanization with an example of studies in Kenya and Togo.

2
TI TITLE: Symposium: alternative technology and mechanisation options in Third World agricultural development.

3
TI TITLE: The prospects for small-scale farming in an industrial society: a critical appraisal of Small is beautiful.

Continued

319

Figure 18.3 Continued

4
TI TITLE: Doing things together.

PRESS ENTER FOR NEXT SCREEN, A SCREEN NUMBER, EXPAND A DOCUMENT (EG, E;5) OR ENTER A COMMAND-->

ANSWER   2   CABA   SCREEN   2 OF   3

5
TI TITLE: Appropriate technology: report by the Ministry of Overseas Development Working Party.

6
TI TITLE: 5. Technology and change.

7
TI TITLE: Some thoughts on intermediate technology and rural transport.

8
TI TITLE: Energy for rural development. Renewable resources and alternative technologies for developing countries.

PRESS ENTER FOR NEXT SCREEN, A SCREEN NUMBER, EXPAND A DOCUMENT (EG, E;5) OR ENTER A COMMAND-->

ANSWER   2   CABA   SCREEN   3 OF   3

9
TI TITLE: Economic research and farm machinery design in Eastern Africa.

10
TI TITLE: Agriculture and the choice of technology.
END OF REQUEST

ENTER E TO EXPAND A DOCUMENT (EG, E;5), ENTER SCREEN NUMBER, S TO RESUME SEARCHING, OR A COMMAND--> **pc**

ENTER ANSWER NUMBER--> **2**   [ONLINE PRINTING – CONTINUOUS MODE]

ENTER TI (TITLE ONLY), S (SHORT FORMAT), M (MEDIUM FORMAT), L (LONG FORMAT) TD (TAILORED DISPLAY)--> **1**

ENTER DOCUMENT NUMBERS--> **8**

8
AN ACCESSION NUMBER: 77R342243. 7700.
HC HARDCOPY:
 World Agricultural Economics & Rural Sociology Abstracts RECORD NO. 0R019–04517.
TI TITLE: Energy for rural development. Renewable resources and alternative technologies for developing countries.
CA CORPORATE AUTHORS: USA, Panel on Renewable Energy Resources, Advisory Committee on Technology Innovation, National Academy of Sciences.
SO SOURCE: 1976, xii + 305pp.
PB PUBLISHER: Washington, D.C., USA; National Academy of Sciences.
LG LANGUAGE: English (EN).

Continued

Figure 18.3   Continued

AB ABSTRACT: The report focuses on small-scale energy technologies, not based on conventional fuels, which while having little impact on the overall energy economy of a country, could contribute to the improvement of rural and village life in situations where conventional fuels had not yet penetrated or were too expensive. The report is in two sections, a technical and a non technical, both of which examine economic as well as technical constraints of the various energy sources. Both sections are in three parts (1) direct uses of solar energy, (2) indirect uses of solar energy (wind power, hydropower, photosynthesis as an energy source, microbiological conversion of plant material to liquid fuels), and (3) other techniques (geothermal energy, energy storage).
DE DESCRIPTORS: energy. rural-development. intermediate-technology.
SC SEQUENCING CODES: 0R17000054.
YR YEAR: 1976.
DT DOCUMENT TYPE: Unnumbered Whole (UW).
END OF REQUEST

RETURNING TO SEARCH
ENTER SEARCH TERMS, COMMAND, OR H FOR HELP
SEARCH 3--> o [LOGGING OFF]

CONNECT TIME   0:09:21 HH:MM:SS   0.156 DEC HRS   SESSION 2506

diphosphate, dipolyphosphate, orthophosphate, trimetaphosphate and so on. Sometimes truncation may be operative on both ends of a stem. So, for example, *Comput* might retrieve documents indexed under any of Microcomputers, Microcomputer, Minicomputer, Computing, Computers, and so on. Truncation can also be used internally, usually in order to mark alternative spellings, for example:

SUL*UR to cover sulphur or sulfur
PROT*N* to cover protein, proteins, proton

Some systems permit the use of both contextual logic and truncated terms simultaneously, but others only permit their application one at a time.
String searching is a technique for locating a string of characters, even if it is embedded within a larger term. String searching is relatively slow, since the computer searches the sequential file of bibliographic records. Thus string searching is not usually performed on complete bibliographic databases, but tends to be used to search a subset, as perhaps in a previously retrieved set of records. String searching can be used to retrieve records with character strings where these have not been listed in the inverted file. String searching can be particularly useful for refining search profiles, once a fairly large number of documents have been retrieved in response to a fairly broad search profile. Thus terms can be located which might not have been anticipated as future search terms during indexing by first selecting records from the databases according to some broad criteria. Also string searching can be useful in identifying chemicals.

321

18.3.7   Phrases, adjacency and proximity operators

Since phrases occur so commonly in records, it is useful to be able to search on them. For example, a search on Artificial Intelligence may be performed by combining the two terms ARTIFICIAL AND INTELLIGENCE, but this combination may also retrieve many irrelevant documents where the two words are present in a record but not in juxtaposition with one another.

This problem can be overcome with *phrase indexing*. As discussed in Chapter 6, fields can be word- or phrase-indexed, although the latter need to be marked in some way. For instance, a bibliographic record could mark index terms as phrases by inserting hyphens to link terms comprising one phrase, such as Motor-Vehicles or Woollen-Carpets. In order to retrive using such phrases it is necessary to enter the phrase in the form in which it has been stored; for instance, S MOTOR-VEHICLES. This approach cannot be adopted for longer free-text fields because in order for proximity operators to be used, the positions of words in the field need to be stored. Proximity operators can require:

1. that two words appear next to each other. BRS uses ADJ; for example, MOTOR ADJ VEHICLES;
2. that two words appear in the same sentence. BRS uses WITH; for example, MOTOR WITH VEHICLES;
3. that two words appear within the same field or paragraph. BRS uses SAME; for example, MOTOR SAME VEHICLES, or
4. that two words be within a specified distance of one another. IBM's STAIRS indicates the number of permissible intervening words in brackets. For instance, MANAGEMENT(2)HOUSING would require that MANAGEMENT and HOUSING had no more than two words between them.

Proximity searching is often more successful when used in conjunction with search term displays and truncation.

18.3.8   Range searching and limiting

Other operators may permit the selection of documents meeting certain criteria. Thus, in STAIRS the following operators may be used in conjunction with the ..SELECT command:

EQ for equal to	LT for less than
NE for not equal to	NL for not less than
GT for greater than	WL for within the limits
NG for not greater than	OL for outside the limits.

For example, DATE nl 870716 will cause the listing of documents with entries in the date field after 16 July 1987.

DIALOG uses suffix codes to limit sets. For example, the use of LIMITALL/

ENG would cause every subsequent set to include only items written in English. With dates or accession numbers, ranges can be specified. For example, . .LIMIT/4 yr LT 90 in Data-Star would limit the items retrieved in set number 4 to those which had 90 or less in the YR (year)field.

18.3.9 Displaying records

Once a successful search has been performed, it is necessary to display the records. Most systems have different record formats that may be selected. For example, many OPACs first display one-line records, and then allow the user to display the full record. Online search services offer a variety of commands for displaying records on the screen, offline printing and downloading. Default formats are often available, but in both CD–ROM and online search services, user-defined formats are becoming more common. Users may design permanent formats for their own use in conjunction with a specified database, or they may merely specify which fields are to be displayed. Some services offer formats that facilitate subsequent processing of records after downloading. For example, records from BLAISE can be downloaded and displayed with field tags.

Another concern is specifying which records are to be displayed. OPACs tend to let users select records and display them one at a time. CD–ROM and online have commands which allow sets of records to be specified for display.

18.3.10 Search management

In any retrieval system where a search strategy is built up from a series of search statements, it is useful to be able to review the search. Having reviewed the search, the user may wish to delete some of the search statements but save others for reuse on subsequent occasions.

18.3.11 Thesauri in retrieval

As indicated in Chapter 16, thesauri can assist in searching in a number of different ways. More sophisticated facilities for the use of thesauri are to be found in the text information management systems that can be used for in-house applications. Online thesauri are available from some hosts in respect of certain databases. Figure 18.4 shows some of the Dialog databases for which thesauri are available and also demonstrates the use of a thesaurus in searching. Such displays show relationships between terms and also the postings associated with each term.

18.3.12 Classification in searching

Some bibliographic databases include codes from classification schemes. Some of these are special schemes developed to cater for the literature of a special subject

Figure 18.4 Use of thesauri in searching on Dialog

Topic: Using the online thesaurus feature

File 11: PSYCINFO – 67–89/Aug
    (Copr. Am. Psych. Assn.)

	Set	Items	Description

(1) ?expand teenage

Ref	Items	Rt	Index-term
E1	1		TEEK
E2	305		TEEN
E3	690		*TEENAGE
E4	0	1	TEENAGE FATHERS
E5	0	1	TEENAGE MOTHERS
E6	0	1	TEENAGE PREGNANCY
E7	23		TEENAGED
E8	1		TEENAGEERS
E9	118		TEENAGER
E10	690	1	TEENAGERS
E11	1		TEENLINE
E12	3		TEENOOR

Enter P or E for more

(2) ?e e10

(3)

Ref	Items	Type	RT	Index-term
R1	690		1	*TEENAGERS
R2	30051	U	17	ADOLESCENTS
?				

Search continues

1. EXPAND on a term. If the term has related terms, a number appears next to it under the column headed **RT**.
2. EXPAND on the E-number to see the related term(s). An R-numbered list displays.
3. The column headed **Type** provides a code indicating the **type of relationship** between the R1 term and the other terms.

Figure 18.4   Continued

Topic: Using the online thesaurus feature

(4) ?e r2

Ref	Items	Type	RT	Index-term
R1	30051		17	ADOLESCENTS
R2	138	B	26	DEVELOPMENTAL AGE GROUPS
R3	690	F	1	TEENAGERS
R4	0	F	1	YOUTH (ADOLESCENTS)
R5	31	N	5	ADOLESCENT FATHERS
R6	210	N	5	ADOLESCENT MOTHERS
R7	27660	R	2	ADOLESCENCE
R8	376	R	2	ADOLESCENT ATTITUDES
R9	1464	R	10	ADOLESCENT DEVELOPMENT
R10	17403	R	15	COLLEGE STUDENTS
R11	147	R	3	HIGH SCHOOL GRADUATES
R12	10014	R	4	HIGH SCHOOL STUDENTS

Enter P or E for more

(5) ?p

Ref	Items	Type	RT	Index-term
R13	5810	R	4	JUNIOR HIGH SCHOOL STUDENTS
R14	1659	R	9	JUVENILE DELINQUENTS
R15	320	R	9	PREADOLESCENTS
R16	53	R	6	PREDELINQUENT YOUTH
R17	248	R	2	VOCATIONAL SCHOOL STUDENTS
R18	3503	R	8	YOUNG ADULTS

(6) ?s r1,r5:r9/de

		23947	ADOLESCENTS/DE
		26034	ADOLESCENT FATHERS:ADOLESCENT DEVELOPMENT
S1		44588	R1,R5:R9/DE

4. EXPAND on an R-number to see that entry's related terms.
5. Use PAGE (P) as needed to see the complete list of related terms.
6. SELECT R-numbers followed by /**DE** to retrieve only Descriptor terms.

area and have been included in the printed equivalent of the database to assist in the arrangement of printed entries. In MARC records, the Library of Congress Classification and Dewey Decimal Classification codes may be available for searching. For example, in searching BLAISE, the Dewey Decimal Classification codes may be used to expand a search. A useful strategy is to perform a keyword search to identify some records on a topic; develop the search or check its comprehensiveness by examining the classification codes on the retrieved records; and then, if appropriate, perform a search on these codes. A straight search on the classification code may also be performed. Searching on classification codes retrieves a set of related documents, and the search can be developed quite easily by exploring codes for coordinate, subordinate or superordinate subjects. Further comments on projects that have investigated the use of the Dewey Decimal Classification, Library of Congress Classification and Universal Decimal Classification in online searching are reported in Chapter 14.

18.3.13   Advanced display options

Where the records exceed the display capacity of the screen – as is often the case with records in full-text databases – facilities are necessary to support browsing through relevant portions of the document. It is necessary to be able to stop as soon as the screen is filled and to re-start. Also moving backwards and forwards through a document is useful.

One approach is to divide the text into numbered paragraphs; a list of these is screened from which various paragraphs for display can be selected. The search terms are highlighted in the text. Another approach is to use a window which displays bits of text with matching terms surrounded by a sentence or two. This is described as a KWIC facility.

Other facilities aid with display. To avoid re-keying fairly complex display commands, shortcuts may be used to invoke the last display command and then move from a single field to the full text or another field. The ability to have a set of records sorted into order online before displaying can be useful. The fields on which records are to be sorted must be specified. Numeric or financial data may be best displayed in reverse or descending order.

Some financial databases offer statistical presentation and analysis. For instance, tables of data can be compiled from a set of records by DIALOG through the REPORT command.

18.3.14   Multifile searching

The standard facilities for saving searches can be extended to multifile searching where the same search can be repeated on another database. This facility is most likely to be useful in accessing online hosts, where a number of databases might be searched in one undertaking. Database indexes can aid in the selection of the databases to search. Greater refinement can be achieved if a search can be rerun in more than one database without re-entering the search strategy. It is better still if the system makes adjustments in the search strategy to cater for the different databases and then produces an amalgamated list of retrieved records, with duplicates eliminated. Dialog OneSearch offers such a multifile search facility.

18.4 Searching of full-text databases

The searching of full-text databases presents some special problems that can usefully be reviewed briefly here. Many such problems arise from the searching of large quantities of natural language text. This section illustrates the use of the retrieval facilities described earlier in the chapter to handle natural language searching of full-text databases. Problems that need to be considered include the following:

1. Identifying the database
The first step must be to decide upon the full-text source. A specific source, such as the *Wall Street Journal,* may be available from a number of different hosts and, to compound the problem, less current or up-to-date sources may also be available on CD–ROM. Ideally this problem could be resolved by a gateway service – where the user could go online with the title of a journal and be directed to the appropriate host. But in the meantime, directories of full-text databases must be consulted.

2. What's in the database?
Not only are some sources available from more than one host, but the offerings from different hosts are different. Full text does not mean the same thing in every instance. Because of such factors as licensing arrangements, royalty considerations or editorial policy, the online version of a periodical might not include syndicated columns, obituaries, editorials or letters to the editor. Sometimes all feature articles and sometimes only major ones are available online. An individual article may include tabular data or simply a note that the print version contains a table. Again, boxed text and sidebars are sometimes excluded and sometimes indexed as separate records. Graphics and photographs are excluded from online but may be included on CD–ROM.

Currency and start dates are a further source of variation. Entire issues might be missing from the database. The definition of up-to-dateness can vary from 90 seconds to 48 hours or longer.

3. Searching
The fundamental difficulty in searching full-text databases is that there are more words to search, which tends to lead to a greater number of hits, but a smaller number of relevant hits. It can be difficult to perform a sufficiently precise search.

327

Some strategies that can be adopted to compensate for this lack of precision include the following:

1. Avoid the use of AND; the association of terms from anywhere in a full-text document will produce too many false drops.
2. Use proximity operators and other system features to increase precision and to analyse retrieved records for relevance. A full range of proximity operators is essential for effective full-text searching.
3. Use relevance ranking facilities that are based on the frequency of occurrence of words.
4. Use truncation to allow for plurals, spelling variants and alternative word endings.
5. Use jargon, synonyms and antonyms, and consult thesauri and other sources of alternative and related terms. Online thesauri or equivalency tables can help considerably in reviewing available terms.
6. Restrict search terms to one field or paragraph. In a newspaper database it may be useful to work with lead paragraphs and title or headline fields, although the detail in these fields varies.
7. Run the search in a bibliographic database to take advantage of controlled vocabulary, then switch to the full-text file to retrieve specific articles. This uses the full-text database as a document delivery tool and sidesteps the problems of retrieval.
8. Consider carefully how to display records in full-text systems, since they will almost always exceed one screen in length and may sometimes be as long as a book. The searcher should be able to view the parts of the document that contain the search terms – available as a KWIC display in Dialog. Some indication of length at the beginning of each record is useful. A brief format is valuable for browsing a number of records quickly before final selection. Review using brief formats must be performed before examining the full text. It is useful to be able to scroll a complete article or series of articles.

18.5 Search strategies

Searching must make use of the retrieval facilities outlined above. The searcher will develop a search strategy – the total set of decisions and actions taken throughout the conduct of a search. The aims of the strategy are to:

- match the desired number of relevant records,
- avoid matching irrelevant records,
- avoid set sizes which are far too large and
- avoid set sizes which are too small or even empty.

Two central tasks are the need to broaden or narrow searches. These can be

Figure 18.5   An online search demonstrating searching of full text files on Dialog

Topic: searching full-text files
   Locate stories of food tampering cases

   File 632: Chicago Tribune – May 88–89/Oct. 13
      (Copr. 1989 Chicago Tribute)

	Set	Items	Description
(1)	?s food?(w)(sabotag? or tamper?)		
		10815	FOOD?
		346	SABOTAG?
		290	TAMPER?
	S1	3	FOOD?(W)(SABOTAG? OR TAMPER?)
	?s food?		
	S2	10815	FOOD?
	?s sabotag? or tamper?		
		346	SABOTAG?
		290	TAMPER?
	S3	629	SABOTAG? OR TAMPER?
(2)	?s s2(5n)s3		
		10815	S2
		629	S3
	S4	11	S2(5N)S3
(3)	?s s2(s)s3		
		10815	S2
		629	S3
	S5	24	S2(S)S3
(4)	?s s2 and s3		
		10815	S2
		629	S3
	S6	82	S2 AND S3

Search continues

1. The 'With' (W) operator is usually too restrictive.

2. The 'Near' (N) operator allows more variations in the phrase.

3. The Subfield or (S) operator requires that the terms appear within the same paragraph.

4. ANDing terms together is too risky in full-text files because the terms may be separated by many pages.

Figure 18.5   Continued

Topic: Searching full-text files
Locate stories of food tampering cases

(5) ? set hi *
HILIGHT set on as '*'

(6) ?t s1/6,k/all

1/6,K/1
00294785
Copycats complicate British baby food case
TEXT:
. . .reward of 100,000 pounds ($170,000).

In northern England, a new report of apparent *food* *tampering*
surfaced when a family was taken to a hospital for treatment after eating
hamburgers contaminated. . .

1/6,K/2
00294299
More baby *food* *tampering* being reported in Britain

1/6,K/3
00219286
Council delays action on gay rights, property taxes
TEXT:
. . .food from sealed containers in grocery stores. The ordinance is
intended to protect consumers from *food* *tampering*, said its sponsor,
Ald. Bernard Stone (50th).

Search continues

5. Use SET HI command to have SELECTed terms appear in a brighter type, reverse
video, or surrounded by a chosen character (in this case, an asterisk (*)).

6. TYPE records using pre-defined Format 6 and KWIC to see the main topic as well as
the SELECTed terms.

Note: *The DIALOG accession number appears when a predefined format is used or
when the AN display code is used in a user-defined format.*

Figure 18.5   Continued

Topic: Searching full-text files
Locate stories of food tampering cases

?s s6 not s5
                82   S6
                24   S5
        S7   58   S6 NOT S5
?t s7/3,k/1

    7/3,K/1
00337041
 Gorbachev fails to get full strike ban

Chicago Tribune (CT) – WEDNESDAY October 4, 1989
By: Vincent J. Schodolski, Chicago Tribune
Edition: NORTH SPORTS FINAL   Section: News   Page: 1   Zone: C
Word Count: 679
 Gorbachev fails to get full strike ban
LEAD PARAGRAPHS:
 . . .agreed on a temporary strike ban in key sectors of the economy to
ensure winter *food* and fuel supplies.

The Supreme Soviet, or parliament, also voted overwhelmingly to tell
Azerbaijanis blocking. . .
TEXT:
 . . .has imposed on Armenia, a blockade that has cut the shipment of
important goods, including *food* and fuel, by nearly 90 percent.

It said unless the blockade–the latest twist in. . .deteriorating quickly. The
earthquake occurred last December.

"There is no petrol at all, and the *food* situation is getting worse and
⑦ worse," said Leon Aramjants, chief spokesman for the Armenian Foreign
Ministry.

He confirmed that trainloads of cement, destined for the reconstruction of
buildings had been *sabotaged* in Azerbaijan.

.
.
.

7. ANDing terms together may add a few appropriate records, but the inappropriate
   records far exceed the 'good' retrieval.

achieved by changing the search terms and combining them in different ways using the retrieval devices outlined above. A search strategy is not only concerned with the final search statement which results in the desired document set, but is also concerned with the way in which subsequent search statements are input to develop the searcher's knowledge of the number of postings under various terms and the appropriateness of specific search terms in the context of the search and the database. The development of effective search strategies requires experience with the subject, its literature and the database being searched (in particular its indexing strategies).

Research into search strategies has identified four strategy models: Briefsearch, Building blocks, Successive fractions and Citation pearl growing.

1. *Briefsearch* uses AND to retrieve a few articles crudely and quickly. These may be used as the basis for a further search.
2. *Building blocks* takes the concepts in a query and extends them by synonyms or related terms using OR. All concepts are then ANDed to produce the final set. This is a comprehensive approach, but it may be time–consuming and involves considerable keying.
3. *Successive fractions* is a method for reducing a large set already created by using AND and NOT as set narrowing devices. This may be used during the final stage of a strategy.
4. *Citation pearl growing* starts from a small set or even just one document and uses any suitable terms (including names and subject words in the original citation) to identify other documents.

Recommended reading

Note: Many of the readings in Chapters 19, 20, 21 and 23 are relevant to the theme of this chapter.

Basch, R (1989), 'The seven deadly sins of full-text searching', *Database*, August, 15–23.

Basch, R (1991), 'My most difficult search', *Database, June, 65–67.*

Beaumont, J and Cox, J P (1989), *Retrospective conversion: a practical guide for libraries*, Westport, CT and London: Meckler.

Boyce, B R and McLain, J P (1989), 'Entry point depth and online searching using a controlled vocabulary', *Journal of the American Society for Information Science*, **40**, 273–76.

'Nexis offers Turbo searching', (1991), *Information World Review*, **57**, March, 10.

PART IV
SYSTEMS

19 Online information retrieval systems: external services

19.1 Introduction

Online information retrieval services, which permit users scattered around the world to search databases held on a central computer, started to develop in the late 1960s and the early 1970s. There are now over 4600 databases extending across science, technology, business, social science and the humanities, mounted on a number of computers spread at various locations throughout the world. Users are able to use terminals many miles distant to search the computer database of their choice, with the support of a telecommunications network to link terminal to computer. This can be summarized as:

Workstation—Telecommunications network—Computer

19.2 Equipment

Workstations for use in online searching may be dumb terminals but are usually microcomputers. An intelligent terminal such as a microcomputer has a number of advantages. Its memory can be used to prepare a search strategy before connecting it to the host computer and to download results onto floppy disc. In addition, microcomputers are widely available in offices and may be used for applications other than online searching. Microcomputers require an asynchronous communications adaptor in order to be able to communicate with other computers. More advanced monitors can accommodate full colour and an advanced graphics adaptor card slotted into the computer. Such facilities allow the selection of a combination of background and typescript colours and the use of windowing environments.

19.2.1 Telecommunications

In order that computers many miles distant from each other can communicate, or that a terminal can send messages to a computer, there has to be a medium for communication. This is usually achieved primarily through a telecommunications network. There are two components of such access – the telephone and national and international networks.

It is possible to link directly to a host via a telephone network, but this is expensive. It is cheaper to dial into a telecommunications network or Public Data Network (PDN) such as PSS in the United Kingdom or INTELCOMFRANCE in France. PSS can be accessed at several points or nodes or Packet Switching Exchanges (PSEs) by dialling the number of the closest node.

In order to use PSS, it is necessary to have a Network User Identity or NUI, which is a network password. The host will supply a Network User Address (NUA) and a password to enter its system. Access to international telecommunications is available through PSS and IPSS. Some hosts, such as ESA-IRS and DIALOG, have their own private data networks that can be used instead of PSS and IPSS. These can either be accessed directly, or the user may dial into PSS and be routed to the private network. These are cheaper than the public networks.

Permanent datalines can be installed between a workstation and the PSS/IPSS network. This saves the time and money involved in accessing PSS. Large organizations may have their own computer network, with connections to PSS; such networks will offer better quality data transmission.

19.2.2 Modem

A modem converts the digital signal which is sent out from the terminal into an analogue signal which can be transmitted along a telephone line. A further modem at the host computer end of the line converts the signal back into digital form. With the growth in ISDN, modems will become redundant, but most users currently still require one.

There are several types of modem available. The most basic are used with a telephone handset on which the number is dialled. Better modems allow the user to enter the number at the workstation keyboard. More sophisticated modems, when used with a microcomputer, can log on automatically to specified hosts.

Modems may operate at different speeds, as measured by the baud rate. There are four rates currently available: 300 baud (sends or receives at 30 cps), 1200/75 baud (sends at 75 cps, receives at 1200 cps), 1200/1200 baud and 2400/2400 baud, with a move towards 9600 baud in the near future. Modems can be set at different speeds.

Transmission of data can be duplex or half duplex. In duplex mode, data are transmitted simultaneously in both directions. In half duplex transmission is in one direction only. Modems must be set to be compatible with the mode used by the host. Most hosts use full, but some use half duplex.

19.2.3 Printer

To make a copy of any data that is displayed on the screen, a printer is necessary. The options need to be evaluated for cost, print quality and speed. Compatibility and noise should not be overlooked.

19.2.4 Software

Microcomputers require software which enables them to act as terminals; this software is known as communications software. The most straightforward software simply sets the microcomputer as a terminal, whilst the more complex versions support logging on and the entering of search strategies in the microcomputer before going online and forwarding to the host computer. Another facility is the downloading of results to floppy or hard discs. There are also some host-specific packages such as Dialoglink and Orbitmaster. These offer host-specific features such as the storage of records of costs and databases used. More advanced packages translate various host command languages either into standard language or into the host language of the user's choice. Examples are ACOM 2.0 from Information Automations and TransNet from EduSoft SA.

19.3 Online search services

Online search services – sometimes known as online system suppliers, hosts or online service spinners – are responsible for mounting databases upon a computer and making the arrangements necessary for such databases to be searchable from a large number of remote user terminals. Some database producers are also vendors. For example, Mead Data Central both compiles and provides access to LEXIS and NEXIS. Cuadra (1988) lists well over 500 such service suppliers. The marketplace for hosts has been very volatile recently. Many new entrants, including Reuters and Jordans, have been accustomed to providing information directly to the end-user which has fuelled a general trend towards end-user services. In addition to new entrants there have been a number of mergers and acquisitions in the last few years. Thus to be fully conversant with available services, it is necessary to monitor current service suppliers and what they offer.

Many major databases are available through what are known as supermarket hosts or vendors. Such hosts purchase or license databases from producers and convert data into a uniform format with standardized element names so that the basic commands and search techniques apply across all the databases they offer. Hosts also provide various support services such as manuals, search aids and training facilities.

Most supermarket hosts offer a range of 50 to 300 plus databases. (For more details of the range of databases see section 19.7.) In order to have access to the databases offered by a specific host, it is necessary to sign on as a user. Most information managers start by signing with two, three or four main suppliers, familiarizing themselves with their systems before progressing to a wider range of services and databases. Once a user is registered, a password will be issued which

337

provides access to all or most of the databases offered by the host as and when the user wishes. Many of the major databases are available through more than one host. It is necessary to select both the most appropriate database for any given search and also the most appropriate host. The comparison and evaluation of hosts will be considered further later, but first some of the major service suppliers are briefly reviewed.

DIALOG

DIALOG Information Retrieval Services Inc was operated by Lockheed Information Systems of Palo Alto in California until it was sold to Knight Rider in 1988. Over 308 databases are available. DIALOG was one of the first services to operate commercially, commencing in 1972, and has established a position as a market leader. DIALOG databases span:

- science and technology: CERAMIC ABSTRACTS, COMPENDEX PLUS, CURRENT TECHNOLOGY INDEX, INSPEC
- bibliography: BOOKS IN PRINT, LC MARC, ULRICHS INTERNATIONAL PERIODICALS DIRECTORY
- reference: DATABASE OF DATABASES, EVERYMAN'S ENCYCLOPEDIA, BIOGRAPHY MASTER INDEX
- business: D + B – CANADIAN DUNS MARKET IDENTIFIERS, KOMPASS UK, MOODY'S CORPORATE NEWS – US
- news: APNEWS, MIDEAST FILE, WASHINGTON POST ELECTRONIC EDITION
- social sciences and humanities: A-V ONLINE, ERIC, PSYCINFO, SOCIOLOGICAL ABSTRACTS.

DIALOG continues to add new databases and to diversify into new markets. Enhancements to search software are also announced from time to time. Examples of services include:

1. Knowledge Index, a low–cost evening and weekend service for accessing about 50 of DIALOG's databases;
2. DIALOG Business Connection, an easy-to-use, menu-driven service for business people;
3. DIALOG Medical Connection, a similar service for biomedical researchers and health professionals;
4. Dialmail, an electronic mail service;
5. DIALOG onDisc, various databases on CD–ROM with DIALOG search software;
6. DIALOG Menus, a menu-based service that offers access to many Dialog databases;

7. DIALOG Alert, a current awareness service, and
8. DIALORDER, a document ordering service.

ESA–IRS

The European Space Agency's Information Retrieval Service (ESA–IRS) was first established in the form of the European Space Research Organization's Space Documentation Service in 1965. Based at Frascati in Italy, ESA–IRS was one of the first organizations to offer online search facilities. Databases originally focused on space science and technology, but ESA–IRS now offers access to over 130 databases, mostly still in science and technology. Apart from this core, other areas in which databases are offered include:

- business and finance: ABI/INFORM, BUSINESS SOFTWARE
- corporate intelligence: CHEM-INTELL, JORDANWATCH, NTIS
- health and safety: HSELINE, NIOSH
- patents: COMPUTERPAT, PATSEARCH
- news: BIS INFOMAT, MIDEAST.

Software has been developed with the introduction of DOWNLOAD, ZOOM (for analysing terms in retrieved sets) and QUESTCLUSTERS (for searching multiple databases). Other developments include Mikrotel, which assists users with micro-computers in linking into the service, an electronic mail service and the facilities by which users can create their own menu interface. ESA–IRS is widely used in Europe where a network of national centres provide local support and training. ESA–IRS can be searched using ESA–QUEST commands and also using the European Common Command Language (CCL). Many CCL commands and features can also be used whilst in ESA-QUEST mode. Hyperline was introduced in 1990; this is a hypertext tool which allows users to jump from one block of text to another.

DATA STAR

DATA STAR, mounted by Radio-Suisse, also make a range of databases available. Examples are:

- business: ABI/INFORM, PREDICASTS, MANAGEMENT CONTENTS, ICC DIRECTORY OF UK COMPANIES, HOPPENSTEDT (FRG, AUS-TRIA, BENELUX)
- biomedical: MEDLINE, AIDS DATABASE, PSYCHINFO
- chemical: CASEARCH, TOXLINE
- engineering: NTIS, INSPEC AND COMPENDEX
- news: DOW JONES, PHARMECEUTICAL AND HEALTH CARE INDUSTRY NEWS.

BRS Information Technologies

BRS Information Technologies of New York was established in 1977. The service provides access to over 130 databases (including reference and source databases) 45 of which are exclusive. Acquired by the Maxwell Group in 1988, the BRS database catalogue is being developed to complement those available from other Pergamon ORBIT Infoline hosts. BRS has a strong collection of medical databases including the AIDS Knowledge Base, MEDLINE, EMBASE and BIOSIS PREVIEWS. Other databases mounted cover:

- busines: ABI/INFORM, HARVARD BUSINESS REVIEW/ONLINE
- social science and humanities: ARTS AND HUMANITIES SEARCH, SOCIAL SCISEARCH, SOCIOLOGICAL ABSTRACTS
- multidisciplinary: MAGAZINE INDEX, BOOKS IN PRINT, NEWS-SEARCH.

The search software BRS/SEARCH is command driven and is marketed for the establishment of in-house databases. A menu approach is available through the BRS/Brkthru service. BRS/After Dark offers subscribers access to a selection of BRS databases at a low rate. BRS/Europe has developed the BRS/Search software to be compatible with CD–ROM databases. BRS/Colleague, containing the full texts of various journals and books, uses a menu-driven interface which accepts search terms in natural language English.

Profile information

Profile, part of FT Information Online (and previously known as Datasolve), specializes in full-text online information tailored to the requirements of specific business sectors. Over 100 sources are available including major newspapers, other international news services, international business magazines and specialist publications. McCARTHY ONLINE is also available.

STN International

Scientific and Technical Information Network (STN) International is a cooperative venture between the Japan Association for International Chemical Information, FIZ–Karlsruhe and the Chemical Abstracts Service. STN mounts around 70 databases.

QUESTEL

QUESTEL is a French online host. A subsidiary of the COGECOM Group, it handles approximately 60 databases on topics such as patents, chemistry, trademarks, medicine, science and technology, business and news. As well as international databases, there is strong representation of French-language databases and databases compiled in France. The Questel software is designed to be adaptable for various types of end-user. Questel Plus is a more powerful interface available for information retrieval specialists; DARC is a chemical substructure system introduced in 1979.

ORBIT Search Service

ORBIT Search Service is now a division of Pergamon ORBIT, having been acquired from the Systems Development Corporation which initiated the service in 1972. It concentrates on science, technical and patent information. Patent information databases include INPADOC, WPI, CLAIMS, JAPIO and USPATENTS. Technical databases include several from British research associations such as AQUALINE, PIRS, RAPRA ABSTRACTS AND WORLD SURFACE COATINGS ABSTRACTS. Approximately 100 databases are available. A special telecommunications link, referred to as ORBITNET, enables European users to access directly the ORBIT computers which are based in McLean (Virginia).

PFDS (Pergamon Financial Data Services)

PFDS is a further division of Pergamon ORBIT Infoline and prior to 1988 was known as Pergamon Infoline. PFDS specializes in services to the European business community, with databases in:

- marketing and sales prospecting: DUN AND BRADSTREET KEY BRITISH ENTERPRISES, DUNS MARKET IDENTIFIERS, INDUSTRIAL MARKET LOCATIONS and IRISH COMPANY PROFILES.
- finance and credit checking: JORDANWATCH, INFOCHECK
- corporate intelligence: BIS INFOMAT, NEWSFILE, WHO OWNS WHOM, CHEMICAL AGE PROJECT FILE and DATAMONITOR (FULL TEXT REPORT)

Searching is via the BASIS software, with a front-end menu option to assist less experienced searchers, such as end-users.

Mead Data Central

Mead Data Central is part of the American Mead Corporation. LEXIS was introduced in 1973, a full-text online database intended for lawyers. NEXIS was launched in 1980 as a full-text business and news database.

341

Figure 19.1 Smaller online service providers

Provider	Country	Database Coverage
BELINDIS	Belgium	Belgian databases, INIS
CED	Italy	Italian law
Dialcom	United Kingdom	Business
Data–centralen	Denmark	Various
DIMDI	Germany	Biomedical, German language
Dow Jones News/Retrieval	United States	Business, investment support
Fiz-Technik	Germany	Engineering and industrial management
ICC DIRECT	United Kingdom	Company finance
INPADOC	Austria	Patents
JOIS	Japan	Various, Japanese language
KOMPASS ONLINE	United Kingdom	Company
Meridian Systems	United Kingdom	Various, POLIS
TNO	Netherlands	Shipping

ECHO

ECHO, the European Commission's Host Organization, has offered access to databases and data banks either wholly or partially sponsored by the Commission of the European Communities. Databases are mainly of a European nature and many are multilingual.

This section has reviewed some of the significant online service providers and demonstrated the ranges of databases offered by these hosts. (Some other online service providers are listed in Figure 19.1.) These examples should demonstrate that:

1. Some online service providers offer a very wide spectrum of databases, whilst others focus their offerings in specific market sectors.
2. In terms of the number of databases offered, the size of the online service providers varies considerably; over the past five years, however, all providers have significantly increased the number of databases that they offer.
3. Many of the large service providers are based in the United States, with a wide range of smaller hosts operating in Europe.
4. In addition to the basic online search facility, the providers offer other services such as electronic mail, menu-based interfaces, document ordering facilities and current awareness services.
5. Many databases are available from more than one online service supplier.

19.4 Hosts-points for comparison

Database hosts must be compared and contrasted in order that a sound selection of host may be made for any specific search. Obviously, the overall objective is to retrieve as many relevant documents, and as few irrelevant documents in the minimum time and at the least cost and user inconvenience. Although hosts offer similar services, and the pressures of the marketplace mean that any vital facility must be offered by all of the major hosts, there are differences between the services offered by the different hosts. Apart from the different databases available from the different hosts, there may be differences in the way in which any given database can be searched under various hosts. For some databases the selection of the database will determine the hosts, but on other occasions other factors must also be considered. Specifically, then hosts may vary in respect of:

1. *The databases offered* As already explored, the numbers of databases offered by any specific host will vary, as will the subject coverage and languages of the available databases. Also, different hosts may have different time spans with regard to any given database available for online searching.
2. *Search facilities* The elements of records that can be searched may differ from one host to another. Certainly the field formats may vary and fields names may differ. (See Chapters 5 and 6.) Some systems offer more extensive facilities with regard to contextual or proximity searching and truncation. For non-bibliographic databases, various special facilities may be required.
3. *Command languages* Command languages are an essential feature of the search facilities of any given host. (Figure 19.2 summarizes and compares some differences between different hosts.) A command language is the language with which the search proceeds; the commands are the instructions that the searcher can issue to the computer. Different hosts have different command languages depending upon their search software. Command languages are considered in a little more detail in section 19.6.
4. *Formats for records* Various formats are available for viewing the details of retrieved references. Sometimes it is possible for the searcher to select the elements that he requires, but in searching other hosts only a few standard formats are available.
5. *Additional facilities* Many hosts offer other facilities in addition to the basic online search facility. Often SDI or document delivery services are available. These may become increasingly important as hosts seek to match the needs of users more closely. User-friendly interfaces can be helpful for inexperienced searchers; these include BRS/Menus or the simplified command language offered by Dialog's Knowledge Index. Electronic mail and online document ordering are also available.
6. *Support services* Most hosts offer some support and training services. Help desks, training courses, manuals, newsletters and other search aids can

343

enhance a searcher's effectiveness. Good training and careful instruction can often increase a searcher's efficiency with even the most complex searching systems and databases. The availability of such support services must be considered, but availability is not the only factor. Support services must be effective, accessible (for example, training courses in the searcher's own locality) and reasonably cheap.

7. *Time availability* Most hosts are not available 24 hours a day, seven days of the week. Some down time is necessary for maintenance and updating of the files. Hosts are available for a variable number of hours in the day, and a variable number of days in the week. For example, DATA–STAR is available on Mondays from 10.00 to 18.30, and on Tuesday to Fridays from 8.00 to 18.30 (Central European Time). Times should be sought which coincide with the user's requirements.

8. *Cost* The cost per search using a specific database can be difficult to assess, but is obviously an important aspect of the searching process. There will be special rates for additional services such as SDI or document delivery. Normally, costs will comprise database connect charges and print charges per reference. The cost of telecommunications should also be considered, and this may vary between and within countries. The database connect charges sometimes include database royalty charges, but for other hosts these will be charged separately. Print charges are usually per reference retrieved, with online and offline prints often attracting different tariffs, and different record formats being charged at different rates. But matters are not as straightforward as merely analysing the direct costs. If extensive use is likely to be made of a particular database, discount charges are available by contracting to buy a predetermined number of connect hours per year.

9. *Experience* The searcher's experience with a specific host may be an important factor in determining his search effectiveness. Thus, from the searcher's point of view it is important not only to assess the specific features of the host, but also to examine his own skills.

19.5 Command languages

A command language is the set of commands or instructions that the searcher uses to instruct the computer to perform certain operations. Negus has identified 14 basic functions for which commands must be present in any online command language. This set of commands forms the basis for the EURONET Common Command Language, which is available for searching on some European hosts. These same functions are also seen to be important in framing the International Standard for Command Languages.

These command functions are:

CONNECT	to provide for logging on
BASE	to identify the database to be searched
FIND	to input a search term
DISPLAY	to display a list of alphabetically linked terms
RELATE	to display logically related terms
SHOW	to print references online
PRINT	to print references offline
FORMAT	to specify the format to be displayed
DELETE	to delete search terms or print requests
SAVE	to save a search formulation for later use on the same or another database on the same system
OWN	to use a system's own command when the general system, in this case EURONET, does not cater for a specialized function available on a particular system.
STOP	to end the session and logoff
MORE	to request the system to display more information, for instance to continue the alphabetical display of terms.
HELP	to obtain guidance online when in difficulty.

In comparing the commands of several hosts, Figure 19.2 demonstrates clearly that there is no standard command language. The different command languages are associated with the different retrieval software used by the various hosts. As far as users are concerned, standardization of command languages is highly desirable. The need to become familiar with different command languages for different hosts is a considerable barrier to effective retrieval. In particular, when a command means one thing in one system and something else in another, confusion ensues. Hosts are less keen to standardize, although the EURONET Common Command Language has been adopted by some hosts such as ESA–IRS. Although there is some recognition of the potential benefits of standardization, progress is slow. The picture is further clouded by the introduction of menu-based and natural language interfaces.

19.6 Databases

The array of databases available through one or other of the online hosts has expanded rapidly. As mentioned in Chapter 5, there are reference databases and source databases. The subject areas that such databases cover may range from relatively narrow interests to interdisciplinary concerns.

The number of source databases which have been created is a matter for open speculation, the majority being private. Many private databases and databanks are consistently supported and updated by individuals and organizations on micro-computers, mini-computers and mainframes. Here we are concerned only with publicly available databases. In this realm, there are data banks covering, for instance, business statistics and government series, chemical dictionaries and direc-

345

Figure 19.2 A comparison of some common commands from various online hosts

CAS ONLINE Commands – Comparison Chart

COMMAND FUNCTION	PROFILE	DIALOG	HOST ORBIT	BRS	ESA/IRS
Prompt	>	?	USER:	-;	?
Change files	SELECT	FILE BEGIN	FILE	..CHANGE/	.FILE BEGIN
Execute a search	GET PICK	SELECT SELECT STEPS COMBINE	– (enter term)	– (enter term)	SELECT COMBINE
Precedence of Boolean operators	1. OR (,) 2. AND (+) 3. NOT (–)	1. NOT 2. AND 3. OR	1. AND 2. NOT 3. OR	1. AND 2. NOT 3. OR	1. NOT 2. AND 3. OR
Look at inverted index	EXPAND	EXPAND	NEIGHBOR	ROOT	EXPAND
Specify level of postings detail	– – –	------	AUDIT	..SET DETAIL	------
Restrict search	(date ranging)	LIMIT	(date ranging)	..LIMIT	LIMIT
Save information for later use	SAVE	SAVE	STORE	..SAVE	END/SAVE
Remove saved items from storage	REVIEW (name)	.RECALL (name) .RELEASE	RECALL (name) PURGE (name)	..PURGE PS (name)	.RECALL (name) .RELEASE

Look at answers online	CONTEXT HEADLINE TEXT TITLE	TYPE	PRINT	..PRINT	TYPE
Print answers offline	OFFLINE	PRINT	PRINT OFFLINE	..PRINTOFF	PRINT
Cancel offline print order	– – –	PR-(set no.)	(Done within PRINT command)	..PURGE (print no.)	PR-(set no.)
Order original document	– – –	ORDERITEM	ORDER (Supplier)	..ORDER	ORDER
View session history	REVIEW	DISPLAY SETS	HISTORY	..DISPLAY	DISPLAY SETS
Restart session	– – –	BEGIN	RESTART	..PURGE	BEGIN
Send message to vendor	MSG	------	COMMENT	MSGS (address BERS)	
End the online session	END	LOGOFF	STOP Y or LOGOFF Y	..OFF	LOGOFF

tory files. In some subject fields, notably business, there may be both bibliographic and source databases covering different aspects of the same topic.

Significant variations exist both in the size of databases and also in the types of databases available across subject areas. For example, full-text databases are dominant in business and legal information, but less central in science technology. There are a number of directories of online databases (e.g. Williams, Hall, Britline, Armstrong and Large). The directories of the major hosts, such as Dialog, are a vital source of information on the range of databases available and their scope.

Databases can be produced by three types of organizations:

- government bodies, for example, CHILD ABUSE AND NEGLECT from the Children's Bureau of the National Center on Child Abuse and Neglect (US), and AGRICOLA from the US National Agricultural Library, and others.
- professional societies, for example, INSPEC from the Institution of Electrical Engineers (UK), WORLD ALUMINIUM ABSTRACTS, from the American Society for Metals, and MLA Bibliography from the Modern Language Association.
- commercial organizations, for example, SCISEARCH and SOCIAL SCISEARCH, from the Institute for Scientific Information, and D&B–DUNS FINANCIAL RECORDS, from Dun & Bradstreet.

Figure 19.3 will repay full consideration. It is more than a list of databases. It demonstrates that some, but not all, have a printed equivalent, and it identifies some of the various types of databases.

19.7 A checklist of features to consider in comparing and evaluating databases

As earlier sections and Figure 19.3 amply demonstrate, there is a great deal of choice with regards to databases. No two databases are identical. There are usually only a limited number of databases covering any given subject field or type of literature. However, even if two databases appear to have similar coverage, they usually differ in some other respect. In general the appropriate selection of database is important for effective retrieval. In order to make such a selection it is necessary to become familiar with the range of databases that any specific librarian or information worker might be asked to consult so that searching can proceed effectively. Such familiarity can be cultivated with experience. Despite the plethora of databases, the searcher will frequently find that there is no ideal database for a specific search and that two or more databases may have to be consulted before a search is complete. Some of the factors to consider in the selection of databases are as follows:

Figure 19.3   Some examples of databases available on Dialog

Subject	Examples	Producer	Printed equivalent/ comment
Chemistry	CA SEARCH	Chemical Abstracts	Chemical Abstracts/very large
	Fine Chemicals Database	Chemron Inc.	Chemical Products/full text
	HELLBRON	Chapman and Hall	Dictionary of Organic Compounds; Dictionary of Organometallic Compounds etc./full text
	SEDBASE	Elsevier Science Publishers	/Full text; analysis of drug side-effect literature
Biology, Medicine, Toxicology	MEDLINE	US National Library of Medicine	Index Medicus etc/very large
	BIOSIS PREVIEWS	BIOSIS	Biological Abstracts
	EMBASE	Elsevier Science Publishers	/Various, e.g. anatomy, anthropology
	TOXLINE	US National Library of Medicine	/Toxicology
	Health Devices Alerts	ECRI	Reports on medical device problems/full text
Energy and Environment	ENERGYLINE	R R Bowker	Energy Information Abstracts
	ENVIROLINE	R R Bowker	–
Engineering and Physics	COMPENDEX PLUS	Engineering Information Inc.	Engineering Index/
	ISMEC	Cambridge Scientific Abstracts	/mechanical engineering
	INSPEC	Institution of Electrical Engineers	Science Abstracts/physics, electronics and electrical engineering, computer science
Agriculture, Food etc.	CAB ABSTRACTS	CAB INTER-NATIONAL	Various e.g. Agricultural engineering abstracts/
	AGRICOLA	US National Agricultural Library	Agriculture
	FOOD SCIENCE & TECHNOLOGY ABSTRACTS	International Food Information Service	Food Science and Technology Abstracts
Geology, Geophysics	OCEANIC ABSTRACTS	Cambridge Scientific Abstracts	Oceanic Abstracts/ oceanography
	GEOARCHIVE	Geosystems	

Continued

Figure 19.3   Continued

	GEOBASE	Geo Abstracts Ltd	Geographical Abstracts etc./
Social Sciences	SOCIAL SCISEARCH	Institute for Scientific Information	Social Sciences Citation Index
	PSYCINFO	American Psychological Association	Psychological Abstracts
	SOCIOLOGICAL ABSTRACTS	Sociological Abstracts Inc.	Sociological Abstracts
	EXCEPTIONAL CHILD EDUCATION RESOURCES	Council for Exceptional Children	
Humanities	HISTORICAL ABSTRACTS	ABC–CLIO Inc	Historical Abstracts/
	ART & HUMANITIES SEARCH	Institute for Scientific Information	Art & Humanities Citation Index/
	ART BIBLIOGRA- PHIES MODERN	ABC–CLIO Inc.	/irregular updating
	MUSIC LITERATURE INTERNATIONAL	International RILM Center	/twice a year
Business	INFORMAT INTER- NATIONAL BUSINESS	Predicasts	/bibliographic
	INSIDER TRADING MONITOR	Invest/Net Inc.	/insider trading filings/ daily update
	ICC INTERNATIONAL BUSINESS RESEARCH	ICC Stockbroker Research Ltd. and Key Note Ltd.	/Stockbroker research reports etc; full text
	INDUSTRY DATA SOURCES	Information Access Company	/Bibliographic data on sources of financial and marketing data
	HARVARD BUSINESS REVIEW	John Wiley & Sons Inc.	/full text
News	FINANCIAL TIMES FULL – TEXT	Financial Times Business Information Ltd.	/full text; updated daily
	FACTS ON FILE	Facts on File	Facts on File World News Digest/news summaries
	REUTERS	Reuters US Inc.	Text of new releases
Others	PASCAL	Centre de Documentation et Techniques Scientifiques	79 Pascal journals/ wide science coverage; bilingual file

Continued

Figure 19.3   Continued

NTIS	National Technical Information Service	/government sponsored research – wide subject coverage
DISSERTATION ABSTRACTS ONLINE	University Microforms International	Dissertation Abstracts International etc.
WORLD PATENTS INDEX	Derwent Publications Ltd.	World Patents Index
CLAIMS/US PATENTS ABSTRACTS	IFI/Plenum Data Corp.	Official Gazette of US Patent Office
INPADOC/FAMILY AND LEGAL STATUS	INPADOC, Vienna	INPADOC Patent Gazette (microfiche)/patents

Note: Those titles listed as the printed equivalent are not necessarily exact equivalents. Often only the major printed source has been indicated. For example, BIOSIS Previews contains citations from Biological Abstracts, Biological Abstracts/Reports, Reviews, Meetings and BioResearch Index.

1. Coverage: does the database provide access to the appropriate subject field: Is it comprehensive? To what extent does the coverage of the database overlap that of other databases in similar subjects?
2. Type of database and the information supplied, including bibliographical information, full-text information, facts or figures.
3. What is the currency of the file and the frequency of updates (for example, monthly, daily)? Some databases, such as those containing stock exchange information, are updated continuously (in real-time); bibliographic databases are often updated monthly.
4. How easy is the database to use, and has the user experience of searching this database, and is s/he therefore likely to achieve effective retrieval?
5. Output, both on screen and in hard copy. What are the options for the record content? Is there an abstract as part of the record? Is there a full-text record available on the database?
6. Indexing language: is it controlled or natural language or both? What are the extent and specificity of indexing, and so on? Are all of these factors appropriate to the desired retrieval performance in this specific instance?
7. Cost.
8. Documentation and search aids available to support searching on the databases; this includes classification schedules, printed or machine-viewable thesauri, and so on.

9. Any biases which might adversely affect search results (for example, emphasis on US or European published material).
10. Time span: length of database available online or its starting date.
11. The host through which the database and its facilities are available (see 19.3).

19.8 Managing the online information service

This section briefly reviews some of the key issues that need to be resolved when a library or other organization considers offering an online information service to end–users. As discussed earlier, many of the external online search service vendors or hosts also market their services directly to end-users; in many organizations some access to these hosts is centralized and operated through a library or other intermediary agency, whilst access by other users to other hosts may be direct. Centralization brings some benefits associated with financial control and coordination of the facilities being used within an organization. Central expertise can be developed, training can be coordinated and expertise shared. In addition, the centralized facility is likely to cater both for the occasional searcher and for frequent searchers who wish to use a different database or host from that with which they are familiar. An organization needs to decide on the extent to which centralization is appropriate. Assuming that some facilities at least are offered centrally, there are a number of decisions to be made during the implementation phase of a service.

First it is necessary to establish which databases are best accessed online, as opposed to on CD–ROM or in microform or printed form. Once these databases have been identified, consideration can be given to the hosts that offer the best access to the combination of databases required. It is likely that one or more of the popular supermarket hosts will be amongst the first that an information manager will sign with. The factors for comparing hosts are listed in section 19.4. Once the hosts have been selected, contracts can be signed.

Telecommunications will be another consideration. The organization may already have a direct link to the national telecommunications network. If not, arrangements must be made to dial the nearest access points or nodes of that service. A direct line that does not pass through a switchboard is preferable for online searching.

Attention might then turn to the workstation for online searching. The three components of the workstation – the microcomputer, search software and modem – have been considered at the beginning of this chapter. The workstation may already be in place. It is certainly likely that an appropriate microcomputer will already be available within the organization; it may be necessary to decide whether a dedicated microcomputer is needed. Communications software and a modem may need to be acquired specially. If new equipment must be purchased, it is wise to adhere to organizational standards and to acquire a reliable workstation with suitable maintenance arrangements.

Once the basic configuration has been selected, there are a number of management issues concerning the way in which the service is to be offered for resolution. These include:

1. *Location of workstations*   There may be one or several workstations; indeed, services may be available to users in their own offices. The number of workstations and their location need to be decided. If a workstation is to be placed in a public area, such as in a library, the location should be quiet to aid concentration. Documentation for several hosts will be bulky, which will probably restrict availability to one location.

2. *Searchers*   Who are to be the searchers? End-users or staff? If the service is based on information staff acting as intermediaries, how many staff should be trained? The greater the number of staff who are trained, the more practical it is to integrate online information retrieval with other services offered to users. On the other hand if too many staff are trained, it is difficult to coordinate the services offered and to keep all staff up-to-date.

3. *Charging and Fees*   Practices with regards to charging vary. Some libraries feel that online searches should be free to users in the same way as other services are free. Other library managers more aware of the pressure to recoup costs would argue that users place greater value on services for which they have to pay. Whatever policy is adopted in respect of charging, costs of online searching must be met one way or another. A further possibility is to charge certain categories of users, such as students, and to make services free to other categories, such as staff.

4. *Record Keeping.*   Careful records must be kept of searches performed which should be checked against accounts submitted by the search service supplier. Records also generate management information for monitoring the use being made of the service.

5. *Documentation*   Documentation includes looseleaf manuals, thesauri, directories of databases and newsletters. This must be organized, made available and kept up-to-date. A procedures manual can also help control the way in which searching is performed. An in–house procedures manual might indicate which search services are available, access routes, passwords and current policy concerning the offering of online searching to users.

6. *Impact on Other Services*   Searching bibliographic databases is likely to generate a demand for documents that are not available in the local library. Interlibrary loans requests will probably increase, and it may be necessary to review the local collection.

7. *Review*   All aspects of the online service should be kept under review. The service suppliers and databases available change, as do the needs of users. Continuous monitoring with a formal annual review is appropriate.

353

19.9   Recent and future trends for online

Recent years have witnessed an upsurge in acceptability to society of computer-based access to information. As part of the infrastructure of the information society, online services are likely to benefit from increased interest in computer-based information; on the other hand, they must retain their market niche in the face of competition from new media such as CD–ROM. There is still scope for the extension of online into other countries, such as the Eastern bloc and Third World countries. This may lead to more databases, more hosts and a more complex marketplace.

The online industry has been subject to a number of takeovers and buyouts which affect the orientation of the service suppliers. DIALOG was sold in 1988 to Knight Rider, resulting in a shift towards business information and full-text databases. QUESTEL split from the French state-owned system Telesystemes in a management buyout. Robert Maxwell added ORBIT to his stable in 1987. INFO-LINE became PFDS, retained its business databases and gained some from ORBIT. ORBIT retained all science databases and gained those on INFOLINE. Maxwell also bought BRS in 1990.

The industry is ripe for further changes and developments which can be expected in the following areas.

1.   Interfaces
Many menu-based interfaces have been introduced, triggered by increasing emphasis on full-text databases and end-user services. Users have become accustomed to the type of interface available in business software and CD–ROM, and expect the same quality of interface from online services. Standardization of command languages is a long running issue; Garman argues that more progress should be evident soon. Other work has focused on the development of intelligent interfaces which support natural language searching. TOMESEARCHER (TOME) from Tome Associates is one such product which was initially intended for use with the INSPEC database. TOMESEARCHER formulates the user's search strategy using a question–and–answer dialogue; the search topic is accepted in natural language and the search strategy constructed with the aid of a built-in thesaurus.

Gateway services are likely to be of further interest since they help users locate a relevant database with the intercession of a cross-host index. EASYnet is a system which, using a menu-based approach, switches searchers automatically to a suitable database. About 13 search services can be accessed through EASYnet. European access to EASYnet is through sponsors such as INFOSEARCH in the UK. Gateway services which specialize in a given discipline are also available. One example is MEDICInet which covers biomedical databases on a number of hosts. The Manchester Host, launched in 1991, will offer easy and low-cost access to electronic messaging of all kinds and to national and international databases. It will also encourage businesses and other local users to put their own information online. The system will work via GEONET, an established feature of which is INFOTAP's Intelligent Interface to 200 databases on 20 hosts. This kind of development should open up a new market to smaller users and integrate use of online hosts with other electronic messaging.

2. Telecommunications
The digital telephone network ISDN (Integrated Services Data Network) will not need a modem. This network should be faster, with more accurate transmission of data. ISDN has been launched in several countries such as Britain, France, United States and Germany, but progress has been slow.

3. Databases
The general trend away from bibliographic databases towards full-text, statistical and other numeric databases is expected to continue. Some news and business databases are being updated in real time, rather than periodically; real-time updating could be extended to other databases where currency is crucial.

4. Cross-File Searching
Cross-file searching has been available for some time on a number of service suppliers, but has resulted in the combined set of references being duplicated. DIALOG has recently introduced a command to identify and remove duplicates.

5. Charging Algorithms
Charging strategies are likely to become more complex during the 1990s in order to reflect such factors as connect time, baud rate differentials, the number of fields searched and online and offline displays.

19.10   Teletext and videotext

Teletext and videotext services can be viewed as a specialized form of online access to information which has developed along separate lines. There are a number of fundamental differences between teletext and videotext and other online services. Since the former were developed with a view to capturing the domestic mass market, the emphasis has been on technology that is easy to use and information that is likely to be of wide interest to the general public. This has led to specialized technological development and a distinctive style of screen display which mixes text and graphics and makes use of colour. Interaction with these services is through menus. Although they have a number of characteristics in common, it is more straightforward to examine the development of teletext and videotext separately.

19.10.1 Teletext

Teletext transmits text-based information using the spare lines in the television signal. The broadcast signal is received and decoded by a suitably adapted television set. The information to be transmitted is formatted into pages on the broadcasting organization's computer which are broadcast as a continuous loop. The user selects the page he wishes to display by entering the page number via a numeric keypad. The decoder grabs the appropriate page the next time that it is broadcast and then displays it on the screen. The user thus interacts with a broadcast signal and not the computer. Teletext has become relatively popular in the domestic market in some countries because it is free to users. Its main limitation is the amount of data that can be handled. If more than about 2000 pages are transmitted, the delay inherent in the selected page being available for grabbing is such that the response time is unacceptably slow.

Teletext was developed in the United Kingdom by the British Broadcasting Corporation (BBC) and the Independent Broadcasting Authority (IBA). Both BBC's CEEFAX services and the IBA's ORACLE (Optional Reception of Announcements by Coded Line Electronics) commenced operation in 1976. CEEFAX offers 400 to 600 pages of information, and ORACLE 1000 to 2000 pages. The information broadcast is of general interest such as news, financial information (including exchange rates and commodity prices), sports news and results, weather and travel news, and information related to television and radio programmes. Searching is with the keypad, via menus. Although there is some dispute as to the effectiveness of the menus, research on ORACLE suggests that users tend to memorize page numbers (Videotext Ind Yearbook 1987).

In addition to the provision of information, ORACLE and CEEFAX are used for other purposes including sub-titling of television programmes and broadcasting and downloading computer software. IBA is experimenting with 4-Tel which will provide a range of programme-related support services, while BBC is offering Datcast, a data-transmission service for private organizations.

In 1983, CBS introduced Extravision and NBC Tempo, both national American teletext magazines. Significant government involvement with teletext and videotext in France and Canada has fuelled developments in these countries. The French teletext service, known as ANTIOPE (Acquisition Numérique et Télévisualisation d'Images Organisées en Pages d'Ecriture) has developed a number of services intended for specialist user groups. For example,

- ANTIOPE-BOURSE transmits financial information to brokers in Paris and Lyon.
- ANTIOPE-METEO is a national weather information service.
- ANTIOPE-ROUTE broadcasts road information to road information centres and service stations.

• ANTIOPE-SNCF provides tourist information from the French railways.

The Canadian Department of Communications has supported the development of Telidon, the Canadian teletex service. In 1982, the Canadian Broadcasting Corporation (CBC) introduced a 300-page bilingual teletext service. Since 1983, the Ontario Telidon network has provided a 100-page teletext service carrying general and local news.

19.10.2   Videotex

Videotext services make use of the telephone network in conjunction with a television set which is used as the terminal. Information is stored in the computer of the telephone service supplier which in most countries is the national telecommunications authority, but can be a private company (as in the US). The information originates with the information providers (IPs) – the equivalent of the online database producer. IPs embrace organizations established in the information industry, government and companies who are using videotext as an avenue through which to market goods or services, such as mail order catalogue and insurance companies.

Information is stored as pages, with each page being divided into one or more frames. One frame is equivalent to one screen of information which is presented on the screen in a style similar to that used for teletext display. French videotex and teletext systems use a single standard. The British and French method of character and graphics display is known as alphamosaic; it has crude graphics capabilities which produce a tiled or mosaic effect on the screen. The Canadian Telidon service uses a different method of display; referred to as alphageometric, this achieves higher quality graphics but requires more expensive terminals.

The original concept was that the television should act as a terminal, and the telephone line provide the telecommunications link. Although it is still possible to use a standard television set to receive videotex, dedicated videotext terminals are now available for the business user. The domestic user can also take advantage of software which allows domestic microcomputers to act as videotex terminals.

The first videotext service was developed in the United Kingdom by British Telecom (BT) and was known as PRESTEL. This was launched into the domestic market on the mistaken premise that there was a significant latent demand for information services in the home. BT now markets PRESTEL to specific sectors. The information that is offered includes general news, sports news, weather forecasts, travel news, leisure activities and information specific to particular market sectors such as agriculture, business, banking, education, insurance, microcomputing, teleshopping and travel.

Uptake of videotex in France has been significantly greater than elsewhere. This is largely because the French government, through its PTT (Postal, Telegraph and

Telecommunications Authority), has acted as a catalyst. The telephone directory was provided as a teletext service, and videotex terminals were offered free to all users who preferred this option to the printed directory. This move has led to a large base of installed terminals in France, which in turn has encouraged information providers to offer a wide range of services.

Gateways and other facilities   A gateway is a means to link one computer to another, and thus to access different services. Gateway developments were led by Bildschirmtext, the videotex service offered in the Federal Republic of Germany. In PRESTEL, gateways are used to provide access to education information. The French Minitel system offers a gateway to the online search service Telesystemes-QUESTEL. Other gateway developments include those between PRESTEL and a cable television company in the UK, and those which support banking transactions in Holland, Italy and Norway.

Another major area of interest has been private videotex – the use of videotext within an organization or specific user group. Private videotext systems have been implemented in the travel, trade, banking, insurance, motor trade, chemical industry, electrical and electronic industry as well as in retailing, national government, local government and education. A similar development is the Closed User Group which makes use of public videotex services to provide information to a restricted group of users.

Transaction processing facilities and electronic mail (which support teleshopping, holiday booking and other transactions) are likely to have a major influence on the future of videotex.

Searching   Searching in videotex systems is essentially menu-based. Since menus are arranged in a hierarchy, it is often necessary to go through several menu pages, up and down menu trees, before the information that is sought can be located. One of the main problems with this elaborate hierarchy of menus is navigating through the menu tree. It can be difficult to choose the correct option and, once some information has been located, users may neither remember how they arrived at it (for future reference) nor be sure whether or not additional information exists in the system on the topic of interest. In recognition of the need for a more direct route to information, other options have been explored. Many systems allow users to key in a specific page number, which they may have been able to locate in an index. PRESTEL introduced a simple keyword search facility in 1987. Single keywords or combinations of keywords using the implicit AND may be input. For example, a search under GERMANY AND TRAVEL goes straight to a listing of companies which offer travel information about Germany. Keyword searching offers greater flexibility, but cannot be performed with a numeric keypad since it requires a keyboard.

Recommended reading

General

Armstrong, C J and Large, J A (eds) (1988), *Manual of online search strategies*, (Second edition 1992), Aldershot: Gower.

Bater, P and Parkinson, H (1987), *Business and company databases*, London: Aslib.

Bates, M J (1988), 'How to use controlled vocabularies more effectively in online searching', *Online*, November, 45–56.

Boyce, B R and McLain, J P (1989), 'Entry point depth and online searching using a controlled vocabulary', *Journal of the American Society for Information Science*, **40** (4), 273–76.

Convey, J (1989), *Online information retrieval: an introductory manual to principles and practice*, 3rd edition, London: Library Association.

Cuadra directory of online databases, New York: Cuadra/Elsevier (twice per annum).

Database directory, New York: Knowledge Industry Publications (updated).

Database of databases, New York: M E Williams (updated).

Dialog database catalog 1991, Palo Alto, Calif: Dialog Information Services.

Efthimiadis, E N (1990), 'Online searching aids: a review of front ends, gateways and other interfaces', *Program*, **44** (3), 175–286.

Farbey, R (1987), *Medical databases*, London: Aslib.

Foster, A and Foster, P (1990), *Online business sourcebook*, Headland, Cleveland: Headland Press.

Foster, P (ed) (1990), *Online business information*, Headland, Cleveland: Headland Press.

Hall, J A (1986), *Online bibliographic databases: a directory and source book*, London: Aslib.

Hartley, R J et al. (1990), *Online searching: principles and practice*, London: Bowker-Saur.

Hawkins, D T (1989), 'In search of ideal information pricing', *Online*, **13** (2), 15–30.

Horter, S P (1986), *Online information retrieval concepts, principles and techniques*, Orlando: Academic Press.

Hunter, J A (1991), 'MEDLINE on BRS, DATASTAR and DIALOG – does it make a difference?', *Database*, February, 43–50.

'International Online Information Meetings (10th–14th), London, 1986–1990', Oxford: Learned Information.

Marchant, P (1988), *Patents and trademarks databases*, London: Aslib.

O'Leary, M (1988), 'Price versus value for online data', *Online*, **12** (2), 26–30.

Online international command chart, Weston: Online Inc (updated).

Online searching in science and technology: an introductory guide to equipment, databases and search techniques, London: British Library Science Reference and Information Service, 1991.

Oppenheim, C (1990), *The relationship between online hosts and database producers'*,

London: Library and Information Technology Centre (Library and Information Briefings no 24).

Palmer, R C (1987), *Online reference and information retrieval*, 2nd edition, Littleton, Colo: Libraries Unlimited.

Parker, N (1991), *Online management and marketing databases*, London: Aslib. (Other databases in the same series are on building, construction and architecture, the environment, medicine, law, and business and companies.)

Scanlon, J M *et al.* (1989), *Business online: the professionals' guide to electronic information sources*, New York and Chichester: Wiley.

Starkey, H and Thwaites, B (1989), *Going online 1989*, London: Aslib.

Summit, R K (1987), 'Online information: a ten-year perspective and outlook', *Online* **11** (1), 61–64.

Tenopir, C (1988), 'Users and uses of full-text databases' in 'Online Information '88': Proceedings of the 12th International Online Information Meeting, Oxford: Learned Information, 263–70.

Trenner, L (1987), 'How to win friends and influence people: definition of user-friendliness in interactive computer systems', *Journal of Information Science*, **13** (2), 99–107.

Tuck, B *et al.* (1990), 'Project Quartet', London: British Library (Library and Information Research Report 76).

Webber, S and Baile, C (1991), *UKOLUG quick guide to online commands*, 3rd edition, London: UKOLUG.

Teletext and Videotex

Binder, M B (1985), *Videotex and Teletext: new online resources for libraries*, Greenwich, Conn: JAI Press.

Buscain, A (1985), 'Videotex systems and data access methods: a state of the art review', *Aslib Proceedings*, **37** (6/7), 249–56.

Forster, W A (1987), *Buyer's guide to videotex equipment*, Hatfield: Cimtech.

'The key to PRESTEL', *Connexions*, May/June 1987, 53–54.

Martin, J (1982), *Viewdata and the information society*, Englewood Cliffs, NJ: Prentice Hall.

Pollitt, S (1985), 'End user boolean searching on viewdata using numeric keypads', in Proceedings of the 9th International Online Information Meeting, Oxford: Learned Information, 373–79.

'Questel to make money via Minitel', *Information World Review*, **25**, April 1988, 1.

Rowley, J E (1983), 'PRESTEL and hierarchical classification: an examination of menu-based information retrieval systems', in Proceedings of the 7th International Online Information Meeting, Oxford: Learned Information, 185–97.

Videotex industry yearbook (1987–), London: Spicer and Pegler.

Yates-Mercer, P A (1985), *Private viewdata systems in the United Kingdom*, Aldershot: Gower.

Yeates, R (1988), 'Prestel indexing from the user's point of view', *The Indexer*, **16** (1), 7–10.

20 Optical disks

20.1 Introduction

The number of databases available on optical disks expanded considerably during the 1980s. Optical disks represent another medium for the storage of information: they can be used instead of online access to external databases via telecommunications networks and possibly also pose a challenge to the printed book. All three media are likely to continue to coexist, each carving its own market niche and fending off other emerging media over the next few years.

If optical disks can be viewed as just another information storage medium, why is a separate chapter necessary? Optical disks offer an alternate means of accessing information. They are akin to the printed word in that the end-user can be expected to consult the source without the aid of an intermediary. In addition, they offer many advantages over the equivalent printed source, particularly in relation to the flexibility of retrieval. Since optical disk products such as CD–ROM offer easier retrieval of information than has previously been available to the end-user, their introduction may have repercussions on other library and information activities such as inter-library loans, photocopying and more generally on the image of the library as an information provider.

This chapter commences with a brief review of the existing range of optical disks in order to provide a context in which to explore other issues. Subsequent sections discuss the range of databases available on CD–ROM, the CD–ROM workstation, searching CD–ROM, and issues associated with the management of CD–ROM. Finally a brief review of the future for CD–ROM and some case studies of specific products are offered.

20.2 Optical disks – what are they?

An optical disk is a data storage medium where data are recorded and retrieved from the disk using a laser. Such disks have high storage capacity when compared with equivalent magnetic media. Optical disks are particularly appropriate for the storage of images, graphics and video images, coupled with sound. There are a number of different kinds of optical disk which fall into the following categories:

1. *Read-Only optical media*
    These disks are a publishing or distribution medium. The publisher encodes the data on the disk and the end-user receives a read-only disk that is placed on an appropriate player to read data, text audio or video information on disk. We will return to read-only media below.
2. *Write Once Read Many disks (WORM)*
    WORM disks are suitable for archiving in-house databases. WORM users can record their own data onto disks; all disks are master disks and are thus relatively expensive. Problems exist with standards since each WORM only plays on one drive and is not recordable or readable on the drive from another supplier. When standards are established, WORM could complement read-only disks for publishing, with WORM disks being used on a mainframe to provide multi-user access to the database. Alternatively, publishers could build image databases on WORM and distribute on CD–ROM.
3. *Erasable optical disks*
    Erasable optical disks offer interesting potential for the future. Data can be recorded, read, erased and re-recorded. Such disks are seen as an alternative to magnetic media for storage in computer systems.

Of these three types, the read-only disks are of most interest and can be further subdivided, as follows:

1. *Videodisks* These were developed to compete with videocassettes and are used for the distribution and display of pre-recorded video. Lacking any recording facility for the user, they have not become popular as a home device but are used in education and training.
2. *Hybrid videodisks* These are used to store digital data in analogue form or a mixture of digital data and analogue information. Their main advantage is their ability to store different types of information – including text, data and high–quality video – on one disk. The BBC Domesday disks are hybrid disks. They are not widely used due to the high cost of hardware and lack of standardization.
3. *Compact disks* Compact disks (CDs) are very popular consumer products, competing with gramophone records for the audio playback market. A low-power laser beam is shone onto the disk's recorded surface; the intensity of the reflected laser beam is detected by photocells and constitutes the raw digital signal. Any computer peripheral based on the CD format (such as CD–ROM) can take advantage of the low-cost components associated with CDs.
4. *Compact Disks Read Only Memory (CD–ROM)* CD–ROMs represent a direct adaptation of the CD system for publishing and data processing appli-

cations. CD–ROMs are mass produced using the same mastering and replication processes as CDs. They have the same physical dimensions and chemical composition, and operate at the same speeds. Having a storage capacity of 55Mgb, each disk can store the equivalent of 500 to 1000 floppy disks or 200,000 pages of text created on a word processor. CD–ROMs are widely used in publishing and are therefore the central focus of the remainder of this chapter.

5. *Compact Disk Interactive (CD–I)*   A development of the CD–ROM format, CD–I is a set of standards concerning the storage of multi-media information (text, audio, graphics and video) on a Compact Disk. CD–I has been developed by Philips and SONY, and the standards are defined in the Green Book. CD–I is intended for the consumer entertainment and education market. CD–I disks require special CD–I drives.

6. *CD–ROM Extended Architecture (CD–ROM XA)*   CD–ROM XA is a set of standards for storing multi-media information on CD–ROM and is related to CD–I. Unlike CD–I, however, CD–ROM XA disks will be playable on any suitably modified CD–ROM drive.

7. *Digital Video Interactive (DVI)*   DVI is a powerful compression and decompression system for digital video and audio. DVI enables more than 60 minutes of full-screen, full-motion video to be stored on a CD–ROM; without compression a CD–ROM can only store 30 seconds of video.

8. *Multi-media disks*   Multi-media disks store a combination of text, colour or black and white photographs (not line drawings), sound, animation (anything in motion) and video. To be described as multi-media, the disk must hold at least two of these data types.

20.3   Databases on CD–ROM

Databases available on CD–ROM form most of the main categories of databases introduced in Chapter 1. More specifically, the databases available on CD–ROM are of five types, as follows:

1. *Bibliographic databases*, with or without abstracts, which offer access to the literature of a subject field or list a type of publication, such as patents.
2. *Catalogue and book trade databases* are a special category of bibliographic databases. They can comprise the records in the catalogue of a specific library or list items published during a given period. These tools may be used either to identify the location of particular documents or in collection development.
3. *Source databases* contain the total contents of a document, including the full text, numeric data, computer software, images or sound and maps and charts.
4. *Quick reference databases* are a type of source database. They offer directory-type facts and figures.

Figure 20.1 Subject distribution of CD-ROM titles (from *1991 TFPL Directory*)

Combined subject index 1991

	TOTAL	%
Biomedicine, Health and Nursing	187	7.6
General Interest, Leisure & Recreation	172	7.0
Science & Technology	168	6.8
Banking, Finance & Economics	157	6.4
Government Information & Census Data	149	6.0
Business & Company Information	145	5.9
Computers & Computer Programs	141	5.7
Earth Sciences	125	5.1
Arts & Humanities	122	5.0
Crime, Law & Legislation	120	4.9
Advertising, Design & Marketing	108	4.4
Maps, Map Data & Geography	108	4.4
Chemicals, Drugs & Pharmaceuticals	93	3.8
Agriculture & Fisheries	85	3.5
Libraries & Information Sciences	85	3.5
Transport & Transportation Systems	85	3.5
Languages & Linguistics	77	3.1
Education, Training & Careers	74	3.0
Life Sciences	52	2.1
Directories	48	1.9
Social & Political Sciences	44	1.8
News, Media & Publishing	44	1.8
Military Information & Weapons	27	1.1
Architecture, Construction & Housing	27	1.1
Manuals	15	0.6

5. *Mixed disks* defy categorization because they contain a mixture of bibliographic data, full-text and quick reference data. For example, Oncodisc is a
fully integrated oncology reference source comprising the Cancerlit bibliographic database, PDQ treatment protocols, directories of physicians and
organizations, as well as a few important textbooks. The McGraw Hill Scientific and Technical Reference Set has both full text and images. The Nimbus
Music Catalog has text, graphics and sound.

Nicholls and Elshout estimated that in 1987, over half of the databases available
on CD–ROM were bibliographic. The growth in other types has been such that, in
1989, bibliographic databases comprised only 31 per cent of the total.

TFPL's 1991 Directory contains 1522 CD–ROM titles compared with only 816
listed a year earlier, an expansion which reflects the growth in the market. The
subject content of these databases is analysed in Figure 20.1. The greatest percent-
age is aimed at the medical profession, followed by general interest titles. Maps

and map data, chemicals and pharmaceuticals, banking, economics and finance have all experienced significant growth in numbers of titles. The entries in Figure 20.2 show the range of different types of databases.

The 1991 TFPL Directory lists some 1840 companies involved in the industry, including distributors and branch offices of major publishers. Some key publishers and the software that they use are summarized in Figure 20.3. Most publishers are not prolific, however; in 1989 Nicholls reported that 60 per cent of publishers had only a simple product. This included Groliers' Electronic Encyclopedia and CCOHS's CCINFOdisk. Although a wide range of publishers are involved in CD–ROM, really only a core are responsible for several products. The databases in the TFPL Directory can be analysed in respect of their countries of origin, thus: US 59%, Germany 6%, UK 6%, France 5%, Italy 5% and others 21%. (Note: the total sums to greater than 100% since several disks have co-publishers in different countries.)

Disks using CD–I, CD–ROM XA and DVI formats are beginning to enter the marketplace. The number of multi-media disks continues to grow, a significant proportion of them designed to run on the Apple Macintosh. The future for CD–ROM is clearly in delivering full-text databases with graphics, video and sound, and not in bibliographic databases.

20.4 Workstation configurations

Workstation configurations have a significant impact on the way in which CD–ROMs can be managed and exploited. For example, many installations start with a stand-alone CD–ROM workstation that provides single-user access to a single disk. This kind of configuration clearly has limited utility in a large organization where networks are widely used to provide access to shared databases. The ideal CD–ROM configuration would offer multi-user access to many databases in a manner that provided for the integration of CD–ROM based applications with other information systems in use in the same organization. Most existing configurations fall short of this ideal. The configurations that are in use today include the CD–ROM drive linked to a stand-alone PC, to a microcomputer network and with access to multiple disks.

20.4.1 CD–ROM drive linked to stand-alone PC

The basic components of the stand-alone configuration are: a stand-alone PC, a CD–ROM drive, appropriate software and, if required, a printer.

The microcomputer is most commonly an IBM or 100 per cent compatible PC; a basic microcomputer is sufficient, but machines with 286, 386 or even 486 processors provide better response times and are growing in popularity. The microcomputer needs at least 640K random access memory, a hard disk and a floppy

Figure 20.2 Some examples of CD-ROM database titles

Agriculture	AGRICOLA AGRIS Food Science and Technology Abstracts
Arts and Humanities	Art Index Image Gallery Sport–ROM The Independent on disc UK Museum Databases Project
Book Trade	BNB on CD-ROM Backfile Books in Print Cumulative Book Index Ulrichs Plus
Business Information	ABI/INFORM Ondisc Dun's Businessline F + S INDEX plus TEXT Lotus One Source PAIS on CD-ROM SilverPlatter COMLINE
Chemistry	Beilstein CD-ROM CLAIMS/Patents CD Dialog OnDisc Kirk-Othmer Encyclopedia of Chemical Technology OSHROM/MHIDAS Science Citation Index
Dictionaries	English–Japanese, Japanese–English Dictionary Information Finder by World Book McGraw Hill CD-ROM Science and Technical Oxford English Dictionary on CD-ROM Reference Set Webster's Ninth New Collegiate Dictionary
Directories	CD-Expert New Zealand Business on Disc The North American Facsimilie Book Phone Disc TELEROM
Games	Games Data ROM Children's Bible Stories 1 – Noah's Ark (CD-I) Dark Castle (CD-I) Space Quest IV
Medicine	AIDS Information and Education Worldwide BRS Colleague Disc, MEDLINE Excerpta Medica CD-Cardiology Journal of the American Medical Association MEDLINE CD-ROM POPLINE
Library Catalogues	Boston Spa Serials on CD-ROM Iowa Locator LC-Marc – English New England Law Library Consortium CD-ROM Union Catalog Venezuelan Bibliography

Figure 20.3   Key CD-ROM publishers and their search software

Publisher	Software
SilverPlatter	MultiPlatter
H W Wilson	Wilsondisc
ALDE	InnerView
OCLC	Search CD450
Space Time Research	Supermap
Bowker Electronic Publishing	Opti-net
Dialog	Dialog
Kronos Editrice	BRS/SEARCH

disk drive. Memory requirements are expanding as disks become more powerful, flexible and user-friendly. The hard disk merely holds the operating system, windows (for windows-based applications) and the CD–ROM search software. Most CD–ROMs make use of colour and some of graphics in their display, so a high resolution monitor is essential. The microcomputer needs a spare expansion slot or floppy disk drive into which to insert the CD–ROM drive or via which the drive can be linked.

CD–ROMs are played on a player referred to as a CD–ROM drive. Single disk drives come either as:

- stand-alone drives which are linked to the microcomputer by a cable which plugs into an interface card which has been fitted into a spare expansion slot in the microcomputer; or,
- built-in drives, which sit in the microcomputer in the position of a floppy disk drive.

Most drives run with the IBM PC and compatibles, but Apple has launched a drive for the Apple II and the Macintosh. Some drives hold the disk in a caddy so that it is protected.

A printer is essential for making hard copy print-outs of the results of a CD–ROM search. Choice of printer depends on the environment and the relative priorities attached to noise, print quality and price. Dot matrix, inkjet and laser printers are the prime candidates.

Finally compatibility was initially a significant problem. The situation has improved immeasurably, but when a workstation is being selected it is important to check the compatibility of all of the hardware components with each other, and with the software, as described below.

In addition to the operating system of the microcomputer, there are three different types of software necessary for a CD–ROM system:

- *Device driver software* tells the microcomputer that a CD–ROM drive is connected and how to interact with it. Microsoft's MS–DOS CD–ROM

367

Extensions software (MSCDEX) is a standard drive software package which has improved compatibilities between disks and players. MSCDEX was developed for use with disks produced according to the High Sierra and ISO 9660 formats. These standards specify the physical format of the disk and how data is organized, conceptually and logically, on it. MSCDEX has two functions: to load the CD–ROM device driver automatically when the microcomputer is switched on, and to extend the MS–DOS file size limit of 32 Mb to handle the large file sizes found on the CD–ROM disk. There are different versions of MSCDEX in use and, again, compatibility between these versions and specific CD–ROM disks can be an issue.

- *Retrieval software* is supplied by the producer of the individual CD–ROM product, with different producers using different retrieval software. A number of traditional text retrieval packages can be applied to CD–ROM products (such as BRS/SEARCH, BASIS and STATUS), but purpose-written software is becoming popular; this is either developed from one of the text retrieval packages or written specifically to accommodate retrieval from CD–ROM.
- *Installation software* takes control of the installation of the product on the user's equipment. It supports the setting of configuration options, such as user-defined formats, password control and other equipment details.

The configurations described above are the simplest but only support the use of one disk at a time by one user. In order to use more than one, disks need to be handled which in busy environments may lead to damage or loss of the disk.

20.4.2   CD–ROM drive linked into a microcomputer network

This configuration has the attraction that several people at different workstations can operate the same CD–ROM simultaneously. A number of products have entered the marketplace relatively recently. These include:

1. SilverPlatter's *Multiplatter system*, a stand-alone CD–ROM network that will allow users to access several CD–ROM drives.
2. Meridan Data's CD *Net System* which can be installed on to existing Ethernet, Novell and Token Ring networks. The system is available in four models to cater for different kinds of systems with different numbers of workstations.
3. *Opti-net* from Attica Cybernetics Ltd, which will support several users on a network; unlike CD Net, it does not require a dedicated file server just to handle the CD–ROM application.

20.4.3   Access to multiple disks

Systems that can handle a number of CD–ROM disks ease the problems associated with swapping disks. There are a number of possible solutions to many-disk access:

- daisy-chained drives with several drives linked together with cables,
- stacked systems, with more than one drive in one housing, and
- jukebox systems, which will work in the same way as a jukebox for records, by selecting the required CD–ROM and inserting it in the player. Multi-drive jukeboxes would allow disks to be loaded in advance, thus saving time in swapping between disks.

The prospects for optical disks are exciting. They have the potential to compete with other media, but their position will be stronger when systems offering multi-user access to multiple disks become more widespread.

20.5   Criteria for the selection of CD–ROMs

As the number of CD–ROMs increases, the need to exercise judgement in their selection becomes more pressing. Many individuals, organizations or libraries start with one obvious choice, such as the CD–ROM of a heavily used database or printed reference source. Experience gained with this first implementation is then used as a basis for further plans. Ultimately many organizations and certainly large libraries need to subscribe to a collection of disks to satisfy a range of requirements. Local considerations must not be overlooked, but some criteria are applicable to most environments. A checklist of key general criteria for the selection process would include the following:

1. *Database contents*
   The contents of the database must be a first priority; it is the information and not the medium that is sought. The options for types of databases are considered further in section 20.3. If the product is a CD–ROM version of a printed document or an online database, it is important to establish whether it is a complete and faithful version of the original. Does it include illustrations?
2. *Scope and currency*
   The time period covered by the database may be crucial. How current is the information? How frequently are updates issued? For some directory-type information, currency may be a prime consideration. Online databases are often more current than their equivalent CD–ROMs. With bibliographic databases, the backfile extent of the database may be important. Are all backfiles available on CD–ROM? A comprehensive backfile of a large database will occupy several disks. How are the files split between disks?
3. *Retrieval software and indexing*
   Software should be user-friendly, efficient and effective. The extent to which CD–ROM has found favour with users is an indication that the retrieval software is greatly improved compared with its predecessors. Indexing must have sufficient flexibility to satisfy various user needs. The software must

accommodate both the novice and the experienced user who may wish to conduct more sophisticated searches. Indexing consistency is also important, since items will not be located if they are inappropriately indexed or the index terms are spelt incorrectly. Online tutorials, customer support and documentation are also welcome adjuncts to aid in the effective retrieval of information.

4. *User interface*
The user interface provides the means for the user to learn what the disk contains, to find and retrieve data and to manage whatever processing needs to be done. Since the user interface merits special attention, this is developed further in section 20.7. User interface design is an area of current research interest, some of the most ambitious experiments being in the design of interfaces for use with CD–ROM products.

5. *Post-processing*
Once the appropriate information has been identified and viewed on screen, the user may want to transfer it to another storage medium such as paper, floppy or hard disk. It may be necessary to integrate this downloaded information with information from other sources, such as other databases or graphics generated by a graphics software package. CD–ROM can support post–processing either by including the tools on the disk itself or by accessing them from a magnetic disk.

6. *Data access time*
CD–ROM players operate more slowly than hard disk drives but, once a track is located, a larger chunk of data can be accessed. Therefore, a CD–ROM search can appear slow.

7. *Costs*
There are a number of issues associated with costing and economics that are relevant to the use of CD–ROM. Costs fall into two categories: set-up costs related to the acquisition of the hardware, and subscription costs in respect of the acquisition and updating of disks. Fixed costs associated with subscriptions (rather than the pay–as–you–go approach associated with access to online hosts) can be easier to manage in the context of budgeting. CD–ROM unit costs (that is, costs per search) decrease with use. There remains much uncertainty as to the eventual level of costs; producers are still wrestling with marketing strategies and pricing structures, attempting to balance the relative economics of their online, paper and (sometimes also) microform products.

8. *Standardization*
Every part of the workstation must be compatible with every other part. Compatibility problems are more likely to be encountered if a number of disks are being acquired from several suppliers. Standardization must be considered in respect of the physical, logical and application levels.

- *Physical standards* have been laid down by Philips and Sony in what is referred to as the Red Book. This specifices disk size, rotational speed, recording density (including the layout of tracks), number of data blocks, their length, and the location and timing of error codes. The Yellow Book further specifies standards that apply to CD–ROM disks and drives.

- *Logical-level standardization* is concerned with the conceptual representation of information on a disk, including volumes, files, records and other data elements and their organization according to directories, paths and tables. This is important if the computer is to access the data. The High Sierra standard has become widely accepted and is embodied in ISO 9660.
- *Application-level standardization* focuses on the manner of representation of the information elements within the logical and physical conventions. NISO is working on standards in this area.

Some key selection criteria have been outlined above. Desmarais offers an alternative checklist of the features of software and hardware that should be considered in the selection of CD–ROM products (see Reading list).

20.6 CD–ROM management

When CD–ROMs are introduced into any environment, the implementation process and the subsequent CD–ROM based services need to be managed. Here we explore some of the management issues surrounding the use of CD–ROMs in libraries.

1. *Terms of use of the CD–ROM*
   Many CD–ROMs are only leased from suppliers. When a subscription is cancelled, the disk must be returned to the supplier, thus denuding the library not only of current information, but also of its backfiles. Restrictions on the downloading of data may also be imposed. The small print needs to be scrutinized carefully in order to establish the details of the ownership situation.
2. *Resources*
   One of the main barriers to the more wholehearted adoption of CD–ROM is simply the cost of its products. Funds may often be found only by releasing resources from other budgets or by generating additional revenue. Such options can include:

- cancelling the hard copy subscription;
- cancelling subscriptions to primary journals;
- transferring resources from the budget for access to online hosts;
- identifying a special grant or drawing additional funds from enthusiastic users, or
- charging users for access to CD–ROM.

As always all of these options have unpalatable consequences; there is no easy formula for the allocation of appropriate resources.

371

3. *Staffing implications*

   In the wake of high CD–ROM use in a library, librarians may be surprised to find that their role has undergone a subtle change. The librarian ceases to be an intermediary using the information tools on behalf of users and becomes, instead, a trainer and educator. This change in role can improve the library's image and enhance communication between staff and users. Staff need to be adequately trained, both in how to use the hardware and how to search effectively, and in how to teach others. Most of the staff responsible for readers' advisory work or information work are likely also to be involved in user training, so that a large proportion of the staff need to be confident in operating CD–ROM.

4. *User training*

   Despite the user-friendliness of CD–ROM interfaces, users still need some introduction to searching a CD–ROM. Planning for a training programme must address a host of questions.

   - Which users are to be trained?
   - When?
   - How can users for training be identified?
   - Should training be compulsory?
   - What level of skill can be expected of users before and after training?
   - Should users be trained individually or in groups?
   - When should training sessions be scheduled?

Training programme design must start with the identification of objectives and proceed to the scheduling and detailed planning of sessions.

5. *Day-to-Day management*

   As with all library materials, CD–ROM must pass through all of the processes of acquisitions, cataloguing and issuing. With disks that may be updated monthly, receipting is likely to require the same kind of control as is exercised in respect of serials. Workstation location also needs consideration. A noisy printer may dictate that the workstation be located in a dedicated room. Some means of disk control and issue may be necessary in order to prevent disks from being lost. A booking system may be unavoidable if CD–ROM facilities are in heavy demand. Also, disks need regular clearing to delete stored searches.

6. *Effects on other services*

   The nature and scale of the impact on other library services will be influenced by the type of database on the CD–ROM and the way in which a number of the other management issues explored above have been resolved. The arrival of CD–ROM is likely to have positive benefits for the image of the library as a provider of information.

   The bibliographic database on CD–ROM will alert users to documents whose existence they would not otherwise have suspected. There will probably be increased and better exploitation of existing library resources, as well as more demand for access to documents that are not within the collection of a particular library. This is likely to increase the inter-library loan workload. The increased use of resources is also likely to contribute to a higher level of photocopying activity.

Demand for online searching might be expected to decrease with the introduction of CD–ROM. This effect is not usually as dramatic as one might expect. CD–ROM and online appeal to different user groups. Some users even discover and progress to online after successful experiences with CD–ROM.

7. *Integration with other information technology applications*
   The integration of CD–ROM into the wider information technology environment needs to be considered. Some of the central issues have already been identified in section 20.4. Other typical questions are:

- Can the CD–ROM be accessed through an existing local area network?
- Does the CD–ROM application require special hardware or software?
- Can the same microcomputers be used for CD–ROM and other applications, or is dedicated equipment more satisfactory?

Integration is likely to improve over the next few years.

20.7 Interfaces and searching on CD–ROM

It is appropriate to explore the information retrieval facilities available on CD–ROM in more detail. Both the style of the interface and the retrieval facilities may influence search strategies and the effectiveness of retrieval. We have already established that the user interface for CD–ROM products is relatively user-friendly and has been designed to appeal to the end-user without the assistance of an intermediary.

When a database is available on more than one CD–ROM, the quality of the interface must be considered as a selection criteria alongside the content and cost. Most of the interfaces are menu-based, but beyond this there is little standardization except among the products of a given supplier. Training considerations may inhibit an organization from acquiring disks from more than one supplier since users need to become familiar with each different interface that they encounter.

There is no standardization in CD–ROM menu design: some disks use a main menu across the top of the screen; some use a menu bar at the bottom of the screen; some offer a single list of options in a window, while others use a series of pull-down or pop-up menus. This variability in screen display is compounded by the lack of standardization in keyboard functions. For example, it is common to use the F1 key for Help, but this is not true for all products.

Windows-based CD–ROM products will become increasingly available. Windows interfaces have been described in section 18.2. Essentially they are characterized by icons, pull-down and pop-up menus, direct manipulation and windows. The use of windows does not replace the operating system, but surrounds it with a user-friendly interface. For example, in order to copy a text file, the mouse can be used to move a pointer to the icon of the file cabinet, to list the available files, to choose the file to be copied and finally to execute the copy command. This operation does not require any prior knowledge of the operating system copy command and uses only a few key strokes.

Multi-tasking is a major feature that is available through Windows. For example, if a searcher were using UMI's Business Periodicals Ondisk and chose to search ABI/INFORM online for the most current information, without Windows the searcher would need to exit Business Periodicals Ondisk and connect to ABI/INFORM. In a Windows environment the searcher could connect to ABI/INFORM without leaving the CD–ROM database. Another facet of multi-tasking is that further searches can be conducted on a disk whilst printing the results of an earlier search.

Further study of the interfaces available on disks can be achieved by examining how some disks actually function. The next section looks at a specific search on the INSPEC CD–ROM and examines both features of the interface and the retrieval facilities.

There is potential for development in interface design. In the future interfaces will be defined by the end-user and not by the publisher of databases. Function keys and commands will fade into history with the further development of interfaces that support the association and development of ideas and the use of natural language.

20.8 Document delivery and CD–ROM

CD–ROM is essentially a delivery medium which can provide the full texts of documents. Several more ambitious projects have been the subject of investigation. Adonis, Project Quartet and DOCDEL are described briefly below. With the potential for integrating optical disk technologies with networks, developments may take one of several possible directions.

1. *Adonis* is designed to study the problems of document delivery. The project has stored articles on CD–ROM which can be accessed via a special workstation for printing out or direct transmission to a group of four fax machines, thus providing an on-demand document delivery service.
2. *Project Quartet* has as its aim the improvement of communications in the

academic community through the use of new technology, communications networks, optical storage, high resolution displays and computer conferencing. Activities include the development of a document ordering and delivery system, using electronic mail for ordering and fax for delivery. The document store will take the form of a large collection of CD–ROM disks which are accessed through a jukebox-type reader.

3. The EEC has also sponsored a number of projects to look at document delivery based upon optical storage.

Transdoc, part of *the EEC's DOCDEL programme*, was set up to investigate electronic archiving and distribution of documents using microfilm and digital optical disks. EORODOCDEL has attempted to investigate alternative delivery systems, including optical disks, satellite transmission and high quality videotex. Projects of this kind demonstrate that there are often alternative ways to achieve an activity such as document delivery; what is the most appropriate technology for any particular purpose remains debatable.

20.9 An example of searching a CD–ROM – INSPEC on CD–ROM

In partnership with University Microforms International INSPEC has attempted to design an interface with special features which cater for all searchers, both end-users and information professionals. The interface offers clear on-screen displays and context-sensitive help. Other facilities of the interface have been described by D. Richards in her article, 'INSPEC Ondisk – design considerations' (in *Aslib Information*, June 1991, 221–23) from which she has kindly given permission to quote the following:

Free-text and field-specific searching   The basic screen contains a search-terms box at the top with a larger scrollable box underneath which can contain up to 100 retrieved sets. Free-text searching, that is if the user does not specify a particular field to be searched, will automatically search the 'Basic Index'. This contains words and phrases from the title, abstract, thesaurus and free-indexing fields. The software assumes word adjacency if a phrase is entered into the search box. The usual Boolean and word proximity operators are available and intermediate set results are created for terms combined with Boolean operators (Figure 20.4(a)).

Field-specific searching can be carried out for 29 fields. For example, to search the thesaurus term field for the term 'hypermedia' you can type: **DE(hyper-media)**. The codes for each field can be found in the help screens. An easier alternate search method is to select the required term from the appropriate inverted index.

Plurals and British/American spellings   Although the INSPEC database is produced in the UK and uses British spelling for the controlled indexing, nearly 50 per cent of the literature covered is published in the USA. INSPEC does not alter the spelling of words in the title and abstract fields, so there are many American spelling variants of words in

375

the database. It can be difficult even for experienced searchers to remember to include the different spellings, so the British/American spellings search option can be very useful. When switched on, it automatically looks for both British and American spelling variants of terms. For example if you select 'colour', records containing both the words 'colour' and 'color' will be retrieved.

To assist the end-user in particular, another search option is available which automatically finds simple plurals of all selected words.

Both of these search options can be switched on or off independently of each other from the search options box.

Library holdings   The Library Holdings facility is a feature that many of our customers have requested. Each year, INSPEC scans over 4,200 journals, about 1000 conferences and many books, dissertations and reports, so it is unlikely that a library will possess all the items that a user may find as a result of a database search. The Library Holdings module allows you to mark most source documents which your library holds, and whether they are available in paper or microform. This list is then transferred to the search software directory on the computer's hard disk and is matched with all retrieved sets of records. Figure 20.4(b) shows a typical INSPEC record screen. The holdings details appear at the bottom of the screen on a bar which overlays the record display box. The text message can be customised to tell users where they should go for further assistance in the library.

It must be pointed out that the Library Holdings module only works for items that have a unique identifier such as an ISSN number in the case of journals.

INSPEC thesaurus   Each INSPEC record is indexed using controlled terms to provide a powerful search aid. The *INSPEC Thesaurus* now contains over 6,000 terms and about 7,000 synonyms or cross-references. The CD–ROM version of the Thesaurus can be used to browse through hierarchical structures and select the most suitable terms for searching.

The first entry screen is a Term Index consisting of a list of permuted preferred and 'used-for' words and phrases. Selection of a particular term takes you to the Thesaurus screen which for each term, shows the narrower, related, broader and top terms. (If a synonym or 'used-for' term is selected from the Term Index, the system takes you directly to the entry for the appropriate thesaurus term). For regular users of the printed thesaurus, the main screen should be familiar (see Figure 20.4(c)). Terms can be marked for searching purposes by using the space bar or F9 function key as a toggle. It is also very easy to move to different thesaurus terms by either highlighting a term seen on the screen and pressing the Return key, or selecting another term from the Term Index.

Full hierarchical structures can also be browsed on an additional screen (see Figure 20.4(d)). Terms can still be marked in this screen, but in addition, there are function keys which allow you to mark all broader or narrower terms to the term which you have highlighted with the space bar. Up to 25 terms can be marked and if you forget which ones you have picked, these can be viewed in an overlay box which also allows you to delete any of them. On returning to the search screen, all selected terms are placed into separate search sets. A final set is also created which automatically combines all selected terms by the Boolean 'OR'.

Future Enhancements   INSPEC and UMI plan to enhance the product with many more features. By the end of 1991, the new features that will be added include the sorting or output, user-defined output formats, the INSPEC Classification linked to the Thesaurus, automatic units conversion for searching the numerical indexing field, and an order module which places bibliographic references into a document request form which can be customised for a library's own ordering system.

Figure 20.4 INSPEC on CD-ROM
(a) INSPEC On disk: search screen

```
ProQuest              CD-ROM Retrieval        Version 0.7E
INSPEC Jul 1990 - Mar 1991          F1=Help  F2=Commands

┌───────────────────── Search Entry ─────────────────────┐
│                                                          │
│  Search Term(s): apple mac                               │
│                                                          │
└─ Press ↵ to view results ──                              │
                                                           │
┌──────────────────── Previous Search ────  Indexes ──────┐
│                                          Basic Index (BI)│
│  Num   Search                            Authors (AU)    │
│                                          Title Words (TI) │
│  #1    ibm pc                                            │
│  #2    apple mac              Thesaurus Terms (DE)       │
│                               Free Index Terms (FT)      │
│                               Classification Codes (CC)  │
│                               Treatment Terms (TC)       │
│                               Chemical Index (CH)        │
│                               Numeric Index (NI)         │
│                                                          │
│                               Document Type (DT)         │
│                               Language (LA)              │
│                               Publication Year (YR)      │
│                               Country of Publication (PC)│
│                               Journal Name (JN)          │
│                               Corporate Source (CS)      │
└──────────────────────────────────────────────────────────┘

Use ↓↑ to move, then ↵ to select.              ESC to exit.
```

377

(b) INSPEC Ondisk: library holdings display

```
                        Item 2 of 4 in this Search
INSPEC 3683490 A90107864              Journal Paper
Title:        Atmospheric transmission in the far-infrared at the South
              Pole and astronomical applications
Authors:      Townes, C.H.; Melnick, G.
Affiliation:  Dept. of Phys., California Univ., Berkeley, CA, USA
Journal:      Publications of the Astronomical Society of the Pacific
              Vol: 102  Iss: 649  p. 357-67
              Date: March 1990
              Country of Publication: USA
              ISSN: 0004-6280  CODEN: PASPAU
Language:     English
Treatment:    Application; Experimental
Abstract:     The combination of low atmospheric water vapor, high
              altitude, and low temperatures makes the South Pole and other high
              interior parts of the Antarctic continent particularly suitable
              locations for certain types of infrared or millimeter-wave astronomy.
              The authors survey information available on the atmospheric column
This item available in: Paper, Microform             Press F7 for Notes
```

Use ↓↑ to scroll. Press ↵ to switch formats.   ESC to exit.

378

(c) INSPEC Ondisk: thesaurus screen

ProQuest   CD-ROM Retrieval   Version 0.3
INSPEC Jan 1989 – Dec 1989   F1 = Help   F2 = Commands

```
_____ Thesaurus _____

Term:      information centres
           Used For:        information analysis centres
                            information analysis centres
                            information centres
           Broader:         information science
           Top Term:        computer applications
           Related:         information analysis
                            information services
                            libraries
           Class:           C7210 (Information services and centres)

Term:      information dissemination
           Used For:        dissemination of information
                            SDI
                            selective dissemination of information
           Broader:         information science
```

Use ↑↓ to move, SPACE to mark choices.   ESC to exit.

(d) INSPEC Ondisk: thesaurus hierarchy

ProQuest   CD-ROM Retrieval   Version 0.3
INSPEC Jan 1989 – Dec 1989   F1 = Help   F2 = Commands

```
_____ Thesaurus – Hierarchical D  |    Commands
computer applications                 |
.  administrative data processing     |  New Search        F3
.  . distributive data processing     |  Review Marks      F5
.  .  . goods dispatch data processing|  Mark Narrower     F6
.  .  . stock control data processing |  Mark Broader      F7
.  .  . warehouse automation          |  Thesaurus Entry   F8
.  . educational administrative data processing | Mark/Unmark   F9
.  . financial data processing        |  Clear Marks   SHIFT + F9
.  .  . accounts data processing      |  Restart          F10
.  .  . bank data processing          |  Change Disk  ALT + F10
.  .  . budgeting data processing     |  Exit        SHIFT + F10
.  .  . corporate modelling           |  Howto
.  .  . EFTS                          |
.  .  .  . automatic teller machines  |  Marks All Narrower Terms
.  .  . electronic trading            |
.  .  . insurance data processing     |
.  .  . payroll data processing       |
```

Use ↑↓ to move, then ↵ to select.   ESC to exit.

Figure 20.5   Details of Some CD–ROM Titles

51   AGRICOLA

Publisher: OCLC (Online Computer Library Center Inc)
Information Provider: US Department of Agriculture, National Agricultural Library

Sources: AGRICOLA (online)
Type: bibliographic
Coverage: international
Subject: agriculture, aquatic sciences, biotechnology, consumer information, economics, environment

175   BNB on CD-ROM Current File

Publisher: The British Library National Bibliographic Service
Information Provider: The British Library National Bibliographic Service

Sources: Blaise Line
Type: bibliographic
Language: English
Coverage: United Kingdom
Subject: books & serials, library aids, library & information science

180   BOOKBANK

Publisher: J. Whitaker and Sons Ltd
Information Provider: J. Whitaker

Sources: Books in Print (print)
Type: bibliographic, addresses
Language: English
Coverage: Europe
Subject: book trade, books & serials

Contains more than 500,000 books in print, from over 14,000 publishers and distributors in the UK and Western Europe.
Covers in-print, recently out of print, and forthcoming books.
Also covers maps available through book publishers.
Searchable through three levels of access – novice, intermediate and expert. Based on the Whitaker's Books in Print database. Interface to Teleordering is available.

Computer: IBM PC or compatible
OS: MS-DOS 3.1 or higher
Memory: 640K RAM
Drive: Philips, Hitachi, Sony
Software: BRS/Search (BRS Software Products)

380

Recommended reading

Akeroyd, J (1989), 'CD–ROM usage and prospects: an overview', *Program*, **23**, (4), 367–76.

Akeroyd, J *et al.* (1988), *Using CD–ROM as a public access catalogue*, London: British Library Research and Development Department.

Armstrong, C J and Large, J A (1990), *CD–ROM information products: an evaluative guide and directory*, Aldershot: Gower.

Barden, P (1989), 'Developments in a CD–ROM jukebox for the ADONIS system', *Program*, **23** (4), 437–41.

The CD–ROM directory 1991, 5th edition, London: TFPL.

'CD–ROM: what you need to know about equipment', *Library Micromation News*, **23**, 1989, 2–4.

Desmarais, N (1989), *The Librarian's CD–ROM handbook*, Westport, London: Meckler.

Goddard, J and Armstrong, P (1986), 'The 1986 Domesday project', *Transactions of the Institute of British Geographers*, **11** (3), 290–95.

Gunn, A A and Moore, C (1990), *CD–ROM: a practical guide for information professionals*, London: UKOLUG and Library and Information Technology Centre.

Halm, J Van (1986), 'The ten DOCDEL experiments: an evaluation of user aspects' in F Mastroddi (ed), *Electronic publishing: the new way to communicate*, London: Kogan Page for CEC.

Lyon, E (1991), 'Spoilt for choice? optical disks and online databaes in the next decade', *Program*, **25** (1), 37–49.

Nicholls, P T (1991), 'A survey of commercially available CD–ROM database titles', *CD–ROM professional*, **4** (2), 23–28.

Nicholls, P and Van Den Elshout, R (1990), 'Survey of databases available on CD–ROM: types, availability and content', *Database*, February, 18–23.

Oppenheim, C (ed) (1988), *CD–ROM: fundamentals to applications*, London: Butterworths.

Roth, J P (1986), *Essential guide to CD–ROM*, London: Meckler.

Saffady, W (1988), *Optical storage technology: a bibliography*, London: Meckler.

Saffady, W (1988), *Optical storage technology: a state of the art review*, London: Meckler.

'The selection of a microcomputer for a CD–ROM workstation', *Library Micromation News*, **27**, 1990, 6–9.

Stern, B T and Campbell, R (1988), 'ADONIS: the story so far', in C Oppenheim (ed), *CD–ROM: Fundamentals to applications*, London: Butterworths, 181–219.

21 In-house information retrieval and cataloguing systems

21.1 Introduction

Information retrieval systems were first developed in the late 1960s and early 1970s in special libraries and information units which sought to exploit the advantages of computer processing in the maintenance of local indexes, databases and current awareness services. Many of the early systems were perceived as replacements for manual techniques including, for example, the preparation of card indexes, the maintenance of post-coordinate indexes on cards, abstracts and other current awareness bulletins. These retrieval systems offered a more cost-effective approach to the control of information, often permitting greater quantities of information to be sifted and directed to the appropriate end-user than would have been possible with manual systems. Many of the early systems ran on mainframe computers, in batch mode. Now, systems are available to run on all types of computers and all sizes, and most systems operate primarily in online mode. However, it continues to be the case that one of the great advantages of such systems is the opportunity to input data once, and then to reformat it to produce a range of products each tailored to a specific need.

When computers were first harnessed for information retrieval and cataloguing applications, both the information retrieval systems and some of the cataloguing systems developed in different environments. In the libraries which were engaged in large-scale cataloguing, cooperation was central to developments, as outlined in Chapter 22. These cataloguing cooperatives developed software which would support joint cataloguing. Probably the importance of being able not only to share the development costs of the software, but also to share the database which comprised catalogue records, – that is, a union catalogue database – determined developments in this area. Thus the networks discussed in Chapter 22 emerged as computer-based systems. In information retrieval applications it was more usual for one organization to carry most of the burden of development of the system and then to market it to others. Thus, as others adopted systems, user groups subsequently emerged, but were not usually responsible for the original design of the software package. Once established, however, these user groups often exerted an important influence in the further development of systems.

Thus there have been different influences in the development of cataloguing and information retrieval software packages respectively. These two are nevertheless treated together in this chapter, because in some respects there is convergence of systems. Cataloguing modules appear in packages originally designed for information retrieval, and also in packages whose primary purpose is library management.

Our emphasis in this chapter is on systems and software that can support the creation of databases for information management. These are primarily reference or, less frequently, source databases. One major category of database that may be maintained by an organization or a library is the bibliographic database which may offer access to any of the following:

- the documents in a library or network of libraries, as in a catalogue database which lists the items in that library or network of libraries;
- the documents in a library or network of libraries, showing not only the volumes in the library, but also the contents of periodicals, conference proceedings and reports, or
- information on a subject of special interest to a given organization.

The creation of such databases is frequently the first component in a computerization programme and often forms the foundation on which other applications can be based. A library catalogue database may constitute the first step in the implementation of a library management system, offering circulation control, acquisitions and ordering, and serials controls, as well as management information. Within a business, commercial, educational or industrial organization, databases are likely to be widespread, with database software finding a plethora of different applications – from mailing lists to complex integrated databases offering financial control and image processing. This chapter commences with an overview of the different types of hardware configurations and software packages currently in use in organizations. This will provide a context from which to focus on library management and text retrieval systems, which are viewed as central to the theme of this text.

21.2 Hardware options

Hardware and software are the central components of any computer system. A stand-alone microcomputer can support a libary or information retrieval system, but where the databases are large and the number of simultaneous users many, more ambitious hardware configurations must be sought. The options can be briefly summarized as follows:

1. *Shared mainframe or large minicomputer*
   If an information manager has already installed an organization-wide

computer system, the system can exploit this main computer. There are three advantages of this solution. Only limited additional hardware – mostly workstations – need be purchased, while on-site expertise should be available to support hardware and possibly software. Most significantly, the databases on such a system can be made available through all of the workstations linked to the system so that information services can be offered at the user's desk. A library management system is often one of the more demanding applications on a shared mainframe. A circulation control system, for example, must be available for all of the hours that the library is open. Software, designed to run on a large computer and to support large databases, may be expensive. These and other political constraints have led to the shared mainframe losing popularity.

2. *Dedicated minicomputer*

A dedicated computer for text retrieval database creation or for a library management system offers a relatively powerful processor. Such hardware will support large databases and a large number of simultaneous users. Some such systems may be purchased as hardware and software separately; others are sold as turnkey packages, incorporating both hardware and software. The great attraction of a turnkey system is simplicity of relations with the supplier: both hardware and software are purchased from one source. A turnkey system may not always be appropriate and may lead to incompatibilities between hardware for the system and other hardware used in the same organization. The organization may impose constraints on the hardware to be acquired.

3. *Stand-alone microcomputer*

Stand-alone microcomputers are satisfactory for one–person–at–a–time access to one workstation. The microcomputer can be used for a range of applications, including word processing, desk-top publishing and management information, as well as for database creation, maintenance and searching. The selection of a microcomputer should be guided by considerations of compatibility and expandability. In due course it may be desirable to link a number of stand-alone microcomputers together in a network. It is helpful if an existing microcomputer will link into a planned network, but it is more important that the database created in a stand-alone microcomputer, single-user environment be transferrable to a multi-user environment.

4. *Networked microcomputers*

A network of microcomputers is intermediate between a stand-alone microcomputer and a dedicated minicomputer; in practice, the choice for hardware is often between a network of microcomputers, possibly with a very powerful microcomputer as the file server, or a dedicated minicomputer. There are a number of different configurations with different kinds and numbers of workstations, more or less powerful file servers and different networks. Microcomputers are usually networked in order to take advantage of shared databases, networked software and access to other hardware such as printers and CD–ROM drives.

21.3   Software options

Software likely to be appropriate in information management can be divided into five categories: (1) database management systems, (2) text retrieval systems, (3) library housekeeping systems, (4) general business software, and (5) communications software. Many of these types of software are concerned with the creation of databases, so that if, for example, the information manager is embarking upon the creation of a catalogue database, packages from a number of these categories may merit further examination. This makes it important to distinguish between the various types of software. Unfortunately it is not always easy to assign a software package to a category.

BookshelF could be regarded as a library management system in that it offers all of the standard functions for library management. It also supports text retrieval, with a full range of search facilities and a thesaurus module. Also some packages are available in different versions for different markets. For example, CAIRS is marketed as CAIRS-LMS (Library Management System), CAIRS-TMS (Text Management System) and CAIRS-IMS (Information Management System).

The main categories of software can be characterized as follows:

1. *Database Management Systems* (DBMS) are general database packages designed to support the creation of databases and are used extensively by organizations to build and maintain databases. DBMSs handle essentially tabular data and originally catered primarily for fixed-length fields. Searching involves looking for specific characters in a specified field. This works well with fixed-length data where searching can be conducted on pre-assigned keywords, but is less suitable where the data is of variable length and searching is on the natural (and unpredictable) text of the record. Text retrieval software is specifically designed for this kind of application. DBMSs are essentially programming frameworks and incorporate programming languages which support the development of specific applications. Some of the library management systems currently on the market are based on a DBMS. For example, Data Trek Integrated Library Management System, from Data Trek SMS, is written in dBase III +. DBMSs are designed to support the relational databases described in Chapter 6.

    An important feature of a DBMS is its ability to work with several linked databases, drawing data from or adding data to several databases simultaneously.

2. *Text information management systems* are also designed to create databases. It could be regarded as special-purpose database software which is designed to handle textual data. Such software offers variable-length fields to accommodate variable data, and sometimes repeating fields to handle multiple authors and subject indexing terms. Usually only one database or a series of independent databases is supported. Search facilities need to cater for the unpredictability of natural languages. On most systems, an inverted file of all potential search terms is maintained to store the location of terms within records. In addition, a text retrieval system is characterized by relatively sophisticated search facilities such as Boolean logic, search refinement, thesaurus support, truncation, contextual searching, nesting and bracketing, range searching, text string searching, adjacency searching and field-directed searching. Text retrieval packages are used both to build in-house databases and to support databases available through international online hosts. The distinction between text retrieval software and DBMS is not as rigid as it once was. Some DBMSs are capable of handling variable–length fields and offer improved searching facilities, but the lineage of a package is likely to determine the emphasis given to different features of the software. Figure 21.1 is a checklist of some of the features that might be sought in any text retrieval or database package. This is a somewhat idealized list, in that few packages offer all of these facilities and in most applications not all of them are necessary. Figure 21.2 is a list of some text retrieval packages and their suppliers.

3. In *Library Management Systems* the software normally supports the following functions:

   - ordering and acquisitions,
   - cataloguing, including online public access cataloguing,
   - circulation control and
   - management information.

In larger libraries the motivation for computerization is often rooted in the benefits of more effective circulation control. In the smaller library the catalogue is often the function which provokes computerization, the library wishing to generate records of its stock and to offer flexible access to that data. Unfortunately, although there have been significant developments in online public access catalogues over recent years, it remains necessary to examine catalogue modules carefully in order to confirm that they offer adequate retrieval devices. Ideally a catalogue module should offer the same range of facilities as text retrieval software. Where this quality of interface is not available, the main motivation for opting for library management software in preference to text retrieval software will be the need to support other functions, such as circulation control, within one software package.

Figure 21.1   A Checklist for the evaluation of database and text retrieval software

1. **Inputting data**
   Are the screens
   - preformatted?
   - user-definable?

   Are word processing facilities available?
   Can you amend existing records? Can you delete existing records?
   Does the package work with:
   - variable-length fields only?
   - fixed-length fields only?
   - a mixture of variable- and fixed-length fields?

   Do field lengths need to be specified when creating a database?

2. **Indexing**
   Are there any constraints on indexing terms?
   Is there a stoplist? Is it user-definable?
   Is there a golist? Is it user-definable?
   How are personal names handled in the index (e.g. inverted)?
   What facilities are available for selecting index terms?
   How are fields with index terms in them to be defined?
   Are the following facilities included:
   - a thesaurus?
   - synonyms?
   - homonyms?
   - broader term?
   - narrower term?

3. **Information retrieval**
   Is there an online help facility?
   Are the following facilities available:
   - Boolean search operators?
   - field directed searching?
   - proximity searching?
   - truncation?
   - range searching?
   - search history?
   - free text searching?
   - save search?

4. **Output facilities**
   Are the following facilities included?
   - screen display?
   - printed output?
   - user-defined output formats?
   - any special facilities for SDI?

5. **Security**
   Are the following facilities included?
   - passwords?
   - user ids?
   - limited access?

6. **Display the index**
   Can this be done?

7. **Setting up databases**
   How is this achieved?
   What parameters need to be specified at database definition?
   What parameters can be modified later?

8. **Relational Databases**
   Is there a relational facility?

9. **User-friendliness**
   Are the following included:
   - manual?
   - help system?

   To what extent is it easy to use?

Figure 21.2   Some text retrieval systems and their suppliers

(a) Microcomputer systems

Supplier	System
Associated Knowledge Systems	ASSASSIN PC
Logical Choice	BOOKSHELF PC
Business Simulations	CARDBOX-PLUS
Byte Smiths Associates	CONCORD
Compsoft	DELTA
Telesystems Questel	MICRO-QUESTEL
Blyth Software Ltd	OMNIS 3
Personal Bibliographic Ltd	PROCITE
Cuadra Associates/Online Information Services	STAR
HARWELL COMPUTER POWER	STATUS/PC
SOUTHDATA	SUPERFILE
Zylab/Primary Process Software	ZYINDEX

(b) Mainframe/minicomputer systems

Supplier	System
Associated Knowledge Systems	ASSASSIN 6
Information Dimensions	BASIS
BRS	BRS/SEARCH
Leather Food Research Association	CAIRS-TMS
Pyramid Computer Systems	CALM
Information Dimensions	DM
Henco Software/Doric Computer Systems	INFO-TEXT and INFO DB+
Inmagic/Head Computers	INMAGIC
Infodata Systems/Thorn EMI Computer Software	INQUIRE/TEXT
Pergamon ORBIT Infoline	ORBIT
QL Systems Ltd	QL/SEARCH
Harwell Computer Power	STATUS and STATUS/IQ
Information Dimensions	TECHLIB
Chemdata/Associated Knowledge Systems	TEXTO
IME	TINLIB

Figure 21.3 offers a checklist of some of the functions that are covered by most library management systems. Figure 21.4 is a list of some library management systems, their suppliers and the functions covered.

4. *Business software* is a broad category. Since the information manager will be working in a computerized environment, a range of general software is also likely to be useful and available. This may be integrated or interfaced with a database or other package or may be used for a completely distinct function, such as the generation of a newsletter or control of the budget.

    The three main strands of business software are: database, word processing and spreadsheets.

    ● *Database software* has been discussed in the previous sections. Simple

Figure 21.3   Functions of library management systems

Acquisitions

Ordering
Receipting
Claiming
Fund accounting
Enquiries
Reports and statistics

Circulation Control

Setting parameters e.g. renewal
    policies, calendars
Issue
Return
Renewal
Fines
Reservations
Short-term loans
Borrower file maintenance
Enquiries
Notices
Reports and statistics

Cataloguing

Data entry
Authority control
Downloading

OPAC and Access

Online access
Public access interface
Hard copy

Serials Control

Ordering
Check-in
Renting
Claiming
Binding
Fund accounting
Enquiries
Reports and statistics

---

microcomputer database software may be described as flat-file, in that it will only support independent databases and not relate databases like a true DBMS.

- *Word processing software* is difficult to avoid, the latest versions of the standard packages offering a very competitive range of features. Word processing packages support the creation, storage and, later, recall and modification of text. Typical applications are standard letters, reports, forms, compilation of lists and manuals. Word processing packages must support the manipulation of text (including, for example, alignment of margins, deletion and insertion of sentences, lines, words and paragraphs), back-up files, underlining, and arranging for the text to be appropriately placed on the page. Most software also merges files, arranges records in a file in order according to some criterion, and searches for specific strings within small files.

- *Spreadsheet packages* facilitate the manipulation of tabular or numerical data. A spreadsheet is a large table which contains a number of cells arranged in rows and columns. Since numbers or text can be entered in these cells, a spreadsheet can be used to store words but is primarily intended to handle numerical data. The software includes the ability both to rearrange data in rows and columns and to transfer data

389

between spreadsheets, but more important is its facility to perform various arithmetical operations on the data. Often facilities for drawing graphs, histograms, pie charts and other graphical analyses of the data are also incorporated into the software. Spreadsheet packages can be useful for manipulating library management information such as loans statistics or financial data.

A number of packages on the market are available as integrated packages. An *integrated package* should integrate two or more other functions that might otherwise be found in separate packages. Typically, an integrated package offers word processing, databases, spreadsheets, graphics and possibly communications in one package. The strength of an integrated package of this type is that it should be easy to generate documents comprising a mixture of numerical, textual and graphical data; since these divisions are artificial, this can be a great asset. Also price may be attractive, and only one system needs to be learnt. The problem with such packages usually lies with the quality of each of the components. For example, often the database facilities offered as part of an integrated package are relatively rudimentary and only suitable for building small databases. When examining an integrated package it is important to establish that the facilities offered in each of the components are adequate for the purpose for which it is intended. The other problem with integrated packages is that they may take up a lot of storage space on the computer. The value of integration has been eroded in the last two or three years as increasing numbers of the main business packages have become more compatible with one another.

Desk-top publishing packages are an attractive option for the in-house publication of documents and the improved presentation of overhead projector slides. Typically they will support the creation of documents, including text and graphics, or the importing of documents from word processing and graphics packages. The desk-top publishing package takes the document and allows the user to create effectively presented documents by such means as modifying layout on the page, with columns and inserts; choosing typefaces and fonts; inserting and highlighting headings, and establishing standard page formats.

Output from database packages can be handled with a database publishing package; alternatively, if output is a report from the database package, it can be handled as an ordinary document by a desk-top publishing package. Desk-top publishing may assist in the generation of a number of documents such as bulletins, newsletters, notices, plans, bibliographies or guides. It is important to remember, however, that manipulating a document with a desk-top publisher requires two commodities: time and design skills. Desk-top publishing does not always lead to quicker publication than by outside agents; moreover, considerable design skills are necessary for a truly professional product. Desk-top publishing is best viewed as a tool for simple improvements to the presentation of in-house documents, rather than as a means of cutting the cost of external printing.

5. *Communications software* may be employed to access external computers. A wide range of such software is available both from business software suppliers and specialist online information retrieval software outlets. This software supports access to external hosts by:

- storing logging on procedures,
- supporting the downloading of data from the external host and
- supporting the local development and storage of search profiles so that searches can be more quickly executed.

Some communications packages are part of a family of software packages which includes a database package; this database package can be used to store, manipulate and retrieve the downloaded data.

21.4 Software evaluation

This section reviews the chief factors that must be taken into account in selecting an appropriate software package. This is followed by some brief comments on a representative, but far from comprehensive, selection of the software packages used for information retrieval and cataloguing.

The most important and perhaps obvious factor is to establish that the package is compatible with the machine on which it is to be used. Indeed, in some instances, the hardware may be chosen to match the selection of software, but where this degree of flexibility is not possible, obviously the machine may constrain the options available considerably. Some packages are portable and are available in different versions. CAIRS is a good example of such a series of systems which will run on a number of different machines, including both minicomputers and microcomputers of various capacities. The early systems were mainframe, developed in the late 1960s and early 1970s. Hence, many of these systems are now well established in the market; they have been thoroughly tested and have sound maintenance arrangements. Some minicomputer packages came onto the market in the mid-1970s, whereas microcomputer packages in general emerged during the 1980s. In the microcomputer range, two types exist: the cheap single-user package and the more expensive multi-user package.

In general, the costs of packages vary considerably, but it is usually the case that you get what you pay for. Although there are some notable bargains, in general as one goes up the price range from microcomputer packages at £100 to minicomputer and mainframe packages at £30,000, there are improvements in capacity and retrieval facilities together with other factors listed below.

391

Factors to consider in opting for a specific software system

There are a number of factors which must be considered prior to making a commitment to a specific software package. These could be grouped into four basic categories:

1. *General*
    (a)   Cost.
    (b)   Extent of use of the software by other libraries and information units, and their experiences with the software.
    (c)   Whether the software can produce the required ouput from the given input in a reasonable time.
    (d)   The producer and the supplier of the software may be two different agencies. Plainly it is worth seeking both reputable suppliers and producers since both have an interest in offering a sound product.
2. *Technical*
    (a)   The software must be written in a programming language which is available on the computer being used.
    (b)   The operating system required by the software must be available on the computer system to be used.
    (c)   What is the hardware configuration required by the software available; for example, amount of storage, number and capacity of disk drives, addressable screen cursors etc?
    (d)   Is other software (such as sort programs, edit programs and word processing programs) necessary before the software can be used?
    (e)   Are there any limits on the types of data that can be input? For example, are there limits on the total storage capacity of the system; that is, the number of records and the sizes of records or fields? Are both fixed and variable fields possible?
    (f)   Ease of use – is the software supporting a system which is straightforward to understand and user-friendly?
    (g)   Format in which the software is supplied. Formats could include disks and tapes of varying sizes. Often a variety of formats is available for any given system, but one format must be suitable for the hardware configuration to be used and must be specified.
3. *Support*
    (a)   What documentation is available? Documentation should include a user manual, an operations manual and a detailed description of how the software works.
    (b)   Personal support in the form of advice and maintenance facilities will also be important. Training in the use of the software, advice on its implementation and the sharing of expertise through membership of a club or existing users can all be valuable.

4. *Legal factors*
   (a)   Is there a warranty?
   (b)   Is the contract satisfactory?

21.5   Catalogue modules in library management systems

The library management systems listed in Figure 21.4 all have a catalogue maintenance module and an OPAC module. These modules are concerned with the
creation and maintenance of, and retrieval from, catalogue databases. These two
modules will be examined more closely below.

The cataloguing maintenance module

The cataloguing module must support the entry of records into the system.
Records may enter the system by direct online creation of records, by loading of
MARC records from tape, and by the downloading of records from a bibliographic utility. Authority control to support the creation of high quality records is
also offered by most systems. These facilities are listed in Figure 21.5.

All systems support online creation of records by means of formatted screens or
prompts. Full screen editing is increasingly being provided, with some systems
incorporating word processing type facilities. Library defined screens are also
another possibility.

A number of systems now include the use of MARC as an option in the system;
this sometimes involves maintaining two records on the system – one in MARC
format and the other in the internal format (for transaction and display purposes).
A few systems are totally MARC-based; they require input in MARC format and
can, as a result, output MARC. For all systems, MARC records can be used for
converting to the internal format, but cannot be reconstituted for output. Most
systems allow libraries to define the fields to be included in their bibliographic
records; at the least, they allow field labels to be changed. Once a record has been
created, most systems allow for retrieval immediately on all keys, although some
have overnight updating of indexes.

Authority control is important to ensure accurate data. Most systems provide
authority control in one of two ways: a separate authority file to control headings
added to the main bibliographic file; or bibliographic records derived from data
held on authority files. Some systems allow libraries to define which fields are to be
authority controlled. Provision is usually made for cross references to be added to
the authority file, which are usually displayed on the public access catalogue. Some
systems also provide a thesaurus which can be accessed during data entry.

An increasing number of systems provide for downloading records from bibliographic utilities rather than loading them from tape. In the case of BLCMP and

Figure 21.4 Some library management systems, their suppliers and functions covered

Larger Systems

Supplier	System	Acquisitions	Cataloguing	OPAC	Circulation Control	Serials Control
ALS	System 88	✓	✓	✓	✓	Under dev
BLACKWELLS	ISIS	✓	✓	✓		Under dev
BLCMP	BLS	✓	✓	✓	✓	✓
CLSI	LIBSIOO	✓	✓	✓	✓	✓
DAWSON TECHNOLOGY	DATATREK	✓	✓	✓	✓	✓
DIGITAL DESIGN	ADLIB-2	✓	✓	✓	✓	✓
DS	GALAXY	✓	✓	✓	✓	✓
DYNIX	DYNIX	✓	✓	✓	✓	✓
G & G SOFTWARE	LENDING LIBRARY	✓	✓	Enquiry	✓	✓
GEAC	GLIS	✓	✓	✓	✓	Within acquisitions
IBM	DOBIS/LIBIS	✓	✓	✓	✓	✓
IME	TINLIB	✓	✓	Enquiry	✓	✓
Information Dimensions	TECHLIB/STACS	✓	✓	✓	✓	✓
Leatherhead Food Research	CAIRS–LMS	✓	✓	Enquiry	✓	✓
MCDONNELL DOUGLAS	URICA	✓	✓	✓	✓	✓
PYRAMID	CALM	✓	✓	Enquiry	✓	✓
SCSS	BOOKSHELF	✓	✓	✓	✓	✓
SLS	LIBERTAS	✓	✓	✓	✓	✓
UNISYS	PC/PALS;U/PALS	✓	✓	Enquiry	✓	✓

Smaller Systems

Supplier	System			
Dolphin Computer Services	Dolphin Library System		Enquiry	
Emtek Computers	LIBRA	✓	✓	
Eurotec Consultants	LIBRARIAN	✓	✓	Under dev.
Floyd Ratcliffe Consultancy Services	LICON	✓	Enquiry	✓
Head Computers	ELROND		Enquiry	Under dev.
Information Systems Design	LIBRARYAPAC	✓		✓
Logical Choice	BOOKSHELFPC	✓		✓
Micro Librarian	MICRO LIBRARIAN		Enquiry	
Top-Tech-Systems	MICRO-LIBRARY SYSTEM	✓	Enquiry	✓

Source: Based on a table in J. Leeves (1989), *Library systems: a buyers' guide*, 2nd edition, Aldershot: Gower.

Figure 21.5   Functions of cataloguing modules

Cataloguing

Data Entry

- online creation of records using formatted screens and/or prompts.
- library defined data fields and display.
- provision for entering records in MARC format.
- provision for loading external MARC records.
- check for duplicates and facility for adding new copies.
- provision for transferring or upgrading order record.
- provision for editing and amending records with minimum of retyping; *full screen editing.
- provision for different types of material, e.g. a-v, serials, etc.
- immediate retrieval on all keys.
- automatic conversion to MARC on input and output.

Authority Control

- provision for maintaining an authority file online accessible during data entry for checking/selecting headings.
- provision for new headings to be added to authority file, either automatically or following review.
- provision for creating 'see' and 'see also' references.
- provision for global changes of heading.
- thesaurus control.

Downloading

- provision for accessing external databases for downloading of records, either directly or via intermediary files.

Access and catalogue provision

Online Access

- online access for staff and public enquiry.
- library-defined indexes for staff and/or public.
- self-teaching, menu-driven facility for public; provision of more sophisticated facilities for staff, e.g. input of commands.
- library-defined displays.
- provision for keyword and phrase searching.
- direct display of record if only one match.
- display of copy/status information through minimum number of screens; staff access to more detailed loan information not available to public, e.g. borrower or reservation information (or via circulation enquiry).
- index display if no match.
- provision for browsing backwards and forwards in index and/or catalogue.
- library-defined help messages; *context-specific help.
- use of Boolean operators (implicit and/or explicit).
- truncation of search terms (implicit and/or explicit).
- limiting searches, by search qualifiers, e.g. date, type of material; searching one location or all.
- different 'views' of catalogues according to type of users.
- offsite access to catalogue.

Public Access

- provision of a suitable interface for public searching, incorporating appropriate elements of the above.
- provision for placing reservations by public, if required.
- and for public to display own borrower information, e.g. books on loan.

Hard Copy

- provision for COM, cards, printed catalogues and listings.
- provision for a variety of sequences.
- layout etc. library-defined.

Source: J. Leeves (1989), *Library Systems*, Aldershot: Gower.

397

SLSS, provision for accessing and downloading from their respective databases is incorporated into their local systems.

The OPAC module

All systems provide online access in some form or other. Some provide an enquiry function, but most provide an OPAC and a separate staff enquiry function which provides more sophisticated facilities than the OPAC. The OPAC can usually be library-defined in a number of respects. The library can identify menus for staff and public use; dialogue and messages can be defined accordingly, as can display of information and help texts. Help is increasingly context-specific so that an appropriate message can be displayed at whatever point has been reached in the search. Some systems allow the library to define which fields are to be indexed for staff and public, and also allow keyword indexing to be specified for certain fields. Often staff can use commands to bypass menus and to display information not available to the public.

Most systems offer both phrase and keyword searching. For phrase searching, there is usually implicit right-hand truncation; for keyword searching, a truncation symbol is normally input if required. Keyword searching is sometimes across all specified subjects and sometimes limited to specific fields.

The display of retrieved records varies. Some systems always display the index before a record; others show the record directly if there is only one match. Usually the record display includes holdings information; with some systems it is necessary to refer to another screen for loan status. For non-matches, some systems show the index. Browsing of the index and/or the retrieved records is normal.

Other search facilities offered are various and system dependent. Boolean operators can be offered, sometimes implicitly, for use in handling phrases as search terms. Use of truncation symbols and qualifiers, together with the availability of a command-based interface (possibly only for staff use), are becoming more common.

In addition to providing access to bibliographic data, increasing numbers of systems allow users access to their own borrower data as well as to place reservations.

Access to catalogues in hard copy form is still useful as a back-up. The quality of this output varies. Some systems allow library definition of format, content, layout etc, and some can produce COM catalogues.

21.6   Current developments and the future for library management systems

Over the past few years the marketplace of library systems suppliers has grown and consolidated. Continuing growth can be seen at the smaller end of the market, whilst larger systems suppliers have concentrated on consolidation.

The larger systems market is quite stable, many suppliers having been active for a number of years. Systems are being enhanced and suppliers are attempting to extend their customer base. CLSI has become UNIX based, and GEAC is marketing Advace which runs on a range of industry standard machines.

The major growth in recent years has been in the smaller systems, the number of implementations having also grown significantly. Some of the fully integrated comprehensive microcomputer-based systems make use of windowing, colour and graphics and can be networked to provide multi-user applications. Recent changes in microcomputer systems include the entry of Dawson Technology marketing, firstly the Data-Trek Integrated Library System and later OASIS. Fretwell–Downing have purchased Lending Library from G + G Software, and DS has acquired a shareholding in Pyramid. Soutron was formed to market the Sydney Library System (formerly MicroLibrary) and has developed Bibliomac for the Apple Macintosh.

Developments which are likely to signal future trends include:

1. improvements in the design of the OPAC interface;
2. greater degree of user definition;
3. an increasing dependence on the MARC record format;
4. improvements in facilities for downloading;
5. the further development of communication facilities so that users can access other OPACs through the OPAC of their local library;
6. interfaces with CD–ROM, both for access to CD–ROM databases (such as bibliographic databases on CD–ROM) and also for catalogue production on CD–ROM;
7. introduction of image processing systems, so that images can be linked to the catalogue database; and
8. links between acquisitions modules on local systems with databases maintained by the book trade, which will not only facilitate book selection and ordering, but also have implications for the creation of catalogue records.

Most of these areas impact upon the catalogue and OPAC modules and confirm the central position of the catalogue module in the library management system. More than ever the catalogue database is the central database of the library management system.

21.7 Information retrieval in text information management systems

By definition, a text information management system has sophisticated searching facilities. It is these search facilities that distinguish text-based systems from other database systems. The many facilities they offer include Boolean search formulation, search refinement, truncation and text string searching, stop lists or common word lists, and synonym recognition or thesaurus support. In fact, these systems provide most of the facilities described in Chapter 18. Of course, the interface style will vary from one system to another, as will the precise nature of the retrieval facility.

21.8 Current developments and the future for text information management systems

Many of the trends that have been identified above in respect of library management systems are echoed in text information management systems, despite the divergence in their fields of application. The last five years have been characterized by an increasing shift in application towards the total information management system, where it is no longer appropriate to divide documents into text and non-text. Systems are becoming capable of handling the complete document including text, line drawings, tables and pictures. Early applications of text information management systems were described as indicative text (ITX) and created bibliographic databases in a special library environment. The trend is now towards full text (FTX) databases handling both databanks and electronic documents. Organizations may use these systems to manage their document collections. These systems tend to be managed centrally within an organization by computer centres rather than by the library, with users having direct access through widely distributed workstations.

The market for text management systems has been relatively stable for the larger systems in recent years. Some key microcomputer systems are now well established as multi-user systems, but there is still some volatility in this sector of the market.

The changing environment in which the software is being used has caused suppliers to think more creatively about the design of the human computer interface. Help systems and OPAC interfaces with improved search facilities have become more widespread. Systems have generally introduced a novice-mode for searching which is menu-based. STATUS/IQ, described below, uses a natural language interface, and other systems, such as Personal Librarian, make use of relevance ranking. Some systems, notably BASIS, make use of windows. There is a general awareness that these systems must be as user-friendly as other business software.

Image processing has been a further area for development, with optical storage being used to store multi-media databases.

21.9 Management of inhouse cataloguing and information retrieval systems

All systems pass through a lifecycle, each phase of which challenges management in different ways. Often within an organization there are several computer systems in operation with several interrelated subsystems. Each of these separate systems or subsystems may be at a different stage in its systems lifecycle, and therefore the manager is often involved in more than one phase of different lifecycles at any one time.

The phases in the lifecycle are:

1. Analysis, when system needs are analysed and functions determined;
2. Design, when the system is designed to meet identified needs;
3. Implementation, when the system is first put into operation;
4. Operating Evolution, when the system is doing the job for which it was intended. Evaluation and maintenance will be essential to ensure that the system continues to do its job, and
5. Decay, when the system starts to deteriorate and planning for a new system should be underway.

We will consider the management issues associated with each of these phases in more detail.

Analysis

Analysis is intended to define the objectives or system requirements for the new system. This includes:

*   evolving guidelines and objectives against which later project progress can be measured;
*   establishing communication and appropriate involvement and commitment to the plans for the new system;
*   preparing a draft specification of requirements, and
*   preparing a study proposal to request funds for further investigation of the project.

The second step is likely to focus on information gathering, with consideration of:

*   gathering information about systems and other applications from suppliers, courses, other systems, users, exhibitions and other sources, and
*   developing a checklist of desirable features, or even a final systems requirements specification, possibly a logical model of the existing system.

The management of the analysis phase is concerned with establishing effective communication and project management.

401

Design

If a new system is to be written, the design phase is concerned with building a logical model of the system and developing it. Where a software package or turnkey system is the solution, the design phase is concerned with putting together such features as will meet the requirements specification. This may involve exploring a number of hardware configuration and software options. Compatibility is a watchword during this phase.

Implementation

Implementation is concerned with getting the system up and running. Implementation needs to consider a number of issues that also need to be revisited at times during the operation of the system.

Implementation starts with a review of the way in which the new system will affect the existing operation of the organization, including its impact on working practices. This is followed by:

- site preparation,
- hardware installation, including links to telecommunications networks,
- software installation and testing, including user evaluation,
- creation of databases,
- preparation of user documentation and
- changeover to new system.

During the implementation phase, training and security need to be considered. A training programme needs to be planned which satisfies the needs of all potential users. The objectives of the training programme need to be clearly identified, and scheduling of the training sessions must be integrated into the work rota. As new staff join an organization, they need to receive training, and existing staff may need a refresher course from time to time to prevent them from acquiring bad habits.

Security is important and must be considered in relation to all aspects of the system, including hardware, software and data. Breaches of security in respect of hardware are likely to lead to its being stolen or damaged. Breaches in respect of software are likely to lead its ceasing to operate in an appropriate way. Data can be corrupted, or errors may arise during data input. Most software has various security devices to protect the data including passwords, user ids and data encryption. Some users are often allowed write access to a file; others may only be permitted to read a file or parts of a file, while another group may not be permitted to access certain files or parts of files at all.

Operating evolution

Once the system has been successfully implemented, it should operate satisfactorily for some years until system requirements change or until the hardware or software becomes unreliable. Enhancements in both hardware and software are to be expected from time to time, and these need to be introduced with the minimum of disruption.

Maintenance arrangements for both hardware and software are important in keeping a system running and in offering some support when the system fails to work as it should. Various different kinds of contracts can be signed for maintenance; a choice should be made in light of the impact on the organization of the system being down for any significant period of time.

Monitoring and evaluation should indicate whether the system is operating as it should. A log of both problems and usage can provide a useful source of information.

User support needs to be available to help users with any problems.

Documentation must be reviewed at intervals and updated as appropriate.

Decay

Once the system starts to fail to function satisfactorily, a new system must be sought. It is important when first selecting a replacement to choose one with a clear upgrade path in an attempt to satisfy anticipated future needs. Above all else, remember that all systems have a limited life and that planning for new systems should commence before the old system has totally collapsed.

21.10   Some examples of systems

Dynix Automated Library System

Dynix is installed in over 300 libraries worldwide and is portable across a wide range of hardware from PCs to supermini computers. Since 1990 Dynix has been available to run under UNIX. Its modules encompass the following functions:

Public access	Management reports
Cataloguing	Circulation
Reserve book room	Acquisitions
Serials control	Backup/mobile library

The catalogue maintenance module provides the primary means for building and maintaining the bibliographic database. The system supports MARC and non-MARC records simultaneously, and accommodates every MARC format required

403

by the library. It is possible to maintain both full and brief bibliographic records. Data is automatically verified; any field in the bibliographic record can be indexed and retrieved; holdings for all locations are linked to one bibliographic record. Other facilities include automatic creation of holdings records, spine/pocket label production as well as help screens and prompts.

Authority files for author, title, subject, uniform title entries etc are automatically generated from the library's bibliographic files. They are easily created through the normal cataloguing process or added and updated online. Authority files also have the following features:

- automatic verification of authorized forms
- global updating
- restricted access to updating functions
- creation and updating of see and see also references
- help screens and prompts
- automatic checking of new authority records against forms already authorized on the system.

An existing database can be loaded from machine readable tape. During loading there is automatic deletion of duplicate records, automatic indexing and an automatic authority check. Direct interfaces are available to BLAISE, OCLC, RLIN, WLN, MARCIVE, Bibliofiole and other systems.

Bibliographic authority records and local indexes (e.g. fiction, newspapers, general information etc.) are retrieved quickly with easy-to-use search methods. Displays can be in MARC format and/or in library-specified labelled format. Access points are library–specified and may include author, title, subject/subject keyword, ISBN/ISSN, class number or other bibliographic fields. Search strategies can use keyword in context, exact entry, truncation, Boolean AND and OR. Displays are library defined, and forward and backward browsing are possibilities. Searches can be limited by date, material, type, language, etc.

Reports and statistics can be produced. Typical examples might include: additions, and withdrawals, subject bibliographies, authority lists, use statistics or unauthorized access attempts.

Multi-level security can be set. Access is controlled both by operator IDs and passwords and by dedicated terminals.

Public Access Module

The library can specify access points and define the types of displays required. The system will operate with touch screens if desired. Non-touch terminals have coded function keys for entering commands with a single keystroke.

Typical access points are author, title, subject, ISBN/ISSN, call number, contents notes and added entries. Again search strategies can use keyword in context, exact entry, truncation, Boolean AND and OR, and forward and backward browsing. Initial search results can be progressively narrowed. If more than one item is found, a list is displayed; items can then be selected from the list or other search commands can be entered. Any item can be viewed in a library-specified formatted display or in full MARC format. The catalogue integrates brief records and fully catalogued items. Location and availability of information are displayed for copies. Search results can be printed out. Public access reports provide information, and statistics are available regarding numbers of searches by type of search, text of searches, material selected and holds placed.

STATUS from Harwell Computer Power

A leading text management system, STATUS has over 1000 installations, plus several thousand more on optical media. Central to STATUS applications is the text file, which is the text of the document in its original form. STATUS does not impose associations or relations between items of information. In order that searching can be performed, an index file is created. The main components of the index file are:

- an alphabetic list of each word that occurs in the text file, and
- a reference pointer to record the position of every single word.

STATUS is used for a large number of different applications, wherever it is useful to keep the text of a document as a computer database. These could include parliamentary information systems, legal transcripts, film library, patents control, technical documentation, company standards, archives and market analysis.

STATUS runs on a wide range of hardware platforms and operating systems, from mainframes to minicomputers to microcomputers. STATUS/PC is a PC version which runs on IBM and compatible PCs. STATUS/LAN is a network version for microcomputers. STATUS/UNIX is a UNIX-based version. STATUS applications are portable from one platform to another.

STATUS holds documents in the STATUS textbase. Text which is put into a STATUS textbase may fall into one of four optional categories:

- Chapter – information category as a subdivision of a textbase; allows information to be categorized into information types that can be searched all at once or in any combination;
- Article – document;
- Paragraph – definable area within document, and
- Word – character string.

There are four standard interfaces to STATUS:

1. STATUS 4GL command language with STATUS commands and user-defined commands;

405

2. User customized menus, which can be created to fit a particular application, or may be general;
3. Screen based question-capture panels, where the user just fills in the boxes, and
4. Natural language interface, where questions can be submitted in plain English. Documents are ranked in terms of their relevance to the question.

Information retrieval techniques include:

- searching for concepts, words or phrases
- proximity searching
- keyword and synonym/thesaurus facilities which cater for normal unstructured or structured text
- truncations
- Boolean logic searches
- question refinement abilities
- range searching, e.g. on dates, and
- macros facility.

Security is available at the level of textbase, chapter, extended chapter, named section and document title, so that it is possible to specify exactly if particular users have different levels of access to different parts of a database.

STATUS has been used for several electronic publishing projects. STATUS/EP has been specially developed for use with optical media, and has been optimized for CD–ROM/WORM systems. CD–ROM services include data capture, textbase design and loading, user interface creation, CD–ROM simulation and CD–ROM production.

STATUS can integrate with other software. External software functions can be called from within a STATUS menu. Software that might be accessed includes Email, ISPF, screen editors, SAS, image processing software and word processors. STATUS can accommodate a range of word processing mark-up systems, which allows a document to be imported into STATUS, indexed, and then exported with no loss of integrity.

STATUS Screenmaker is a data entry system. It offers full screen working with multi-screen forward and backward paging, scrolling within all fields and the ability to hide and protect STATUS mark-up and keyed field names. Other features include user designed prompts and tailoring of screens; full validation of all special fields; use of user defined defaults and full word-wrap and WP style editing within scrollable fields.

STATUS CORA has been designed specifically to help manage registries, archives and record management centres. The facilities control the management of files from their creation in registries or other offices, through a period in archives and on to eventual destruction or transfer.

TECHLIB

TECHLIB is an application of BASIS plus the new text retrieval system launched in 1990 to replace BASIS. BASISplus boasts a relational architecture and real time updating of files. TECHLIB was also launched in 1990 and is aimed at the larger special library. The system may run alongside a BASISplus application or as a stand-alone system. The base system comprises BASISplus, PAC and cataloguing/maintenance. Optional modules are circulation, serials and acquisitions. There is also a system for inter-library loans which operates on a separate database called BILLplus.

The system may be customized to local requirements. The databases can be designed to suit local practice so that for each library various parameters relating to circulation can be set up. The ability to handle multiple libraries is a feature of TECHLIBplus. There are global parameters, such as the definition of collections and material types. The user can write plug-in functions for local processing, and these are maintained between releases. There are also BASISplus utilites which can be used to change fields, screens, help, texts, etc.

The system is menu-driven, although it is possible to exit to BASISplus command mode from most menus to perform tasks that cannot be performed by the menus; this is especially useful in searching since the complete range of BASISplus retrieval facilities are available. Help texts can be changed by the user and are context specific. On each screen there is an action bar with a default action highlighted. Throughout the system activities associated with a given routine are clustered, and various activity screens show the current state of processing. Each module has a reports menu.

The catalogue database comprises a number of different record types. The cataloguing maintenance function not only provides access to the catalogue records for different material types (books or serials), but also gives access to other record types (such as copy records or acquisition records). There is a MARC processing option which maps MARC fields to TECHLIBplus fields. The MARC records can also be stored on the database and displayed in that format.

There are different cataloguing maintenance screens for the different material types. Screens are supplied as standard, but can be modified. Each screen is divided into two parts, the top part for bibliographic details and the lower part for copy details. The level of a catalogue record can be defined, as can the format which will appear on the OPAC.

There is an optional Thesaurus Manager. All records are added to the database in real-time and are immediately available on the OPAC.

The default OPAC introductory screen provides for the searching of all libraries for all materials. Function keys are used to limit searches to given libraries or materials. At any time context specific help can be summoned using a function key and is displayed in a pop–up window. Function keys are also used to move between screens.

Every field in the system is keyword indexed. The user enters a search on a form which provides for searching by author, title, subject, keywords and call number; other fields can be added by the library. Boolean operators can be used to link terms so that when the user enters a phrase, by default the OPAC finds all records where all of the words in that phrase appear in any order. This default, together with others, may be changed by the library.

If a search results in several matches, a summary screen is displayed showing the number of matches and a brief citation; records can be marked for a fuller display. This display gives copy information, though further display options are available.

The user can make a request for an item via a pop–up window which allows name and address to be entered; this is not a reservation, but creates a record for the librarian to respond to.

21.11 More on OPACs

An important component of library management systems is the online public access catalogue (OPAC). Since the theme of this text is information retrieval, it is appropriate to focus on the way in which users can access catalogue databases. An OPAC is a library catalogue accessed via a computer terminal for the benefit of library users. All library management systems offer an OPAC module.

The OPAC has had a fundamental effect on user access to library catalogues. The OPAC could be viewed as just another physical form of catalogue, but the consequences of their introduction have been much more significant than those associated with any other physical form of catalogue. First and foremost, research has confirmed that users use OPACs when they would have eschewed the card or microfilm catalogue. Secondly, OPACs can be searched from a workstation within the originating library, at a terminal elsewhere in the organization, or remotely via national and even international telecommunications networks. The OPAC is a shop window on a library's collection and can facilitate a better awareness of information sources and a fuller utilization of stock, both within a library and beyond it to other libraries and document collections. The OPAC is part of a stable of developments that includes networking, inter-lending and sharing of resources, all of which are set to have far-reaching implications for collection management.

The development of OPACs

The development of OPACs in operational systems has progressed alongside research into OPAC design. This section focuses on the former leaving consideration of the latter to Chapter 23. Although a somewhat artificial divide, it has been adopted in order to place research on OPACs in a more general context of information retrieval with which it has many techniques in common.

As Hildreth has stated, 'The online public access catalog is the first major development that brings the benefits of automation directly to the user: as a means of expanded access to library collections and as a means of organising and presenting bibliographic information for effective self-service access.' Attention started to focus on online public access systems in 1980. Dowlin (1980) reported a pilot study at Pikes Peak Public Library. In June 1980, the Council on Library Resources commissioned a joint planning study by OCLC and the Research Libraries Group (RLG) to identify the issues, problems and priorities in designing, developing and operating patron access online catalogues. The recommendations from this project led to a set of CLR-sponsored research projects to analyse user requirements and the performance of existing public access systems. 1980 saw the installation of OPACs in several institutions, and for the next few years they spread through American libraries. Progress in the United Kingdom followed. Seminars held by the Centre for Catalogue Research in 1983 discussed the development and implementation of online catalogues. Attention focused on GEAC systems, other systems such as OCLC, and in-house systems such as CATS at Cambridge University and CIRCON at St Andrews University.

The three generations of OPACs

Further discussion of the development of OPACs is best structured in accordance with the three generations of catalogues witnessed to date.

1. *First-generation OPACs* were derived from traditional catalogues or computerized circulation systems. Access keys mirrored those of their predecessors, such as author or title (as a phrase), classmark and possibly subject heading (as a phrase). In addition searching was available by acronym key such as an author-title key containing the first four letters of the author's surname and the first four letters of the first significant word in the title. First-generation OPACs expected exact matching of search terms and were intolerant of user mistakes. They were generally acceptable for known item searching, such as might be performed in an author search. Many first-generation OPACs were menu-based, but offered only limited search facilities through the menu.

   When there was not an exact match, first-generation OPACs usually displayed records that were a close match. It was possible to browse backwards and forwards through a sequence, which subsequently could lead to a successful hit. Often subject searching was on the basis of classification numbers or one keyword in a title. Such a search could be successful if the classification number or keyword were specific, but would often lead to large numbers of items being retrieved.

   Searching in a first-generation OPAC had too many of the characteristics of searching printed and card catalogues, and there was not much improvement in the search facilities available.

2. *Second-generation OPACs* began to rectify some of these evident limitations.

409

Systems designers looked for inspiration to other text-based retrieval systems, such as text information management software, and the software used by online hosts. Second-generation OPACs then offered much better search facilities based on keyword searching and post-coordination of keywords. Usually these OPACs could also be operated by a simple command language which allowed the system designer to offer a greater range of search facilities, including the opportunity for search refinement.

Although second-generation OPACs were a great improvement, two problems still needed to be addressed. Browsing through records remained difficult, while the large size and wide subject coverage of many catalogue databases led to too many false drops.

3. *Third-generation OPACs* use a natural language interface so that users may input their search strategy as a natural language phrase. Most third-generation OPACs are research prototypes. OKAPI, for example, uses keywords and phrases in searching; the user sees a natural language interface but the search mechanism remains invisible.

OPACs and the future for catalogues

The emergence of the OPAC has reopened debate about the nature of a catalogue. We could revisit Cutter's functions and assess whether they stand the test of time. Alternatively, Kaske and Ferguson offered an early definition of what an OPAC must do:

> A public access online catalogue must at least provide the bibliographic record content, retrieval functions and access points similar to, and understandable in terms of, a card catalog. Therefore, the record content will include entry information, notes information and tracings information. The user must be able to locate, in the database, all works by an author, all editions or other versions of a work, all works on a given subject, and a work or works with a specific title.

This basic definition could be supplemented to include:

1. authority control over name and subject headings;
2. cross-reference structures linking variant forms and related headings;
3. keyword access to titles and subject headings, and
4. easy-to-use Dialog options for the untrained, unassisted user.

This definition clearly emerges from a perspective limited by the card catalogue. Even though second-generation OPACs and beyond are beginning to shake off the heritage of the card catalogue, OPAC design has still been conditioned by this environment. A complete review of the appropriate approach to OPAC design would involve a total rethink of the way in which catalogue records are created, stored and can be accessed, with concomitant implications for AACR2R, classification schemes, indexing practices and record formats. Research is beginning to consider more radical OPAC design, but there is a long way to go.

A first step towards an examination of design is to look at the three fundamental components of the OPAC, as follows:

1. *data contents* such as records, files and their structure and organization. Questions to be considered are associated with the enhancement of records to include more analysis of content and even full-text records of some documents. Do records and files need a structure? If they do, what is the best structure?
2. *access points and retrieval methods* including subject, title, author, but what else? What about hypertext and other new retrieval strategies? Can images be used fruitfully (the red book with the picture of a crane on it)?
3. *user interface characteristics* including how data is made available to the user? Considerations are ease of use, comprehensible displays, help systems, WIMP interfaces and natural language interfaces.

Searching in a second-generation OPAC

Much of the power and flexibility familiar to users of online information retrieval systems is now to be found in OPACs. Many OPACs support the ability to restrict searching to specified record fields, to perform character masking and/or right-hand truncation and to limit the results by date, language, place of publication, etc. Also bibliographic records may be viewed and printed in a number of different display formats. There are, however, some key differences between OPACs and other online information retrieval systems, including the following:

- the OPAC must be usable by untrained and inexperienced users who may need online assistance to help with the mechanics of searching;
- records in the catalogue database lack abstracts or full text, so subject indexing is based on a limited number of terms whose vocabulary is often not representative of current terminology; and
- the catalogue database contains information on a wide variety of disciplines and subject areas.

These differences have been recognized in OPAC design, first, by providing precoordinated phrase searching and browsing options and, second, by providing

411

keyword and Boolean capabilities which give more and more online user assistance in the form of menus, help displays, suggestive prompts and informative error messages.

Recommended reading

Library management systems

Anley, C and Mullner, K (1989), 'Dynix at Kensington and Chelsea libraries', *Program*, **23** (3), 231–46.

Arfield, J A (1991), 'CLSI's LIBS-100 at Reading Univerity Library', *Program*, **25** (1).

'Automation and electronics for libraries of the 1990s' *Library Review*, **39** (3), 1990.

Battin, P, 'The effects of information technology on library management', in *Libraries after 1984: Proceedings of the LAA/NZLA Conference 1984*, 244–56.

Bawden, D (1988), 'Specific roles for microcomputer software in an information department', *Aslib Proceedings*, **40** (1), 1–8.

Bawden, D and Blakeman, K (1990), *Going automated: implementing and using information technology in special libraries and information units*, London: Aslib.

Bawden, D and Blakeman, K (1990), *Information technology strategies for information management*, Sevenoaks: Butterworth for IIS.

Blunden-Ellis, J (1987), 'A market study of library and automation systems in the UK', *Program*, **21** (4), 317–82.

Blunden-Ellis, J (1989), 'A UK market study of large library automation systems vendors 1987', *Program*, **23** (1), 55–64.

Blunden-Ellis, J (1991), 'The UK market survey of library automation systems vendors (January 1989–January 1990), *Program*, 25 (2), April, 133–49.

Burton, P F (1987), 'Microcomputer applications in academic libraries II', London: British Library Board (Library and Information Research Report no 60).

Burton, P F and Petrie, H F (1990), *Microcomputer for information management*, 4th edition, London: Chapman Hall.

Clayton, M (1987), *Managing library automation*, Aldershot: Gower.

Computers in Libraries international conferences (1st–5th), 'Proceedings, conference chairman John Eyre, Westport and London: Meckler, 1987–1991.

Cowley, R (1988), *ALS: a guide for librarians and systems managers*, Aldershot: Gower.

Dickmann, J (1990), *Introducing IT in the library: some management issues*, London: Library and Information Technology Centre.

Dyer, H and Gunson, A (1990), *A Directory of library and information retrieval software for microcomputers*, 4th edition, Aldershot: Gower.

Dyer, H and Morris, A (1990), *Human aspects of library automation*, London: Gower.

Foster, W (1990), *Library automation: an introduction*, Birmingham: BLCMP.

Fryer, R K *et al.* (1991), 'Criteria for selecting mainframe database management systems', *Database*, **14** (2), 54–57.

Griffiths, P (1989), 'Entity-relationship analysis, the operational requirement and a buyer's view of the market for automated library systems', *Program*, **23** (1), 13–28.

Guy, R F (1990), 'Evolution of automation in a national library: the experience of the National Library of Scotland from 1978–1989', *Program*, **24** (1), January, 1–19.

Jones, K E and Rea, G A (1989), *URICA: a guide for librarians and systems managers*, Aldershot: Gower.

Leeves, J (1989), *Library systems: A buyers guide*, 2nd edition, Aldershot: Gower.

Leeves, J and Manson, P (1988), *Guide to library systems for schools*, London: Library and Information Technology Centre.

'London Borough of Bromley: from ALS to GEAC in six months', *Vine*, **75**, 1989, 4–7.

Manson, P (1989), 'Integrated automation systems for cataloguing, circulation and acquisitions on microcomputers: an overview of functions and products on the UK market', *Program*, **23** (1), 1–12.

Manson, P (1989), 'Turnkey systems marketplace: ten years on', *Vine*, **76**, 3–8.

Matthews, J R (1985), *Directory of automated library systems*, New York: Neal-Schuman.

Nelson, N M (1990), 'Technology for the 90's: microcomputer in libraries', Research contributions from the 1989 Computer in Libraries Conference, Westport and London: Meckler, 1990.

Nicholson, D M (1987), 'Choosing a library system', *Library Review*, **36**, 48–56.

Ramsden, A (1988), 'Micro software for library and information work – an overview', *Aslib Proceedings*, **40** (1), 9–18.

Richardson, I *et al.* (1990), 'In-house library systems development at the University of Lancaster', *Vine*, **81**, 24–26.

Rowley, J E (1987), *Info-tech?: a guide for young professional librarians*, London: AAL.

Rowley, J E (1988), 'Basics of information technology', London: Library Association.

Rowley, J E (1990), 'Guidelines on the evaluation and selection of library software packages', *Aslib Proceedings*, **42** (9), 225–35.

Rowley, J E (1990), *Systems analysis and design for information managers*, London: Library Association.

Sippings, G (1987), 'The use of information technology by information services: the Aslib Information Technology Survey 1987', *The Electronic Library*, **5** (6), 354–57.

State of the art of the application of new information technologies in libraries and their impact on library functions in the UK, London: Library and Information Technology Centre, 1987.

Stubley, P (1988), *BLCMP: a guide for librarians and systems managers*, Aldershot: Gower.

Tedd, L A (1987), 'Computer-based library systems: a review of the last twenty-one years', *Journal of Documentation*, **43** (2), 145–65.

Thomas, D (1988), 'Moving from locally written systems to turnkey systems: the story of automation at Brunel University Library', *Program*, **22** (3), 209–21.

Westlake, D R and Clarke, J E (1987), *GEAC: a guide for librarians and systems managers*, Aldershot: Gower.

Text management systems

Ashford, J A and Willet, P (1989), *Text retrieval and document databases*, Bromley: Chartwell Brat.

Beiser, K (1987), *Essential guide to dbase III in libraries*, Westport, Conn: Meckler.

Citreon, C (1989), 'Microcomputer software for information retrieval: how to make a well-founded choice', *Program*, **23** (2), 141–50.

Crane, J A (1991), 'Selection of a text retrieval system in two user environments', *Journal of Information Science*, **17** (1), 93–104.

Datta, V K (1987), 'Use of CAIRS at the Tropical Development and Research Institute Library', *Program*, **21** (4), 360–75.

Dowlin, K (1980), 'Online catalog user acceptance survey', *RQ*, **20** (1), 44–47.

Frey, C (1987), 'Microcomputer software packages for information management: an Australian perspective', *Microcomputers for Information Management*, **4** (1), 11–37.

Gillman, P (ed) (1990), 'Text retrieval: the state of the art', Proceedings of the Institute of Information Scientists Text Retrieval Conference: The Users Perspective (1988) and Text Management (1989), London: Taylor Graham.

Gillman, P (ed) (1991), 'Text retrieval: information first', Proceedings of the Institute of Information Scientists Text Retrieval Conference, London, October 1990, London: Taylor Graham.

Ingebretson, D L (1987), 'Information management software: a selected bibliography', *Database*, **10** (6), 27–34.

Jackson, A E (1991), 'Prototyping a text information management system', *Aslib Proceedings*, **43** (5), 173–87.

Kazlauskas, E J (1987), 'Information management software: guidelines for decision making', *Database*, **10** (6) 17–24.

Kazlaukas, E J (ed) (1987), *Directory of information management software for libraries, information centers, record centers 1987–8*, Studio City, Ca: Pacific Information.

Kimberley, R (1986), 'Integrating text with non-text – a picture is worth 1K words', Proceedings of the Institute of Information Scientists Text Retrieval 1985 Conference, London: Taylor Graham.

Kimberley, R (ed) (1990), *Text retrieval: a directory of software*, 3rd edition, Aldershot: Gower.

Kimberley, R *et al.* (ed) (1985), 'Text retrieval in context', Proceedings of the Institute of Information Scientists Text Retrieval 1984 conference, London: Taylor Graham.

414

Lundeen, G and Tenopir, C (1988), *Managing your information: how to design and create textual databases on your microcomputer*, New York: Schuman.

Oxborrow, E A (1986), *Databases and database systems: concepts and issues*, Bromley: Chartwell Bratt.

Pape, D L and Jones, R L (1988), 'STATUS with IQ – escaping from the Boolean straightjacket', *Program*, **22** (1), 32–43.

Rowlands, I (ed) (1987), *Text retrieval: an introduction*, London: Taylor Graham.

Rowley, J E (1986), 'Text retrieval systems – an outline' in P I Zorkoczy (ed), *Oxford Surveys in Information Technology*, vol 3, Oxford: Oxford University Press, 211–45.

Saffady, W (1989), *Text storage and retrieval systems: a technology survey and product directory*, Westport and London: Meckler.

Willet, P (ed) (1988), *Document retrieval systems*, London: Taylor Graham for IIS (The Foundations of Information Science vol 3).

OPACs

Akeroyd, J *et al.* (1988), *Using CD–ROM as a public access catalogue*, London: British Library.

Bates, M J (1986), 'Subject access in online catalogs: a design model', *Journal of the American Society of Information Science*, **37**, 357–76.

Burton, T *et al.* (1989), 'OPACs and JANET: a simple technique for easy user access', *Program*, **23** (3), July, 257–68.

Cochrane, P A (1985), *Redesign of catalogue and indexes for improved online subject access*, Phoenix, Ariz: Oryx Press.

Ferguson, D and Kaske, N K (1980), 'Online public access to Library bibliographic databases: developments, issues and priorities.' Final report to the Council on Library Resources (ED 195 275).

Foster, W and Wellings, R (1989), 'Development of BLCMP's online public access catalogue', *Program*, **23** (2), 151–62.

Hildreth, C R (ed) (1989), *The online catalogue: developments and directions*, London: Library Association.

Kinsella, J (ed) (1986), 'Online access to library files', Proceedings of the Second National Conference (University of Bath, April 1986), Oxford: Elsevier.

Markey, K (1985), 'Subject searching experiences and needs of online catalog users: implications for library classification', *Library Resources and Technical Services*, **29** (1), 34–51.

Matthews, J R (1985), *Public access to online catalogs*, 2nd edition, New York: Neal Schuman.

McSean, T and Smith, N (1989), 'As simple to use as a card catalogue: can you put your library catalogue on CD–ROM', *Vine*, (**74**), August, 25–30.

Mitev, N N *et al.* (1985), 'Designing an online public access catalogue', London: British Library (Library and Information Research Report no 39).

Potter, W G (1989), 'Expanding the online catalog', *Information Technology and Libraries*, **8** (2), 89–104.

'Public access online catalogues', *Library Trends*, **35** (4), 1987.

Slack, F (1988), 'Subject searching in OPACs: a general survey of facilities available on OPACs in academic libraries in the United Kingdom', *Vine*, **72**, 8–15.

Walker, S (1988), 'Improving subject access painlessly: recent work on the Okapi online catalogue projects', *Program*, **22** (1), 21–31.

Walker, S and Jones, R M (1987), *Improving subject retrieval in online catalogues*, London: British Library.

22 Cataloguing systems: networks

22.1 Introduction

Networking is a term used by information professionals to describe various co-operative activities. Increasingly these activities are based on physical networks of computers linked by telecommunications. Here we adopt Dempsey's definition of networking which is 'the use of physical networks to describe library services'. Molholt outlines the confusion:

> there is constant confusion in the library and information community regarding the dual nature of networking, particularly as two meanings or functions intertwine so strongly in today's libraries. Most of the references to networking in the library literature refer to the resource-sharing aspect of the term, despite the fact that the enabling mechanism for such sharing is telecommunications.

This quotation identifies the two strands of networks: (1) resource sharing, and (2) the telecommunications that facilitate the resource sharing. Many of the developments in resource sharing in recent years have been due to the opportunities offered by improvements in information and communications technology.

The early networks that prompted developments in library and information science were those of the bibliographic utilities and the online hosts. The online hosts have been described elsewhere; here we focus on the bibliographic utilities and associated activities. These had their origins at a time when networks were single purpose and associated with the services that they made accessible. As the use of networking becomes more pervasive, as the infrastructure becomes available which makes data transfer much more common, and especially as library and information services are delivered to end–users over networks, it will become increasingly difficult to identify one network from another. Networks will be tightly interlinked, and various routes through the networks will be available to users. Barriers will be less defined by the limitations of physical networks, and more by licensing and access agreements. Library networking envisages the use of the diversity of telecommunications networks for communication between libraries, between libraries and other organizations and between libraries and their users.

In this fully networked world of the future, the objectives of a library network will be:

1. to reveal the contents of a large number of libraries or a large number of publications, especially through accessibility of catalogue databases; OPAC interfaces will be able to reveal the resources of any number of individual libraries.
2. to make the resources thus revealed available to individual libraries and individual users when and where they may need them, such as at the end-user's workstation.
3. to share the expense or work involved in making these resources available through exchange of records and associated activities, in order to control the costs of these activities to individual libraries and users.

It is impossible to describe in detail all of the potential applications of networking in library and information management in this chapter. Potential applications include:

- value added services such as electronic mail, directory services and file transfer,
- exchange of bibliographic records,
- inter-library loan,
- distribution and publication of electronic documents such as electronic journals.
- end-user access via the integrated OPACs of several libraries, and
- end-user access to other databases such as those available on the online hosts and others.

This chapter examines the provision of these facilities by considering the role of the main existing agencies in library networking. First it is useful to review the context from which today's activities have evolved.

22.2 Background and development – cooperation and centralization

Libraries have long recognized the benefits of cooperating in catalogue production. There seems little point in hundreds of cataloguers in separate locations wading through cataloguing codes and classification schemes in order to create a variety of catalogue records for the same work, unless the local situation requires specific features in respect of cataloguing or classification. Both centralized cataloguing systems and cooperative networks are means of sharing cataloguing effort and information. Their objectives are however slightly different, even though in any discussion of computerized cataloguing systems, cooperative networks and centralized cataloguing are inextricably linked. Most libraries exploit the fruits of centralized cataloguing in some way, and it is difficult to envisage a cooperative network which does not make use of centrally produced records.

Centralized cataloguing is the cataloguing of documents by some central organization such as the British Library for the British National Bibliography (BNB), or the Library of Congress. The main purpose of centralized cataloguing is to create a standard and acceptable record that can be inserted into the catalogues of a large number of independent libraries.

In *cooperative or shared cataloguing* a number of otherwise independent libraries share the work of producing a catalogue for their mutual benefit. In particular, a central feature of cooperative cataloguing is the union catalogue, which is intended to permit improved access to and exploitation of the resources of the libraries in the cooperative. A *union catalogue* is a listing in one sequence of the holdings or part of the holdings of two or more libraries. Usually some indication of the location of the documents will be given in the catalogue.

Apart from participating in a cooperative cataloguing scheme and exploiting centrally produced cataloguing data, libraries have one other possible strategy in the creation of catalogues. This is to opt for local cataloguing, using either a purpose-designed software package or a standard software package. This option is considered in more detail in Chapter 21.

Many large library systems have some contact with shared and centralized cataloguing activities, but may also resort to local cataloguing for specific kinds of materials. In general, the larger public and academic libraries exploit centralized and shared cataloguing for most of their monograph cataloguing. The situation for the cataloguing of serials varies considerably, and there are notable differences in practice between the US and the UK. Nonbook materials are more likely to be catalogued locally, although many shared and (increasingly) centralized cataloguing systems do cater for nonbook materials. In general, then, there are many options in selecting a system for the production and maintenance of catalogue records.

22.3   Centralized and shared cataloguing

Centralized and cooperative cataloguing could generally be described as shared cataloguing. There have always been certain requirements for shared cataloguing to be viable, the benefits of the earlier non-computerized systems still forming the basis of many network activities today. Networks have evolved from earlier cooperatives. It is worth rehearsing the motivation for shared and cooperative cataloguing.

Centralized and shared cataloguing should remove duplication in cataloguing effort. In order that this can be achieved it is necessary that:

1.   Libraries should catalogue and classify a document in the same way (that is, without shared cataloguing there would be exact duplication of cataloguing decisions). For this to happen requires some standardization in cataloguing

419

and classification practices. Generally, if the economic aspects are favourable, the availability of shared cataloguing records will encouarge uniformity, but a readiness and a trend towards consistency are a prerequisite to the success of shared cataloguing. If different libraries have very different requirements of catalogues, then shared cataloguing will not prove attractive. Generally, libraries have been able to accept uniform bibliographic records which they will then amend or supplement with other data according to local needs. Typical local data might be locations, loan status or items in special collections. Less standardization has been achieved with regard to the subject approach to documents than with the description and the author/title approach.

2.   A number of libraries must acquire the same document. In fact, extensive duplication only occurs in respect of a limited number of documents. Many libraries have special collections of foreign, unpublished or unusual materials which include items unlikely to be acquired by other libraries. It is relatively economic to produce shared records for documents which many libraries acquire. Thus, for instance, popular fiction that is included in the collections of a large number of public libraries can easily be handled by a centralized service. It is less obviously effective to aim to generate a shared catalogue database to cover all the materials acquired by a range of libraries. If some records are required by only a limited number, it will be difficult to recoup the cost of creating and maintaining these records. Almost inevitably then, many libraries will have some acquisitions for which records are not available in a shared cataloguing service. The relative proportion of new material covered and not covered by a shared cataloguing database will be a significant factor in that library's decision whether or not to participate. Thus, some materials, in particular books, are likely to be covered to varying extents by shared cataloguing services, while other materials will never be covered by them. At the present time these include periodical articles, the individual papers in conference proceedings and other items which might possibly be revealed by analytical cataloguing. The bibliographical control of such items is primarily the province of in-house indexing, analytical cataloguing, abstracting and indexing services and associated databases.

3.   A mechanism exists whereby the cataloguing agency or agencies can view new documents, preferably prior to publication or at least very soon thereafter. It is essential for the agency to be able to provide records for new documents as soon as a librarian receives them, otherwise stock will have to wait in cataloguing departments until the appropriate records do become available. If there are excessive delays in the record becoming available and if long delays become a common phenomenon, the librarian who is anxious to make new stock available for the user as soon as possible will resort to local cataloguing. Thus excessive delays in the availability of cataloguing records will negate much of the value of a shared database. Usually a central cataloguing agency is based

upon a national library or copyright office, where publishers are required by law to send at least one copy of every book published in that country. Cataloguing-in-publication can also assist in reducing delays, and this is considered separately below. Other shared records may be produced by the members of cooperative networks.

Merits of shared cataloguing

A quick list of the merits of centralized cataloguing is useful in summarizing some of the features of these services:

1. Economy of effort, particularly in eliminating unnecessary duplication of cataloguing decisions.
2. Superior cataloguing may result, since more consistency and closer adherence to standard codes are likely to emerge with cataloguers who spend all of their time cataloguing, than with a librarian who tackles cataloguing as one of various professional tasks.
3. Uniformity of cataloguing between a number of libraries who are all using shared cataloguing records will help readers and librarians. This advantage must be tempered by the fact that the standard record may not always be consistent with local requirements, and local modifications are likely.
4. In some instances the exploitation of shared cataloguing records contributes to more prompt cataloguing since less local cataloguing needs to be performed. However, delays in the generation of records can be a considerable nuisance.
5. Availability of the shared database as a basis for resource sharing and inter-library loans.
6. Sharing in the development of other services and of expertise in these areas, especially in relation to information technology-based developments.

22.4 Agencies in networking

The various agencies involved in networking offer similar facilities to one another although there are some differences. Most agencies offer several of the following:

- online access to large databases of catalogue records which contain a common bibliographic record, with local holdings information,
- the databases, based on the MARC record format, can be made available to participating libraries,
- catalogues in printed, card and other formats can be produced for participating libraries, in accordance with individual library specifications,
- access to authority files, such as those of the Library of Congress Name and Subject Authority Files,

- support for inter-library loan,
- subject search facilities,
- microform catalogues,
- automatic built-in authority control,
- stand-alone library management systems and
- CD–ROM products.

The next few sections briefly review the activities of some of the key agencies in library networking. The Library of Congress and the British National Bibliography offered centralized cataloguing services before the age of computers. Their major contribution now is in maintaining and providing access to major bibliographic databases, although (as described below) they also have other major contributions to make to networking activity. The national libraries or national bibliographic agencies of other countries also perform a similar role, but the Library of Congress, followed somewhat later by the British National Bibliography, were the first services and remain central players.

Other networking organizations have emerged from shared cataloguing and cooperative ventures. Since developments in the United States have again led the world, these are described in more detail than developments elsewhere.

22.4.1   The Library of Congress

As an early centralized cataloguing service, the Library of Congress (LC) started to distribute printed catalogue cards in 1901 and still plays a central role in library networking.

The MARC Project, initiated in 1966 to examine the possibility of generating machine readable cataloguing data and distributing it to user libraries, led to the establishment of the MARC Distribution Service in 1969. The MARC database is central to LC's activities. The LCMARC database is based on the Library of Congress' cataloguing of its own collections, with additional records from cooperating libraries. The databases therefore reflect the interests of a major library collection. The LCMARC database can be accessed online via a number of hosts. Cards are still printed from MARC records, either on demand or via the 'Alert Service'. For instance, a particular library can establish a profile consisting of the subject areas that are of interest. Then, when the LC enters a bibliographic record into its database that matches this profile, a catalogue card will automatically be printed. CD–ROM services are also being developed. CDMARC Subjects and CDMARC Names have already been mentioned in the context of authority control in Chapter 8. CDMARC Bibliographic is planned which will put the complete LC bibliographic file onto compact disk.   Retrospective conversion of records for pre-1966 publications started with the RECON project and is ongoing. A related project is REMARC which is mentioned below in the section on UTLAS.

LC has also played a major role as a coordinator of networking. In the mid-1970s a Network Development Office was established, followed by the Network Advisory Committee. Various major cooperative ventures have been undertaken, including the following:

1. *CONSER* (Cooperative Online Serials) has involved the LC together with some other US libraries, the National Library of Canada and OCLC in building a machine readable database of serials cataloguing information. Participating libraries can upgrade their records and add information to the OCLC Online Union Catalogue in accordance with CONSER standards.

2. *Linked Systems Project* (LSP), initiated in 1980, aimed to establish a national network where systems are linked by a standard interface. Thus a subscriber to one service or utility is able to search the database of other services or utilities without having to learn the search procedures of that system. The participants are the LC, the National Library of Canada, UTLAS, OCLC, RLIN, WLN and library automation vendors such as Geac.

   The Authorities Implementation, the first of the LSP applications, was introduced in 1981 as the Name Authority File Service (NAFS); this became the Name Authority Cooperative (NACO) in 1984. Within NACO, the LC, RLIN and OCLC contribute records to and receive records from the national authority file using the Standard Network Interconnection (SNI) – the telecommunications component of LSP. Records contributed by LSP libraries are available to subscribers to MARC tapes.

22.4.2 British National Bibliography

The British National Bibliography (BNB), which is now the responsibility of the British Library Bibliographic Services Division, was established in 1950 under the auspices of the Council of the British National Bibliography. The service was originally based upon books received by legal deposit in the British Museum, and later upon those received by the Agency for Copyright Libraries. The British National Bibliography is a weekly printed list with entries classified and arranged by the latest edition of DC. Separate author/title indexes and subject indexes are included. BNB has two four-monthly cumulations per annum which are superseded by an annual volume and then triennial cumulations. From 1991, the classified section is in two parts: the first consists of forthcoming titles and the second of titles recently received on legal deposit.

A MARC distribution service began in 1969; currently some 200 UK libraries and other organizations use BLMARC records for local cataloguing and associated purposes. The BL introduced a licence to use British Library Records in 1986 in an attempt to ease restrictions on access to records. All organizations intending to use BL records in machine readable form require this licence which entitles them to obtain BLMARC records by whichever supply method is most convenient and to distribute them to other licensees without restriction.

The BNB is also available on CD–ROM as a backfile covering 1950–85 and as a current file for records from 1986 onwards.

An interesting recent development is the copyright libraries Shared Cataloguing Project, in which the BL, the other UK legal deposit libraries and Trinity College (Dublin) are cooperating. The other five libraries have agreed to share the BL's cataloguing burden and to contribute records to the BNBMARC files. This project, which is concerned with the creation of a major database, needs to be considered in the context of the Linked Systems Project and CURL (described later in this chapter).

22.4.3   BLAISE

BLAISE, the British Library Automated Information Service, became operational in 1977 and now has three components: BLAISE-LINK, BLAISE-LINE and BLAISE-RECORDS. BLAISE-RECORDS is responsible for records supply from the BL databases, whilst BLAISE-LINE and BLAISE-LINK offer the services of an online host in supporting access to a number of bibliographic databases.

BLAISE-LINK is operated collaboratively with the US National Library of Medicine (NLM). It offers access to biomedical and toxicological information (on databases such as MEDLINE, TOXLINE and RTECS) and to records of books and serials held by the NLM (as are found in CATLINE and SERLINE). GRATEFUL-MED is a microcomputer–based software package which provides an extremely user–friendly interface to all of the databases on BLAISE–LINE. GRATEFUL-MED was developed by the NLM and has been in use in the US since 1987 and in the UK since 1989.

BLAISE-LINE is the British Library's own service. It offers access to bibliographic data such as is found in the following databases: BNBMARC, Whitaker, BLISS (British Library Information Sciences Service), BL Catalogue Preview (entries so far converted in the BL Catalogue Conversion Programme), Document Supply Centre Catalogue, Humanities and Social Sciences Catalogue, Science Reference and Information Service Catalogue, LCMARC, University of London Catalogue, AVMARC, Cartographic Materials, HELPIS (audio-visual materials database produced by the British Universities Film and Video Council), Music Library Catalogue, Conference Proceedings Index, SIGLE (grey literature), HMSO (UK government publications), NSDC (UK National Serials Data Centre), ESTC (Eighteenth Century Short-Title Catalogue) and Register of Preservation Microforms. BLAISE-LINE is now connected to JANET, which will make access easier for academic users and eventually for others.

BLAISE-RECORDS manages record supply facilities from the various BLAISE-LINE databases. Records are supplied via downloading or magnetic tape. If a record cannot be located on BL files, it can be sought on the OCLC databases. All records can be delivered on tape in UKMARC format, but down-loaded records may be in UKMARC or LCMARC depending on whether they have been downloaded from BL or OCLC databases. Records selected via BLAISE-RECORDS could formerly have been added to a LOCAS file. Introduced in 1974, LOCAS (Local Cataloguing Service) maintained a local MARC-based catalogue file for each participant; libraries were able to specify the type of catalogue required. LOCAS was withdrawn in 1988 and ceased operations in 1991.

22.5 Other US networks

OCLC (Online Computer Library Center Inc)

OCLC, founded in 1971 by a group of Ohio College libraries, was originally known as the Ohio College Libraries Center. OCLC has played a major role in the US and beyond in record supply, research and sharing of expertise. There are now over 10 000 libraries in 26 countries that make use of OCLC's various services. OCLC has a European office in Birmingham.

The OCLC database is the largest of its kind in the world. Records are held in the OCLCMARC format which is similar to that of LCMARC. The database is available for searching online. Records can be downloaded, while the Micro Enhancer software package facilitates offline editing and printing. EPIC is an online service which offers subject access to a variety of databases including the Online Union Catalogue. A Selective Record Supply Service allows libraries to extract and use OCLC records without requiring any input in return. Cards, sheaf slips, COMfiche, magnetic tapes, spine labels and accession lists can be supplied. Online access to LC Name Authority and Subject Authority files is available. OCLC also has an inter-library loan subsystem.

Search CD450 provides various databases on CD–ROM. A stand-alone local system, LS2000, is marketed, and CD–ROM cataloguing is available. Recently, a packet-switched network was introduced which will offer improved facilities for cataloguing, searching and authority control and will also support future developments in facsimile transmission and linking with other systems and networks.

WLN

WLN was previously known as the Western Library Network and earlier as the Washington Library Network. WLN was formed in 1967 when the Washington State Library took responsibility for developing a network. Nearly 600 libraries now make use of WLN's services, with 40 per cent of these subscribers in the state of Washington.

WLN provides shared cataloguing and catalogue maintenance and offers an automated acquisitions facility. There is a large central database which also acts as a union catalogue. An agreement with RLIN to exchange records enhances the breadth and depth of the database, which also contains authority control records, notes and cross-references. LC name authority records are transferred to WLN electronically via LSP, and subject authority records are received from LC and other sources.

MARS (MARC Record Service) is a database upgrade service. Authority records, including cross-references, are available on tape. Customized CD–COM catalogues can be produced using the LaserCat software. WLN's CD–ROM LaserCat system, containing records for the holdings of 250 libraries, was introduced in 1987 and is available for current cataloguing and retrospective conversion.

RLIN (Research Libraries Information Network)

RLIN is the responsibility of RLG (Research Libraries Group), a consortium of research libraries dedicated to resolving common problems in collection development, management, access and preservation. RLIN's central files are divided into segments for books, serials, music, sound recordings, visual materials, maps, computer files, and archives and manuscripts. The book file contains 80 per cent of total records. The database is an online union catalogue of the holdings of the system's participants which can have records converted to MARC format magnetic tape for input to local systems. Printed card and book form catalogues are other options. LC name and authority files can be accessed, as can other selected databases. Online acquisition and inter-library loan subsystems support these activities for participating libraries.

UTLAS International (formerly University of Toronto Library Automation System)

UTLAS merits mention both because it is a major utility and also because it operates in both French and English. Based in Canada, UTLAS commenced in 1973. Now a for-profit organization, UTLAS serves more than 2500 institutions in Canada and the US, and is very dominant in Canadian research and university libraries. A high-speed data link installed in Canada and Japan in 1982 allowed the Maruzen Company (one of Japan's largest book companies) and the International Christian University to connect to UTLAS, so that it is also used by a number of Japanese libraries.

The UTLAS database contains over 50 million records, of which 10 million are unique. The database forms the basis for the Cataloging Support Service (CATSS) and is comprised of CANMARC (the Marc Québecoise database produced by the Bibliothèque Nationale in Quebec), the Centrale des Bibliothèques database of records for monographs and audio-visual materials, and the Canadian Institute for Historical Microreproduction (CIHM) database. Also available are LCMARC,

UKMARC, Bibliothèque Nationale and the US NLM databases. The REMARC database, which includes records for items published prior to the MARC programme, is also available. The REMARC database was created in the late 1970s and early 1980s by Carrollton Press which was subsequently merged with UTLAS International.

UTLAS offers online cataloguing and OPACs, acquisitions control, retrospective conversion and serials control. Good authority facilities are available. Book, card and COM catalogues can be supplied, as well as machine readable records on magnetic tape. CD–ROM products based on CATSS are available; CD–CATSS offers a multilingual cataloguing system.

Other US developments

There are a number of regional organizations, some of which depend upon OCLC for their systems. SOLINET (South Eastern Library Network) and DALNET (Detroit Area Library Network) are examples. Other interesting networking activities incorporate full resource sharing.

1. *CARL (Colorado Alliance of Research Libraries)* became a not-for profit organization in 1978 and introduced its first system in 1981. The aim was to develop a cooperative, shared resource treating the collections of the member libraries as one. The six original members were Auaria Library, Colorado School of Mines, Denver Public Library, University of Colorado at Boulder, University of Denver and the University of Northern Colorado. The CARL system has six modules: database building, PAC, circulation, bibliographic maintenance, acquisitions and serials control. The public access catalogue has been designed to be particularly easy to use, and several catalogues may be mounted and searched with a single set of commands. The system has been implemented on other sites, all of which are linked.

2. *ILLINET Online (IO)* is now one of the largest automated library systems in the world. IO is composed of two linked components:

   • LCS (Library Computer System) which supports the circulation activities of 35 academic libraries and provides inter-library lending facilities to Illinois. Short circulation records for 35 libraries are included.
   • FBR (Full Bibliographic Records) is a state-wide union catalogue which contains records for over 800 libraries in Illinois which use OCLC.

   IO is one element in a wider strategy which also includes local library systems automation programmes, the Inter-library Delivery Service, and the Cooperative Collection Management programme. IO has pioneered automated resource sharing and has made extensive resources directly accessible to users.

427

3. *OLIS (Ohio Library and Information System)* is a statewide resource-sharing network that is being developed in Ohio and should begin services in 1991. Initial members will be 17 academic libraries in Ohio linked to appear to the user as a single resource. The network will have three components: local library services; OLIS Central, a central facility with union catalogue and other functions; and controlled access to national and other networked resources. OLIS is a new initiative which should be able to take full advantage of the latest technology.

4. *MELVYL* is the online union catalogue of the University of California. Fully operational since 1983, MELVYL has developed into one of the biggest systems in the world, covering items in over 100 libraries as well as the California State Library. A pioneer of second-generation online catalogues, it has continued to evolve innovative indexing and searching techniques to cope with the problems of end-user access to very large databases. Also a private network has been constructed in order to access MELVYL, and considerable expertise has been developed in the implementation of these networks.

22.6 United Kingdom developments

BLCMP

Originally Birmingham Libraries Cooperative Mechanization Project, BLCMP is a cooperative venture which embraces both network and stand-alone services. Formed in 1969, the first operational system was implemented in 1972–73. Today BLCMP offers services to a large number of libraries in the UK, including public and academic libraries and others.

BLCMP maintains extensive MARC databases, including records for audio-visual items, music and serials. Databases include Whitaker's Books in Print, UK and USMARC databases and records produced by the participating libraries. BOSS (BLCMP Online Support Service) provides a fully integrated online acquisitions, cataloguing and access system. The online cataloguing system allows users to search for, edit and create records which are of two types: general bibliographic records and local records containing information pertaining to a particular library. An extensive name authority file is maintained. BLCMP produces union and individual library catalogues, these last being available in a range of formats.

BLCMP's stand-alone Circulation Control system (CIRCO) is integrated with the stand-alone OPAC facilities. All stand-alone systems may be linked to provide access to central databases. Networking is also available between libraries, and access can be provided to and from local systems via networks such as JANET.

LASER

LASER (London and South Eastern Region) is an organization for library cooperation within Greater London and various counties in the south east of England.
LASER operates an interlending service based on its union catalogue. The LASER
union catalogue database contains well over one million bibliographic records
which represent the holdings of the 57 member libraries located within the LASER
geographical area.

VISCOUNT (Viewdata and Interlibrary Systems Communications Network),
which became operational in 1988, provides online search, retrieval, location find
and electronic mail facilities. VISCOUNT is available to all public library and
major non-public library members of LASER; investigations are also underway
into the implications of extending VISCOUNT to other regions. A first-stage
search reveals the holdings of libraries in the region and the BLDSC; a second-
stage search shows holdings in other participating regions. When an item has been
located, electronic mail can be used to request a loan.

Other UK developments

In addition to BLCMP and LASER, there have been other regional developments
in the United Kingdom.

SLS (Information Systems) began life as SWALCAP (South West Academic
Libraries Cooperative Automation Project). SLS's chief product is LIBERTAS, a
sophisticated library management system which includes modules for acquisition,
cataloguing, circulation and serials control. The product has an OPAC that uses a
natural language interface that is particularly worthy of note. SLS also maintains a
shared database.

SCOLCAP (Scottish Libraries Cooperative Automation Project) started in
1973. After various attempts to develop a library management system and much
exchange of expertise, SCOLCAP ceased to exist in 1990.

The UK has not benefited from the kind of national coordination of networking
activities that the Library of Congress has offered in the US. Nevertheless there
have been various attempts to coordinate activities and to create a national
bibliographic database.

1. *The Cooperative Automation Group (CAG)*
This was formed in 1980 under the auspices of the British Library, with the
objective of coordinating the work of the main UK utilities and networks with a
view to planned and coordinated development. Membership included representatives from the BL, all major UK networks and other interested parties. At an early
stage the group decided to direct its efforts towards the creation of a common
database. The CAG proposed that the UKLDS (UK Library Database System)
was to have two key objectives: (1) to make bibliographic records available for

429

cataloguing, and (2) to provide locations which could be used as a basis for reference or inter-lending activities. Lack of resources and conflicts of interest of the participating parties meant that the UKLDS never materialized. The CAG turned its attention to the development of standards. The CAG Study Group on Bibliographic Standards produced a proposal for input standards for UKLDS in 1983, which was revised in 1984.

2. *CURL (Consortium of University Research Libraries)*
CURL succeeded in creating a major machine readable catalogue database. The CURL database incorporates the catalogue records of the UK's seven largest university libraries. The records are available for shared cataloguing and are distributed on tape, using file transfer and by capturing session logs. The database is available to non-CURL libraries via JANET.

3. *JANET (Joint Academic Network)*
JANET is a network that provides communications links between users of computing facilities in over 100 universities, polytechnics, research establishments and other institutions; approximately 1000 computers are connected to the network. JANET commenced operations in 1984, but only more recently has its potential started to be exploited. JANET offers electronic mail, interactive access, file transfer and job transfer. Gateways are available to other networks such as EARN (European Academic Research Network), Internet (US) and to public data networks. Over 50 OPACs can be accessed via the network.

4. *UK Office for Library Networking*
The UK Office for Library Networking was established in 1989; it is funded by the British Library and based at the University of Bath. Its function is to support the development of networking activities amongst UK libraries by

1. representing the needs of libraries to the computing and telecommunications industry, and
2. promoting effective use of existing and developing networking infrastructures in the UK and abroad.

22.7 Cataloguing-in-Publication and related activities

Cataloguing-in-Publication (CIP) is the cataloguing of documents prior to their publication so that cataloguing data can be printed within the document itself. The data may also be used in databases such as those of the book trade, so that libraries and other purchasers may select documents prior to their publication from lists of CIP records.

The Library of Congress implemented a CIP programme in 1971. Catalogue

Figure 22.1 Some examples of networks

Acronym	Name	Country of Origin	Notable Features
ABN	Australian Bibliographic Network	Australia	started 1979. National bibliographic utility for shared cataloguing; uses WLN software; database based on WLN LCMARC, AUSMARC, UK MARC and CANMARC
PICA	Project for Integrated Cataloguing Automation	Netherlands	academic library network. National cataloguing database and local systems. Includes LC and UKMARC records. Uses thesauri of names and subjects
NACSIS	National Center for Science Information System	Japan	established 1986 from earlier initiatives; automated union catalogue of library materials; provision of bibliographic and other information
LIBRIS	Library Information System	Sweden	research libraries union catalogue; database contains local, UKMARC and LCMARC records
BUMS	Biblioteksjanst Utlaningosch Mediakontroll System	Sweden	started as a circulation control system; also has a union catalogue database; generates catalogues on CD-ROM (CD-KAT)

cards are printed from CIP records whenever full MARC cataloguing is not available. CIP entries differ from full MARC cataloguing in that they are shorter, with pagination and size omitted. Brazil implemented cataloguing-in-publication in 1971, and similar programmes now operate in many countries.

In 1976 the British Library Bibliographic Services Division began to provide brief catalogue entries on the verso of the title page of British publications from cooperating publishers. The scheme required the publishers to supply advance information to the BL, so that it could perform the cataloguing and return details to the publisher. CIP entries began to appear in the BNB and on the MARC database in 1977. CIP records were upgraded in 1985, from which time CIP records in BNB were to level 2 AACR2 description and carried full subject data. This avoided the necessity of upgrading CIP entries on publication and meant that full records could be made available quickly. By 1990 well over 1000 British publishers were participating in the scheme, increasing their marketing opportunities and offering libraries early information. In 1991, however, the BL ceased to create CIP records from advance information supplied by publishers. As an interim arrangement, the BL will buy in CIP records from Book Data Ltd. These CIP records appear in a separate section of BNB approximately six weeks before the expected date of publication. As soon as the book has been received by the BL, it creates a full authoritative record and switches the title to the main sequence of BNB. Whitaker will supply CIP data to the BL from 1992.

Another facet of cooperation with the book trade is exemplified by the work done by BEDIS (Book Trade Electronic Data Interchange Standards Committee), set up by the MARC Users Group in 1986. BEDIS has produced recommendations concerned with the communication of bibliographic and commercial data amongst libraries and booksellers. These recommendations have

1. identified a range of data elements that publishers are asked to make available to other users of bibliographic information. These elements have been categorized into mandatory, highly desirable and optional.
2. suggested that software houses should provide UKMARC conversion packages and that the BL should expand the UKMARC format to include those few bibliographic elements required by publishers.

Further developments to facilitate the handling of pre–publication records and links between systems beyond those of the individual library into the acquisitions modules of library management systems would facilitate the processing of documents.

22.8   Current developments and future trends

Each network is unique and the current picture is complex. There is a collection of national and international utilities offering different services, some of which overlap one another and some of which depend on the products of other networks or centralized cataloguing agencies for effective operation. Networking is clearly of increasing importance, but it is difficult to predict who will be the players on the network stage in ten years time or what their roles will be. There are a number of trends that can be discerned. The utilities place significant emphasis on the database as a resource and are concerned to improve its comprehensiveness and coverage. The delivery of other reference and information services is increasingly supplementing the basic bibliographic services. Utilities are also exploring how to distribute some processing to the local level, how to establish links between central and local systems and how to maintain the value of the central system resource. Issues that have already emerged and which are likely to continue to preoccupy the networking agencies include the following.

1. Linking of utilities
Cooperation and exchange of records are already evident to some extent and are likely to be extended. UTLAS has recently agreed to act as an OCLC regional network affiliate for OCLC services in Canada. RLG and OCLC have participated in the Linked Systems Project, described earlier. RLG and OCLC agreed in 1990 to work closely on the development of OSI library application protocols and are investigating the use of the ILL protocol to enable inter-library loan requests to be transmitted between their systems.

2. Maintenance of the databases
The databases of the utilities are unique sources of bibliographic data; this is a strength that the utilities will wish to preserve. Pricing structures are likely to encourage the contribution of records. Linking of local and central systems will also facilitate database maintenance.

3. Reference and information services
Additional databases intended for end-user access will increasingly become available via the utilities. These may complement or compete with the databases available on CD–ROM and via the online hosts. RLIN already make available a number of information sources in addition to the union catalogue. It is also developing a user-friendly interface with a view to offering more end-user information services. OCLC has recently launched Search CD450, a series of databases on CD–ROM, and EPIC, an online reference service aimed at the end-user.

4. Electronic documents
Various projects have investigated the electronic delivery of the full text of documents such as journals. OCLC has, for example, participated in the AAAS/OLC project which investigated the delivery of an electronic journal. AAAS (the American Association for the Advancement of Science) would be responsible for the contents of the journal, whilst OCLC (through EPIC) would take care of access

and delivery. The Mercury Project at Carnegie Mellon University has several research programmes investigating aspects of electronic text management.

5. Distribution of processing load
User interaction with the utilities has to date been largely through terminal access to a central host. This can be expensive, making other options such as CD–ROM more attractive. OCLC and UTLAS have each introduced a CD–ROM based cataloguing service. More dramatic is the redesign of the basic network. OCLC and RLG are redesigning their online systems to run as separate software components with standardized interfaces. Eventually, the software (providing the user interface, data manipulation and display facilities) may run on local workstations, with the central computers functioning primarily as a database server in a wide area network. RLG is developing software for an ILL workstation and OCLC's new online system PRISM (together with various reference services) will be mounted using the same Newton search engine.

6. Linked systems
OCLC and RLIN are cooperating to specify common interfaces to local library systems so that local cataloguing can be represented without delay in the union catalogue. Unfortunately the vendor implementation of protocols that make this possible is slow.

7. Network development
OCLC and RLIN are switching from systems based largely on dedicated terminal networks to those based on private X.25 networks. Networks now need to offer flexible links in an integrated way to local area networks, local systems and workstations, and offer the potential for distributing processing and data, and delivering a range of electronic information services. X.25 networks provide platforms for fuller integration of local and central systems and distribution of processing responsibilities. These offer higher-speed, lower-cost networks with greater flexibility.

8. Reciprocal catalogue access
Library users are increasingly likely to have access to the OPACs of other libraries. Full access implies libraries acting as an integrated group, with the OPAC and document delivery services appearing seamless to the user. CARL, MELVYL and ILLINET Online have been described elsewhere. Tentative moves in this direction in the UK include SABLIN, a project of major Scottish libraries jointly to examine their collection strengths, and CURL. Essex, Norfolk, Suffolk and Hertfordshire are discussing the possibility of allowing users within one local authority to search for books in another and initiate inter-library loan requests. Libertas' InterLibertas Access and Transfer module allows users at one Libertas site to access databases at other sites and for the transfer of records between them.

9. Extension of cooperation with publishers and the book trade
Cataloguing-in-publication programmes are well established. Further record creation and delivery services may be originated by the book trade, BEDIS having
examined some of the possibilities in the UK.

Recommended reading

Adams, R (1991), *Communication and delivery systems for librarians*, Aldershot:
    Gower.
Adams, R and Collier M (1987), 'Local area network developments at Leicester
    Polytechnic Library', *Program*, **21** (3), July 273–82.
'ADONIS: a new era in document delivery', *Interlending and Document Supply*, **16**
    (2), 1988, 65–69.
Arms, C (1990), 'Using the national networks: Bitnet and Internet', *Online*, Sep-
    tember, 24–29.
Arms, C (ed) (1988), *Campus strategies for libraries and electronic information*,
    Bedford, Mass: Digital Press.
Brindley, L (1987), 'Planning for library and information services over a campus–
    wide network', *Netlink*, **3**, 4–9.
Brindley, L (ed) (1989), 'The electronic campus: an information strategy', 'Pro-
    ceedings of a conference held on 28–30 October 1988 at Banbury, London:
    British Library (Library and Information Research Report 73).
Boss, R W (1990), 'Linked systems and the online catalog: the role of OSI', *Library
    Resources and Technical Services*, **34** (2), 217–28.
Buckland, M K and Lynch C A (1988), 'National and international implications of
    the Linked Systems Protocol for online bibliographic systems', *Cataloging and
    Classification Quarterly*, **8** (3/4), 15–33.
Buxton, A (1988), 'JANET and the librarian', *Electronic Library*, **6** (4), 250–63.
Cailloux, J M (1989), 'Proceedings of the workshop dedicated to the use of OSI for
    libraries', Luxembourg: Commission of the European Communites (EUR
    12436).
'Campus of the future: conference on information resources', Wingspread Confer-
    ence Center, June 1986, Dublin, Ohio: OCLC, 1987.
Cawkell, A E (1991), 'Electronic document supply systems', *Journal of Documen-
    tation*, **47** (1), 41–73.
Collier, M (1985), 'Microcomputer networks for library applications: research at
    the Polytechnic of Central London', *Microcomputers for Information Manage-
    ment*, **2** (1), 33–42.
Collier, M (ed) (1988), *Telecommunications for information management and
    transfer*, Aldershot: Gower.
'Connecting the networks', Proceedings of the Joint Library of Congress Network
    Advisory Committee and EDUCOM Meeting, 5–7 December 1988, Wash-
    ington, DC: Library of Congress, 1989 (Network Planning Paper 18).
Danczak, J (1989), *Cable and satellite: the potential for the information market*,
    London: British Library Board (British Library Research Paper no 59).

435

Dempsey, L (1991), 'Libraries networks and OSI: a review with a report on North American developments', Bath: UK Office for Library Networking.

Dempsey, L (ed) (1990), 'Bibliographic access in Europe', Proceedings of a conference organized by the Centre for Bibliographic Management, held at the University of Bath, 14–17 September 1989, Aldershot: Gower.

Greenwood, D (1989), 'OPAC research in the United Kingdom', in 'OPACS and beyond', Proceedings of a joint meeting of the British Library DBMIST and OCLC, 17–18 August 1988, Dublin, Ohio: OCLC, 1–16.

Lynch, C A and Berger, M G (1989), 'The UC MELVYL MEDLINE system: a pilot project for access to journal literature through an online catalog', *Information Technology and Libraries*, **8** (4), 371–83.

Machovec, G S (1989), 'Locally loaded databases in Arizona State University's online catalog using the CARL system', *Information Technology and Libraries*, **8** (2), 161–71.

Matthews, J R (ed) (1986), *The impact of online catalogs*, New York and London: Neal-Schumann.

Molholt, Pat (1988), *Library networking: the interface of ideas and actions*, Washington: US Department of Education.

Packham, K (1991), 'Installing LANs in the British Library', *Aslib Proceedings*, **43** (1), 19–22.

Smith, C H (ed) (1988), *Open systems interconnection: the communications technology of the 1990s*, Munich: K G Saur.

Smith, P (1987), 'The Viscount Project at LASER', *Vine*, **68** 11–18.

Stone, P (1990), 'JANET: a report on its use for libraries', London: British Library Research and Development Department (British Library Research Paper 77).

Tedd, L A (1987), 'Facsimile in libraries project', London: British Library (British Library Research Report 57).'The CURL database project', *Vine*, **73** 1988, 4–8.

Tuck, B (1989), 'Networks update', *Aslib Proceedings*, **41** (5), 191–96.

PART V
GENERALIA

23 Research and the future

23.1 Introduction

The development of systems for the organization of knowledge and information retrieval has reached a plateau, with many of the fundamental systems characteristics now tried and tested. It would not be accurate to say that there has been no progress. Significant advances in recent years are evident in the evolution of OPACs, CD–ROMs and full-text databases, together with the continued expansion of networking activities (all of which have been mentioned previously). Nevertheless, many of the core concepts – such as the heavy reliance on Boolean logic in the framing of search strategies, the use of inverted files to aid in retrieval and the organizational context in which many systems operate – have not been revised for 20 or 30 years.

Researchers have pursued a variety of approaches in their search for better systems. Research may broadly be categorized into that which focuses on:

1. systems design, where the general objective is to improve the efficiency and effectiveness of the system, including its storage requirements and its retrieval speed and effectiveness;
2. retrieval facilities and strategies, to improve methods for matching document descriptions with query descriptions; and
3. the human computer interface, where the objective is to improve the quality of interaction between users and the computer so that the former can be more successful in extracting what they require.

Work in all three of these areas has been conducted in relation to different types of systems. We are concerned here with work related to text retrieval systems as are used in online access to external hosts, CD–ROMs, in-house text information management systems and OPACs. Work in all three of the above areas is also being conducted in the context of general database design, and some of the progress in this area will influence the systems under consideration. Some text information management software is an integral component of a database management system, and library management systems may be constructed using general database software.

Most recent research and development in information retrieval have been conducted within the ambit of computer-based systems. This willingness to embrace the opportunities offered by technology has led to a dearth of research in other areas of information retrieval, such as the design of classification systems and the way in which users browse in a library.

It is often asserted that there is too wide a gap between research and practice in information retrieval systems. To some extent, the nature of research dictates that not all investigations and prototypes will lead quickly to improved operational systems. The gulf between research and real systems is perhaps narrowing. One of the objectives of this chapter is to identify some of the major research initiatives that have been undertaken over recent years and to draw these to the attention of the new and intending information manager. A further objective is to gather into some kind of framework the areas which might benefit from research and innovation. Future developments in specific areas of information retrieval, such as CD–ROM and OPACs, have already been explored. This chapter seeks to identify general trends that may affect the overall direction of the development of information retrieval systems. It attempts to identify areas that show potential for development, not only in theory, but by recounting some of the key research that has been undertaken.

23.2   Research into systems design

Research into systems design is concerned to offer alternative methods of constructing the system so that information can be retrieved more efficiently and effectively. Work in this area seeks to overcome the limitations of the inverted file by developing fast methods of scanning the contents of a database. The inverted file requires a considerable amount of storage, while overheads are associated with the generation and maintenance of indexes. Also some pattern-matching operations (such as left-hand truncation, variable length don't care and embedded substring searches) are difficult to implement efficiently in an inverted file. Serial files are attractive in that they are economic in terms of storage, require little processing and accommodate new records by placing them at the end of the file.

Researchers felt that it was worth revisiting serial files and re-examining mechanisms for text scanning. Work falls into two categories: that which seeks improved text scanning algorithms on conventional hardware, and that which explores the potential of parallel processors and other hardware with new architectures.

23.2.1   Text scanning algorithms

Retrieval in serial files is based upon pattern matching – that is, the comparison of the words or stems in the query with those in the documents in the file. If the efficiency of scanning could be improved, this method might offer hidden promise.

Research has focused on two main techniques: pattern-making algorithms and text signatures.

1.   *Pattern matching algorithms* place the string of characters that is being sought (the pattern) alongside the start of the string (text string) in which it is being sought. The first character of the pattern is then compared with the first character of the text string. If these match, the second characters are compared and so on until either a mismatch is found or the entire pattern is located. If a mismatch occurs between a pair of characters, the pattern is shifted by one position towards the right end of the text string and the matching process is resumed, starting again at the beginning of the pattern.

   With this simple pattern-matching algorithm a very large number of matching operations may be necessary. More sophisticated string search algorithms reduce the number of character comparisons required to not more than the number of characters in the pattern and text strings. These algorithms involve a pre-search analysis of the pattern strings and the construction of auxiliary tables to control the character comparisons. Boyer and Moore (1977) and Aho and Corasick (1975) have been responsible for two potential algorithms.

   The Boyer and Moore algorithm compares the text from the right-hand end of the pattern. Each time a match is found a left shift is made until either the start of the pattern is reached, indicating that the pattern has been found, or a mismatch occurs. When a mismatch occurs, the pattern is shifted to the right by the larger of two pre–computed functions 1 and 2. 1 is a function of the text character at which the mismatch occurs and is equal to the shift necessary to achieve coincidence with the current text character if that character is also in the pattern. 2 is a function of the position in the pattern at which a mismatch occurred. Thus knowledge from the previous scanning is used to reduce the number of pattern matches. The Boyer-Moore algorithm is effective for patterns of six characters or more.

   The Aho and Corasick algorithm is based on finite state automata. A finite state automata (FSA) is a conceptual machine that can determine whether or not an input sequence matches a specified pattern. At the start the automaton is in state B (beginning state). Whenever a character arrives the rules R are used to determine the next state of the FSA. This process continues until a final state (F) is reached when a desired pattern has been matched. A FSA scores over other pattern-matching algorithms because it can be used to recognize many words input at the same time; thus the text string can be matched against all of a set of query patterns simultaneously. The efficiency of this algorithm has led to interest in hardware implementations of the method.

2.   *Text signatures* seek to eliminate some documents from the pattern-matching search and thus reduce the size of the file to be scanned. A text signature is a fixed-length bit string in which bits are set to describe the contents of the document. The bit string is created by applying an operation to each of the keywords or descrip-

441

tors that characterize the document, causing one or more bits in the string to be switched on. Once a file of signatures has been created, queries that are presented to the database may be searched using a two-stage retrieval mechanism. In the first stage, the query signature is compared with the set of document signatures. Matching using strings of bits is generally quicker than matching based on characters, since the bits comprising a computer word can be inspected in parallel, so that several bits can be examined at once. This stage quickly eliminates most documents; the second stage uses a pattern–matching procedure on the remaining documents.

Other advantages accrue from the brevity of the text signatures compared with the original document, so that processing is conducted on a much smaller file. If large full-text documents are being searched, then to make the signatures distinct from one another it may be necessary to divide the documents into smaller units such as paragraphs and to assign a signature to each unit.

Several methods are available for the creation of text signatures, the development of efficient and effective text signatures being an active area of research (for instance, by Croft and Sarvino). Some methods are word based, with one bit being generated for each non-stop word in a document; in other methods, each word is used to set several bits by developing signatures based on substrings.

23.2.2   Hardware solutions

Conventional hardware and its architecture have inherent limitations in text scanning:

1. they can only execute a single instruction at a time, and each instruction only operates on one set of data at a time; additional loop control structures are therefore required if the same operation is to be applied to several data items;
2. systems are designed for computational tasks rather than for text comparisons, and
3. all data to be processed must be moved into the main memory before it can be processed; secondary storage devices are slow, and much irrelevant material has to be brought into the main memory for processing.

Three main options have been developed to overcome these limitations: database machines, array processors and transputer networks.

1. Database machines have been designed specifically for database searching. Most of these machines provide content addressability by associating processing logic with the read/write heads of a disk unit; this allows database searching and processing activities (that would otherwise have been performed by the central processor of the host machine) to be performed by the read/write heads. Thus only relevant data are passed to the host machine. Several small search processors are usually provided, each executing the same search and processing commands on different parts of the database. This parallel processing reduces the time for serial scanning.

Many database machines are only research prototypes; the chief exception is ICL's *Content Addressable Filestore* (CAFS). CAFS is a commercial product which consists of a cooperating group of special hardware units operating in conjunction with a conventional disk controller. The disk controller carries out normal file transfers in which data is either read or written in blocks, whilst the CAFS units scan stored data in a continuous stream from disk, passing back to the host only that small subset of the datastream that satisfies the query.

ICL has built CAFS into a number of diverse software products. QUICK-BUILD supports the rapid development of analysis and reporting applications for corporate and strategic data. INGRES is a relational database suite. STATUS and ICLFILE support text databases. INDEPOL, originally developed for police and defence information systems, bridges data and text.

2. *Array processors* also rely upon parallel processing to scan large quantities of text. An array processor contains a large two-dimensional array of identical and very simple processing elements or PEs. An individual PE consists of a single memory chip and a bit-serial arithmetic and logical unit; this allows high-level instructions (such as 32-bit additions) to be built up from cycles of basic one-bit instructions. This basic design allows all of the PEs to carry out the same operation in parallel. The control unit of an array processor carries out many of the functions of the control unit of a conventional computer in that it is responsible for the tasks of instruction fetch, decode and modify by registers. On the other hand, it does not generally execute instructions since most of the decoded instructions are sent or broadcast to the array of PEs; each PE then executes the instructions sequence on its own locally-held data. An array processor is an example of the class of computer referred to as *Single-Instruction stream, Multiple-Data stream* (SIMD), where the same instruction is executed simultaneously by a very large number of independent processors. Two examples of array processors are the Distributed Array Processor (DAP) by ICL and the Connection Machine (CM) by Thinking Machines Inc.

3. *Transputer networks* comprise another type of parallel processor – *Multiple-Instruction stream, Multiple-Data stream* (MIMD) machines. Here many low-cost, high-performance microprocessors are linked in a network; each processor can execute its own programs simultaneously as well as communicate with other processors to meet the requirements of a particular application.

Ideally the factor by which scanning is increased in speed should be equal to the number of processors in the network. Unfortunately, communication and scheduling take some processor power, and this, together with a limited amount of parallelism in the algorithm which is being executed, can lead to a sub-linear

443

increase in the processing speed-up as more processors are added to the network. In order to minimize this problem, commercial mainframe multi-processors typically contain only a few processors. It is asserted that the new generation of microprocessors is less affected by the speed-up problem. The use of text compression algorithms – to effectively increase the bandwidth of the data communications pathways in the network – may improve performance further. Also, onboard memories with increased capacities mean that the text can be stored adjacent to the processor so that only queries need to be distributed across the network.

Hardware techniques such as those described above offer interesting possibilities for the future, especially when used in conjunction with some of the software-based algorithms, as in the implementation of text signature searching on an array processor. If it can be shown that serial searching can out-perform searching based on the use of an inverted file, then future systems may have very different file structures.

23.3   Research into retrieval facilities

Research into the retrieval process has focused on the development of substitutes for Boolean searching. Boolean search logic was introduced in the earliest systems and is widely used, but has certain limitations including the following:

1. end-users need training in the formulation of queries;
2. there is no control over the size of the output produced by a particular query; when a query produces too many or too few records, the searcher must just try again;
3. retrieval results in the partition of the database into two discrete subsets: those records which satisfy the query criteria and those which do not. All retrieved records are assumed to be of equal importance; and
4. there is no means by which one can reflect the relative importance of different components of the query. On the other hand, Boolean searching does allow complex multi-faceted subjects to be defined very explicitly; moreover, the use of AND provides a mechanism for the partial identification of word phrases.

Three major lines of development in offering improved retrieval facilities are automatic indexing, best-match searching and hypertext.

23.3.1   Automatic indexing

Early work in information retrieval focused on automatic term selection. Luhn suggested that terms describing the contents of a document could be obtained by selecting words from the text and that this extraction could be based on frequency information. This was further developed by Salton and others. An investigation of the relationship between term discrimination values and collection frequencies reveals that terms of low-to-medium frequencies should be used to represent the contents of documents and queries. However, more recent work claims that the least frequently occurring terms are the most useful (Willett). However, there is still disagreement as to the best method for the selection of terms, and the tendency in operational systems is to index every term, except those very frequently occurring terms that are included in the stopword list.

23.3.2 Best-match searching

Best-match searching, also known as nearest neighbour or ranked output searching, uses statistical information concerning the frequency of occurrence of terms in records as the primary input to the retrieval algorithms. A best–match search is based on the matching of a set of query words against the sets of words associated with each document in the database. A measure of similarity between the query and each document is calculated, and then the documents are sorted into order of decreasing similarity with the query. A typical measure of similarity is the number of terms in common between the query and a given document. The output from the system is a ranked list in which those documents having most terms in common with the query are at the top; these documents should have the greatest probability of being relevant.

The major attractions of the best-match approach are:

1. there is no need to specify Boolean interconnections, and the query is simply a list of keywords;
2. there are no problems with the volume of output; users merely scan as far down the list as they wish to go; and
3. it is possible to take into account weighting information concerning the relative importance of query terms.

Systems to support best-match searching can be based on an inverted file with an additional pointer list corresponding to the terms in a query. When a document identifier is encountered for the first time in a pointer list corresponding to some query term, a counter is allocated to the document and set to one. This counter is incremented by one each time that document is encountered in subsequent pointer lists. When all of the lists have been processed, there will be a new list containing identifiers of all of those documents that have at least one term in common with the query, together with the actual number of common terms for each such document. Thus the calculation of similarities involves access to the pointer lists only.

The input of a query to a best-match retrieval system requires a natural language statement. This may be a string of keywords, a sentence-like string of words or the text of a known document. Each of the words in the input is identified and compared with a stopword list. Thus in a query such as 'The evaluation of online catalogues in public libraries', the query keywords would be 'Evaluation; Online; Catalogues; Public; Libraries.

The most obvious limitation of best-match searching is the loss of semantic information, such as the position of words in a phrase. The automatic identification of phrases by linguistic techniques has proved difficult. Sparck Jones and Tait (1984) use a natural language parser to generate grammatically acceptable noun phrases from sentence-length natural language queries. These phrases are then searched for in the records in the database.

A further problem encountered in best-match searching is word form variants. These are handled by a conflation algorithm, a procedure which reduces all variants of a word to a single form for use in retrieval. Term conflation is achieved by the user in operational online systems through truncation. The most common automatic conflation procedure is the use of a stemming algorithm which reduces all words to a stem or root by removing derivational and inflectional affixes. Most algorithms work with suffixes only, using a dictionary of common word endings such as -SES, -ATION, -ING. Provided appropriate checks are conducted to ensure that, for instance, S is not removed from GAS, and FORGETTING becomes FORGET and not FORGETT, these algorithms work well. However, stemming does not cater for all word variants, and several investigations have tested other conflation mechanisms. One approach involves the calculation by the system of a measure of string similarity between a specified query term and each of the terms in the dictionary component of the inverted file, based on three character substrings.

The most important component of the similarity measure used in best-match searching is the term weighting scheme which is used to allocate numerical values to each of the index terms in a query or a document in order to indicate their relative importance. Weighting schemes have attracted much attention. Most have focused on the weighting of query terms, with documents being characterized by binary (either present or absent) indexing. Sparck Jones (1972) introduced the concept of collection frequency or inverse document frequency (IDF) weighting. This involves assigning weights to the terms in a query which are in inverse proportion to the frequency of their occurrence within the documents to be searched. Of course, any frequently occurring terms will also appear in many irrelevant documents. Infrequently occuring terms have a greater probability of recurring in relevant documents and should thus be considered of potentially greater importance for retrieval purposes. Thus a weight can be of the form

$$logN(N(I))$$

where I is a term and N(I) its frequency of occurrence in the N documents in the collection. The IDF scheme produces better results than best-match searching with unweighted query terms.

The weighting algorithm can be further refined by incorporating relevance feedback. Once an initial search has been carried out and the user has inspected a few documents and evaluated their relevance, these relevance judgements can be used to calculate a new set of weights. Robertson and Sparck Jones (1976) proposed a weight of the form

446

$$\log < [R(I)(N-N(I)-R+R(I)]/[(R-R(I))(N(I)-R(I)] >$$

for a term which occurs in R(I) of the R relevant documents. This incorporates relevance judgements and therefore assumes that relevance information is available for each term and query. If this is not available, then an initial search is conducted using IDF weights and relevance judgements collected from the user to estimate R(I) and R. Relevance weights can also be used in query expansion, by calculating relevance weights for terms in documents chosen as relevant.

Best-match searching has been the subject of many research studies; an overview is available in Salton and McGill (1983). The techniques are used in STATUS IQ, mentioned in section 21.10. OKAPI also uses automatic term conflation and best-match searching in an OPAC.

23.3.3 Hypertext and related developments

Ted Nelson coined the term hypertext or non-sequential writing to describe non-linear text. Nelson had a vision of a single online database of the entire library corpus; this he named Xanadu.

Work on Xanadu identified the basic concepts and problems of hypertext. The first operational hypertext system was developed by Douglas Engelbert at Stanford Research Institute in the early 1960s. This system was known as the Online System. There are two essential components of a hypertext database:

- the items or units of information which are to be associated, and
- the links between those items or units.

The same components also form part of hypermedia systems which integrate text, data, images and sound on a single database using hypertext principles.

The units to be associated are often arranged in blocks or nodes which contain different types of digitized information such as text, graphical or other types of image (including photographs or maps) and audio or video data. The nodes can be linked hierarchically, non–hierarchically or both. Some systems, such as Hypercard, permit only one node to be displayed on the screen at a time; others, such as Notecard, allow simultaneous display of the contents of a number of nodes.

In a hypertext system, nodes are connected by links. Links can be

- structural links, which maintain the underlying skeleton or structure of the hypertext, or
- user-defined links, which allow the user to create new associations in the hypertext.

The originating or starting point of the link, such as a word or sentence, called the link source, usually acts as the reference; the destination or endpoint, called the link destination, acts as the referent. In addition to connecting nodes, links can also be used to:

447

1. connect a document reference to the document itself,
2. connect a comment or annotation to the text about which it has been written,
3. provide organizational information,
4. connect two successive pieces of text, or a piece of text to its immediate successors, or
5. connect entries in a table or figure to description or to other tables or figures.

Movement from node to node in a system is via links; thus the system must not only be able to recognize links and follow them, but also movement between nodes must be accomplished quickly and easily. A user should be able to move from one node to another with one or two keystrokes or mouse movements, and with only a one or two second delay.

Hypertext is essentially non-linear. One problem with interaction in such a database is disorientation; users forget where they are and how and why they got there. To alleviate this problem, many systems provide a 'graphical browser' or similar facility which gives an overview of the network structure. The graphical browser is a node which contains a diagram of the network nodes. Zoom or global facilities enable the user to move to the portion of the network to be displayed.

Paths and filters can also help reduce disorientation. Paths are ordered sets of nodes which guide the user through the hypertext along routes which might be considered useful or logical by the author. Filters suppress detail and allow the user to skip quickly from one node to another without having to examine the full contents of each node traversed.

Interest in hypertext has been stimulated by the new opportunities that it offers for moving between concepts. In particular, with hypertext,

1. references can be followed forwards or backwards;
2. new references, annotations, comments or links can be created, so that the user can develop a personalized network of links;
3. hierarchic and non-hierarchic structuring of information is possible;
4. documents can be customized to suit different applications, and
5. there is no need to duplicate points in different places.

On the other hand, hypertext has some less desirable features:

1. users can become disorientated and may have difficulty with hypertext documents;
2. users may suffer from cognitive overload when working on a number of simultaneous tasks or trails, and
3. hypertext documents can take a considerable time to prepare and index.

Hypertext principles have been embedded in a number of card-based and text-based systems as well as in catalogues. Several of these are described below.

1. *NoteCards and hyperCard* are card-based hypertext systems which use non-decomposable data structures otherwise called cards. Each card can be defined in terms of the different types of data they contain (such as text, graphics, audio or video) and the operations which can be performed on them.

NoteCards was developed by Xerox PARC to aid in the gathering and organizing of information on a topic for report production, but it is a general-purpose package. The cards in NoteCards can be text sketch (drawings) or graph (diagrams). Card are held first in FileBoxes and then in NoteFiles. It is possible to trace down through hierarchies of FileBoxes as long as they are in the same NoteFile. NoteCards makes extensive use of Windows; each card has its own separate window, and scrolling allows large cards. The cards contain icons which indicate links with other cards.

HyperCard was developed by Apple for the Apple Macintosh. Cards are held in stacks, equivalent to files. Related ideas are contained in cards held in the same stack. Each card is made up of a background, which may be shared by a number of cards in the stack, and a foreground, which is specific to that card. In general each card contains one screenful of information. Hypercard makes no use of windows; only one card can be displayed at a time.

A card can contain pictures, buttons (used to initiate a HyperCard function) and fields (which display text or can accept text input). The author can set different types of access rights for users of the stack. One application of HyperCard has been in Glasgow Online, a community information resource for use by residents of the city, tourists, researchers, educationalists and potential investors.

2. *Text-based systems* are epitomized by Guide, now marketed by Office Workstations Ltd (OWL). This works with an hierarchically structured text, with additional cross-reference connections across the text hierarchy.

Text, graphics or pictures can be used as databases for Guide, which essentially operates as a system for converting machine readable documents into Guide hypertexts, referred to as Guidelines. These Guidelines appear as a continuous scrolled display, but actually consist of a hierarchy of blocks of text; lower levels in the hierarchy are accessed for display using Replace buttons embedded in the higher-level text. Guide also uses Glossary and Cross Reference buttons. The former provide explanations of terms (displayed in sub–windows) whereas the latter enable the user to access text across the hierarchy.

One application of Guide has been the development of a prototype integrated information retrieval system called JUSTUS. JUSTUS runs on a Sun workstation and automatically creates a hypertext database in Guide format from machine readable versions of legal texts.

Another application of Guide has been in the context of Project Quartet which built and evaluated a hypertext journal. The articles formed a database and were structured using Guide, with a front-end browser being written using HyperCard.

3. *The Hypercatalog project* is an international venture between the Library and

Department of Computer and Information Science at the University of Limkoping (Sweden), the Department of Library and Information Science, University of Tampere (Finland), and Informatics Management and Engineering (IME) of England. It is envisaged that by using hypertext, the Hypercatalog will enhance the traditional catalogue by the following means:

1. supporting browsing and navigation;
2. providing for conventional searching;
3. offering alternative means for presenting information,relations and structures;
4. providing ways of establishing relations and following trails;
5. allowing users to specify and save personal views of the library;
6. containing information relating to links and relations between fields, records and files, and
7. containing information on collections as well as on individual items.

The database of Hypercatalog would comprise bibliographic descriptions of items with their reference lists, reviews and other information pertaining to individual items. The individual items would be connected in a network by their citation and other types of links. Works by the same author or in the same journal, or citations to a particular work or author could be identified by links; other forms of presentation (such as contents pages of journals or publishers lists) could be provided for in separate linked nodes.

Further exploration into the use of hypertext in catalogues may soon lead to some interesting developments.

23.4 Research into the human computer interface

Another approach to improving retrieval in online systems is to focus attention on the quality of the interface or dialogue between the computer and the searcher. Work in this area has focused on the development of a front-end or intermediary computer system between the user and the retrieval processes. Microcomputer-based software packages that provide pre-search query formulation and storage, automatic logon, downloading and menu-based interfaces are all well established and have been described in Chapter 19 (which deals with online searching of external databases). More recent research has turned to front ends that simulate a best-match retrieval system or even model the actions of a human intermediary. This research uses knowledge-based techniques from the field of artificial intelligence. Two main lines of enquiry have been pursued: simulation of best-match searching and knowledge-based front ends.

23.4.1 Simulations of best-match searching

This research develops interfaces based on best-match searching to a public online host that is using Boolean retrieval. CIRT (Robertson *et al.*) develops this approach. CIRT runs on a front-end minicomputer which accepts natural language queries and allows best-match searching of the DataStar implementation of the MEDLINE database. It uses both LDF and relevance weights. One of the major problems of designing a best-match interface to work with a host using Boolean retrieval is the translation of the weighted-term search into a Boolean search. CIRT uses an algorithm to generate a number of Boolean combinations which together result in the same output as a conventional best-match search. Documents are thus retrieved and displayed in order of decreasing similarity to the query, using either IDF or relevance weighting.

23.4.2 Knowledge-based front ends

Knowledge-based techniques have recently been adopted in the implementation of expert intermediary systems or expert systems for referral. There are two strands: first, systems which aid in the formulation of Boolean search queries (such as CANSEARCH and PLEXUS) and, second, research into the nature of the interaction that takes place between a human search intermediary and the enquirer in determining the enquirer's needs (such as MONSTRAT, I^{3}R and CODER).

CANSEARCH facilitates end-user searching of cancer therapy literature in the MEDLINE database by providing a systematic way of leading users to those MeSH (thesaurus) terms that best describe their query. Appropriate subsets of the MeSH thesaurus are displayed at the terminal to allow users to choose terms. Terms are arranged in a hierarchy, so that the choice of one term causes the system to display an additional frame in the hierarchy from which the user selects additional frames. The frame hierarchy thus coaxes the user to make a series of choices between terms from which the system generates MEDLINE search statements for use in searching. Evaluation of CANSEARCH suggests that whilst it is no substitute for a trained searcher, it can help end-users perform more effective searches.

CANSEARCH uses two types of knowledge-based processing. The subject knowledge of a trained indexer is made available through the MeSH displays, which act as a knowledge base. Also, the search statements are developed via a rule-based approach with many rules covering the selection of frames, the processing of the results of term selection, the generation of search statements and the handling of the interaction with MEDLINE. The system uses a Blackboard which is divided into sections or boards which are consulted and updated by the rules as they are fired, and which act as a record of the data captured during the dialogue with a user.

The PLEXUS system is more ambitious than CANSEARCH, since it aims to simulate an intermediary acting in the context of a searcher with a range of sources. PLEXUS is an intelligent front-end interface that supports question formulation and modification.

Query formulation in PLEXUS takes the user's natural language input and analyses its meaning. First, all terms (except stopwords) are stemmed and then assigned to a semantic category in accordance with the meaning of the stem. PLEXUS has 11 semantic categories (objects, parts, operations, processes, interactions, instruments, attributes, environments, use, time, locations), subdivided further into 40 sub-categories. These stems are contained in the PLEXUS dictionary.

The system then goes through a problem-modelling stage in order to generate an initial search strategy in the form of stems linked by Boolean operators. This Boolean query is then input for searching a small database; the initial search strategy is modified until an appropriate number of items has been retrieved. The initial search strategy may be broadened or narrowed by entering related descriptors from the BSO classification, dropping existing query stems, adding synonyms or changing ANDs and ORs. The way in which the query is modified is determined by a set of rules based on the encoded knowledge of the way in which the query has been constructed.

PLEXUS has been incorporated into the product TOME SEARCHER to support the searching of the INSPEC database.

MONSTRAT concentrates on the nature of the interaction between an enquirer and an intermediary in attempting to determine the user's needs. The nature of the interaction is characterized as two-way model-building, with the user building a model of the intermediary and vice versa. The functions that the intermediary performs are:

- determination of the Problem State and Problem Mode,
- generation of the User Model and Problem Description,
- choice of Dialogue Mode, Retrieval Strategy and appropriate responses to the user via the Response Generator, and
- provision of Explanations of the systems experts and vice versa via the Input Analyst and Output Generator.

Within these broad functions, different subfunctions were identified. In the design of the system, each of these functions was handled by a different expert system. This distributed expert-system approach is based on detailed specification of the individual functions, as well as specification of the knowledge resource required for each function, the nature of the interaction between the different functional experts and the form of the dialogue between the user and the system. Two major issues need to be addressed in relation to the interaction between the different experts in a distributed-expert system: the mode of communication and the control structure. Communication can be direct or indirect. With direct communication the experts need to know what the other experts need and can provide.

Indirect communication operates through a shared database or blackboard through which messages are distributed. Control may be concentrated or distributed. If control is concentrated, it is the responsibility of one or a few experts; if distributed, control is shared amongst the expert systems.

452

The model developed in MONSTRAT has been tested and fared well.

23.4.3   Intelligent intermediary for information retrieval (I^3R)

I^3R builds on previous experience with statistical approaches to retrieval, but also enhances the query by adding domain knowledge. Domain knowledge is acquired from individual users in respect of specific queries; this sidesteps the probable need to specify all possible domain knowledge relations for all possible queries.

The system builds a request model which consists of concepts derived from information from the user's initial query and from domain knowledge. The request model is then employed to retrieve and rank documents using two different statistical techniques – one probabilistic and the other a clustering algorithm.

Following the initial search, the user examines the documents retrieved and identifies both which documents are relevant and which terms or phrases describing the documents are important. This information is then used to refine the request model. Alternatively, the user can commence the search by specifying a particular document; details of this document can be used to start building the request model.

At the heart of I^3R system are a number of expert systems, each containing information relevant to one aspect of the total problem. In the most recent version of I^3R, there were six experts: user model builder, request model builder, domain knowledge expert, search controller, browsing expert and explainer.

The I^3R system remains a prototype, requiring more work on the implementation of the system experts.

23.4.4   Composite document expert/extended/effective retrieval (CODER)

CODER represents a testbed for the application of artificial intelligence techniques to information retrieval. The approach is similar to that of MONSTRAT and I^3R in that the CODER system uses sets of experts operating via blackboards and exchanging information relating to users, documents and other lexical items.

The principle focus of the work is the representation and analysis of the types of documents sent by electronic mail; a test collection is being developed.

Various projects have looked at the application of artificial intelligence techniques to information retrieval. However, Brooks concludes that 'for several reasons . . . information retrieval does not seem to be an ideal domain for an expert system application. It is a domain that is neither well bounded nor narrow nor homogeneous; . . . it seems that it is not feasible at present to think of building an expert system that carries out intelligent retrieval.' Whatever the future for this research, it has been useful in focusing attention on the interaction between the system and the user.

23.5 Research into OPAC design

Research into OPAC design in the 1980s has proceeded side by side with OPAC development and has largely been performed in a field setting. Research into OPAC design has taken a number of different forms, but always the central concern has been to facilitate effective searching in the OPAC. Indeed, the need to cater for inexperienced users in searching a large database poses a significant challenge.

Today's second generation OPACs are self-service interactive online information retrieval systems. A fresh perspective is required if the new design opportunities are to be moulded to the advantage of library users. OPAC design should be guided by what can be learnt about searching strategies and user behaviour.

Since much OPAC research has been integrated with the development of operational OPACs, it would be impossible to attempt a complete review of OPAC research in this chapter. Instead a few key projects are listed below in order to demonstrate the direction of OPAC research.

1. The Dewey Decimal Classification Online Project at OCLC studied the DDC as a searcher's tool for subject access, browsing and display in an experimental OPAC. This project has been described in Chapter 14.
2. Various projects have investigated the use of Library of Congress Subject Headings for subject searching in OPACs. Users do not exploit such headings very successfully. Further research has indicated that they have difficulty in matching their search terms with those used in indexing. Users cannot identify terms that are broader or narrower than their topic of interest and have difficulty in developing search strategies.
3. OKAPI is a long-running series of OPAC research studies initiated in 1982 at the Polytechnic of Central London. The Okapi research programme uses an evolving demonstration OPAC which is permanently placed in one of the Polytechnic's libraries. The aim has been to build an OPAC that requires no training to use, yet which offers powerful retrieval facilities. Relevance ranking, natural language interfaces and other techniques described elsewhere in this chapter have been tested in Okapi projects. Further work on the use of expert systems in interface design is underway. Since 1986 research has focused on the problems associated with subject searching. Faulty-term matching of conventional OPACs has been alleviated by the introduction of automatic search-term stemming routines, automatic cross–referencing using a synonym table, and semi-automatic search-term spelling correction.
4. Extended OPACs may offer functional extensions or data extensions. Various projects have evaluated the possibility of providing access to databases similar to those available from the online hosts. One such project was based on the LCS/WLN OPAC at the University of Illinois. A software interface was designed which could be integrated into the local OPAC at its IBM PC user

terminals. The new interface has assisted untrained users with the selection of search terms, the development of search strategies and the formulation of Boolean queries.

5. HYPERcatalog, developed at the Linkoping University Library in Sweden, has been mentioned previously in this chapter in the context of hypertext research.

Hildreth has listed the limitations of existing second–generation catalogues which, according to him, do not accomplish the following:

* sufficiently assist with the translation of entered query terms into the vocabulary used in the catalogue,
* provide online thesaurus aids useful for subject focusing and topic/treatment discrimination,
* automatically assist the user with alternative formulations of the search statement or execute alternative search methods when the initial approach fails,
* lead the searcher from successful free-text search terms (e.g., title words) to the corresponding subject headings or class numbers assigned to a broader range of related materials,
* provide sufficient information in the retrieved bibliographic records (such as tables of contents, abstracts and book reviews) to enable the user to judge the usefulness of the documents,
* rank the citations in large retrieval sets in decreasing order of probable relevance or 'closeness' to the user's search criteria, and
* facilitate open-ended, exploratory browsing through following pre-established trails and linkages between records in the database in order to retrieve materials related to those already found.

This lists constitutes a challenge for current and future research into OPAC design.

23.6   And, finally. . .

This book has reviewed many aspects of the organization of knowledge and information retrieval. It has been an ambitious task to attempt to draw together into one volume topics such as OPACs, online access to external databases, library management systems, text information management systems, cataloguing networks, videotext and CD–ROM developments. Indeed, some readers may have found the individual treatment of these topics to have been frustratingly superficial. I have tried to focus on key issues, but have necessarily mentioned other topics only briefly.

There is, however, a very important reason for offering this kind of broad

455

overview. Ideally, the information user would like access to information at a workstation in his office. There may be a limit to the tolerance of users to the diversity of avenues for gaining access to information that the information professional has devised. The user would prefer to transfer easily from searching an OPAC to an online search of an external database, to the use of a videotext service, and then back to consultation of a database on CD–ROM. Currently, the user has difficulty in moving between the searching of one external online host to another due to incompatibilities in command languages, let alone dealing with other media. There are numerous other avenues for development (many reviewed above), including possibilities for enhancements to CD–ROM, online OPACs and other information retrieval systems. It is appropriate to conclude this book, however, by identifying the progress that will be necessary to deliver more integrated information services to the user. End-user information services are growing in importance, and the role of the information professional will increasingly be in the realm of database creation and maintenance, database design and end-user support and training.

The level of user-friendliness implied by an integrated workstation involves progress with standardization in relation to both hardware and software. The user would prefer to be able to sit at one workstation (either in the office or at home, or even on the move) and access the catalogue database, the CD–ROM database and online in-house and external databases. Provided that his terminal is connected to the appropriate networks, this is technically possible. In practice, however, organizational factors often militate against this ideal. Users may need to consult the OPAC in the library, may not have free access to external databases (which may only be available to specified users) or may need to book access to CD–ROMs. Another major limitation of all current systems is the restricted amount of text that can be displayed on the screen. The large high-definition displays becoming available in in-house text information management systems may eventually come into more general use.

Furthermore, in relation to software and interfaces, the user would appreciate the same search facilities offered for access to all databases; better still, standardization (as far as is compatible with function) in interface design with respect to features such as screen layout, menu design, key functions and command languages. There is currently quite a divergence between OPACs, CD–ROM and online because they use different software that has evolved in distinct contexts. Improvements in interfaces based upon natural language interfaces and artificial intelligence techniques are possible in the longer term. Interface design in CD–ROM has much to offer online and OPACs but, in these environments, data transmission associated with improved displays needs to be considered. On the whole search facilities are best in external and inhouse online systems, with scope for more sophistication in OPACs and CD–ROMs. Once users can connect to the various databases of their choice, they wish to be confident that they can perform the kind of search those databases require.

Recommended reading

Aho, A V and Corasick, M J (1975), 'Efficient string matching: an aid to bibliographic search', *Communications of the ACM*, **18**, 333–40.

Baird, P *et al.* (1988), 'Cognitive aspects of constructing non-linear documents Hypercard and Glasgow online', in Proceedings of the 12th International Online Information Meeting, Oxford: Learned Information, 207–18.

Baird, P and Percival, M (1989), 'Glasgow Online: database development using Apple's HyperCard', in R McAleese (ed), *Hypertext: theory into practice*, London: Intellect Ltd, 75–92.

Bawden, D (1990), *User-oriented evaluation of information systems and services*, Aldershot: Gower.

Belkin, N J *et al.* (1983), 'Distributed expert problem treatment as a model of information system analysis and design', *Journal of Information Science*, **5**, 153–67.

Belkin, N J *et al.* (1984), 'Simulation of a distributed expert-based information provision mechanism', *Information Technology: Research, Developments, Applications*, **3**, 122–41.

Belkin, N J *et al.* (1987), 'Distributed expert-based information systems: an interdisciplinary approach', *Information Processing and Management*, **23**, 395–409.

Boyer, R S and Moore, J S (1977), 'A fast string searching algorithm', *Communications of the ACM*, **20**, 762–72.

Brooks, H M (1987), 'Expert systems and intelligent information retrieval', *Information Processing and Management*, **23**, 367–82.

Brooks, H M *et al.* (1986), 'Research on information interaction and intelligent information provision mechanisms', *Journal of Information Science*, **12**, 37–44.

Conklin, J (1987), 'Hypertext: an introduction and survey', *Computer*, **20**, 17–41.

Cringean, J K *et al.*, 'Efficiency of text scanning in bibliographic databases using microprocessor based multi-processor networks', *Journal of Information Science*.

Croft, W B (1987), 'Approaches to intelligent retrieval', *Information Processing and Management*, **23**, 249–54.

Croft, W B and Savino, P (1988), 'Implementing ranking strategies using text signatures', *ACM Transactions on Office Information Systems*, **6**, 42–62.

Croft, W B and Thompson, R (1987), 'I3R: a new approach to the design of document retrieval systems', *Journal of the American Society for Information Science*, **38**, 389–404.

Daniels, P J (1986), 'Cognitive models in information retrieval: an evaluative review', *Journal of Documentation*, **42**, 272, 304.

Davies, R (ed) (1986), *Intelligent information systems: progress and prospects*, Chichester: Ellis Horwood.

Duncan, E B (1989), 'A faceted approach to hypertext', in R McAleese (ed), *Hypertext: theory into practice*, London: Intellect Ltd, 157–63.

Fox, E A (1987), 'Developments of the CODER system: a testbed for artificial intelligence methods in information retrieval', *Information Processing and Management*, **23**, 341–66.

Freund, G E and Willet, P (1982), 'Online identification of word variants and arbitrary truncation searching using a string similarity measure', *Information Technology: Research and Development*, **1**, 177–87.

Frisse, M (1988), 'From text to hypertext', *Byte*, October, 247–53.

Gostick, R W (1979), 'Software and algorithms for the Distributed Array Processors', *ICL Technical Journal*, **2**, 116–35.

Hillis, D (1985), *The Connection Machine*, Cambridge, MA: MIT Press.

Hjerppe, R (1985), 'Project Hypercatalog: visions and preliminary conceptions of an extended and enhanced catalog', in *Proceedings IRFIS 6: intelligent information systems for the information society*, Amsterdam: North Holland.

Hjerppe, R (1989), 'Hypercat at Liblab in Sweden: a progress report', in C R Hildreth (ed), *The online catalogue, developments and directions*, London: Library Association, 177–209.

Hsiao, D K (1980), 'Database computers', *Advances in Computers*, **19**, 1–64.

Hsiao, D K (1983), *Advanced database machine architecture*, Englewood Cliffs, NJ: Prentice Hall.

Hyatt, E (1988), 'Hypertext: a review and evaluation', M.Sc. Dissertation, University of Sheffield.

Keen, E M (1991), 'The use of term position devices in ranked output experiments', *Journal of Documentation*, **47** (1), March, 1–22.

Luhn, H P (1957), 'A statistical approach to mechanised encoding and searching of library information', *IBM Journal of Research and Development*, **1**, 309–17.

McKnight, C et al. (1991), *Hypertext in context*, Cambridge: Cambridge University Press.

Nelson, T H (1967), *Getting it out of our system: information retrieval: a critical review*, Washington DC: Thompson Books.

Nelson, T H (1974), *Computer lib*, Chicago: Nelson.

Nelson, T H (1980), 'Replacing the printed word: a complete literary system', in S H Lavington (ed), *Information processing 80*, New York: North Holland, 1013–23.

Nelson, T H (1981), *Literary machines*, Swathmore: Nelson.

Nelson, T H (1988), 'Managing immense storage', *Byte*, **13**, 225–38.

Paice, C (1986), 'Expert systems for information retrieval', *Aslib Proceedings*, **38**, October, 343–435.

Pollitt, S (1987), 'CANSEARCH: an expert systems approach to document retrieval', *Information Processing and Management*, **23**, 119–38.

Radecki, T (1988), 'Trends in research on information retrieval – the potential for improvements in conventional Boolean retrieval systems', *Information Processing and Management*, **24** (3), 219–27.

Robertson, S E and Sparck Jones, K (1976), 'Relevance weighting of search terms', *Journal of the American Society for Information Science*, **27** (3), 129–146.

Robertson, S E et al. (1986), 'Weighting, ranking and relevance feedback in a front-end system', *Journal of Information Science*, **12**, 71–75.

Salton, G (1975), *A theory of indexing*, Philadelphia: Society for Industrial and

Applied Mathematics.

Salton, G and Buckley, C (1988), 'Term weighting approaches in automatic text retrieval', *Information Processing and Management*, **24**, 513–23.

Salton, G and McGill, M J (1983), *Introduction to modern information retrieval*, New York: McGraw-Hill.

Schneiderman, B and Kearsley, G (1989), *Hypertext hands-on: an introduction to a new way of organising and accessing information*, Reading, Mass and Wokingham: Addison-Wesley.

Smith, K E (1988), 'Hypertext – linking to the future', *Online*, **12**, 33–40.

Smith, L C (1987), 'Artificial intelligence and information retrieval', in *Annual Review of Information Science and Technology*, **22**, New York: Elsevier Science Publishers, 41–73.

Sparck Jones, K (1972), 'A statistical interpretation of term specificity and its application in retrieval', *Journal of Documentation*, **28**, 11–21.

Sparck Jones, K and Tait, J I (1984), 'Automatic search term variant generation', *Journal of Documentation*, **40**, 50–66.

Vickery, A (1986), 'Developing an expert system for referral', in *Proceedings of the second International Expert Systems Conference*, Oxford: Learned Information, 285–301.

Vickery, A (1980), 'The experience of building expert search systems', in *Proceedings of the 12th International Online Information Meeting*, Oxford: Learned Information, 301–13.

Vickery, A and Brooks, H M (1987), 'Expert systems and their application in library and information systems', *Online Review*, **11**, 149–65.

Vickery, A and Brooks, H M (1987), 'PLEXUS: the expert system for referral', *Information Processing and Management*, **23**, 99–117.

Wade, S J *et al.* (1988), 'A comparison of knowledge-based and statistically-based techniques for reference retrieval', *Online Review*, **12**, 91–108.

Willett, P, 'An algorithm for the calculation of exact term discrimination values', *Information Processing and Management*, **21**, 225–32.

Willett, P (ed) (1988), *Document retrieval systems*, London: Taylor Graham.

Willett, P (1991), 'The ranking of paragraphs as an access mechanism for full-text documents', in *Text retrieval: Information First*, Proceedings of the Institute of Information Scientists Text Retrieval Conference, London, October 1990, London: Taylor–Graham, 34–45.

24 Filing order in indexes and catalogues

24.1 Introduction

Earlier sections have considered in some detail the headings and search keys to be used in catalogues and indexes. In any situation where a number of such headings are to be displayed one after another, some well-recognized filing order must be adopted. Thus in printed, card and microform catalogues and indexes, the filing order is important in assisting the user in the location of a specific heading which may be intermixed with other headings. In computer-based systems, displays of headings, index terms or search keys are sometimes encountered, and here it is also useful to work with a defined filing order. However, such an order is less essential since online searching of computer databases is normally supported by facilities which make scanning through sequences easier than in printed lists. If no filing order is recognized, the only way in which appropriate headings and their associated records can be retrieved is by scanning the entire file.

Since most headings in catalogues or indexes comprise primarily numbers (usually Arabic numerals) and letters of the Roman alphabet, it is these characters that must be organized and for which a filing order must be defined. All the careful work of a cataloguer or indexer is to no avail if, a heading having been assigned and a record prepared, that record is not filed in the expected place in accordance with its heading. A user needs to know, for instance, whether a work by John McMillan can be found before or after one by Eli Marner. Equally, a set of subject headings such as:

Faith,
Faith, Confessions of
Faith healing
Faithfulness

could be filed in a number of possible orders, and the adopted order needs to be declared. The arrangement of headings into an overall sequence is important; an order which is erratic, unpredictable or with which the user is not familiar can lead to poor retrieval in any printed, card or microfilm index or catalogue.

Although filing has traditionally been regarded as part of the catalogue or index creation process, and its status in this respect was more than obvious in large card

460

catalogues, filing orders today are more important for the searcher than the indexer. Prior to computerization of the production of catalogues and indexes, considerable clerical effort was expended in filing index and catalogue cards. One of the biggest and most evident advantages of computer production of catalogues and indexes is the elimination of the need for filing. The computer, once instructed on the desired filing order, is eminently suitable for filing, achieving a level of consistency which was a remote dream in the days of human filers. Increasingly, information workers do not need to know how to file a given heading, but rather to predict where a sought heading is likely to have been filed in a sequence. Thus familiarity with normal filing orders becomes an important factor in complete and speedy retrieval from almost all printed sources.

With the onus on the searcher to achieve familiarity with filing orders, there are other factors that need to be considered.

The most common order is alphabetically by letters of the Roman alphabet arranged in their normal order. Other possible orders may be numerical, chronological (by periods of time), geographical (grouping places within a country or region together) or classified (according to a classification scheme, and ordered in keeping with the notation of that scheme). It is important to recognize that some of these orders will be more self-evident than others. Alphabetical order can present problems, some of which are discussed in succeeding sections. For some audiences, even the straight 'a to z' sequence of alphabetical order may present serious difficulties. Schoolchildren, students and others whose native language is written in a non-Roman script may find alphabetical order according to Roman characters an almost insurmountable hurdle in the use of catalogues and indexes. Consider, for example, that in order to arrange a set of words alphabetically, it is necessary to consider each letter of each word in turn. So although alphabetical and to some extent numerical order are common (as we shall see), it should be recognized that some people will have difficulty with these orders; therefore as much help and assistance should be given within the catalogue or index and outside it as is reasonably possible.

For classified catalogues or the shelf arrangement of non-fiction according to a classification scheme, it is necessary to establish a filing order for the symbols used in the notation. (For further details on this, see Chapters 13 and 14 on Classification.) The filing order for notation in classification schemes is normally given in the text of the scheme, so the comments that follow relate primarily to alphabetical indexing.

In computer-based information retrieval systems, the importance of filing orders varies considerably. The characters to be arranged may vary, but many of the access points used in such systems are basically alphabetical in nature. In systems where documents can be retrieved according to search keys on a string search basis, few problems arise. Order is not important since any specific string of characters can be located directly. Sometimes displays of alphabetically close terms may be used in a search in order to review all the possible variations on a key word (for example, to note in a natural language index that documents may be indexed under any of photogenic, photograph, photographic, photographs, photography and so on). Here, unusual orders may mean that search terms which might have been helpful are overlooked.

Display of hits in computer-based catalogues may show short records. If the user seeks to scan through a large number of such records, their order can become critical and filing is significant.

In menu-based information retrieval systems, alphabetical order may be important especially if the menu asks a user to identify the alphabetical range within which he expects a term to fall. Thus, a user will have difficulty in locating Allen and Unwin if this is filed either under G. Allen and Unwin or under George Allen and Unwin. Whichever of these headings is chosen will necessitate the user initiating a search into different parts of the sequence.

24.2 Filing codes

Just as in the establishment of headings for use in catalogues and indexes, a code was deemed useful in maintaining consistency between catalogues and cataloguers, so a code is a wise precaution in any search for standard filing orders. The object of such consistency is to improve the coincidence between the order expected by the user and that actually encountered in the index or catalogue.

An 'a to z' sequence would apparently offer little possibility of confusion. However, reflect that every character or form of heading which might feature in a catalogue or index must have a uniquely defined place in a sequence. For example, does London, Jack file before or after London Bridge, and where will a title such as 'All the 9's' file? Filing codes are primarily concerned with guidance on how to interfile difficult cases into a basic alphabetical order.

Unfortunately, libraries and other agencies engaged in filing entries in printed indexes and catalogues do not adhere to one filing code. Even when a specific filing code is adopted, local deviations can be expected. Given the diversity of filing practices, it is at least as important to recognize the most common filing dilemmas and to review some of the possible solutions as to learn the provisions of one code thoroughly. However a quick review of the major codes will help to provide a context for later discussions. No attempt is made here to provide a full comparative study; for this, the reader should consult Hunter (1991: see Readings to Chapter 1).

1. *Cutter's Rules for a Dictionary Catalog* contains rules for filing in a dictionary catalogue. Later cataloguing codes have tended to regard filing as a separate issue, instituting special codes for filing.
2. *ALA (American Library Association) Rules for Filing Catalog Cards* (1942) was essentially a summary of various acceptable methods of filing as practised

in American libraries at the time. The nature of the compilation of the code led to limited consensus and many alternative rules, which together made it rather confusing. The second edition of the *ALA Rules for Filing Catalog Cards*, issued in 1968, aimed to take account of developments in cataloguing rules and practice. This edition specifically attempted to recommend straight alphabetical order, keeping exceptions to a minimum. An abridged edition of the ALA 1968 Code was also published. Both were extensively used both in America and, in more restricted contexts, in the UK.

3. *ALA Filing Rules (1980)* supersedes both the first and second editions of the *ALA Rules for Filing Catalog Cards*. These rules follow a general trend in filing practices in endorsing the 'file-as-is' principle outlined below. These rules aim to be more widely applicable than their predecessors to many types of bibliographic displays and thus could be a significant influence upon filing practices. The introduction to this code certainly repays reading, containing sensible advice, not so much on recommended filing orders, but on how to make a filing order amenable to the public.

4. *BS (British Standard) 1749: Recommendations for alphabetical arrangement and the filing order of numerals and symbols* was originally published in 1951 as a specification for 'alphabetical arrangement'. An intermediate standard was published in 1969 as 'Specification for alphabetical arrangement and the filing order of numerals and symbols'. The 1985 revision consolidates much British filing practice. This standard is designed to take account of computerized filing and covers alphabetical arrangements in lists of all kinds, including bibliographies, catalogues, directories and indexes. In preparation of the 1985 revision, the BLAISE rules, the ALA and LC rules were all considered. The British Standard does not however choose between word-by-word or letter-by-letter filing, but maintains that 'the nature, purpose or tradition of a list may determine the choice of filing method'.

5. *The Filing Rules for the Dictionary Catalogue of the Library of Congress*, first published in 1956, has been influential in American filing practice, contributing to the development of the ALA rules. These LC rules were revised in 1971 to be more amenable to computer filing. This code was used in the Library of Congress in a number of its computer-produced files and catalogues, but was superseded in 1980 by the *Library of Congress Filing Rules*. These are more elaborate than the ALA rules, twice as numerous, and exhibit a tendency to adhere to traditional classified arrangements (which is in keeping with stability in Library of Congress catalogues).

The British equivalent to the LC rules is the *BLAISE Filing Rules*. Published in 1980, these rules summarize British Library filing practice as embodied in its various MARC databases. These rules were drafted according to principles developed by the International Standards Organization, and have their origins in the report of a Working Party on Computer Filing set up by the

Figure 24.1 Basic alphabetical filing orders

Word-by-word filing	Letter-by-letter filing
Child abuse	Child abuse
Child artists	Child artists
Child neglect	Childbirth
Child psychology	Childnapping
Child welfare	Child neglect
Childbirth	Child psychology
Childnapping	Children
Children	Children and civil rights
Children and civil rights	Children in poetry
Children in poetry	Children's books
Children today	Children's hospitals
Children's books	Children's plays
Children's hospitals	Children today
Children's plays	Child welfare

Library Association Cataloguing and Indexing Group. Other computerized cataloguing networks also have filing rules and conventions.

24.3 Problems and principles in filing

The emphasis in this section will be on major filing problems and their potential solutions, rather than any type of systematic review of the different solutions offered by specific codes. A fully comparative account of recommendations for filing orders is likely to prove confusing until the reader has attained some familiarity with the general problems and solutions offered by one code. It is important to note, however, that solutions to problems do vary between codes.

24.3.1 Basic orders

There are two basic orders that can be adopted for alphabetical sequences of headings. These are word-by-word or letter-by-letter. Figure 24.1 shows one set of headings arranged according to both systems. Word-by-word files one word at a time and exhausts all headings containing a specific word before proceeding to longer words with the first word as part of them. Thus Child will always file before Children. One way of indicating the requirement to adhere to word-by-word filing is to file a space before any letter. Letter-by-letter filing takes no account of spaces, but requires filing in alphabetical order merely in response to the letters in the headings.

Subjects which are closely associated and have similar names may be grouped by word-by-word filing. Inadvertent variations in authors' names may also be grouped by this approach. Letter-by-letter filing, on the other hand, groups variations of the same word; for example, there would be no difference in filing position between on-line, on line and online. Word-by-word filing is generally used in catalogues and bibliographies, although some dictionaries, directories and encyclopaedias use letter-by-letter filing.

24.3.2 The file-as-is principle

Modern codes have moved towards the file-as-is principle. This means that headings are filed exactly according to the characters in the heading in the order in which they are presented. Some earlier codes would have filed some headings in a 'standard' form; for example, abbreviations and numerals would be filed as if they were spelt out. The file-as-is principle would lead to Mc being filed as Mc and not as Mac, so that these two forms would appear at different places in the sequence. The same goes for other common abbreviations such as St and Saint.

The file-as-is principle makes for relatively simple computer filing procedures, which has undoubtedly been one of the reasons for its growing popularity. Although a computer can be instructed to file Mc as Mac, the instructions will be simpler if it is not necessary to list a number of such specific cases, but rather rely upon a blanket instruction to file the characters as they are found in the text of the heading. Filing according to the file-as-is principle can also be helpful to the user. The user who knows the common form of the name for which he is searching will find retrieval straightforward. Thus with the file-as-is principle, the user who seeks MIT or MS London, but is ignorant of what the abbreviations mean, will be relieved to find these headings filed under their abbreviated form rather than under a spelt-out or complete version. Had the heading been filed according to its full form, the user would have been unsuccessful in his search unless appropriate references were provided from the abbreviated form. Another important limitation to any set of filing rules that require spelling out is that they must either specify at some length how abbreviations or numerals are to be spelt out or accept that variations may arise in the way in which specific headings can be expanded. Whilst indexers may be expected to familiarize themselves with spelling out procedures, searchers are rarely likely to be fully conversant with these.

One reason why headings have not always been filed as they appear is that this approach splits sequences of similar names written in a different form. Thus, if filed as they appear. St Joan and Saint Joan will be separated from each other by Sin, Slavery, Soils, Soldiers, Sonata and Space, to list only a few of the intermediate words. Of course, in a catalogue or index where the headings are closely controlled, St Joan and Saint Joan would be unlikely to appear. One form would be chosen and used on all appropriate occasions. If such consistency in the establishment of headings exists, this removes or minimizes many filing dilemmas. The cataloguer can also alert the user to unexpected filing orders by the judicious use of references.

In a filing sequence where natural language terms or titles are being filed, it can be more difficult to avoid inconsistencies in the form of headings.

The file-as-is principle means that collocation of similar headings is provided by the consistent use of uniform headings and does not rely upon inspired filing. This shifts responsibility for headings and their arrangement into the arena of cataloguers and indexers.

24.3.3 Some other filing problems

1. *Sequencing different characters* It is necessary to define the filing value of all characters that might be found in headings in a catalogue or index. The BLAISE rules define the preferred filing order of characters as:
   - (a) spaces, dashes, hyphens, diagonal slashes, all of which have equal filing value,
   - (b) ampersands,
   - (c) Arabic numerals and Roman numerals arranged in numeric order interfiled,
   - (d) Roman alphabet letters arranged according to the English alphabet and
   - (e) other alphabet letters arranged in their commonly accepted order within each alphabet.

   This basic order is similar to those recommended in the ALA and LC rules, except that the latter two add full stops to the first group of punctuation symbols; also ALA either ignores the ampersand in filing or files it as if spelt out.

2. *Numerals* can either be filed as recommended in BS 1749 or filed as if spelled out. Earlier rules, as discussed in 24.3.2, tended to prefer the numerals to be filed as if spelt out, but this required codes to specify the nature of spelling out. For example, does 1984 read as nineteen-eighty-four, or as one thousand nine hundred and eighty-four, or as one nine eight four? The filing of numerals also presents other problems which are nicely treated in the ALA rules. These include guidance on how to file:

   - punctuation; for example, The 5,000 fingers of Dr T,
   - decimals; for exampe, 1.0 für Dich
   - fractions; for example, 3/4 for 3
   - non-Arabic notations; for example, Louis IX
   - superscript and subscript numerals; for example 1^3 is 1, and
   - dates.

3. *Diacritical marks* such as umlauts, accents and disaereses may either be ignored or be assigned a filing value. For example, ü may either be filed as u or as ue.

4. *Punctuation, signs and symbols* Punctuation and other signs and symbols must be considered. In both the ALA rules and BS 1749, punctuation is

ignored except where specially mentioned or where a filing value has been defined for a specific piece of punctuation.

5. *Initial articles* It is well-established practice to ignore initial articles when they occur as the initial word of a title or subject heading, so that unwieldy sequences do not evolve under such words. Thus 'an', 'the', 'a' and 'der' and 'la' will be ignored in filing headings where these are the initial words. In order to be able to execute an instruction that requires such initial articles to be ignored, it is necessary to be able to recognize initial articles in many languages; this applies whether the filer is human or a computer. Initial articles associated with name headings are sometimes ignored, but on other occasions are used in filing. Often cataloguing codes require that such initial articles should not be included in headings unless they are essential for identification. Thus AACR2 allows 'The Club', but prefers 'Library Association' and not 'The Library Association'. Here it would be sensible to include the initial article in filing if a deliberate decision has been made to include it in a heading.

6. *Abbreviations and single letters* Abbreviations present problems in filing primarily because different forms of abbreviation may have been established for the same name. A catalogue may include entries under both MEDLARS and M.E.D.L.A.R.S, and under SDC, S.D.C. and Systems Development Corporation. The instinctive reaction is to attempt to frame filing rules which will result in all of these variants filing together. A number of options exist for the filing of abbreviations and acronyms. Abbreviations may be filed as spelt out, but it is more common these days to file initials as separate one-letter words (for example, B.B.C. comprises three one-letter words) and to file acronyms as one complete word (for example, BLAISE is one word).

This is a satisfactory distinction provided it is possible to fit every set of initials or abbreviations into either 'initials' or 'acronyms'. Such a categorization may depend rather arbitrarily upon whether stops have been used between letters or not.

7. *Subject entries* Subject headings beginning with the same word may be interfiled in different ways according to the filing value given to inverted headings, phrase headings and subdivided headings. Frequently the filing value accorded to a subdivided heading may be different from that for inverted headings which may lead to deviations from the strict and most obvious alphabetical sequence. Figure 24.2 demonstrates this.

24.3.4 Arrangement of different kinds of headings beginning with the same word

Headings may arise as author, title and subject, and all types of headings may commence with the same word. 'Black', 'Rose', 'London' to give but a few examples could all be entry words in any of the three main types of headings. The problem is whether to opt for strict alphabetical order or whether the user would

Figure 24.2 Filing orders for subject headings

Crime
Crime, sex
Crime – United States
Crime and narcotics
Crime prevention
Crime syndicates
Crime victims
Crimean War
Crimes
Crimes, military
Crimes, political
Crimes against public safety
Crimes against the person
Crimes without victims
Criminal assault
Criminal investigation
Criminal justice, administration of
Criminal law
Criminal procedure
Criminal psychology
Criminals
Criminals – drug use
Criminology

find it helpful to have types of entries with the same entry word grouped. In this case, all subject entries would be found together, and all personal name entries be kept in a separate sub-sequence. Many catalogues do seek to achieve some type of grouping of types of entries. However, once a decision has been made to group similar types of entries, other difficulties emerge in defining the categories. Amongst both subject and author (or name) entries there will be different types of entries. Name entries, for example, may include personal names, corporate names and geographical names and their subdivisions or qualifiers.

24.4 Arrangement of entries with the same heading

It is quite common under some headings to have a number of entries and references listed. A prolific author may be responsible for a number of books, or a particular subject heading may be assigned to several books which discuss the same subject. Any given subject heading may be associated with both entries and references. The preferred sequence of these multiple entries, all with the same heading, needs to be established. First, it is normal to distinguish between references and added entries, and then to group references at the beginning of the sequence associated with a given heading. Next, it is necessary to order the works for which entries are made under a specific subject or author heading. Often, the title will be used for this purpose, but on occasions when the title is not appropriate for use as a filing element, a chronological order of entries according to the date of publication of the document may be preferred.

The comments in this chapter should illustrate that filing is not as straightforward as it first appears. Familiarity with filing orders cannot be assumed. Further, although there is now reasonable agreement as to how to compile catalogues and which headings to use, there is less unanimity concerning the arrangement of catalogues and indexes. Perhaps one of the main strengths of online access to a computer database is that problems of arrangement become less significant if string searching is available.

Recommended reading

American Library Association (1968), *ALA rules for filing catalog cards*, 2nd edition edited by P A Seely, Chicago: ALA.

American Library Association (1980), *ALA filing rules*, Filing Committee, Resources and Technical Services Division, Chicago: ALA.

Ayres, F (1979), 'It's not as easy as ABC', *Catalogue and Index*, **54**, 1–3, 8.

BLCMP (1971), *Code of filing rules*, Birmingham: BLCMP.

British Library Filing Rules Committee (1980), *BLAISE filing rules*, London: BLAISE.

'British standard recommendations for alphabetical arrangement and filing order of numbers and symbols', Hemel Hempstead: BSI (BS 1759:1985).

Hines, T C and Harris, J L (1966), *Computer filing of index, bibliographic and catalog entries*, Newark, NJ: Bro-Dart Foundation.

Library Association, Catalog and Indexing Group, Working Party on Filing Rules, 'Filing by computer', *Catalogue and Index*, **27**, 1972 (Complete issue).

Library of Congress (1980), *Library of Congress filing rules*, prepared by J C Rather and S C Biebel, Washington DC: LC.

25 Document arrangement

General principles

Documents in libraries or resource centres must be physically stored. Normally these documents are organized in a way that facilitates retrieval. With closed access collections the choice of arrangement may present only limited problems, since the librarian will act as an intermediary between the stock and the user. Thus, complex and irrational arrangements can be tolerated, since only relatively experienced staff need to be able to locate items. Open access environments, where the public are expected to locate documents for themselves, are different. Documents must be arranged or physically stored in an order which is self-explanatory, and which preferably coincides with the way in which the public normally seek to retrieve a document. For example, if the users of the library in a College of Education normally ask for slides sets by subject, and serials by title, then subject labels (such as classification numbers) and titles are, respectively, serious contenders for arrangement of the documents concerned. Some type of sympathetic arrangement is not only important for the location of specific documents, but assists users in browsing. A helpful arrangement supports browsing by grouping documents which have some characteristic in common; for example, author, subject, age.

Shelf arrangement and supportive guiding are important in information retrieval. For small collections document arrangement may be the only retrieval device available, particularly in bookshops, small public libraries and small specialist collections. Even where a catalogue or index to a collection is available, users do not always consult these tools, and may prefer to locate either individual documents, or documents with specific characteristics by inspection of the stock. In larger collections it may seem more difficult to browse effectively, but even where browsing a complete collection is a daunting prospect, subsets of the collection may be examined by browsing. Hence, although document arrangement, often in the form of shelf arrangement, may be a very unsophisticated information retrieval device it is probably the most widely used such device, and thus deserves special attention. Equally, shelf arrangement is easy to overlook as an information retrieval device. Special attention has to be devoted to the creation of an index or catalogue and its maintenance but the maintenance of orderly shelf arrangement is often considered an unimportant chore.

470

Why is shelf arrangement popular in information retrieval? Shelf arrangement fails to permit a document to be represented at more than one place in a sequence (unless there are multiple copies), and thus does not allow any given document to be approached from various different angles, or with requirements specified in terms of different characteristics. It may be that, apart from the simple pleasure of browsing, documents arranged on shelves, filing cabinets and so on may be more easily examined in terms of characteristics of documents which are rarely reflected in catalogue or index records. The physical format of a document (for example, a book, filmstrip, poster), the quality of production, the design of the cover, the apparent age of the document, are all factors which can be ascertained on examining the actual document, but which are unlikely to be fully evident from a catalogue.

25.2 Characteristics for shelf arrangement

The document or shelf arrangement in a library or information materials collection is unlikely to follow one sequence for all types of material, and different libraries and users groups may merit different approaches to document arrangement. Two factors determine the type of order which might be adopted in any given application:

1. user convenience
2. library convenience.

Usually, the convenience of the user must be given priority, but on occasions it is necessary to adopt an order or arrangement which supports other library functions (for example, inter-library loan or quick reference) or which leads to the efficient utilization of space.

There are a number of characteristics which can be used in determining document arrangements, and in any given collection a mixture of these might be applied. Some common characteristics for arranging books are:

  author
  title
  subject
  physical form
  nature of the information stored in the book
  audience level
  extent and nature of use of the collection.

Some of the above characteristics are employed in order to differentiate between sequences, whilst others are more appropriate for determining the order within

471

sequences. For example, audience level may be a criterion which is applied in order to divide a collection in a children's library into material suitable for different age groups. The nature of the information, on the other hand, may determine its inclusion in a special collection of statistics or quick reference materials. Titles may be used to determine the alphabetical order of documents, which perhaps have been primarily grouped as being serials or non-serials, or fiction or non-fiction.

Physical form is often used to divide documents according to their physical format. A music library is a good example of an environment where an array of physical forms is available. The library may have music scores, books on music, sound disks and sound tapes, to mention but a few of the possible media. These different media can all be arranged together in one integrated sequence, or separate sequences may be established for books, scores, tapes and disks. An integrated sequence permits book scores and recordings of Beethoven's music to be stored in proximity to one another. Some libraries will find this kind of integrated approach helpful to their clientele, in that it draws items together by their content, irrespective of their physical form. However, integrated stock certainly can present problems in terms of physically housing the items, and keeping an assortment of media in a tidy sequence. Imagine, for example, attempting to interfile maps and charts with books on a specific country. Unless maps were folded it would be almost impossible to file them in an integrated sequence in such a way that they were preserved for a reasonable period of use. Many libraries, then, opt to file different physical forms in separate sequences, and may, for example, rely upon a catalogue to draw attention to the range of media in which a given author or subject might feature.

Apart from separate sequences for completely distinct physical forms (for example, maps, slides, sound discs), sometimes separate sequences are also maintained for different sizes or types of one physical form. The classic and well-known example of such a distinction is that which is frequently found in libraries where books are arranged in separate sequences according to their size – for example, octavo, quarto and folio. Sound recordings will often be divided into disks and cassettes, and then each of these media may be represented by more than one sequence according, for instance, to the size of disks.

Common characteristics on which to base document arrangement are author, or author equivalent, title and subject. To take some common examples, fiction is often organized by author, periodicals by their titles, and non-fiction by subject. These arrangements are compatible with the normal approach of readers to these types of documents, and this to a large extent accounts for the frequency of their occurrence. Fiction is sought for its style and form, which is often characterized by an author's name, whereas non-fiction is sought for the information that it can provide, and information is usually located according to its subject. Serials may be sought by title as part of a specific search for a given part of a periodical, or used for current awareness where each new issue is a means of updating the knowledge gleaned from the first.

472

Greater difficulties arise when there is no plain arrangement which will suit all users.

A number of more unusual arrangements have been tried, but none have met with wide approval. One reason for this is that many of the experimental approaches to shelf arrangement abandon the basic requirement of a shelf arrangement system, which is that each document has a unique place in the sequence, so that not only is browsing possible, but also specific documents can be retrieved. Any shelf arrangement systems which do not permit ready location of specific documents are cumbersome for the user or member of staff seeking a specific document, but on the other hand may eliminate the need to keep documents in a closely defined order.

Reader interest arrangements have been tried in public libraries. These are really a type of arrangement by subject, but the subject categories into which documents are organized are usually broad and do not follow the discipline-oriented approach of many major classification schemes. The categories are usually chosen locally, to be consistent with the interests of library users. In public libraries, these categories are likely to represent major leisure interests.

A similar approach to arrangement, but one which is less radical than reader interest arrangement, is to rely upon broad categorization rather than detailed specification. A number of small public and school libraries opt for broad subject categories which follow the main subjects represented in, say, DDC and organize the subjects in the same sequence as in DDC. This can easily be achieved by effectively using the second or third summary of DDC as a basis for classification; that is, assigning only two or three digit numbers, depending on the degree of specification required. Thus, for example, all aspects of Music might be classified at the one number 780, and the number 630 used for every document concerned with Farming and Agriculture. Obviously, such categories may be totally adequate to divide up the stock of a small general collection. Compared with reader interest arrangement, this approach based upon one of the major classification schemes has the advantage of being compatible with the approach that users and staff will encounter in larger collections, and may for instance permit all libraries in a public library system to exploit the same classification scheme, regardless of their size. On the other hand, adhering to one of the major schemes carries with it all of the disadvantages of that major scheme. In particular, some would argue that the discipline-oriented approach of such schemes is unsuited to many applications, and that public libraries, for instance, need to take account of the leisure use that they receive.

Service in-depth abandons subject arrangement altogether, and seeks to arrange documents in categories according to their popularity. Arrangements vary, but one possibility is to place more popular books near to the counter, and less popular subjects in more remote areas of the library. Sometimes this is based on locating complete subject areas with respect to their popularity, but it is impossible to treat

473

individual books in this way. Depending on the precise arrangement the objective may be to serve two different types of clientele. For example, books close to the door and the circulation desk may be intended for the user who merely wishes to make a swift selection of items to take away and read elsewhere. Books further into the library may be those judged suitable for detailed study within the library building, and may be stored adjacent to study space.

25.3   Limitations of document arrangement as a retrieval device

Document arrangement labours under some inherent limitations as a document or information retrieval device. These can be briefly enumerated as:

(a)   Documents can be arranged in one order only. Any one document may be required by author, title, subject, form or other characteristic, but this one document can only be grouped according to one of these characteristics at any one time. Thus, a non-fiction book which has been placed in a sequence according to its subject content is difficult to locate if only its author is known (without resorting to a catalogue, or scanning the entire collection).

(b)   The second limitation follows from the first. Not only can any given document be only placed in one sequence, but that document can only be placed with respect to one category for any given characteristic. Thus a book on 'the history of naval warships' may be sought under history, navy or warships, but can only be placed in a subject sequence according to one of these features, that is with other books on history, or with other books on warships, or with other books on the navy. Equally, a document with several authors can only be arranged in an author sequence according to one author's name.

(c)   The document arrangement adopted is often broken, in the sense that documents in libraries are rarely shelved in one single and self-evident sequence. The physical constraints of the library building may lead to sequences continuing on other floors, or sequences being broken by certain subsections being removed from the shelves. Parallel sequences may be established. Consider sequences of reference works, pamphlets, periodicals, outsize material, all shelved according to the same subject sequence (for example, the same classification scheme) then these will constitute parallel sequences. The user is presented with much walking around shelves, and altogether a formidable task if he wishes to gather all documents on a given subject.

(d)   Only part of a library collection will normally be visible on shelves, in filing cabinets, in map cabinets, and so on. Documents which will not be evident to the browser of shelves, but which nevertheless are available through a library include: documents out on loan, documents which might be obtained by inter-library loan, and any collections which are kept in closed access. Thus the browser may miss valuable items, although some browsers are primarily

474

concerned only with items that are readily and currently available for loan, and will find browsing a perfectly adequate method of gauging the extent of a library collection.

Plainly, catalogues do not suffer from the above four limitations of document arrangement, and indeed are intended to provide the facilities that document arrangement cannot offer. Although document arrangement has limitations, it is important not to forget its popularity, and therefore to attempt to make document arrangement as effective as possible as a document retrieval device. Guiding is important in enhancing the effectiveness of document arrangement.

Recommended reading

Apted, S M (1971), 'General purposive browsing', *Library Association Record*, **73** (12), 228–230.

Carey, R J P (1974), *Library guiding: a program for exploiting library resources*, London: Bingley.

Donbroski, L (1980), *Life without Dewey: reader interest arrangement of stock in East Sussex Library*, Catalogue and Index 57, 3–6.

Fosket, A C (1970), 'Shelf classification – or else', *Library journal*, **95** (15), 2771–2773.

Green, R J (1977), *The effectiveness of browsing*, College and Research Libraries, 313–316.

Hyman, R J (1980), *Shelf classification research: past, present – future?* Illinois: University of Illinois Graduate school of Library Science (Occasional papers 146).

Sawbridge, L and Favret, L (1982), 'The mechanics and the magic of declassification', *Library Association Record*, **84** (11), 385–386.

26 Physical forms of catalogue and index

Introduction

The physical form of a catalogue or index imposes constraints upon the way in which these various tools may be used. In fact some of the distinctions between the computerized databases and printed indexes derive from their very different physical forms. Some aspects of the retrieval characteristics which are normally associated with particular physical forms have already been reviewed in earlier chapters. Indeed, since OPACs have been treated in some detail in other parts of this book, they will not be considered further here. This chapter focuses on the physical characteristics (rather than the retrieval features) of the various physical forms of catalogue and index.

26.2. Physical forms of catalogue and index

Amongst the physical forms that catalogues and indexes can take are ultrafiche, microfiche, microfilm, computer book form, conventionally printed book form, looseleaf book form, guard book form, sheaf, card and online terminals. The more important physical forms for the future are those which can most effectively be produced from computerized cataloguing systems; however since manual cataloguing and indexing are still performed, it is too early to dismiss the physical forms associated with them. Physical forms must be evaluated when starting a new index or catalogue or when processing methods are changed.

In practice many larger libraries contain indexes in many of the above physical forms for different applications. The library catalogue of one library alone may be available in different physical forms for different locations (for example, computer book form for branches and microfiche for the central library), or to cover different periods of time (for example, an early catalogue may be in card form, superseded for recent stock by an online catalogue). If a user finds it necessary to use a range of information retrieval tools in any given library, his search is likely to bridge tools in several different physical formats. This variety of physical forms presents unhelpful complexities to a user who, in even relatively simple searches, may have to contend with a computer print-out in book form, conventionally printed indexes, microfiche and online indexes and catalogues.

Some of the more popular forms of catalogue and index are now considered in more detail.

26.3   Requirements of a physical form of catalogue or index

Ten points can be introduced in order to identify a suitable physical form of catalogue or index:

1.   Flexibility to allow easy insertion and withdrawal of records, so that the catalogue can be amended to reflect the current state of a library's stock.
2.   Compactness, so that valuable space which could be occupied by other library material is not given over to bulky catalogues.
3.   Immediate access when required by users and staff, preferably several users at the same time.
4.   Portability, for ease of comparison with other bibliographic listings and the documents themselves, either within the library or beyond (this feature can be a mixed blessing – things which can be moved have a habit of disappearing!).
5.   Availability of multiple copies for branches, additional locations and other interested parties.
6.   Convenient, cheap and quick to reproduce, so that copies may be supplied as required for branches, other libraries and so on.
7.   Quick, easy and accurate to use.
8.   Inexpensive to maintain.
9.   Compatible with cooperative ventures, specifically in permitting the compilation of union catalogues and international indexes.
10. Usable in conjunction with bibliographies and indexes.

Not surprisingly, no one physical form meets all these criteria. Different criteria are relatively more important in various applications and the physical form appropriate for any given application must be assessed with the assistance of the ten criteria.

The requirements of a physical form of catalogue can be divided into two categories: those which are primarily in the interests of the catalogue or index maintainer, and those which mostly affect the catalogue user. Those primarily concerned with maintenance are numbers 1, 2, 6, 8 and 9, whereas the remainder of the list have a more direct impact on use.

26.4 Cards

Card catalogues or indexes comprise a set of cards often 5 × 3 inches (122 × 72mm), with each entry on a separate card. Cards are filed in drawers, approximately 1000 cards per drawer which, when stacked together, may form a catalogue cabinet. Rods may hold the cards in the drawer and stops may prevent drawers from falling out of the cabinet. Various mechanisms for displaying and holding cards are possible, including revolving drums and platforms. Cards, although often a standard size, may sometimes vary, and for some post-coordinate indexes may be printed with various codes and grids.

Card catalogues and indexes were popular before computers were as well established as they are now. Cards will remain useful for small and personal indexes.

26.5 Computer book-form catalogues and indexes

Computer book-form catalogues and indexes are one of the products of computer processing of records. The output may be in the form of a raw computer printout or may be computer typeset and presented in a form more akin to a conventionally printed index.

Book form has always been used for abstracting and indexing publications and for other published indexes and directories, but was generally regarded as too inflexible for library catalogues, especially since they require regular updating to cater for continuing and gradual expansion of the collection. Conventionally printed book-form indexes (often without the intercession of the computer) are of course still usual in printed directories, monographs, conference proceedings, reports and individual periodical titles. In these applications it remains important that the index be in the same physical form as the document that it indexes.

26.6 Microform catalogues and indexes

Microform catalogues are a common output from computerized cataloguing systems. They have many advantages, not the least of which is their low per copy cost. Since the early 1970s various forms have been used extensively for catalogues, and other forms less frequently for printed indexes. For published indexes, microform is often offered as an alternative to the hard copy; this is known as simultaneous publication of microform and hard copy. Some dictionaries, directories and other reference works are also available in microform.

Most microform catalogues and indexes are produced by COM bureaux which specialize in such products. There is often a range of options for format, type, size and so on. As an indication, the following forms are common for catalogues and indexes:

1. microfiche, usually 208 or 270 frames per fiche, in a piece of film and with a reduction ratio of 42 or 48:1;
2. microfilm, in either 35 mm or 16 mm roll film, usually but not always packaged in a cassette, and
3. ultrafiche, an extra-high reduction ratio fiche with a reduction ratio of 150 to 200:1.

26.8   Other physical forms of catalogue

The four major categories of physical forms outlined above account for most of the published indexes and catalogues. Cataloguers have been inventive, however, producing a plethora of physical forms. Most of these are variations of some type, either upon card or printed book-form indexes, but have been deemed specifically suitable for particular applications.

Visible indexes, strangely, are normally used for catalogues. There are two types:

1. those holding cards with only a certain depth of card visible so that, for instance, headings can be scanned; or
2. those made up of narrow strips about ¼ inch (6mm) wide which are mounted one below another in a frame. In the finished frame the strips are displayed like the lines on a complete page.

Type 2 is usually found as brief entry periodical catalogues or subject indexes to classified catalogues, possibly for the main stock of the library. Type 1 is used as periodicals accessions registers, in which it is possible to record details of receipt and so on, and sometimes for catalogues of other items such as filmstrips.

The *guard book catalogue* is a book-form catalogue with several entries on each page, each entry inserted by pasting slips onto the stout pages of the book. The British Museum had a large guard book catalogue, and some academic libraries used this form. Although bulky and time-consuming to maintain, it does offer a book-form catalogue in which entries can be inserted and withdrawn.

The *sheaf catalogue* comprises sets of slips held in small looseleaf binders. Slip size is typically 7¾ by 4 inches (19 × 10cm) and each binder holds a few hundred slips. Each slip normally carries a separate entry, so the form is both flexible for insertion and withdrawal, while also in 'book form'. Each of the binders is portable and can be separately studied. Because duplicates can be easily made, sheaf catalogues were popular in applications where multiple copies were desirable, such as union catalogues, but the need to maintain large sheaf catalogues has been largely superseded by the products of computer processing. The slips are cheaper but less durable than cards.

Recommended reading

'Bath University Comparative catalogue study: Final report', Bath: University of Bath, 1975 (BLR&D Report 5240–5248).

Bryant, P (1980), 'The catalogue', *Journal of Documentation*, **26** (2), 133–153.

Butler, B (1979), 'Library and patron response to the COM catalog: use and evaluation', Report of a field study of the Los Angeles Public Library System, rev. edition, Information Access Corp.

Diaz, J (ed) (1975), *Microforms and library catalogs: a reader*, Westport, Conn.: Microform Reviews.

Folcarelli, R J *et al.* (1982), *The microform connection*, New York: Bowker.

King, M (1980), 'On costing alternative patterns for COM–fiche catalogues', *Program*, **14** (4), 25–30.

Needham, A (1974), 'User reactions to various forms and orders of catalogues', Bath: Bath University Library (Bath University Comparative Catalogue Study: Final Report, paper no 8).

Glossary

This is not a comprehensive glossary covering all the terms used in this text. Since this is an introductory text that covers a wide subject area, a comprehensive glossary would be extremely long and would probably be totally indigestable. Instead, this glossary is intended to aid the reader by identifying some of the key concepts covered in this book. In particular, concepts that are likely to be encountered in a number of different places in this text are listed. Also the definitions offered are not formal definitions, but rather quick working explanations that should aid understanding. The definitions offered here reflect the use of the term in this book. In the interests of effective communication, the author has attempted to use terminology consistently, although many terms may be used with a number of different meanings in the literature. No attempt has been made here to review all these meanings, although where the different uses of a term may cause confusion this is explained in the body of the text. Abbreviations that are listed in the List of Abbreviations are not repeated here.

Abstract   A concise and accurate representation of the contents of a document, in a style similar to that of the original; a type of summary.

Abstracting service   An organization that prepares abstracts, and usually includes them in a bibliographic database which may be accessed online. Alternatively the abstracts can be used as the basis for a printed abstracting journal.

Access device   A device or method whereby a document may be found, such as an index, bibliography, catalogue, or database.

Access point   An indexing term or heading in an index, catalogue or database, which may be used as a means of identifying specific records or entries in a file.

Acquisition   The process of obtaining books and other documents.

Added entry   A secondary catalogue entry (see also Main Entry). The entry may be an abbreviated version of the main entry.

Adjacency   The proximity of two or more words specified as a requirement in an online search statement, so that phrases can be located (see also Proximity).

Alphabetical subject catalogue   A catalogue arranged alphabetically by subjects: headings are subject headings.

Alphabetical catalogue   A catalogue in which the entries are arranged alphabetically. Usually includes author, title and subject entries. Also called a Dictionary catalogue.

Alphabetical subject index   An alphabetical list of subject index terms or headings. Used to describe:
    a subject index, as in a card index to a collection of documents;
    a subject index to a classified catalogue;
    a subject index to the published schedules of the classification scheme.

Analysis

1. (Cataloguing) What has happened to a book when an Analytical Entry has been created.
2. (Classification) Breaking down a subject into its facets.
3. (Information retrieval) Identification of the concepts within a document that are worthy of indexing.

Analytical cataloguing   The creation of analytical entries.

Analytical entry   An entry in a catalogue for part of a book, periodical, or other publication, article or contribution of separate authorship or subject in a collection. Analytical entries are made in addition to the Main entry, and may be made under authors, subjects or titles.

Analytico-synthetic classification scheme   A scheme which is based upon the analysis of subjects into one concept subjects, and the later synthesis of these subjects in order to create a notation to represent the compound subject.

Annotation   A note included in an entry in a catalogue, bibliography or like tool to offer further information about the document.

Area   A major section of a bibliographic description.

Array   The series of coordinate subdivisions which are obtained by dividing a class or division according to a single characteristic of subdivision.

Article   A contribution written by one or more persons for publication in a periodical.

Articulated subject index   A subject index generated by a computer on the basis of a title-like subject statement.

Audio-visual materials   Non-book materials such as records, tapes, slides, film-strips and video-tapes.

Author   The person or corporate body that can be regarded as intellectually responsible for the content of a work. Authors may include writers, illustrators, performers, producers, translators and others.

Author catalogue   A catalogue of author entries arranged alphabetically under authors' names, or with authors' names as access points.

Author entry   A catalogue entry under an author's name.

Author heading or access point   The heading under which an author entry is made, or the name by which a record may be identified.

Author statement   Part of the description in a catalogue entry; a part of the title area.

Author-title catalogue   A catalogue which contains both title and author entries.

Authority control   The control of heading or access points, usually through the application of an authority list.

Authority list or Authority file   A list of author names, and uniform titles that are used as headings or access points in a catalogue. May also refer to a similar list of classification codes or subject headings.

Automatic indexing   The process of using computers to assign index terms, based on the text of the document.

Auxiliary schedules and tables   Tables of subdivisions which supplement the schedules of classification schemes, and which can be used to synthesize notation for specific subjects.

Baud   Measurement, in bits per second, of the speed with which data can be transmitted.

Bibliographic database   A database which includes citations and possibly abstracts of the printed literature. Such databases indicate the available literature.

Bibliography   A list of materials or documents which is restricted in its coverage by some feature, such as subject, or place of publication. Bibliographies may be printed or held as computer databases.

Boolean search logic   The use of the terms AND, OR and NOT in framing search statements.

Broader term   A term that represents a concept that is broader than the specified term. Used in thesauri.

Browse   To investigate without any clearly defined strategy the contents of a document collection.

Card catalogue   A catalogue whose entries are made on cards and stored in a specified order. Each card contains a single entry.

Card index   An index whose entries are made on cards and stored in a specified order. Each card contains a single entry.

Catalogue   A list of the materials or items in a library with the entries representing the items arranged in some systematic order.

Catalogue code   A set of rules offering guidance in preparing entries for catalogues, so as to encourage consistency in cataloguing practices.

Cataloguing   The process of making entries for a catalogue. May also be used to include classifying items and generally preparing items for use.

Cataloguing in Publication   (CIP) – or in the USA Cataloging in Source – Bibliographic data is provided for new books in advance of publication, so that it can be included in the publication, and thereby be easily available to libraries.

CD-ROM   Compact Disk Read Only Memory. Plastic disks with a reflective metal coating which are read by a small laser beam. A wide variety of databases is available on CD-ROM.

Centralized cataloguing   Cataloguing where catalogue records are created by some central agency, such as a major library or bibliographical service.

Chain   In a classification scheme, the succession of divisions subordinate to one another.

Chain indexing   An alphabetical subject indexing system, based upon the analysis of the chain of subdivisions in a classification scheme. The system is widely used to produce subject indexes to classified catalogues.

Characteristic of classification   A distinctive property or feature by which a class is defined.

Circulation control system A system for maintaining records concerning the circulation of library stock. Usually computer-based.

Citation A reference to a document, or part of a document, giving identification of the document.

Citation index An index that lists articles on the basis of other articles that they have cited. The method has been most widely used in Science Citation Index, Social Sciences Citation Index and Arts and Humanities Citation Index.

Citation order The order in which subjects are synthesized to make a composite subject statement. May be applied in both classification and alphabetical subject terms or headings.

Class A group of concepts or things assembled by some common characteristic. A major division of a classification scheme.

Class mark or Class number The classification notation assigned to an item and used in catalogues, databases and on an item for document arrangement.

Classification The arrangement of things in logical order according to their degrees of likeness.

Classification scheme A scheme for the arrangement of library materials in a systematic sequence, according to their subject and, to a lesser extent, their form.

Classification schedules The main published subject listing of a classification scheme.

Classified catalogue A catalogue with three or four separate sequences: an author/title catalogue or index, a classified subject catalogue and a subject index to the classified catalogue.

Classified subject catalogue A catalogue in which the access points are classification symbols, which have been drawn from a classification scheme.

Collation That part of the description of a book which describes the book as a physical object in terms of, for instance, its number of pages and size.

COM Computer Output Microfilm/Microfiche. Output from a computer database on to microfilm or microfiche.

Combination order (see also Citation Order). The order in which the single concepts in a compound subject heading are arranged.

Command language   The set of commands or instructions that the searcher uses to instruct the computer to perform certain operations.

Common subdivisions   Form divisions that are used throughout a classification scheme to sub-divide any subject. The tables that list these divisions are known as auxiliary tables in Dewey Decimal Classification and the Universal Decimal Classification.

Composite subject   A subject that includes more than one unit concept. The terms complex and compound subject may be used with the same meaning.

Controlled language indexing   Indexing where the terms that may be used as index terms or headings in the index are controlled. Such terms are usually listed in an authority list such as a thesaurus or a subject headings list.

Cooperative   A group of libraries and other information organizations formed in order to share resources or share the work associated with bibliographic record creation.

Cooperative cataloguing   The sharing by a group of libraries or other agencies of the work of cataloguing.

Coordinate subjects   Subjects which are at the same level in the hierarchy in a classification scheme, or the same level of specificity.

Corporate author   A corporate body such as a government or government department or other organization which authorizes the publication of documents and whose name is used for author access points in a catalogue.

Corporate body   An institution, or group of people which has a collective name.

Cross classification   Incorrect subdivision in a classification scheme, where subdivision is conducted by applying more than one characteristic of subdivision at one stage. A poor structure of subjects will result from it.

Current awareness   A system for notifying current documents and information to users of libraries and information services. Includes selective dissemination of information, bulletins and other indexing services.

Database   A collection of similar records with relationships between the records. A database may contain bibliographic data, numbers, statistics or graphics and images.

Database management system   A software package for the creation and maintenance of databases.

Date of publication   The year in which a document was published. For serials it may be more specific and give the day, month and year of publication.

Decimal notation   A notation that can be infinitely subdivided by inserting subdivisions using the next decimal place. Used in the Dewey Decimal Classification and the Universal Decimal Classification.

Descriptor   A subject indexing term. Traditionally used to describe a one-concept subject term.

Dialogue   In computer-based systems the interchange between the computer system and the user, usually guided by the information displayed on the screen. Various dialogue styles are possible including WIMP, Menus and Commands.

Dictionary catalogue   A catalogue with only one sequence which contains author, title and subject entries interfiled.

Distributed network   A network in which processing power is distributed at several different locations in the network.

Distributed relatives   Related subjects that have been scattered by the process of subdivision adopted in a specific classification scheme.

Division   The process of dividing classes or groups of a classification scheme into more specific groups. Also used to refer to the group defined by this process.

Document   A record (in the general sense) that stores and conveys information. Documents were originally text based, but now include graphic, acoustic, video and alphanumeric data. A document is a package of information that may be acquired by and stored in a library.

Downloading   The transfer of data or software from one computer to another.

Edition   All the copies of a work published in one typographical format, printed from the same type or plates, and issued at one time or at intervals.

Edition statement   That part of the description in a catalogue entry which describes the edition of the book being catalogued.

Electronic document delivery   The transfer of information from publisher or library to user by electronic means. Includes CD-ROM, videotex, electronic mail and online databases.

Electronic publication   The use of electronic means of communication to make information available. Uses the same means as electronic document delivery.

Entry   The record of a document in a catalogue.

Enumerative classification   A classification which enumerates all subjects that might be encountered in a collection. Since complete enumeration of all composite subjects leads to very long schedules, most enumerative schemes are selective.

Exhaustivity   The number of themes that are indexed in a document.

Expert system   A computer system that incorporates a knowledge base and rules which are used to simulate the decision-making processes of a human expert.

Facet   The sum total of isolates formed by the division of a subject by one characteristic of division.

Facet analysis   The analysis of a subject to identify appropriate facets and the division of isolates into these facets.

Facet indicator   A symbol which separates parts of the notation of a classification scheme, so that it is possible to identify the facets from which parts of the notation have been drawn.

Faceted classification   A classification scheme in which subjects are divided into facets. Composite subjects are specified by the scheme by drawing together notation from different facets. Such a scheme is Analytico-Synthetic.

False drop   A record that has been retrieved as the result of a search but which is not relevant. Derives from edge-notch card based systems when retrieved cards dropped off the needle. Cards which represented documents that were not relevant were called false drops.

Field   A part of a record in a database. Fields tend to accommodate individual data elements, such as a title or person's name.

File   A collection of records or documents dealing with one organization, person, area or subject. Files may hold paper documents or be computer-based. A computer file is part of a database system.

Filing   The process of arranging documents, papers, records and other items into a pre-specified order.

Filing code   A code of rules that determines the filing sequence, for, say, entries in a catalogue, or records in a catalogue display. Codes may be intended for manual sorting or computer sorting.

Filing order   The order for arranging documents or records. Filing orders are usually alphabetical, or numerical, or in accordance with the notation of a classification scheme.

Finding list   A catalogue with very brief entries. The entries support the location of items in the library, but do not give much information about the items.

Free language indexing   Indexing where there are no constraints upon the terms that may be used as index terms.

Full text searching   Online searching in which all or most elements of the records may be used in searching. Sometimes also called free text searching.

Go list   A list of terms which are to be used as index terms. Used in a computer system during natural language indexing to indicate which terms should be selected as index terms. Opposite of a stop list.

Heading   The sequence of characters at the beginning of an index or catalogue entry or record; these characters determine the position of the record within the filing sequence. Headings are most commonly authors' names, subject terms, notation from a classification scheme or titles.

Homonym   In the context of subject terms, a word that sounds the same, and is possibly spelt the same as another word, but has a different meaning.

Hospitality   The ability to accommodate new subjects, as in a classification scheme. The hospitality of a classification scheme is determined by the underlying subject analysis and also by the notation.

Host   An online service supplier which mounts a number of databases on a computer and offers access to these databases over national and international networks.

Hypertext   A system for handling non-linear text. A hypertext database includes items of information, and links between those items. Hypermedia systems use the same principles but integrate text, data, images and sound in one database.

Identifier   An indexing term. More specifically used for a proper name that is used as an indexing term, such as an acronym, a name of a geographical location or the name of a person.

Imprint date   The year of publication as specified on the title page.

Index   A pointer or indicator, or, more fully, a systematic guide to the items contained in, or the concepts derived from a collection or database.

Index entry   The entry that is included in an index.

Indexing   The process of compiling an index.

Indexing language   The index terms that are used in an index, or the terms or notations that might be used as access points in an index. Alternatively, the vocabulary and the devices for handling the relationship between the terms in the vocabulary in a system for handling index descriptions.

Indexing service   A service which generates an index to literature. Such indexes may be printed publications or updates to databases.

Information retrieval   The process of finding documents or information.

Information system   An organized procedure for collecting, processing, storing and retrieving information. Most commonly used to refer to computer-based systems.

Inverted file   An index type file in a computer-based system which stores index terms and their location in records in the database. Used by the computer system to locate a record containing the search term.

Inverted heading   An index or catalogue heading which has the order of words inverted from its natural language order.

Isolate   A single concept subject. Used in the context of facetted classification schemes.

Keyword   Word indicating the subject discussed in a document. May be used to describe an index term, but strictly a one-word index term. Used in association with KWIC and related indexes.

Known item searching   Searching for a document that the user knows exists prior to the commencement of the search. Usually the searcher knows something about the document, such as its author or title.

KWIC   Acronym for Keyword In Context. A method of permuted indexing which uses a computer to permute words in titles of, say, periodical articles, in order to produce one index entry under each of the words in the title. Variations on KWIC are described as KWOC, KWAC and KWOT indexing.

Library management system   A computer system supporting functions associated with the basic processes of the library such as ordering and acquisitions, cataloguing, OPAC, circulation control and management information.

Literary warrant   The subjects that have appeared in the literature or are present in a library collection. Used as a basis for determining the subjects to include in a classification scheme or an indexing language.

Local area network   (LAN) A network linking computers and associated devices within a restricted geographical area.

Machine readable   Information in a form that can be input into a computer system.

Main class   The principal division of a classification scheme.

Main entry   The chief catalogue entry, which has the fullest details in the description and may bear the tracings, or the indication of the headings for other entries.

Mainframe   A large computer system.

MARC record format   A special record format used for machine-readable catalogue records.

Menu   A type of user interface on a computer system which permits the user to select one of a number of options that are offered.

Microcomputer   A small computer, usually suitable for desk top use or even portable.

Microform   A microrecord based on film. A generic term to cover microfilm, microfiche and microcard.

Minicomputer   A medium sized computer, suitable for many applications such as supporting a library management system.

Mnemonics   Notation in a classification scheme that has been designed to be easy to remember.

Modem   Modulator-demodulator. A device that converts a digital signal from a computer to an analogue signal that can be transmitted along a telephone line, and vice versa.

Monograph   A separate treatise on a subject. Used in cataloguing to distinguish such documents from serials.

Multimedia   Either a collection of materials that includes various materials, such

491

as non-book materials, audio-visual material and non-print material, possibly, as well as books; or an optical disk, such as CD-ROM which carries a combination of text, graphics, sound etc.

Name authority file   The list of names of persons or corporate bodies that are used in a catalogue.

Name catalogue   A catalogue arranged according to the name of persons or places or both. The names may be names of subjects or authors.

Name index   An index arranged according to the names of persons, those persons usually being authors.

Narrower term   A term that denotes a concept which is narrower than the concept described by another term. Used in thesauri.

Natural indexing language   An indexing language which is essentially the language of the documents being indexed. Natural language indexing may be based on titles and abstracts, or on the full text of the document being indexed.

NEPHIS   Acronym for Nested Phrase Indexing. A computer-based system for producing printed indexes, based upon index strings designed by the indexer.

Network   Either a system of physically distinct computers linked by telecommunications. Or, a group of libraries and associated institutions that have agreed to resource share. See also Cooperative.

Non-book media   Library materials that are not books. Examples are sound recordings, filmstrips, motion pictures, computer software and video-recordings.

Notation   The symbols which stand for the divisions of a classification scheme. The purpose of notation is to mechanize the ordering of subjects wherever the scheme is applied.

Nothing before something   Alphabetizing word by word, counting the space between one word and the next as nothing.

Online information retrieval system   A system where a user at a remote terminal can interrogate the databases on a computer system.

Online public access catalogue   A catalogue whose database is stored on a computer, and to which the public has online access via terminals.

Online search service   Alternatively known as online systems suppliers, hosts or

492

online service spinners, are responsible for mounting databases on a computer and making the arrangements necessary for such databases to be searchable from a large number of remote terminals.

Optical disk   A disk made of plastic with a reflective metal coating that is read using a small laser beam. Read only optical discs are a publishing medium. Types are CD-ROM, laser disks and videodisks.

Pagination   That part of the description in a catalogue entry or bibliographical citation which specifies the number of pages in a document.

Permuted indexing   A method of generating a number of index entries under different entry words, by using the computer to re-arrange the terms in an index string.

Personal author   The person responsible for the intellectual content of a work. Authorship has been the responsibility of the individual, and could not be regarded as a work of corporate authorship.

Phoenix schedule   A new development of part of a classification schedule.

Place of publication   The town or other location in which a publisher's office is located.

Pre-coordinate indexing   Indexing where subjects are represented by headings that coordinate a number of single concepts into one heading.

Post-coordinate indexing   Indexing where subjects are represented by a series of single concept headings in the index, and some mechanism exists whereby these single concepts can be coordinated to make a composite subject description during searching. Also called Coordinate indexing.

Postings   The number of records retrieved by a search statement.

PRECIS   Acronym for Preserved Context Index System. A subject indexing system that uses role operators to arrange terms into an index string. The string is then computer manipulated so that a series of entries is produced under different index terms.

Precision   The precision ratio of a system measures the relevant documents retrieved as compared with the total number of documents retrieved.

Preferred term   A preferred term is the term that will be used in an index, possibly in preference to a number of synonyms or near synonyms. Used in the context of a thesaurus.

Recall   The recall ratio of a system measures the relevant documents retrieved as compared with the total relevant documents in the system.

Record   Either a document that preserves information, or, in computer systems, a collection of related items of data; for example, the information relating to and describing one document.

Reference   A direction from one heading to another. References may be see or see also. See references are made from an unused access point to a used access point, ie between two synonyms. See also references are made between two related used headings. References may be made between two titles, subjects or names.

Related term   A term that is coordinate to another term, ie at the same level in the hierarchy. Used in thesauri.

Related work   A work that has a relationship with another work. Typically a continuation, supplement, index, extract.

Relational database   A database where data is held in a number of separate files, which are linked by the use of common keys, so that data can be drawn from several of the files simultaneously.

Relative index   An alphabetical index, usually to the schedules of a classification scheme. The index draws together aspects of a subject that would otherwise be scattered by the classification scheme.

Relevance ranking   A searching technique which uses weights to signify the importance of various concepts either in the document or search profile, and produces a list of retrieved documents in an order that reflects their weights. The most relevant documents should be at the top of the list.

Retrieval   The process of finding something, such as information that has been stored and indexed.

Retrospective conversion   The conversion of records from an existing catalogue into machine readable form.

Schedule   A list of the subjects in a classification scheme set out in such an order as to display the relationships between the subjects.

Search statement   A search comprising search terms linked by logic operators.

494

Search strategy The way in which a searcher performs a search. Typically involves framing a series of search statements.

Search term A word or phrase or piece of notation input by the user to locate those documents that have been indexed under that term. Index terms form the set of available search terms.

Searching The process of looking for something, such as information or a document.

Selective dissemination of information (SDI) A current awareness tool in which users are able to specify individual interests in an interest profile, and then receive tailored notifications of new documents and information.

Semantic relationships Relationships between subjects that are reasonably stable and which reflect the consensus of opinion concerning the relationships between subjects.

Serial A publication issued in successive parts, appearing at intervals, usually regular intervals, and usually intended to be continued indefinitely.

Series entry An entry under a series title in a catalogue or index.

Series statement The part of the description of a catalogue record which shows the name of the series to which a document belongs, and the number, if any, of the publication within the series.

Shared cataloguing Where a number of different agencies share the creation of a catalogue database.

Shelf arrangement The arrangement of library stock on shelves, so that it can be viewed and selected by users.

SLIC index An index based on Selective Listing In Combination, where a set of terms are chosen to describe a document, and these are rotated in the index entries to produce a number of different entries from the one set of terms.

Source database A database that contains the source data. Includes numeric databases, full-text databases and text-numeric databases.

Special classification A classification scheme which is limited in its coverage by subject or purpose.

Specificity The extent to which a system or indexing language allows the user to be precise about the subject of a document.

495

Stop list   A list of words or terms, or character strings that are considered non-significant for information retrieval, and therefore will not be represented in the inverted file. Such words are known as stopwords.

Subdivision   The process of dividing a subject into more specific areas, and the areas created by his process.

Subheading   A secondary heading, used in conjunction with a main heading, to qualify that main heading.

Subject   An area of interest, or an area in which an individual writes or works, or an area of knowledge that is studied. Can also be viewed as the theme of a document.

Subject authority list   The list of subject headings that have been used in a given catalogue and which are acceptable for use.

Subject catalogue   A catalogue arranged by subject. Could be in alphabetical or classified order.

Subject entry   An entry in a subject catalogue or index, where the access point or heading will be an alphabetical subject heading or a classification number.

Subject heading   A heading from a list of subject headings which defines the controlled indexing language to be used in the catalogue or index. A subject heading is a word or group of words which is used as the access point in a subject catalogue.

Subordinate subject   A more specific subject to a subject that is described as superordinate. A subject at a lower level in the hierarchy.

Superordinate subject   A more general subject, to a subject that is described as subordinate.

Synonym   A term with the same or similar meaning to another term. In controlled indexing languages only one synonym will be preferred and used.

Syntactic relationships   Relationships that arise from the context of subjects in specific documents, or from the syntax. Two concepts may appear together in one document, but not in another.

Tag   A character or digit which is attached to a record or to a field in a record, for purposes of identification. Used in the MARC record format to indicate fields in the record.

Teletext   Broadcast videotex, based upon using an adapted television as a receiver.

Term   Used to describe an index term, or a term in an indexing language.

Text information management system   A computer based database system which specializes in the management of textual data.

Thesaurus   A compilation of words and phrases showing synonyms, hierarchical and other relationships and dependencies, the function of which is to provide a standardized vocabulary for information storage and retrieval systems.

Title   The word or words by which a document is designated, for example on the title page. The title distinguishes the work from others, but may not be a unique identifier.

Title catalogue   A catalogue consisting of title entries.

Title entry   An entry under a title in a catalogue or index.

Truncation   The process of shortening or cutting off part of a search term so that it can be matched against other terms with the same stem.

Uniform title   The distinctive title by which a work which has appeared under a number of different titles may be known, and which is used in a catalogue as an access point.

Union catalogue   A catalogue showing the stock of a number of libraries, who may be members of a network or cooperative.

Unit entry   A standard catalogue entry offering relatively full details, which can be used in different sequences in a catalogue, by adding different headings such as authors' names or classification notation.

Uniterm   A one concept term.

User interface   The interface between the user and a computer system. Incorporates data input and output means, and a significant component is the dialogue which is displayed on the screen.

Videotex   A system where information is made available by a television monitor. Embraces teletext which is broadcast videotex but also includes systems which use a telephone line to transmit messages.

Wide area network   A data transmission system linking several organizations. The network may be national or international in scope.

WIMP   Acronym for Windows, Icons, Mouse and Pointer. Describes a type of user interface.

Window   Part of a computer display screen acting like a window so that text or menus can be overlaid on other items already on the screen.

WORM   Acronym for Write Once Read Many. Describes optical discs that can be used to record data once, but then read many times. Used widely for archive applications.

Index

ARK BABY

BY THE SAME AUTHOR

EGG DANCING

ARK BABY

LIZ JENSEN

BLOOMSBURY

First published in Great Britain 1998
Copyright © 1998 by Liz Jensen

The moral right of the author has been asserted

Bloomsbury Publishing Plc, 38 Soho Square,
London WIV 5DF

A CIP catalogue record for this book
is available from the British Library

ISBN 0 7475 3526 4

10 9 8 7 6 5 4 3 2 1

Typeset by Palimpsest Book Production Limited,
Polmont, Stirlingshire
Printed by Clays Ltd, St Ives Plc

FOR MICHEL

Natural selection is daily and hourly scrutinising, throughout the world, every variation, even the slightest; rejecting that which is bad, preserving and adding up all that is good . . . we see nothing of these slow changes in progress, until the hand of time has marked the long lapse of ages, and then so imperfect is our view into long lost geological ages, that we only see that forms of life are now different from what they once were.

Charles Darwin, *Origin of Species*, 1859

Forgive, O Lord, my little jokes on Thee, And I'll forgive Thy great big one on me.

'Forgive, O Lord', Robert Frost, 1962

PROLOGUE

In the beginning, the ocean. Huge. Ink-dark beneath a black sky. The sunlight chinking through: bright, dangerous. Beneath the bunching clouds, rain slashes the waves, walls of glass that crash in brutal shards against the *Ark's* hull. The vessel is a speck on the face of the deep. A toy of wood and string.

The air rumbles.

Inside his padded leather cabin in the *Ark*, the Human awakes lurching in the gathering storm. Flings out an arm, grasps the hip-flask, glugs at blood-red claret. Then splutters and curses. His language: the Queen's English.

'Buggeration.'

Something's wrong below deck. The Human can sense it. Listen: from deep in the sarcophagus of the *Ark*, come screeches, yowls, grunts; whistles, growls, barks; snarls, baying, primal hoots. The Human fumbles in his breast pocket and peers at his greasy fob-watch. It's four o'clock. This racket is the usual feral cacophony of feeding time – but the beasts have already devoured their hay and slop. And Higgins, Steed and Bowker administered them their phials of laudanum an hour ago. The creatures should be comatose, drugged into quiet. They've slept through storms before.

Yes: something is awry.

Sniffing the air, the Human begins to sense the creatures' panic. He can smell their fear, too. And then, suddenly, his own, prickling from his armpits into his ruffed shirt.

He mutters a word to himself. The word is 'mutiny'. As if

1

he has been waiting for this moment. As if he has known it would come.

A sudden wave jolts the ship, and the Human's hip-flask falls to the floor with a tinny clang, bounces and skids under the bunk.

The Human jangles the alarm bell for Higgins and the crew. The men know the drill. As the clomp of running feet fills the gangways, the Human notices how the animals' smell has changed. Mingling with the odour of his own sudden fear, it permeates the whole vessel, insinuating its way through cracks in the wood and snaking into his nostrils. It is sweet and violent. Urgent and metallic. Fresh blood.

The noises from below grow louder and more ominous. Baying, growling, yapping, squawking. And the shrill scream of a woman.

The Human pulls on his thigh-high boots. Reaches for a metal-and-glass syringe. Charges it carefully with praxin. Screws on a sturdy needle. Sways to his feet. And descends with a clatter to the hull.

As insurrection explodes below deck, outside, the storm breaks with a murderous thud.

A month later, when the Travelling Fair of Danger and Delight was encamped in Riverside Fields, the Frozen Woman arrived at the Greenwich Workhouse with her cloak turned to ice, a rigid tent. Beneath it, the skirt of her ballerina's tutu stuck out horizontally from her hips. It was 5 December 1844 and the air was so cold that ravens were dropping dead from the trees like wasted fruit, thwopping into the snowdrifts in tiny, efficient acts of self-burial. She was a little stick of a woman, an icicle herself.

'Where have you come from?' asked Sister Benedicta, aghast.

'The ocean. I swam. Then got caught in a fishing net. The others drowned,' she croaked.

That was all she could say. Her tutu had to be cracked off her. The nuns plonked her naked in a metal tub of lukewarm water, averting their eyes. But Sister Benedicta could not help taking a peek.

'Call the midwife, somebody,' she gasped, as the peek became a wide-eyed stare. 'She's in the advanced stages of a delicate condition!'

'She opened and closed like a pair of nutcrackers,' the midwife reported afterwards. 'It just wasn't natural,' she added, expressing her astonishment at the Frozen Woman's pelvic control – due in part to her double-jointedness – and the unusual ease of the birth. She'd just squatted down and out he came. As if to echo her anxiety, a sickly wail and a stream of vomit emerged from the baby's mouth.

Word soon spread through the Workhouse that the Frozen Woman's offspring was the child of the Devil. Inspecting the newborn infant, and consulting his Bible, the Principal, a man of girth and gravitas, made the same assessment. Ponderously informing the new mother that he ran a Christian establishment, he then had two man-servants throw her out into the winter night. What the Frozen Woman called over her shoulder to the Principal as she left came as further proof, they all agreed, of her Satanic connections.

'See you in Hell, you fat bastard!' she yelled, as she picked her way through the snow towards the twinkling lights of the Travelling Fair of Danger and Delight, the swaddled baby stuffed under her arm askew like a parcel. She was wearing only the torn remains of her tutu, and a pair of thin ballet shoes on her small feet.

The next day the Travelling Fair of Danger and Delight decamped and headed north.

The Frozen Woman was not seen in Greenwich again.

CHAPTER 1

2005: IN WHICH A ROGUE MALE ESCAPES FROM THE HERD

Boundless hope; that was what flooded my heart as I pressed my foot on the accelerator of my spanking new car, and headed north towards my spanking new life.

Boundless hope, and the bright motorway up ahead. I slipped in a CD and flooded the car with Elvis: 'Blue Suede Shoes'. I sang along. A few pints inside me, and I'll do you a good impression of the King.

> *Ah you c'n burnah mah hous-ah, stealah mah car,*
> *Drinkah mah wiskha fromman ol froojar . . .*

He died the day I was born. 16 August 1977. Like a phoenix, he was just waiting for me to come along, I reckon. Knowing he could hand over. But unfortunately I'm not much of a singer, which is why I'm a vet.

Snakes shed their skin at least once a year. You find their faded, papery husks caught on bracken, gorse, or heather long after the creature inside has slipped away. I'd sloughed off my old Vauxhall at the Motormart and emerged in a sleek little Audi Nuance. A bit of whoosh, a bit of poke. That's me sorted.

On the map, Thunder Spit just looked like a scramble of broken veins two centimetres above Hunchburgh, but driving out of London I was already building up a clear mental image of my destination, based on nostalgic memories of camping holidays on the seashore in the 1980s: glorious summers of seagulls pecking at ice-cream cones, we boys ritually burying Dad in sand and fag-ends while Mum sat cooped in the tent, drinking thermosed vodka and listening to the Weather; the smell of chicken nuggets, sun-cream, popcorn, piss. Who said there was no such thing as society?

How was I to know, as the North Circular receded in my driving mirror, and the M1 hove into view, that my future was about to be hijacked by someone else's past?

> *But uh-uh, honey, lay off of my shoes, er don't you,*
> *Ah steppon mah blue suede shoezah . . .*

And how could anyone have predicted, as I slid back the sun-roof and inhaled the smell of freedom, that the Victorian legacy unearthed in the attic of the Old Parsonage would change the course of human evolution?

> *You c'n doanythin-ah-ba-lay offamah blue suedah . . .*

And how could –

No. Switch off Elvis. *Begin at the beginning, go on until you come to the end, and then stop.*

All right then.

The beginning wasn't actually the day I revved up the car, but the previous month, when Giselle, the catalyst for my upheaval, arrived in my surgery for her appointment with death. What's that saying, 'Never work with animals or children'? I did both.

It was only October, but the sun was sinking earlier every day over Tooting Bec, and Christmas had already muzaked its way into the shops. Giselle was one of my afternoon clients; a moody-looking, low-slung macaque monkey. She was wearing a pink dress, with the obligatory nappy beneath, and was clasping the hand of a bloke in a cable-knit sweater. It's something of a commonplace in the veterinary profession that the owners resemble the pets and vice versa, so Mr Mann's appearance was a surprise. That he was male, for starters; since the Fertility Crisis, primate owners were 92 per cent female, according to *Pets Today*, to which my surgery was a reluctant subscriber. Plus there was nothing low-slung about him at all; on the contrary, he was quite high-stepping and angular. More of a dog type, I'd have said: red setter, bordering on the whippet. He probably owned one once upon a time, back in the old days.

The monkey was sucking her thumb.

In the last couple of years, since the National Egg Bank closed its waiting list to women over thirty, I'd been seeing ten or twelve macaques a week. Plus chimps, spider monkeys, orang-utans, even the occasional gibbon or baboon; the usual specimens that doting pseudo-mums brought in, freshly shampooed, complaining of bowel blockage and needing a psychiatrist. The real fanatics would shave them, and openly breast-feed in the waiting-room. It made my flesh crawl.

Sure enough, it quickly emerged that Giselle wasn't Mr Mann's at all, but belonged to his wife, who was away on a business trip. When I inspected the monkey, I remembered the wife clearly: brawny but petite, fanatical-looking, clumpy heels. That figured.

'No need to examine her,' Mr Mann announced bluntly, lifting the macaque on to my op table. 'I want her put down.'

Giselle's hairy legs, poking out absurdly from her pink dress, dangled over the side, and she swung her feet experimentally. She was wearing ankle socks and a pair of the expensive elasticated trainers that were all the rage in primate fashion.

'Humanely,' Mr Mann added, as though it were an afterthought. As though there might be a messy, non-humane option, involving torture, and available for a lower fee.

As I went to the cupboard and selected the usual carbo-glycerate of praxin concoction, I wondered idly what his reasons were. She was a good specimen; probably about three or four years old. The Fertility Crisis dated back to the Millennium, so none was over five. When I turned back with the loaded syringe, I saw that Giselle had now swung her feet back up on to the table, and rucked her dress up to expose her muscular tummy, which she was grooming busily. So much for instinct, I thought.

Holly was standing by with the paper towels and the self-sealing incinerator bag, trying to stop the tears. She liked animals. Primates especially. She was a temp.

'Nope,' said Mann. 'No particular reason. Just, as I said, the wife's away.'

'You mean, if she were here you wouldn't be asking me to do this?'

'Got it in one, mate.' He stood there, expecting me to join in the joke. He was smirking, as though betrayal were a clever new idea that he'd developed and patented, and he was just waiting for the dividends. He began to stroke Giselle clumsily on the head, and she paused from her grooming to look up at him with the surprise and gratitude that only females can muster in these situations. Then she handed him a flea.

'I can't do it,' I said. 'Not if you're not legally the owner. Did you bring the licence?'

I should have asked him all this before, of course. As her name suggests, Holly can be a bit prickly. She gulped a bit, and I noticed her eyes hardening up in the way they'd taken to doing when she reckoned 'human rights' were involved, but she kept quiet, thank Christ. I didn't want her thinking she had some kind of moral hold just because we'd crumpled her duvet together a few times. It had been a busy morning, and she knew it: there'd been a massive cat-fight in Sainsbury's car-park the previous night and I'd already seen to six of the injured and had to deal with their owners, too. The waiting-room reeked of cat-spray. A cockatoo, an innocent psittacosis booster case, passed out in shock when the squalling started, and I'd had a dud batch of spider-monkey flu vaccine, and bugger me if the surgery wasn't out of nitrate capsules. I put my head round the door; I was going to ask those with baskets to wait outside, but just then an obese, growling mastiff with testicular cysts

7

came in, which solved the caterwauling problem but gave rise to others, namely an IOU from the owner, and a pool of piss on the lino.

'Licence?' Mann was saying. 'Didn't know I had to bring it.'

'New regulations,' I told him. 'Since the Fertility Crisis.'

'Don't know where she keeps it.' He said this accusingly, as though I should have telepathically intercepted his thoughts and phoned to warn him about the paperwork before he left home.

'Primates, dogs and horses have licences,' I told him. There was a silence, during which he sucked in his cheeks and rocked to and fro on his heels a bit, so I elaborated. 'Cats, no.'

Mann then said pointlessly, 'Well, I don't have a cat. I've got a monkey, though.'

'So I see,' I said, and winked at Holly. Giselle, crouched docilely on the operating table, emitted an odour. Holly blushed.

'No,' Mann was saying. 'I mean I've got *another* monkey. *My* monkey. Used to belong to my sister but she –'

He stopped. He didn't need to say it. The post-*fin-de-siècle malaise*, they called it. No babies, no future. Did she do it dramatically, I wondered, from a cliff-top? Or quietly at home, with chemicals?

'We live in terrible times,' I said, shaking my head. I wasn't kidding; we did.

'Ritchie's a macaque, too,' Mann was saying. 'Not a pedigree, like Giselle here, but –'

I always practise faces in the mirror after I've brushed my teeth. So now I tried out quizzical on Mr Mann. Like I didn't know what he was getting at.

'Well, couldn't I just bring *his* licence, instead? Wouldn't that do?' He was asking me like a boy asking his teacher. 'They don't get on, see.' And now his tone was becoming dangerously confessional. 'Her and him. Giselle and Ritchie. They fight, see. Ever since my sister – well, ever since Ritchie's been living with us, he's been disturbed. Bereaved, like. And he tries having a go at Giselle here – mounting her, sorathing, wanting sex, like – but she don't want it. She's neutered, see. So she's like frigid.'

8

I remembered neutering her now. Mrs Mann had been insistent that Giselle had never been with a male, and that there was no risk of her already being impregnated.

'She's virgin territory, I assure you,' she'd said smugly.

But of course when I operated, I'd found twin foetuses clinging to her uterus. I always charged extra for that.

'Ritchie's just a frisky lad,' Mann was pleading. 'What he needs is a playmate, not some stuck-up little thing that's always going to spurn him.'

There was a desperate look in his doggy eyes: he needed a chocolate drop, a pat on the head, a rubber bone to chew on, a stamp of approval for the churning cauldron of petty emotions that functioned as his intellect.

I remembered Mrs Mann's expression when she'd come to collect Giselle after the operation; the delicate little jaw set firm, the victorious smile nudging at her mouth as she wrote the cheque. I told her about the foetuses.

'Not such virgin territory after all, you see,' I'd said. 'Your Giselle here isn't as innocent as she looks.'

Mrs Mann adjusted her face.

'Well, I came to you in the nick of time, then,' she said finally, with a brisk smile. It struck me, her decisiveness, the cool way she took it. (The way the mastiff man had behaved over the cysts this morning, it was like his own bollock I was planning to cut open.)

'She's too young to be a mother,' she'd added brightly. I'd heard that one before. It was a fairly standard remark, uttered by women who bought themselves a baby-substitute, then got jealous when little Miss Primate became a teenager and got knocked up. 'Giselle couldn't possibly cope,' she said. 'She comes from a very sensitive pedigree, you know.'

I remember snorting, and exchanging a glance with Holly. Someone out there – probably the same bloke who designed the elasticated trainers – was whacking up a fortune with this pedigree scam. But there was no point telling Mrs Mann that the monkey family-tree business was a load of shite;

9

she had that appalling look of conviction on her face that people have when they've been nourished from birth on pure gibberish.

Mr Mann was still looking at me expectantly. So was Giselle. 'Well? Will you do it?'

I didn't reply. I pretended I hadn't heard.

'I'll pay you an extra five hundred Euros.'

Holly looked at me.

'Cash,' he said, interpreting my lack of response correctly. There was no shame in his voice, and no shame in mine when I answered.

'A thousand, and I'll do it.' It seemed a risk worth taking. 'But mind you find that licence and destroy it as soon as you get home. I won't be answerable.'

I shook the clammy hand he offered me, and he gave me the Euros then and there. Giselle watched as he counted it out; she mimicked his hand movements, and moved her lips like he did, as though she were counting it, too.

It was all there.

'Right, Giselle, I'd like you to roll up your sleeve now for me, will you, darling?' I murmured. She complied obediently.

Mann turned his face away while I found the vein on her hairy little arm. It was his right, I suppose. After all, he'd just paid me a thousand yo-yos not to do the honours himself. Holly turned away, too.

Giselle didn't. She watched closely, interested in the procedure.

'See?' I said, squeezing the syringe. 'It doesn't hurt. Night-night, then, baby.'

She nodded, as though she understood the transaction. She even flashed me a toothy smile. Then went out like a light, the little pink frock crumpling beneath her as she sagged, then horizontalised. Her tail twitched briefly, then hung limp.

Mann made a choking noise.

'Too late for regrets, mate,' I told him. His face had faded to a chalky white. He mumbled something I couldn't make out, then

10

stumbled out of the surgery faster than you could say verbal contract.

Afterwards, Holly bagged up the stiffening but still-warm Giselle, and said she was handing in her notice.

'What you did was wrong,' she snivelled, 'destroying that lovely little girl, and the guy wasn't even the legal owner. What'll you do when she comes in? The wife?'

I was annoyed. Holly didn't normally question me. But she was new, I had to keep reminding myself.

'Look, she wasn't a *girl*,' I said, nudging at the body-bag. 'She was a sodding macaque monkey.'

This stuff was old, old hat to me. I explained to Holly how, having been in the veterinary business now for ten years, five of them since the Fertility Crisis and the quadrupling of domestic animal ownership that it had engendered, I was used to the charade-playing of pet-keepers.

'The psychology of pet-ownership has undergone a sea-change, since the Fertility Crisis,' I told her, quoting verbatim from an editorial I'd skimmed in *Pets Today*. Holly nodded impatiently; she'd clearly read the same article. 'Certain animals have almost literally become children to certain people. Especially the primates.'

Anyone could have told you that.

'Mr Mann was defending his nephew-substitute against his stepdaughter-substitute,' I analysed for her. 'He's following his own human instinct to protect the nearest he's got to his own genes. His sister's offspring, or offspring substitute, is closer to him, genetically speaking, than his wife's child-substitute that she bought before they met. It's all imaginary, so it's bollocks, but it means a lot to their subconsciouses.'

'OK, Mr Super-Intelligent Psychologist,' goaded Holly, still upset. 'But how's Mrs Mann – or should I say her *subconscious* – going to react?'

I outlined the forthcoming scenario to her simply: how in the next few days Mrs Mann would come in on a weekday morning surgery with her husband's dead sister's monkey, Ritchie, to

11

exact revenge. How she would instruct me to destroy him, and probably offer me some extra money to forget about the licence. How she'd of course be bitter with me over the Giselle thing, but would have the sense to bite her tongue if she wanted Ritchie to join Giselle up there in Great Bananaland.

'And you'd murder Ritchie, too?' Holly spat out the histrionic word 'murder' with the unaccustomed venom of the recently innocent. 'You'd really do it?'

I took her by her plump little shoulders and kissed her very long and very hard, the way my temps always seemed to like it. Holly was a sweet thing. I found the puritanical taste of her toothpaste, combined with her naivety, arousing, and Sigmund stirred in my boxer shorts. It was the end of the day, and the last clients had shuffled out of the waiting-room. I was tempted to have Holly then and there, but she wrenched herself away. Her face was still half-angry, but half-admiring, too. I could see that she was as ready for sex as Sigmund and I were, but Ritchie and Giselle were preying on her mind.

'You'd really do it, wouldn't you?' she repeated. Her brain seemed to have stuck in a groove.

'There's no point in lying,' I said. A whopper in itself, of course. There's *always* a point. 'Yes, I would.' But honesty wasn't going to budge her. So I added, with sudden inspiration, 'Don't you see? I'm actually assisting in the mercy killing – the *euthanasia* – of something much bigger.'

That got her thinking.

'Like what?' she asked. She didn't get it, but she wanted to. 'Like what, exactly, Bobby?'

'Like a failing marriage, Holly,' I said. Sigmund was straining at the leash. 'Like a marriage in the throes of death.'

She understood then, because she didn't resist as I undressed her and laid her naked on the operating table. Very slowly, I parted her legs and began to lick between them. I felt the origami folds of her flesh thicken; she didn't move.

But I was wrong about Mrs Mann. I was wrong about Holly, too.

12

The phone rang in the kitchen at home the next morning. I'd just finished defrosting half a dozen sausages in the microwave, and was opening a tin of sliced mushrooms. I picked up the phone, still clasping the tin by the tin-opener, and holding three eggs in my other hand. Not a good idea, because what the woman said made me drop one of them.

'I'm lodging a formal complaint.' Splat, on the lino. I sat down heavily on a chair, and nursed the mushroom-tin in my lap.

'Who is this?' I asked, to buy a bit of time, though of course I knew. I remembered those hard little eyes of hers: what I'd taken for sexual repression was clearly something more dangerous. 'How did you get my private number?' I wondered about my pulse-rate. It was probably way up around the hundred-and-forty mark.

'From your assistant. Holly, isn't it? Lovely girl. You don't deserve her.'

'No,' I said. *Holly?* I felt my heart squeeze up and bang against my rib-cage, like a fist. 'I *don't* deserve her.'

'What you don't understand,' said Mrs Mann, 'is that Giselle –'

I knew what was coming. I was a killer. I had murdered her baby-substitute in cold blood.

'Giselle was a *person*,' she said. She'd been crying, I realised, and was now struggling to keep her voice level.

'Mrs Mann –' I began.

'Yes?'

'Mrs Mann, I –' (This could develop into something absurd, I realised. It was also, at the same time, quite serious. So now I'm going to put down my remaining eggs, and my tin of mushrooms, very gently, on the floor, and put into action that phrase women hate. Here goes.) '*I can explain.*'

'Go on, then,' she challenged. Her voice still had that deranged crack in it, a fault-line that could suddenly become a chasm. 'Explain.'

'Your husband told me –' I started. But she didn't play by the rules: she butted in.

'I know what happened. He paid you off. You're – you're just

13

a cheap contract killer! *A thousand Euros*? Is that all a child's life is worth to you, Mr Sullivan?'

She used the word 'child' without a trace of irony.

'Mrs Mann,' I said gently, thinking: Those yo-yos are going towards my spanking new Audi Nuance, missis, so don't knock it! And then I said her name again, even more gently. 'Mrs Mann. As far as I was concerned, it was a perfectly standard procedure. I put down at least five primates every working day.'

This was a wild exaggeration, I'll admit. It was one a month, max. As I spoke, I was beginning to wonder if I could tell her that Giselle had been terminally ill. That when I'd inspected her, I'd found inoperable bowel disorder, of the kind monkeys are prone to when they've been fed the wrong diet. That Holly, being a temp, had misunderstood. It might get me off the hook. She might even be grateful. But too late: Mrs Mann's crazed voice was veering up at me again.

'I'm going to fight you all the way,' she said.

Some instinct made me glance over at the doormat in the hallway. I peered at the single white rectangle that lay on it. The envelope was addressed to me in Holly's schoolgirly hand-writing. That did it. I'd been caught in a pincer movement.

'Bugger off,' I told the Mann woman, and slammed down the phone.

Holly's letter was hand-delivered and brief. She was leaving 'for ethical reasons', and 'would not hesitate' to give evidence against me in an inquiry.

It was that phrase, 'would not hesitate' that pissed me off the most.

I lit the gas-ring and cleaned up the mess. As I stabbed away at the sausages sizzling gently in the frying pan, I thought about Giselle, and the excruciating Manns, and the silly Holly, and the statement that she would make on Mrs Mann's complaint form. It was generally true, I realised, that, apart from the fleeting exoticism of a sick tarantula or a truly challenging road-accident case like the paralysed collie whose hind legs I'd replaced with little wheels the previous year, my life had become a banal treadmill of feline vaccinations, mauled rabbits, cracked terrapin shells and primate psychiatry. But the Giselle incident was excitement of a kind I didn't need.

And then, watching the little flecks of sausage-fat hitting the tiling behind the hob, where they congealed opaquely, a sudden, simple and quite mind-blowingly compelling thought came to me. Primates were a metropolitan thing, largely.

So quit the jungle.

Leave them all behind. Holly, and the Manns, and the apes and the monkeys. I could let the surgery to some starry-eyed newcomer, and be gone within the week. A change of scene. Some outdoor stuff. Cows, sheep, geese; the kind of animals that paid their keep, and were brutish, messy and unappealing enough to keep human sentimentality at bay. A place with farms, by the sea. Slurry lagoons. The seaside. Burying Dad in sand and fag-ends. Pissing into the waves. The smell of popcorn. Sex on the beach. Crabs.

I felt light-hearted and light-headed. As I turned the sausages in the frying pan, I noticed that I had begun to whistle a tune: 'It's Now or Never'. Telling, that. And I hadn't whistled in weeks. Elation was whirling through me like a snort of ether. Then I prodded at the sausages. Yum, yum! My mouth waters just thinking about them. They were prime pork, flecked with dark-green spots of sage. I inhaled, and my heart soared. They smelt of freedom.

Boundless hope, and the bright motorway up ahead. As my car whooshed northwards to Thunder Spit, I was filled to giddiness with the knowledge that the future was mine.

15

CHAPTER 2

IN WHICH A MISTAKEN
PIGLET HOVERS NEAR
DEATH

They sed it wuz not POSSIBEL, the Frozen Woman wrote years later, with her splattery peacock quill. *But I PROOVD it WUZ, tho I never SETTE OUT to do so, as I hav no lernin of SYENSE, and at that TYME I had not herd of Mister DARWYNNE'S beleefs.*

The onion-skin parchment on which she laboriously penned her garbled testimony (in blood? In mud? In a hideous mixture of the two?) is now cracked and split with age, and the text itself is smeared with Parson Phelps' snotty tears, which were to flow and flow in the Sanatorium, before dissolving into the sudden, insane laughter of pure joy.

All I REKOGNYZED, she wrote, *wuz that I had ikkstreemlie BAD LUK in LUVVE.*

She could say *that* again.

It is perhaps necessary to state, at a time when fiction is rife, that the account of my life that I deliver here is punctiliously reported, and scrupulously faithful to both truth and fact. That stated, shall I begin?

Picture first Thunder Spit: a peninsula in the shape of a herring, its tail nailed to the mainland, head straining out to sea. A God-fearing, wave-slapped place, an outcrop of harsh winds and cowering, gnarled trees and shrubs that hug the land like devilish suckers. Follow the promontory: follow the line of the herring's back and find the dorsal fin, a beach of grey bleached sand and grey bleached rock. Look back across the fish's belly, past the flat shimmer of the River Flid, and see the grey slate roofs of the town like a mesh of scales. Further west, see the Church of St Nicholas, a spike its skull. The smell of salt, and thyme, and rock, and seaweed, and rotting fish. Sea-water washing and sloshing at you from north and south. There are floods each year, when the tide spills too far.

Thunder Spit; this was home, the home I still wear inside me like an extra ventricle, pounding away: Thunder Spit; a village famed for its annual bare-handed Thistle-Pulling Contest, for which a special field is set aside; a village where men have always been raised to seek out discomfort, and to thrive on it, striving to maintain the rigorous hair-shirt mentality of their forefathers. My foster-father, a moon-faced, passionate man who encouraged this approach to hardship, always used to say, 'Coddle yourself, Tobias, and you slip away from God.' On Fridays, he would stuff marbles into his shoes: he believed in paying penance whether you owed it or not. But my foster-mother, who suffered from bunions, and who would have liked to coddle herself and slip away from God once in a while, perhaps into a little brushed cotton, made a rigid horizontal of her lips and said nothing. That was her way.

Thunder Spit, home of the herring gull, the kittiwake, the storm petrel, the guillemot, the Lord Chief Justice sheep, the Hildamore cow, the famous Thunder Spit tortoiseshell cat, a variety of dogs, and three hundred and twenty-three of God's human citizens.

Soon to be three hundred and twenty-four.

This is how the story goes: I heard it often enough. The white light, the piglet, the doctor, the infection, the gift-from-Heaven nonsense. The story changes, with the appearance of the umbilical cord, but that's for later. The happy part first: my famous arrival in the Year of Our Lord 1845, as recounted by the God-fearing gent who was to become my father, for better and for worse, and despite himself.

Parson Phelps was well aware – sometimes most painfully so – that miracles did not often come to Northumberland, much less to Thunder Spit. Quasi-occult dabblings involving tea-leaves and chicken-droppings, accusations of witchcraft against Mrs Boggs' idiot cousin Joan, moral transgressions of the adulterous variety, calves with two heads, yes. But miracles, never, if he was honest with himself. (And when was he not?) The biggest excitement for months had been the Travelling Fair of Danger and Delight, which rolled out of Judlow yesterday, leaving the usual hot and silly mess of yearning in its wake. Parson Phelps had preached against it, as he did every year, and all the more fervently when he had heard that this year's exhibits included a Man-Eating Wart-hog, a Ten-Foot Woman, and a Latvian hermaphrodite with a fan of ostrich plumes poking out of its exposed anus. The Fair, with its spangle-maned horses and Mechanical Millipede and dizzying bravura, always left the villagers goggle-eyed and addle-brained. Last year, a Judlow lad, drunk on exotic decadence, had sailed away on a Chinese skiff, and was now living among the heathens of Xiang, doing fancy basketwork and *tai chi*. The Fair always gave rise to a desire among the young to cast off their scratchy hessian, to popinjay themselves in silk and taffeta, to escape and see the world. Even though, as the Parson repeatedly told them, bellowing from his honest and unadorned wooden pulpit until he grew hoarse, all of God's kingdom was before them, here beneath the vast flat open sky which is God's window, and the salt ocean which is the residue of his tears, water which is both cruel and angry and beautiful and full of the triumphant sardine, the Lord's own fish. Search no further than your own doorstep to find magic! It is already here, all about us, in God's creation!

Slosh, slosh, went the grey North Sea as the Parson hell-fired and brimstoned his message to the fisherfolk.

Oh yes? thought the young men, their hands sore from thistle-pulling and scraping out lobster pots. Is that a fact? mused the young women, wiping their bloodied hands on rough aprons after a hard morning's work, gutting fish and singing, cracked and tuneless, the rhythmic ballads of drudgery that were passed down from mother to daughter in these parts: 'Hey-a-Minnie,'

18

'Bobby Shafto', 'The Crab's Lament'. Their lives were hard and thankless. No wonder they craved fairgrounds. Who in their right mind would say no to a toffee apple?

It was the day after the Travelling Fair of Danger and Delight left Judlow that I arrived in the church.

'No coincidence,' went the village whisper.

St Nicholas is the patron saint of fishermen, which is what most Thunder Spitters were. The Cleggs with their rolling seaman's walk, the squint-eyed Lumpeys, the silent Peat-Hoves, the literal-minded Balls, the crabby Barks, the Morpitons with their tendency to exaggerate the size of every fish, the stubborn Tobashes: these were all net-heavers and lobster-pot-wielders down the generations, and proud to be so. The church that bears the saint's name is constructed of sea-flint, with a black slate roof. Its darkness makes it a perpetual silhouette, even in bright sunshine, when the slates become a sheet of mirror and God's home lurks beneath. Inside, as a rule, a somewhat gloomy darkness reigns within its thick stone walls, but today the rules are broken, for on this particular and momentous morning, as the Parson enters his cherished domain, he is suddenly aware of a cloud of glittering light, a ball of luminescence, an unaccustomed and dangerous brightness which comes whirling at him so hard that he feels his heart might be in spasm. In such a mischievous manner, he knows, does the great queller and provoker, God, sometimes see fit to manifest Himself.

It was this vision of white, Heavenly light, tinged with pink, he reported to his wife Mrs Phelps afterwards, that convinced him there was something special about me, even after I had bitten him and the whole episode had turned to vinegar.

At first he just saw the light (hallelujah!); then he saw the feathers. They gathered in a mighty white cloud, billowing in transcendental swirls, refracting the shafts of sunlight that came in through the wide-open door. Humbled by the glory, and afflicted by a weak left knee, Parson Phelps backed his be-cassocked rump cautiously into a pew and watched the feathers float down, recognising a message from God when he saw one.

19

As the import of what he was witnessing became embedded in his consciousness, the Parson, humbled and amazed, sank down from the pew to the lower level of the floor, where on his knees he now began to pray in a most fervent and passionate manner. And as he prayed, more feathers flew, and more and more and more, *like unto a whirlwind*, he thought, and although he knew that there was something miraculous going on, he now began to grow increasingly aware that there was also something plain odd, so he begged the Lord to forgive him for interrupting his own prayer, but might he just hurry over and inspect what kerfuffle was taking place in the vicinity of the altar? For he had begun to hear the strangest little grunts that came as though from a young swine.

And sure enough, through the flying feathers, the Parson could now make out something small and reddish-pink at the epicentre of the movement. Yes: a piglet, or perhaps a goat, attacking a goose-down pillow. So much for God-given messages. So much for miracles. He suddenly felt somewhat disappointed and not a little foolish for having wasted the Lord's time, not to mention his own, with a prayer of thanks, when there was nothing to be thankful for, and he would now be better employed, God help him, summoning Mrs Phelps for a dustpan and brush, and Farmer Harcourt to catch the piglet, left there no doubt by some naughty village boys, pleasure-seeking pranksters for whose idle hands the Devil had found work.

But now the feathers were flying more wildly, and the noises becoming more acute, like a furious squealing snowstorm doing battle with its own self.

Alarmed and dismayed, Parson Phelps resolved to catch the creature with his bare hands. He had seen Farmer Harcourt do it, with a sudden grabbing movement, plunging down, and bagging the beast for market. He could then throw it out, and let it trot away. No; that lacked a sense of charity towards its owner. Tether it, then, from the birch tree, until Farmer Harcourt came to fetch it. Or, more Christian still, incapacitate it by swaddling it in the altar-cloth, and carry it over to the farm himself. Yes;

this, surely, was the option the Lord was most likely to favour, containing as it did elements of consideration to both man and beast, not to mention a level of inconvenience to himself that would elicit a merry glow of innocent satisfaction later.

'So be it, young swine!' he boomed aloud. 'Parson Phelps is a-coming to get you!'

The piglet was still ripping at the pillow, so the Parson decided to take advantage of the creature's violent preoccupation to swipe downwards with both hands, the feathers flying. Choking on them, he managed to grab the beast. Its flesh was hot. Parson Phelps, blinded by feathers, spat and choked. He breathed a scatter of fuzz-fringed plumes in through his nose and sneezed explosively, the hot little animal wedged against his knee and still squirming in his hands.

'Ouch!' A sharp pain ripped its way up the Parson's leg. The creature had bitten him, suddenly and hard, on the shin. He dropped it and kicked at it; it landed on the devoured pillowcase with a noise that went *thwonk!*, and lay there twitching. And now the Parson felt a wetness on his cassock. He looked down, and saw blood.

Blood that came pouring from the piglet.

A piglet that was not a piglet.

It was, by God and by merciful Christ in Heaven, who gave His life for us that we may be saved, and by the Holy Ghost, and by the saints also, the following thing: a human baby, armed with a full set of sharp milk-teeth.

A miracle after all. (Have you guessed, gentle reader?)

It was Tobias Phelps!

Me!

That not-quite-nativity scene in the church is what I call the mistaken-piglet episode. Like the Morpiton family, from whom they had both individually descended five generations back, the Parson and his wife were prone to exaggeration, so how accurate their representation is, I cannot say, although I convey the spirit of their reports as faithfully as I am able, I do assure you.

21

Near death comes next.

This section of the story unfolds as follows: my bloody wound, consisting of a lacerated lower back, was so terrible that the Parson and his wife feared that by morning I would be dead. But being blessed by God (though in a later, more cynical version this changed to 'cursed by the Devil') I made it through the night, sweating furiously, and as hot as a cooking pot. Dr Baldicoot arrived in a cloud of seaweed pipe-smoke and inspected my wound, and took note of my other physical oddities, and shook his head, but he refrained from voicing his thoughts in front of the Parson, knowing they would be interpreted as a slap in God's almighty face. What Dr Baldicoot thought was that it would be kinder to let me die. Was this what God called fairness? Who, or what, could have been the cause of my ghastly mutilation? And what mother could have abandoned a baby with such an injury? In a cold church?

As I look back in time, I find that I harbour no resentment of the good Dr Baldicoot within my heart. He knew the odds were grievously stacked against my survival. I have since consulted Professor K.G. Hornblast's weighty tome, *The Rudiments of Spinal Injury*, which states categorically that a wound of this nature affecting the lower vertebrae means that the victim, in the rare event of his recovery from inevitable infection, will never walk straight. Not that my gait would ever have been normal in any case. There exists another weighty volume, *Congenital Abnormalities below the Knee*, which discusses, *inter alia*, deformities of the foot. Club feet, flat-footedness, the hereditary long toes of the egg-scavenging cliff-climbers of the Orkney Islands, et cetera. My flat feet, and the somewhat thumb-like big toe, emerging at a right-angle, which made them resemble nothing so much as a pair of squashed and rather hairy hands, fitted into several of these categories, though none exactly. But as J.M. Bellowes, its author, points out, 'The variations are as many and varied as *Homo sapiens* himself.' (So where does *that* leave us?)

Dr Baldicoot was a simple country doctor, with little room in his bulging bag of instruments for books, weighty or otherwise. So he puffed on his pipe, administered a large dose of morphine, and shook his head. Apart from the formalities of greeting and parting, he remained taciturn. As the room filled with Dr Baldicoot's noxious seaweed smoke, Parson Phelps' heart filled with anger. He had not read *The Rudiments of Spinal Injury* either, but he had read the thoughts that boiled beneath the doctor's silence. He diagnosed pessimism, born of lack of faith.

'I shall cure him myself,' he stormed, breaking Dr Baldicoot's pungent silence. It was a Friday, and the marbles were afflicting him.

Dr Baldicoot, in turn, had also divined the Parson's mind: arrogance, born of ignorance. He knocked his pipe out into the fireplace, bade my parents goodbye, and stepped out of the Parsonage into an east wind, which blew his cloak up into a great dark bubble. As the wind-buffeted doctor wobbled off into the night, Parson Phelps sat down heavily to take the weight off his bad knee at last, and took his wife's hand. He said, 'God has given us a chance.'

They were both forty-six. A baby at last. A foundling babe whose own mother has attacked it and thrown it from the nest like a vicious herring gull, thought the Parson, stroking my cheek, which was covered with a soft down of rust-red baby-hair. As he was fond of remarking, herring gulls can be the worst parents in the world, after humans. He resolved in that moment, he told me later, to be the best father a boy ever had, and Mrs Phelps made a similar vow concerning motherhood. This solemn promise undertaken, she made the sign of the cross with her blunt, practical finger, and took out her needle and thread, and a roll of hessian. I would be needing nappies.

Years later, when my foster-mother was delirious and dying, I discovered why she and Parson Phelps had no children of their own. It was due to a private incompetence of the Parson's male object and related accoutrements, dating back to a childhood incident. He had discovered a live snake – an adder – in his knickerbockers, and had been obliged to strangle it with his bare hands. The trauma had tragic consequences, for as he passed through adolescence and into adulthood, every time his object stirred, Parson Phelps saw the adder in his mind's eye and was forced, despite himself, to remember its strangulation – the effect of which was to quell whatever tentative excitement had occurred well before any occasion between himself and Mrs Phelps could be risen to.

'And that's a true fact, Tobias,' she breathed to me hoarsely on her deathbed. 'That killjoy creature had a lot to answer for, in our bedroom.'

Had they not been so desperate for a child, would they have taken me in? I cannot tell you, but they were good people, and until the moment of my father's great madness, they did not wish me ill.

But I digress.

Back, instead, to the thrust of my memoir, which has begun, in the traditional manner, with the story of my coming into the world, insofar as I am able to convey it. Yes, Ladies and Gentlemen, I was a foundling. But a fortunate one; Parson and Mrs Phelps took me into their home, the Parsonage, Thunder Spit, near Judlow, Northumbria, England. There was nothing to be done about my mis-shapen feet, so they applied clean bandages to the wound at the base of my spine and prayed for a week. My foster-father, like a champion player of the bagpipes, did not lack stamina when it came to communicating with the Lord. Together, my adoptive parents removed my bandages, applied seaweed and dandelion poultices that the Parson made with his own hands, sealed them with oatmeal mash, and prayed some more. Within six weeks, their prayers were answered. The skin began to heal over the wound, creating a bulbous and jaunty scar over the coccyx.

Now, on his knees, Parson Phelps forgave the adder its treachery and thanked the Lord: 'This is Thy mission for us, O mighty one, for we had given up hope, but now Thou hast sent us a baby, though I mistook it for a piglet, which as Thou canst imagine, is easily done when the creature is surrounded by cushion-feathers, to raise in Thine honour, Lord, and in Thy worship, here in Thunder Spit, home of St Nicholas's Church, and home also of three hundred and twenty-three, nay now three hundred and twenty-four, human souls. Not to mention beasts of the sea, such as the mackerel, and the octopus, and the whale, and last but by no means least, Lord, the sardine, Thine own fish. And the birds of the sky, among them the cormorant and the noble kittiwake and at the risk thereuntofore of losing the thread of my prayer, Lord, I, that is to say me and Mrs Phelps my dear wife, even though our marriage is not strictly speaking consummated in Thine eyes, on account of the ignoble adder incident, we thank Thee most profoundly for the unexpected but most welcome addition to our family. Praise be!'

So, Edward Phelps, thought Mrs Phelps. This foundling creature is the least you can give me, being such a dolt in bed. She said nothing, but merely smiled at her husband in that half-weak, half-heroic way she had, and sighed in queasy gratitude. Surely, any child is better than no child when one is nearing the change, she acknowledged, as she pursed her lips and changed my scratchy nappies. My stool didn't seem normal to her, appearing greenish and a smidgeon cowpatty; Mrs Phelps wasn't accustomed to children, but she was a willing servant of the Lord, and when she investigated the soilings more closely, she knew what needed to be done. She bundled me in a cloth so that I wouldn't wriggle, and gamely nestled my little thin-lipped mouth and squashed-up nose against her floppy dug, and let me suck. If ever there was a consummate example of the triumph of blind faith over human physiology and reason, it was this. For three days, nothing came, and Mrs Phelps' forty-six-year-old nipples were sore and cracked, despite the camomile cream she applied day and night. But then, suddenly, just as she was about to give up, another miracle: full-cream human milk sprang from her bosom and I began to gorge myself and thrive and grow a head of fiery red hair, thick and coarse as a donkey's. So my parents lurched down on their knees on the embroidered pew-cushion placed on the stone floor for just such spontaneous exultations, and praised the Lord, even after I had nearly bitten off my mother's nipple.

That's the story.

Like Jesus, and many other small boys whose parents dote on them, I grew up being told that I was 'a gift from Heaven'.

Later, this changed to 'a curse from Hell'.

What is a man, I wondered then, but a conglomeration of skin and skeleton, his giblets and his kidneys trapped inside? And what is this thing, his brain, but a mere giant overgrown walnut in a case of bone? What is his heart, but a mere organ?

As for his soul –

CHAPTER 3

CUISINE ZOOLOGIQUE

In London, it is a chill February. The year is still 1845, but it is a very different 1845 from the simple churning of Nature's seasons that constitutes the twelve-month in the tiny nowhere of Thunder Spit, where Tobias Phelps has just arrived. This is a metropolitan, sophisticated, and worldly 1845, an 1845 of monumental historic changes and fierce political and social debate, an 1845 of philanthropy and commerce, Empire and oysters, multiple petticoats, child chimney-sweeps, grocery deliveries and boiled breast of mutton with caper sauce. A bright, shining 1845, full of hope and grandeur, with not a little debauchery and grime at the edges, a year in which we are now crossing the capital in an imaginary Montgolfier balloon, gazing queasily down at the lumpy grey quilt of London spread below. There's St Paul's Cathedral, a great blackened dome, peeking out through the lurking cloud of chimney-smoke. And there's the Thames, twisted like a cobra with appendicitis, and Tower Bridge, and the Houses of Parliament, both fortressy and cake-like, and the great thrust of Big Ben.

Oi, can anyone steer this thing?

If so, float west now, and guide our craft over elegant Belgravia, and here pause a moment to admire the crescent curves of white-painted brick and the shiny black doors, the forbidding doorsteps and the potted boxwoods of the exclusive cul-de-sac called Madagascar Street. And hover here a moment, by the third-floor window of number fourteen, to observe a pair of two-legged mammals in their natural habitat, the home, a

27

nest that is also a den that is also a warren that is also a lair, a repository for food, a rearing site and a thinking parlour. What a strange creature is man! Strange, too, that unlike many mammals, the human animal has no particular mating season. All the luckier, then, that we have arrived here on what will turn out to be a momentous day.

Peer through the ground-floor window first and observe Dr Ivanhoe Scrapie, taxidermist, in his workshop, engaged in the complex process of stretching the skin of a Chilean bear over a plaster cast he has made of the carcass in the ridiculous, sentimental position chosen by the Queen. The creature is to stand upright, Victoria has commanded, with its paws together, as though at prayer. In keeping with all animals destined for her Royal Highness's Animal Kingdom Collection, its genitalia must be excised completely; as a double measure of prudery, the creature will also, later, be clad in custom-sewn breeches. Furthermore, as per usual, the Monarch has commanded Scrapie to endow the beast with eyes that are 'blue, a sort of eggshell blue, such as you gave our other royal mammals'. But, she had specified, 'somewhat larger than the normal for a bear of this kind, which should, we feel, be gazing Heaven-ward as though in holy contemplation'. The idea being to transform the bear into a sort of noble, brutish creature of piety, fit to join the growing ranks of beasts in her whimsical bestiary: a whole Arkful of stuffed and de-sexed mammals, absurdly clothed, and in the posture of religious maniacs. As though, Scrapie is fond of remarking, Buckingham Palace were not such a vessel itself.

'Buggeration and damnation,' he mutters now, through a mouthful of pins, then lifts one foot off the floor and raises a haunch, to facilitate the emission of a thunderous fart, which echoes through the workshop and out into the hall, as he bellows, 'To Her Majesty Queen Victoria, Royal Hippopotamus and bane of my life!'

Meanwhile upstairs in the drawing room, Mrs Charlotte Scrapie, wife, mother, and celebrated medium, has sprinkled lavender-water in an attempt to drown the stench of that noble medicine, laudanum, which fuels the engine of her psychic thoughts. Observe, through the chintz, this: that her daily dose has had its narcotic effect. That despite an unappetising luncheon, cooked by Mrs Jiggers, there is something aphrodisiac in the air. That suddenly Mrs Scrapie's husband, finally bored by the silence and wire and sawdust of his workshop and fed up with the increasingly ludicrous demands of the Monarch concerning her Animal Kingdom Collection, tired of the jars of camphor and the little trays of glass eyes and the rows of pegs and steel pins, and the sheaves of notes and the skins and the little rubber noses that are the tools of his trade, is ascending the stairs.

For there is only one thing to do when you are in this sort of mood, in Dr Scrapie's experience. Impose the needs of your reproductive organ upon your wife, Charlotte Scrapie, affectionately – and sometimes not so affectionately – known as the Laudanum Empress. Whether or not she is drugged.

And there is only one way to respond to such a mood on the part of Dr Scrapie, if you are his wife, and in a laudanum daze: succumb.

There is nothing shameful in a little voyeurism. So adjust your balloon until the basket is level with this sash window here, and peer through the curtains of the drawing room. And witness the following things: a *chaise-longue*, a tumbler of whisky, a glimpse of curved breast, and a stiffened male object. Catch sight of a whalebone corset being cast to the ground like the chrysalis of a metamorphosing grub. See what might or might not be two semi-clad human bodies groping for balance upon the *chaise-longue*. The windowpane having now – infuriatingly – steamed up, press your ear to the glass and hear instead a series of noises: a whispered cajoling, a languid rejection, a thick-voiced insistence, an acquiescent sigh, a jostle of petticoats, an unclipping of braces, a fumbling and a slapping, a grunting and panting, a squeaking and a moaning, an increasingly rapid rhythmic thudding, a lion's roar, a little moan, a big, heavy sigh.

A quiet couple of minutes. After which, the mission of his male object accomplished, Dr Ivanhoe Scrapie returns to his workshop, to do battle with a Highland stork, while his wife, surrounded by a cloud of psychic particles which shape and re-shape ghostly images of the Great Beyond, sinks back into the shadowy dreamland of her addiction.

Then, as your balloon floats upwards into the night, imagine, in the light of the full moon that is emerging through the London clouds, a period of hormonal risk beneath the Scrapie corsetry. A meeting of sperm and egg deep inside the Scrapie anatomy. A fertilisation within the confines of a Scrapie fallopian tube. And then –

Abracadabra! An embryo! An embryo which –

But no! Quick, let loose more hot air, I beg you, into your Montgolfier, and chuck out a sandbag! Let us leave the embryo Violet Scrapie there, going about her homunculoid business, and fly rapidly to London docks, where her future guru, the man who is to shape her – quite literally – into the majestic woman she will become – awaits us on board a ship named *HMS Beagle*.

A beagle, as we all know, is a breed of hunting dog. An odd name for a ship.

You'll need binoculars at this point. The docks are far, far below; night has given way to morning and the bevy of vessels crammed into the dockside is tinged with an orange glow – among them Captain FitzRoy's ten-gunned three-masted *Beagle*. She is berthed there next to the *Paradigm* (cargo: linen, peacock feathers, liquorice, candle-wax, nuts, bolts, and Brazil nuts). The *Beagle* is a serious, non-profit-making vessel, a vessel that, until several years ago, contained a small group of respectable scientists doing a difficult and painstaking job, but more recently, has housed only the melancholic captain and his brooding whims. Yes; all the scientists, Mr Darwin included, have long since departed to their personal residences and taken their bulky microscopes and notebooks with them. The heyday of the *Beagle* is past, and she has set sail only a few times since then, for survey work in the North Sea. Now, today, Captain

FitzRoy has wandered off, mad and alone, leaving only his crew on board. The sea was rough during their most recent trip, and the seamen are laid low from sickness, bad food and exhaustion. The *Beagle* has a mixed crew, mostly English, but with a few Spaniards. And a Belgian. Let the English and the Spaniards stew in their own juice: it's the Belgian who's our man. Land your balloon on the dockside, alight from the basket, and meet Monsieur Jacques-Yves Cabillaud, a seasickness-sufferer who this morning, having cooked breakfast porridge for twenty men and received no thanks for his pains, has thrown down his oat-choked ladle and declared, '*Ça suffit.*'

A proud man. An ambitious man. A man about to do a bunk.

These are the facts that are known about Jacques-Yves Cabillaud's past:

1. That his father sent him to sea during the Belgian potato blight, forcing him to leave behind a sweetheart named Saskia whom he feared he would not see again. (He was right there; she married his cousin Gustave, a baker, whose croissants won prizes).

2. That the young Jacques-Yves became first a cabin-boy on a whaler in the North Sea, and then a cook on board a French merchant ship.

3. That in Cape Town, he answered an advertisement for a chef on a zoological research vessel, the *Beagle*, and was taken on.

4. That when the *Beagle* sailed all the way to the Galápagos and then to Tahiti, Cabillaud was both so seasick and so lovesick that he never even bothered to look out of a porthole.

5. That the only thing that relieved his physical and mental torment was the occasional request, from Mr Charles Darwin, to concoct recipes for the various exotic meats the scientist brought on board from his shore visits.

6. That this made a change from the usual seaweed-and-biscuit diet Cabillaud was forced to serve up, and once

the seas were calm, despite his melancholy state he became increasingly excited by the possibilities of what he termed '*Cuisine Zoologique*'. Emu, iguana, finch, snake – some of the ugliest and humblest of God's creatures, he realised, could, with the appropriate garnishes, be a culinary delight.

7. That this was a hypothesis that he went on to prove with great aplomb, to the delight of the not-yet-famous Mr Charles Darwin, who personally gave his compliments to the chef on several occasions.

8. That as a result of his experimentation, and the compliments he has received, Jacques-Yves Cabillaud discovered within his bosom the seed of a great ambition.

Now, finally, staring out at London docks, bereft of his beloved Darwin these six years, and left only with the crazed FitzRoy, he is grimly considering his future. Surely the knowledge he has gained of the skinning of lizards, the grilling of ostrich meat, the handling of rodent liver and the braising technique required for giant turtle cannot – *must not* – be wasted?

Certainement pas! With this in mind, he shoulders his knapsack and heads for the Zoological Gardens. So let us land our imaginary Montgolfier, tether it to this handily situated monkey-puzzle tree, don our walking shoes, and follow him on foot.

The city into which the absconding Cabillaud queasily stumbled from aboard the *Beagle* was a metropolis reeking of parsnips, cabbages, coffee-stalls, the putrefying flesh of poisoned rats, freshly cut flowers, rotten herrings, oysters, and smoke from charcoal burners. Down alleyways, in open sewers, excrement wound its way towards the Thames and thence to the sea, while in the sky, as ever, a thick pall of smoke hung low like a throttling blanket. God knows how Cabillaud managed to leave the *Beagle* unnoticed on his wobbly legs. Nor how this small, intrepid, stubble-jowled man came to stagger halfway across the capital, jostled by an unruly

March wind, and enter the elephant enclosure in the Zoological Gardens. And above all to remain there, unnoticed, for a week, nursing a fever and eating only swill, straw and mouse-droppings. Or how it was that the chief zoo-keeper, Mr Gardillie, rather than tipping him back on to the streets, took a perverse liking to him and, once Cabillaud had explained that his *Beagle* experience had accustomed him to wildlife, offered him a job shovelling elephant shit. Cabillaud, who took a long view of things and possessed a formidably stoical side, accepted the job with the humility required, retreated to the enclosure of Mona the elephant, bided his time, hatched his plans, and shovelled. And lo and behold! After three weeks of negotiating with elephant turds the size of the moon, the kind of opportunity he had been hoping for – as a first step on the glittering pathway of his dreams – arrived on a plate. On a plate, in the form of an irascible-looking man who one morning entered Mona's enclosure without so much as a by-your-leave, and set up a step-ladder.

The surly gentleman, who is none other than the bipedal mammal we spied earlier from the Montgolfier, mating with his drugged female in Madagascar Street, ignored the Belgian completely. But Cabillaud scrutinised the taxidermist closely. He had already heard much about Dr Ivanhoe Scrapie from the head keeper. Scrapie was one of several taxidermists who often came by the Zoological Gardens, like a vulture in search of carrion. News of Mona's stomach upset, which was keeping Cabillaud busy round the clock, must have spread to the museum, where Dr Scrapie was not only chief taxidermist, but in charge of Her Majesty's own personal bestiary of stuffed animals. Which the Monarch was anxious to enlarge in proportion to her growing Empire. Mr Gardillie had told Cabillaud about her proposed Animal Kingdom Collection, which would contain a stuffed example of every living creature in the world, clad in human clothes and depicting pious scenes. Impressive. And now, here, was the man who was by all accounts charged with stuffing the things; all fifteen thousand or so of them. No wonder he looked haggard and distracted. (The Animal Kingdom Project was indeed to blame, but only partly; there was also the fact that the Laudanum Empress was wearing her pregnancy badly, and even at this early stage, arising sixteen times a night to empty her bladder.) Cabillaud, his mind racing with possibilities, leaned on his giant shovel, and observed Scrapie with interest, as the tall thin man reached the pinnacle of the step-ladder, and raised a lamp to Mona's ear. She flapped it like a gigantic wing, irritated, and Scrapie wobbled precariously.

'Monsieur,' announced Cabillaud, who had by now decided upon his plan of attack. Scrapie slowly looked down, annoyed at the interruption. Then, realising the social stature of the man who had addressed him, he took out his magnifying glass and peered through it at the human insect on the floor.

'I sweep out elephant's piss, I clear away *merde* all day,' Cabillaud informed him by way of self-introduction. 'And all night, also, now, because ze creature is *malade*.'

Scrapie polished his magnifying glass on a hanky.

'Zis,' Cabillaud elaborated, indicating the shovel and the sloppy lagoon of *ca-ca* that Mona's breakfast had engendered, 'is not my natural position on ze ladder of nature, Monsieur.'

Scrapie, tottering on his own ladder, leaned forward to peer closer at the elephant-keeper. He could see nothing much: just a black-and-white blur, and some facial hair in close-up. Cabillaud continued, 'I am not slave of elephant creature, I am *artiste*. Give me to spend one day in your kitchen, Monsieur. I zen will show you what is in true fact *la gastronomie*.'

Mona, swinging her trunk, shifted silently and ominously on her umbrella-stand feet, and Scrapie, sensing danger, disengaged himself jerkily from the step-ladder and re-arranged himself on to the straw next to Cabillaud. This time he drew up close, applied the magnifying glass to Cabillaud's face and inspected the man again: he noted five days of stubble, a torn and infected ear-lobe from which an earring had clearly been forcibly ripped, a foul odour, and a huge brown eye, larger than a cow's. An overseas specimen, he concluded. Nothing rare. Probably

European in origin. Satisfied with his diagnosis of both species and genus, Dr Scrapie pocketed his magnifying glass.

'Well?' he said.

Cabillaud recognised an order when he heard one. His life-story, as relayed to the taxidermist, necessitated holding the shit-shovel between his knees, clamped as in a vice, so that the hands were free to gesticulate their accompaniment to the tale. Cabillaud described how he was destined for great culinary fame (a reaching on high of the right hand), but had mistakenly ended up on board the *Beagle* (here Scrapie pricked up his ears), a terrible vessel (a thwack of spittle aimed at the water-butt), full of Englishmen (a turning-down of the corners of the mouth), on which since leaving the Galápagos, apart from his experiments in *Cuisine Zoologique* (Scrapie looked puzzled; he had no French), all he had been required to cook was porridge, pickled herring, and seaweed (more phlegm). Dishes containing, sometimes, when the sea was rough – *Dieu me pardonne!* – his own seasick vomit.

'Seaweed soup, seaweed fishcakes, fried seaweed, mashed seaweed. I make seaweed *gratin* one time, because some cheese falls off another ship, I fish out, I make *gratin*, zey send it back, say no good. You English, you would take the choice to eat human *ordure* if it had lumps in it unchewable *suffisamment* to your taste of like.'

It was a challenge. Hands on hips. *Fini. Voilà.*

'I'll consider the matter,' said Scrapie, eyeing up Mona once more, and estimating her weight to be approximately two tons. As every taxidermist can tell you, it's not the stuffing so much as the skinning and the construction of the armature that are problematic in such cases. Not to mention the space constraint imposed by one's workshop. Scrapie's conclusion: Forget it, Your Majesty. She's overly gigantical; discussion over.

Mona shifts uneasily, as if telepathically interpreting Scrapie's train of thought, which is now moving on (she sighs a big windy sigh of relief) to the subject of the Monarch, who lurks permanently at the back of the taxidermist's brain like a constant

35

nagging headache. Bloody woman! Scrapie is thinking. Bloody, bloody woman! Look at her, with her pink-splotched map of the world and her Animal Kingdom nonsense! Only a woman as rich and unhinged and as grandiose as she is would come up with such an idea. And only a man like Horace Trapp could have the audacity to persuade her that he could actually bring a thousand foreign species home intact, in a single vessel. A royal Ark! What hubris!

'Bloody woman!' says Scrapie aloud.

'*Comment?*'

'The Queen. I told her not to. I said it was a bad idea. More than bad. Noah did it, but that was in the Bible.'

'Ah,' murmurs Cabillaud, doing his best to look sympathetic, and wondering how he is to steer the conversation around towards his own goals. He is also preoccupied with a parallel train of thought: Would the acidic tang of a gooseberry *coulis* go well with the succulence of raccoon?

'Everyone knows that Trapp is nothing but a fool,' Scrapie is saying. 'A dangerous fool.' Blast him, thinks Scrapie, his exhausted brain churning with rage. The man has a whole history of entrepreneurial disaster behind him. Not to mention the slavery business. It was well known that the only reason he'd been forced to quit trading in humans was because a whole ship-load had died on him for want of food. Bloody hell! What possessed the Hippo to put her faith in such a man? What wild promises did he make her? (I must have some sleep. Sixteen times in a single night! And she had drunk no liquid!)

'A dangerous fool,' echoes Cabillaud, not having a clue what Scrapie has been mumbling so angrily about, but hoping to please. 'I too have heard zis same thing. Dangerous, and a little bit deranged also, zis man Tropp.'

'Trapp,' Scrapie corrects him wearily, patting Mona on the big leather wall of her thigh. 'Horace Trapp.'

'Yes,' rejoins Cabillaud with enthusiasm. 'That's iz name! Trapp! Complcte madman! Complete *idiot*!'

Scrapie remains lost in thought. It is now two years since

Trapp and his entourage set sail for Africa, and needless to say, nothing has been heard since. Just as well, maybe, the taxidermist reflects. For it is he, Scrapie, who will be in charge of stuffing the creatures on their return. As if he doesn't have his hands full already. (The Laudanum Empress is no help to him. Pregnancy sends her into a nine-month trance, broken only by her nocturnal sorties to the Crapper.) Meanwhile, Horace Trapp appears to have taken the royal money and run.

'And that's no surprise,' says Scrapie.

'No, no it is surely not,' agrees Cabillaud. 'Not one bit surprise at all, I sink.'

'Bugger the Queen!' concludes Scrapie.

'And bugger Trapp, also!' says Cabillaud with gusto. 'Bugger him utterly, zis madman who I hate with all my heart and my very soul also! And ze Queen also who is nothing but a big, big, big, big, big –'

'Hippopotamus,' finishes Scrapie.

Mona snorts through her trunk in agreement, and begins to work her way through a bale of hay.

Then Cabillaud, emboldened by his own vehemence on a subject about which he knows nothing, ventures; '*Vous acceptez, donc, ma proposition, Monsieur?*'

Scrapie takes out his magnifying glass again and stares the man in the eye. Yes: they appear to speak the same language.

'I'll give you three days in my kitchen.' And he turns to leave.

'Thank you, sir,' whispers Cabillaud, barely able to contain his joy. His heart is all set to leap out of his very chest! 'You will not *regrettez*!'

Scrapie folds his step-ladder and swings himself over the gate. 'Three days.'

Cabillaud and Mona watch him as he makes his way down the gravel path past the monkey enclosure, a tall, lanky figure with a rolling walk.

Then they see him turn. Cabillaud blanches. Can the man have changed his mind?

37

The taxidermist is cupping his hand over his mouth to yell something.

'Any objections to cooking unusual meats?' comes his voice, faintly, over the chattering of chimps. 'The casualties of the Zoological Gardens have a tendency to come my way. Waste not, want not!'

Mon Dieu!

'No objections at all, sir! My very own delight!'

He is grinning so widely, he realises, that his jaws hurt. When was he last so happy? He kisses Mona on her trunk, which she curls around him affectionately. Then like the lady she is, she lifts her keeper clear of the ground and high into the air like a little toy, and gratefully opens her bowels.

The dusty old peacock feather bobbed in the gaslight as the Frozen Woman scratched away with its quill on a sheet of onion-skin parchment.

My first mistake, she wrote, *woz to BELEEV that wen a man sez he has a DREEM, that DREEM is to be TRUSTID and must command RISPECT. It is NOT. The things He spoke of were*:

1. *Distant CUNTRIES were I wud be a QUEEN.*
2. *Fame and RICHIS.*
3. *A new kind of WURLD to be made, wer nobody haz to WURK.*

He twurld his MUSTARSH, and I beleeved him.

She paused, and fingered the nib of her quill, then bent her head again, and continued her laborious scratching. *Wel, He wuz gud to me wen we furst met, I was dansin at the Kings Arms, nites, then. E see me an He wont me, that's wot E sed.*

E sed, you do the SPLITS like that for me?

Posh talking. Munny in iz vois, I thinks. He stands me on the table.

Now do the SPLITS, E sez.
No, I sez. Cant. Legs gone. So SKARED I cud piss.
He just sits ther, twurls His Mustarsh. Waitin.
HORIS, wuz is furst name. Then comes the TRAPP.

CHAPTER 4

2005: IN WHICH THE
ROGUE MALE EFFECTS
METAMORPHOSIS

The Nuance was in her element on the motorway. She purred with oil like a randy lioness, and before I knew it, I'd covered a hundred and fifty kilometres, and had entered a transcendental travel limbo. There's nothing like having A behind you, and B ahead.

> *Lovah me tender, lovah me trewah* [I sang.]
> *All my dreams fulfiyul*
> *For my darlin, I love yewah . . .*

Nah.

I turned on the radio. It was one of those programmes where grown-ups get paid for indulging in opinionated argy-bargy. They were talking about the Fertility Crisis again.

'My feeling is that we reached an evolutionary cul-de-sac,' pontificated an earnest woman. I imagined her: reading specs, dangly earrings, a Ph.D., halitosis, a brooch. 'We'd gone as far as we possibly could, in terms of sophistication, civilisation, humanity –'

Then a bloke, a religious type, cut in. No-no-no-no-no. Sorry, sorry. Ha-ha. Lovely idea, Susan, blah-blah, he was saying, but with all due respect, the facts couldn't be plainer. I pictured him, too: dog-collar, dentures, sensible Y-fronts, dumpy wife at home trying to tune in but not being able to find the right wavelength. The Crisis happened, he was saying, because the Lord had become angry with the world, just as He had done once before. He'd sent the Flood then – he quoted something here – bla-de-blah – and *unleashed mighty waters*, et cetera, so that only the meek should inherit, bah blah, and it was all our own doing.

'If I could just cut in here –' the Ph.D. brooch woman began, but he was on a roll.

'– *Not* because we were so sophisticated, civilised, morally advanced, and humane as a species, but the very OPPOSITE. We didn't honour what He had done for us. We, here in Britain. This once great nation.'

'Susan? Would you like to come in here?' said the radio man. He was just a voice.

'Yes. Well, what we experienced was hardly a flood,' the earnest woman remonstrated. 'You can't possibly call it a real flood! It was no more than a few inches!'

She was right there, I thought. The hallelujah types liked to call it a deluge, because of what happened after, but it was hardly what you'd call a big deal. New Year's Eve, 1999 – very apocalyptic, of course. They all seized on that. But it was just a bad shower, maybe; no more. 'A noxious squall,' the Met Office called it at the time. The surgery got swamped, but it was nothing that a couple of *Sunday Timeses* couldn't mop up, in the end.

'Now come on. You can't deny that it changed our lives,' said the radio man. 'Flood, heavy shower, call it what you will, things haven't been the same since.'

'Nobody's claiming they *have* been,' said another man. He had that reasoned, slightly chewing voice that scientists use when they're on the radio. 'I'd be the *last* person to say that the sudden infertility of the human egg in Britain isn't a national catastrophe. As for whether the flooding on the night of the Millennium was the cause of it –'

'But Professor Hawkins,' butted in the woman. 'I don't frankly *care* about the cause of the problem. I care about the *solution*. We've got to remember that if it weren't for the National Egg Bank, the British would already be headed for complete extinction. All *I'm* saying is –'

'Should we really be that pessimistic?' said the radio man. 'After all, the Government's telling us that in fact it's only a matter of time till the fertility curve swings up again. And in the meantime, we've got the stored eggs to tide us over, so –'

'But there are nowhere near enough pre-Millennial eggs in storage to deal with the queues!' The women was getting quite shrill. 'Look at the evidence. There hasn't been a single natural conception since New Year's Day 2000! Five years of sterility! I say release ALL the eggs now, and get the girls pregnant as soon as possible, and –'

'Big mistake,' said the religious man. 'Look, if God had *wanted* us to store human eggs, he'd have *designed* us to store them. It's this very type of scientific intervention we were being punished for in the first place.'

'*Punished!*' squawked the woman. 'You think –'

'Yes, *punished*. You don't like that word, do you. It's not very liberal-friendly, I'm afraid.'

'Well, you can't deny it's incredibly *value-laden.*'

'I can't, and I won't. I say, *What's wrong with values?* And if I may make another point, I don't call two inches of rainfall 'just a shower'. I call it a flood.'

'So you're saying God just wants us all to fizzle out, then, does he? You lot are quite happy to witness our decline? It's all right for you. You've had your children, haven't you? Boys, I'll bet. If you had girls, you *certainly* wouldn't be taking that line. When I see my daughter taking hormones so she can breast-feed an orang-utan, my heart breaks. If you take away the human eggs that were put in storage before the Millennium, you're killing their only hope of becoming mothers. Not to mention the future of Britain as a nation.'

'*God* knows what He is doing,' the dog-collar man said complacently. 'I'm confident that He'll offer us some hope, if we show humility. Can't you see it? This is a *test*! *A challenge for us all!* We will arise from the ashes of our impurity, as Christ arose on the third day!'

But it wasn't going to be like that, and he knew it. Everyone

42

knew it. I remembered the sequence of events, when the Fertility Blip officially became no longer a blip, but a crisis. First, when it became clear that male sperm were not affected, only female eggs, there'd been a whole spate of hastily arranged marriages to foreign imports. The women arrived here, fine, amid much domestic resentment, but within a couple of months, it became clear the new pregnancies weren't going to materialise. Nature had played its wild card; their eggs seemed to have died as soon as they passed Customs. The whole country was an egg-killing zone. A nation of ovarian doom. The quickie divorces followed, and the Sperm Drain began. The tourist industry collapsed completely, and overnight, we became a third-world leper colony. Europe poured millions of Euros into fertility research, but was desperate to get shot of us.

'How can anyone be resurrected, when half the men have left?' snapped the woman. She was becoming quite strident. 'Even the frozen eggs in the Egg Bank are only 50 per cent viable. I suspect it's less. When did you last see a baby?' she accused. They were getting rarer than hen's teeth. It was like the Lottery used to be; anyone who benefited from the Egg Bank had to go into hiding. 'Unless something's done soon about the Sperm Drain,' the woman was saying, 'there'll be no men left!'

True. A lot of blokes were leaving, now that it was clear the country was blighted. There was nothing wrong with British sperm, after all. Or foreign eggs. Emigration restrictions for men were on the cards; there was a rumour that, come next year, you wouldn't be able to leave unless you could prove you'd fathered a genuine *Homo Britannicus* before the Crisis.

And that there'd be Loyalty Bonuses for men who stayed.

Was it the prospect of that, that stopped me going abroad? Not really. The fact was, I didn't give a monkey's about the future.

Carpe diem, I say. Seize the day. Grab it by the throat and rattle its bollocks.

Before I left London, I phoned the Veterinary Society to inform them of my change of name by deed poll. I spoke to a Mr Jenks. I told him I needed confidentiality. Should anyone, such as a woman called Holly Noakes, or Mrs Patricia Mann, for example, try to contact me by the name Bobby Sullivan, he was to inform them that I was no longer on their books. I could hear the sound of a Jenks eyebrow being raised.

'There was a sort of vendetta against me,' I explained.

'A vendetta?' Jenks asked.

Oh Christ, I realised. He's interested now. I've used a foreign word. He wants details.

'A client with a grudge,' I said, going for a spot of honesty. Busking it. I pictured Mrs Mann with a little silver revolver pointed at me over Giselle's body-bag. 'A dead-monkey scenario. Husband gets me to put the animal down, licence in order, all legal and above-board, wife comes along, threatens me. Bad marriage, baby-substitute, the old story. You feel more like a shrink sometimes.'

'A common complaint,' Jenks sympathised. When I assured him that I was completely in the clear, and (stroke of genius, this) that I was taking out a legal injunction against the deranged pet-owner concerned, he became even more understanding. 'There's a lot of it about,' he confided. 'We had a member shot with a crossbow last year, over a bushbaby. Claims and counter-claims, insurance hoo-ha and now the Court of Appeal. It's the anthropomorphism,' he mused. 'Gets people carried away.'

There were several possibilities, Mr Jenks explained, clicking away at the vacancy file on his computer. A Saudi Arabian zoo, for instance, if I was interested in sunshine, but there was a strict no-women-no-booze clause which wasn't everyone's *cup of tea*, as it were. 'Not many reproductive possibilities there, I'm afraid,' he said. 'Most men opt for Holland or the Far East.'

'Anything closer to home?' I asked. 'I'm not bothered about reproduction, myself.' This was true. Unlike Elvis, I'd never felt the urge to pass on my genes. No rock-a-hula baby for me.

'Well, there's a locum going up north,' he said. 'A suburb of

44

Judlow called Thunder Spit. By the sea. Famous for a breed of sheep called the Lord Chief Justice.'

'Sounds interesting,' I lied. But the idea of the coast appealed. I thought of those camping holidays, with sun-cream and popcorn.

'I'll put in an application, then,' I told him.

'An excellent choice of name, if I may say so,' said Jenks, when I spelled out my new identity for the records. I was pleased with his reaction.

'You'll be hearing from us soon, Mr de Savile,' Jenks said. 'Or may I be among the first to call you Buck?'

'It's a tragedy,' the brooch woman was saying, as my windscreen wipers swished me past Axelhaunch, Fibber's Wash, Blaggerfield. Viking names. I'd heard a couple of blokes speaking Danish once; they sounded like clogged drains.

'But to go back to the central point, as long as we have our stored eggs, then we have hope, surely?' put in the radio man. He was paid to make sure people didn't get too depressed. A difficult job. As the discussion took its usual apocalyptic course, the earring-and-brooch woman's voice grew ever more quivery with emotion, and the hallelujah man with the Y-fronts and dentures became more and more triumphant, and the reasonable professor sounded more and more like a herbivore chewing old cud, and I thought: Desperate times. And desperate women. Hence the primates. No self-respecting woman over thirty could afford to be without her cute little companion. That's what it said in an old copy of *Cosmopolitan* in the surgery waiting-room, anyway. I had a sudden clear picture of Giselle, the doomed macaque, handing Mr Mann a flea.

Desperate times, but a bonanza for vets.

My involvement with animals began with blood, meat, and a gizzard stone.

I am six. Unexpectedly, I visit the butcher's shop with my mother.

'Why not the supermarket, Mum?' They had a popcorn machine, and photo booth where you could have your picture taken with the Terminator.

'Because he's organic.'

She walks fast, dragging me by the wrist, to buy lamb cutlets for her actressy dinner party, at which she plans to call them *côtelettes d'agneau*. The year is 1983, and the shop is one of those expensive old-fashioned London butcher's you rarely came across, even back then. (You see extinction everywhere, when you look for it.)

Meat hangs from hooks and languishes in little bloody trays; crimson sawdust confettis the floor. I gob in it and rake it about with my toe as I stand in the queue next to Mum. Then suddenly the butcher is heaving down towards me, holding something out in his palm. It's a stone. I take it. It feels smooth and slightly oily.

'From a chicken's gizzard,' says the butcher. 'For you, mate. Freebie!'

I clasp it tight. In my innocence, I recognise I belong here.

'When I grow up, *I* want to be organic,' I say as we leave the shop.

'Oh Bobsy-Wobsy, how horrible,' says Mum, popping the plastic bag of bloody *côtelettes* into her shopping net. 'Meat's so grisly, darling.'

'I like that. I like grisly.'

'Well, be a surgeon, then,' says Mum. 'You can open up people's bodies, and take out the bits with cancer and sew them up again.'

'I don't want to cut up people.' I am fingering the gizzard stone in my pocket. And there, by the Norwich Union Building Society, the enormity of it stops me in my tracks.

'I want to cut up animals.'

There's nothing abnormal in this.

When I was twelve, I built a rat-trap, and then one for squirrels, because in those days the Council, which still deemed them urban vermin, gave you 50p for every tail you brought in. I

46

dismantled the bodies the way my friends dismantled toy cars or aeroplanes. I kept a plastic box of animal bits in the far corner of the fridge, and another in the freezer. Mum never really noticed. As long as her ice and lemon were within reach, she paid no heed. Mum rested a lot, 'Because actresses just bloody do,' and because of her migraine sessions. It was left to Dad to see us boys through. He raised us efficiently, and he raised us to be men.

At fifteen, I was spotty and sweaty, with limbs that seemed roughly modelled out of plasticine and a penis likewise. All were embarrassing and unmanageable. It was this version of myself that began work as the organic butcher's assistant. My mother hated the idea, and went off for one of her migraines. She was having them daily by this time. Dad was seeing another woman, Jilly, who wore tight-fitting jodhpurs and was married to a fox-faced man who skulked in the City all week. Fact: Jilly caused Mum's migraines. Dad's version: Jilly had 'come into his life' (he said it like she was Jesus) because Mum was always drunk.

But when I started work at Mr Harper's, Mum made it clear that today's migraine extravaganza was for me.

'You'll chop off a finger!' she screeched through the door. 'Or worse! You could lose a whole arm in those electric slicers!'

But this did nothing to put me off. In fact, the idea that I'd be working with lethal instruments increased the thrill. I pictured feeding my right index finger into the greedy blade, and saw it emerge in wafer-thin strips of pink flesh with a central spot of pellucid white bone. From behind the door, the familiar whiff of Amontillado sherry and the sound of heartbreak. Like all Mum's noises, it had a thespian ring to it: Mrs Sullivan, stage left, falls to floor, clasps magnificent bosom, dies in sorrow. Exit spotty teenage son running, head in hands.

Things evolved from there, and before I knew it, I was at vet school.

The radio discussion had degenerated into a phone-in: a woman

47

from Cleethorpes was wanting to know why it was *Britain* that had been affected by the Crisis.

'It's so unfair!' she wailed. 'Why not the whole of Europe? After all the kow-towing we've done to Brussels!'

The brooch-woman gave a piggy snort.

'Well, the infertility is certainly very *regionalised*,' said the radio man, covering for her. 'Do you have an explanation, Professor Hawkins?'

'Well, if you look at it globally,' he droned, 'it's perhaps unfortunate that it should have just hit our archipelago of islands, but in evo*lut*ionary terms, it's not unusual for a disaster to be contained in this way.' He paused, chewing on his words. 'Islands are well known for housing species that aren't found elsewhere in the world. But by the same token, their populations are *also* prone to be wiped out in accidents such as this. Be they caused by rainfall, triggering a genetic malfunction, or something else which we don't yet understand. The end result, of course, being –'

I switched off the radio. *Extinction*. I'm fed up with that word, I thought. Let's put on our blue suede shoes and dance like we did in the good old days, before I was born! I have twenty-nine virtual Elvis concerts on tape.

I peer through the windscreen: outside, the land is as flat and bare as a splat of emulsion, and the few trees seem to be cringing from something. As I drive past the hypermarkets, car-phone warehouses, carpet wholesalers, discount shoe shops, DIY stores and bungalows that herald the outskirts of town, a sign enlarges ahead of me. WELCOME TO THUNDER SPIT.

Which is the cue for the butterfly that is Buck de Savile, emerged from the caterpillar that was Bobby Sullivan, to press his foot harder on the accelerator and speed into town.

Yo! *Homo Britannicus* is dying, but the son of Elvis is going to live!

CHAPTER 5

FATHER OF THE MAN

Dr Baldicoot said I would die, but I lived. The Parson and his wife christened me Tobias, and I formally took their surname, Phelps. A solid name, evoking oakwood and rainy autumns and English brawn, passed down through many a generation in Thunder Spit.

But I was not as sturdy as the name I bore. Unlike the Phelpses who had gone before, whose graveyard epitaphs spoke of long, industrious and healthy lives, I was small and sickly; they said that all the energy of my babyhood seemed to be put into growing more hair. My head was a great thick tangled clot, and I had copious body hair from an early age, which promised great manliness, my father said wistfully.

Others took a different view.

'His real parents must've been infidels,' I heard Mrs Tobash say once, as she and Mrs Fletcher gutted fish at the harbour market. 'There's nothing Christian about body hair.'

My hair was rust-red.

'Another sign of evil,' asserted Mrs Fletcher, throwing some mackerel innards down for the tortoiseshell cats to gobble. 'He's crawling with fleas, too, they say.' This much was true. 'I reckon he's witches' spawn.'

'And *I* reckon he's from the Fair,' said Mrs Tobash. 'He's a misbegot. One of them freaks. He'll never be a man.'

I ran and hid in my mother's skirts.

I will be frank with you, reader: I grew up with a distinct sense that all was not well.

Proud though I am now of my eloquence and literacy (if you will forgive me a moment of self-praise), it may come as a surprise to you that in childhood my lack of speech was the cause of great anxiety to my foster-parents. It was clear to them that I was not unintelligent (indeed, I was quite the opposite, although it is perhaps immodest to mention it) but it was evident that some inexplicable blockage was preventing me from uttering a single sound other than a squeak or a grunt, which bore no relation to the human language. In the opinion of the good Dr Baldicoot, the matter was related to my general sickliness at birth, and the trauma caused by my unfortunate mutilation.

'For who knows,' he argued, puffing on his vile-smelling pipe, 'what effect such an attack may have had upon the psyche?'

My father had a more theological explanation for my silence.

' "*I speak in the tongues of men and of angels*," ' he would quote from the Bible, comforting his worried wife. 'He is an angel. These grunts are angelic discourse.'

My foster-mother, who had the task of dressing me every morning and knew with intimacy the extent of my physical oddities, including my singularly un-angelic hairiness, was not so sure.

'Speak to me, Tobias,' she would wail. 'In God's own English, I pray!'

It was not, in fact, until my fifth year that words finally emerged from my mouth. I remember the occasion well, for it was my official birthday. My true date of birth being unknown (a common problem with foundlings), we celebrated the event on the anniversary of my parents' wedding. See them there, at the big kitchen table, every knot of whose oak surface I know with intimacy, their hands clasped; it is the thirtieth year of their marriage. My father moon-faced, earnest, his bushy brows turning to grey; she quiet and unassuming, like a friendly potato or a lardy bun. And see their smiles of parental pride as they gaze lovingly at the child sitting opposite them, the linen napkin

tucked beneath his chin, a fried sardine before him on his plate.
I am their darling, their joy.

'Happy birthday, Tobias! May the Lord bless you and keep
you!' booms Parson Phelps.

I smile. In my lap, I finger the wheels of a toy train they
have given me. It is made of wood, carved by the cobbler, Mr
Hewitt.

'Eat up,' whispers my mother, her eyes bright with excitement,
her mouth trembling with delight. 'And then you shall have your
surprise!'

Dutifully, I pick some more at my sardine, and leave the spine
on the side of my plate.

'Now shut your eyes,' whispers Mrs Phelps, 'and make a
wish!'

I close them, and (my imagination being limited, and the
hair-shirt mentality of Thunder Spit prompting luxurious urges
in me even at this early age) I pray for a magnificent cake.

It has already been established that miracles did not often
come to Thunder Spit. So when two came into the Phelps
household within the space of five years, there was joy to be
had indeed, and a feeling of extra-special blessedness. There is no
physical explanation for what happened (although the good Dr
Baldicoot did his best to come up with a diagram of a larynx that
had been blocked and then suddenly unplugged, due to a sudden
stimulation of the psyche, thus confirming his theory) but – for
what it is worth – it is my belief that at that same moment that
I was wishing for a cake, my mother was making a wish of her
own. How else to explain what next transpired? In her neat and
careful script, my mother wrote down in her diary that night:

> The sequence of events, as Parson Phelps and I recall it,
>   was thus:
> Firstly, the child opened his eyes, and saw the cake.
> Secondly, he blew out the candles, one by one.
> And thirdly, clear as a choirboy, Dear Lord be thanked, the
>   CHILD SPOKE!

At the bottom of the page, in writing that was a mere scrawl, and jittered with emotion, she had added: *Fourthly: I shall die a happy woman!*

My first words – 'Words we will cherish for ever,' declared my delighted father – came suddenly, unbidden, from my mouth.

'What a delicious-looking cake,' I said. 'Please, dear Mother, would you kindly be so good as to cut me a slice?'

A child prodigy! And so polite with it!

'Manners maketh man,' choked my father, then joined my mother in weeping with joy. As I helped myself to another slice, I smiled at the pleasure I had given them, and watched them hauling out the prayer-cushion and flinging themselves on the floor to thank God. Their prayers were so long and passionate that I managed to polish off the whole cake before they got to their feet again.

From that day, I never squeaked or grunted again, and so proud were my parents of my newly acquired talent that they encouraged me to read long passages of the Bible aloud, and to memorise tongue-twisters: *Peter Piper picked a peck of pickled pepper, Miss Mosh mashes some mish-mash, Betty Botter bought some butter*, and the like. My ability to surmount difficult verbal challenges such as these has been much remarked upon throughout my life, and remains a source of pride. Needless to say, soon my father was training me to read aloud long passages from the Bible in church, and the congregation marvelled at my sudden precociousness.

But in a community as small as ours, I was still the foundling boy, the outsider. People stared at me and jeered when I ventured into town. (They said redheads smell different, but if you're one yourself, how can you tell? And even then, what can you do about it?) The villagers accused me of frightening the sheep and the cows in particular, and I was banned from Harcourt's farm because of the havoc I once wreaked in his paddock when I accompanied my mother to buy eggs. The whole flock of poultry refused to lay for another two weeks. I was also the cause, according to the farmer, of his favourite horse throwing a nervous fit. Dogs growled at me, too. My unfortunate effect on the animal population of Thunder Spit soon earned me a bad name, and some villagers began to mutter biliously about an 'evil eye'.

This enraged my father. I was the Lord's own chosen child, and my love of God and the Scriptures was proof of it; how could anyone who had heard my readings in the church – to a packed and admiring gathering of Christian brethren – think otherwise? How could a boy who sang hymns so eagerly and with such a clear and angelic voice be anything other than special to the Lord? But after the epileptic-horse incident, I avoided Harcourt's farm, and walked a lonely path to school, where the creatures would catch no whiff of me. My trips to the cobbler were the source of deep shame, and I always kept my socks on to hide the unnatural shape of my feet. Mr Hewitt's shop was poky and dank, and it stank of badly cured leather, a smell I have come to associate with death and fear. Here he made me special shoes, with leather and bark soles. They looked like fishing boats. Over the years, perhaps to counteract my natural inclination to crawl somewhat crab-wise rather than to walk, and to disguise the oddity of my gait, I began to tread slightly on tiptoe.

In the village, they called me Tobias Trotter.

At every school, there is an unattractive boy who lurks in a corner of the playground, fiddle-faddling with a stick or a stone, who is unruly, who sometimes reverts to scrambling on all fours, who has no great talent to compensate for his oddity. In Thunder Spit, that boy was me.

And yet do not pity me, gentle reader, for I was not unhappy; far from it. My parents loved me, and my memories of those early childhood days are golden, because I had the sea, and its astonishing contents. It was a huge toy-box to me, and every day it spewed forth a new miracle. See me there, on the grey beach, a speck of humanity beneath the great unrolled carpets of sky and ocean, sitting on a sand-dune with my bare toes dug in deep and my soul unlocked, watching.

The sky turn from coral pink to pale gold, the clouds flattened against the sea, the pearl waves rolling into green. The rocks grey, cold, shimmering with sea-salt like sacred dust. There, alone, I would stare into rockpools; for hours, I gazed in deep, watching the vague clutchings of sea anemones and the swirl of jellyfish and the little light-explosions made by shoals of baby herring. Plunging my arm in deep, I captured crabs, minia-ture lobsters, crayfish, shrimps, mussels, cockles, quillsnappers, aquatic and semi-aquatic feats of engineering that wear their skeleton on the outside like armour. Searching tenaciously, I found bigger and better rockpools, bigger and better crabs; picking them apart, I found inside a maze of inter-connecting meat-chambers, like Parson Phelps' church organ decked with knuckles of calcium, yet the divisions as smooth and papery as the internal walls of a Japanese samurai's abode. 'God's doodlings', my father called them, inspecting what I brought home in my tin bucket. His belief was that molluscs and other sea-creatures were drawn from the margins of the Lord's great sketchbook, in which the masterpiece was man.

He certainly broke His nib the day he drew me, I thought, as I looked wistfully at my reflection in the rockpool. The squashed-up face, too crammed with features for its size, with thin lips and round, dark eyes like two raisins shoved deep into a burnt cake.

But, 'Beauty is in the eye of the beholder,' my mother always said, and I came to believe her.

To most Thunder Spitters there were two types of Nature: the Nature man could vanquish, and the Nature that vanquished him. The Nature we conquered had long been domesticated for us, by previous generations of Thunder Spitters: our famous cats, that were black-and-red-patched like cows, with a distinctive stripe down the nose, and always fled when I entered the room. Or the skinny sheep who scattered at my approach, or the cows whose milk I was alleged to curdle, or the dogs that so loathed me: mostly sheepdogs, collies and whippets which inter-bred like the families here, the Peat-Hoves, the Balls, the Cleggses:

54

long lines of intermarriage and gravestones to match. But the other Nature always remained: wild Nature, the Nature we couldn't guard against; the Nature that was always erupting and rattling around us. The swarms of stinging jellyfish, the Portuguese men-o'-war that could kill you or, as in the case of Robbie Tobash, lose you the use of an arm; the floods and the winds that knocked over our boats like paper hats, the giant octopuses that grabbed men overboard in the night, the potato blight and the centipedes and lice and silverfish in the sacks of corn, and the fleas that attacked us, and the parasites we bore within.

My mother had a theory that I was inhabited by a particularly tenacious tapeworm, which had been my lodger since babyhood. She claimed this sordid stowaway was the cause of my sphincter trouble, and she spent much of her time thinking up new ways to purge me of it.

'This'll do for you, you evil creature,' mother would murmur, her plain potato features wincing in concentration as she forced the foul concoctions down my gullet. She christened my tape-worm Mildred. The name was also – 'By pure coincidence,' she said – that of a woman my father had once been sweet on in his bachelor days. But try as she might, my mother could never abolish my invisible passenger. Or the fleas, or the bats, or the toe-fungus that haunted us all.

Yes, Nature infested us, and we fought it off. But it came back. We fought it off again and it came back again. It was like the fizzing waves on the shoreline, leaving a lacework of foam and history that clung to our lives.

'Father, how exactly, how *exactly*, did God make this?' I remember asking Parson Phelps one day. I was brandishing a mermaid's purse at him, a black dogfish egg with twirling strands protruding extravagantly from its four corners.

'By His holy craftsmanship,' the Parson explained patiently. I pictured God in a sort of workshop, like that of Mr Hewitt the cobbler, puzzling over the engineering. 'And what is more, he created all this, and more, in a mere day. The fourth day.

Remember, Tobias? Remember your scriptures? What did God do, Tobias, on the fourth day, that is so apt to your question? God said let *what* bring forth *what*?'

I had scriptures coming out of my ears.

'God said, "*Let the waters bring forth abundantly the moving creature that hath life, and let fowl fly above the earth in the open firmament of Heaven,*" Father.'

'Well remembered, Tobias. A sound memory is a blessing.'

'But, Father, did he really make it all out of nothing?'

It just didn't make sense.

'He made it out of the void, Tobias. "*For the earth was waste and void –*"'

'"*And darkness was upon on the face of the deep,*"' I finished. I was mesmerised by the beauty of it.

Like him – like all of us – I believed the words of the Bible implicitly, just as I believed Herman's *Crustacea*. Neither book had ever given me any cause for doubt. God was as real to me as my tapeworm, Mildred. Both were invisible, but housed within. Both made their presence felt in a hundred small ways.

'"*And the spirit of God moved upon the waters. And God said let there be light,*"' intoned the Parson. I loved his big voice. It boomed with righteousness.

'"*And there was light,*"' I replied.

When you live near the sea, all this is obvious. As I discovered later, it's in towns and cities that your soul is caught unawares.

'And,' continued the Parson, but in his other voice, his less appealing, thinner, somewhat nagging voice, 'returning to your dogfish detritus, not to mention your crab collection and your cuttlefish and your sea-beetle and your dead cormorant, which your mother spied on Wednesday in your chest of drawers and threw out, Tobias, because it was smelling foul, what else did God do on the fourth day? He created the great sea-monsters, Tobias, and every living creature that moveth, which the waters brought forth abundantly, after their kinds, and every winged fowl after its kind – and what did God see, Tobias? What did he then see, son?'

'He saw that it was good, Father,' I replied, picking at a sea-urchin spine that had lodged painfully beneath my thumbnail.

'Precisely. Which is more than can be said of your smashed limpets, and also your lobster shell, which I found lurking in the vestry, when tracking down the source of a vile odour. I saw then, and smelt, that it was *not* good. Not good at all. No more carcasses in our house, son, or in God's.'

'No, Father. I promise.'

'Good boy.'

'Father.'

'Yes?'

'What is this?' I thrust my stone at him. There were many such stones on the beach, and I had never understood them. This was a wonderful specimen, its dark whorl with radial stripes reminiscent of a shell.

'That,' said Parson Phelps, stopping in his tracks, 'is one of God's jokes.'

'God makes jokes?' I questioned, aghast.

'Yes. Some big, and some small. On scientists.' My Father hated scientists. They were responsible, he often claimed in his sermons, for much of the world's confusion. They were a scourge, and ranked as low in his estimation as rude children and fallen women. 'Your stone is called a fossil,' he continued, 'and God planted them in the earth to muddle a certain breed of scientist known as a geologist. He knew exactly what He was doing.'

'A geologist? What is he?'

'A man who dares to question the truth of Genesis,' my father replied. 'These fossils are red herrings, planted by God, to trick geologists into believing they are right. And thereby wasting their time on a grand scale.' He laughed, sharing God's joke. 'Do not forget, son, that he is a *jealous* God!'

My father seemed to find this most mightily amusing, and chuckled at God's holy sense of humour, but I was merely confused. I believed passionately in the Lord, but His fossil joke and other holy eccentricities led me to question His divine purpose on more than one occasion. Another question vexed me, too.

'Father.'

'Yes, son?'

'Who made God?'

Well? Is that such a foolish question? What *were* his origins?

My father had the answer, though. 'God is self-made,' he said finally. 'Like a self-made man. But God.'

'I see, Father,' I said. But I lied, for I did not, and it remains to me a puzzle.

After I dun the SPLITS for Him, the woman wrote, *Trapp claps his hands, cals me to His tabel to drink WINE.*

He was hansom enuf. Big MUSTARSH, with wax tips, keeps TWURLIN and TWURLIN away at it. Sumthin about Him. Dont no wot till later.

I likes you, He sez. You hav nacherel GRASE, animal GRASE.

I has wot? I arsks.

Exept wen you speeks, He sez. So I kept my mouth shut mostly arfter that remarke. HE was in business, He says, but He doesnt say wot.

He takes me home. I dont object to THAT, wot with my lodgings at Mrs Peersons, the BICH. The hous is big and shabby but posh, no mistake. Grand PIANNA in the drorin room, big chairs, big PIKCHERS on the worls. Pikcher of him, Trapp, standing on top of NELSONS COLUM in TRAFALGA SKWER. He sez its Him, anyway, THE FACT IZ the man is too smorl to see and He is SPITTIN on the crowds below. Thats wot E sez, but thats too smorl to see as wel.

I enjoyed that IMENSELY, He sez. An EXELENT evenin that wuz. See that PIANNA, He sez. I wonts you to stand on top of it an DARNS for me.

So He plays the PIANNA, and I darnsis, and He has teers in his eys after, I SWER IT. That was a good nite, that furst nite with Trapp, but it didnt stay good.

UNFORCHENATLY FOR ME.

My next mistake woz to moov in with Him as a servant, but to liv with Him as a wyfe, and thus to lern all about SLAVERIE.

CHAPTER 6

HEADS WILL ROLL

As Tobias Phelps pursues his lonely childhood in Thunder Spit, let us now catapult ourselves back in time to observe the beginnings of a parallel childhood: that of Miss Violet Scrapie. The normal gestation period for *Homo sapiens* is nine months, and it is now November 1845, forty weeks to the day since we bore voyeuristic witness to the scene of marital union enacted by Dr Ivanhoe and Mrs Scrapie behind the chintz curtains of Madagascar Street, Belgravia.

Time for some screaming!

'AAAGH!'

That is the Laudanum Empress, in the early stages of childbirth.

And some cursing!

'Buggeration and damnation!'

That is Dr Ivanhoe Scrapie, reacting to this piece of ill-considered timing on his wife's part; he is battling with an awkwardly lopsided yak which refuses to conform to the structural requirements demanded by the armature. He is loath to leave his workshop to hang around outside the bedroom door; he will stay here, he decides, and fiddle with the armature, and smoke a cigar, as is traditional. Damn the whole business, he thinks, surveying the yak. He has approximately seven other children, if his memory serves him. Aren't they all more or less grown-up by now? He thinks so. Many have surely departed abroad, or have married, or both. And now – just as the Queen's Animal Kingdom Collection is weighing him down

60

with work (eighty-one animals completed; fifteen thousand-ish to go) another wretched child!

The screams are getting louder. Scrapie hears the midwife calling for more water. He hears Cabillaud shouting *merde*. He puffs at his cigar.

'AAAGH!'

The Laudanum Empress again. Unlike other mammals, who bear their offspring in silence, *Homo sapiens* has a tendency to scream in agony. This is due to bad design on the part of God. He wished to give man a large brain, but forgot to give woman a proportionately structured pelvis.

'*Merde alors!*'

That is Jacques-Yves Cabillaud.

Symbiosis describes a relationship in the natural world by which two creatures very different in nature and characteristics come to a mutual accord of assistance. This is the status that the two human animals, Jacques-Yves Cabillaud and his employer, Dr Ivanhoe Scrapie, have quickly reached in Madagascar Street. At the heart of the exchange is the use of the carcasses of other, non-human animals – largely mammals, but embracing also bird-life, reptiles and fish – and the motto, beloved of Nature itself, *Waste not want not*. And thus it is that while Dr Scrapie puffs on his cigar and adjusts his lopsided yak in the taxidermy workshop upstairs, Monsieur Cabillaud, in the basement kitchen, has been preparing a hearty yak-meat stew, which he is now forced to leave on the back burner, while he heats vast quantities of water for the midwife attending Mrs Scrapie in the throes of childbirth.

Merde encore!

He fills another kettle. But it must be said that, apart from today's interruption, Cabillaud is pleased – more than pleased, with his lot. His instincts on the day Scrapie walked into the elephant Mona's enclosure had all been sound, and now, the initial territorial disputes with Mrs Jiggers sorted out (a common occurrence when one animal low in the pecking order is ousted by another who presumes to be slightly higher), Cabillaud has assumed his role as dominant male in the Madagascar Street kitchen, and by pure force of his culinary talent, has revolutionised the Scrapie diet.

Doing his best to ignore the sounds of childbirth which can still be heard, faintly, from the Scrapie bedroom two floors above him, Cabillaud settles the kettle on the hob and pokes at the simmering yak stew.

Mais oui, he reflects, he has the world at his feet, *quand même*! He had arrived at the Scrapies' home in Madagascar Street armed with a dead wallaby from the zoo, and that very evening, had furnished Dr and Mrs Scrapie with their first decently cooked meal. Decently cooked? May he presume to say that it was in fact unparalleled? The meat was neither burnt, nor stone-cold, nor tough – the three idiosyncrasies that had been the hallmarks of Mrs Jiggers' cooking. Cabillaud had been declared a genius (a fact he was already aware of), and Mrs Jiggers relegated to housekeeping duties. Because how, having tasted *wallaby aux dix-neuf oranges*, could the Scrapies ever look back?

'*Mais bien sûr que non*,' murmurs Cabillaud, fishing out a ladleful of stew-juice and sniffing something to which the adjectives *majestueux* and *formidable* might well (though it is not for him to say) apply.

'AAAGH!'

That is Mrs Scrapie once again. How did she come to be in this sorry mess? And is she now about to pass to the Other Side? She remembers nothing of the episode that triggered her condition. Phantoms whirl in a miasma about her head, and in the middle distance, her cloud of psychic particles shimmers ominously. As Mrs Jiggers trickles more laudanum-water into her mouth by means of a sponge, the Empress sees the cloud's inner recesses writhing into strange shapes. Is that a piglet among all those flying feathers? Is that a child sitting on a beach? Surely that's a swarm of seagulls, over there! And is that a fossil? And surely *that* is a sardine?

What does all this mean?

She wails again, as her ravaged womb contracts once more. As the pain lunges through her and appears to rip her very soul apart, the particles swirl and re-form. From a high corner above her bed, she observes herself sprawled horizontally, her legs aloft, Mrs Jiggers mopping at her brow, the midwife prodding at her nether regions. And as the particles shimmer, the future dances before her: she sees a monkey in a short pinafore dress, and a man with a syringe; a gleaming motorised vehicle shooting along a huge wide road; an immensely fat woman dressed as a meringue, a pair of identical female twins, an odd-looking man in extraordinary shoes hopping on a doorstep – *her* doorstep – Her Majesty the Queen wielding a scimitar and splitting in half the belly of a –

'AAAGH!'

The doorbell clangs. Two minutes later, the door of Scrapie's workshop is suddenly flung open by a flushed Mrs Jiggers, whose apron is falling off and whose hairpins are dangling skew-whiff across one eye.

'Boy or girl?' asks Scrapie, laying down his skinning-knife.

'Neither, sir. She's still in labour. But there's a messenger arrived from the Palace, sir! Says he's the Queen's equerry! He awaits you downstairs!'

With some reluctance, Scrapie stubs out his cigar. Mrs Jiggers wipes her hands on her apron and dances about nervously. It's not every day there's this much activity in the house. Or such news arriving! The good woman cannot contain herself.

'He's come to tell you, sir, that Horace Trapp's *Ark* has landed at the docks!'

Scrapie groans. Two years and five months behind schedule! The nerve of the man!

'Oh, and I'll be needing more water, sir,' Mrs Jiggers frets as she pants her way along the hallway, Scrapie striding purposefully in her wake. 'It won't be long now.'

'Cabillaud will see to it. What else does he say, this equerry?'

'Oh. Just one thing,' says Mrs Jiggers, stopping in her tracks

63

and turning to look down with excitement at her employer. She wipes her hands feverishly on her starched apron, and bites her lip, scared and thrilled in equal measure. She has not felt this way since the Travelling Fair of Danger and Delight passed through London last March, and she rode on the Mechanical Millipede.

'Well?' barks Scrapie.

'He says that Horace Trapp is missing, sir. And that all the animals are dead!'

And she gathers up her skirts and rushes out.

Our imaginary Montgolfier awaits us; let us therefore abandon the Laudanum Empress to her ghastly screaming (which will continue for several more hours) and follow Scrapie, Cabillaud, and the equerry to the docks, to witness the scene of devastation that is Trapp's *Ark*. The Hippo's equerry, a man of a certain femininity and nervous energy, has been voluble on the subject of Trapp, as they made their way, post-haste by hansom cab, to the docks.

Rumour had it, he said, that Trapp had fled.

Rumour had it, the equerry claimed, that Trapp had abandoned the *Ark* in order to marry a foreign princess.

Rumour had it, the equerry counter-claimed, that Trapp had drowned.

Rumour had it, the equerry mused, that Trapp had gone back into the slavery business, and was working out of Georgia.

Rumour had it, too, that –

'Shut up,' said Scrapie tersely, descending from the halted hansom cab. 'Just show me the bloody ship.'

Silently, the nervous equerry leads Scrapie and Cabillaud to the *Ark*. The balloon goes like the wind. Before we know it, we too have arrived.

The *Ark* is berthed next to *HMS Barcelona*, and is in comparison a sorry sight indeed. A huge hole gapes in its hull, its sails are torn and bedraggled. It lolls in its berth, its belly ragged as an old husk.

'Jesus Christ on a penny-farthing!' exclaims Scrapie, who has quickly scurried on board and is now heaving open the door of the cavernous beamed hull. He is hit full-force by an atrocious stink. The *Ark* is a former galley ship, a slave-trader, and the first things the taxidermist can make out in the gloom are the rows of manacles chained to the wooden planking of the walls.

Now, pinching their noses, Scrapie and Cabillaud peer through the darkness, attempting to decipher what they can. Cabillaud, who after his miserable seafaring experience is less than keen on ships, lurches out on to the gang-plank to inhale fresh air. Dr Scrapie, who is made of sterner stuff, notes that the smell of putrefaction means that many of the specimens – in the unlikely event that they are not completely ruined – are beyond taxidermic hope. The rest must be frozen immediately. The equerry hovers in a corner, shifting nervously from foot to foot. This place gives him the creeps, and he doesn't mind who knows it.

Cabillaud now returns from the quarter-deck, staggering, and grabs Scrapie's arm. As they accustom their eyes to the darkness, both men blanch, for neither has ever before witnessed such a terrible scene of destruction. Every door of every cage, large and small, has been opened. The carcasses are strewn everywhere. Fur, feathers, reptilian skin, broken bones, staring eyes. Huddled, stiff little shapes. Wings awry. Dry crusts of maroon-coloured blood.

'*Merde!*' yells Cabillaud suddenly. He has tripped on something, which now rolls slowly across the planking to land at Scrapie's feet. A rotten old coconut, by the look of it, its hair long and matted, and stinking to high Heaven. Scrapie is about to kick it away, but something stops him. Instead, he squats, holding his nose, to inspect the object at his feet.

'My God,' he murmurs. 'It is a head!'

It is indeed a head. The head of a human. Months old. Reeking.

Despite its rottenness, Scrapie recognises the moustache. And the excellent teeth.

'God Almighty,' he whispers. His voice is hoarse, a mere croak.

This head is Horace Trapp's.

Scrapie has long prided himself on his lack of squeamishness, but his normally cast-iron belly now turns to gelatine, and he lunges forward, grappling with the door, to escape. Outside on the deck, Cabillaud and the equerry, who have swiftly followed him, both vomit copiously over the side of the *Ark*, and Scrapie tries to calm his frayed nerves by reciting to himself a smorgasbord of logarithms. Finally, he pulls himself together.

First things first.

'Tell the Queen,' he orders the equerry, 'that Trapp has been murdered. And that as far as the Animal Kingdom Project is concerned, I shall be needing a ton of Arctic ice shipped over immediately. Immediately is in fact an understatement. I need ice NOW. I will commandeer her supply until my own arrives. Understood? There is no time to lose. We have work to do.'

That, too, was an understatement.

The project Scrapie was about to embark on would take him twenty years.

'AAAGH!' comes a faint cry from the bedroom. The Mont-golfier has whisked us back to Madagascar Street.

In the nick of time!

Welcome, Miss Violet Scrapie! Welcome to the world!

As the Laudanum Empress sinks back on the pillow and retreats into the comfort of her psychic particles, the newborn Violet yells lustily for the milk that is her birthright.

The other Scrapie children had the small bones and delicate features of the Laudanum Empress, a famous belle. The four sisters were beautiful. The two brothers were handsome.

But now, into this collection of valuable Society china, charged the big-boned Violet.

Crash, thump, disaster. What had gone wrong? There was no rhyme or reason to it, as far as Dr Scrapie could tell, when he returned, badly shaken, from the débâcle that was Trapp's *Ark* and inspected his newborn infant. It was a bad day altogether.

First, all the Animal Kingdom nonsense, then Trapp's severed head rolling about like a pustular football, and then another bloody girl. Skeletally, the child was definitely bovine. So much so that the Empress, for whom the act of union had been just a vague interruption of her normal psychic trance, wondered whether she could perhaps have been impregnated by a visitor from the Other Side, and she surreptitiously inspected the *chaise-longue* for signs of ectoplasm. Meanwhile odd visions still swirled among her cloud of psychic particles, and she remained puzzled by their import.

Time passed, and the baby grew, and grew, and grew, a great greedy cuckoo in the Scrapie nest. Neither of her parents was sure when it was that Violet decided to up sticks and descend into the basement kitchen, to live with Cabillaud. Was she perhaps three or four? Or maybe as young as two? Both were too preoccupied with their own doings to pay the girl much attention, that much is certain, and it was a good month before they noticed her absence, prompted by hints and mutterings from Mrs Jiggers, who did not approve of the new arrangement. It was wrong for a child born to be a lady, a member of the upper classes, to descend to the level of servants. It upset the natural order of things. Being uneducated, Mrs Jiggers had not heard of the word *hierarchy*. But it is the word she would have used, to explain what it was that was being overturned, in her humble view.

But no one listened to her. Least of all Violet herself. It was Cabillaud to whom she was drawn, as though by magnetism. And to his domain, the kitchen.

So while Tobias Phelps spent his boyhood years climbing trees and digging his unusual toes in the sand of the beach, Violet Scrapie spent her childhood on the floor of the kitchen in Madagascar Street, playing with pots and pans, and gobbling up whatever tasty morsel the Belgian chef Cabillaud threw her way. For he had soon spotted the child's unseemly preoccupation with ingestion, and her vocation as a gastronome.

Nature or nurture? Who cares!

'*Ouvre la bouche, ferme les yeux, ma petite chérie!*' Cabillaud would order, and the child Violet would duly comply, her cherub's mouth agape, like a baby seal waiting to receive a herring from its mother. When she opened her eyes, she would have to guess what delicacy Cabillaud had popped through her parted lips.

What better training for a fine palate?

How many children have the good fortune to be able to distinguish, by the age of five, between fifteen different types of poultry? A whole genus of rodents? A hundred different herbs and spices? And how many children can claim to have access, via the carcasses in the ice house at the bottom of the garden, to a whole arkful of frozen meat, including such exotic rarities as the smooth savannah rhinoceros, the Mediterranean spotted turtle, the lesser quaggar, the two-headed Goan snake, the black-footed rabbit, Humboldt's penguin, Rufous Tinamon, the Surinam toad, and the Gentleman Monkey?

Answer: not many!

Time passed, and Violet cooked and cooked and cooked. And ate, ate, ate.

By the age of ten, she was fast turning into a human pyramid, a heavy wedge that moved about the house from kitchen to dining room, from dining room to kitchen, sweating like a great cheese on castors, a stack of cookery books a permanent fixture under her arm. The Empress was at her wits' end, and repaired with increasing frequency to the comfort of the Ouija board and the seance.

'The girl's a mystery!' she confided in the spirits. 'She reads a cookery book the way she eats a plate of cake. Blink and it's over!'

The spirits shrugged their shoulders.

Could Violet perhaps be shipped off to somewhere like Australia? the Empress wondered.

Crash! The breaking of a mixing bowl.

Sloop! the licking of a sauced finger.

Yum yum. *C'est bon.*

'Or might New Zealand be further, as the crow flies?'

The spirits shrugged again. 'Wait and see,' they said.

'Fat lot of good *you* are,' muttered the Laudanum Empress, crumpling up a page of automatic writing and hurling it into the fire.

She bought Violet her first corset at the age of eleven. The child was popping out all over the place; her body had to be put under control. One day she actually fainted from constriction in the street, and collapsed on to a grocer's cart, knocking a thousand carrots off a precarious pile. With considerable difficulty but even more exasperation, the Empress took her by the scruff, and they stumbled through the sea of rolling orange veg, the grocer's boy yelling, the Empress flinging a sovereign behind her as you might throw salt over your left shoulder to ward off evil.

To Harrod's, pronto!

'Bring us the biggest corset you have,' ordered the Empress, 'and be ready to add gussets.' And she made a thin, tight line of her perfect mouth.

'A relative?' asked the assistant, as Violet disappeared to try on the hosiery.

'No,' responded the Empress quickly, checking the mirror, where a fine figure of a woman – a creature of remarkable beauty, in fact, to whom the word 'paragon' could be applied without exaggeration – greeted her gaze. 'Just a child I happen to know.'

From the changing room, the sound of huffing and puffing, and the distinct odour of adolescent perspiration.

'I despair of you,' hissed the Laudanum Empress later, as they sat before a plate of cinnamon muffins in the tea shop downstairs. What could a mother do with such a child? Having felt lately the call of the Other Side, she knew she was not much longer for this world. Could she perhaps have some influence in death, which she had so signally failed to have in life? It was worth trying.

'You'll be the death of me, Vile,' she warned, stirring sugar into her tea with an angry clatter.

There's nothing wrong with *me*, thought Violet, as she crammed another muffin into her face.

Even then she had a sense of purpose – that rare sense of purpose that comes to children who instinctively know part of their destiny. She didn't play with dolls. Or hoops. Or marbles, bats or balls. She watched Cabillaud, studied the recipes of Mrs Beeton and Miss Eliza Acton, and hatched grown-up plans.

CHAPTER 7

IN WHICH THE ROGUE MALE
ATTEMPTS INTEGRATION IN
THE STONED CROW

Thunder Spit relished its heritage, both ancient and modern: its ancient chalk soil, its spanking new community centre, its fame among amateur botanists for its wide variety of sedges ('the sedge capital of England', according to the *Outdoorsman*), its proximity to the Gannymede power station, its sugar-beet and parsnip polyculture, its history of unprecedented cowardice during the plague of 1665, its tortoiseshell cats, its two petrol stations, its River Flid, winner of the Pollution Challenge Award of 1997, its mobile video-hire service, its post-modern vicar, its intolerance of New Age travellers, its prehistoric fossil heritage, its electronic speed-sensitive road-signs which flashed the words SLOW DOWN, YOU ARE GOING TOO FAST at vehicles that drove through the high street at over 50 k.p.h., its Great Flood of 1858, its early and wholehearted commitment to agricultural phosphates.

All this I learned from Norman Ball, my first Thunder Spitter. I met him in the Stoned Crow. I arrived at 6 p.m., and thought: First stop, a beer. I gave the Nuance a little pat on the arse. She'd done well. I parked her round the back of the pub, near the quay. Across the car-park I saw a driving-test centre and a billboard advertising Lucozade, both dwarfed by sky. Too much sky, I thought, as I locked the car – chk! – with the remote-control doo-da. So much sky, compared to land and buildings, that it seemed to be pressing down on you. Agoraphobia is probably quite similar to claustrophobia that way. I looked across to where I reckoned the sea should have been, but there was a huge

71

concrete barrier in the way, covered in strangely hopeful-looking graffiti:

DON'T DRINK AND DRIVE – TAKE CRACK AND FLY
ROSE AND BLANCHE ARE SLAGS
URBAN CHAOS

Forget the geography, I told myself, as I pushed open the swing door of the pub. Concentrate on the social life.

So it was through the cheery cigarette fug of the Stoned Crow that I caught my first real glimpse of the town that was to be my new home. The pub windows had that thick Olde Worlde glass, but through a more transparent section I could see the black, gloomy silhouette of a church spire, and a row of bollards. I watched a woman in a sou'wester being dragged by a border collie across the high street. The lead she was holding had a handle like a giant trigger. The dog was wearing a bright coat with a spaceship design; the sort of thing a boy of six might have specified if his granny had offered to knit him an exciting woolly. Bloody hell, people and their pets, I thought. At least I'll be dealing with farm animals here. I remembered Mr Jenks at the Veterinary Society saying something about Lord Chief Justice sheep. What the hell were they? I downed my beer, and was just telling myself to go and buy another, when I saw a fat man at the bar waving at me.

'A stranger in our midst!' he called across. 'What's the betting you're the new vet?'

He was coming towards me now with two pints of bitter, foam frothing down the sides of the glasses and on to the red-patterned carpet, walking carefully, like he was giving his own blubber a piggy-back. He planted the pints on little flannel mats, then eased himself down next to me. The red velour stool shuddered.

'Welcome to Thunder Spit, mate. You're among friends.'

'It's an honour to be here,' I said, though what I'd seen of Thunder Spit had yet to enthral me. 'I'm a big fan of the

72

countryside. Used to come up this way on camping holidays as a kid. Plant flags on sandcastles. Cool stuff.'

We shook hands.

'Buck de Savile,' I said. I was pleased to notice that he looked impressed.

He told me that Norman Ball was the name. 'Good journey? Saw you drive up while I was in the little boys' room, pointing Percy at the porcelain. Noticed your Audi.' He gave me a thumbs-up sign. 'Nice one. Nuance, if memory serves?'

'Yup. Turbo.'

Despite the burp smell, you couldn't help warming to a man who'd buy you a beer and could appreciate the thrill of a shiny red chassis. Norman told me he was in insurance, and that, for his sins, he commuted to Hunchburgh. As well as being an active member of the village council, he was a keen DIY-er.

'A fanatic, you could say. I'm a dab hand with a router, though I say it myself. So need any advice, just give me a tinkle.' Something about the way he spoke made me feel that I knew him already, but I couldn't put my finger on what it was. 'So, young Buck,' said Norman. 'To what do we owe the pleasure?'

I had known this question would pop up at some point, and I'd formulated a few Giselle-free replies on the journey up, while trying out some of my new faces. Knowing the veterinary complaints procedure well, I reckoned I had at least six months' leeway *vis-à-vis* Mrs Mann. If not more. According to my enquiries, most complaints were dropped as soon as the pet-owner acquired a new baby-substitute. Boundless hope.

'I got fed up with pets,' I told Norman. 'They were too –'

'Tame?' Norman guffawed. I couldn't help laughing, too.

'After the wild stuff then?' Norman asked. 'I'll give you wild stuff. My wife Abbie was clearing out the loft, doing a big old spring-clean-and-chucking-out job, cos the planning permission came through to refurbish. It's a listed building, the Old Parsonage, so we had a helluva wait. Anyway, what do we find up there?'

73

I realised he was waiting for an answer, and racked my brains.

'Some of that vintage Japanese pornography?'

'Not even close, mate.'

'A skeleton in a cupboard?'

'Hey. Getting warmer. A collection of stuffed animals, as a matter of fact.'

My heart sank: I knew what was coming next.

'Heirloom of Abbie's, bless her heart,' Norman is saying. 'Dates back to the nineteenth century sometime. Reckons there must've been a taxidermist in the family, way back. She says they're a dust-trap, wants the whole lot binned. Fancy a squizzerooney?'

You come across this in all jobs, I suppose. You're a lawyer, and they ask if you've ever had to defend someone you knew was guilty. You're a dustman, and they enquire whether you've ever come across a wad of banknotes in a rubbish bin. You're a doctor, and people want you to look at their piles. You're a vet, and they demand an inspection of Great-Aunt Ethel's stuffed menagerie.

'It'd be a pleasure,' I said, groaning inwardly. 'I did a bit of taxidermy myself at vet school. It's quite an art. Not one I ever mastered myself, I'm afraid, though,' I told him, remembering a succession of botched squirrels and rabbits with wire sticking out in unhelpful places. We were taught by an ex-con, who said it was his way of putting something back into the community. 'It's the ears,' I added. 'They're a bugger. So what've you got? Any interesting specimens?'

'Most of them birds and small mammals, by the looks. Oh, and an ostrich. Blue eyes, rather human. And they're all wearing old-fashioned frocks and breeches and stuff, like something out of a kinky costume drama. There's a monkey, too. Wearing pantaloons.'

I had a sudden picture of Giselle in her pink frock and her nappy, stiffening with rigor mortis on my operating table, and felt a chill creep over me.

'You all right, mate?' he asked. 'You look like you've seen a ghost.'

'I'm fine,' I mumbled.

'Talking of ghosts,' he said, 'we've got one back at the Old Parsonage. Victorian lady. Quite a beauty. She'd be fanciable, I reckon, if she had a bit more flesh on her. The Laudanum Empress, she calls herself. Wears a lot of petticoats. Abbie reckons she popped out of the same wardrobe she found the animals in. She's been wreaking havoc with our telly.'

That was another post-Millennial thing. I'd read about it. Supernatural sightings had gone up by 300 per cent. This, I thought, does not bode well.

'Fancy some nibbles?' Norman's asking. 'Pork sushi? Cheese Loons?'

And he's wheeling his bulgy bottom across to the bar.

What did Norman and I discuss that night, before the momentous newsflash?

The usual things: how United were doing, my virtual Elvis collection, the new freak strain of ulcerative arthritis in Spain, the pros and cons of the new Windows software, the fact that it was quite a year for aphids but you could zap them with that new eco-chemical, the latest on the Fertility Crisis. It made Norman glad he wasn't my age. He had two grown-up girls, he said, his 'Gruesome Twosome'. Rose and Blanche. The names somehow rang a bell.

'We've had twins in the family since way back when,' Norman is saying. 'My side of the family, that. My mother was a Tobash.'

He might as well have told me she was a Martian, for all it meant to me.

It was that evening, from Norman, that I learned that Thunder Spit, population fifteen thousand, had once been a herring-shaped peninsula, but a land-reclamation scheme back in the late 1980s had knocked sense into its impractical geography, rendering it more a suburb of Judlow than a separate town.

'Some folk were against it being rationalised,' said Norman.

'But not me. Include me out, I said. Me and the hard core on the Council stuck to our guns. It put paid to the barmy one-way system for a start.' He had a weak bladder; as he wobbled off for yet another 'Jimmy Riddle', he called over his shoulder: 'Show me a man who says he isn't proud of being a Thunder Spitter, Buck, and I'll show you a liar!'

While he was gone, I wrote a mental list:

1. Sort out the surgery.
2. Check out the farmers.
3. Get laid.

Norman returns with two more beers, slosh, slosh, and another fistful of plastic-wrapped snacks. He plonks the lot on the table, and beer-foam whudders down the sides of our glasses.

'Cheers.' He slurps a big mooshful of bitter.

And then, as though intercepting item number three on my list: 'Women. I love 'em to bits, but do I understand them? The hell I do!' There is a pause, as I nod and he ruminates. 'Woman's a mysterious creature,' he pronounces finally. 'And we're entranced by her mystery, aren't we, Buck, as men?' I try out one of my new agreeing faces. 'I saw a documentary about it,' he continues. 'It's all to do with the DNA business.'

Here we go, I thought. Another spouter of gobshite putting in his ha'p'orth on the subject. There's nothing worse than a scientific ignoramus with a biological theory. They pick them up like verrucae. Norman's telling me it's all in the genes.

'DNA's simplicity itself, Buck. I reckon that, in a nutshell, it's all about history having to replicate itself. Enigma variations on a theme, type-of-thing. Bit of this, bit of that, chuck it all in the melting-pot. You've heard about these new pig-heart transplants. Their DNA's been doctored so's we don't reject them. Amazing, eh? And Jessie Harcourt, she's got a llama's pancreas. You know what I reckon about this Fertility Crisis,' he said. 'I reckon our time's up. That's the bottom line. Look at the

dinosaurs. They died out, didn't they? Same thing's happening to
Homo Britannicus.' He paused to burp. 'We've evolved as far as
we can, mate.'

That's what the woman on the radio had said, too.

As a child, I used to try to imagine how the earth looked
when it all began, those millions of years ago. The whole
planet was just a wilderness of mares' tails and dinosaurs and
stagnant pools, back then. And the wind wasn't so much wind,
as a load of blue steam whirling about. I used to dream about
earthquakes splitting the crust of the earth, like a failed soufflé
of my mum's, or eczema. I'd read those science-fiction comics.
They'd show artists' impressions of lower life-forms squabbling
for supremacy. They were always bulbous, with little eyes on
stalks, and they'd be submerged in a kind of churning primordial
gloop. I had a vision of time speeded up, and dwarfy creatures
with fins – not animals, but not plants either, a kind of horrible
in-between thing – wriggling and twisting. Eating one another
and being eaten.

'I once watched a praying mantis eating a beetle,' I told
Norman. 'Its jaws crunched from the side. They're like mechanised clamps, an insect's jaws.' I demonstrated with my thumb
and index finger, making pinching motions at Norman's nose,
and he shrank back in mock-fear, laughing. 'The beetle put up
quite a fight,' I said. 'It was still trying to defend itself when
it only had one leg left, hanging by a thread.' It had really
impressed me. Things like that do, when you're six. Then you
forget about them, until suddenly they snap into your head one
evening, years later, in a pub, after a few lagers. 'Kicking and
struggling to the very last. In the end, all that was left was a
back foot, waving.'

Norman was looking at me sideways.

'Well, that's us, isn't it?' I continued, remembering why I'd
thought about the mantis. 'We're that foot, waving. We're being
eaten alive. Swallowed up by time.'

He nodded slowly. 'Point there, Buck. Bit of a philosopher,
then, are you?'

To counteract this flattering but way-off-the-mark impression, I did him one of my brooding Elvis looks, and he guffawed.

It was my dad who told me about evolution, or rather his idea of it. I don't suppose that either of us realised, then, how important it would become.

Even before the gizzard stone and, later, my Saturday job at Harper's, I'd had a passion for skeletal biology, fuelled by the discoveries I made in the back garden, a long, narrow sliver of land subsiding towards the canal, black as Coke, which flowed sluggishly in a diagonal across the south of the borough. Both garden and canal were flanked by thin privet hedges and dust-filled urban weeds – bastard forms of dandelion, burdock, teasels, and rosebay willowherb which had mutated to outwit the weedkiller my father used to attack them. Every September, around the time the school term started, the cotton-wool tufts of willowherb drifted aimlessly on gusts of wind and settled on the lawn like lint, stirring up that strange feeling of melancholy that accompanies the changes of season in a city. At weekends, while my brothers helped our father fight weeds or prune hydrangeas or tackle rhubarb, I'd pick my way over the upturned earth, avoiding the lumps of half-buried cat-shit, to exhume the more ancient detritus of nature: snail-shells, cow's teeth, old sparrow-skulls, a dog's femur as drilled and pocked as a hard sponge. By the canal I found dried beetles, dead dragonflies, stiffened birds, and once, three-quarters of a fox. I became obsessed with this jetsam of calcium, and the audacity of its design.

'Daddy, how did they make this?' I ask, thrusting part of a shrew up at him.

My father's spade is an extension of his foot, a submerged stilt. He's digging a trench for beets. 'Make what?'

'This bone. Look, it's teeny-weeny. Look, Dad.'

'It made itself, Bobby. The shrew grew in its mummy's tummy.'

'But who made the mummy shrew?'

'The mummy shrew's mum and dad.'

'So, Dad, who made the first ever shrew, then?'

'Evolution. It developed from another type of creature.' Dad heaves his weight down on the spade, makes an '*Eurkah*' noise, wipes sweat from his upper lip, stands back, and looks love-hatingly on his tiny, fenced kingdom. The beet-trench has thrown up a negative of itself: a long bulbous spine of earth.

'What kind of creature, Dad?'

'The elephant, I believe. Now help me with this root.'

'And the elephant?'

'From the pig.'

'And the pig?' I'm enjoying this; it's like that game where you keep asking *why* until they give you some money for sweets.

Dad sighs. 'There were little fishy things. They crawled out of the water and lost their fins and learned to breathe and eventually became pigs.'

'And the fishy things? Where did they come from?'

'From the sea.'

'But how did they get in the sea, Dad, in the first place?'

'They grew from plants. Plants that –' He looks uneasily about, checking that no neighbours are in earshot, perhaps sensing that he is on shaky ground. He lowers his voice slightly, just in case. 'Plants that developed from tiny underwater mushrooms.'

'And the mushrooms?'

Dad looks up at the sky and frowns. A pigeon whizzes past, as though on a mission. 'There was a big bang in space, and they burst out of nowhere.'

Even at the age of seven, I suspected that this was bollocks.

Norman's still talking about DNA. I haven't really been listening.

'Anyway, this documentary I saw, on BBC 2 – no, I tell a lie, it was Channel Four – there was a bloke saying the mystery of woman is actually just a mystery of DNA. And once we've unravelled the conundrum, the women's eggie things'll get back to normal, and they'll start getting pregnant again, and we'll be laughing. But in the meantime –'

Here he threw up his hands and made a face, and I made a face, too, and laughed.

'Crying, more like,' I joked, picturing Holly and Mrs Mann huddled together over the complaint form, with a little urn containing Giselle's ashes stood next to them on a plinth.

'Anyway, *chez moi*,' says Norman, 'for mysterious, read infuriating. Take my Abbie: illogical is putting it mildly. She tries to set the video to record the Lottery, right, but she wants to watch something else while it's on. So what does Madame do? I call her Madame sometimes, Buck,' he confided, 'cos she's a French teacher. Well, French and home economics, actually, *pardonnez-moi, Monsieur*. Anyway, she records the thing she's *watching*, then acts all surprised when she discovers she hasn't recorded the *other* thing. And d'you know what she says to me? "Stupid machine," she says, and I quote: "I thought it could record two programmes at once, but all I've got is a blank tape." Woman's the eighth wonder of the world, I reckon. Mind you, joking apart,' says Norman (''Scuse I') belching, 'I'll give credit where credit's due. My two gals – Tweedles Dum and Dee, I call 'em, my daughters – they've never had any problems with technology. If there's one thing they've learned from yours truly, it's how to use an instruction manual.'

As I was to discover for myself, some weeks later, when they expertly demonstrated to me the workings of their vibrator.

I was in the middle of my Elvis impression – 'Jailhouse Rock', as I recall – when the barman shouted at me.

'Hey, you! Shut up over there! Shut up!'

Norman and I whirled round on our stools; so fast, in my case, that I had to grab hold of the table to stop myself spiralling into lift-off. When I regained my bearings, I saw that everyone in the pub had suddenly congregated around the television above the bar, and was gawping intently at the screen.

'Newsflash!' mouthed the barman through cupped hands,

80

and turned up the volume so that the television was blaring at full pitch.

The whole screen was filled with a scene of devastation. Dust falling. Firemen at work with hoses, shooting water and foam at the twisted metal-and-concrete armature of a multi-storey building in flames. A reporter in a hard hat and gas-mask picking his way through the smoking debris.

'This is all that remains of the National Egg Bank tonight, after it was blown up by a massive Semtex bomb,' he said. Even through the gas-mask, you could tell he was almost in tears.

We all gawped at the screen.

The reporter couldn't go on. After some more shots of fire-fighting and smoking detritus, all he could manage, through a muffled sob, was, 'Back to the studio.'

Where a tougher news nut took over. 'Britain's hopes for the future were dashed tonight,' the newscaster said, 'when a huge explosion ripped through the National Egg Bank. The building – and its contents – were completely destroyed. No organisation has claimed responsibility for the attack, but religious fundamentalists are suspected of being behind tonight's blast.'

The pub went completely silent as the news continued. There was now not a single British egg left in the world.

We watched, Superglued to our seats, to the very end of the extended news programme. Then the barman stood up and flicked off the TV. Still no one said anything. But the implications of what had happened must have sunk in to all of us at about the same time, because suddenly, as though choreographed, we all reached for our beers and downed the remains in one.

Then Norman spoke. 'Looks like that's the end of Albion, then, folks.'

Which was as good a cue as any to get rat-arsed.

CHAPTER 8

IN WHICH
DISEASE STRIKES

I did the splits agen the next nite, the woman wrote, *even tho sumthin about Him makes me scared enuf to piss. Him on the table an He kissis me an wen He stops I feel lik Im in luv but still scared.*

Wot els can you do, He asks me.

Revers crab, I sez. Scorpion. Headstand. Handstand. Human notte.

Bed, He sez. You is cumin to bed wiv me now.

Only after that I find out Hes rich.

It was on the beach that I looked up from a rockpool one morning and saw a boy. He was a stocky little figure, standing on the shoreline in the distance. He was wearing a strange knobbled head-dress, which I was curious to inspect more closely. When I approached, holding a crab in one hand like a gift but also, just in case, like a weapon, I saw a tough, confident face, topped by a huge lump of seaweed. Sandhoppers were shooting out of it hysterically in all directions.

'This is my warrior's helmet,' said the boy. He had a stone in his hand, which he threw and caught, threw and caught. I was frightened he might throw it at me: I was an easy target in the village. Only the week before, a four-year-old girl, Jessie Tobash, had called me Prune-face.

'I can see a little wentletrap in it,' I said, in a conciliatory way. Thanks to Herman's *Crustacea*, I knew the name of everything, from abalone to Nilsson pipefish, from dog cockle to sand-smelt.

From this distance the boy's helmet looked like the sort of hat Mrs Simpson wore to church, all precarious-looking and featuring cornucopias of foodstuffs and flowers made of felt: more a market scene than a piece of headgear. I recognised him now, from the playground at school. He was Tommy Boggs, the blacksmith's son. The Boggses were a rough, threatening family. They had loud voices and they shouted unstintingly, as if it was their job, and the father, Matthew Boggs, was often drunk: not quiet-drunk, like the fishermen, or happy-drunk, like Farmer Harcourt, or even tipsy-tottery drunk like Mrs Sequin, but wild and angry drunk like no one else. The Boggses were heathens, too, according to my father. I never once saw them in church, not even at Christmas or Easter. Their aunt read the future in tea-leaves, a sure sign, my father said, of spiritual wantonness.

As Tommy approached, I dug my toes into the sand to hide them. But he was looking at me questioningly.

'I collect crustacea,' I blurted, by way of conversation, hoping that words might defend me from him in case he saw fit to attack me. But the boy said nothing; he simply stood there in his seaweed get-up and stared, a human fortress. I felt the opposite – vulnerable without my shoes, like a hermit crab that's left the shelter of its shell.

Still the boy said nothing. He neither threatened me, nor shrank away.

In fact, he smiled.

And then, because I must have felt, suddenly, that I could trust this boy, and because I was lonely enough, despite my self-sufficiency, to feel the need of a young friend my own age, I did a desperate and unprecedented and foolishly brave thing: without warning, I withdrew my toes from the sand, and showed him the sad deformity of my feet.

'There,' I said. My soul was at that moment laid barer than it had ever been, and inside I quailed at the risk I had taken with this boy whom I did not know, and partly feared. What had possessed me? To this day, I am not sure, though I like to believe it was an inner instinct that guided me.

Tommy gazed down at my feet. Sea-water was lapping at them, leaving little bubbles that popped and died. He noted my flat-footedness, and the way my hairy toes sat all wrong.

'I can't run fast,' I told him. 'But I can beat my mother in any race, because of her bunions.' Still he said nothing, so I went on: 'And on Fridays I can beat my father, too, because of the marbles in his shoes.'

Tommy looked puzzled, but interested. He was clearly unacquainted with the Parson's weekly idiosyncrasy. He was still staring at my feet.

'I like them,' he said finally. 'They don't look too foolish to me. In fact, I would say they are magnificent.'

My heart somersaulted in joy, and I felt the tears sting in my eyes.

'But please tell no one,' I whispered.

'Our secret, then,' he said.

From that moment, Tommy and I were friends. Apart from the secret we now shared, we had other things in common: Tommy also had fleas, and an aggravating tapeworm, he told me. His was called Benedicta, but she mostly kept herself to herself.

My own tapeworm, Mildred, was a cruel mistress, however. Knowing her likes and dislikes to some extent, I did my best to appease her. Fortunately I shared her love of fruits, fungi and sweet berries – and it was Tommy who taught me where to find them. Sugar was unknown in Thunder Spit, though Tommy assured me that the streets of London were paved with hundreds of minuscule sugar-cubes like Roman mosaics, depicting the glories of Empire. But there were fruits aplenty. We went searching in the early mornings, before school, the cows staring at us as they always did with that resigned look they cast on humans, then trundling away, mucus trailing from their noses, when they caught a whiff of me. In summer, there were raspberries, and in autumn, we'd trawl the hedgerows and copses for hazelnuts or cram our mouths with wild strawberries.

Tommy and I became firm friends. When it rained, or during

the winter months when only a crazed fool would step on to the frozen beach, choked with salt and ice and lashed by a screeching wind, I used to visit Tommy and we would play together at the back of Mr Boggs' forge, where the furnace kept us warm. We'd spit on the dirt floor, full of iron filings, and rake the resulting grey-flecked mess about, while watching Tommy's huge muscular father bashing at red-hot steel as if it had done him some terrible wrong.

'That'll be me one day,' said Tommy, with that careless certainty of his, that was as part of him as his shadow.

Later, it was Tommy who taught me how to spill my seed, and I soon became expert at it, though I knew it to be wrong, because the Lord had said so, and my father had reinforced this message with another, more immediate threat; that the profane activity would blind me. Every time I indulged in my foul habit, I pictured my vision blurring until all I could see were little pinpricks of light in the firmament, but this never happened. In fact, the opposite; I always had the impression that my eyesight was clearer afterwards, as though a blockage had been removed.

Looking back, I can try to see myself as they saw me.

A boy with a need to ask questions.

A boy with a low-slung walk, a love of cliff-climbing, and a coarse thatch of red hair, always in his eyes.

A boy always small for his age, but surprisingly strong and agile, and with a natural love, said Parson Phelps, of the blessings of the physical world. (Also a natural love of throwing tantrums and playing practical jokes, such as placing a dead hedgehog on the seat of the Parson's chair at Sunday school. For this misdemeanour he was forced to administer three blows of the cane, to set an example to the other children.)

A boy who puzzles and infuriates his adoring parents with his need to show off by climbing dangerous rocks.

A boy who has become a little unruly.

And then, suddenly, a boy whose mother has developed an alarming cough.

A boy who, terrified by this cough, and hoping to take some of God's punishment on to himself, has now, at the age of thirteen, taken to extreme naughtiness.

The ship was a whaler *en route* to Hunchburgh, dragging an entire whale skeleton destined for Queen Victoria's wardrobe. I can still see it: the huge vessel lolling slowly out on the ebb tide, dragging the great bobbing stinking creature behind her as she drifts with the tide. And I can still recall the scene the next morning, and the ensuing cries and screams when the whole village realised what had happened: that Tommy Boggs and I, having stolen a file from Mr Boggs' forge, had cut the vessel loose from its moorings. By the time the sailors aboard ship worked out what had happened, and scolded the night watch for falling asleep, they were a league out at sea. It took a whole day to manoeuvre the ship back.

When you grab something, such as the attention of a whole village, you pay for it later. They put us in the village stocks and pelted us with wodges of goose-dung. And then, when the sun went down and we were released, our fathers came to collect us; Mr Boggs angry, and brandishing the metal bottom-whisk, Parson Phelps sorrowful, ashamed, and preoccupied with distressing events at home concerning the cough.

And now it is his turn to punish. I have been called a naughty jackanapes, and sent to my room, and locked in, but I feel safe, my world condensed to the span of this one room. And now I am here, eating stale bread and with only a drop of water left in my pottery bowl, unsure of why it came upon me to perform this act of naughtiness, and wondering whether the recent upheavals in the house – upheavals I have done my best to ignore – could have provoked me into an odd kind of madness.

For the sound of the cough has been getting worse.

If I close my ears and my eyes, time will stand still, and I will be safe.

My room is an attic they have arranged for me at the top of the Parsonage. There's a criss-cross of low beams, ideal for gymnastics, a writing desk, bed, a chair, and a simple rag rug, woven by Mrs Phelps in my favourite colours, mauve and green. And on the wall a picture I love: of Noah and his animals of the Ark. Noah stands on the deck, with his three sons and his nagging wife, and below him is spread the hierarchy of creatures, from mighty elephant down to humble ant. Looking down on them all from the top right-hand corner is the face of an elderly gent whose white beard dissolves into the grey storm-clouds of the Great Flood. Behind his head, a silver Heaven gleams. This is God, who has made us all. I am snuggled into my goose-down quilt, looking at the picture. A sea-beetle has crawled across its canvas surface, and is making its way inexorably towards God's Roman nose.

At last, I hear the rattle of the key in the door, and my father enters, pale-faced. Silently, I pray that he has simply come to punish me some more. But I know in my heart as I look at his drawn features and the set of his eyes that, next to what lurks downstairs, my misdemeanour with Tommy will pale into insignificance.

If I shut my ears and my eyes.

'Your mother is unwell,' he blurts out. 'I should have told you before, but I could not. I hoped that if I ignored it –'

I say nothing.

'Tobias! Did you hear me?'

Then I speak. 'So according to this picture, man's place is between God and the animals.' What I am thinking is that I would like to bring some warmth to his cold face. I notice on the Ark picture that the sea-beetle is now attempting to tunnel its way up God's left nostril, but to no avail. 'Why is that?'

'Why is a big question,' says the Parson, smiling stiffly. 'And it has a big answer. It's because we have souls, and the animals do not.'

'What does a soul look like, Father?' (Downstairs: cough, cough.)

'Well, some are bright and shining, if they are righteous, and others are blackened and shrivelled, if their owners have committed foul acts.' (Cough, cough.)

87

'If you cut up a man's body, would you see his soul?'

'Yes, son, you most assuredly would. It is situated above his heart, where it forms a translucent canopy.'

Later in life, when I had cause to reflect upon the nature of the human soul, I would wonder how Parson Phelps, who was not a stupid man, came to dream up such lunatic twaddle.

Then, from the floor below, the terrible sound comes again. I will remember it for ever. This time it is too loud to ignore. Loud and brutal.

'That is nothing like her usual cough,' I venture.

And he takes me to his breast and holds me tight.

That night I dreamed I was aboard a vessel that was like a whale inside. I was Jonah but a son of Noah, too. My job was to feed the caged beasts that surrounded me – tigers and hippopotami and giant wingless birds – but I could not for I too was caged, and manacled like a slave.

My foster-mother was always good to me. I remember her bent over the stone sink, scaling fish, the plainness of her face, the redness of her hands, rough from heavy work. Or forcing down my throat a new purgative she'd invented to oust our mutual enemy, Mildred. Or standing by the stove, frying barley flip-cakes for my tea. Or at the scrubbed-pine table stripping the perfumed seeds off sprigs of lavender, to stuff into little bags and put in my underwear drawer. The trouble she took to make a fine man of me, knowing how much harder I would have to struggle in life than my contemporaries! She must have known, deep in her soul, as she watched me clambering up the huge oak tree outside the door, my crazy shoes slipping on the bark, that I would one day have dire need of those little civilising touches that make a God-fearing gentleman.

I suspected it myself, too.

My mother's cough could no longer be hidden; we lived with it every day. We saw it doubling her up. Tearfully, one day, she informed me that she had become possessed by a Thing.

'If only I could cough the Thing out,' she said, 'I feel I should recover, Tobias. It is crushing me from within.'

But the Thing stayed put, and grew; every day her breathing became shallower, and her suffering racked the whole house.

At night, I lay in bed watching the sea-salt twinkling on my collection of shells, listening to the cawing of sea-birds above my attic room, and my mother's wild cough coming up from below. It mocked us all. It was like a demon's laugh. I prayed, but a little pang at the base of my spine told me that prayers were no use.

Mother took a whole summer to die; I measured out her wasting in the progress of the vegetable plot which grew lusher and more abundant every day, as though it were a parasite siphoning off her vitality and growing fat on it. And I was a conspirator in this process: for two months I tended the vegetable patch with a fury and an intensity that startled me. I was surely searching for something other than earth, but I never did discover exactly what. We moved my mother's bed to the window, so that she could see me working. The sight of it pleased her, but I felt she was watching me digging her grave.

I was thirteen, that age of reckless physical sprouting and transcendental uncertainty, which provided me with a new cross to bear: a permanent uncouth urge in my loins, which I did my utmost to quell. I worked harder and harder, hoping to exhaust myself thus. As Mrs Phelps drank thin soup, and spluttered into a handkerchief, I planted potatoes, and grew crimson radishes whose furious sting punished the mouth, bulging Cinderella pumpkins, skinny haricot beans, and purple-veined, crinkle-leafed cabbages. While her mind wandered back repeatedly to the goose farm of her girlhood, and to the incompetence of the Parson's male object (it was from her delirious ravings that I caught my first inkling of the human mating process), I killed slugs with sea-salt collected from rockpools, and planted garlic to keep the snails at bay. Autumn came, and as Mrs Phelps lay skeletally dying in her bed, I harvested a bumper crop of sprouts, and carrots as thick as a bull's horn, and an ornamental gourd, knobbled and useless, stippled pale and dark green.

One day she waved her hand at me, summoning me to her bedside. When she spoke, her words were wheezed out like air from a stiff pair of bellows, and her inhalations were winded gasps of pain. I put my ear close to her mouth.

'I love that gourd,' she croaked. 'It is a freakish vegetable, without obvious purpose, but it has its place in our garden. God knew what he was doing when he made the gourd.'

There was a pause, as she breathed in and out a few more times, raspingly. I wished I could breathe for her. But all I could do was watch.

'That gourd, in its oddity, and freakishness, reminds me of you,' she said finally. If this was supposed to be a compliment, it was sadly misjudged, I thought. Oddity? Purposelessness? Freakishness? A gourd? I'd have preferred her to use her precious breath on something a little kinder.

She fell asleep again. It was midnight when she woke up, or seemed to, and sat rigid and suddenly attentive. Then she said, 'Listen to me carefully, Tobias. I have some requests I must make of you before I go to Heaven.'

'Yes, Mother,' I whispered. 'Tell me what you want. And I will do it.'

'Firstly,' she breathed, 'I want you to plant that gourd upon my grave so that I can take the memory of you with me where I go.'

'I will, Mother.' I would have agreed to anything, at any level of absurdity, to make her happy.

'And Tobias,' she croaked. I put my ear to her lips again, to hear. 'I would have liked to purge Mildred,' she mustered. 'Perhaps I tried too hard. When I am gone, do all you can to coax her out, Tobias.'

'I will, Mother. I swear.'

'And Tobias.'

'Yes, Mother?'

'Remember that God does not like a man to be naked.

Keep your body covered at all times, son. For the sake of modesty.'

'Yes, Mother. It goes without saying.' It had always been an unspoken rule in the Parsonage that one should always keep as much clothing on as possible, even when washing. I had never so much as glimpsed myself naked, and would not think of doing so.

'And there is something else,' my mother croaked. 'We do not know where you came from,' she whispered. 'But promise me that you will never visit the Travelling Fair of Danger and Delight.'

The Fair came once a year, and though I had always been forbidden to go, I had longed one day to taste its illicit pleasures. My mother's mention of the Fair – and of my unknown origins – puzzled me. Had my parents not always told me that, unlike other children, who were brought by storks or found beneath gooseberry bushes, I had been left at the altar of St Nicholas's Church by none other than God himself? This was the first time I had thought otherwise, and then and there, a seed of curiosity was planted deep within me.

'Promise me,' my mother repeated.

'I promise,' I told her. *We do not know where you came from.*

'Good boy,' she said, and fell back into a painful twitching doze.

'She wants to be buried beneath a gourd,' I reported to my father the next morning. He had been cleaning his shoes at the kitchen table, waxing them with great care with black wax polish, and buffing them, bashing the brush against the leather in the same particular motion and rhythm that he always used. Now it was his turn to look surprised and pained. I remember him standing there, a buckled shoe in one hand, the little black brush in the other, the smell of black shoe-polish, vinegary and burnt.

'And holding the Bible, of course,' I added quickly. The lie seemed to help.

91

The next day my mother coughed suddenly, and very hard, and the Thing that had been tormenting her shot out of her mouth and on to the white sheet. We stared. My father groaned.

'What is this?' she mouthed faintly, picking up between thumb and forefinger a purple-black object, leather-like and riddled with holes. She held it aloft. 'Look, dear Edward, dear Tobias, I have coughed up my own soul and it is all shrivelled with sin, and as black as night! Forgive me, O Lord!'

Two minutes later she was dead.

The Parson and I did not believe the Thing could be her soul. It was too solid, and it stank. So when the doctor told us it was a cruelly diseased lung, we were enormously relieved.

'For if that poor good woman contained an ounce of evil,' sobbed the Parson, grinding his teeth in sorrow, 'then I contain three thousand tons.'

And I five thousand, I wailed inwardly, thinking of the pleasurable but unholy habit Tommy Boggs had taught me in the privacy of the sand-dunes, and at which I now had considerable and shameful expertise. There was no more talk of translucent canopies after that. We buried my mother in the cemetery beneath a huge mackerel sky, the sea-salt mingling with our tears, the sand-grass prickling our ankles, the kittiwakes squalling, the sea roaring wide as a whale's yawn. The next summer, a gourd plant was to appear on the grave, but the gourds were not of the same variety as the knobbled green one I had planted. These fruits were orange, with a frilled rim, and yellow stains; Parson Phelps said he found them miraculous but disturbing, a sign that God's plan for Nature had veered off course.

As indeed it had.

CHAPTER 9

THE SCRAPIE DINOSAUR

'There will be two world wars,' murmurs the Laudanum Empress, yawning over her untouched cup and saucer. It is the heyday of her psychic particles. 'As a result, a million skulls will be strewn all over France.' She pauses, squinting sideways. 'But on the more positive side, there will be something known as long-life milk.'

Since the birth of her bovine daughter Violet, the particles have not ceased to swarm about her head like a cloud of angry mosquitoes, and the slightest peripheral glance on her part can conjure up a dizzying maelstrom of flotsam from the future. Even Dr Scrapie, a strict non-believer in hocus-pocus, has recognised the presence of the famous particles.

'Pardon?' he says irritably. He hates being interrupted while reading the paper, and this morning he has been engrossed in several articles of interest. A more experimentally inclined scientist might have been inspired to harness the Empress's particles to his research, but Dr Scrapie's imagination is sadly limited. Of what concern is the future to him, he argues, when the present is proving so problematic? The Scrapies are taking breakfast with their daughter Violet. Time has passed, as it does; the child is now sprouting two majestic bosoms.

'There will be heat-seeking missiles, and split-crotch panties,' says the Empress. 'Not to mention a substance called Play-Doh.'

Scrapie grunts, and shuffles his newspaper. She's talking balderdash again. Violet butters some more toast, pours green

Gunpowder tea into bone china, swirls in milk, applies her spectacles and skims an article on a page her father has discarded about how slavery on the American plantations is a cruel and inhuman thing, and must be stopped. She bites into a beef mushroom. All men were born equal, the writer argues. Then a sliced tomato, somewhat underdone for her taste. Rich and poor, Negro and white man. But we must beware of taking things too far. This butter is rancid! Women, for example, might anticipate sharing these equal rights. But if we accept that, as some strident females in our midst are urging, what next? Children? Dogs? Macaws? Woodlice?

'There will be gambling machines called one-armed bandits,' says the Laudanum Empress. 'And artists will display their own excrement in galleries.'

'Pass the marmalade, will you, please?' says Violet, sipping more tea, as she glances at her mother, all madness and beauty and draped shawls and shimmering particles and glistening jet beads.

'Marmalade,' murmurs the Empress. Her heavy-lidded eyes have turned inward again, speaking silent volumes: *Daughter – bother me not, for I am not at home.* Aerial buzzings, automatic writing, Ouija boards, phantom scraps, whisperings and groans from the past and the future; these have been the stuff of Mother's life for as long as Violet can remember. How much is drug-induced, how much the result of insanity, and how much real, Violet has never fathomed; all she knows is that Mother is very much elsewhere, and always will be. Returning to her article on human rights, Violet fails to notice the dish of marmalade levitating itself. Or making slow but efficient progress across the table in her direction, as per her request.

'Do you know,' whispers the Laudanum Empress softly, 'that there will still be beggars on the streets of London in two hundred years' time? Progress is a dangerous myth, I can assure you. If my particles are to be believed, the world is moving not forwards, but backwards. I see men and women dancing and cavorting in the open air half-naked, like savages.

I see a vehicle called the Audi Nuance. I see the entire nation fizzling into extinction!'

'Come along now, Mother,' says Violet briskly, patting the Empress's arm and adjusting her shawl like an invalid's. 'You are getting hysterical again.'

'Hysteria is in the eye of the beholder. Your orange conserve has arrived.'

'Thanks, Mother,' says Violet, as the dish settles itself on the table before her.

The Empress sighs. We see only what we wish to see.

Dr Scrapie shuffles his newspaper. There is an article in it about old maids. Distressed spinsters. Their financial cost to the family. Their social status. Their general undesirability. As he observes his daughter Violet consuming her usual gargantuan breakfast, a terrible note of doom strikes within the heart of Dr Ivanhoe Scrapie, and shudders there for several minutes.

'According to this newspaper article, a girl like Violet will never marry,' he announces bleakly.

'I don't trust the word *never*,' declares Mrs Scrapie. 'Especially in print. My spirits say that Violet's actually in with a chance.'

'No,' says Scrapie firmly. 'Impossible. Never in a thousand years. Just look at her. She'll never marry because she's *completely unmarriageable!*'

'Good,' thinks Violet, dusting toast-crumbs from her two newish breasts. 'That's one thing Father and I *can* agree on.'

Violet is opposed to marriage – or rather, to the act of union it legitimises. It was only last week that she witnessed Jacques-Yves Cabillaud coitally occupied in the chopping room with Maisie, the scullery maid from next door. She shudders as the scene revisits her: Maisie is crouched on the chopping-table, her skirt over her head, an apple in her mouth like a stuck pig. Cabillaud rocks behind her, as if he is steering a boat, his face wild and throttled.

'Water will cost more than wine,' the Empress is droning.

95

'And there will be a Millennial flood that rains down poison!'

Violet sighs, as the Empress's wretched particles spew forth their usual crazed concoctions, relayed by the channel of her vocal cords. 'A cobweb of misinformation and gossip will buzz all over the world like an aura,' she continues, 'but it will be corrupted by a giant lunatic headache, and sink into mist.'

'She'll never marry because she is a dinosaur,' says Ivanhoe Scrapie, ignoring his wife and expanding angrily on his old-maid theme, fuelled by the spinster article in *The Times*. 'Look, Charlotte. Observe the quantities. She eats as much as a bloody dinosaur.'

Mrs Scrapie jerks out of her trance of future particles and gives a faint smile of acknowledgement.

'Did that man over there say something?' she questions vaguely. Her voice is slurred. Scrapie rustles his newspaper angrily; there's another article here that's getting his goat, concerning a newly recycled zoological rumour that's doing the rounds. Meanwhile Violet remains silent: it's impolite to speak with your mouth full. Besides, she agrees with her father. She *is* like a dinosaur, in that she is developing a thick skin.

'It's what's inside that matters, Father,' she grunts, finally, wiping her mouth on a napkin and patting her satisfied stomach. Her celebration of the alimentary canal, aided and abetted by Cabillaud, has given her a wisdom beyond her years.

A wisdom, and a certain kind of odd grace.

Don't laugh: despite the uncooked-pastry aspect of her face, and her somewhat buck teeth, which render her not a *traditional* beauty, she has grace, and there's no explaining it. You either do or you don't. All sorts of things can be embedded in fat. Grace is one of them.

Violet, under the auspices of Jacques-Yves Cabillaud, has been continuing to expand her childish girth. At two she had already been pronounced a heffalump; by seven, she was the size and shape of a barrel. And now –

'Why do her very expensive dresses always manage to look

like an old rug thrown over a milking cow?' the Empress murmurs, sipping her laudanum.

But yet – deep down, deep, deep within, there is grace.

'I said a *dinosaur*,' repeats Dr Scrapie, returning to the subject of spinsters and society.

'Yes, dear,' murmurs the Empress, whose particles are now receiving some unusual signals from the ghostly and unappetising future, concerning freeze-dried coffee granules. 'A dinosaur. That's what you said.'

Dinosaurs were the talk of the town; the terrible lizard had the educated world a-jitter with excitement. Bones of these lumbering and monstrous creatures had recently been discovered in the chalk soil of Lyme Regis, and fossilised dragons had been unearthed in China. A new and frightening light was being shed on the makings and doings of the earth. Minds boggled. Dr Scrapie had attended a banquet in Crystal Palace, inside a concrete replica of the iguanodon, where afterwards, in a japonica bush, he had come across a set of false teeth stuck in a meringue. The incident had marked him. Meanwhile a Czech monk called Gregor Mendel had made some alarming discoveries about reproduction in peas, which might or might not disprove the existence of God, and there were rumours that Darwin's *Beagle* voyage, on which his own chef Cabillaud claimed to have been a crew-member, had gathered enough zoological information to challenge the Creation story itself! Furthermore, in this morning's *Times*, Dr Scrapie has just read that Lamarck's Theory – that it is possible for a child to inherit characteristics acquired during its parents' lifetime, such as a liking for mulligatawny soup, or an ability to play scales upon the pianoforte – is once again being resurrected, and that as a result (oh foolish clowns!) London is now rife with allegations that, as of tomorrow, if a man lost an eye, his son would be born a cyclops like the porcupine in the Zoological Museum's Abnormality Annexe.

'Tosh!' Scrapie now yells, having finished the article, and flinging down *The Times*. 'I stuffed that porcupine myself! Its

97

father was completely normal, and I have the paperwork to prove it! It's all a pack of bloody lies!'

'That's where you are wrong,' says the Empress languidly. 'There's something in the air. I can feel it wafting past me.'

Violet, future distressed spinster, butters yet more toast with a practised hand.

'But these gaps in the fossil record,' muses Scrapie. 'There's no explaining them. It's not enough for Darwin to say that they will be *filled* one day, that the geologists of the future will *find the missing pieces*. We want to know the answers *now*, dammit!'

'They will never find them,' says the Empress suddenly, and sharply. 'The gaps will remain just that, Ivanhoe: gaps. I've seen it. They are evidence of sudden, rapid changes. Transformations. There is . . .' but here she trails off.

Scrapie lights a noxious Havana cigar, and the Empress sinks back into her cloud of particles, which is now exhibiting the collapse of the worldwide Web.

'A bloody dinosaur,' repeats Scrapie, his glance once again scaling the human Himalaya that is his youngest child and twiddling his pencil over a diagram he is working on. He is having a table made out of fossilised dinosaur turds, sliced through and arranged in a mosaic pattern.

I am the child of mad people, reflects Violet Scrapie, scribbling a note of the ingredients for this evening's dinner on the table-cloth.

'Tell me about the Gentleman Monkey, Father,' she says. 'Cabillaud and I are planning to stew its flesh tonight. With coriander and a rather unusual shrimp sauce.'

Over the years, thanks to the imaginative genius of Jacques-Yves Cabillaud, the willingness of Violet, and the ready availability of exotic animal carcasses, the Scrapie diet has grown ever more refined, audacious and splendid. Violet has learned how to baste and pickle and stuff and jelly and devil, and to make forty-five different kinds of pastry. She has also thrown herself wholeheartedly into the waste-not-want-not philosophy of *Cuisine Zoologique*. By the time the second shipment of Arctic ice arrived for the ice house, she and Cabillaud had prepared material for the first three chapters of Cabillaud's book, *Cuisine Zoologique: une philosophie de la viande*. Cabillaud would cast his mind back to Brussels and remember dishes he had seen through the windows of restaurants, or smelt wafting from beneath the doors of imaginary châteaux, castles of air. Reminiscing and imagining, he would describe and then re-formulate, and together with his young assistant, concoct recipes that grew increasingly unusual. Cabillaud was particularly inventive when it came to sauces – so much so, Mrs Scrapie had the nerve to complain in one of her more practical moments, that one was never sure what kind of meat or fish one was actually eating, so drowning was it in an artful mix of flavours. By now he and Violet had invented successful recipes for a variety of creatures salvaged from Trapp's *Ark*. They had eaten zebra and boa constrictor and walrus, experimented with mongoose and emu and Goan lizard, partaken of tiger, and conjured up budgerigar mousse *à la Grécque*. And tonight they are planning to cook another primate carcass – the umpteenth casualty of the Trapp *Ark* débâcle. It is in the chopping room at this very moment, defrosting after its years of residency in the bosom of the Arctic iceberg.

Violet sips more tea. 'I said the Gentleman Monkey, Father.'

'Oh him. Yes. Fascinating creature,' replies Scrapie, pleased that his daughter is finally taking an interest. 'Quite strikingly human in appearance. Almost shocking. I'm working on him today. The Hippo wants him as a bloody towel-holder for the ladies' powder room in the banqueting suite, so I've done an armature with an elbow bent crooked, so they can hang the towels off that.'

'But I thought it was part of the Animal Kingdom Collection,' objects Violet. 'Aren't they all supposed to be stuffed in positions of prayer?'

'Mostly, yes. But she's taken a liking to the primates. She doesn't want them in the Museum, she says. She wants them dressed more like servants, helping out at the Palace. You know.'

Violet nods. She gets the idea. She finds it mildly unsettling – like the article in the newspaper – but cannot identify why.

'He's animal number three thousand and eight, if I recall,' Scrapie is sighing. 'You can come and have a look if you like. He's not finished, but it'll give you some idea. Good specimen. The last in the world, apparently. From a Moroccan menagerie, originally, according to the paperwork, such as it is. Trapp got about all right. Do you realise, he followed the same course as the *Beagle* in that old slave tub of his?'

'He went all the way to Australia?'

'He most certainly did. No wonder it took him so long. He went bloody well everywhere. South America, the Galápagos, Mauritius, Tasmania, North Africa, South Africa – bloody lunatic. If that man was ever a naturalist, then I'm a pink-footed goose.'

'How exactly did he die, Father?' asks Violet.

The chef, Cabillaud, has told her the story of the human head a thousand times. How, on the day of her birth, he had boarded Trapp's *Ark* with Scrapie to examine the damage, and stumbled over a rolling, rotting thing that had once been attached to a human body. How Scrapie had squatted down and stared into what remained of its face, and recognised Trapp. How he and the equerry had both rushed out on deck to be sick, while Violet's father had remained level-headed and iron-stomached enough to report Trapp's murder to the Royal Hippopotamus in the same breath as ordering a ton of Arctic ice.

'Nobody knows,' returns Scrapie darkly, recalling the same scene. Trapp's bruised and broken face, caked with blood and filth, a ghastly ball of gristle with a human brain within, is an image that he, too, has found it hard to dispel over the years.

'They never found the rest of him,' he said finally. 'And the crew had all disappeared. Higgins, Steed, and Bowker; they were gone, too. Along with the lifeboats. They say there was a woman, too. A ballerina. Quite a mystery.'

100

For a moment Scrapie sits there silently, brooding on the doomed expedition. Then he snaps out of his dark reverie. 'Come up to the workshop after lunch and I'll introduce you to the monkey.'

Violet stifles a burp. 'Thank you, Father.' It is important to know what one is eating.

'And people will one day have mechanical hearts implanted by a surgeon operating through a keyhole,' warns the Empress, reaching for her medicine bottle with a fluttering hand. Dr Scrapie rolls his eyes Heavenward.

Trapp wuz givin me a job, the woman wrote. *I wuz His mistris and His dancer. Big house, and He giv me munnie. Gents cumin and goin. I DANCIS for them wen E sez. I dont see nufin at first, cos most of the dors is LOKD, but I herd stuff at nite. Screems, LARFIN, Trapp and gents havin there way wiv girls. I lys in bed and I crys one nite. Trapp cums in. He is the wors for DRINK. But insted of hitin me He sez He LUVS me, and taks me in His arms. Dont no wy, but my will is gon. Ther is somthin you must do for me, He sez. Wot, I say. E shows me a big emptie CAGE.*

CHAPTER 10

IN WHICH THE
ROGUE MALE SEARCHES
FOR A MATE

The first client at my new surgery was a bloke called Sequin, who thought his border collie might be gay. It didn't bode well, I thought. Overnight, people seemed to have become more morose, introverted, and prone to obsession. The whole country was succumbing to a kind of mourning process after the bomb at the Egg Bank. No one could seem to see the wood for the trees.

'I prescribe a holiday for Chum-Boy, Mr Sequin,' I said. 'Get him out and about a bit. Take him to a national park and play fetch. It might do *you* some good as well.' He skulked off, looking doubtful.

I'd stayed in the Stoned Crow the first week, then set up shop in the surgery of my predecessor on Crawpy Street. The house was attached: a small cottage overlooking the River Flid. Norman Ball told me that a few years back, the Flid had won the Pollution Challenge Award (north-east section), but looking at it now, you got the sense that it was no longer a contender. From time to time, Norman warned me, it would bear a batch of foamy-scummed fish, which he referred to as 'eels flottantes'. There was a chemical factory at Fishforth, fifty miles upstream, specialising in detergents. Sometimes the water frothed violet, like something in an extravagant technicolour cartoon. It didn't really matter any more, how much we screwed up the earth, I thought. Or at least our part of it. The rest of Europe will probably use the whole island as a nuclear dumping ground, once we're gone. And who can blame them? Strange, but the fertility thing hadn't bothered me till now. In fact, I'd felt quite cavalier about it.

I didn't any more. I felt strangely coshed. I kept thinking: I wish I'd been born in the good old days. I wish I'd been alive before Elvis died. I wish I could've seen him perform on stage, just once, in the flesh. I'd have been one of those fans that tried to catch some of the sweat that flew off him, to keep in a little bottle. Try capturing *that* virtually. I wish –

Oh well. As Norman said: life must go on. What would Elvis have done? He'd have rocked around the clock, that's what.

But no matter how loud I played my virtual concerts, I couldn't quite get in the mood.

I reckon urban man must have evolved lungs that needed a certain degree of environmental contamination: I experienced positive withdrawal symptoms during my first week in Thunder Spit, and felt quite nostalgic when I caught a whiff of exhaust. The air, as well as being cleaner than in Tooting Bec, was a couple of degrees colder, and it took my nose a while to detect any smells at all. But when I did, they were pleasant enough: wood-smoke, fresh tarmac, the salt wind. I still hadn't actually clapped eyes on the sea. The concrete barrier that hid it had been erected, Norman told me, in the 1980s, when they'd done the rationalisation project. Before the land reclamation, Thunder Spit had been prone to flooding: back in the nineteenth century, the water had sometimes come in as far as the church. He said if I looked hard, I'd see the water-line at the back of the pulpit, but I said I'd take his word for it. I'm not into history. After I'd made the first round of phone calls and goodwill visits to a few local farmers – Ron Harcourt, Billy Clegg, Charlie Peat-Hove – I felt I had the measure of the place. It was turning out to be an easy locum. I'd heard rumours about my predecessor; phoney BSE certifications and kickbacks, among other things. He couldn't be a hard act to follow. If the cuddly stuff – domestic pets like Giselle – had represented a form of chaos, then farm livestock represented the opposite: here were working creatures with a pre-determined lifespan who paid their keep by ending up as

103

leather or meat, and producing milk and eggs in their lifetime; functional beings you could respect, not the slaves-cum-mental-health workers that urban domestic pets had become, sad breeds of prostitute for the lonely and confused human. From now on the budgie-neutering would be restricted to the population of one town. As bad luck would have it, I had to perform an operation on an Indonesian iguana belonging to a little girl – the daughter of some Healthplan bigwig called Baldicoot – on day two, but I put out word in the pub that Buck de Savile was more into the rugged outdoor stuff. It fitted his image, I reckoned. And sure enough, when I visited the farm of the silent Johnny Peat-Hove, I found that I liked pigs. Visiting the squint-eyed Mr Lumpey over at Hawthorn Farm, I discovered I liked the Lord Chief Justice sheep, too – even though, disappointingly, their only difference from ordinary sheep turned out to be a diminished brain capacity and a tendency to fight. I saw to Mrs Harcourt's addle-brained chickens, which kept drinking from the slurry lagoon and poisoning themselves, and prescribed Narcomorph – a mild hallucinogen with healing properties – for Mrs Clegg's disturbed foal.

Despite my overall *Weltschmerz* – this was the big buzz word to describe the current national mood since the Egg Bank exploded – I felt pleased with myself on a practical level. Within a week, I'd crossed the first two items off the mental list I'd written that first night in the Stoned Crow. Only one remained.

It was in the unromantic setting of the hypermarket in Judlow that I first clapped eyes on the girls. When I first saw Rose, or was it Blanche, I remembered item number three: get laid. Then I spotted the other one, and invented a new item. Number four: get laid again.

I was near the checkout, where a huge sign flapped: BUY THE SAUSAGE AND ONION LATTICE PIE, GET THE COLE-SLAW FREE! I was conscious of dithering about which queue to join, aware that there was a petite, attractive, rusty-haired girl on each. They stirred a strange feeling of recognition in me, though I couldn't have put my finger on who or what it was they reminded me of.

You see, I didn't notice, at first, that the girls were identical, and that they were actually reminding me of *each other.* To my eye, all checkout girls, frankly, are much of a muchness, insofar as women tend to break down into a few basic but useful categories: young and attractive, old and attractive, young and unattractive, mother-type (drunk: avoid!), Holly-type (betraying: avoid!), available, unavailable, et cetera. These categories could all be subsumed into two broader sets, if you were in a hurry: the shaggable and the unshaggable. These two, despite their rather charmless orange-and-white chequered uniforms, were eminently shaggable, so here I was, torn between two checkouts. The shopper nudging at my back with a chariot of wire decided me, and I veered towards Blanche with my mesh basket of essentials: margarine, razor blades, frozen dinners, cans of lager, crisps, ice-cream, socks – a basket which I reckon should have yelled out Buck de Savile's eligible bachelorhood without him having to say a word.

I strewed my consumer items on the conveyor belt with manly assurance. But reaction came there none. Blanche didn't even look up. So feebly, I tried to make conversation ('Wanted to buy that pie, you know, the sausage and onion lattice one, but couldn't find the coleslaw'), but she ignored me. Like her sister, she was in a round-eyed trance. As I was paying, I had another stab at it ('Do you take Visa, darling?'), but she barely reacted to my presence. When I'd finished loading my carrier bag, I turned to have another look at Blanche, and saw she had switched checkouts. She'd been on number nineteen. Now she was on number twenty. Except that when I looked at nineteen, I saw her again. I looked carefully again at both of them. Scrutinised them thoroughly. No, not double vision, I suddenly realised. Identical twins!

It was then that I remembered something. Norman had twin girls, didn't he? Double Trouble, he called them. Or the

Gruesome Twosome, or Two Peas in a Pod, or Tweedles Dum and Dee.

I stood there with my two shopping bags, just staring first at one, and then the other. They still didn't notice me. The hypermarket was busy, and I was impressed with the deftness of their movements as they weighed plastic bags of fruit on their electronic scales, whisked the bar-codes over the infra-red, and dealt with credit cards and loyalty vouchers. It intrigued me, the way their hands could be so busy when you could tell that their minds were blank.

On the way home, I couldn't stop thinking about them. And that night they must have crept into my dreams, because by the following morning, they were under my skin, like an itch.

As Buck de Savile, formerly Bobby Sullivan, spiritual son of Elvis, busies himself with his veterinary tasks and worries away at his desire, the two young women who are causing his pleasurable discomfort are now sitting on bar-stools in the Pig and Whistle in Hunchburgh. Rose and Blanche Ball, conceived of a single bifurcated egg and born on Midsummer's Day, 1985, more or less simultaneously by Caesarean section to Abbie Ball, née Boggs, home economics and French teacher, are enjoying a glass of Liebfraumilch, which their personal tutor Dr Bugrov has told them means 'the breast-milk of spinster virgins'.

'Cheers,' says Rose.

'Here's to the end of the world as we know it,' adds Blanche grimly. The *Weltschmertz* thing has hit them both hard; like all girls their age, their names have been on the Egg Bank waiting list since the beginning. Norman and Abbie hadn't wasted a moment getting them enrolled. Fat lot of good *that's* turned out to be. Oh well. They've earned a hundred Euros this morning.

'I'm a lucky man,' smiles Dr Bugrov, with the smile of a man who knows about cash well spent.

'And we're lucky girls,' says Rose, smiling sweetly at the balding professor, while her sister takes advantage of his back being turned on her to waggle two fingers at her throat in a being-sick gesture. Rose sniggers.

In the beginning, the man who is now their genealogy teacher had been a bit of a long shot, a lonely old git they'd taken pity on in the cinema queue because it had been a day or two since they'd had any excitement in their lives. Dr Bugrov – 'Call me Sergei,' he'd insisted, but they couldn't – had proved a disappointment, and not worth the gamble, until he came up with an unexpected proposal, in the form of cash. A hundred Euros to do it regularly; say, once a week? They didn't dislike him. His accent was quite sexy if you shut your eyes. And he'd been intelligent and practical enough to recognise straight off that they weren't going to do it again for free. After a few sessions, he had offered to throw in genealogy, too, as a bonus.

'Like a Loyalty voucher?' asked Rose as they lay in bed doing special studies.

'Like two Loyalty vouchers, my dears,' Bugrov had smiled, squeezing Blanche's tit. 'I'm in charge of a module.'

The whole enterprise had seemed like a reasonable idea, since they were always short of money, and Dad had been saying he may be sticking his neck out here, gals, but wasn't it time they got themselves some gainful employment, instead of forever scrounging off the state? What's more, Dr Bugrov led them to believe that genealogy could lead to financial self-sufficiency – wealth, even. Now that the whole of the British race was headed for extinction, everyone was looking backwards, rather than forwards, he told them. Ever since the bomb at the Egg Bank had hammered the last nail in the coffin of the British, the whole nation had gone ape-shit. Everybody was in shock. The crisis lines were jammed solid, the worldwide Web was overloaded, all flights out of the country were fully booked.

A side-product of this madness, Bugrov predicted, was that there would suddenly be millions of gullible Americans wanting to trace their roots, before those roots completely shrivelled. Enter the twins.

'You could set up a service,' Dr Bugrov advised them. 'Once

107

you have your diploma. You offer to trace their families. You produce a brochure. Three hundred Euros per generation for the first three generations, then four hundred Euros per generation after that. Anything they don't like, history of madness, criminality, sex changes – you offer to doctor it for a surcharge.'

They had liked the idea of a weekly 'grant packet' from Dr Bugrov, who was indeed connected, in some tangential way, to Hunchburgh University's Department of Human Sciences. He was fifty, and he always smoked a pipe of Three Nuns after sex. Like many of the men captivated by Rose and Blanche, he was excited by the idea of two women catering to his sexual whims simultaneously. And intrigued by the way that when one of them climaxed, the other would, too, as though by proxy. It was telepathy, they explained. Everything was interchangeable, with them. Plus they had a strong natural urge. 'We're animals,' they purred sexily. And then spoilt it by sniggering. But Dr Bugrov wasn't complaining. Like many before him, he would lie back and close his eyes and feel their hands creeping over him – Rose's right, Blanche's left – and imagine it was just one woman doing all this to him, an octopus-woman who could kiss him on the mouth and suck him off at the same time. Sometimes he didn't even want to do it, but just lie there and stroke their four bored tits and reminisce about academic politics, departmental meetings he had attended, and witty ripostes he claimed he had made to deans of this or that institute of higher learning in Britain or America – ripostes so heavily overwrought that it was clear even to Rose and Blanche that they were only remarks he wished he had made, dreamed up years later when nursing the ancient wounds of missed opportunity.

They'd wash the Three Nuns out of their hair afterwards, and spend the grant money on the usual things: depilatory creams, leg-waxes, or electrolysis.

Heigh ho. They knew all about unwanted heredity, thank you very much. Witness the hair problem that they battled with on a daily basis, and the toe thing they had. Thank God for those new elasticated trainers that were all the rage for pets. Shoes had been quite a headache, till then.

'More Liebfraumilch, my dears?' offers Bugrov. He pronounces it elaborately, stressing the *ch* ending.

'We wouldn't say no,' says Rose.

'In fact we'd say yes,' asserts Blanche.

They are twenty years old, and they have the world at their slightly deformed feet, and they know it. Nobody can take that away from them.

'And some soya balls,' adds Rose.

'Here's a pink one,' the obstetric surgeon had said when the girls were born, holding up a screaming female baby by the ankle with his left hand. At which point, according to family legend, Abbie murmured in French, 'Rose.'

'And here,' announced the surgeon, wielding a second baby in his right hand, 'is a white one.'

'Blanche,' croaked Abbie, and fainted, thinking the baby was dead, because she was so pale and uttered no sound. And from that day, it was always Rose who spoke first of the two.

Blanche didn't stay white and Rose didn't stay pink: the colours melded until they were both equal parts peaches and cream beneath a down of coarse body hair that was to be the cross they bore through life, requiring leg-waxes once a week and extensive electrolysis. Blanche and Rose, beloved twin daughters of Abbie and Norman Ball, citizens of Thunder Spit, England and the world. Marital status: single, but looking! Blanche and Rose, who grew from rock-climbing tomboys into nubile teenagers, who were attractive in a wild, buck-toothed, unclassical sort of way, who had, after leaving school and maturing physically, been to secretarial college and who now worked Saturdays on adjoining checkout tills in the hypermart in Judlow, who kept their socks on during sex so that no one should see their embarrassing feet, who were identical except that Rose always spoke first and was right-handed, while Blanche always spoke second and was left-handed; and

109

who now, in the Pig and Whistle, are watching the elderly Dr Bugrov ordering more Liebfraumilch and soya balls from the bar.

'Oh, and some calorie-free peanuts, please!' Rose yells across.

'Boring old fart,' mutters Rose, as Bugrov returns bearing brimming glasses of spinster virgins' breast-milk, and crackling half a dozen packets of nuts, and plonks himself between the girls. He is basking in pleasure. And who wouldn't be, with beauty to the right, more beauty to the left, a morning of sexual gratification behind him, and more just like it ahead if he can only get to the cash machine?

'Here, look, there's going to be a reward,' says Rose. She has chosen her CD track from the juke-box terminal at their table and is now flicking through the Internet news pages. 'Five million Euros for the first British pregnancy!'

'What?' says Blanche, grabbing the mouse. 'That'll get things moving again,' she predicts, scanning through.

'How d'you prove it's British, and not foreign?' asks Rose.

Blanche reads some more. 'Cos it has to be born in Britain. Look, read the details,' she says, handing over the mouse. 'Nothing's born in this country any more. Look at Harcourt's Filipina. He paid a fortune to have her sent over, and she hasn't produced doodly squat.'

'It's a blasted heath, this nation,' muses Dr Bugrov, pulling out his reading glasses and peering at the news on the screen. 'Your culture has died and now you are dying, too. Money is not going to fix it.'

Rose darts him a sharp look. 'It fixes some things, though, doesn't it, Dr Bugrov?'

A pause, as Dr Bugrov pretends to be more deaf than he is, and fights to open a packet of peanuts.

'We need a new bloke,' murmurs Blanche, reading her sister's mind. Dr Bugrov looks up. There is no disguising the pained look on his face.

'Some young blood,' agrees Rose pointedly, just loud enough for him to hear.

Time, perhaps, to cash in those Loyalty vouchers?
The twins look at each other.
Yes. A new man.
Now where on God's earth are they going to find *that*?

CHAPTER 11

THE FLOOD

'Now, Tobias. What can a squid do?'

'Shoot ink to a trajectory of fifteen feet, Father.'

'Describe an isosceles triangle.'

'Two sides the same length, one not.'

It is a December evening, and I am studying at home, at the kitchen table, with my father. My education had been haphazard since the age of ten, at which age the local school washed its hands of children. The other boys began work on the fishing boats then, or on their fathers' farms, or in Tommy's case, at the forge, but I remained at home, at the mercy of my Father's well-intentioned but scatter-gun pedagogical techniques. We would do mathematical puzzles, and he would order me to memorise maps of the world and parts of the Bible, and I read daily from Hanker's *World History*, which ended in 1666 with the Great Fire of London.

'Has the mystery of the *Marie Celeste* ever been solved?'

'No, Father.' I look out of the window: the sky is suddenly turning black.

'Pay attention, Tobias. Can you name the parts of a flower?'

'Petals-fruit-stamen-pollen-stalk.'

'What did Donne say?'

' "No man is an island." '

'Good boy,' said my father, himself now glancing worriedly out at the yellow pall which hung over the sea. 'That colour bodes ill,' he announced. 'Now clean your quill and put away the ink. Class dismissed.'

An hour later the River Flid gurgled ominously, there was a restlessness among the cows, and Farmer Harcourt found the milk had curdled to cheese in their udders. The goats, bleating in their panicky way, and craving shelter, made lunatic compasses of their tethering-posts. The sheep huddled in groups, scattered across the land like fallen clouds. The women herded the beasts off the promontory, and into fields in Judlow belonging to relatives of the Peat-Hoves and the Morpitons.

'Close all the windows,' commanded my father. 'And then go and spread a horse-rug on your mother's grave.'

I went about this and other duties; by mid-afternoon, a threatening mass of foggy air, gun-grey, had congealed on the horizon, the wind had grown heavy and dank, and the herring gulls became self-destructive and reckless and infanticidal, tearing their own nests from the cliff-face and sending the eggs hurtling down to smash on the grey rocks below, streaking them with yellow. After the gulls' display of panic-induced violence, it was apparent that this year, God's wrath was going to be mighty indeed. The sky stayed black. When the clocks said it was night – though no stars appeared and only a thin rind of moon hung in the blackness – the villagers loaded themselves and their belongings on to boats, and sailed to Judlow.

But Parson Phelps and I stayed, along with a scattering of men – Bark men, Hayter men, Balls and Tobashes – who were determined to defend their homes, come what may.

'We are remaining here,' Parson Phelps said, 'because it is God's will.'

And the Lord's word, as usual, was final.

'But –' I faltered.

'God objects to the word *but*, with a great intensity,' Parson Phelps warned. He was intimate with God's opinions about vocabulary, as they were uncannily congruent with his own. 'We shall not abandon the church!' He thundered this at me as though I were Satan trying to drag him bodily away. The wind was banging at the windowpanes of the Parsonage, like the Devil himself knocking.

113

'But God can surely fend for himself,' I argued. 'He is omni-present and omnipotent, and everlasting, Father – but we are mortal! We cannot even swim! The church is just a building! It's *people* that matter!' My tapeworm Mildred appeared to agree with me on this issue, for she was giving me holy hell as I spoke and turning my bowels to water.

'There are other people staying, too,' my father replied. 'They are my parishioners. My flock. How can I leave them?'

'Because they all own boats, and we do not!' I answered. But he turned his deaf ear on me, and when I pursued it further, he cast me aside and pointed in the direction of the harbour, where the fishing boats were being loaded with passengers anxious to leave.

'So go, then!' he shouted, so that my ears hurt. 'Leave your father to the mercy of God, and to the flood-water that riseth!' But I couldn't leave him, mutinous sphincter or no.

Outside, the lightning cracked and the thunder rolled in a sky of a dingy and malicious purple hue. But it was only when the rising sea-water began to insinuate itself beneath the oak door of the Parsonage that we wrapped ourselves in oilskins and left our home; I with a sinking feeling of dread, my father swept along by the frightening tidal wave of his own faith. Carrying an ember from the dying fire with us in a puffball, we stumbled past the wind-whipped trees and through the flattened bracken to the church. Here we made our camp; first by the altar, where fourteen years earlier the Parson had mistaken me for a piglet, and then, as the water rose, to the pulpit. We watched as the waves sloshed beneath the door and swished up the aisle. I remember the sight of Parson Phelps, as he stood in the pulpit like Canute, his hand willing the flood to abate. But despite the force of his will and his character, it did not, and the level of the water continued to creep ever upward. We stayed there all day and all night, drinking from a hip-flask of rum and eating raw the stray sardines that slapped on to the pulpit. At first, my father would only allow us to burn two candles at a time.

'One for light, and one for heat,' he explained solemnly.

On the second day, it was just one. By evening, the last candle guttered and died, and we just had a thin impression of daylight though the stained-glass window by day, and by night, the ghostly, fungal phosphorescence of plankton in the nave.

It was here, over the course of those three days and three nights that my father chose to tell me about the world. Sometimes I would ask a question. But mostly, he just talked. It was cold enough to freeze a toad, and mostly dark, and looking back, I realise that it was his passion for life, combined with the rum, that kept both our hearts from stopping. Every article that he had read in *The Times* over the past quarter of a century was now being hauled up from the vast archive of his memory and filtered through the prism of his faith until it formed clear shafts of light by which I might see God's truth; I remember that I listened gratefully and attentively, and that for the three days that we were to live in the besieged church, my father kept us both alive with alcohol and with the earnest and fortifying bagpipes of his informed discourse, while I made paper boats from the pages of a collapsed hymn-book and sent them bobbing across the water in search of land and safety.

As the waves slapped at our ankles in the pulpit, he told me about the Monarchy and the hierarchies of the Kingdom in which we lived, starting at the top with Her Majesty and working down the ladder through dukes and archdeacons and Sir Thises and Sir Thats, as laid down through the ages, down to humble us, Parson Phelps and Master Phelps his son. As we heard the wind screaming around the church spire, and the rusty weather-vane spinning wildly on its axis, he spoke about a man, Cromwell, who in history had once attempted to overthrow the Monarchy. An ugly man with warts on his face, and a wart for a heart, said my father. He told me, too, as we rescued an exhausted cormorant, about the heinous slave trade in America, and the slave-traders who had pillaged Africa for its manhood and shipped the poor savages half-dying to labour in the sugar plantations so that vainglorious trollops in London

115

could sweeten their cakes, as if honest honey from the noble bee wasn't good enough for them. And as dawn broke on the second day, about happier things: the invention of the hot-air balloon by a Frenchman, Montgolfier, and about the conquest of the Empire, and the conversion of millions of native savages who, were it not for Queen Victoria, would still be hopping around worshipping baboons and practising cannibalism. That night he told me about Galileo and his charting of the planetary system, which had once been seen as heretical, but was now an accepted truth. He named the Planets for me, and though we couldn't see the stars through the stained-glass window, he described them to me, and even now, when I look at the constellations, I remember his words. ('Three fingers to the right of the Plough . . . a little southerly from the North Star . . . draw a diagonal line directly left of the Milky Way and you will discover . . .') He waited till dark to inform me, in a vigorous but incomprehensible way, with many praise-thees and therefores, about the reproductive process, as enacted by a type of Highland cattle not seen in this part of the world. He made no mention of the human equivalent, and I dared not ask. Nor did he mention the adder in his knickerbockers which had prevented him from pleasuring his wife – but he reminded me, in the anonymity of darkness, of the brimstone and hellfire that would come raining down on me and strike me blind if I were to practise the deadly vice of onanism. On the third dawn he told me the history of the sea-storm in 1822 in which three boats capsized, killing fifteen fishermen from two families in one fell swoop, and of how Mrs Firth's idiot cousin Joan came to live with her, having been hounded out of Judlow accused of being a witch, after she had vomited on the floor and the regurgitated stew created a puddle in the shape of a five-legged sea-monster, complete with horns.

Then he told me, not for the first time, that no man was an island. It was a favourite theme of his.

'"No man is an island, entire of itself!"' he thundered.

'– self, elf, elf, elf!' his voice echoed in the dark rafters.

116

(Ironically enough, during this evocation of Donne's topological conceit, we were now actually marooned on the very geographical feature in question. Though we did not know it, the peninsula had been cut off from the mainland, turning our speck of land into a small and threatened oval, like the back of an engulfed spoon.)

'Every man is a piece of the continent, a part of the main!'

'– main-ain-ain-ain!' the church replied.

It was at that moment that the pulpit broke, and we fell into the water.

I recall little of what immediately preceded my holy vision: only that I saw a jellyfish wobble past me, its trailing skirt a-jingle with tiny bubbles. That a herring collided with my nose. That a crab pinched my finger. That for a moment my floundering sent me bobbing up to the surface, where my father floated serenely, turning slowly in a whirlpool, his cassock expanded around him like a big bubble of faith.

That he announced, 'Have courage! The Lord has seen fit to challenge us, Tobias, and we shall rise to His command!' And that then, instead of rising, I sank like a stone beneath the surface.

And here, deep in the freezing waters of the flood, I met an Angel.

It is said that a dying man sees his life pass before him in the form of a small morality play, so that when he reaches St Peter's Gate, he may humbly accept whatever direction the saint commands him to follow. This thought only came to me much later, as an explanation for what I experienced while I drowned.

The Angel before me is beautiful, and I love her instantly.

She is dressed like a ballerina, in a white garment with a skirt of stiff fabric sticking out horizontally from her waist, and white stockings on her small legs. Her wings must be folded behind her, or perhaps they are transparent as gossamer, for I do not see them. Her face is pale, and in her dark hair she

117

wears a band of gold. A stream of silver bubbles pours from her mouth.

Sunlight is streaming in on us from somewhere high above. The Angel smiles at me. In the background, I hear people laughing and cheering. I am in a golden cot, with bars. A huge bristle-haired animal is on the other side. Its snout is soft, its eyes are ochre-orange, the irises vertical slits. I hear a high, grating song in my head, like a distant echo of something long gone.

> *Rock-a-bye-baby, on the tree top,*
> *When the wind blows, the cradle will rock . . .*

'O Lord do not take him from me, I beg you!' a man's voice is crying. It is far away, as distant as the moon. 'Hold on!' yells Parson Phelps, louder this time. My Angel trembles, like a reflection in a pool. Then something grabs me and yanks me upwards with a wrenching pain. I break the surface and scream, and the water takes me again, this time to Hell, where I see –

Other things. A cage. Teeth. Blood. The Angel, screaming. Broken glass.

And worse.

My father was slapping my face, hard. The water sloshed about us.

'Now wake, Tobias! Wake up!' And he slapped me again. 'Wake-up-up-up-up!' echoed the church. The vision of Hell disappeared in a flash, and only the swirling waters remained.

'You are delirious with hunger and exhaustion,' my father said at last.

'I saw a vision of a Holy Angel,' I spluttered.

But I had seen Hell, too.

When the Flood finally drew back, and the sea was calm, the church was strewn with seaweed and oysters and clams, I was weak from too much knowledge on an empty stomach, and shaken by my visions. Parson Phelps had lost his voice completely by now. He could only croak his praises and his heartfelt thanks to the Lord in a ragged manner. We staggered up the aisle, gathering fish in the collection bucket, fighting off the gulls that swarmed in, and headed for the Parsonage.

We were met with a shock. The whole exterior of the house, from top to bottom, was covered in giant barnacles, which clung on with an awesome force. (I had never seen such huge specimens; later Tommy and I would lever them off with crowbars.)

My father laughed shakily. 'God has cracked a joke,' he explained. 'For his own almighty pleasure!'

And God had more pranks up His sleeve, because when my father opened the Parsonage door, a huge wall of sea-water came hurtling out, knocking him sideways. He lay there as it flooded over him and spent itself in the sodden earth. Then he stood up, and laughed, and said, 'Praise be, for the Lord is in good humour!'

Ever the optimist. Personally, I did not think much of God's sense of humour. Then or later.

That morning, as the villagers came rowing and sailing back, there was a sky as capricious as oil, conjuring itself back and forth from light to dark under a wedge of lemon sun. The heavy salt-bearing wind still racketed in from the east, and in the harbour, the masts and sails of the returned fishing boats danced and glimmered in a chaotic mirage. That's how I remembered Thunder Spit, after I left it. Strewn about in pieces like a smashed glass bowl, after the storm. Later, in the city, when I was lost, if I put my whelk to my ear, I could hear it, smell it, taste it. Wind and fish, fish and wind, salt and spike-grass and gulls.

Home sweet home!

Sweet, but sour, too. The Parsonage never fully recovered from the Flood, and the first of the jokes that God was to play on us. Most of the house was ravaged, and was to remain so for several years; from then on, when we needed to salt our food, we just scraped a kitchen flag-stone with a penknife. In

119

the meantime, sea-life rotted in corners, and for months the larder was a rockpool, containing a variety of living creatures, including a blue starfish, an array of clams, and four lobsters. We spent the rest of the year trying to repair the damage, and every fine day we would haul out our furniture and belongings in an attempt to dry them out.

Look: there's the sofa steaming in the warmth of a spring morning.

And listen: crrrkkk! That's the sound of the mahogany dresser splitting suddenly, and gaping soggily apart to reveal a lumpy mass of disintegrating jellyfish on its floor.

Don't inhale: hold your nose! Pffffwah!

'God moves in a mysterious way,' boomed my father, the eternal looker-on-the-bright-side, as he chopped up the useless furniture wood, 'His wonders to perform!'

If my father was distraught at the damage the sea had inflicted upon my mother's grave (the blanket he had bade me lay upon it had been carried off by the waters), he hid it well. The waves had churned up the earth, and all the shrubs and plants we had so carefully tended were destroyed. Or so we thought, until the following autumn, when the gourd plant appeared.

'Praise be, for the life that sprouteth from Thine earth!' he shouted, when I told him that I had identified a gourd shoot among the nettles and sand-grass.

He must have felt vindicated after all for his meek acceptance of the damage at the time. We cared for the plant as I will warrant you no plant has ever been cared for before or since, including those in Her Majesty's own greenhouses. My father would collect horse-dung from Harcourt's farm, a mile away, every day, including Marble Friday, and drip pure spring-water into its roots from a glass pipette he received by courier from a medical supply shop in Hunchburgh, to mimic God's rain falling drop by drop. And I must confess that there were some startling results to be had from this method. It's a well-known fact that gourds hate a salty climate, and do not normally thrive north of London. They are a Mediterranean quasi-fruit, quasi-vegetable, and they crave the sun, which was always in short supply in Thunder Spit, but the plant, nourished by manure and goodwill, thrived in an almost obscene way, and when its yellow flowers fell, ten fruits began to swell. And what gourds they turned out to be.

It was only years later that I heard about the monk Gregor Mendel, and his experiments with peas. By selective breeding, Mendel could create green peas from yellow, and tall from short. Within a mere two generations, he showed that a species of plant can abandon the inheritance of its forefathers, and create a new legacy all its own. Our gourds must have decided to take such a step – alone. For on inspection, it could be seen that they bore little or no relation to the original green-striped gourd my mother had so admired. They were whorled in orange and yellow, with bulbous protuberances and a distinctly hairy leaf.

– this big emptie CAGE.

Get in there, He sez.

Wot for, I sez, steppin in. Ther is a BUKKIT on the floor, and a sort of bed, like a litel shelfe. There is a bole of WATER, that is all.

To see if it is the rite SIZE, He sez.

The rite size for WOT, I sez.

The rite size for you and SUMWUN ELS.

He loks the door and puts the kee in His pockit.

Good gerl, He sez. We will be leevin next week, so get acustomd, ay.

I forls to the flor and I crys and crys and crys.

Wot a stupid cow, ay? Wot a stupid –

CHAPTER 12

THE EMPRESS TAKES
HER LEAVE

'Phew! Oomph! Whuuur! Huh!'

The primate carcass now chopped and its flesh marinating gently in the coriander-and-lemon preparation, Violet Scrapie is huffing and puffing her way up the stairs to the workshop, where her father is smoking a cigar.

'You need to get some exercise,' he tells her as she flops in, panting. The child is bearing far too much weight. Completely overloaded. Her skin will overstretch itself. Her internal organs will be squashed. Her armature will give way. 'A bit of walking. That'll do the trick.'

'Yes, Father,' says Violet dutifully, peering through the fug of cigar-smoke at a small, humanoid creature perched on the table. 'Is that the Monkey?'

'Most of him, yes. One arm and a pair of buttocks missing for now. Made a mistake with the cutting. Bloody annoying. Had to re-do it. And the tail's a bugger. Take a look.'

Violet manoeuvres her bulk around the table, and surveys the half-finished creature, some of whose skin hangs loose, falling away from the sawdust-sprinkled wire of the armature. The animal is bigger than she expected from the bits of carcass Cabillaud had chopped earlier. There hadn't been much in the way of meat, once you'd eliminated the bones and gristle. Its tail rises behind it like a question mark.

'A handsome beast,' she comments. 'There's something very *noble* about him, considering he's just an animal. You can actually begin to see why he's called a Gentleman.'

'Yes,' agrees Scrapie. 'Intelligent, too, by all accounts. Shame they're extinct. They were a very under-researched species, unfortunately. A type of ape, according to some, but the tail sets them apart. And then they died out, so there's bugger all way of finding out more.'

'Definitely handsome,' repeats Violet, musingly, stroking the creature's hairy arm.

'He will be, when he's finished. Such a waste. Not a mark on him, though. Still haven't fathomed how he died.'

This was true. Of all the creatures Scrapie had chosen from the remains of the *Ark* menagerie that day, the Gentleman Monkey had been the only one without any traces of violence on his body. Odd, that. As though he'd died of something else altogether.

Violet glances down and sees a pair of blue glass eyes on the table.

'The Hippo still wants them all to have blue eyes?'

'She does indeed, God blast her.'

'And the –?' Violet blushes; the subject is rather intimate.

'Yes. That, too. No genitalia of any kind. And then the pantaloons on top, to discourage the curious. Bloody woman.'

Every time he thinks about the Monarch, Scrapie becomes enraged. He twiddles with the glass eyes, doing his best to calm himself, and then observes his youngest child once more. She really is enormously fat. Almost a young woman, and as distressed a spinster as you could ever wish to meet! Will he be stuck with her for life?

'What you need,' Scrapie tells Violet with sudden inspiration, 'is a dog.'

Later that afternoon, his mind still preoccupied with the distressed-spinster issue, Scrapie left the house and returned with a corgi pup, spared from a vivisector's laboratory by his charm.

'Here,' he says now, shoving a wooden box at his daughter, with a snuffling thing inside.

'Thank you, Father,' she replies dutifully, wiping her hands on her bloody apron and peering down into the wooden box.

She has no interest in pets. A small puppy looks back up at her with large brown swelling eyes.

'Hello, dog,' she says doubtfully, calculating the creature's weight with a practised eye.

'What are you going to call him?' enquires Scrapie. There is an edge of annoyance in his voice. As far as he can recall, the creature is the only gift he has ever presented to his daughter. She might at least attempt a little gratitude.

'Suet,' she replies vaguely. What is actually on her mind is a recipe for Alsatian, of which suet is a major ingredient.

Scrapie sighs in exasperation, and returns to his workshop to do battle with the monkey towel-holder.

The newly christened Suet whimpers in his box.

'We'll need to fatten you up a bit, eh?' murmurs Violet, lifting the creature out. There is even less of him than she had thought; he can't weigh more than two pounds. She and Cabillaud have developed a marvellous canine repertoire. Dog (in case you have not partaken of it, gentle reader) tastes similar to fox, which is in turn not unlike rat, though with more of a venison twang.

And nothing at all like Gentleman Monkey, as the Scrapie family discovers that night when they take their first taste of the extinct, de-frosted primate. The flavour is strong and slightly musky – though by no means offensively so. The flesh, they agree, is tender, almost veal-like in consistency. Of the parts of the carcass Cabillaud and Violet have removed from the ice house and chopped, the thigh and rump were certainly the best cuts, followed closely by the ribs.

'Excellent!' pronounced Dr Scrapie.

'Delicious. I haven't enjoyed flesh so much for a long time,' agreed the Laudanum Empress.

But under the table, the puppy Suet whimpered.

'He must be hungry,' murmured Violet, retrieving the last remaining scraps of the braised primate from her mother's plate and chucking them on the floor. But instead of snapping them up, as any normal dog might have done, the ungrateful Suet merely growled suspiciously at the meat.

'Oh well,' said Violet. 'Suit yourself, stupid.'
But Suet's canine instinct turned out to be astute.

It was the following day that gastric illness struck the Scrapie household. Violet and Dr Scrapie were doubled up with acute diarrhoea, and Cabillaud took to his bed. On the *chaise-longue* in the drawing room, the Empress's psychic particles dispersed, and the shadow of death took their place.

'I see a town called Thunder Spit,' the Empress muttered feebly, her eyelids flickering. 'I see a jar on a shelf. I see a gourd plant, and a rockpool, and a ballerina and a –' The Empress never finished her sentence.

She had officially crossed to the Other Side.

Cuisine Zoologique had claimed its first victim.

CHAPTER 13

GONE TODAY,
HERE TOMORROW

'Food poisoning?' asks Abbie Ball, aghast, when the Victorian phantom has finished recounting the circumstances of her death. As a home-economics teacher, Abbie is more aware than most of the dangers of unhygienically prepared food. 'Most likely to have been salmonella, I expect. Or E coli. Well, I suppose you didn't have fridges and clingfilm in your day. Things can't have been as developed then as they are now, Mrs Scrapie.'

The phantom sighs. This silly woman, Abbie Ball, in whose home she has recently had the misfortune – thanks to something called a 'loft conversion' – to find herself, appears to be convinced that the world has improved in the hundred and fifty years since her death – although a quick glance at the year 2005 is enough to inform one that this is far from so. Why, the whole British race is becoming extinct, according to the electronic spirits inhabiting the crystal box in the living room. Only last week, the news spirit told her that religious fanatics had destroyed something called the National Egg Bank – making a disaster out of a crisis. Can this really be called progress?

'Actually, it wasn't the flesh that was poisonous,' she tells Abbie, adjusting her petticoats and sipping at the glass of Pepto-Bismol that is her one physical indulgence in these godforsaken times. 'It was the praxin the creature had been injected with before death. My husband did an analysis of the remaining meat. Suet was right not to touch it.'

'Suet?'

'My daughter's dog.'

'The stuffed corgi in the attic? Is that him?

'Well observed, Mrs Ball,' murmurs the Empress.

'Oh do call me Abbie.'

'I'd rather not, if you don't mind. Now please excuse me for a moment; I do believe *The Young and the Restless* is showing on your crystal box.' And she floats off into the living room. Seconds later, the signature tune of her favourite soap opera blares out.

Abbie winces. 'I wish she'd keep the sound down,' she mutters.

When, a month ago, Abbie Ball had first spotted the Victorian wardrobe up in the attic, she had assumed that it contained the outdated camping equipment of her late parents, Iris and Herman Boggs, who had been tragically killed in a Swiss avalanche ten years previously. The huge second Empire *meuble* towered over her, two metres high and almost as wide. It was made of a darkly polished walnut, lovingly adorned with cherubs, bulging of thigh and cheek, bearing fruit and trumpets and little scrolls tied with ribbons. Abbie had not been keen to re-awaken memories of her beloved parents, but her domestic urge to clear up the loft overcame her hesitation, and she prised open the wardrobe's vast door, which creaked and wheezed with age, and leaked from its ancient hinges the bitter dust of woodworm. Imagine her surprise when, instead of finding the poignant items she had anticipated, to wit, a chemical loo, aluminium pots and pans, folding camp beds and a portable gas cooker, she had instead unearthed a collection of stuffed mammals, ranging in size from small (a guinea-pig) to large (an entire ostrich), an ancient cookery book, an old painting of Noah's Ark, a fossil, a scientific treatise about evolution, and a curious flask in the form of a crucifix, smelling faintly of rum.

'Norman!' she had wailed.

Her husband came heaving breathily up the stairs and followed the direction of her accusing finger. 'Look at all this junk!'

'Blimey,' said Norman, sitting down heavily on an old laundry basket. You could have knocked him down, he said, with a proverbial feather.

127

'What d'you reckon, love?' he asked Abbie. 'Worth a call to the Antiques Hotline?'

Neither of them spotted the phantom till later. The ghost – dressed in myriad petticoats – took a day to materialise, and then another day to declare herself fully.

'My name is Mrs Charlotte Scrapie,' she had announced, wafting into the room one Sunday teatime. 'Although my family knew me as the Laudanum Empress, because of my unfortunate enthralment to a certain opiate. Is there a chemist's shop in the vicinity? I feel the need of some pink medicine.'

And with that by way of introduction, she had allowed herself to solidify sufficiently, as a presence, to polish off four of Abbie's barley flip-cakes. Her attention then turned to the execrable dress sense of her hosts, which she criticised in no uncertain terms.

'What's this?' she had accused, snapping at Abbie's elasticated waistband. 'And what are those?' she groaned, pointing at Norman's giant frog slippers. 'In my day we stuck to whalebone.'

By the following morning she had solidified completely, installed herself on the settee in the living room, and promptly substituted her laudanum dependence with an addiction to Pepto-Bismol and television.

As uninvited guests go, she was something of a pain, but there was no getting rid of her.

'She's one of those *après-fin-de-siècle* phenomena whatsits,' pronounced Norman, after reading an article in the *Sunday Express*. '"*A tangible symptom of the Zeitgeist*", in boffin-speak. They reckon there's more and more of them about, with the Extinction Crisis. People looking backwards, rather than forwards. Going a bit doo-lally over history.'

Abbie made a face. 'Well *I* certainly didn't invite her here,' she said firmly. 'As far as I'm concerned, she can get straight back in that old wardrobe and stay there. All she does is criticise.'

'I heard that,' the Empress called through from the living room. 'And by the way, your upholsterer should be shot.'

The Balls had mentioned the Old Parsonage's new inhabitant

casually to the Vicar at the Twitchers' Association AGM, but they were disappointed; he said he was only interested in her as an artefact of their joint psyche. Later, in the pub, Norman had discovered that the Vicar had said exactly the same thing, *vis-à-vis* the Peat-Hoves' poltergeist, and the Morpitons' haunted barn. 'These sodding marriage-guidance counsellors,' he grumbled. 'They've got a one-track mind.'

So for lack of a means of exorcising her, the Laudanum Empress had, in the last month, become a fixture at the Old Parsonage. Apart from costing the Balls a small fortune in Pepto-Bismol, she made no real demands, Norman finally conceded, and reached the conclusion that they should be grateful for small mercies. Every cloud has a silver lining, after all.

'And every silver lining has a stinking great cloud,' muttered the Empress, who wasn't keen on her side of the deal, either, but didn't share Norman's natural optimism. She would *gladly* go back in the wardrobe, if only they'd finish emptying it of stuffed animals, and would supply her with a portable crystal box.

Today Norman and Abbie are occupied with their Saturday jobs: he Black-and-Deckering at an intransigent piece of skirting in the upstairs toodle-oo; she preparing her weekly TV rehearsal. The Empress is still in the living room, engrossed in a soap opera. She'll get square eyes if she doesn't watch out. Meanwhile Rob Morpiton's huge red setter has found its way into the garden of the Old Parsonage. Sensing the presence of the supernatural, it has now begun to bark frantically.

'Sodding dog,' mumbles Norman, fiddling with his drill-bit. 'If that hound does a *mea culpa* on my lawn, I'm phoning Ron to come round with a pooper-scooper pronto. There's a limit to goodwill, and it's just been reached.'

But as well as inciting Norman's anger, the red setter has also prompted animal connections in Norman's brain, because after a couple of minutes, he remembers something, and wheezily plods his way down to the kitchen.

'Getting to know the new vet,' he tells Abbie. 'He's become quite a regular at the Crow. In fact, as regards my hangover the morning after the explosion at the Egg Bank, I can confidently tell you that the finger of blame points at him.'

'Hope he's handsome,' Abbie remarks. 'That'll be a nice treat for the girls.'

'How about a nice treat for me?' Norman ogles at her, forgetting Buck de Savile's rendition of a string of Elvis Presley hits, his drunken monologue about a macaque monkey called Giselle and an insane woman called Mrs Mann, and the workings of the veterinary complaints procedure, and remembering instead how, last night, after the pub, beneath Abbie's nightie – brushed cotton in winter, plain in summer – her White Cliffs of Dover had allowed themselves to be attacked by his eager earth-moving equipment. Norman's *jeu de mots* concerning earth movements was in tribute to Ernest Hemingway's famous *oeuvre*, *For Whom the Bell Tolls*, in which the leading lady says, after having it away, 'The earth moved.' Sometimes, as a variation on the same linguistic theme, he would ask afterwards, 'Did I toll your bell all right for you, then, love?' Abbie would always smile and say, 'Yes thanks, Norman,' and pull the nightie back down over her bony knees. She wasn't bothered about not having her bell properly tolled: she always used the time to think up a new dessert recipe. Last night had been a gratifying experience for both of them; Norman's earth-moving equipment had scraped through its MOT again, and Abbie had dreamed up a new way with profiteroles.

'What?' says Abbie, oblivious to Norman's sexual reverie.

'What d'you mean, what?'

'You said something.'

'Did I?'

'Yes. About the vet.'

'Oh,' remembers Norman. 'Nice bloke. He says he'll look at the junk in the loft for us.' He reaches for the biscuit tin. 'He says he might have a book on taxidermy antiques. Reckons if they're vintage, and a professional taxidermy job, they could well be worth something. Expect it depends on how they're mounted.' He chuckles, and wiggles his eyebrows up and down. 'As 'twere!' he adds, popping a barley flip-cake into his mouth.

'I'd better have another look,' sighs Abbie. 'And give them all a good dust. How many are there, d'you reckon?'

'Well, there's the famous ostrich, for starters,' says Norman through a mouthful of flip-cake. 'Plus a wombatty-looking job, a big monkey, and what looks like a badger. Oh, and a dog. He's got a whatchermacallit on his collar with SUET engraved on it.'

'That name rings a bell,' says Abbie, taking out her notepad and adding DUST CREATURES to her list in her neat script. 'I think the Empress said it was her daughter's dog.'

'The girls've enrolled on another course at the university,' Abbie says, when Norman returns from chasing the red setter off the lawn. She checks the percolator. 'Special studies, they call it.'

'What's that, when it's at home?'

'Something modern, by the sound.'

'So they're going intellectual on us again,' smiles Norman, twirling a three-centimetre screw between finger and thumb. 'Bless their cotton socks.'

As Norman returns to his DIY, picture his wife Abbie now a million miles away in her kitchen, reading, as she does every day, from the Recipe for Happiness. The recipe, writ large on a poster featuring cherubs with cooking pots, is dear to her heart; its homely kitchen philosophy has served her well:

Take one ounce of goodwill, and mix with a measure of frankness. Add a pinch of lovingkindness and stir in well with humour, the spice of life. Sprinkle generously with open-mindedness and courtesy. Add sympathy and optimism to the melting-pot, and apply warmth until a merry glow is achieved. Serve with a dash of glee and garnish with hope. Note: this is a dish for sharing, and is very more-ish!

It never fails to make her smile, and to put her in the mood for the task ahead. For which observe her now, checking her utensils for the morning's full dress rehearsal of minestrone *suivi par* artichokes Riviera, *ensuite* potted pears *avec* cinnamon custard. Some people have things in their blood: she has food in hers. She'll be trying out another of those Victorian veggie recipes later, from *The Fleshless Cook* by Violet Scrapie. The Laudanum Empress says they'll be disgusting because they're her daughter's recipes, but what sort of taste does a self-confessed drug-addict have?

Pots, pans, knives, casserole, whisk, scissors, sieve, garlic-crusher, colanders, baking tin, all present and correct, standing by Worktop A ready for Camera One. And soup ingredients to the ready: pre-prepared stock, vermicelli, seasonings, peas, beans, carrots, Parmesan, white wine. The artichokes Riviera and potted pears ingredients are to stay in the fridge until after the commercial break. Camera Two, as always, she pictures perched several centimetres above the microwave, for the wider shot. Quite a flattering angle; she's checked it from a step-ladder, narrowing her eyes and picturing the on-screen effect. It's absurd, but despite her years of cooking experience, she still feels a little nervous.

Yes; nervous. The big day is right around the corner. She can feel it in her bones.

The scenario for the big day is as follows: an independent television producer's car breaks down on the A210, and because his mobile phone is also on the blink, he walks to Thunder Spit where he smells a wonderful smell coming from the Old Parsonage. He rings the doorbell, and Abbie answers its chimes, her apron still on. The television producer, whose name is Oscar or perhaps Jack, wonders if he can use her phone to call the AA, as his mobile isn't charged up. While they are waiting for the AA man to arrive, Abbie offers Oscar or Jack a cup of freshly brewed coffee and some of her home-made Apfelkuchen, and he is so bowled over by the Apfelkuchen, and the elegance and poise and *je-ne-sais-quoi* of Abbie Ball herself, that he enquires whether she has ever considered working as a television presenter, and would she do him the great honour of accompanying him to the studio for a screen test?

132

After that, the rest will be history.

But now, today, is pre-history, and Abbie stands framed for the opening shot of her rehearsal.

'Hello. Now it's easy to get into a bit of a tizz when you're thinking minestrone,' she begins. 'But just remember that the secret of success is to take it one step at a time.'

Minestrone is a good metaphor for Abbie's life, she reflects, as she runs through the list of ingredients for the benefit of the imaginary viewer at home: full of bits and pieces of interesting things, swirling about in the family pot. Like genes passed down through the ages, some items will crop up more frequently, and others sink to the bottom. One night, she, Norman and the Empress had all watched a programme called *Death of a Nation*; the extinction of the British was all down to DNA, apparently. Bad thoughts, good thoughts. Traits from Norman's side, traits from her own side. Look at Rose and Blanche: the red hair; that's definitely a Boggs characteristic. But their manual dexterity; that's surely Norman's side of the family? The Tobash feet, poor dears, and the over-developed coccyx – though they haven't got it as badly as Granny had, and that was in the days when they wouldn't operate so readily if it didn't affect your gait. The excess body hair: guilty again, as charged: that's the Tobash side, but the cosmetics industry has come up trumps there. I came off quite lightly myself, but thank God for hot wax! The trouble with so many ingredients in the gene pool, in the pot of thoughts and memories, is that there are always a few that you find less appetising than others, and some which are so downright appalling that you force yourself to gulp them down without looking too hard.

'Now a cook's best friend is her chopping board,' says Abbie gaily, smiling at the imaginary Camera Two. 'And as you can see, I use the traditional wooden kind, though if you're thinking kitchen hygiene, the plastic variety is best, to be honest. Nice sharp knife' (she holds it up to the imaginary Camera One and lets it glisten in the light) 'and you're ready to go.'

The Laudanum Empress, her soap opera finished, has been

133

watching Abbie, transfixed. Noting the woman's passion, her exhausting single-mindedness, and her slightly buck teeth. And thinking.

'You remind me of my daughter,' she says suddenly. Abbie looks up in shock at the opaque phantom perched on the draining-board. 'Could you by any chance be related?'

Outside, the sky is a jovial cobalt blue, and the trees are punchbags for a wild, irrational wind. While Abbie has been rehearsing, Rose and Blanche have travelled back from Hunchburgh by bullet train, and are now stomping purposefully up Crawpy Street in their elasticated trainers, past the giant Lucozade billboard, up a little alley decorated with dog-shit and old Coke cans, and squeezing their way through a rusty turnstile, past a big FOR SALE sign, into the graveyard of St Nicholas's Church. A cluster of teenagers – the twins recognise Clinton Tobash, Cameron Mulvey, and Jade Yarble, regular truants from Abbie's home-economics class, among them – sit on a gravestone smoking and kicking at the long grass and nettles. Nearby, an ancient Lord Chief Justice sheep nuzzles about the gravestones like a self-operated Hoover, the mobile nozzle of her lips wiggling to reach the most succulent dandelions: the new ecclesiastical administration, to establish its green credentials, had insisted on not buying a new church lawnmower, but had instead persuaded Ron Harcourt to contract out one of his flock to graze. Rose and Blanche pat the sheep. Then nod at the kids, remembering their own tendency to come here when skiving off school. History repeats itself, they think, as they pick their way past the crumbling gravestones.

'Look,' said Rose, pointing to a grave from which sprouted a mass of indecently sprawling vegetation with yellow flowers.

'Eugh,' said Blanche. 'Creepy.'

'It's a gourd plant.' A long-haired, ineffectual-looking man stepped out from behind a gravestone. 'I looked it up. It's famous for its adaptability. Repeats itself every four generations. Green one year, yellow the next, then orange, then mauve, then back to green. Amazing, eh? The Lord moves in a mysterious way. I'm Josh – remember?'

'Hi, Josh,' said the girls.

They did remember. He helped organise things like the Thistle Festival. They'd seen him at the Yard of Ale Contest, and he and Dad had taken turns to MC the Karaoke nights at the community centre. And wasn't he the bloke who did that embarrassing cabaret thing for the Birdspotters' Association? Yes: the Vicar.

'We wanted to look at some old church records, for our genealogy module,' said Rose, stepping carefully over the tendrils of the gourd plant. At the base of each yellow flower, an odd-looking purplish fruit was beginning to swell.

'See who married who, in Mum's family,' added Blanche. 'And then put it in a diagram. Family trees are all the rage in the States. We're going to set up a business.'

'Do a sort of trace-your-roots service,' Blanche elaborated.

'Yeah, charge a fortune,' suggested Rose.

'Uh-huh? Well, follow me,' said Josh. They stepped into the gloom, where after a moment the mournful shapes of some dingy pews began to loom into view. A bucket of whitewash stood on the floor in the middle of the aisle. 'I'm trying to get rid of the water-mark,' explained Josh. 'It dates back to the Great Flood of 1858, but now we're selling up, the estate agent wants it looking marketable.'

'Selling soon, then?'

'Hoping to. We've had a few nibbles from a McDonald's franchise. It makes financial sense; we can't compete with the satellite services. I'm off to the States, myself.'

So, think the twins. Another wanker exports himself.

'You'd better get a move on,' said Rose, 'before the Emigration Restriction.'

'The clergy are exempt. I'm doing an ecclesiastical MA in Louisiana, home of the water-melon.'

'So where's the marriage register?'

'Over here,' said Josh. Then, suddenly inspired: 'Ten Euros, and it's yours.'

Rose and Blanche exchanged a glance.

'Let's have a look, then,' said Rose.

They wandered into the registry and inspected the book. It was old, thick and faded, its pages oddly bulbous.

'Another victim of the Flood,' commented Josh. 'Nowadays we put it all on disc, of course, and send it to the Office for National Statistics.'

The girls leafed through the tattered pages. The ink had run on many of them, rendering them illegible. 'It's a bit shop-soiled,' complained Rose.

'That's history for you,' said Josh with a smile. 'Take it or leave it.' He was looking forward to his three-year creation-studies course.

'Five Euros, and you're on,' said Rose.

They settled for seven Euros fifty.

All right if I invite him to a barbie, then?' asks Norman, popping his head round the kitchen door.

'Invite who?' asks Abbie.

'The new vet. Buck, he's called. Buck de Savile.'

'Ooh, a Frenchman?' enquires Abbie hopefully, putting away her imaginary TV equipment. She'll be able to flex her subjunctives.

'Seemed as English as beef to me,' says Norman.

'Oh well. We'll soon find out. Tell him the Saturday after next,' says Abbie.

'Tell who the Saturday after next?' call Rose and Blanche, slamming the front door behind them. 'No one boring, we hope.'

'Ah, the return of Double Trouble,' comments Norman.

'The new vet,' says Abbie. 'Nice man, according to your father.'

The twins exchange a glance of amused contempt.

'Age?' they ask together.

'Oh, youngish to middle-ish. Told me he was born the day Elvis Presley died, so work it out for yourselves. Drives an Audi Nuance. You can't say fairer.'

Rose and Blanche exchange another look; this one more optimistic.

'Any more ideas about earning your keep, you two?' Norman is asking. 'Sorry to raise the subject, but there's been a lot of hoo-ha about the pensions issue, since the Egg Bank. The P-word, they're calling it. Your mother and I aren't the only parents racking their brains about how you're going to cope financially when we're six feet under.'

'We're planning to get pregnant,' announces Rose. 'That's *our* P-word!'

Norman and Abbie exchange a God-help-us glance; they've also heard about the Reward on the news.

'Along with twenty million other bounty-hunters!' sighs Norman, in frustration. This Reward thing is a big mistake by the Government, he and Abbie have agreed. All it's going to do is raise hopes, start off a national rutting fever, spread a lot of venereal disease, and break young hearts.

'Have you tried thinking of anything on a *practical* level?' sighs Abbie. 'Just in case you *don't* manage to become the first British girls since the Millennium to get pregnant by natural means?'

'Yes, as a matter of fact,' says Rose. 'We're going to research the Ball family tree.'

She and her sister dump their handbags and a crumpled carrier bag on the hall table. Keys, cigarette packets and chewing gum spill out.

'It's part of our genealogy module,' says Blanche.

'Module?' asks Norman. 'As in space module?'

'That's education jargon for you,' says Abbie.

'Dr Bugrov reckons that with the British becoming extinct, the family-tree market is going to be the next big money-generating thing. We're going to get into it. We've got to start off by making a sort of chart, showing the Ball family's ancestry.'

'Get the Empress to help you,' suggests Abbie. 'She reckons her daughter might be a great-great-great something or other of ours. *She* was a famous cook, in her day.' The twins groan in unison.

'No thanks,' says Rose.

'In any case,' adds Blanche, 'oral testimony isn't allowed.'

'Certainly not phantom oral testimony,' adds Rose drily.

'Yeah,' agrees Blanche. 'It's all got to be in writing. Empirical, it's called.'

'We've got hold of the Thunder Spit marriage register,' says Rose, pulling it out of a crumpled carrier bag and waving it at her parents.

'We'll be using that,' says Blanche.

'To make a chart,' continues Rose. 'Showing who's related to who.'

'Whom,' corrects Abbie, scooping the girls' belongings back into their handbags. 'It's not who,' she says. 'It's whom.'

'For whom the bell tolls,' says Norman, winking at Abbie.

'Pardon?' say the twins together.

'Ernest Hemingway,' says Norman, slapping Abbie on the bum. 'She's a thoroughbred, your mum. Ask not for whom the bell tolls, it tolls for her.'

The twins groan in unison and do their puke-face.

'Now on to matters serious,' announces Norman, aligning his belly over his belt and rocking on his shoes. 'Have any of you three gorgeouses nicked my strimmer? Because in case it has slipped your collective memories, it's the Thistle Festival next week. And there's no peace for the wicked!'

138

CHAPTER 14

THE ORIGIN OF SPECIES

There is no peace, Parson Phelps always maintained, for he who is pure in heart. 1859 was the year that Charles Darwin's book, *Origin of Species*, was published, and it was a date which also marked the decline into melancholy and madness of many a theologian – including Parson Phelps.

He and I laughed at first. The idea that we were descended from monkeys and apes was not new, Parson Phelps informed me, but this was the first time it had been voiced with such apparent authority. It was only when he realised the extent to which otherwise sane people were actually taking the scientist's beliefs seriously, that my foster-father's outrage began in earnest. He was not alone in deciding that the ungodly book was the last straw in a long and uncivilised barrage of assault upon the Lord's word by his great bugbear, that unseemly vehicle of destruction, science. The whole Christian world – or that part of it that Parson Phelps and I represented, i.e. the humble common clergy of the land – was still weary and frustrated from all the geology battles over fossils, but we rose up against it, stones in a great wall of faith that united us all.

These were heady days in the Church, and every day, including Marble Friday, my Father walked to Judlow to purchase the *Thunderer* and keep abreast of developments in the Great Debate. But he was no passive participant. His sermons at that time took on a force and a passion I had never seen before, and it was thanks to his stormy sermons from the pulpit that Charles Darwin – hitherto a complete stranger to all Thunder Spitters –

became such an object of public contempt in the village that he replaced Guy Fawkes in effigy on Bonfire Night. Shortly after its publication, Parson Phelps appeared in the church brandishing a copy of the infamous book, and during the service ripped out and tore page after page. If the congregation had been permitted to cheer in God's house, they would have done, but instead they smiled and allowed their faces simply to shine encouragingly in support of Parson Phelps as the pages went fluttering to the floor.

'This is my message to all heretics,' warned my father. 'That he who dareth to challenge the word of God, as evidenced in the words of Genesis, may be treated as a worshipper of the Devil himself, and punished accordingly!'

The congregation had come to adore such scenes – but afterwards Dr Baldicoot looked worried, and shook his head.

'I fear he may have a brain tumour,' he confided to me. 'He is taking this evolution debate too seriously.'

I disagreed. I knew my father, after all. He was simply a man of deep conviction, and I loved him for it. Besides, I knew him to be right, and shared his beliefs most passionately myself. Of all the books of the Bible, that of Genesis was the one that I had always held most dear to my heart, and I felt its truth deeply. The Earth had been without form, and void, and darkness had been upon the face of the deep! And then man appeared! For me, there was simply no denying it, and science could hang.

'I believe that time will show you, Dr Baldicoot, that it is Mr Darwin – and certain sections of society – who have a malfunction of the brain,' I said. 'Five years hence, I do assure you, this ridiculous craze will have died away, and the crisis we are living through will appear as nothing more than a season of ill-judgement and fashionable whimsy.'

Dr Baldicoot shrugged and poked at his abominable pipe, and said we would see what we could see, and I smiled to myself, proud of my father's stand. For the controversy over the *Origin of Species* united our small family of two most happily, and some of my fondest memories of him, before madness struck, date from that year, when together we spent many hours poring over Darwin's profane tome, by the light of the candle in the kitchen, the flag-stoned floor twinkling with salt. And as we read, our concern about his heresies grew.

For was Mr Darwin not making three uniquely dangerous propositions?

1. God's word in the Book of Genesis was a lie.
2. All life – including human life – developed by a gradual and haphazard process of evolution, from basic, humble life-forms such as the sardine, and that man himself was by implication but a glorified baboon.
3. That – *quid erat demonstrandum* – our faith and my father's life's work was as nought.

It was the third item on this list that was soon to plant the seed of madness in Parson Phelps' poor brain. Had I only heeded the words of Dr Baldicoot, and pulled my father back from the edge of the abyss! But I had not known he was standing there, and I with him. I had thought we were safe.

But the world had begun to tilt.

There is a fallacy among city dwellers that goes as follows: there are four seasons in a year. Yet as anyone who lives outside a city knows, there are not four seasons in the year, but twelve. Each of the main seasons, spring, summer, autumn and winter, is divided into three distinct sections: the beginning, the middle, and the end, stretches of time in which certain preordained natural miracles occur, such as the forsythia blooms, the razor-bill mates, the beech-leaf falls, or the bat hibernates. I explain this to demonstrate how regulated our lives were in Thunder Spit; how governed by the wheel of the calendar. It was early autumn, for example, when my mother died. It was mid-autumn the following year, when the Flood came and I experienced my disturbing visions and the gourd plant sprouted. And it was early winter – November – when the first frosts were biting, that the Travelling Fair of Danger and Delight came to Judlow. And it

141

was there, in a single minute of a single hour of a single day, that a portcullis slammed down behind me, marking the close of that season of my life called childhood.

My age: fifteen. It is a Sunday afternoon, and for my own subversive reasons, I have just told my unsuspecting father a triple untruth: that despite the winter chill, I wish to go to the schoolhouse to meditate, and conjugate Latin verbs, and read the Bible. Far from arousing his suspicions, Parson Phelps' reaction to my elaborate lie is one of surprise and pleasure. He ruffles my coarse thatch of hair with his hand.

'I admire your dedication, Tobias,' he says. He is gutting sardines to make a pie. 'It does a credit to the upbringing your mother gave you.'

I bite my lip at his mention of my mother. 'We do not know where you came from, Tobias,' she had whispered to me on her deathbed, ravaged by the cough, eaten alive by the Thing, and clasping her precious gourd to her breast. 'But promise me that you will never visit the Travelling Fair of Danger and Delight.'

Which was precisely what I was about to do. For why would a mother make a child swear to such a thing, if the Fair did not house a secret? Conscious of my imminent betrayal of her deathbed wishes, I hang my head. But Parson Phelps misinterprets the gesture.

'And modest, too,' he says fondly, making the sign of the cross first over me, and then the sardines. Yet as I gulp back my shame, my spine tingles with the anticipation of the illicit.

It is only natural, is it not, for a child to be curious about his origins?

It was only this morning that my father had delivered his annual sermon – to a crowded congregation – about the evils of triviality, to coincide with the arrival of the Fair, an event which came a close second to the great enemy, science, as a target for his personal wrath. The church-going families of Thunder Spit – the Tobashes, the Peat-Hoves, the Balls, the Mulveys, the Barks, the Hayters, the Harcourts, the Cleggs and Mrs Sequin had all listened attentively, as my father, preaching at full volume, his breath leaving him in chilled puffs and mingling with the sunlight that streamed through the stained glass, held forth with passion. Tommy and I, somewhat less attentive than the others, sat crushed in a back pew; we had been to the far end of the Spit to collect conkers from the gnarled little horse-chestnut tree, which had produced a bumper crop, and our pockets were full to bursting.

A certain Godless event was taking place in Judlow, my father was telling his flock. An event which marked – in God's eyes – a low point to an otherwise wholesome year of toil. An event which should be avoided in much the same way as one might avoid a venomous snake.

The congregation nodded sagely.

'The magic is here, in Nature and in our hearts,' Parson Phelps had warned solemnly. 'We have no need for man-made entertainment; it is all around us, God-given, for which we thank Him.'

I had heard it all before: about how birdsong is God's way of making music for us, and lobsters are for our nourishment but also for our entertainment because of the way they change colour in boiling water, and wave their claws at us. About how God thought of Man first, when He created the animals, sending camels to live in the desert where they can function with precious little water and so be of use to the desiccated bedouin, and keeping lions in the jungle, well out of our way. Why, my father argued, should anybody need to look at a painting, when he can gaze at the wing of a butterfly? Et cetera: he never mentioned the Fair by name, but he took care to damn it with his every word.

'He has never been to it,' Tommy muttered to me, as we shuffled about under our pew, retrieving the rolling conkers that had spilled from our bulging pockets. 'So how does he know?'

For my own part, to house such a thought in my own bosom would have been heretical; I was only just now beginning to question my father's omniscience, and every time I did so, I

143

felt guilty and ashamed. But as I returned to my hard seat and polished my largest conker with my handkerchief and listened to the continuation and climax of Parson Phelps' righteous drone, I realised that my father's sermonising only increased my desire to venture into the forbidden land of the Travelling Fair, whose very toffee apples spelt moral depravity.

And so it came to pass that on that same afternoon, despite God's most specific wishes on the subject, Tommy and I set out for Judlow, a town that boasted nine shops, a pub, a mayor, a Sir Eustace and Lady Antonia Yarble living at the Big House, a slaughterhouse, and a newfangled closed sewer system, that sent the town's waste trickling into the sea. I had not visited Judlow more than ten times in my life, and on each occasion it had felt like venturing abroad. (The thought of going to Hunchburgh, where my father had studied theology, was even more daring, like voyaging through Parson Phelps' vision of space to the constellations. From Hunchburgh, I imagined, one could look down on the world like the Man in the Moon.) But although the excitement of our adventure gave me additional energy, my gait hindered me, and it soon became abundantly apparent that I could never keep pace with Tommy for the full three miles of our journey.

'Hop on my shoulders,' he suggested, when we had left the village behind us. 'Else we'll never make it before dusk.'

How I loved this! My unorthodox transport, coupled with the guilty pleasure of transgression, charged the atmosphere of the day with a tingling light. Swaying up there on Tommy's shoulders, I could see for miles: the sparkling sea, the whirling ridges of cloud, the distant hum of the town – all filled my blood with the sharp, unrivalled thrill of freedom. At the edge of the promontory, the hawthorn and the bracken stopped, and other shrubs began. Mainland shrubs.

'I can smell it!' I yelled. 'I can smell the Fair!'

Here Tommy set me down, and we sniffed the air. Sure enough, we caught the scent of animals and rotting straw and burnt sugar. As the wind gusted towards us, it bore with it, too, the faint sounds of screaming and laughter.

Ten minutes later, we entered the swirling, chattering crowds, and I immediately lost sight of Tommy. I began to panic, leaping up to catch a glimpse of my friend over the heads of the milling strangers, but the next thing I knew, there he was, back at my side, thrusting a famous Danger and Delight toffee apple under my nose. He had stolen two. The toffee apple contained real sugar, he told me, harvested by manacled slaves in cruel overseas plantations. It was the best thing I had ever tasted. The Ten-Foot Woman swung past us, smoking a clay pipe and showering everybody with confetti, and I giggled with joy. Walking arm in arm with Tommy, licking my toffee apple and surveying the scene, I soon realised that there were faces here from my father's congregation. Tommy spotted them, too.

'Look! There's Johnny Clegg at the coconut shy!'

'And Ron Tobash! Over there! He's guessing the weight of that pumpkin!'

We saw others, too: Mr Mulvey scolding his son Johnny, and Farmer Harcourt and his family braying with laughter as they descended the helter-skelter, and Mrs Sequin arguing with an urchin who she claimed had stolen her purse. Seeing all these citizens of Thunder Spit enjoying themselves thus, it seemed that my father's sermon had had the opposite effect to that intended. I felt ashamed on his behalf, and, conscious of my own betrayal, pulled my hat low over my brow.

'Let's look at the Two-Headed Snake,' I suggested to Tommy, eager to remain incognito. We paid a farthing each, and the one-eyed man in charge of the Snake whipped back a curtain to reveal a glass case with a tangled rope-like creature coiled within.

'It's two snakes bound together,' Tommy pronounced, after inspecting the reptile closely, 'with some kind of glue.'

'Time's up,' snapped the man, and whipped the curtain back. Disappointed in the fraud, we headed for the world-famous Mechanical Millipede, an iron and wood construction which was so big that, had it been transported into the church at Thunder Spit, it would have obliterated the altar and spilled out into the nave and the vestry. We rode on this contraption three times, so that Tommy could understand its engineering, which, he informed me, wriggling out from underneath it later, involved a system of interlocking cog-wheels and a steam-powered piston accelerator mechanism, designed by a genius.

'Oi, Tobias, come here!'

Tommy was now hopping about at the edge of a big crowd standing around a pen that contained a piebald horse. I joined him: I stood on tiptoe, and Tommy peered through the elbow of the man in front of him. A red-faced gent was yelling questions at the horse, and the creature was answering by stamping its front hooves on the earth.

It was fed sugar lumps as reward for its intelligence.

'It's incredible!' said Tommy, commenting on its arithmetic abilities.

But I wasn't so sure. 'It's a trick,' I told him. 'No animal is that clever.'

We wandered off.

According to my recollection of that day, it was when we visited the Man-Eating Wart-hog that the nervousness began to engulf me – a nervousness so strong and so sudden as to have an odour all its own. There was a high enclosure of sticks, which we entered. And there the creature was, slumped in a filthy cage, licking its hairy accoutrements next to a pile of fetid meat-chunks. He looked up, and although I had the time to note, in a rational manner, that he resembled in many ways the illustration I had previously seen of such an animal in *Hanker's World*, its eyes unnerved me immediately. They were a colour midway between orange and ochre, with vertical irises, like narrow doors into another world. The smell that emanated from him made me shudder. It was the raucous odour of captivity and rotting meat, which though hitherto alien, seemed suddenly as familiar to me as the scent of wax candles in the church. As

Tommy and I approached, toffee apples still in our hands, the creature, a pig-like animal covered with hideous carbuncles, stared at me, sniffed, and gave a sudden, low grunt of hatred.

I was by now well accustomed to animals reacting disfavourably to my presence, but the reaction of the Wart-hog – perhaps because I knew him to be a man-eating beast – unnerved me. My nervousness deepened, and I felt faint, as though at the periphery of my vision, beyond my control and my comprehension, something invisible and dangerous swarmed. I caught my breath, and grabbed Tommy's arm.

'It's all right,' he said. 'He's only a big piggy-wig. Eh, porky?' And he laughed.

My head spun. As the Wart-hog's ugly bristle-covered snout and tusks rammed up close to my face, and his unblinking orange-ochre eyes stared me out, I shuddered. Then, as the creature grunted ominously again, I felt my hackles rise in a sudden, unaccountable fear. Why did this hideous, grunting creature seem suddenly familiar to me in a way I could neither fathom nor describe?

Puzzled and shamed by my now raging sense of anxiety, I tugged my eyes away from the Wart-hog's gaze, and turned to leave. Tommy was already walking out, oblivious to my discomfort. 'Come along,' he said. 'There's a show starting in the Tent of Miracles.'

We do not know where you came from, she had said. I regretted coming here, and I wanted nothing more than to go home, but I dared not tell Tommy this. As we turned our backs on the creature in his cage, and headed towards the tent, the nervousness came with me, and I could not shake it off.

By the time we arrived at the Tent of Miracles we had no money left, of the shilling Tommy had stolen from his father, risking the metal bottom-whisk. When the guard's back was turned, we slipped inside; Tommy out of curiosity, and I out of the feeling that here, away from the Wart-hog's orange-ochre eyes, I might find shelter.

Foolish hope.

Inside the darkened tent, a crowd stood around a small podium, staring at the creature upon it. It was her face that you saw first: it was alarmingly beautiful, and ageless, and wild. Her hair shot upwards, scraped into a tight knot that sat balanced upon her head like a ball. At first, her head seemed simply to float there, in boxed suspension, white against the darkness of the sheeted backdrop, but as our eyes grew accustomed to the gloom, I realised that the dark frame that housed her face in fact consisted of her own black-clad legs and feet. From her neck, an oval locket hung down, trembling and catching the light, flashing it around the room. Tommy and I drew a breath and looked at one another. No wonder Parson Phelps had preached against this place from the safety of his pulpit. There was an aura of disgrace about the little ballerina, but pride, too, and a feral quality which increased my nervousness enormously. Tommy, too, was jiggling at his conkers in a disturbed fashion. We stared at the spectacle of the little figure, her legs arched up from behind her, her back bent like a scorpion's. We stared at her for a long time. Then slowly, as the tent filled up, she began to loosen the grip of her shins and feet, and move slowly, slowly, and with great precision, to unwind herself. It was absurd, and frightening, but also gracious and miraculous, like watching a camel successfully passing itself through the eye of a needle.

As she emerged slowly from her scorpion position, we saw that she was of diminutive stature. Her whole torso, like her legs and feet, was clad in the tight-fitting black of an unbroken silhouette, except for the stiff little skirt which stuck out horizontally from the waist. Something physical and visceral stirred within me, twisting my guts.

'Mildred is punishing me,' I told Tommy. 'Let's go.'

'No. I'm staying,' said Tommy firmly. 'Look, she's tying herself in another knot!'

And sure enough, she is on her belly again, balancing a tray on each foot. On the trays are tiny glasses of Madeira sherry. It seems you can pay twopence to come and take a glass, and drink it, then put it back on the tray. 'Sherry comes from Spain,' whispers Tommy. 'It makes you drunk just to sniff it.' I try to refrain from breathing at all; God forbid that Parson Phelps should discover me intoxicated! Now, still balancing her tray and a dozen little glasses, and still bunched in her uncomfortable knot, the woman has launched into song. I strain to listen over the babble of voices. There is a tune to it, of sorts, but no words, and for some reason I find her singing unspeakably unsettling and poignant. She has a small, cracked voice, and the clatter of notes that emerges sounds oddly familiar, though I cannot place them.

Maybe it was that lonely, wordless singing. Or maybe it was what happened afterwards. Either way, unaccountably, I found myself suddenly in tears, a curious, nagging sensation of sorrow mixed with happiness tugging at my innards and infuriating Mildred.

She had stopped, suddenly, mid-note. At first I thought she had merely missed a beat, and would resume her song, but it was as though she had lost interest in her own performance, and simply switched herself off, for there was a jagged hush. A few murmurs began to swell among the small crowd, and Tommy shifted from foot to foot.

'Get on with it then,' he muttered.

I drew in a sudden breath, and swayed on my feet. She was looking at me! Staring into my eyes! I could swear it!

It was when she flung her tray to the ground that I began to shake uncontrollably. It felt as though I were drowning all over again. I wasn't alone in my fear, for I heard several women scream as she hurled the tray. It flew high into the air as though slowed down by an invisible hand. Then it reached the height of its arc and with a brutal suddenness, went crashing to the floor. There were more screams and gasps as the sherry glasses smashed, tinkling and sending up a spray of golden droplets that smelt sweet and harsh and forbidden.

'Oh dear God!' I murmur.

Now she is unwinding herself, but in a hurried fashion, pulling at the knot of her own body with impatience. Her limbs free,

149

she's sniffing the air, ignoring the crowd who are beginning to shuffle about nervously, and to hurl little balls of paper and gumdrops in her direction.

It is then, in the space of a single second that seems to last an hour, that I am drowning once again. I am dashed back into the flood-water of St Nicholas's Church, and the memory returns to me as vividly as a blow to my stomach.

My Angel is near. I am in a cot with golden bars, and I can hear the sound of a woman's voice singing a lullaby. *Rock-a-bye baby on the tree top* . . .

A bristle-skinned animal with orange-ochre eyes guards me.

Then I hear Father's voice calling me through the flood-water, begging me to return. I remember bobbing to the surface, and seeing the Parson's cassock balloon about him in a bubble of righteousness. I sink again, and this time visit Hell.

My Angel has disappeared, and my golden cot has become a rusty cage. I am lying in a pool of blood. And I hear a scream, high and shrill, that plays up and down my spine like fingernails screeching across a blackboard.

Yes: I remember this.

And as I do so, my heart begins to thump horribly, banging at my ribs like a caged beast desperate to escape. The Contortionist is pointing at me. On her face is anger, and pride, and wildness, and beauty, and desperation, all in one. Tommy clutches my hand.

Time freezes.

And remains frozen.

It is indeed fortunate that I am in many ways my father's child. For there, stuck in frozen time, I find a mood of sudden calm growing within me, and I feel the presence of Parson Phelps as solidly as if he were there in the flesh. And there, as I stare at the woman staring back at me, the full force of my faith tells me in a sane and measured fashion that there is nothing here that I know. The face, the ballet shoes, the little tutu whose skirt sticks out horizontally: nothing about the Contortionist is familiar to me in any way. Nothing, I realise, could in fact be further from my world, and the calm and ordered life of Thunder Spit: that I can swear with my hand on my heart. A heart which, although it is still thumping within me madly, witnesses no swirl of recognition, feels no stirring of memory, and experiences no instinctive rush of hatred or of love. None. Nothing.

Just a desire to run away and return to my father, and the church, and God, and all the safety and security of home.

'Come along, Tommy!' I croak. I have grabbed his arm so hard that he yelps in pain. 'Let's go!'

So from that place of horror and depravity, gumdrops flying around us, the smell of sherry in our nostrils, the memory of a tuneless, wordless ballad ringing in our ears, we flee.

– stuk ther. Nothin to do. NOTHIN, ever.

Then I waks up one day and am SUMWER ELS. Dark. I ratles the CAGE. I screems and screems. Wer am I, I screems.

London Doks. This woz a SLAVE SHIPPE, says Trapp. I used to keep slaves in it. Afrika, and Gorgia. Gorgia, and Afrika. To-in and fro-in, like that. NOW it is sumthin els. Much mor CUMFTERBLE, He sez. Lots mor roome! It is an ARKE. And he is gon, larfin.

Ther is a man cald Higgins, feeds me, changis my BUCKIT. Wen do we sail, I arsks. Wer to.

He dusnt no, or says not.

But He tels me their is a LIST, and wen we hav got everythin on the LIST, we can cum home agen.

Wot kind of things is on this List, I sez.

Animals, He sez. The animals went in two by two, HURRA!

A few lines are obliterated here. But further down the page, the writing continues:

– so they brings me FOOD, and water. Empties my buckit of piss and shit. Then TRAPP cums bak. Cumfterble? He arsks. Barsterd.

We will go to DISTANT CUNTRIES wer you will be QUEEN, He sed, that nite wen we met, wen I was DANSIN at the kings Arms. Long Ago.

151

Let me out of this CAGE, I sez. I am screemin and cryin. Wot is this for, I sez. Wy cant you treet me like a lady.

Becos you is an ANIMAL now, He sez.

I am an animal alrite, I sez, I am a COW, I sez, I am a stupid COW. He stil has a hold of me. Dont no wy. I luvs Him stil, even wen He shuttes the dor of the CAGE and leevs me in the darke agen.

Its WOT YOU WONTS, He sez. Wimin DREEM of this.

I opens my mouth to speek but ther is no words ther for wot I feel. And not a thing in the WURLD that I can do. Becos by now the ARK is aflote.

CHAPTER 15

LONG LIVE DEATH

Which guests to invite and which to shun, what type of frilled smocking would best suit the bridesmaids, whether there will be enough champagne to go round, how the in-laws will get on: from as young as three, a normal healthy young girl will spend a fair proportion of her time, in the company of her favourite doll, agonising over the details of her hypothetical future wedding. Mrs Charlotte Scrapie being neither normal, nor healthy, nor a young girl, and in addition being already married, and indeed also dead, had long been concerned with a ceremony of the more gloomy variety, involving not white lace, but black. The happy hours she had spent preparing for this day! Earth to earth, ashes to ashes, dust to dust! Ding-dong, loud and long and tragic may the bells toll! A time to live, a time to die, a time to love, a time to hate, a time to bawl your eyes out and blow long and hard into a big black hanky!

'It was a marvellous funeral,' bragged the Laudanum Empress to Abbie Ball, a hundred and fifty years later. 'Far be it from me to boast, but it was certainly one of the most moving occasions I have ever attended.'

In accordance with her wishes, set out in detail in a document of some twenty-five pages, the ceremony was a grandiose affair, involving acres of pungent waxen lilies, hymn after tear-inducing hymn, black confetti, white faces, a fawning tribute to the deceased penned by the Empress herself and read by a hunch-backed vicar, and much booming organ music. Many of the Empress's grateful former clients – from both sides of the Great

153

Divide – sat in rigid and respectful attendance. In the front row of the church, Violet Scrapie, clad in mourning garb, dabbed at her eyes as the coffin was borne in, heaped with a mountain of lilies topped with the Empress's favourite old fox-fur.

'I'll let you into a secret, Vile,' murmured the dry-eyed Scrapie, sitting next to her. 'I gave her that fox because I botched it. It was unstuffable. Too many bullet-holes.'

Suet, reprieved from his fate as a dinner of the future, wheezed at Violet's feet. For him at least, something positive had emerged from the calamity: from now on, the kitchen would be needing an official food-taster. Neither Scrapie nor Violet noticed the presence of the psychic particles hovering above their heads. It was an extraordinarily moving service, Mrs Scrapie felt, allowing her own ghostly bosom to shudder and a single human tear to roll down her pale cheek as she listened to the hunchbacked vicar's heartfelt eulogy. 'Mrs Charlotte Scrapie, adored by all who knew her – gone, but still with us!' The tear fell upon the nose of the dog Suet with a plop. Crouching low with fear, he licked it off and whimpered.

'Farewell, Mrs Charlotte Scrapie!' intoned the vicar. 'May you rest in peace!

Rest in peace? Fat chance!

It is a well-known fact that grief can set all manner of other emotions shooting off in odd directions. The result of Mrs Scrapie's untimely death by food poisoning was to cause a deep doubt to hatch within the breast of Violet Scrapie. The week after the funeral, Monsieur Cabillaud, in an effort to relieve the child's troubled spirits and take her mind off her bereavement, urged her to resume her hitherto tireless work on his great tome *Cuisine Zoologique: une philosophie de la viande*, but she refused outright.

'I'm having nothing more to do with the wretched book!' shouted the blubbering Violet, distraught. 'I have poisoned my own mother!'

Cabillaud had the common sense to button his lip, but at the back of his mind lurked rebellion. Should his life's work grind to a halt, just because of a single, isolated misadventure? Should *Cuisine Zoologique* fail, just because a lone recipe within it had proved (in one case only) fatal?

There is a saying that goes: Too many cooks spoil the broth. Did too many, in the Scrapie houschold, now mean two? Was the Scrapie kitchen, spacious though it was, large enough to contain two consciences as afflicted as those of Violet Scrapie and Jacques-Yves Cabillaud? Both were volatile. Grief hung over them like a pall.

A philosopher such as Confucius might have said, 'We witness before us here an imbalance of yin and yang.'

But a young woman such as Violet Scrapie said instead, 'This is unbearable. I'm going out. Find your lead, Suet, and follow me!'

Cabillaud, kicking the stove, said, '*Merde!*'

Was it the ghostly presence of the Laudanum Empress and her cloud of psychic particles that steered Violet and the faithful Suet in the direction of Oxford Street that day?

Or was it simply fate that caused them to barge past the stalls selling roast-chestnuts, past the organ-grinders and the charlatans and the hansom cabs, and clatter straight, slap-bang, into a placard on which the following words were printed: MEAT IS MURDER?

The placard was attached to a man. The man in question – now cast in the role of victim, picked himself up off the pavement, and patiently awaited the apology he deserved. He was accustomed to abuse from strangers, but being a Christian, he also made a point of always hoping, most fervently, for the best.

'I am most terribly sorry,' said Miss Violet Scrapie. She said it with simplicity and grace. The man noted that, despite her quite monstrous size, she had a pretty, sad face, and was wearing mourning garb. So feeling suddenly sorry for her despite the shock she had caused him, he smiled at her, and began to speak.

'Your apology is – OUCH!'

He yelped in pain. He had been assaulted a second time.

Violet never knew what it was that came over Suet. So far his canine instincts had been proved utterly sound – witness his refusal to eat the braised primate that caused the death of the Laudanum Empress – but surely this was utterly out of character? It was not in his nature to hurt a fly. It will take more than another gracious apology to fix this, Violet thought, as she whipped out her black lace handkerchief – still sodden with funeral tears from a week ago, that's how much she had cried – and began dabbing at the wound on the man's curiously skinny leg.

'Suet's never attacked a human before,' Violet mustered. 'I don't know what's got into him. He's gone after rats, but . . .' Her voice trailed off in confusion. 'Look, can I escort you anywhere?' she offered the bleeding man.

'As a matter of fact you can,' he told her, mopping furiously at his shin. 'You can be good enough to help me stagger to a meeting I am about to hold in the public chambers.'

'What's happening there?' asked Violet, picking up the MEAT IS MURDER placard and propping it against a railing.

'A meeting of the Vegetarian Society,' he replied. 'Let me introduce myself. My name is Henry Salt, and I would like to invite you, miss, and your dog, to be my guests.'

'I am Violet Scrapie,' she said, proffering her hand. 'And this is Suet.' She kicked the creature lightly, and he hung his head. Going to the man's wretched meeting was the least she could do, she supposed, as she half-carried the limping Mr Salt to the public meeting hall, the reluctant Suet pitter-pattering along in their wake. The hall was dusty, and as Violet seated herself, it was filling up with an odd selection of people, all spectacularly thin. Violet shuddered, grateful for her own padding on these hard little chairs.

'Silence, please!' called Mr Salt, standing before them with his hands in a supplicating gesture. 'I would like to welcome a newcomer to our gathering! Please allow me to introduce Miss Violet Scrapie!'

There were murmurs of acknowledgement from the crowd, and a woman next to Violet, who looked like a bony fish, piped up, 'Pleased to meet, you, miss, I'm sure!'

Mr Salt's speech was a lengthy one, during which he exhibited himself to be most passionate about his fellow beings. More particularly those with feathers, fur and scales. Violet, who had seen the carcass of many a fellow being, and cooked and eaten not a few of the more exotic ones, thanks to *Cuisine Zoologique*, listened with irritation to his evangelistic discourse. It was clear to her, glancing briefly round the half-empty hall, that Mr Salt was preaching to the converted. His argument was contorted, wordy and earnest, but boiled down – reduced, as you might reduce a stock – its central argument was simple: men are hypocrites.

'Look at us,' he stormed, 'cherishing our pets, and treating them like humans,' here he cast a glance at Suet, who retreated further beneath Violet's chair, 'and then destroying a whole class of animal for our ghoulish consumption.' Suet began to wheeze unhappily. Violet, meanwhile, recalled her father's work on the Animal Kingdom Collection, and the Royal Hippo's insistence that the stuffed beasts be clothed in breeches and the like, and conceded that Mr Salt had something of a point here. 'Anthropomorphism makes cannibals of us all,' he continued. 'The only solution is to abandon our lust for the carcass, and eat herbs of the field!'

Now here, they parted company.

'We are the most complex and highly developed creatures on earth,' he proclaimed. 'Yet despite our thousands of years of civilisation, we pander to our primitive urge to feed on flesh. Is this the pinnacle of humanity, to breed creatures in order that they may be killed for our consumption? Are we no more than uncivilised fatteners of calves?'

As Mr Salt delineated the rights of God's beasts, and the holiness of St Francis of Assisi, and the inhumanity of man, a guilty tear rolled down Suet's cheek, but Violet's mouth remained set in refusal. After Mr Salt's speech had ended, there was much applause from the group of undernourished-looking people, and the bony-fish woman next to Violet rose to her feet, reached beneath her chair, and whisked a linen cloth off a platter. Violet began to concentrate, sniffing the air as the thin woman sidled round with the platter, bearing lumpy vegetarian pies. Violet took a single bite, then spat.

'That's disgusting,' she said.

'Any chance you might be interested in becoming a member?' asked the thin woman, apparently undeterred. 'Vegetarianism is excellent for the figure.'

'No chance at all,' said Miss Scrapie, suddenly peckish and feeling the urgent desire for a pork chop. Dragging the distressed Suet behind her, she swept her huge bulk out of the hall, and headed for the butcher's.

Again: was it the ghostly presence of the Laudanum Empress and her cloud of psychic particles, or was it fate, that gave her this desire for a chop? Or was it simple, straightforward human greed?

Whatever the cause, Violet Scrapie finds herself, minutes later, peering through the window of Mr Samuel's shop, where a plaster statuette of a pig, whose chubby, cheeky face displays no irony, proffers a platter of chops, sausages and bacon rashers. Violet enters, dragging Suet behind her. But – what idiocy has entered the creature's foolish brain? He's whimpering! What's going on?

'Shut up, you silly dog,' Violet hisses, and kicks him again. He squeals on the blood-stained sawdust. In the crowded butcher's shop, upside-down poultry hangs from hooks, exuding that seductive and atrocious smell of death, so familiar to Violet from an early age, when she played on the floor of Cabillaud's chopping room. The butcher, like Cabillaud on his chopping days, wears a murderous apron and Violet notices how his fat fingers, mottled with blood and cold, are indistinguishable from the chipolatas he holds bunched for wrapping in paper for his customer. It's as though he has wrapped his own severed hand.

'Lovely piece of meat, there, madam,' he murmurs, handing it over to the woman in a little bloody parcel.

The invisible ghost of the Laudanum Empress hovers above Violet as she gazes about her, taking in the scene – so similar to the chopping room back home, but suddenly so alien. What's come over her, all of a sudden?

Suet squeals again, and whimpers, pulling on his lead to get out. 'Herbs of the field . . . cannibals of us all . . .' These are Mr Salt's words. Why are they coming back to her now? Why here? Still rooted to the floor, Violet gawps as the butcher now serves his next customer, a little coughing man, with a rack of lamb; watches as he wields the chopper, slamming it down with a crunch, brutally cleaving the gristle and holding up half a rib-cage for the man's inspection. She turns, and sees dead pigs hanging gaped open like small pianos, alongside calves' heads, mutton thighs, trays of kidneys in puddles of ink-dark blood, slobbery white brains and strips of tripe, thick and pale as undercarpet.

'Good afternoon, miss,' says the butcher, addressing Violet, who has suddenly reached the front of the queue. He offers his bloody hands. 'How can I help you?'

She stares for a while at the butcher. 'You can't,' she says bluntly. Something is choking her. 'There's too much blood.'

'Begging your pardon, miss?'

Silence. Then a strangulated gulp. Suet, flooded with a sudden audacity, seizes the moment and tugging on his lead, drags Violet Scrapie forcibly from the shop.

Violet Scrapie has since argued that it was indeed that chance meeting with Mr Salt in the street, and the eye-opening visit to the butcher's shop that was the first step on her road to Damascus. For that afternoon, sweaty and disturbed after her adventure, Violet returned home to find that, despite herself, the words of Mr Salt were still ringing in her head. 'Anthropomorphism makes cannibals of us all,' he had proclaimed. 'If we truly believe that animals have souls, then we should refrain from eating our brothers! And if they do not have souls, then why, I pray, does the elephant shed tears and the mother leopard lay down her life to save her cub?'

Violet heaved her way up the stairs in Madagascar Street, with Suet anxiously scampering in her wake. She flung open the door of her father's workshop and gazed upon the scene before her. Her father lay slumped over his work table, fast asleep and snoring gently. An eviscerated squirrel dangled on a hook above his head, and in front of him, pinned to the wall, was a diagram of a jaguar's skeleton and musculature. Suet drew in a sharp breath; it was his first foray into this chamber of horrors, and doggy memories swirled in his brain: long-forgotten inhumanities performed upon him at the laboratory as a pup came floating into his consciousness, and he shuddered and whimpered. Violet, sensing his unease, took a step back, and stumbled over a jawbone. A crocodile lay belly-up, slit open on Scrapie's stuffing table, its flesh and a wobble of unspeakable viscera gleaming in a pile beside it. Violet recalled Cabillaud's blood-stained chopping room, and felt, for the first time in her life, a pang of remorse.

Those dishes they had prepared together had indeed been a delight – but a price had been paid, in the form of lives. Animals' lives – and now that of a human. What's more, her own mother! Could there not be some other way? She stroked Suet, deep in thought. Mr Salt's words began to haunt her. Imaginary tastes turned to ashes in her mouth. And imaginary smells – smells that had once made her mouth water – now began to make her retch.

She descended to the basement kitchen, from whence the odour of walrus tripe was wafting ominously.

'There is a problem,' Violet announced.

Cabillaud looked up from his cooking pot. 'Ah, *chérie*. You have returned. I am making ze mustard sauce with ze peppercorns, and a little tiny hint of sweetness, in ze form of my own rosehip *compote*.' Cabillaud had not yet noticed Violet's stony and tear-besmirched countenance. 'This walrus, he has need of lifting a little from his unhappy heaviness of taste.'

'I said a problem.'

The chef looked up, saw the finality on the face of his protégée, and read some of her thoughts, for was she not an open book to him? Was she not his own little Violette, whom he had personally perched on his weighing machine a million times, and to whom he had fed the best morsels of everything! His own little Violette, whom he had single-handedly educated in the pleasures of the palate!

'Meat is murder,' she announced.

His own little Violette, now turning against him? *Mon Dieu!* How could she?

'But ze human being is a carnivore!' countered Cabillaud. 'Ze animals, is not ze peoples! Zey have no human rights, *chérie!*'

One thing has a terrible tendency to lead to another – and sure enough, this sudden, bitter exchange proved to be but the *hors d'oeuvre* to a whole menu of conflict, whose main course was the marinated and long-simmered substance of Violet's grief, accompanied by an ethical dispute on animal rights featuring *mille-feuille* and crushed garlic and coriander, leading into a rich, repercussive meringue and sherry trifle of a debate on personal morality, an argument with scalloped icing and raspberries, a confrontation of furiously clashing flavours, multiple toxins, and flagrant disjunctions of taste. Tears were shed on both sides. A pan was thrown. Knees were got down upon. Belgian beseechings were to be heard. Pages from *Cuisine Zoologique* were spat upon and shredded out of pique. And finally, sobbing but victorious, the mistress of the house, the loyal dog Suet at her side, dismissed her former guru. Violet Scrapie. No longer a girl, but a woman. And what a woman.

As Violet Scrapie experiences her coming of age in the basement kitchen, a banging rhythmical noise is emanating from the taxidermist's workshop on the ground floor. *Thump, thump, thump.* It is the sound of flesh on wood. Fist on table, to be

161

more precise. It's a busy life, being dead, reflects the Laudanum Empress; satisfied with Violet's progress, she drifts upstairs clutching her phantom petticoats to discover Dr Ivanhoe Scrapie in a state of utmost distress.

'Why, why, why?' he wails, his voice catching. As she passes through the closed door of his workshop, the Empress pats her hair and adjusts her ghostly face. She is briefly touched by his display of emotion, but also somewhat piqued; could the man not have tried a little harder to summon up such feelings while she was alive? But her sympathy is short-lived; it soon becomes apparent that the emotion we are witnessing here is neither grief nor remorse over the death of Mrs Scrapie; it is that green-eyed monster, professional jealousy.

'Bastard!' he moans, thumping harder on the table. 'Damned, bloody man!'

When the findings of the great scientist Charles Darwin had been published yesterday, Dr Scrapie's reaction, after he had stayed up all night reading the scholarly work, had been even more extreme than that which we are now witnessing. They had involved his forehead, and a marble mantelpiece. Human blood had been shed.

And why not? For he had been an idiot, a buffoon, an intellectual amoeba!

'Thirty years in zoology – *how could I not have seen it*?' he growls. 'It's so *obvious*! Any child who has visited a bloody *farm* could have spotted it!'

The hideous fact at the epicentre of Scrapie's misery is this: Darwin's *Origin of Species*, charting and explaining the great ladder of Nature, has made the sum of his own life's hitherto not inconsiderable achievements look suddenly so unambiguously lightweight that they almost fly into the air of their own accord. His historically successful stuffing of an earthworm, the publication of his paper *On the Epidermis of the Chameleon*, his appointment as Taxidermist Royal, his work on the Animal Kingdom Collection and the defunct specimens of Trapp's *Ark*, his discoveries about the rhino's hip-joint: all are as nothing compared to Darwin's spectacular triumph! Dr Ivanhoe Scrapie will now be consigned for ever to the dustbin of history! The grotesque injustice of it leaves him winded. His whole career blotted out by another's fame! It is all so monstrously galling!

He slumps over the table and breathes heavily, his chest shuddering, as though it houses a volcano instead of a heart. A volcano now on the verge of a most dangerous eruption. Oh, God! If only *he*, during his long career, had made a discovery of similar note! If only *he* had ventured forth on the *Beagle*, journeyed to the Galápagos, and, when drunk on ship's rum (how bloody well else?) imagined a stretch of time over which scales became feathers, fins mutated into legs, legs metamorphosed into wings, and swim bladders fashioned stomachs of themselves, all through the vagaries of chance. Instead, he had stayed here in London all these years, working for Her Majesty's absurd Animal Kingdom Collection, and faffing about with the carcasses of Trapp's *Ark*. In short, spending years of his life cleaning up another man's mess, to feed the whimsy of a crazed monarch, and a woman to boot! Why? Why? Why?

'Bloody book!' he yells, now flinging the tome to the floor in frustration, rage and pique.

'It's *obvious* that human beings are primates! I always *knew* we were! It's *obvious* that we evolved from monkeys and apes! So why didn't *I* come out and say so? Instead of messing about stuffing the buggers and putting breeches on them?'

'Calm down, Ivanhoe,' soothes the Empress, floating away from the shelter of the moose antlers to hover opaquely above him. 'I foresee that this kind of violent emotion will be the death of you.'

'*Charlotte*?' he murmurs. 'Charlotte? Is that you?'

'You will blow a gasket in your heart,' predicts the Laudanum Empress.

'A gasket in my heart?' he breathes. He must be hyperventilating, he concludes. Dreaming. Overworked. Something.

'If you think Mr Darwin's revelation is shocking, let me inform you, my dear Ivanhoe, that there is far worse to come! Don't say you haven't been warned!'

'Worse to come? What? Charlotte, what are you talking about? Are you there?'

But she's gone. Vanished. Skedaddled. That's the trouble with ghosts.

CHAPTER 16

THE FEEDING
RITUAL

It was a time of national panic. The Fertility Crisis was now officially a disaster, and the Sperm Drain became so intense that the Government decided to launch the Loyalty Bonus Scheme immediately. Overnight, I found myself eligible for an extra hundred yo-yos a week. In the meantime, the Pregnancy Reward had been announced. There's nothing like greed, is there? Five million yo-yos aren't to be sneezed at. The plus side of it all, of course, was that Britain was a lad's paradise. I was in with a chance now, I reckoned. A bloke could have any girl he wanted.

Or girls.

The Saturday of the barbecue came. Norman and his wife Abbie were in their element there on the patio, he fussing with charcoal pellets and firelighters and wind direction, she all flushed with mother-hen excitement at the prospect of a new palate to tempt at her elegant pale-green plastic flexi-table.

'Meet the harem,' said Norman proudly. 'This is Abbie' (I shook her flour-covered hand) 'and these are Tweedles Dum and Dee.'

'Buck de Savile,' I said. The girls looked at each other and giggled. There was a glamorous but rather eccentric-looking woman in white petticoats hovering about in the doorway; I caught a whiff of mothballs.

'And who's this?' I asked.

'Oh, she's just our ghost,' said Norman. 'The skeleton from the cupboard. I told you we'd been invaded by Victoriana. She came with the stuffed animals. Don't mind her.'

I laughed. 'Nice one, Norman! I hear they're all the rage!'

The eccentric woman made a sour face, and slunk back indoors.

'Nice cuts of pork you've got there,' I said, eyeing something marinaded. Those teenage Saturdays working at the butcher's hadn't been entirely wasted.

'Oh, call me Abbie,' said the head of the harem. 'Much friendlier. The pork's organic, because you never know, do you? I'm a bit of an ingredients nut.'

'She likes food that'll respect her in the morning,' put in Rose, reaching through the window for a pot of dip, then joining her sister to confederate next to a concrete urn. They kept looking in my direction, and I couldn't help wondering if I was the topic of their whispered conversation. Rose and Blanche were both wearing dresses, one white, one pink. Sigmund stirred, and I imagined them –

'That's my two lovelies,' says Norman, as though intercepting the vision. 'Sociable is putting it mildly.'

'Can I help you with anything, Norman?' I asked quickly.

'No, mate, just you relax. Abbie is just finishing off her TV rehearsal in the kitchen, bless her. She'll be along with the rest of the or doovers in half a tick. I'm off for some more of these charcoal pellets; the gals'll keep you on the straight and narrow in the interim, won't you, gorgeouses?'

'TV rehearsal?' I said. 'I didn't know Abbie was involved in television.'

'She isn't,' said Norman. Then added, loyally, 'But she will be, if there's any justice in the world!'

The twins snorted.

'Food's her thing,' says Rose.

'There's nothing she doesn't know about food,' adds Blanche. 'Food allergies, the origins of food, the sociology of food, food and music, the nutritional value of food, how to cook food, when and how to re-use the leftovers, storage of food, how to tell if something's edible or non-edible –'

'And she's an expert on food symbolism,' says Rose.

166

I wasn't entirely sure what food symbolism might be, but I nodded knowingly.

'Food and love, food and the post-war generation, food and cutlery,' continues Blanche.

'Food and discipline,' adds Rose.

'Food and God,' counters Blanche.

A pause.

Then Rose blurts, 'Only she's never really made it.'

There's another pause, and then Blanche adds, 'Never will.'

Food and failure, then.

'Well, Buck. What's your real name, then?' asked Blanche, or was it Rose, when Norman had disappeared from view. Not a great start.

'Buck de Savile *is* my real name,' I insisted. I'd have to think on my feet here.

'Pull the other one,' said Rose, or was it Blanche. They were nothing if not direct.

'My father was French,' I lied. 'That's where the *de* comes from. It's what's called an aristocratic prefix, I'll have you know. *Voulez-vous coucher avec moi ce soir*, et cetera.' They giggled. So they liked the idea, too. 'And the Buck is short for Buckingham.'

'There was a young Frenchman called Buckingham,' began one of them.

'Who always kissed girls before –' giggled the other.

'I've seen you both,' I intercepted. 'In the hypermarket in Judlow.'

'Saturday job,' the Roseblanches said in unison, and sniggered some more.

'But you didn't notice me,' I said ruefully, teasingly. Flirtatiously. They laughed.

'We're the living dead in there,' said Rose.

'Yeah,' agreed Blanche. 'If God himself walked in, we'd just treat him like any other customer.'

'I'd prob'ly ask him if he wanted extra carriers,' laughed Rose.

167

'I wouldn't even notice if he signed his cheque GOD in big letters,' added Blanche, enjoying the fantasy. 'Or if he didn't pay for his shopping at all but just wheeled his trolley right through the checkout area, past the redemption desk, and out into the car-park.'

'And then flew up into the air with it.'

'To His celestial home beyond the clouds,' finished Rose.

They certainly had a vivid imagination.

Then the conversation moved on to wildlife.

'I'm just a glorified plumber with a stash of drugs,' I told them, when they begged me for details about which was the cutest fluffy animal I'd ever cured of cancer. Norman was under a similar illusion about my veterinary knowledge; he'd been going on about the stuffed-animal collection again, and had insisted that I take a look at it this afternoon. Frankly, I had other things on my mind.

'We had a hamster called Mohammed,' Rose was telling me.

Uh-o, I thought.

'He used to run about loose in our bedroom,' sighed Rose.

And together: 'He was so sweet!'

'He'd sit on your shoulder, and stuff his cute little cheeks with sunflower seeds,' remembered Rose.

'They'd be so bulging that sometimes he got overloaded and keeled over like a little wheelbarrow,' added Blanche.

'Then Dad trod on him by accident,' said Rose.

There was a brief pause as they exchanged a glance, recalling their shared mini-moment of tragedy.

'But we're going to get another one,' offered Blanche. 'A female, because we want babies.'

Disaster ahoy!

'But we'll need a male, too,' suggested Rose.

'You'd better watch out or you'll create a plague of them. One day soon there'll be more hamsters in the world than humans.'

Their faces went suddenly serious.

'It might just be a blip, like they say,' I said, to break the sudden silence that had fallen. The subject of extinction was quickly turning from an obsession into a taboo. I'd heard a stammering psychologist on the radio saying that since the b-b-b-b-bomb, we were going through a d-d-d-d-denial phase. 'You never know,' I added weakly.

The signs were indicating the opposite, though, and we all knew it. Funnily enough, the less people suddenly talked about it, the more it began to hit home that we might actually die out.

'It's because we're badly designed,' said Rose ruefully.

'Especially us,' offered Blanche, exchanging a secret look with her sister. For some reason, they both glanced down at their shoes. They were wearing oddly shaped trainers that looked familiar, though I couldn't place them.

'Two friends of ours have tried committing suicide over it,' offered Rose.

'And everyone's having sex like crazy,' mused Blanche, giving me a sly look.

'Is that an offer?' I asked, flashing them a smile.

'Might be,' they said together.

Which I took as a yes.

During the course of the meal, despite my promise to myself to avoid fluffy-animal fans, I found myself charmed by the twins' unity as sisters, their team-spiritedness, the way they took it in turns to speak, the way they held my attention like something in a pair of pincers. I noticed, too, their habit of biting their rather narrow lower lip and letting their round, quite deep-set eyes go slightly out of focus. I observed their innocence, their gaucheness, their fun-loving turn of mind, which I guessed – rightly, as it turned out – was the outward manifestation of a fun-loving turn of body. The smell of their flesh, which I now began to detect beneath the protective layers of cheap perfume, was unusual, almost feral, and marvellously tantalising. I had to admit that by the time we'd finished the meal, I was completely under their extraordinary spell.

I have had cause to ask myself since then, in my more

philosophical moods: Was it because I was two men, Bobby Sullivan and Buck de Savile, that I was so inevitably drawn to two women? What if it had only been one girl? Would I have felt the same way about her?

Does one feel differently about broken scissors? Were lives revolutionised by the first photocopiers?

Buy the sausage and onion lattice pie, get the coleslaw free.

'Delicious, Abbie,' I told their mum, when I finally pushed away my plate. 'Mouth-watering, unusual, and satisfying. And very attractively presented.' I winked at the girls. I was talking about the food, but I meant them, and they knew it. 'I'm sure you noticed that I took double helpings of everything,' I added.

They giggled.

'And now,' said Norman firmly, steering me indoors, 'you're coming with me. I'm luring you up to the loft for an hour to inspect Abbie's stuffed menagerie. There are some beasts up there that are sorely in need of a professional assessment, mate,' he informed me, as I followed him upstairs, resigned to my fate.

As it turned out, the Victorian stuffed-animal collection in the attic turned out to contain some interesting stuff, including a corgi named Suet – obviously someone's pet, because taxidermically speaking it wasn't a great specimen – a few birds, all rather greasy but worth a bit if you sold them in the right place, i.e. some kind of fayre – and a weird primate, strangely humanoid and dressed in red velvet pantaloons. The brass plate underneath was labelled 'The Gentleman Monkey'. If that was its species name, it was a new one on me, I thought – but then it's all too easy to forget that there are more than two hundred and fifty species of primate, other than us. I must admit, though, that I shuddered when I looked at it. It was the clothes that did it. I couldn't help remembering Giselle, in her little pink frock and her nappy, and Mrs Mann, and her threat to –

'Abbie says they're worthless,' Norman was telling me. 'She

called the Antiques Hotline, and now she wants me to bin the lot.' He patted a stuffed wombat on the head absent-mindedly. It was wearing a frock-coat. 'That's the danger of your loft refurbishment. Bugger of a house, if you'll pardon my franglais. Jellyfish in the larder, salt all over the flag-stones, and there's sweet FA you can do, cos of the blinking listed building malarkey. Thank God for charity shops, say I. A bit of recycling doesn't go amiss, eh, Buck? Or maybe we could flog 'em at a car-boot sale. There's a big Firework Night do at the community centre looming on the horizon; we could do with some funds for a few bits and bobs.'

I was staring at the primate. No; it was nothing like Giselle. There were similarities with the macaque family – the shortness of the tail, the humanoid expression of the face – but it didn't fit into any of the categories I'd seen. And Christ knows, back in Tooting Bec I'd seen quite a few. I'm not a specialist by any means, but I knew enough to recognise that this was an unusual specimen. It had ape-like characteristics, a strangely human-looking head, and was stuffed in an upright posture – a posture which the angle of its pelvic girdle indicated wasn't a mere whim of the taxidermist, but the creature's natural stance. I was immediately fascinated. It appeared to be more of an ape than a monkey, but there was a tail sticking out of its pantaloons like a question mark. It didn't make sense. And its glass eyes were blue; an unlikely colour, and also over-large, I reckoned, for any of the primates.

'Keep it,' I told Norman. 'I've got a hunch that it's rare.'

'Can't,' he replied. 'Boss's orders. Everything's got to go.'

'I'll take it back to my place, then,' I told him. I'd taken a liking to the thing. There was something familiar about its features that I couldn't place.

'Abbie says it looks like her grandmother,' said Norman, reading my thoughts. 'Gives her the creeps.' I peered at the creature again. Now that he said it, you could even see something of Abbie in it, when you looked. The odd pelvis, and the deep-set eyes. I laughed.

171

'Not flattering,' I said. 'Best get her Gentleman friend out of the house, then, mate.'

Norman helped me load the monkey on to the passenger seat of the Nuance, and I took him home. I tried him in various rooms, then finally opted for the bathroom. I hung a towel off him. His arm was crooked in just the right position.

It was almost as though he had actually been stuffed with that in mind.

CHAPTER 17

A COMING OF AGE

Higgins feeds me throu the bars.
  Let me out, I wispas. I wil do anything.
  Cant he sez. Wer on the SEA. Nower to go. NOWER. Exept
DIE in the wavs.
  Then I wil throw myself out and DIE, I sez. I dont care.
  (Here another stain obliterates a few lines of the text.)
  – stil in darkness. The giraf cums on in TANGEER. And the
turtels and the wulvs and the smaller creechers. Higgins feeds
them. They grunt and they howl. Thats wy its DARK, to mak
them sleep mor. Lordnum for all of us.
  Im sleepin all the tyme. Sleepin away my lyfe. DREEM
sumtymes that sumwun wil cum and SAVE me.
  But fat chance of THAT.

I did my best to forget what had happened at the Travelling Fair
of Danger and Delight, and I swore Tommy Boggs to secrecy.
But the Contortionist began to haunt my dreams, and barely a
night passed without some terrible visitation from her or the
Man-Eating Wart-hog. In one dream, she was slitting open her
belly to reveal writhing tadpoles. In another, Parson Phelps was
nailed to the cross, and she and the Wart-hog were lapping up
his blood. In another, she was an Angel again, but when she
spread her wings, they were no more than dusty, battered old
cobwebs.
  It was perhaps in an effort to banish such dreams from my
thoughts that I ventured to take part in the Thistle-Pulling

173

Contest for the first time. Perhaps I hoped that the experience would purge me. Or make me a man. After all, my fifteenth birthday having passed, I was now eligible for manhood – defined by Thunder Spit as showing the ability to skewer oneself alive on thistles without complaint.

'Now you're to start on a count of three!' yells Farmer Harcourt. 'You're to grab 'em with your right hand, and pull 'em by the root, and may the best man win!'

The villagers cheer. Down by the gushing Flid, beneath the scraggy junipers, a little Boggs boy, Tommy's youngest brother, takes a straw and blows a live frog into a balloon until it pops. The Thistle-Pulling Contest might easily be defined as a pagan ritual, but Parson Phelps has nevertheless always given it his blessing, for it tallies well with his 'Marble Friday' principles of self-denial and sought-after hardship. And as his sermon this morning reminded us, the thistle is part of the glorious function of Nature, designed by God to serve man in a myriad ways. 'Just as birdsong is God's way of making music for us, and the herring gull is there to serve us as a warning not to ill-treat our children, and sardines are there to remind us of the loaves and fishes, and the horse He provided for us to ride as transport, and the sheep for wool, so the thistle' – here he gave one of his famous four-second pauses – 'the thistle is there to remind us that there is pain in His glory as well as delight.'

Thunder Spit has been holding Thistle Day, in the same scrubby field by the Flid, 'since the beginning of time', according to Mr Clegg, who was eighty-three. His own great-grandfather was a champion, in the days when, according to nostalgic memory, the thorns were the size of bodkins, and the plants themselves grew to five feet.

Everybody is here; old Mr Clegg and his entire family – four generations, all with the same rolling seaman's walk, the squint-eyed Lumpeys, Mrs Sequin with her hat made of felt and papier mâché, the silent Peat-Hoves, the literal-minded Balls, the crabby Bark twins, the stubborn Tobashes, and the exaggerating Morpitons, with their dancing eyes.

174

And I, the freak, the foundling, the cuckoo, whose sphincter is being cruelly tortured by Mildred at the very thought of grasping these brutal weeds that jut like threatening weapons before me. A pang of envy overcomes me as I spot Tommy on the far side of the field, rubbing his hands together as if they were a pair of tools.

'One, two, three, GO!' yells Farmer Harcourt, and the agony begins.

'Get on with it, Tobias!' yells Parson Phelps from the hawthorn hedge. 'You owe it to your Saviour!' As usual, it isn't quite clear whether he is referring to himself or to the Lord. Dutifully, I flail about, praying that the world's first thornless thistle will suddenly appear before me. Beside me, young Charlie Peat-Hove, bloodstained and tearful, has already pulled his first thistle. Parson Phelps' voice is thundering at me now.

'Shut your eyes, son, and God will be with you! He will preserve you from all pain if you only have faith!'

I shut my eyes, and think of the Lord, who resembles the portrait in my Noah's Ark picture; a gentle-faced, Roman-nosed gent with a long white beard and a toga-like cassock flowing down. A man in the clouds. And close my fist around the thistle's stalk.

'OUCH!' It was like being stapled through with steel bolts.

'Go on!' shouts Parson Phelps again. 'Have courage! Think of Christ and His crown of thorns!'

'AAAGH!' I wail, and pull another one. Is it faith in the Lord, or the desire to please my father, that triumphs at this point? Either way, the thistle pulled, and my hand gushing bright blood, I can stand it no more, and withdraw from the game. Parson Phelps arrives and mops busily at my bleeding hand, applying camomile nipple-cream in silence. The words milksop, sissy and coward are not uttered, but they hang in the air between us as we witness Thunder Spit's bravest toiling amid the whirling thistledown to prove their manhood.

'Perhaps next year, I will be a man?' I offer. But my father sighs; I have let him down.

175

Within half an hour, Farmer Harcourt's thistle field was plucked clean as a chicken. The contest was won by Tommy, who had by now started as an apprentice to his father in the forge, and who had calluses on his hands as tough as bull-hide. He had become a hero; that night, the mountain of dead thistles was dragged down to the beach and set alight to cook the feast of clams and lobsters and sardines; as the great bonfire took light, illuminating the grey sand and grey bleached rock with an orange glow, I prayed that next year I, too, would pass the test of manhood.

That night I dreamed of her again – more vividly than ever. She was standing on top of a burning pyre of dead thistles, her face calm. Out of the smoke, she rose like a phoenix or an Angel. Her great wings flapped as she flew off into the night.

Despite my failure to become a man at the Thistle-Pulling Contest, I think of that time as my coming of age. It was also more, and worse. It was a fall from grace. I have always thought that it's in the nature of childhood to misunderstand. To witness adult behaviour and, because there is no reference in the child-world, to invent a story around that thing which turns out to be a completely garbled and inaccurate concoction. But I was no longer a child. I was a fifteen-year-old who stared, and wondered, and made assumptions, and who signally failed to do the one thing he should have done, which would have possibly saved him so much grief. I did not insist on knowing.

In short, I was a coward. And I was a coward because I feared the truth. And this, as you will see, dear reader, has been my story. A fear, a lack of courage, because of a further fear, that the thing itself, the truth, will be so unacceptable that –

'That what?' she asked me, years later, as we stared into our favourite rockpool.

'That I will be rejected. And that you will not love me. That no one will.'

My dream was prophetic. It was a windy Friday after the Thistle Contest. Tommy Boggs and I were returning from the harbour, where we'd been helping with the lobster pots. It was my task to tie their claws together once we had heaved them from the pots, and then hurl them into the lobster bins to take to Judlow. I kept getting pinched. Tommy, being stronger, had the job of ripping the seaweed from the pots and flinging the pots into the boats. When we had finished, Mr Tobash handed me and Tommy each a bunch of sardines on a string, flipping and flashing in the sun. Clutching them like heavy jewellery, we headed home through the buffeting wind: I to the Parsonage, to cook the sardines for our tea, and Tommy to the forge, where his father was teaching him how to make fancy whorled doorknobs to sell in Judlow. St Nicholas's Church had just come into view, and it was as we were rounding the corner by the gnarled chestnut tree, where Tommy's path diverged from mine, that we saw Parson Phelps standing in the graveyard with a stranger.

Tommy and I stopped in our tracks and stared. The smell of fresh fish. The lash of the wind.

You couldn't see her properly. She seemed to be a tiny woman – so small I thought at first that she was a child – wrapped in a hooded cloak that flapped wildly. They stood a foot or so apart from one another next to a thick tombstone, my father stooping slightly to catch her words, but clutching his hands behind his back in a nervous mannerism that I recognised. It was apparent immediately that they were engaged in an intense and heated discussion.

Tommy now gestured to me to creep towards the low hedge that separated us from the graveyard; we crouched against the briars, near a blackbird's nest with four blue eggs in it. Suddenly Tommy grabbed my shoulder and pulled me down.

'Shhhh!' he said. 'Listen!'

My father had begun shouting, and gesticulating furiously as he did so. As the words flew, I strained to catch them.

'Foulness'. 'Evil'. 'Slander'. 'Whore'. I recoiled. How could this unknown woman have so induced his wrath? 'Devil himself'. 'Dare you'. 'God's name'. Then he shook his fist in her face. Surely he could not be about to attack her? I flinched.

Then suddenly, perhaps recognising how close he had come to violence, he stopped. His arms hung loose by his sides, and his shoulders slumped in a dismal triangle.

'Look!' said Tommy. 'She's reaching in her cloak!'

I squinted. 'She's giving him something.'

'What is it?' asked Tommy, peering, too.

'Looks like a bottle. Or a jar of some sort.'

Whatever it was, it appeared to be heavy and unwieldy, and after lifting it to his face for inspection, she stood it on the tombstone. As he stared at it, his upper body still in the same sad posture of defeat, the woman reached in the folds of her cloak again, brought out a white rectangle of paper, and thrust it in his hand.

'An envelope,' breathed Tommy. 'She's giving him a letter.'

Without taking his eyes from the jar, my father took the envelope and shoved it deep into the pocket of his frock-coat.

We could see even from this distance that his face was unnaturally pale.

Then he said something to her, and lifted the jar from the tombstone. Holding it in outstretched hands, as though it might explode, he turned, and walked stiffly into the church. The woman stayed outside. She had her back to us now, a huddled figure amid the gravestones. She didn't move, but just stood there as the daffodils bounced wildly about her feet. After a few minutes, my father emerged from the church. He no longer had the jar. He walked like a frail ghost. Mechanically, he pulled something from his waistcoat.

'Money!' exclaimed Tommy. 'He's counting out notes, look!' And so he was. On and on, until a whole wad of money – where did this come from? From his own savings? From the church's funds? – had passed from his left hand to his right. He said something to the woman, who held out her hand, and he gave her the wad.

Then, suddenly, my father had sparked back into life and was shouting once more. 'Ever again', I heard. 'Wrath of the Almighty'. Then, 'Forbid you, ever'. The other words were

178

indistinct but their despair and rage carried over to us, and we were afraid. Even Tommy looked suddenly smaller and quite white. The blackbird came back and hopped around her nest. Taking my eyes off my father, I stared at the perfect symmetry of her four blue eggs, and my tapeworm Mildred writhed within me. I do not know how long I stared at these eggs; a minute or an hour. When I lifted my eyes again, my father had turned on his heel, and was disappearing into the church. The woman was stuffing the wad of money into the folds of her cloak. Then turning suddenly, she was walking down the path towards the church gate.

It was then that Tommy and I saw her face and gasped.

I swear to this day, and Tommy swears, too, that it was the expression we recognised, rather than the face itself.

She swept past us and was gone.

We stayed there in silence for a while.

'I'll come and see you tomorrow,' said Tommy finally. 'I'm on my way to the forge, and Dad'll beat me if I'm late. You be all right?'

'I'll be all right,' I lied. I was half-crying by now. Somehow I managed to stagger home, and began to gut and fry the sardines. Father still didn't return, so I put the fish aside and made my way to the church, to find him on his knees, sobbing before the altar.

'Father –'

He swung round, his moon-face streaked with tears. 'Go home!' he shouted. 'Go home now, and lock yourself in your bedroom! Read from Genesis, and do not come down until I return and call you!'

'Father – who was that woman?'

'You saw her?' he whispered. His face was waxy pale.

'I saw you argue with her.'

'And what else?' he mustered. The tears had suddenly dried, giving way to a hardness I had not seen before.

'Nothing else,' I lied. 'I was just passing. I went home. Then I sat and waited for you, because I had prepared four sardines

179

for our supper, God's own fish, but when you didn't come, I came looking for you. The sardines are burnt now, father. They are now far from triumphant.'

'The sardines be damned, Tobias!' Parson Phelps was suddenly quivering all over. 'Go home now and pray.'

I turned and left. I had no courage. My spine ached.

At home, I prayed more fervently than I had ever done. Life had changed shape. My hands shook. I opened my Bible at the Book of Genesis.

'*The earth was without form, and void, and darkness was on the face of the deep,*' I read. '*And God said let there be a firmament in the midst of the waters.*' Yes. That is how it had been, in the Beginning. I could picture it happening quite clearly. Who could not, when they read these words? My eyes swam down the page. '*And the earth brought forth grass, herb yielding seed after its kind, and tree bearing fruit, wherein is the seed thereof, after its kind.*' I looked at the gourds I had collected from the plant that grew on my mother's grave. I kept them in my bedroom, in a wooden bowl. This year the fruits had not been green and stippled, as my mother's original gourd had been, nor yellow and frilled, as last year's had appeared; they were orange and warty, with little black flecks. I shivered.

'*And God created the great sea-monsters, and every living creature that moveth, which the waters brought forth abundantly, after their kinds, and every winged fowl after its kind: and God saw that it was good . . . And the Lord formed man of the dust of the ground and breathed into his nostrils the breath of life; and man became a living soul . . . And the Lord God caused a deep sleep to fall upon the man, and he slept; and He took one of his ribs, and closed up the flesh instead thereof; and the rib, which the Lord God had taken from the man, made He a woman, and brought her unto the man . . .*'

Bone of my bones, and flesh of my flesh.

For hours, I listened for the return of my father, and then, after the front door had slammed, to his mutterings and wailings emanating from downstairs. And then, for the first time in

180

my life, I heard my father curse – 'Buggeration and double damnation!' – and then weep. Finally, I fell asleep.

In the morning, slumped in Parson Phelps' chair, was a man I did not recognise. His hair had turned completely white. His skin had washed to the grey of a weak autumn sky. For a dreadful, lurching moment I thought he was dead.

He seemed to sense me in the room, then, because he opened his eyes. When he saw me standing there, he groaned and covered his face with his hands.

'Father?'

Slowly, he lowered his hands and looked at me with an expression of hatred, pity and horror.

'Yesterday,' said the Parson, his voice struggling, 'I met a witch.'

'A real witch, Father?' I whispered.

'As real as you or I.' He gazed at me for a minute, then averted his eyes from my face.

I felt myself flush. Yes; I had recognised her. From my dreams, and my vision during the Great Flood, and from the Tent of Miracles. And Tommy had, too.

She was the Contortionist.

When a leaf dies, its colour changes so gradually from green to brown, its skin shrivels so imperceptibly, and yet with such purpose, that its final dropping from the tree is more a blessing then a sadness. But to observe this process speeded up, and not in a leaf but in a human – ah. There is a pitiful sight, and one I now witnessed day by day as my Father lost his faith. His voice was increasingly bereft of conviction when he said his prayers, and those passages of the Bible which had once been of the most comfort to him now seemed to be the source of some bitter irony. Every day was now Marble Friday, and I winced as I watched him stuffing the glass balls in his shoes with such a look of grim determination as to make you weep. One morning I even spotted him put itching-powder made from rosehip seeds down his own shirt. In his madness he refused to speak of the Contortionist,

181

and every time I opened my mouth to ask a question he would put up his hand to stop me, with an expression on his face so tragic that I had not the heart to pursue my enquiries.

Not the heart, nor the courage, either. For where might my questions lead?

As Parson Phelps turned his broad back on God, his congregation, once solidly packed into St Nicholas's Church, began to thin out. As the weeks went by, his sermons became more and more haunted and rambling.

He talked of the sin of cities, and of corruption so thick you could scrape it off the walls. He said the Bible was a lie.

'Throw each of you your own so-called holy book into the deep, and see its pages disintegrate and fall away,' he hurled at what remained of his congregation one Sunday, namely Mrs Harcourt, Mrs Sequin, Dr Baldicoot, Mr Tobash and myself. 'And if there is a God, let Him work a holy miracle to save His word.'

'The Contortionist has done something to your father,' Tommy said, when I reported this to him. 'She's poisoned him. I reckon she's made him give her all his money, and then drink what was in that jar, and it's a witch's brew that's sent him mad.'

Tommy and I stared at each other.

'It's not our fault,' said Tommy, but his voice was shaking.

That night I dreamed of her again. This time she was slitting her own belly with a knife, and tadpoles were slithering out, surrounded by horrible clots of frogspawn. I touched my own skin, and screamed. I, too, was jelly.

'Something came to me in my sleep,' my father announced to me the next morning. I shuddered; had she crept into his dreams, too? But no. 'When you are seventeen you will go to Hunchburgh,' he announced, 'and become a servant of the Lord.'

God – or what was left of Him – had spoken.

And that was that.

Trapp sez we hav past Cape Horn.

Wer is Cape Horn, I sez. I do not no the shape of the Globe, and all its Places. I have no LERNIN.

He dus not tell me, so I do not discuver wer Cape Horn is. I hav been SEESICKE all nite and all day.

The Queen wants Trapp to bring bak animals for her stuffd colecshun, Rogers sez. I nows this much by now. The Animal Kingdom, its calld. He gets the animals from other zoos, African zoos, Indian zoos, zoos everywer. The hole of Empyre. Brings them bak alive, to London, that's the PLAN. There a man calld SKRAPY will keep them in the ZOO, kill them wun by wun and stuff them. Sooveneer for her Majisty. But they must be kept wel. Nice fur, nice fevvers, no bad spessymens. She wonts kwality.

I am giving you a job, soon, Trapp sez wun Day. A very important job. Wen we get to Moroco.

Wots that I sez. I am SLEEPIN all the Tyme in my cage,. It is the onlie way not to run MADDE. Ther is a DWORF GIRAF arrived next to me, maks fartin noisis in the NITE. Ther is a walrus and an antylope and a big Beaver. Al of them so RARE, says Rogers, that they is practicly the LAST IN THE WURLD.

I dont think I wonts a job, but I sez to TRAPP, wot job? from my CAGE.

Lookin after a certin GENTLEMAN, Trapp sez. You wil LIKE HIM. He is verie Hansum, verie HUMAN.

And he larfs and larfs.

CHAPTER 18

ADIEU

Last night Violet had found herself on a beach of grey rocks and grey quicksand. She was walking and sinking at the same time. The more she tried to struggle, the quicker and more greedily the quicksand gulped her down. Then it changed to soup; a thick, greenish primordial soup, writhing and lukewarm; she slapped into creatures with dark, flapping wings, horned elbows, jutting teeth, razor-edged beaks, gruesome tusks, metallic scales, prehensile talons of rusted iron. Metal-riveted sea-monsters and fowl of the air whirled in the viscous firmament, brandishing curved claws, cruet sets, flippers and dinner forks. They pinioned her to a waterlogged commode, where they bit, and pecked, and clawed, seasoning her with cloves and cayenne pepper, and ripping out the guts from her abdomen like visceral spaghetti. And she watched, helpless, pinned to her useless piece of furniture, as a stream of jeering animals paraded before her, yelping and baying and yowling for her blood. An eye for an eye! A tooth for a tooth! A rump for a rump!

And then she awoke, screaming, in a soggy pool of her own menstrual blood.

She shudders now at the recollection of her dream, and shivers in the cold breeze. All that pain! And now more!

'So not *au revoir*, Miss Scrapie,' says Cabillaud finally, when Violet has finished recounting her carnivore's nightmare.

'No, not *au revoir*.' Both of them, involuntarily, shiver, as the word hangs, unspoken, in the October air outside 14 Madagascar Street.

184

Then falls.

'*Adieu.*'

The yellow-painted cart is almost fully loaded. As Violet watches the frozen kangaroo carcass being slowly winched aloft and placed precariously on the top of the meat pile, she inhales deeply to smother a sob. In all, some forty-odd skinned creatures from Trapp's *Ark* are to accompany the Belgian chef as he leaves 14 Madagascar Street for the last time. Violet will not be sorry to see them go, but the departure of Monsieur Cabillaud is another matter. More personal. Less clear-cut. Messier. Sadder.

'All ready, zen, to go.' The Belgian bows stiffly, and takes Violet's hand, whereon he plants a chilly kiss. Their eyes slide away from each other. Cabillaud vaults atop his stack of frozen carcasses, making a niche for himself within the natural *chaise-longue* created by a half-zebra, its exposed rib-cage glistening with ice. Around them, pale and twinkling, stand the frozen statues of hippo, mongoose and chameleon, wombat and jackal, hammer-headed shark and tiger. Violet Scrapie's uncooked-pastry skin pales further, and she feels a lump forming in her throat. She gulps painfully. Her coming of age, she acknowledges, had been a bitter conflict. A clash of wills and minds, as experienced in families, that had evolved, inevitably, into a broader argument, such as lovers might have, provoking wider disagreements, as enacted by politicians and ideologues, and thence to a huge full-blown opposition of belief systems such as in war. The two sides solidly intractable. But one with a definite edge, formed by her higher social status and class, her position as the man's employer, and her sudden, newfound crisis of conscience. Everything has its price. And I am paying it now, Violet reflects as she watches Cabillaud now, settling himself into his icy seat. The price of principle. And the price of pride.

Violet has heard a rumour, via the next-door scullery maid, his one-time mistress (she of the stuck-pig episode), that Cabillaud's monstrous ambition has secured him a prestigious post in the Palace kitchens. As Cabillaud's cart, pulled by two shire horses, creaks off down the road, Violet is aware of the lump in her throat expanding, as though a walnut is growing within it at great speed, against her better judgement. She swallows with difficulty, but the walnut will not budge. If Cabillaud sheds tears, it is in secret, and they freeze on his face as the yellow-painted cart trundles towards Buckingham Palace with its ghoulish load.

The meeting of the Vegetarian Society in that dusty hall in Oxford Street, and in particular the words of Mr Henry Salt, following hard on the heels of her mother's poisoning, have continued to prey on the distraught conscience of Violet Scrapie – day and night, with a cruelty and relentlessness that beggars belief. Witness her soup dream. Cabillaud's departure, Violet realises, watching as he turns to a speck that vanishes around the corner of Madagascar Street, has done little to alleviate the unspeakable burden of her guilt.

The dream comes back to her again, and she shudders. Then turns, waddles back inside the house, and slams the door in her wake.

A moment later she is seated at her kitchen table, her big shoulders heaving, the tears running freely. Feeling more alone than she has ever felt in her entire life.

Alone? Wait! For is that not the corgi Suet, snoring beneath the table? And is a certain ghostly presence also discernible? Over there, by the door to the larder? Could it possibly be, gentle reader, that the cloud of flickering ectoplasm that is forming on the fourth shelf of the dresser is the Laudanum Empress herself, metamorphosed into phantom form?

'Still wallowing in self-pity, then, Vile?' murmurs a familiar voice.

Violet sits up rigid in her chair and listens intently. Suet stops snoring, pricks up his ears and begins to whimper.

'Mother?' ventures Violet through her tears. 'Is that you?'

'Gone, but still with us!' whispers the petticoated Empress, quoting the epitaph from her own gravestone.

'Mother?' falters Violet. She was so sure that she heard something!

'You wouldn't believe what I can see from here!' the Laudanum Empress is saying. 'A huge grocery store, Vilc. Motorised vehicles driving into its great maw, and emerging with improbable merchandise, wrapped in a substance known as cellophane. A National Lottery. Shoes with wheels, like ice skates. The young ruling the world!'

'Pardon, Mother?' whispers Violet. She can make out individual words, but they do not seem to cohere. Vehicles? Cellophane? Wheeled shoes? She must be having another nightmare. Violet's meaty shoulders slump once more.

'Vile! I'm talking to you!'

But Violet is oblivious. It is all a ghastly dream, induced by guilt! The Empress sighs with frustration. What can one do to nudge her out of this decline? 'And did I ever tell you about the workings of a high-speed food-warmer called the microwave oven?' she offers.

But wild horses cannot drag Violet Scrapie from the misery that is rightly hers. At least, not yet. In her lifetime, Violet Scrapie calculates, she has not only killed her own mother, but cooked and eaten four thousand chickens, twenty cows, nine hundred sheep, a thousand fish, and three thousand sea crustacea. And what of the incalculable? All those creatures from the Zoo and from Trapp's *Ark*, all those jettisoned carcasses from her father's workshop – how do you begin to assess quantities as vast as those? Mammals, fish, reptiles, birds, insects – where, oh where, can one even begin? All that meat. All that blood. All that murder. And for what?

FOR WHAT?

Violet shudders again, and blows her nose loudly into a large lace handkerchief.

'I will atone for all those lives!' Violet snuffles, her eyes red with weeping. 'I will atone for them, in the only way I know how!'

'Ow-ow-ow!' echoes Suet from beneath the table.

'Pure melodrama,' snorts the Laudanum Empress, and floats off.

187

CHAPTER 19

2005: THE MATING
RITUAL

The Thistle Festival was the second-biggest community event in
the Thunder Spit calendar, after the Guy Fawkes Heritage Party
in November, Norman told me. And when I arrived there that
Saturday afternoon I realised he wasn't bullshitting. 'Le tout
Thunder Spit,' as Norman called the clientele of the Stoned
Crow, was represented. Scattered about the famous Thistle
Field I spotted all the blokes from the pub, Jimmy Clegg,
Ron Harcourt, Jack and Ken Morpiton, Charlie Peat-Hove,
Billy Tobash, and a whole gaggle of wives, kids, mobile phones,
dogs and mountain bikes. The Festival was jointly sponsored
by the Baldicoot Medical Centre and the Hunchburgh Echo,
and sure enough, the local nobs were there, too: I spotted
Sir Terence Baldicoot mingling among the hoi polloi – I'd put
his daughter's Indonesian iguana out of its misery – and the
MP Bruce Yarble. He'd called me out to Judlow once to
bandage his racehorse, and now here he was in a tweed
cap, strutting about giving the Who's Who types little salutes
of recognition. Mrs Sequin and Abbie Ball had hired a marquee
for pizzas and chicken nuggets, and Mrs Firth had organised
a crèche and video room for the kiddies. I wandered through
the gathering crowds. Someone had lit a wall of joss-sticks
to counter the reek of dead fish from the River Flid, and
their incense wafted across the field, mingling with the odours
of popcorn, crushed grass and car-grease, giving the whole
event a real buzz of community. I get sentimental about things
like that.

'Not bad, eh,' agreed Ron Harcourt, when I commented on the size of the thistles. 'Thank God for phosphates.'

'Ron managed to wangle two grants for this field, didn't you, you cunning bastard,' said Billy Clegg, appearing beside me and thrusting a can of Guatemalan lager at me. 'A Euro grant not to plant genetic aubergines on it, and a Nature Council one, to stop the thistles becoming endangered weeds.'

'Nice work if you can get it,' said Norman, emerging from the Portaloo behind us.

'Bugger off,' said Ron Harcourt, and fired his stun-gun for the start of the game.

'Hey!' yelled Norman, wrestling with his machine. 'Wait for me, guys!'

Within seconds, the air was filled with the roar of a hundred strimmers. The men charged up and down the field with their excitable appliances – state-of-the-art, in Norman's case – thistledown flying all over the place, little thistle-thorns whizzing through the air at hectic speed. The women, standing in rows by the thorn hedge, jeered and whooped and blew the men kisses, swigging Buck's Fizz out of plastic cups.

Then I spotted the twins.

They were jumping up and down by the electricity generator.

'Get a move on, Dad!' they were yelling. You couldn't call them beautiful, I thought, in any classical sense. Their eyes were too close together, and they had Abbie's slightly bony, tilted pelvis – but nevertheless there was something about the two of them that drove Sigmund wild. I wasn't the only bloke looking in their direction. They must give off some undetectable animal scent, I thought. A sort of musk. Watching them, my resolve kept stiffening. Then they looked up and saw me, too, and smiled invitingly. Hey, Buck, I thought. Now's your moment, mate. I was just wandering nonchalantly over in their direction when Mrs Clegg tapped me on the shoulder.

'About my foal,' she said. Talk about bad timing, missis, I thought.

When I'd countered all her accusations, her son crashed into me with three pints of beer and in the imbroglio I lost sight of Rose and Blanche. Then a huge cheer went up: the last thistle had been mown down.

'And the judges have decided,' farted a megaphoned voice across the field, 'that the winner of the year's strimmer event, and therefore this year's Thistle Champion, is Mr Tom Boggs!'

There was another huge cheer, and some honking of car-horns. Tom Boggs stood on the podium and waved, then burst open a bottle of champagne, slewing everyone near him with froth. I recognised him; he was the young bloke who ran the Texaco garage. The field was suddenly swarming with people carrying candy-floss and talking into their mobiles. After wandering about trying to catch sight of the girls again, I finally gave up and retreated to the beer tent.

'It's a cheap way of getting my field mown,' Harcourt confided. He'd been getting quietly sozzled all afternoon. 'My dad did the same thing. And his dad before him. That's tradition for you.'

'That Tom Boggs' great-great grandfather was a champion, too,' mused Billy Tobash. 'Back in the old days. It runs in his family.'

Ken Peat-Hove said nothing, as usual, but spat on the floor. It could've meant anything. On the way back, I had to stop off at Ned Morpiton's farm, to see to some poisoned Lord Chief Justices, and give his new BSE-free moo-cows the once-over; by the time I drove up the high street, and turned into Crawpy Street, it was evening. I kept thinking about Rose and Blanche Ball. The look they'd given me.

Then I caught my breath. Christ! There they were, just standing there! In the street. The two of them, at the bus stop, right opposite my front door!

Hey! *Yes!*

It was a chilly evening, for spring; they were standing in the bus shelter smoking, and kicking at old blobs of dried-up chewing-gum with their elasticated trainers. Like they were waiting for a bus, but for me, too. Whichever came first.

I drove up slowly.

'Like a kerb-crawler,' they said to me later.

'Where are you going?' asked Rose, as my window wound down.

'Wherever you're going,' I told them. I gave them my sexy grin.

'What are we waiting for then?' asked Blanche. 'Let's go to a club.'

They were dressed in black, with fake jewels twinkling, and wearing the bold red lipstick, dramatic eye-shadow and vicious nail-extensions that I soon learned were their night-wear hallmark. They were temptation incarnate. I opened the doors of the Nuance for them, and gave them one of my Elvis looks, which they missed because they were too busy settling themselves on the back seat, where they sank fragrantly into the soft leather. I say fragrantly, but actually they'd overdone the perfume a bit and once we were on the road I had to keep the window open to prevent myself from asphyxiating. Like good girls, they'd stubbed out their fags first.

'We saw you at the Thistle Festival,' said Rose.

'In the old days, it was like an initiation ceremony,' said Blanche.

'To prove you were a man,' said Rose.

'You want proof, girls,' I said, glancing at them in the mirror, 'I'll give you proof.'

I thought that was quite a witty thing to say.

On the journey to Hunchburgh we talked about their genealogy module, and their mum's loopy idea about some television producer called Oscar or Jack arriving on her doorstep. Then they wanted me to explain how birds digest hard seeds, and why there were so many pet monkeys and apes in the cities, but hardly any in the country.

'It's a fashion thing, I reckon,' I told them. 'I used to get loads of them in my surgery back in Tooting Bec.'

'You had a surgery in Tooting Bec? In London?'

'Yup.'

'Why did you leave?'

Bugger, I thought, remembering Giselle the macaque and Mrs Mann.

'Well?'

'Because I had a sixth sense that, if I came to Thunder Spit, I might meet the two most desirable girls in the whole country.'

They liked that, and giggled.

'And you know something?' I said. 'My sixth sense wasn't wrong.'

They were good dancers. They were exhibitionists. There are plenty of starers in Hunchburgh. Male and female: people who prefer to watch, and comment. As they whirled about under the big glitter-ball, and waggled their peachy arses, I felt special. Special, that everyone was staring, the blokes with admiration and lust, the girls with criticism and envy. The twins were dancing for me, and I felt like a million Euros.

Later, I said, 'Come to my place.'

'Both of us?' suggested Rose, running her red nails up my right thigh.

'Together?' whispered Blanche, nibbling at the lobe of my left ear.

'Both of you,' I said. 'Together.'

Because as well as feeling a million Euros, I felt twelve metres tall and three metres wide.

And Sigmund felt thirty-five centimetres long.

CHAPTER 20

FAREWELL!

I felt small and alone. It was October on our herring-shaped peninsula, and the freezing air crackled with salt. Under a thin sun, slate roofs shone bright with hoar-frost, and the silhouettes of trees stood bare and stark against the churning seascape. Never had Thunder Spit looked colder, or bleaker, and in my heart, a part of me was glad to leave.

'God has cursed you!' Parson Phelps called after me as the silent Mr Peat-Hove flicked his whip and my horse and cart trundled off along the slippery shingle path. 'You can never atone! Begone! Abandon yourself to that cursed metropolis, where the corruption is so thick that you can scrape it off the walls!'

My father appeared to have forgotten that it was his own idea – and God's – that I should go to Hunchburgh in the first place. There was no pleasing him, I thought dismally, as my father's ranting died in the distance. I pulled my wool hat down over my ears, and shivered. In my hand, I clasped the linen bag that contained my most treasured possessions: my Bible, Herman's *Crustacea* and Hanker's *World History*, four dried gourds from my mother's grave, the whelk shell Tommy Boggs had given me as a leaving present, a fish-knife from his mother, and my mermaid's purse.

'Goodbye, dear Father,' I whispered under my breath, as the gnarled trees of the peninsula gave way to mainland shrubs.

My new life had begun.

*   *   *

What I knew of cities amounted to what my father had chosen to relay to me, namely, that they are dens of vice; that they are crawling with women of ill-repute who are receptacles for foulness, and bear infants unblessed by God; that there is neither neighbourly nor brotherly love; that there are beggars in the street with suppurating sores that can never be healed.

My train from Judlow arrived in Hunchburgh, and tipped me out on to thronged streets, where I saw at once what my father had failed to tell me: that there were more people in the world than I had ever imagined. It was market day, and the centre of the city was bustling; a million chattering voices filled the air; the cries of the stall-holders, the shrieking laughter of women, the plaintive whimpers of beggar children thrusting out grubby palms for halfpennies. I wandered through the market, past coffee-stalls and mountains of oysters, butchers' carts and fruit-stalls. The place was buzzing and teeming with humanity – and yet these folk represented just a tiny fraction of the human population of the world! I suddenly felt small and insignificant, and invisible, as I wandered the cobbled streets in search of the Seminary. Nobody stared at me in the way they did in Thunder Spit and Judlow, or laughed at my gait; they were too busy, I soon realised, just going about their business. I saw a man with a painted face, juggling apples, and spotted a young urchin, a pickpocket, jostling the crowd who watched. By the wall of a church, I also spied a huddle of women guzzling gin and showing their bloomers to whomsoever cared to look; heeding my father's warnings, I buttoned my frock-coat tighter and hastened my step, my head whirling with light and sound. O strange and bright and frightening new world! Yet my heart lifted in hope. For here, surely, I could begin life anew!

I found the Seminary near the heart of the city, a red-brick rectangle, curlicued at the corners, and ringed with threatening holly trees, their glinting leaf-spikes flashing in the autumn sun like knives. When I saw the grandeur of the building and its big black shiny doors, I understood why my father had once dreamed that I should come here. For who could attack God, when He was housed in such a formidable fortress? After the chaos of the market, I entered the building with relief, and made my way along echoing tiled corridors to the Abbot's office. I knocked hesitantly on his door.

'Come in,' called a loud, fruity voice. I entered. The room was lined with books and smelt of tobacco.

He was a big red-faced man, with a handshake that nearly lifted me from the ground.

'Welcome to the Seminary, Tobias,' he said. 'Your fame goes before you.'

I quailed. What had he heard? Had my father written to him, telling him I was cursed by the Devil? I would not have been surprised.

But my fame turned out to be of a more quotidian nature, and relayed to the Abbot by Mrs Tobash's cousin, a former Thunder Spitter who was now married to his own cousin's niece. 'They tell me,' said the Abbot, 'that you've been reading aloud in church in Thunder Spit since you were five years old, and can do tongue-twisters like the Devil himself!'

I breathed a sigh of relief, and smiled. 'It's true,' I said.

'Well?' he said, folding his arms.

'Miss Mosh mashes some mish-mash,' I ventured, and he applauded.

'Betty Botter bought some butter,' I went on. 'But, she said, this butter's bitter! If I put it in my batter, it'll make my batter bitter! So Betty Botter bought a bit of better butter and she put it in her batter and it made her batter better!'

'You'll go far,' pronounced the Abbot, slapping a meaty hand on his tattered Bible. 'Now, I've found just the landlady for you. Her name is Mrs Fooney and she is a fine woman, with a very large – er, a large heart,' he said, indicating the curve of a female bosom. I blushed. 'In the meantime, let me introduce you to your fellow students.'

The students were at luncheon, and the refectory echoed with the voices of five dozen noisy conversations. The Abbot led me to a table.

'This is Farthingale,' he said, indicating a weasel-faced youth who was shovelling boiled beans into his mouth with great speed. Farthingale looked up from his plate.

'And, Farthingale, this is Tobias Phelps,' said the Abbot. 'I want you to take him under your wing. He is the son of a parson who attended this very seminary many years ago. Also has a knack with tongue-twisters. Did Betty Botter for me in my office. Most impressive.'

Farthingale gave me what looked more like a smirk than a welcoming smile, and exchanged a glance with a fellow student sitting next to him. 'Pleased to make your acquaintance, Betty,' he said. 'Serve yourself to beans.' And he jerked his head in the direction of a metal pot.

'That's the stuff!' said the Abbot, and slapped Farthingale on the back with a hearty laugh. Then he turned to leave, clasping his Bible in his hand like a brick he was going to plant somewhere. 'Come to my office after lunch, Phelps,' he said. 'Farthingale will make the rest of the introductions.'

'Well, Betty,' said Farthingale, when the Abbot was out of sight. 'Impressed the Abbot already, have we? There's a good boy. Come and meet the new student, Popple,' he said to his neighbour, a podgy lad with crooked teeth. 'His name's Betty Botter.'

And so it was that Betty became my nickname – or rather one of them. My fellow seminarians had smelt meat. During the course of that meal, during which I made the acquaintances of Popple, Ganney, Hicks, McGrath and other seminarians, I was offered further appellations: Fartybockers, and Hobble-de-Hoy among them. I chewed on my beans, and said as little as possible. I had entered this building full of hope – but now, with a lurching feeling of recognition, I recalled my lonely days at school, when I was taunted by the other boys, or played alone in the playground.

'So what brings you here, Betty?' asked Ganney.

'The Church is my vocation,' I mumbled fearfully.

They all laughed like drains at that. By the end of the meal,

Farthingale, Popple, and Ganney had elected themselves my persecutors.

'They're just boisterous,' the Abbot said airily, drumming his big sausagey fingers on his Bible. I had returned to his office after luncheon, and recounted some of the conversation. 'I'm afraid that if you view the Church as your true vocation, you're an exception here,' he explained. I was taken aback by the somewhat breezy manner in which he announced this news. 'Most of the fellows here are either younger sons, failures in other professions, or otherwise here against their will. That's the truth of the matter.' Then he sat back, and made a thick, blunt steeple of his hands. I wondered whether the same applied to him.

'As a matter of fact it does,' he said, reading my thoughts. 'I'd like to have been a builder, but it would have been over everyone's dead body.' He stopped and chuckled. 'So here I am, constructing souls instead. And doing repairs.'

I hung my head, and tried to stifle my tears. 'Look, son, let me tell you something,' he said, when he saw my distress, taking my hand in his large benign paw. 'This is a dying profession. I fear the Church is headed for extinction. And Darwinism hasn't helped. All this stuff about being descended from monkeys and apes has turned people away. In a hundred years' time, this seminary will be gone, and your little church in Thunder Spit will be but an empty shell.'

I said nothing; I just sat there, miserable beyond words.

'But maybe you are different, Phelps,' he said kindly. 'If you have faith, then it's a good thing. Keep a hold of it. Just see Farthingale and his chums as a challenge God has given you,' he proposed. 'You must remember about turning the other cheek, son.'

'Yes, Abbot, I will.'

'And another thing.'

'Yes, sir?'

'I have the impression that you carry a burden, Phelps. Am

197

I correct? You don't walk straight, and you appear to stoop. Your shoes, if I may say so, look like a couple of pancakes.'

I explained to him about my deformities of the foot, and the fact that I had been a foundling, and that my spine had been mutilated when I was a mere babe.

He appeared sympathetic, in his rough and ready way, but had a warning for me.

'You have suffered Tobias, I grant you that. But the way out of this suffering, son, is to witness for yourself how others suffer more, and to help them. If you're serious about this as a vocation – God help you – you'll need to get stuck in. Understand?'

'Yes, sir.'

'So go out there, Tobias, and visit the slums, of which there are many. Go to Mickle Street, and Petersgate, and Upper Hayside, and bring succour and help and faith to the needy of the parish, and thereby forget your own troubles. That's my advice to you. Now go and settle in at Mrs Fooney's, and come to me if you have any problems.'

Although it was by no means what I had expected of my first encounter with my new vocation, I decided to put my worries to one side, and take up the Abbot's advice. If he gave me little solid comfort, at least I found it elsewhere. Mrs Fooney's lodging-house was next to the Seminary, and as soon as I crossed her threshold, I felt at home.

'Come in, young gentleman!' said Mrs Fooney. 'Welcome! Wipe your feet on the mat and let me make you a cup of tea!' Mrs Fooney was as big-breasted as the Abbot had indicated, and also as warm-hearted. Indeed, they are characteristics that have always gone together, in my limited experience of women. You cannot have the one without the other. Needless to say, Mrs Fooney reminded me very much of my own mother, and even offered me barley flip-cakes.

I also met her granddaughter, Tillie, a charming, ringleted, cheeky child of seven who immediately settled herself on my lap and took my hand in hers.

'You're very hairy,' she remarked, stroking my wrist. Suddenly she pulled her hand away. 'Ugh! He's got a flea!'

'Shush, Tillie!' Mrs Fooney rebuked her. 'We all have fleas, child. Even men of God!'

Between them, Mrs Fooney and Tillie lifted my spirits immeasurably. Tillie helped me to arrange my possessions on the mantelpiece in my room, and I let her hold my whelk shell while I read to her from the Bible.

So began my new life.

I am proud to say that I was good at my work; I already knew most of the Bible by heart, and the Abbot praised my diligence and the quality of my fledgling sermons. My first sermon, which concerned fossils, was a treatise condemning Darwinism – a subject close to my heart. He heralded it as a work of genius. I argued, just as Parson Phelps had taught me, that God had planted the fossils in the earth to muddle geologists into believing that the world was much older than it was, and tricked Darwin into developing a fantastical theory about man descending from monkeys and apes.

Towards the end of my sermon, I held up the fossil I had brought with me from home.

'This is God's joke,' I concluded. 'And a fine one it is, too!'

Needless to say, my presentation provoked much derision from my fellow students. However, I persisted with my studies, applying myself with fervour to my library books, thus earning myself another nickname; the Bookworm. In private moments of loneliness, the needs of my male object became ever fiercer, and I spent much time fighting my own bestial urges.

It was then that I thought of my father and his marbles: would that, perhaps, bring me some respite? I bought a bag of these glass balls from a pedlar, and put them in my shoes.

After half an hour, I realised that Parson Phelps must have been mad for longer than I'd thought.

I gave the marbles to Tillie, who thanked me most prettily.

Then she floored me with a strange query, which unsettled me for weeks.

'Mr Phelps, who made God?'

She had arranged her marbles on a plate, and was now stringing beads. The question hit me like a slap, for it was the very same one I had asked my father, when I was her age. I recalled the reply he had given me then.

I cleared my throat. 'God is self-made. Like a self-made man, but God.'

'What d'you mean, self-made?' asked Tillie, her eyes squinting in puzzlement. 'Nothing can *make itself*, Mr Phelps. That would be a very silly idea, I think!'

I considered this for a moment.

'It requires a leap of faith,' I told her finally. 'It requires believing in what you don't understand. It requires believing that everything is connected, like your beads are connected, but with an invisible string.' Tillie looked puzzled. 'A gourd plant sprouted on my mother's grave the year after she died,' I went on. 'And every year since, the gourds it sprouts have been of a different shape, colour and texture. Look,' I said, and took her to the mantelpiece, where I had arranged my dried gourds. 'This was the first one that grew.' I pointed to the green, stippled fruit, now somewhat shrunk from its original size. 'And the next year, this one came from its seed.' I pointed to the gourd with the orange frill and yellow blotches.

'And then this one?' asked Tillie, picking up last year's gourd, which was green and yellow, and striped.

'That's right,' I said. 'See? It looks nothing like it, but this is the next generation.' And then from the seed of the stripy one, came this one,' I said, handing her the gourd I had picked just before I left Thunder Spit. It was knobbled and almost mauve in colour. 'Can you explain that?' I asked.

'No,' said Tillie. 'But there must be a reason.'

'There is. But only God knows it. All we know,' I told her, the thought striking me as I said it, 'is that they are related to each other, as surely as an island is related to the shore. Look deep enough, and you will see that, below the level of the sea, the land is joined.'

I thought of Thunder Spit. I thought of the Flood, which had turned our herring-shaped peninsula into an island. And I thought of my father's words in the church, just before we fell into the water and I saw my vision of the Contortionist. He had quoted John Donne's poem to me, which I quoted to Tillie now.

'"No man is an island,"' I told her, '"entire of itself. But a piece of the continent, a part of the main!"'

The tears came into my eyes most unaccountably as I said these words, and Tillie put her little arm around my shoulders.

'Let's play marbles, Mr Phelps,' she offered gently.

And so we did.

When not occupied with my studies, I haunted the slums. I had taken the Abbot's advice about avoiding self-pity and bringing help to others, and within a few weeks of my arrival in Hunchburgh, I had thrown myself with conviction into my task as a saver of souls and a champion of the Bible. I found Parson Phelps' voice emerging from my larynx as I preached. I trod the bumpy streets with a stride that mimicked his, and grew increasingly confident in my manly gait, thanks, in part, to the well-fitting shoes Mr Hewitt had so skilfully cobbled for me. Slowly I learned to live without my father's words and presence; I recreated him inside me instead. I had no choice; he returned my letters unopened. Turning the other cheek, I continued to send them, in the hope that charity, if nothing else, would prevail.

The misery and poverty of the slums had at first made me gasp: whole families of up to twelve children shoved together in stinking rooms, without enough to eat, and dragon-sized rats constantly on the rampage. I saw many children die, or become orphans. I wondered, in my darker moments, what relief I could possibly bring into this despair, with nothing but my prayer-book and my humble bag of medicines. But lo and behold, my deformities worked in my favour: one woman, Mrs Jeyes, said to me that clapping eyes on a sight as pitiful as me put her own troubles into perspective. I did not know whether to be hurt or grateful.

There was one particular hovel, on Mickle Street, that I visited more often than most, as its need was the greatest; indeed, no other slum dwelling that I knew seemed to match its squalor and decrepitude. I was often to be found there.

'Like a fly to dung,' commented Farthingale, my harshest critic, when he saw me one morning preparing my medicine bag and my Bible for my next visit to Mickle Street.

'He's got a whore down there,' speculated Ganney.

I turned the other cheek so many times with my fellow seminarians, I sometimes became dizzy with it. But I ignored their taunts, and continued my regular visits to Mickle Street, for here dwelled a family by the name of Cove, who seemed to be in permanent need of my attentions. The elder Mr Cove, a former seaman with a pitted face and beery breath, had recently developed an ulceration on his leg, and because he was unable to afford the doctor, I took it upon myself, as my Christian duty, to see to him as best I could. It was in this unlikely setting, and quite unexpectedly, that during one of my visits, I had an encounter with physical temptation that was to create both excitement and turmoil within me, in equal measure.

The object of my desire was a thing of great lewdness.

I didn't even know its name, at first.

'I stole it off a cargo ship,' confided the little Cove boy, a little lad of seven with an elfin face and knickerbockered legs as skinny as a sparrow's.

I had arrived to change the dressings on the ulcerous shin of Grandfather Cove to find the whole family staring and sniffing at a curious object on their table. It was yellow, and about eight inches long, and in circumference, about the same thickness as an engorged male object. As soon as I saw it, I blushed a fierce red, and I felt the base of my spine tingle at the site of my ancient mutilation.

'They was hanging in huge bunches,' whispered the boy, recounting what he had witnessed in the ship's hold, his voice reduced to an awed whisper. 'From hooks. Some bunches was yellow,' he said, his eyes flaring wide with excitement. 'But some was green!'

No one approached the table.

'I went to grab one,' said the boy. The Coves were all listening intently, although I was sure it was not the first time he had recounted his tale. 'But then I saw there was this giant hairy spider guarding them.'

He indicated its size by making a hoop of his thin arms. Bigger than a plate. I knew the wonders of God's earth to be manifold, and some of them even beyond the scope of the redoubtable Hanker's *World History*, but I was beginning to suspect that the boy was telling an untruth. 'So I goes on peering round the place till I sees another bunch, that don't have a spider,' the boy continued. 'And I grab it like this with my bare hands.' He showed me his hands. They were bony and grubby. I nodded to acknowledge his bravery. 'I just took the one. I could've taken more.'

The boy looked suddenly anxious.

'You did right, son,' said his mother. She had a flat face, like a plaice. 'We don't know as it's not poison.'

The thing was dark yellow, and blotchy, and as I have already indicated, obscene in shape. But as I stepped further into the room, I was struck by a sublime and mesmerising fragrance, which pulled me towards it like a helpless magnet.

'Have you ever in your life seen such an ungodly-looking specimen?' the ulcerous Mr Cove asked me, eyeing it worriedly. 'Can the Lord ever have given His holy blessing to it?' He was looking to me for God's answer, and I searched my heart to find the reply that Parson Phelps might give, but my thoughts were in turmoil. I did not know what to make of this thing, but I knew that I desired it more fiercely than I had ever desired anything.

'Beauty is in the eye of the beholder,' I said at last, dredging up something my mother always used to say to me when she caught me gazing miserably at my reflection in the hall mirror. I inhaled deeply, and with every second that ticked by on the ancient grandfather clock in the corner of the room, I succumbed still further to the fruit's exotic lure.

'The boy swears it's edible, but we're not so sure,' said Mrs Cove. 'You'll need to peel off its jacket first!'

She was not to know it, but I was by now so overwhelmed by a desire to eat the thing and to possess it for ever, that I could barely prevent myself from leaping forward and grabbing it.

'I'll try it, if you like,' I offered. I was trembling with a wild urge to cram the whole thing into my mouth. 'I'll just take a bite, and tell you if it's all right.' Cautiously, I removed its yellow skin, and bared its white flesh.

I had intended to take a small bite only, but a sudden and unnatural greed overwhelmed me. My shameful urge at that moment was simply to stuff the whole thing in, but I managed, with extreme difficulty, to restrain myself. Instead I merely took a large bite, which broke the fruit in half. I closed my eyes and ate, transported into Heaven. When I opened them again, the whole of the Cove family was gawping at me. They must have been surprised at how much I had bitten off. The adults said nothing, but the boy let out an indignant, 'Hey!'

It was the best thing I had ever tasted; better, even, than the toffee apple Tommy had stolen for me at the Travelling Fair of Danger and Delight. And as I chewed on it, savouring it, I knew that I must have it again. As its glorious taste spread across my tongue, I even contemplated cheating the Cove family, by twisting my face into an expression of disgust and telling them I thought the thing was poison. Anything to keep the whole fruit for myself! But in the end, God's stern leadership prevailed, and I reluctantly quelled my more selfish desires. I told them, 'It's good.' Then added, weakly hoping it might yet repel them, 'though not to everyone's taste, I imagine.' Reluctantly, I held out the half-fruit to the Cove boy, who sniffed it, then took a bite. He chewed slowly, and a smile spread.

Guiltily, I cornered him on the way out, and slipped him a coin.

'There are more pennies where that came from,' I said, 'if you can get hold of a whole bunch of those things.'

The boy grinned at me, showing broken teeth.

'And mind the giant spider!' I called after him, as he ran off to the harbour.

My new-found passion for bananas – a passion so extreme as to be almost uncontrollable – provided me with inspiration and comfort in my moments of darkness. The Cove boy brought me several bunches of the fruit, which I cloistered in my wardrobe, and I repaid him generously with all the money I could spare from my ever-dwindling supply. Occasionally I worried about the single-mindedness of my diet, and forced myself to eat a little bread or fish to supplement it, but both my palate and my tapeworm recoiled increasingly from such fare, and I returned to the comfort offered by the noble fruit.

Comfort I was coming to need more and more. For events at home had taken a sudden downward turn.

This is Dr Baldicoot's letter. I have it still.

Dear Tobias,

It is with a heavy heart that I write to tell you of your father's removal to the Sanatorium for the Spiritually Disturbed at Fishforth, where he declares he will not see you. It grieves me to tell you this, but it is for the best, I am sure. He is there among men who are similarly distressed by the issue of man's creation, and has learned to knit. If he were in his right mind he would convey his kind regards, for I know he loves you. It was he who fought for your life when you were a baby, though I personally would have given up, if you will pardon my being so blunt.

Yours sincerely,

Will Baldicoot.

PS. The Parsonage is now inhabited by a temporary parson by the name of Gudderwort, of whom none of us is fond, as he has tried to ban our Thistle-Pulling Contest, which he says is paganism. All of Thunder Spit wishes you well in your studies, and awaits your return as Parson, for we are a flock with no shepherd!

PPS. A few ounces of good tobacco would not go amiss, on your next visit.

'Welcome home, my little friend!'

Tommy squeezed me tight against his huge muscled torso, so hard I feared he might crack my ribs, for he did not know his own strength. I hugged him back. How I had missed him! I had arranged a week's compassionate leave from the Seminary, and travelled to Thunder Spit to settle Parson Phelps' affairs. Tommy was a father now; he had a bonny child, a boy, by his wife Jessie. 'We've called him Nicholas,' said Tommy. 'After the church.'

Although she was now a grown woman, I remembered Jessie from childhood days; the little Jessie Tobash who had once upset me by calling me Prune-Face – a cruelty about which she was most red-faced and apologetic as she welcomed me into her kitchen and laid a place for me at table.

'She's expecting another,' Tommy told me proudly, patting her rump as if she were a horse. Jessie served us sardine pie and sloeberry wine, and I gave them a present of a small bunch of bananas, at which they marvelled.

I begged for news of Thunder Spit, and they furnished me with a brisk account of how Ron Harcourt had lost five of his cows, and Tommy's brother Joe had run away to sea, and Mrs Firth's idiot cousin Joan had got her senses back for a week and then lost them again, and the new parson, Gudderwort, had banned the Thistle-Pulling Contest, as Dr Baldicoot's letter had said, prompting the whole village to boycott the church.

'And Hunchburgh?' Jessie begged. 'Tell us all about your life in Hunchburgh!' So as they savoured their bananas, I told them about the Seminary, and about the weasel-faced Farthingale and his henchmen Ganney and Popple, my trio of persecutors. And I told them about my visits to the poor and needy, and about the breezy nonchalance of the Abbot who ran the Seminary, and about Tillie and Mrs Fooney, and the Cove family and my discovery of the banana.

Then I came to the letter I had received from Dr Baldicoot. When I told them its contents, Tommy confirmed that Parson Phelps had indeed gone quite mad.

'Jessie was there, at his last service. 'She saw him.'

'Yes,' said Jessie, sitting down heavily at the table next to us. 'He didn't read aloud from the Bible,' she said, 'but from other books.'

'What books?' I asked.

'Hanker's *World History* was one,' said Jessie, untying her hair and letting it fall across her shoulders. I would one day like a wife who would do that, I thought. But I am Prune-Face. Fartybockers. Hobble-de-Hoy. The Bookworm. Only a blind woman would ever want me as a husband!

'And the Origin of Something,' said Tommy, interrupting my reverie. 'That selfsame book he was always preaching against before.'

'The *Origin of Species*,' I murmured. 'By Charles Darwin.'

'That's the one,' confirmed Jessie. 'We didn't understand a word of it. It was all science and nonsense to us, about the fins of fish transforming into arms and legs. It quite turned my stomach to hear it. And then he tore up his Bible.'

I felt the blood fade from my face. Oh, my poor beloved father! I hated Mr Charles Darwin at that moment, stranger to me though he was, for putting Parson Phelps through this agony. Parson Phelps, and all the others, too! For he was not alone in his suffering, if Dr Baldicoot's letter was to be believed. Had the letter not implied that there was an entire sanatorium in Fishforth, chock-a-block with befuddled souls such as my father's? And that the blame lay entirely at Mr Charles Darwin's feet? I pictured the Bible pages fluttering to the church floor, just as the pages of Mr Darwin's book had once done, at a happier epoch in our lives.

'Then he swore foul oaths at us,' Jessie continued, putting her hand on mine gently. 'And then he called us all sea-slugs and barbarians. And he called you, Tobias, a –'

'Never mind,' interrupted Tommy. 'He is mad.' In the silence that followed, a flea hopped off my wrist and on to the chequered tablecloth. Jessie squashed it with her nail, and continued: 'And then Mrs Sequin got up to leave, and we all followed her. Only Dr Baldicoot stayed.'

'And then?'

'And then the next day, Dr Baldicoot took him away to Fishforth. He was clutching an envelope, but he took nothing else with him, not even a bag of clothes. He left it all behind.' She patted my hand, and passed me a white handkerchief that smelt of fish. I took it, and blew my nose fiercely.

I wondered about the envelope. Could it be the same one that the Contortionist had thrust at him when she gave him the jar? I shuddered.

When I visited Dr Baldicoot the following day, he told me that his diagnosis of a tumour of the brain remained a possibility. Such an affliction, he said, would undoubtedly account for the Parson's odd behaviour over the last few years, and his painful rejection of me.

'Fate is cruel,' he said, knocking out the dead seaweed tobacco from his pipe and filling it, with barely disguised rapture, with the tobacco I had brought him from Hunchburgh. Lighting it with his tinderbox, a cloud of smoke, pungent as a burning haystack, was soon trailing upwards, spreading to fill the whole room.

'Yes!' he exclaimed, sinking back in his chair and savouring the smoke.

A jealous God, my father had said. The smell of Dr Baldicoot's burning tobacco made me dizzy, and I was suddenly filled with an immeasurable sadness, not only that my father might die, but that our relationship should be so soured by principles I could not understand.

'One day,' I coughed through Dr Baldicoot's smokescreen, 'I shall bring him home.'

'I hope that you one day shall,' he replied, laying down his stinking pipe on his desk. 'But for now, I fear he still has no wish to see you. He has developed what I consider to be an unhealthy obsession with your origins.'

'Of what nature?'

But Dr Baldicoot began to fiddle furiously with a sheaf of pipe-cleaners, and would not speak.

The new Parson, Gudderwort, was dry and gaunt and ascetic, with a high, domed forehead, and skin like parchment. He poured out acidic seaweed tea, and I poured out some of my woes to him, but I fear they fell on stony ground. My father had left a legacy of mistrust in Thunder Spit, Gudderwort informed me somewhat accusingly.

'After he'd torn up his Bible in the church, nobody was keen to return,' he said bitterly. He seemed to lay the blame for this on me. Or so I felt.

'Shall we pray?' he suggested, in his mealy-mouthed way, when we had finished our tea.

So we knelt down together on the uncomfortable flag-stoned kitchen floor (Where was the embroidered pew-cushion my father had always used, his one concession to luxury?) and Gudderwort pressed his dry palms and skeletal fingers together, and we prayed for the safety of my father's diseased soul, and my forgiveness of him. And I prayed, secretly, that Dr Baldicoot was not lying to me about the cause of my father's madness in order to make me feel better. Uncharitably, I also prayed that Gudderwort would get water on the knee.

Just as I was leaving, Gudderwort called out to me. He was carrying something in both hands.

'Your father left this,' he said drily. 'Mrs Firth suggested that I not bother you with it, once she saw what it was, but I have no use for it, and it appears to be a personal object.'

And he thrust it towards me.

I felt a lurch of vertigo. The room seemed to contract, and then expand.

The jar.

'So here you are,' prompted Gudderwort irritably, waiting. My hands felt jelly-like as I took the jar from him. Its thick glass was cold, and heavy.

'I found it in the vestry,' said Gudderwort, guessing my thoughts. 'Hidden away beneath his spare cassock.'

I gulped and trembled, summoning the courage to investigate what the jar contained. When I did, I had to squint. It was full of a dark liquid. A dark liquid, with something floating in it. I felt both sick and baffled in equal measure.

'Do you know what it is?' I asked Gudderwort. My voice cracked as I spoke. There was a pause before Gudderwort replied. His parchment lip creased with disapproval and distaste.

'An umbilical cord,' he said finally, depositing the words as if they were small turds. He clearly wanted to be rid of me, and even more, it.

'A what?' I blurted.

'An umbilical cord, according to Mrs Firth,' he said. Mrs Firth was his housekeeper. He was still unable to hide the deep disgust in his voice. What foul parish had he landed himself in, he must be thinking. What bad luck to be obliged thus to mop up the mess of another parson's spiritual crisis!

I raised the jar to my eyes: and sure enough, behind the swirling blur of dark pickle, there lurked a whitish thing.

Suddenly I found myself laughing aloud. But there was hysteria in that laugh.

'Shall I see you to the door?' said Gudderwort with finality. 'I think it best that you be on your way.' Like father like son, he was no doubt thinking. Lunatics both.

I wrapped the jar in a crumpled old fish-paper and took my leave.

Back at the forge I told Tommy what had happened. I showed him the jar, and together we peered at it.

'Mrs Firth told Gudderwort it was an umbilical cord,' I said. Tommy grunted. 'Not poison, then,' he said. 'Let's ask Jessie.'

She'd borne a babe. She would know. Jessie lifted Nicholas from her hip and plonked him on the floor, then wiped her hands on her apron, and peered into the jar.

After a while, she said, 'Yes, I think she's right. An umbilical cord.'

Tommy and I stared at each other. It made no sense. But then, my father had gone mad. Perhaps it made sense to a madman.

As I shook his hand in farewell, the jar wrapped in fish-paper and tucked beneath my arm, Tommy smiled at me stiffly, and slapped my back.

'We didn't half get scared, eh?' he said. 'Over something as small and silly as that?' But his voice lacked its usual hearty conviction, and his words did nothing to quell the anxiety in my heart, or the sudden distress in my sphincter. Until this visit to Thunder Spit, I suddenly realised, the parasite Mildred had been leaving me increasingly in peace. But now she was back with a vengeance. Something was wrong. Just as a strip of seaweed can detect oncoming rain, so my tapeworm could sense ill. I'll say that to her credit.

In the meantime, a question of a practical nature occupied me: should I bury the cord, or burn it? Or just leave it as it was, floating in the jar? The pickled human flesh was, after all, my only heritage, that I knew of. I was faced with a dilemma, though not one of the kind that I was used to grappling with in the Seminary. Fundamental questions there concerned such things as whether or not Adam possessed a navel. Not: What does one do with an anonymous umbilical cord, when it is presented to you in a jar, as your sole heritage?

No two omphalic issues could be further apart.

I sat in the coach on the way back, with my boxes in the luggage rack and the jar clasped to my breast. I pictured the tiny strip of flesh within, that had once connected a baby to its mother.

What baby, to what mother?

211

Why had the Contortionist sold my father the jar?

And why had he kept it?

Did I, even then, suspect the answer to these questions, and deny them to myself?

I was in a woeful state by the time I returned to my lodgings, where Mrs Fooney, remarking that I looked pale, fussed over me with hot-water bottles and cups of tea, and home-made muffins, while Tillie put my whelk shell to her ear, and listened to the sea, and chatted over her dolls on the kitchen floor. But after a while I could bear this scene of domestic contentment no longer; hot tears welled in my eyes, and excusing myself, I tore myself away, clutching my jar to my bosom.

For several days, I shut myself in my room, afflicted by a deep and unfathomable depression of the spirits, staring at the jar, and the jar staring at me. It was a wonder the glass hadn't cracked on the journey from Thunder Spit, or leaked. The pickle was murky-looking; the cord was barely discernible inside: a bulbous, tapering thing, floating in suspension. There was a residue at the bottom, black and gritty-looking. The disintegrated placenta, perhaps? I wondered. I did not know. I was no more familiar with women's bodies, and their workings, than with the geography of the Planet Mars. I should have thrown it out, then and there, perhaps.

But I did not; I kept it there on my mantelpiece, as if it was the only thing I had left in the world.

I am all filld up with a medicin calld lordnum. We hav been at Sea five or six munths, acordin to Higgins. The Arke is getin crowded, and the more crowded it gets, the mor lordnum we gets. Ther is very few cagis left emptie. Howlin and screemin and fartin all nite. Higgins and Steed and Bowker playin cards all day. Trapp drinkin his CLARIT and talkin about the Queen's Collekshun, and his Slave-tradin days.

And how wot we need is a NEW WURLD, wer no-wun will

212

hav to WURK. On and on he goes, about this idea. His Uther Biznis, he corls it.

Then we reech the shors of MOROKO.

Oi, Deerie. Redy to sher yor HOME with a nice GENTLE-MAN? Trapp sez to me, twurlin his MUSTARSH.

CHAPTER 21

METAMORPHOSIS

There's no smoke without fire, is there? That's what they say about rumour. It can begin anywhere there's a tinderbox and a match, or lightning. There is no telling where the flames will spread, or where the smoke will drift.

The latest rumour doing the rounds of London Society is this: that Miss Violet Scrapie, said to be the anonymous joint author of Monsieur Cabillaud's controversial book *Cuisine Zoologique: une philosophie de la viande*, published last week to general bemusement, has become a militant vegetarian!

What's more, the rumour is true.

Mr Henry Salt, who had last seen Miss Violet Scrapie heading determinedly away from the assembled throng of non-carnivores muttering something about her need for a pork chop, had been pleasantly shocked to witness her presence at the November meeting of the Vegetarian Society, an occasion that featured an edifying speech by a guest vegan – a former abattoir-owner – and a display of etchings depicting the horrors of vivisection.

At the end of the meeting, Violet Scrapie, her face creased with anxiety and excitement in equal measure, approached the podium bearing a covered silver platter, and made her announcement.

'My name is Violet Scrapie, and I am writing a book of vegetarian cookery, with which I dare to rival the achievement of Mrs Beeton herself!'

There! Done it! She bit her lip and stared down bashfully at her domed dish.

The audience, who had heard the rumours of Violet's conversion, gasped and exchanged whispers of amazement at the young woman's intriguing combination of modesty, presumption and passion. Suet, unaware of the impression his mistress was making, was scrutinising the poster display. It featured ghastly representations of dogs like himself in cages, and prompted him to recall once again the worst moments of his puppy-hood. His mouth went dry with fear, and he began to pant, his tongue lolling out like a slice of ham.

'Now try this, Mr Salt,' Violet was urging the President, whipping the cover off the platter to reveal an unusual but strangely elegant display of *amuse-gueules* featuring creamed asparagus, celeriac mousse, jellied mushrooms and devilled grapes, garnished with zest of orange, angelica and fern leaves. 'My own recipes!'

The vegetarians gawped at the audacity of her vision, then began to whisper animatedly in little huddles. Their conclusion: Farewell, perhaps, boiled turnips! Let Mr Salt decide our fate!

Mr Salt, no culinary ignoramus himself, tasted. His first mouthful told him that Miss Scrapie had a fluency with garlic. His second, that she had an innate understanding of the wayward vagaries of paprika. His third, that she had expertly married the demands of texture and taste, form and content, raw and cooked. He swallowed, and spoke.

'I declare this young woman a genius.'

When the roars of approval died down, Miss Scrapie, perspiring somewhat from the strain of the occasion and blushing from the roots of her hair, but proud of the impact she had made, announced, 'I shall be inventing and compiling a collection of vegetarian dishes, as mouth-watering as can be imagined.' Mr Salt smiled in benign approval. 'May I beg you for your support in this endeavour?'

The platter was passed round, and within moments, Violet's offerings had been snaffled up.

'You try to stop us!' yelled a woman encouragingly.

Never had herbs of the field tasted so good. It was a moment, they all agreed later, of supreme civilisation.

With one voice, the thin campaigners cheered in approval.

'Hurrah for Miss Violet Scrapie!' proclaimed Mr Salt.

Violet smiled, the first smile of genuine happiness she had been able to muster in recent weeks, and *The Fleshless Cook* was born.

Violet Scrapie, a woman with a mission.

Three hundred miles north from this happy metropolitan scene of conviction, picture another landscape; the landscape of loss. The Fishforth Sanatorium for the Spiritually Disturbed stands high on a hill overlooking the North Sea, the shore on which the Vikings once landed. The Sanatorium, tall and stark and built of grey stone, is perched on the edge of a precipice, as though in sympathy with the mental state of its inmates. Herring gulls and guillemots, oblivious to the symbolic disjunction between land and water, belief and chaos, wheel in the sky overhead, jostled by the sharp salt wind, and screech their hoarse and plaintive cries. Ink-blue, the sea rolls far below, its surface dashed with the startling white of horses' tails on the wave-crests. The looming shadows of giant squid, patrolling the coast, lurk ten fathoms deep beneath in an unknown world.

On the precipice, in a window in the high central tower of the Fishforth Sanatorium, a light burns. Here, in the drawing room, the firelight dancing behind him in the wide grate, the fragrance of cedar-wood filling the high-ceilinged room, Parson Phelps sits alone with his knitting. The wool he knits is dark red, the colour of Christ's blood. The tightly upholstered chair upon which he is seated has an antimacassar to counter hair-grease, and padded wings to protect its occupier's head from evil thoughts and cold draughts. A book, a torn and bedraggled copy of the *Origin of Species*, balances precariously on his once plump, now bony knees. Inside it rests the envelope he brought with him from Thunder Spit when Dr Baldicoot took him away. The envelope contains a crumpled old letter, on onion-skin parchment, and is covered in splattery stains. A useful bookmark.

'She sells sea-shells on the seashore,' mumbles Parson Phelps, slurring on the words whilst recovering a slipped stitch. Knitting does not come easily to him. Nor do tongue-twisters. Tobias used to recite tongue-twisters, he recalls. The Parson winces in pain at the memory of his son. 'Miss Mosh mashes some mish-mash,' he mouths sadly, winding some more red wool around his bony finger. 'Betty Botter bought some butter!' A tear falls.

Despite its forbidding exterior, Fishforth is a far cry from Bedlam. All the inmates here are thoughtful and courteous. Their voices, which once thundered from the pulpit in the confident fortissimo of righteous conviction, are now soft and hoarse with bewilderment, murmuring only the husks of discourse. The gentlemen's table-manners are impeccable, and such homely gestures as the placing of knives and forks, the breaking of bread, or the smoothing of a table-napkin, are performed with simplicity and grace. After lunch, they read poetry or discuss the religious and social issues of the day, while those who are inclined to pray do so in the privacy of the small chapel in the upper half of the tower. Paying homage to God is neither encouraged nor frowned on here, for Fishforth is an enlightened establishment, which sees the dilemma of its inmates as a passing phase, a rite of passage on the journey towards a fuller spiritual maturity. The beliefs of men like Parson Phelps have been shattered by Darwinism – but should their life's work be set at nought as a result? And cannot shattered objects be re-assembled in different ways, like fragments of stained glass in a church, to form a new holy picture: another facet of truth's kaleidoscope? Why, surely they can! As a result of this generous approach, most clergymen recover within a few months of rest, and return to their parishes with a deeper conviction of the Bible's wisdom, or a broader understanding of creation.

'All depending,' says the Principal, a former inmate himself, 'on whether you choose to cling to the solid rock of your already

217

established belief, or to take that leap of imagination and faith that will hurl you into an abyss of chaos and wonder.' Of those who leap, he preached gravely, some crash upon the stony ground of atheism, while others float or even fly.

He personally had stayed on his rock.

While waiting to make his choice of direction, Parson Phelps found himself reasonably content. If you have to be in turmoil, let it be among like-minded men.

'See it as a stage in your spiritual development,' said the Principal. Obediently, Parson Phelps had tried to see it that way. He'd floated weightlessly, as though emptied, through the thinly furnished rooms, and the hallways where bales of wool were stacked. The Sanatorium ran a small cottage industry of carding, spinning, and dyeing; the institution received no payment, but inmates were permitted, in exchange for work, to use the wool for their personal and recreational purposes. Parson Phelps was not the only clergyman here who had decided to seize on this opportunity. He had fond memories of Mrs Phelps knitting. He could picture her now, sitting on a hard chair in the flag-stoned kitchen, knitting a jersey for Tobias in one of the boy's favourite colours, either mauve or green. Tobias, who as a child had seemed such a blessing, such a prodigy! Who had spoken in the tongues of angels until the age of five, and had then astonished them all suddenly with his pure, clear speech! Oh, Tobias! God help you now, in your cruel catastrophe!

And Parson Phelps remembered God, too – God, who had worked His great needles slowly, as he listened patiently, like a second wife, to the Parson's long, baggy prayers. Long ago. It is now two years since the marriage of their true minds began to go awry, and since that time, Parson Phelps has not directed a single word in God's direction.

'There was a jar –' Parson Phelps had said, when Dr Baldicoot first brought him here.

'Shhh, rest now,' they told him.

'I lied to Tobias.'

'Tobias?'

'My son. Or rather –'

'Your son must look after himself. All shall be well. Concentrate on your own needs, Parson Phelps. You have been shepherd to a flock for too long. Now it is time to be a sheep for a while.'

'Baa,' said a young clergyman all the way from Basingstoke, whose head was a gleaming ball of silver-blond hair that fitted him like a cap.

'Baa baa black sheep,' sang his bearded friend. They were making a cat's cradle together, in purple wool.

'A woman came to see me,' insisted Parson Phelps. 'She was from the Travelling Fair of Danger and Delight. She had a jar, and she gave me this letter, too.' He held out a crumpled sheaf of onion-skin pages, and thrust them beneath the Principal's nose. 'She said she was his – Mrs Phelps and I –' A pause. The Parson cast his eyes to the ground, and flicked at a stray piece of yellow fluff with his slippered toe.

'Yes?'

Parson Phelps lowered his voice. 'There was an adder in my knickerbockers as a child. I had to strangle it, and –'

'I see.' This was said very gently. 'You must be tired from your journey.'

'So when Tobias arrived –' Parson Phelps persisted, crumpling the letter back into his pocket.

'Arrived?'

'In the church. By the altar. I thought he was a piglet.'

'A piglet?'

'Yes. A young swine. He bit me.'

'Ah.'

'But it seemed like a miracle, because of all the feathers.'

'Feathers?'

'From the pillow.'

'The pillow?'

'He tore it, and the feathers flew out.'

'Ah. I see. Pillow-feathers.'

'Yes. We thought he was a gift from Heaven.'

'All children are gifts from Heaven.'

'Not this one,' said Parson Phelps, suddenly vehement. 'He is from Hell!'

'Let me show you to your quarters.'

'Baa,' said the blond-headed young clergyman. 'Welcome to the flock.'

He and his friend inverted their hands, and a replica of the Clifton Suspension Bridge was revealed.

'Isambard Kingdom Brunel,' said the blond clergyman. 'The greatest engineer who ever lived.'

'Apart from God,' murmured the Principal.

Parson Phelps said, 'I paid the woman for the jar, and then I paid her some more so that she would go, and never come back.'

'Baa,' said the dark-haired clergyman.

'Lunch is served at twelve, and tea at five. As you see, our main window in here is south-facing, so we have the benefit of a sea view, and plenty of sunlight.'

This was true. During the daytime, the sun's brilliant rays pierced the windows, creating haloes of dust on the furniture, and causing the dark wood table to gleam, Parson Phelps now noted, like the carapace of a great mystical beetle.

'God loves the beetle,' he said, staring at the table. 'That's why He made so many.'

'"*And the earth was without form and void*,"' intoned the bearded clergyman, '"*and darkness was on the face of the deep.*"'

'I had to pay her,' said Parson Phelps. 'Otherwise she'd have told him who his father was.'

'"*Our Father which art in Heaven*,"' droned the blond-haired clergyman, doing something complicated and unsuccessful with the tangle of his fingers.

Parson Phelps asked in a croak, 'Did I do wrong?'

'*Thy Isambard Kingdom come*,' said the bearded clergyman. '*Thy Isambard rum-te-tum.*'

'God will forgive you. You are a lost sheep in distress.'

'Baa-aa,' bleated the blond and the bearded clergymen in unison, untangling the purple Clifton Suspension Bridge.

Charles Darwin had a lot to answer for.

Now, alone, Parson Phelps adjusts his needles and his ball of wool, and commences another row of knitting, but after three stitches, he stops. He can't see for tears. He sniffs a long, shuddering sniff, then wipes his eyes with his ball of blood-red wool. Snatching up his crumpled letter, he rises from his chair, and his knitting falls to the floor. The ball rolls to the other side of the room, dividing the floor with a thin line of red. Parson Phelps stands still for a while. Then he carefully steps over the line, and walks to the darkened window.

Below: the ocean. Huge. Chaotic. Dark as ink. He pictures the slashing rain on the glassy waves, and the *Ark* bobbing. A toy of wood and string.

Clutching the Frozen Woman's crumpled letter in his hand, he stares out into the void, and into the darkness on the face of the deep.

Then, just as we reechis the shors of MOROCKO, I falls ill.

Very ill. Fever.

The Arke rolls and rolls on the wavs, and I thinke: I am in a dreem. I hav been so SIK wiv this Fever that I dont no wen the Ark stops, or wen the GENTLEMAN cums. Just wak up wun mornin or afternoon or wotever, an smel the harber, stil in darknis, and he is ther. I tuches him and I SCREEMS, an he SCREEMS too. I shufles to the other side of the cage.

Storm in the nite. Arke rockin in the dok like its goin to sinke. Giraf forls over an dyes. Rogers sicke like a dog, serv him rite. TRAPP nower to be seene.

Me and him is thrown agenst eech uther. He stil hasnt sed a wurd. But in the storm, suden, we is flung together and he puts his arms round me, stil dusnt sa a wurd. And nor dus I. He just holds me and I feel his HART beeting, beeting, against MY OWN HART.

221

CHAPTER 22

BESTIAL URGES

I could feel a heart beating on either side of me, as we lay in bed. And my own heart a piggy-in-the-middle.

'Polygamy's a natural instinct,' murmured Rose, breaking the silence with a yawn of Sunday-morning contentment.

'A bestial urge,' mumbled Blanche, reaching for the heritage chart on the bedside table. They'd start conversations like that, sometimes halfway through. Like they'd done the first half in silence.

'Look, Buck, we're nearly done,' said Rose, thrusting the chart at me.

'We worked on it last night,' said Blanche, while you were down the Crow with Dad.'

I looked. It was impressive. They'd added some heraldic shields with fleurs-de-lis and lions rampant round the edge since I last saw it, and felt-tipped in the structure of the tree; just the names were missing.

'Hope it's all worth it,' I said. I had my doubts. The more I heard about this Dr Bugrov, the less I liked the sound of him. He'd managed to convince the girls that the American heritage craze, where the newly retired come over in coaches to bore you with their roots, was also going to take a grip on our own dying nation, and make them rich. Though how they'd managed to wangle a grant to research their own family tree was beyond me. Oh well. Maybe he was right. There were certainly a lot of foreign film crews about the place, recording poignant documentaries about the end of an era, like they did in Hong Kong, before it was handed back to China. Voyeurs, I thought. Parasites.

'Look, Mum's mother was a Clegg,' said Rose, shoving a computer printout at me.

'And her mother was a Tobash,' put in Blanche, accordioning it out in front of me. They could be a couple of trainspotters, with a map of a gigantic and rather tedious railway junction.

'And before that, there were Boggses on her father's side, and Morpitons on the mother's.'

'So we're incredibly interbred,' they said together, and made a face.

'Practically a species in your own right, then,' I said. They seemed to like this idea, and did some giggling.

'Just one generation to go,' commented Blanche, yawning.

'God, I feel sick,' said Rose.

'Me, too,' said Blanche.

'Must be those Victorian veggie things Mum cooked,' says Rose, yawning. 'From that recipe book she found in the attic. *The Fleshless Cook*. Puke City.'

'But who's to say when you stop?' I asked, peering at their genealogy chart. 'Surely a family tree can go on for ever?'

'The module only requires five generations,' said Rose firmly, yawning again.

'Then we get our diploma,' said Blanche, yawning, too. Yawning's infectious; suddenly I had to do it, too. I snuggled down under the duvet. Idly, Sigmund stirred. I ran my foot up Roseblanche's shin. Ugh; it was all stubbly. I tried Blancherose's: likewise. Sigmund shrank back. It hadn't been like that in the beginning.

'We haven't shaved lately,' they said together.

'We've been feeling too lazy,' said Rose. 'In fact, we're going to spend the whole day in bed.'

'Because we feel ready to throw up,' finished Blanche.

'You certainly know how to turn a guy on,' I said.

What was it about women? This was a question that was aired from time to time in the Stoned Crow, but no one seemed to have the answer. Charlie Peat-Hove thought it was purely hormonal. Ron Harcourt said it was their mothers' fault. Tony Morpiton said it was to do with the nature of society. But I reckoned they just evolved that way.

'Your turn to make the coffee, Buck!' said Rose, jabbing me in the ribs.

'It's always my turn.'

'Hey, he's observant!' they giggled.

'Except this morning, we don't feel like coffee,' announced Rose.

'We feel like Ovaltine.'

Roseblanche, Blancherose, my Balls and chain, I thought, as I heaved myself out of bed, and headed downstairs to do their bidding.

'Chop chop!' they yelled after me.

'Your whim is my command!' I yelled back. I'd heard it somewhere.

Believe it or not, it had only been a month since they moved in. It had certainly been a novelty in the beginning. I suppose that's the nature of novelties. I hadn't been involved in anything polygamous before. I'd always associated it with baboons and sheiks.

After the nightclub in Hunchburgh, they'd stayed the night at my place. And the next night, and the next. The beauty of it, but the trouble, too, was that there were two of them, and only one of me. I'd always been in charge of things in bed, with other women. But I wasn't, with these two. It wasn't just our limbs that got entangled; it was our roles as well. It was quite a thrill, at first, being outnumbered and manhandled like that. I was the luckiest bloke in the world, I kept telling myself. Not everyone could have hacked it; there was stamina required, after all. I was doing the work of two men, let's face it. At weekends they'd wear me out, so that sometimes, come Sunday night, Sigmund would go on strike. Then they'd insist, and pummel away at me and cajole me with licking and whispers and I felt like their sex object, being pushed and shoved about according to their whims. Afterwards, I'd lie between them and listen to their stereo breathing. But it wasn't just sex they dominated. They kept making bilateral rulings about everything we did. Whose decision was it, that they'd move in with me? Not mine.

You went and asked the father's permission, in the old days.

'I would like to ask you for your daughter's hand in marriage, sir,' you'd say.

Those days are gone.

'Bog off,' was Norman's reaction when I announced that his daughters and I were all three planning to live together on a semi-permanent basis. 'That's what they call it in advertising,' he said, noticing my puzzled look. 'Buy one, get one free. Good thinking, Batman! I'll buy you an emperor-sized bed. There's a flat-pack model down at B and Q. Sorted!'

'Now we'll all be able to breathe,' sighed Abbie happily. It wasn't that it hadn't been a joy having the twins at home all these years, she explained; it was just that with the Pepto-Bismol addict in the lounge all the time nowadays, the place was feeling a bit crowded. 'Plus – don't laugh – I feel ready to spread my wings a bit, TV career-wise!'

We didn't laugh. It was sad.

'Time they flew the nest, anyway, I reckon, if the truth be told,' said Norman. 'No offence, Buck, but we'd been scratching our heads a bit over their future. We reckoned they'd be on the shelf for ever, what with the curtains coming down on Britain, and all the young blokes buggering off like rats leaving the proverbial.'

All had gone well to begin with, I reflected, as I hunted for the Ovaltine and microwaved the milk for the two-headed monster upstairs. It's every bloke's dream, I reminded myself, to have two nubile women squirming all over him like a couple of audacious eels. 'So don't knock it, mate!' I murmured aloud, as I fumbled about with mugs and artificial sweeteners.

Then I stopped. 'Come on, Buck!' I urged myself. 'Get a grip! Isn't it obvious that you're living in paradise?'

I plinked two sweeteners into each mug of Ovaltine.

I realised early on – within a couple of days – that the girls had their eccentricities, but I coped. While I went about my veterinary practice, which consisted mainly of vaccinating cows against BSE and grappling with a dispute over Mrs Clegg's foal, which she claimed had been driven insane by the hallucinogen I'd administered, the twins had been working on their genealogy chart with disconcerting zeal, using the St Nicholas's Church marriage register for what they called empirical data. They'd spent hours poring over it, and copying out entries, and computerising tables. As for their obsession with unwanted body hair – they'd been great leg-shavers in the early days, both of them – it hadn't bothered me unduly. Quite the opposite, in fact, I thought now, ruefully. Call me old-fashioned, but who wants to be scratched all over by stubble, or have his girlfriends look like a couple of dykes? And their phobia about showing their feet – well, Sigmund and I actually found it quite sexy that their feet were a no-go area, and that they insisted on keeping their socks on during –

'The joy of socks,' I called it. They'd made a face, like it wasn't the first time someone had made that quip. Like it was the hundredth, in fact. I'll admit that it did bother me that they'd been round the block somewhat. The twins exchanged one of their secret looks whenever their genealogy teacher, Dr Bugrov, cropped up in conversation, and I got wolf-whistled in the pub, when the word spread that we were a threesome. Ron Harcourt made a 'Rather you than me' sort of face, and Jimmy Clegg winked at me, and Keith Hewitt made the double thumbs-up sign, and Tom Morpiton asked me rather pointedly how I was bearing up.

One night I went out with a spray-can, and attacked the graffiti on the harbour wall. It made me feel gallant, to insert that word NOT, in between the ARE and the SLAGS.

The microwave pinged at the same time as the doorbell rang. It was Abbie, laden with boxes from the Old Parsonage, which she thrust at me with finality. 'If they're moving in with you, they might as well make a thorough job of it,' she announced, taking off her coat and beginning to sort through some of the paraphernalia she'd brought: an array of Barbie dolls, sheets, quilts, thermoses, aspirin, and articles of feminine hygiene. When I saw the economy boxes of tampons, my heart sank; female plumbing always makes me squirm. It's all those rogue hormones.

'By the way, Buck,' said Abbie, smoothing the pristine cuffs of her baby-blue seersucker blouse, 'there's something for you in that box of magazines over there; I thought it might be of interest. I found it stashed away in a corner of that old Victorian wardrobe, the one that had the stuffed animals in.'

I looked at the cardboard box she'd indicated: it was full of women's magazines. I pulled one out; it was covered in headlines about human freaks. MY MUM STOLE MY HUSBAND – AND THEN MY CHILDREN! THIS MAN WAS PREVIOUSLY A WOMAN – TWICE! I PAID MY TEACHER FOR SEX – IN CHEWING GUM! I was getting quite sucked into one of the articles – about a beautiful woman whose plastic surgeon had accidentally amputated both her ears – when Abbie interrupted me.

'There it is,' she said, pointing to the box. It was a yellow, tattered old notebook, bound together with string. 'I thought you might be interested, it seems to be zoological.'

Reluctantly, I abandoned the article about the woman who'd lost her ears (she married the surgeon who did it), and blew some dust off the notebook. The title was hand-written, in faded ink. *A NEW THEORY OF EVOLUTION*, BY DR IVANHOE SCRAPIE. The date at the bottom was obliterated by a smear of what looked like blood.

While Abbie bustled about re-arranging the furniture and running her finger along the mantelpiece to check for dust, I flicked through the treatise. I'm not much of a reader, but there were some pictures in it that caught my attention. They were quite amateurishly done, but I recognised the ink sketches none the less; they were of mammal bones and the skulls of what were undoubtedly primates.

227

'Interesting?' asked Abbie. 'The Empress suggested it would be up your street.'

'Yes. Thanks.' I continued leafing through. It was the ink sketch of the monkey that made me stop and stare.

'Christ Almighty!'

'Buck?' called Abbie faintly from the other room. 'With you in a mo!'

'It's nothing,' I murmured.

But it wasn't nothing. The sketch wasn't just any monkey. It was my towel-holder. No mistaking it. Only in the picture, he was minus the blue glass eyes and complete with male genitalia. The same humanoid stance, caused by the unusual slant of the pelvic girdle. The same fragile-looking ears, the same hair distribution, the same –

Below it, Dr Ivanhoe Scrapie had written: '*The Gentleman Monkey, last remaining specimen of its species, captured in Mogador in 1843, and transferred from the Jardins Zoologique de Mogador to Britain in the zoological research vessel, the* Ark, *in 1845.*'

Well, I'll be buggered, I thought.

'Buck, where d'you want these pillow-cases?' called Abbie. But I didn't answer. By now I was riveted. I kept reading. And I kept turning back to the page with the monkey picture. I barely noticed Abbie leaving, and the twins had to shriek at me for their Ovaltine.

While they lay in bed all day, sleeping or working on their chart, I sat downstairs on the settee, poring over Dr Ivanhoe Scrapie's document. The ink was faded in a lot of places, and barely legible, but by the end of the day, I'd read the whole seventy pages. It was clearly written by a madman. Its main thesis – an absurdly childish and unscientific conjecture concerning the monkey that had turned up in the Balls' attic – appeared to be inspired by jealousy of Charles Darwin. I reckoned that the author, Dr Ivanhoe Scrapie, probably *had* been a taxidermist of some sort, as he claimed. There was no question that he had a sound grasp of taxonomy, and if the specimens in the Balls' attic were his own work, he was clearly an expert. But like many taxidermists, he appeared to be a failed zoologist, and very keen to make his own impact in zoological circles.

It was entertaining stuff, in its way. Complete rubbish, of course.

The thesis itself could be dismissed. But the sketch of the monkey got my brain racing. My appetite was whetted. I needed to know more about this creature. Urgently. Because if Scrapie's claims that the monkey was extinct were true then it might well be worth a lot of money.

A *lot* of money.

I couldn't get the thought out of my mind all day, and it was still rattling about in my head when I strolled into the pub that night.

Norman Ball saluted me as I entered.

'Hail the conquering hero, mate! What d'you make of the news? You must be getting pretty excited, with two of them on your hands.' He gave a big wink.

'What news?'

'You haven't heard?' laughed Ron Tobash.

'It's been on all the news bulletins since five o'clock,' said Tony Mulvey.

'What has? Spit it out!'

'There's a woman in Glasgow who says she's pregnant,' announced Norman triumphantly, handing me a beer. 'Cheers, mate!'

It took me a while to absorb this. 'What, naturally? Not from the Egg Bank, before the bomb?'

'No. It's too recent for that.' His eyes were bright with excitement. 'See for yourself, mate.' And he flicked on the news.

The TV news confirmed what the blokes said about the woman in Glasgow. But went further. The number of pregnant women had now risen from one to –

'*Seven thousand*? What, just in a couple of hours?' shouted Ron Harcourt. We all gawped at the screen.

'Nice ONE!' exclaimed Norman. 'Quite a turn-up for the

229

books, eh? I always said the British were survivors!' He pulled out a tissue from the pocket of his cardigan, and unashamedly wiped away a tear. 'The miracle of life, Buck! Just think! We'll be hearing the pitter-patter of tiny feet again!'

The programme on the news channel showed a map of Britain. Concentric circles were emanating from Glasgow, where the first pregnancy had been reported; it seemed that subsequent reports of pregnancy were coming from areas to the north, south, east and west of the city.

'Look!' cried Ron Harcourt, pointing at the animated graphic. 'It's reached past Hunchburgh! Yo!'

Various scientists, church leaders, and politicians were discussing the reports excitedly. It was a rebirth, they agreed. A triumph. We could begin to plan for the future again.

'We always maintained that it was just a blip,' said a politician smugly.

Only one man – a washed-out-looking academic type with a stammer – was expressing doubts.

'Where's the p-p-p-p-proof?' he kept saying. 'Do we have one case that's actually corroborated by m-m-m-m-medical evidence?' I'd heard him before on the radio. He was some kind of psychologist.

'Seven thousand home pregnancy-testing kits can't be wrong!' said a woman.

'C-c-c-c-can't they?' mustered the weedy man. 'And do we know that they all took home p-p-p-p-pregnancy tests? I don't think we d-d-d-do. We are t-t-t-talking about seven thousand w-w-w-w-women. I don't think there are that many p-p-p-p-pregnancy t-t-t-t-testing k-k-k-k-k-kits in the c-c-c-c-country!'

'Shame on you!' yelled Norman, red in the face with indignation.

The studio audience and the Stoned Crow all agreed with him. There were boos, and calls of 'Get him off the show!' and 'How dare he!'.

'The last thing we need is more gloom and doom,' agreed the

religious man. 'I say we fall on our knees and give thanks unto the Lord for this, folks!'

But the weedy psychologist was quite pathetically persistent. 'I don't like to put a d-d-d-d-damper on the euphoria that's sweeping the n-n-n-n-n-nation. Believe me. I want my wife to have a b-b-b-b-b-baby as much as the next m-m-m-m-man. But we should bear in mind that these k-k-k-k-kits are easily tampered with. And that there's a very b-b-b-b-big reward being offered here.'

'Get him off!' yelled Tony Morpiton.

'There may be some w-w-w-w-wishful thinking going on,' he was saying, but his stammers were being drowned out by a chorus of boos.

'What a d-d-d-d-dog-in-the-manger!' said Billy Clegg indignantly. 'He's suggesting that they're inventing their p-p-p-p-p-pregnancies just for the money!'

Everyone laughed.

'But you must admit it *is* pretty odd,' I said. 'Everyone suddenly getting p-p-p-p-pregnant all at once.'

'It's not everybody,' said Norman. 'Just look at the m-m-m-m-map!' It's Glasgow! It's starting in G-G-G-G-Glasgow, and spreading outwards. Anyway, it's no odder than conceptions just stopping with the M-M-M-M-Millennium.'

I had to admit he had a point.

'Rule Britannia!' shouted Norman. And began to sing. Soon we had all joined in. It made you feel quite patriotic, the whole thing. Blokes together.

'Rule Britannia, Britannia rules the waves!' we sang, lurching about, our arms around one another's shoulders. 'B-B-B-B-B-Britons never never never shall be slaves!'

It was that night, when I staggered home from the Crow, that the twins broke their news to me. They were sitting up in bed surrounded by party balloons, drinking more Ovaltine through novelty straws.

'Buck, we're pregnant.'

'Congratulations, girls,' I said. They were kidding, of course.

They'd seen the news, and they were trying it on. But I felt myself going faint.

'And am I the lucky father?' I tried to keep my voice steady, but what with all the beer and the nationalistic emotions sloshing about inside me, it came out slurred. They sucked on their straws, then looked at me solemnly.

'Yes,' they said together. 'You are.'

'We're going to be rich!' said Blanche.

'I need to sit down for a minute,' I said. And fell into blackness.

CHAPTER 23

THE JAR

It is true that in nurturing me from boyhood to manhood, Parson Phelps had prepared me to follow in his footsteps. Had he and Mrs Phelps not raised me as their son, Heaven knows what path I might have followed. Would I ever have ceased to scramble on all fours? Would I ever have learned to speak?

Yet the expression 'a self-made man' came to my mind with increasing frequency as my stay in Hunchburgh drew to a close. For what had I been, these past three years, but a young man, forced by circumstance, into the process of making of himself what he could? Like the whaling-ship that Tommy Boggs and I had once unleashed from its moorings, I was now a vessel voyaging alone. I had left the captain on the shore. And I had finally (if I may be pardoned the pursuit of this nautical metaphor) landed on an even keel. Or so I thought.

But how quickly and suddenly can a storm break, and fortune change! In my case, it took no more than a few seconds.

It was the winter of 1864, and I was about to become ordained. The ceremony was to be the crowning moment of my two years' stay in Hunchburgh, and as a gift to myself, I had indulged in purchasing from little Jimmy Cove a bunch of eight green bananas, which were just ripening nicely in my wardrobe. I planned to eat them, one by one, after my ordination ceremony, which was the following morning at eleven o'clock, presided over by the Abbot and the Bishop. I was looking forward to both events – though I am ashamed to say that I was by now so in thrall to the banana that the prospect of eating some more of the fruit appeared even more exciting to me than my elevation to the status of Parson.

'Hey, Betty!' yelled Farthingale across the refectory table at me that morning.

I looked up and saw his weasel face.

'We're holding a party in your rooms tonight!' he said. It was a Seminary tradition, he told me, that a sort of 'stag-night' is always held for those students about to enter the Church. My heart sank, for now I understood what all the recent whisperings in corridors had been about. Mrs Fooney was away in Wales with Tillie visiting her cousin, and would not be back for a week; my fellow theologians had clearly discovered this.

'Happy, Fartybockers, that your lodgings have been chosen?' Farthingale asked, smirking. 'Quite an honour for you, eh? And if you're a good boy, you'll even be invited!'

'So what d'you say, Hobble-de-Hoy?' asked Ganney menacingly, joining Farthingale with his plate of soup. I turned the other cheek.

'Hey, listen, everybody!' yelled Popple, standing on the table. 'Fartybockers is inviting us all to a party in his rooms tonight! Meet at Mrs Fooney's lodging-house at eight o'clock sharp!'

At eight, as threatened, my unwelcome guests began arriving, and within half an hour, my two small rooms were swarming with fellow theologians. Soon the place was crammed to bursting; students from other disciplines had caught wind of the party, and before I knew it, five students of botany, a geology student, and several medical scholars who had just finished their final exams decided to turn up, with more hangers-on in tow. The rooms were filled with the pungent haze of tobacco smoke, and I began to feel ill. Soon the party had no choice but to implode, or to spill over into Mrs Fooney's own private quarters. The former not being an option, the latter course was taken, and I was horrified to see my beloved landlady's neatly arranged belongings being scattered to the floor, and the contents of Tillie's toy-box investigated.

234

A group of young men were soon playing with the marbles I had given her, and peeking beneath the petticoats of her china dolls. I was horrified, and from time to time tried to stammer my objections, but to no avail.

'Enjoy yourself for once, Fartybockers!' jeered Farthingale.

'Unless, of course, you would rather celebrate with your whore on Mickle Street,' added Ganney, swigging at a bottle of rum.

'Hey, look at this!' yelled a student from my bedroom. And he emerged bearing the trophy of my cherished bunch of bananas – the very bananas I had been saving to celebrate tomorrow's ordination.

'Bananas!' cried Ganney. 'I tasted one once! Capital! Share them out, everybody!'

I groaned, and could only watch as my prized fruit was torn from Ganney's hands amid big beefy roars of delight. The revellers made quick work of the fruit, and soon there was nothing left of my bunch of bananas but the scattered skins on Mrs Fooney's floor.

'Hurrah for Parson Fartybockers!' yelled out Higgs through a mouthful as he thumped me on the back. 'Most excellent bananas!' A morsel flew out of his mouth and landed on my waistcoat, and I was filled with melancholy. 'Have a drink, sir!'

At this, a bony-kneed boy of about twenty, already quite drunk, had the bright idea of standing on my mantelpiece, which was wide enough to take three men, and proposing further toasts to us all, in honour of our forthcoming ordinations.

Some of my ornaments had to be displaced for this purpose, and I watched nervously as Farthingale swept my whelk shell to the floor, and Ganney fingered the fish-gutting knife that Tommy's mother had given me. My Bible, likewise, was removed, and my mermaid's purse, and my copy of Hanker's *World History*, and Herman's *Crustacea*; my dried gourds were all shoved unceremoniously to one side. My eyes were on my jar;

I did not wish to draw attention to it, but was concerned for its safety. I watched worriedly as Farthingale slid it over to the far end of the mantelpiece, and Ganney gave him a leg-up. But as soon as he was up there, Farthingale must have spotted that my focus was on the jar, for it immediately became a topic of interest.

'What's in here, Phelps?' he asked, picking it up.

I said nothing, but my heart yawned in fear.

'A secret?' asked Farthingale. He could spot any sign of weakness at a thousand paces.

'Yes, tell us what you keep in it!' demanded Popple. 'Is it rum?'

It was he who had once referred to me, because of my cordial respect for the Abbot, (forgive me, reader, for repeating his crude words) as an 'arse-licker'.

'Or pickled herrings?' asked Farthingale. He knew I came from a fishing village. I was dragged over to explain.

'How about the toast?' I managed weakly, but Popple had set his heart on my explaining what was in the jar.

'It's nothing,' I said. 'Just something my father left me.'

But Popple was infuriatingly insistent. I racked my brains for a lie, but untruth does not come naturally to me, having been punished for it so consistently when I was a child, so I could think of nothing.

'Well?' Farthingale was demanding. 'What's the big secret? Is it edible?'

'No!' I cried, shocked. God forbid that they should eat human flesh!

'Animal, vegetable or mineral?' called another student.

'It's animal,' I managed weakly. I just wanted them to stop talking about it. So I blurted, 'It's an umbilical cord. I have reason to believe,' I faltered, 'that it once joined me to my mother.'

At this, the room burst out into a cacophony of jeering, laughing, baying, hoots and whistles, as the jar and its by now distraught and miserable owner both became the focus of their mirth and derision.

'Hand it over here!' called Farthingale, egging them all on. 'Let's have a proper look.'

'Yes, go on,' said Popple. 'Kinnon's a student of medicine. He can give you an opinion as to the health of this intriguing object.'

'There's nothing to see,' I cried. 'Nothing!' This was true enough; the liquid in the jar had reacted to the heat of my fireplace by becoming even murkier than on the day I received it from Thunder Spit. The cord was just a fuzzy blur.

But Kinnon, the young medical student, was adamant that he must inspect the thing, as he was currently most interested in obstetrics and gynaecology (here he winked at his fellow students), and he would hand it back to me as soon as he had had a peek-a-squeak at the object in question.

'Please, I beg you, be careful!' I cried, as my jar – suddenly incalculably precious to me – was handed down from the mantelpiece. I watched it being passed across everyone's heads to Kinnon, who was over by the door next to another student smoking a pipe.

'There may be a risk of fire!' I murmured, feeling faint. Then I sank into a chair and said a silent prayer. Kinnon squinted into the jar.

'May I open it?' he asked, finally beginning to wrestle with the seal.

'Yes!' urged Farthingale. 'Let's all have a look!'

'No, I beg you not to!' I blurted, suddenly gripped by an inexplicable panic. My spine bristled. 'It is an heirloom,' I added weakly.

At this, the whole room fell about laughing again, and the women squealed with derision. One of them, I noticed, had her skirt hitched up high above her waist, and two drunken students were snapping at the elastic of her bloomers. I shot up from my chair and thrust my way through the throng as best I could to grab the jar back. This was going too far. With a sudden force of will, and an unaccustomed courage, I reached across to snatch it, but by now Farthingale had grabbed the jar from the medical student and was holding it high above his head. I could see the sediment in the bottom swirling up, hiding the white organ completely from view.

Farthingale was now standing on the table. 'Shall I open it, everyone?' he yelled.

'Yes!' Many of the students, I now realised, were quite drunk, and I saw that the woman with the bloomers had now reached inside the trousers of one of the men and was fishing about inside. He was groaning.

'No!' I called pathetically, and lurched forward to snatch the jar. I managed to grasp it with one hand, but at that moment I trod on something slippery – doubtless a banana skin – and lost my grip. Farthingale pulled backwards and in the ensuing flurry of hands, the jar went flying through the air.

And smashed, horribly, and suddenly, at Kinnon's feet.

Pandemonium!

A horrendous, pungent stench rose up from the puddle on the floor, and the room exploded into immediate panic as everyone flung their hands to their faces, choking.

'Quick! Get out!' shrieked Popple through the coughing. 'Open the door, before we all suffocate!'

'Fetch water!' Ganney's voice choked. 'Dilute it!'

There was a great rowdy and chaotic surge for the door, and more slipping on banana skins, as screaming, shouting, coughing people, their eyes and noses running, tried to escape the fumes, but I just stood there, my eyes smarting from chemicals and tears, staring at the shattered fragments of glass and at my umbilical cord there on the floor. I groaned.

Kinnon, the medical student, was holding his nose and had crouched down to peer at it. Together, coughing, we stared at the thing.

'A strange mother you must have had, Mr Phelps,' he spluttered, 'to play a trick on you like that.'

'Trick?' I asked shakily. 'How is this a trick?' I felt very faint.

'All right, lad?' enquired Kinnon. 'Shall we get out of here?'

But I couldn't answer just then. Kinnon wiped his mouth and nose with the back of his sleeve and coughed some more.

Finally, 'How's it a trick?' I faltered. My voice was like that of the dying Mrs Phelps. Suddenly I had a vision of her blackened lung on the white sheet. She had thought it was her soul. 'How's it a trick?' I repeated.

We gazed at the thing together as the formaldehyde vapour steamed off it. Kinnon looked at me. 'Because that's no umbilical cord,' he said at last.

'What is it, then?' I managed queasily. I was still choking on the fumes that rose from it.

I need not have asked him, though, for anyone looking at it could have told me.

Help me, God.

'Steady on,' coughed Kinnon. 'She was probably just having a joke.' The base of my spine tingled in a violent, ghastly recognition: I reached across Kinnon and was violently sick into his lap.

Of the fifteen theological students due to be ordained the next morning, one was missing from the ceremonies. For I had fled.

The thing I had seen was a tail.

Wot I beg you to UNDERSTAND, Parson Phelps, the Contortionist wrote, *is that the Cercumstancis woz most partikular.*

CHAPTER 24

A PREGNANT PAUSE

The circumstances were unprecedented; unique, even. That was the world's verdict. Britain, as a nation, had entered a nine-month period of insanity. The first trimester was a shaky time, during which many marriages dissolved amid mutual recriminations.

'It's a war of the sexes,' declared Norman. He was right; the situation was serious. Not least because –

No; wait. I'm telling this all arse about face.

The night the twins made their pregnancy announcement – along with five million other women – I was so battered by alcohol and shock that I'd passed out, unable to digest the news. The next morning, I didn't have to: the nation had regurgitated it on my behalf. It turned out that the whole thing was an out-of-season April Fool's joke. Or, as Ron Harcourt put it, 'A load of hormonally induced female gobshite.'

Within twenty-four hours of the first scare in Glasgow, it had emerged that what we were witnessing was not a sudden wave of fertility emanating from Glasgow, but a sudden wave of mass hysteria, prompted by greed, prompted in turn by the five-million Euro Fertility Reward. The stammering psychologist had been right after all. Not a single pregnancy was real. They were all either deliberate hoaxes, or cases of delusion. And that was official. So official, that the Prime Minister said it three times in the House of Commons. 'Official, official, official.'

'Never in history,' jeered the Leader of the Opposition, 'has a government – or the media in its response – been so disastrously

hoodwinked! The words *headless* and *chickens* spring to mind!'
You couldn't help agreeing. A domino effect set off by one
woman, a certain Mrs Belinda Gillie, was to blame for the
epidemic of delusion and trickery. Her pregnancy – the first
case to be reported – had been a deliberate fake. Mrs Gillie
had persuaded her husband – a doctor – to falsify two tests.
She'd wanted the money from the reward.

'She was so insistent,' pleaded the shamefaced Dr Gillie on
television. 'I just wanted to make her happy.' He paused, desperate. 'You do things like that sometimes, to please someone.'

'Even if you know it's wrong?' jabbed in the reporter.

Dr Gillie hung his head. 'Well, sometimes, yes.'

When the news of Mrs Gillie's 'pregnancy' had spread,
first by word-of-mouth, then by rumour and local radio,
then nationally – other women had latched on to the idea,
subconsciously. All the pregnancies were either copycat hoaxes,
or the result of a contagious mass hysteria whose epicentre
was Glasgow. Everyone had been out for the Reward, was the
analysis. Mass hysteria was common among women in times
of crisis – varieties of Münchhausen's syndrome in particular.
It was practically *de rigueur*. It was a wonder, some speculated,
that it hadn't happened before.

'Still pregnant?' I asked the twins, after we'd switched off the
TV the next morning. They were looking pale and worried.

'Yes,' they insisted indignantly. 'Theirs may be fakes, but ours
are real.' Their voices, I noticed, were quite shaky.

'Well, there's a deadline on this one,' I said. 'Shall we lay
bets?'

They scowled at me, and I left for Clegg's farm. When I came
back that evening, they were still huddled together in bed in
their yellow dressing-gowns, whispering conspiratorially. There
was a special programme on TV about it that night; a national
poll had shown that, despite the quite incontrovertible medical
proof that the pregnancies were fake, 60 per cent of the women
who had claimed to be pregnant at the beginning of the scare
hung on to their delusion.

And therein lay a social problem, the TV experts said, on a massive scale. You couldn't get hold of a pregnancy-testing kit for love nor money, and all ultrasound scans were booked six months ahead. With delusional chaos – either euphoric or depressive – among the female population, male morale was hitting hitherto unplumbed depths. Primate sales had slumped since the mass hysteria struck, according to *Pets Today*, and many apes and monkeys – once beloved child-substitutes – were being found abandoned, now that their surrogate mothers were convinced they were expecting the real thing. In London, they'd set up a refuge for orphaned primates. That's where I'll go, I thought, if it all gets too much up here. Back to the jungle. The threat of Mrs Mann's litigation seemed more distant than ever now; she'd be pregnant with the rest of them.

The weeks passed, and sociologists and social psychologists from all over the globe flocked to Britain with their camcorders and their questionnaires to chart the progress of the new 'British disease'. A whole new industry seemed to spring from nowhere: suddenly there were phone-ins, ante-natal classes, public debates, pram sales, crisis-counselling services, baby books, hypnotherapy, aromatherapy, reflexology, foot massage, divorce negotiation, suicide counselling, and cuddly toys on every street corner. In the Stoned Crow, opinion was divided about how to handle the phenomenon of the mass hysteria. Keith Eaves, the weedy stammering psychologist who had been booed off the television on what became known as the Night of Madness, was now revered as an icon of common sense, and was appearing at charity events, photo opportunities and garden centres up and down the country. When he confessed to having considered abandoning his wife and emigrating to Finland at the beginning of the crisis, he was guaranteed instant hero status and offered his own TV show – *Breakthrough* – as counsellor to the nation. We watched *Breakthrough* regularly in the Crow.

'There are three natural responses to any p-p-p-p-predicament of this n-n-n-nature,' declared Dr Keith Eaves. 'F-f-f-f-ight, f-f-f-f-flight, c-c-c-c-ollusion, or n-n-n-n-non-reaction.'

'That's four,' I said.

'I reckon it's kinder to go along with it,' said Norman. He and Abbie had taken the line – right from the beginning – that it would be unfair to burst the twins' bubble. I disagreed; I thought it should be popped right away – if only I could pop it. I was a fighter.

'Of these responses,' Dr Eaves told us, 'c-c-c-c-ollusion is the most dangerous.'

'Hear that, Norman?' I said.

'Well, I happen to know that my wife *really is* pregnant,' said Ken Morpiton, addressing the TV indignantly. 'So what d'you say to that, Dr Eaves?' We all exchanged a look. Ken was nuts.

'I'm buggering off to my mum's for a few weeks,' confessed Ned Peat-Hove, taking the flight path. 'I can't stand it any more. All the nest-building that's going on. The wife's bought a buggy, and she's knitting like crazy.'

We all agreed – apart from Ken Morpiton – that it was exploitative of the babywear manufacturers to flood the market with all this baby paraphernalia that was going to be unusable. It'd all have to be exported to the Third World, like all that frozen beef a few years back.

'It's greed that started it,' said Billy Clegg. We all – apart from Morpiton – agreed.

'Subconscious, of course,' I added. 'We're dealing with severe delusion here.'

Ron Harcourt favoured the non-reactive approach, which Dr Eaves reckoned was the best way of dealing with the pregnancy delusion; neither confirm nor deny the fantasy. Not difficult, in his case. His Filipina, whom he'd ordered from a catalogue in the days when it was believed foreign women could be fertile in this country, was one of the few wives in Thunder Spit who wasn't claiming to be pregnant. That was because she refused to have sex with Ron any more. He wouldn't tell her he loved her. She couldn't live without love. It had been a bad transaction. She was going back to the Philippines; she

243

was fed up with him. She'd rather live in poverty with a real man, she said.

'Well, what if they really *do* have babies?' persisted Morpiton, shouting over the television. 'What if the doctors' pregnancy tests are wrong?' I exchanged a glance with Ron. Morpiton spotted it, and swung round to poke me in the chest accusingly. 'OK, Buck, so when did your two girlfriends last have a period?'

This was true; the monster pack of tampons Abbie had brought remained untouched.

'At least we won't be suffering any more of that PMT malarkey,' mused Billy Clegg. 'But it's funny, the way they all reckon they're due nine months to the day after the Reward was announced.'

Norman agreed that we were talking loony tunes. That five-million yo-yo Reward had certainly had an impact on the nation's psycho-wotsit. 'If you'll pardon my German.'

Not least in my own ménage. To celebrate the five million Euros – ten million, they reckoned, if they gave birth simultaneously – Roseblanche stole my credit card and went on a spree. Their bogus hormones had turned them into a couple of decorating maniacs, who felt the need to give my rented cottage a complete overhaul: Venetian blinds and a cloggy ochre paint-job in the downstairs loo, too close to shit-colour for comfort, peach and cranberry marble effect in the porch, reminiscent of dog-spleen, a Jackson Bollocky sort of wallpaper in the kitchen, three-piece suites with tassels and framed prints of arty-looking turnips bunging up the lounge. All my virtual Elvis concert tapes were relegated to the garage. As lust triangles go, it was expensive: within a month, they'd run me up a huge overdraft. Abbie, who took the collusion approach to their fake pregnancies, was the high priestess of taste, master-minding the whole operation from the John Lewis catalogue and cooking for the giant freezer she insisted I buy for her gals, to make honest women of them. The labour-saving device stood out in the garage, waiting to be fed with little cling-filmed dishes like a hungry gourmet animal. Meanwhile Norman would call round every day with his toolbox, exhorting me to call him Mr Fixit, and nailing me ever more securely into my coffin of domesticity. By the end of the second trimester, Thunder Spit was awash with waddling women padded with wind, cushions, or genuine fat. Rose and Blanche, who had opted for genuine fat, had swelled to such a size that they could barely squeeze through the doors; the way they shared the weight of their phantom pregnancies, it was like a triplet had joined them. They were still attractive, but only in the way that a sculpture fashioned out of pure lard might be. Like all the other hysterics in the town, they were enjoying their mock fecundity, and flaunting it. They'd all get together in a gaggle for the swimaerobics classes at the leisure centre, then converge on Pizza Hut, which had a special 'Eating for two' discount on pizzas.

'We were born to breed,' said Rose, as she and Blanche returned from their ante-natal session at the Baldicoot Medical Centre. There was another place that had cashed in on the crisis; it had bought St Nicholas's Church and converted it into a surgery, where it ran both pregnancy classes *and* a Denial Group.

'We want to start up a whole tribe,' explained Blanche.

'It's a primal urge,' said Rose authoritatively.

'Since the time of Noah,' added Blanche.

A primal urge which had soon rendered us flat broke. As we neared the second trimester of delusion, Rose and Blanche kept buying things we didn't need; endless electrical appliances – toasters, ghetto-blasters, bottle-warmers – for which Norman, the great colluder, had to come in and make a little shelf. 'I warned you,' he'd say cheerily, dusting down a high-chair or an ancient plastic bath-toy. 'Double trouble!' Then he'd leave.

The twins' bellies grew and grew, and eventually I was forced to vacate the emperor-sized bed for fear of being squashed to death in my sleep. I set up on the sofa-bed in the surgery, where the smell of praxin gave me queasy dreams – dreams in which the macaque Giselle would jabber at me, or whimper, or howl. Was her sudden re-appearance trying to tell me something? It was she, after all, and the terrible Mann woman, who had been the trigger for my arrival in Thunder Spit – a place of refuge, I reflected, which had quickly become a trap. I tried to analyse it. I pictured Giselle with her little upturned face and her hairy legs and her pink frock, but it still didn't dawn on me.

'A lot of m-m-m-m-men have been having anxiety d-d-d-d-dreams as we enter the f-f-final stages of the delusionary ph-ph-ph-phase,' warned Dr Keith Eaves on *Breakthrough*. 'Now I'm going to ask you to look at the c-c-c-c-components of your d-d-d-d-dreams carefully, and try to make c-c-c-c-connections. It might well be the k-k-k-key to the future well-being of your r-r-relationship.'

Time passed; the lambing season turned to the cat-flu season and then the abandoned-dog season; as we entered the third trimester, I dreamed about Giselle with increasing frequency, and tried to make sense of it, as Dr Eaves had suggested, but was still none the wiser. Then, when I was shaving one morning and reaching for the towel, I suddenly made the connection.

Giselle – monkeys – Eureka!

Monkeys!

My towel-holder! The Gentleman Monkey! Dr Ivanhoe Scrapie's manuscript! The sketch!

Money! How could I have been such a moron all this time?

Thank you, Dr Keith Eaves!

The Gentleman Monkey had become so much a part of the household furniture that I barely noticed him any more; he had become reduced to pure function. With all the upheaval over the pregnancy hysteria, I'd put Dr Ivanhoe Scrapie's treatise to one side. Abbie had given it to me the very day the news had broken about that Gillie woman in Glasgow. I'd been meaning to do something about it and then –

Christ. In all the madness about the twins being pregnant, I'd just forgotten about it. Now, I cursed myself for letting it slip to the back of my mind. Hadn't I decided that this monkey might be valuable? Where had I put the treatise? Christ knew. I turned the house upside-down looking for it, then discovered that the twins had shoved it under the kitchen sink, along with my animal-anatomy books and the bleach. I re-read it. It looked like this bloke really believed what he was saying. Just like Rose and Blanche really believed what they were saying. Not hoaxing: pure delusion. But the sketch of the Gentleman Monkey, and the claim that it was extinct – that was still exciting, as a prospect. A financial prospect. And a good reason to pack my blue suede shoes and hit the road.

As their due date approached, I noticed with some satisfaction that the twins were finally beginning to fret about money. Perhaps it was about to dawn on them that they might *not* be about to get the Reward. They even began work on the genealogy chart again – a project they'd abandoned as soon as they were up the imaginary spout. It was the morning they presented me with their four-point financial plan scrawled in lipstick on a sheet of greaseproof paper that I decided that now was as good a time as any to bugger off back to London, take a break from country life, and research the Gentleman Monkey. I'd trawled the Internet for more information, but despite endless E-mails from enthusiastic primate-watchers, I'd been unable to locate anyone who knew about a creature of that name. There's nothing like doing something in person.

I re-read the twins' list of objectives and sighed.

1. Get genealogy diploma and sell roots charts to Americans.
2. Apply for another grant increase from Dr Bugrov.
3. Flog all our old junk at the car-boot sale.
4. Give birth, and win ten million Euros! Hurray!

'I'm thinking of going down to London,' I said.

'Fine by us,' said Rose, holding up a little knitted jump-suit.

'Where are you going exactly?' asked Blanche, putting the finishing touches to a mobile of dangling pastel bunny rabbits and bulbous butterflies.

'To the Natural History Museum,' I said. 'To discover the origins of our increasingly fascinating towel-holder.'

They looked at each other then, and made a face.

'Funny, we've just been talking about that old thing,' said Rose, sniggering. '*Vis-à-vis* our financial plan.'

But she wouldn't tell me what was funny. I went upstairs and packed my things.

'Well, come straight back,' they called after me as I left. 'We're due the day after tomorrow!'

Along with twenty million other women, I thought, chucking the keys to my Nuance in the air like they do in films, but failing to catch them.

I left with the sound of their stereo laughter ringing in my ears.

CHAPTER 25

ON THE THRESHOLD OF
THE FUTURE

Nature red in tooth and claw: who has not witnessed its very particular horrors? Who has not observed Mr Jaws the Beetle crunching up poor Mr Bobby Centipede alive, or Mrs Itsy-Bitsy Spider cannibalising her husband only seconds after congress, or Mr Moggy Cat (Here, Pussy, here Pussikins!) torturing and disembowelling the innocent rodent, Miss Squeaky Shrew? Call it bad design if you will, but this is life!

So the idea of a natural carnivore such as *Homo sapiens* reverting to the allegedly herbivorous diet of his most ancient, primitive ancestors, on the grounds of 'humanity', is no more and no less than an absurd and sentimental whim. And worse, an argument without logic! Take it to its obvious conclusion, Mademoiselle Scrapie, *ma petite chérie*, and you will discover yourself not stepping into your vegetable patch for fear of crushing a garden slug, and holding your breath, for fear of inhaling an innocent germ! If Mr Darwin is right, then surely, the more we evolve, the more frequent, demanding, wide-ranging and imaginative should our visits to the butcher's be! *This* is civilisation!

So run the thoughts of Monsieur Cabillaud, the Belgian chef, as he stirs his pot of guinea-pig broth for Her Majesty's luncheon. Yet he is grateful, paradoxically enough, for the illogical argument and sentimental whim that led Miss Violet Scrapie to lose her wits and boot him out of Madagascar Street. For what turn of events could have engendered a happier outcome?

Being head chef at Buckingham Palace is not to be sneezed

at. Jacques-Yves Cabillaud does not sneeze. He breathes in the sweetly scented air of simmered guinea-pig and freedom. Freedom to, and freedom from! What can be more sublime a thing than to have risen in a few short months through the ranks of Her Majesty's servants, and now to be master of the best kitchen in the land, at a time when one of the greatest ever of Victoria's famous feasts is *en pleine préparation*. Never more so than today. The Banquet approaches, and the Palace kitchen plays host to an odoriferous whirlwind of activity: filleting, sizzling, chopping, basting, kneading, and whisking in readiness for the event, which is, dear reader, none other than the Celebration of Evolution Banquet!

Long live Charles Darwin, guest of honour and excuse for all this kerfuffle!

Cabillaud smiles to himself. Will Mr Darwin recall him now? Will the great zoologist in whose honour the Banquet is being held, recognise in the rounded, confident form of the Queen's head chef the vestiges of the seasick but ambitious young cook who once travelled with him on the *Beagle*? Unlikely, but tantalisingly possible. Darwin, after all, is an expert on the subject of evolution. And what is Cabillaud's life-history, if not a dramatic example of personal transformation over time? What indeed is Cabillaud, dare he suggest it himself, if not a shining example of Nature's quest for – and attainment of – perfection?

''Ere. Take zis.' Shoving his wooden spatula at a callow *sous-sous-sous-chef*, Jacques-Yves Cabillaud points the minion in the direction of the steaming broth, and begins to pace the kitchen, reviewing for the umpteenth time his plans for the Banquet. There is to be a meringue castle, the preparation of which requires fifty dozen eggs. There are to be a thousand jellied eels. A tub of mongoose pâté. Five thousand oysters. Poached desert weasel. A whole field's-worth of strawberries, to be glazed and placed inside individual puff-pastry moulds. Grilled dolphin. The biggest fruit salad ever made in the civilised world. Jackal mousse *à la triomphe*. Kebabbed cat. Fifteen hundred individualised *amuse-gueules* featuring zebra mince and *coulis de tomates*.

Not to mention the Time-Bomb. The magnificent casing of which is being steered into position as we speak.

'A bit to ze left!' orders Cabillaud, rubbing his hands in anticipation.

'Yes, sir!'

'Now to ze right a little!'

'No sooner said than done, sir!'

'And now you will PUSH!'

The hefty *sous-chef* heaves with his bristling fore-arms, and the giant clam shell – measuring a good fifteen feet across – wobbles dangerously, then topples into its pre-ordained horizontal atop the specially designed trolley. Jacques-Yves Cabillaud surveys the clam, a big rocky bowl of calcium deposits, with the critical eye of a connoisseur. It is rumoured that this clam once housed a pearl, a pearl so extraordinary that it has been squirrelled away to a secret pearl room, to which only the Royal Hippo has the key. But Cabillaud doesn't give a hoot about the pearl. It is the shell that is his concern – and its safe arrangement on the trolley.

Why, dear reader?

Because it is to become part of his greatest work of culinary art to date – a work so ambitious that it will eclipse even the glory of his published tome, *Cuisine Zoologique: une philosophie de la viande*, that's why!

The bristle-armed *sous-chef* now stands back, sweating, and awaits further instructions from his master.

'Now you will scrub it clean until it is gleaming!' commands Cabillaud, patting its bumpy surface. 'Until I can see my own face in it!'

'Yes, sir!'

Everything about the Time-Bomb must be perfect. Including its delicate mechanics. When Cabillaud had first heard of the extraordinary Mechanical Millipede, he sent out search parties to locate its engineer, an acknowledged genius.

''E must 'elp me,' Cabillaud insisted. ''E will understand. Only ze best minds in ze 'ole country can do justice to my *idée*.'

It was in this spirit of culinary idealism that the engineer, Mr Hillber, of the Travelling Fair of Danger and Delight, was eventually tracked down, lured away from his regular work in exchange for a fat fee, installed in the servants' quarters, and roped into Cabillaud's grand plan. A major ingredient of which – the giant clam – now stands before Cabillaud, its rocky exterior about to receive the scrubbing of its life, its delicately coloured inner shell hidden, but gleaming with promise. The promise of secrets. The promise of a surprise within a surprise within a surprise.

'What's for pudding?' Cabillaud used to ask his mother as a boy.

'Wait-and-see pudding,' the reply always came.

Amid the clatter of pots and pans, and the hiss of fragrant steam, Cabillaud is once again eyeing the clam critically. It suddenly reminds him of his unhappy days of seasickness and seaweed aboard the *Beagle*, and he shudders.

'All zis seaweed must vanish completely!' he commands. 'If zer is one sing I 'ate and detest, it is ze seaweed!'

'Yes, sir!'

Kashoum, kashoum, kashoum, goes the wire brush, as scraps of stinking weed, along with rotting mussels, limpets and barnacles fall to the floor. Kashoum, kashoum.

Yes: the Time-Bomb requires extraordinary levels of commitment, negotiation, inspiration, technique, fervour, and plain honest elbow-grease. Pistons have been discussed at length, ink diagrams sketched on linen tablecloths, pros and cons weighed, decisions reached, abandoned, and resurrected; promises made and reneged upon; plans hatched and scuppered; hair torn out, nails bitten, brandy drunk, sleep lost, and floors angrily spat upon. *Vive la création*!

'Ah, my dear Hillber!' calls Cabillaud, spotting the Mechanical Millipede engineer. Hillber – so small and wiry he might almost be fabricated from a coat-hanger – skips past a row of pastry-

252

makers in a cloud of flour, and comes to shake Cabillaud's hand warmly. Then he gestures to introduce his companion, also emerging from the flour: he is a sharp and frostbitten-looking man sporting a bow tie.

'Mr Edward Ironside. I believe you have met in the past. He arrived this morning.'

'Welcome, my dear friend!' says Cabillaud, smiling in recognition. It has been many years since they last met, at Dr Scrapie's, when Ironside was a mere stripling, an apprentice taxidermist. It was he who supervised the Arctic iceberg and its safe arrival in the Scrapie ice-house, and now his expertise in the dual disciplines of freezing and taxidermy make him an invaluable member of the team.

'Excellent,' says Cabillaud, shaking Ironside's freezing hand. 'Shall we zen begin? We 'ave ze problem of ze breathing to discuss.'

'And the woman?' asks Ironside. 'The artiste? Has she been informed of our requirements?'

'Yes, indeed,' confirms Hillber. 'She volunteered herself – begged, even – to be a part of it. She has asked me to report that she is honoured to do anything we require.' He pauses, then lowers his voice to an excited whisper. 'Anything, within *or even beyond* reason!'

'*Merveilleux*,' beams Cabillaud, gratified but not surprised at the reaction of the artiste concerned. Who would not give their eye teeth to be a part of his great creation?

'Shall we proceed, zen, gentlemen?' Cabillaud motions them towards a table upon which sketches and diagrams of the Time-Bomb and its audacious contents are pinned. Within minutes, they are deep in discussion, and Hillber is sketching furiously.

'A system of holes?' he suggests.

'Or a periscope solution?' wonders Ironside.

'Perhaps a hosepipe?' offers Cabillaud.

'Or,' ventures Hillber, 'more daring but more aesthetically discreet – a miniature inflatable balloon?'

'Why yes!' The man is indeed a genius!

Kashoum, kashoum, kashoum.

'Zer! Over zer!' yells Cabillaud, glancing up from Hillber's latest drawing and pointing to a barnacle half-concealed beneath the ridged lip of the clam.

The *sous-sous-sous-chef* looks up anxiously from his brushing. 'Yes, sir.'

Kashoum, kashoum, kashoum.

Is it not something, to be master of one's own kitchen, the best kitchen in the whole of Britain?

A something which Cabillaud, who once served seaweed gratin with human vomit in it aboard the *Beagle*, is entitled to celebrate.

And celebrate he will!

Kashoum, kashoum, kashoum.

Jusswannabe
Yurteddyber
Puddachaynarannamahnekkah an leedmi anywayah . . .

Blaggerfield, Norton's Krig, Wipperby. The Nuance purred its way down the motorway, and I yodelled along with Elvis. But it wasn't long before the sound of my own voice began to grate on me, and my singing turned to yawning, and then silence. Outside the car, the green grew greyer, the skyscrapers taller as I journeyed south. It had been almost a year since I'd left London, I realised with a jolt. Christ. For the first time in ages I thought of the surgery in Tooting Bec, and then I suddenly remembered Mr Mann, and the thousand Euros, and Giselle in her little pink frock. And Holly and the body-bag and the letter. And the phrase 'Would not hesitate'. I shuddered. Odd, that I should have left because of a monkey, and was now returning because of another one.

I glanced at the photo of the Gentleman Monkey that I'd perched on the dashboard. I'd thought of taking him with me

254

to London, to show him to an expert at the Museum in person – but then dismissed the idea. He was too bulky. And possibly – exciting thought, this – far too valuable. So I'd borrowed the twins' polaroid camera and taken a few shots. They hadn't come out very well, but I was in a hurry. This was the best one, but it still didn't do him justice. The ruffed shirt and the red pantaloons didn't help; they were the kind of clothes an organ-grinder's monkey might wear. They demeaned him, somehow. I say 'him', but it still wasn't clear to me whether the creature had been male or female. He was dressed in male clothes, but the genitals had been completely done away with. Although Scrapie's treatise claimed the creature was male, you had to take anything he said with a shovelful of salt. A madman with a vision is a dangerous thing. I thought about his bizarre hypothesis: *A New Theory of Evolution*, he'd called it. Nothing if not grandiose. Maybe the idea didn't seem so crazy at the time, I thought: the Victorians didn't know about DNA. And it was another century or so before blokes like Dawkins and Gould evolved.

Looking at the photos now, that feeling of excitement I'd had when I first saw the monkey started rummaging away again. He really was some specimen. I realised that I was curious about this weird, almost human creature in a way I hadn't been since I was a kid, when I unearthed three-quarters of a desiccated fox in the garden, and kept rat spleens in the fridge.

At midday I stopped for lunch at a service station at Grommet Hill. While I was waiting for my order, I spread out the photographs in front of me and inspected them one by one. I also had my eye on the waitress; it wasn't often these days that you spotted a young woman who wasn't sporting the obligatory pregnant belly. She wore a badge on her tit that said I'M PAULA, HOW CAN I HELP YOU? When she came back to my table with my chicken and chips, plus side-salad, I peered at her chest closely.

'Sorry,' I said, when she showed signs of embarrassment. 'I'm dyslexic.'

'It says "I'm Paula, how can I help you?",' she said.

'By getting me a Coke, Paula, my darling,' I told her. And gave her my Elvis look, the one that's designed to make them melt with desire. But she hadn't noticed my curled lip; she was looking at the photographs.

'Aaaw, isn't he sweet,' she said, in a gooey voice. 'I do love children. I've got a chimp. How old is he? Have you had him long?'

Christ, I thought, snatching up the pictures. The whole nation is insane.

'He's dead,' I snapped.

A tear instantly welled in her eye. 'Oh, I am so sorry!' she said, touching my arm. 'How did you – lose him?'

'I killed him,' I said, remembering Giselle. 'I'm allowed to. I'm a vet.'

That sent her packing.

Betty Botter bought some butter . . .

Before I left the north by steam train I said a prayer on the platform: Please God, make this a wild goose chase. As we chugged and stopped at every small town on the way to London, I cheered myself up as best I could with my tongue-twisters, and read the names of the towns we stopped at: Snail's Rump, Hinkley Firth, Knaveswood-under-Gab, Blaggerfield. By the time we reached Grommet Hill, my mind was awash with a flotsam of Viking balderdash.

An elbow kept jamming into my ribs; it belonged to a woman who was knitting a strange pair of leggings for her son. She told me he was a member of a dance troupe. The front gusset was the size of a horse's nosebag.

'He's quite a man,' she said, reading my thoughts, and burst out laughing.

I laughed with her for politeness's sake, but my laughter was hollow. If a male object is all it takes, I thought, then I am human, too.

'What makes a man, in your opinion, madam?' I asked her suddenly.

'That he's a civilised gent is all I ask,' she said, her face looking suddenly weary. 'That he says his pleases and his thank-yous, and if the need arises, he would lay down his life to protect another.'

I scratched my flea-bites for a while, lost in thought.

When I had told Kinnon my story two nights earlier, he had diagnosed madness, and administered first Epsom salts, then castor oil, then laudanum. Now, as the steam train chugged though the flatlands of Northumberland on its journey south, I could feel all three remedies beginning to wear off, and my heart began to shrink in cowardly trepidation.

Norton's Krig, Wipperby, Brill. The trees grew taller, the landscape lusher as we journeyed south. We stopped for half an hour at Nobb-on-Humber, where the sun came out and threw a shaft of sudden wonder into the carriage, and the knitting-woman offered me a bite of her chicken leg. Politely, I said no. I was weak with hunger, I told her, but had to starve today on account of my tapeworm. It was at that point that she spotted my fake dog-collar beneath my scarf, and apologised for her crudeness *vis-á-vis* the mentioning of her son's 'thingummyjig'.

'Not at all, madam,' I said, in my parson's voice. 'A mother's pride is a blessed thing.'

'He's doing *Swan Lake* at the Royal Ballet,' she said, relieved that I had not taken offence. One plain, one pearl. 'He's not a swan, he's one of them other birds.'

A crake? A cormorant? A herring gull? I wondered, remembering the sea-birds wheeling in the skies of Thunder Spit, and Jared, my carrier pigeon, now asleep in his cage, covered with a cloth. I would sooner place my faith in a humble bird than in the Penny Post.

Fib's Wash, Crowtherly, Axelhaunch. I slept fitfully and awoke half-crazed, remembering my dread quest.

'Are you all right, dear?' the woman asked me suddenly, near Gladmouth, jamming her elbow in my ribs as she jerked at her skein. 'You're trembling.'

I said nothing, but pulled my coat tighter around me, like a shell.

London at last: at St Pancras Station, the train disgorged me and I stood on the platform, fingering my whelk on its string. It was indeed soothing, I reflected, to carry the ocean round one's neck at all times. Tommy must have known, when he gave it to me, how much I would miss the sound of crashing waves. I will go nowhere now, I thought, without my precious whelk.

I put it to my ear. Slosh, slosh.

But after a minute standing there on the platform I gave up, and nestled the shell back in the warmth of my greatcoat next to my crucifix rum-flask.

The platform was noisy. My heart was skinned.

'You must forget this nonsense,' Kinnon had insisted, pouring me more castor oil. After my jar had smashed, he had taken me back to his lodgings, and I had shown him the evidence of my feet.

Never, I thought, as we gazed at them together, had they looked hairier or more deformed. 'You need rest, and sleep,' prescribed Kinnon.

He was wrong. I had learned my lesson. What I needed was the truth.

I can't, I protested to myself.

But I will, said the creature within.

I left Jared with the pigeon man at St Pancras, saying I would return in a week to send my letter back north.

In Paddington, I found a boarding-house; the woman who ran it obviously had a sixth sense about her lodgers' finances, because she warned me she'd always need the money in advance. The place was dismal and filthy – a far cry from my cosy bachelor rooms back in Hunchburgh, where Mrs Fooney's motherly warmth permeated the kitchen along with the smell of baking bread and poppyseed.

I slept with cotton wool in one ear and my whelk pressed

against the other. The next morning I found a tick on my shin. I burnt it, but its jaws remained in my flesh.

'And no more screaming in your sleep!' the landlady commanded the next morning, ignoring my mention of the parasite. Unlike the pillow-chested Mrs Fooney, her bodiced torso was as flat and hard-looking as a beetle's carapace, and her eyes were small green marbles of mistrust. 'This isn't Bedlam.'

It was some other little Hell, though. I paid the woman for another night, and she put a mark in her ledger. I knew for a fact that I wasn't the only screamer. Parson Phelps always used to tell me that London was a place where young men from the provinces quickly go insane.

'Or a place they flee to once their madness is a fact,' he'd add darkly.

I found a little coffee gazebo in Regent's Park where I sat, absorbing it all: the deals struck, the philanthropy, the pimping, the Empire-boasting. In the end, homesick for the ocean, I wandered to the docks, but this wasn't water as I knew it. I had seen many a ship out at sea, her sails bloated with wind, but what I saw here were stranded sea-creatures, their great hulls cracked with sunlight, their souls trapped by gang-planks and wheelbarrows and ropes.

As I left my lodging-house the next morning, a fellow lodger joined me; he introduced himself as Hikes. Together we strolled to my coffee gazebo in Regent's Park, and there he listened to my tourist's tales.

'You're nervous,' he said, eyeing me up.

'It's nothing,' I said.

'Here.' He proffered me some brandy in a hip-flask – little knowing what I carried in my hollow crucifix. 'Drink this,' he said. 'Then do what you really came here to do.'

'And you?' I asked.

'I bought an hour's worth of fat whore and gambled the rest.'

We sipped our coffee.

'I'm going to find a man,' I blurted at last, smashing my

cup down on to the saucer and spilling half my coffee in my jitteriness. He raised an eyebrow. 'And I am going to make him tell me the truth.'

'Go on,' said Hikes, shoving his liquor-flask under my nose. 'Get that inside you.'

'I'm normally teetotal,' I lied. But I took it from him and swallowed a large gulp of brandy and it glowed in my upper body like religion.

'The truth about what?' Hikes called after me as I left.

In Portobello Road I stopped and made some purchases: a waistcoat, a pair of scissors, a needle and thread, a small revolver. I mended the waistcoat, and slipped the gun into its pocket. Then I headed for the centre of the city.

That bit of London near the Museum has always been Hell, parking-wise. I'd forgotten that. It was pissing with rain; I eventually found a space in a nine-Euros-a-day multi-storey, then bought a paper and stopped for coffee in a gloomy little roadside caff called The Gazebo. The waiter who brought me my *cappuccino* slopped it into the saucer and didn't apologise; he was wearing a Walkman. My paper reported that hoax calls to the ambulance service had risen by 50 per cent, as the phantom pregnancies reached their barren and inevitable conclusions. In most cases, according to the report, it was an accumulation of wind, and the women felt physically much better once they had released it. Pity the ozone layer, I thought. In the distance I could hear the sirens.

'Intense depression is bound to ensue,' it quoted the ubiquitous Dr Keith Eaves, now the undisputed therapist to the nation's buffeted psyche, 'as we all undergo a period of mourning for what never was.' They'd cleaned up his stammer for him in print. 'In *Swan Lake*, the swan flutters before it dies. What we are witnessing here, in a final act of yearning, disappointment and acceptance, is the dying dance of *Homo Britannicus*.'

You had to hand it to him; he had a way with words.

The article also made the point that the inevitable anti-climax of the largest attack of mass hysteria on record was causing chaos on a practical level, and genuine emergency cases were being forced to wait up to 47 per cent longer than stipulated by their health charter. Some poor sods had even died as a result, I read. Now there was going to be a one-hundred-Euro fine for every hoax call. Enter a small industry in the form of cowboy midwives offering phoney services for bogus events. I thought of Rose and Blanche, with their Ovaltine and their novelty straws and their pathetic industriousness, sighed, and shoved my cup and saucer to one side. The coffee was pure swill.

I left.

In the underground walkway, I fought my way through crowds of Saturday shoppers, street hawkers, homeless and sightseers. I followed the signs like an obedient tourist, climbed a flight of pissy-smelling concrete stairs, and emerged in the open air, next to a life-sized fibreglass triceratops guarding the Museum.

Pray God this is a wild goose chase, I murmured as I approached the vast building. As I entered the arched portals and stepped into the gloom, I thought of Jonah. The Museum's belly was filled with footsteps and echoes and whispers. I looked above me. The cornices crawled with ornamental tiles, and the stained-glass windows refracted and smithereened their colours, stippling the varnished walls with haphazard designs; it was not a whale, I realised, but an Aladdin's cave, monstrous in its grandiosity, not a surface left undecorated. I know what Parson Phelps would have said. He had always hated a decorated surface. Something about the Devil finding work for idle hands. Something about the worship of graven images. He would have made the sign of the cross.

I reached inside my greatcoat, where my hand brushed against the crucifix and the whelk. Still there.

HER MAJESTY'S ANIMAL KINGDOM, said the copper-plate writing on the notice before me. EXHIBITS ON LOAN FROM HER MAJESTY THE QUEEN'S COLLECTION. Following the direction of the sign's pointing finger, I walked nervously into the gloom, my footsteps echoing on the ceramic tiles.

I could feel the eyes before I saw them. They stared from all directions, baleful and disturbing. My spine was bristling, and I felt my heartbeat betray my fear. And then I saw the beasts, and a chill ran through me.

They stood in stiff rows, staring at me from plinths and pedestals.

'Good God!' I breathed. I closed my eyes for a second, hoping that when I opened them again, the vision would have disappeared. But it had not.

The creatures were all wearing clothes.

A giraffe in a long tent-like dress with a fleur-de-lis design towered above me. A lion in pantaloons and braces, wearing a top hat, crouched next to it, ready to pounce. A wildebeest in a white nightgown and matching nightcap stood fixing me with its glare, its hooves clasped in a position reminiscent of prayer. What frozen forest of horror had I entered? Feathers gleamed beneath frilled shirts and frock-coats; fur was flattened beneath petticoats and pinafore dresses. An ostrich wore a frilled hat, like the one Mrs Sequin used to wear to church. A cow sported spectacles. A raccoon in a cassock wielded a walking-stick. The human eyes stared, both knowing and blank.

'A travesty,' I murmured, half-choking with horror. 'A travesty of Nature!'

Scrabbling in my knapsack for my pen and notebook, I copied down the name of the taxidermist from a plinth – Dr Ivanhoe Scrapie – and fled from the Museum like a bat out of Hell.

Christ, what a whopper of a building; big enough, I reckoned, to house umpteen wide-bodied aircraft if the need arose. After queuing up for ages, I had to pay nine Euros fifty to get in, though I noticed that, with a family ticket, it would have been a lot cheaper. The place resounded with the echoes of a million children oohing and aahing in the shadow of a huge brontosaurus skeleton. I hadn't been to the Natural History Museum since I was a kid. I was in for a shock. No stuffed animals, for a start. Apart from the brontosaurus skeleton, it was all acrylic reconstructions and interactive hands-on stuff. A group of schoolkids suddenly poured in and started yelling obscenities. To my left, an ineffectual-looking bloke in a mauve tracksuit put up a hand and called, 'Yo, kids! Let's have a bit of shush, please!'

They ignored him, and carried on yelling and kicking their Coke cans about, and making silly faces. He was their teacher.

The primates were upstairs, in an exhibition all about the evolution of man.

In 14 Madagascar Street, Belgravia, Violet Scrapie is dressing for dinner, and picturing the capture of a whale by harpoon. She has recently seen an Italian *gravura* of such a scene, in which the artist, Rafael Ortona, disturbingly managed to show in the creature's wildly swivelling eye all the agony and indignity of the blubber being stripped from its still-living flesh. In her imagination, she colours in the heart-breaking detail that Signor Ortona has delicately omitted from his *gravura*, yet so vividly evoked: the sea heaves red with blood, while beneath the water-line, the smaller fragments of blubber and flesh float down into the depths.

Nature, like Violet Scrapie, loathes the sight of wasted protein: these fragments will feed whole armies of sea-life. She sees the great sea-cucumber, a living ocean turd, laying claim. She observes the wily scissoring of the lobster's claws as it snatches a hunk of blubber from a passing quillsnapper. And the thuggish gang of sharks attacking the carcass and stripping whole sections of it to the bone as the skeleton is hauled off. Violet knows, having read it in one of her father's zoological treatises, that depending on the swiftness of the action, and the temperature of the surrounding waters, the creature will emit vast quantities of steam from its flesh. Yes, steam. This is the effect of the heart's great pounding motion as the mammal enters into a state of shock, pain and fright.

Imagine!

Imagine, too, how the blood then boils. How the flesh itself is heated, and the bones cook. And how the whole brute edifice is transmogrified into a grotesquely floating stew, a loose scaffolding of hot bones dragged through the choppy waves to Hunchburgh, where it is dismantled much as a ship itself can be dismantled in a shipyard, and the merchants dispatch its cleaned components – ribs, jawbone, tailbone, skull, in tiny quantities relative to the whale's size, to the haberdashers and hosiers and couturiers of the Nation.

It is said that the bodices and hats and fashion accessories of Queen Victoria contain so much whalebone that two skeletons'-worth have not been enough to feed her rapacious wardrobe.

Violet bends asthmatically for the corset, reflecting with some resentment on the Royal Hippo's hosiery supplies. No stingy annual clothes allowance for *her!*

(Should whalebone be boycotted? she wonders suddenly. Why, surely it should!)

The contrast, Violet reflects, is stark: Victoria – wife, Queen, Ruler of Empire, owner of two skeletons worth of whalebone, and mother to a whole litter of blue-blooded royal babes. Violet Scrapie, distressed spinster. Violet Scrapie, daughter of the eminent Dr Scrapie, stuffer of animals By Her Majesty's Appointment. Violet Scrapie, prisoner in her own home:

> *A violet by a mossy bank,*
> *Half hidden from the eye,*
> *Fair as a star*
> *When only one is shining in the sky.*

Huh. *When only one*. And when there are more? Eh, Mr Wordsworth? Ugly as a blasted moon.

On a more positive note, Violet's mission, *The Fleshless Cook*, has been progressing in leaps and bounds. Only this morning, she has taken pride in the preparation of a hearty chestnut soup containing both cinnamon and parsley. Furthermore, she has finished making her last batch of walnut ketchup, invented asparagus and lemon pudding, made a dozen pastry ramekins, fried two giant Jerusalem artichokes for tomorrow's dinner, and perfected a recipe for baked Spanish onions which makes Mrs Beeton's version look laughably naive, and indeed almost inedible. All seventeen stone and five pounds of flesh that is Violet Scrapie stands now in the bedroom in her vast bloomers, staring down at the complex structure that lies at her feet. The Royal Hippo and I have little in common, she reflects: just womanhood, Dr Ivanhoe Scrapie, and whalebone. Or to be more precise, the miracle of soft engineering that is the corset.

Like a clockwork ectoskeletal creature of the deep, Violet now begins the task of assembling the shell of wire and padded whalebone around her stupendous body. First she heaves the heavy black sheath up to her gigantic hips, then twists it so that it lies symmetrically around her pelvis. There are wire hooks that must be aligned, and made to cling together like wrung hands. To do this, she must first draw in her breath and lift her rib-cage so that her waist is elongated, insofar as is possible, a celebration of cause and effect, soon to be reined in by structure. Each breast is the size of a human baby. They quiver and shake, setting up a rolling judder across the great vista of her belly, as – whup! – she hauls up and clasps together, at waist-level, the two sides of the encasing pod.

What are the alternatives? Bamboo? she wonders, exasperated at the effort of it all. Or wire?

'Fasting,' whispers a ghostly matriarchal voice. 'The answer, Vile, is to consume less food.'

'Bugger off, Mother,' mutters Violet, wrenching her carapace into position and tugging at the cords.

Three floors below, a small man with an odd gait and unusual shoes is peering at the numbers on the doors. He, too, has little in common with Queen Victoria, apart from his diminutive stature. Like the head of our great British Empire, he measures five foot two, but there any resemblance to the reigning monarch ends abruptly, would you not agree, gentle reader? After all, Queen Victoria does not have a mutilated coccyx, nor does she wear orthopaedic shoes, or a phoney dog-collar, or house a temperamental tapeworm, or harbour fleas; nor does she have the organs known, in polite society, as a male object and related accoutrements (cock and balls to you), and nor does she urgently need to discover the truth of her origins – because Queen Victoria has a family tree that stretches back centuries, adorned with heraldic plates of Huguenot shields and Plantagenet memorabilia, Battenburg gewgaws and Tudor roses, and Tobias Phelps (for it is he) has nothing but the evidence of his own deformity, and a piece of pickled human flesh, re-bottled for him in Hunchburgh by a medical student named Kinnon.

To read the brass-plated numbers on the doors, he has to squint.

Number two.

His deep-set eyes are wild, haunted.

Number four.

His face is thin-lipped, wrinkled, sad.

Number six.

He is mumbling feverishly to himself. A sharp ear might make out the words to a tongue-twister about a woman called Betty Botter buying some butter but finding it bitter and not being able to put it in her batter.

Number eight.

He clasps his frock-coat about him tightly.

Number ten.

He fingers a whelk shell.

Number twelve.

'Pray God this is a wild goose chase,' he murmurs.

Number fourteen.

Home of Dr Ivanhoe Scrapie.

Tobias Phelps mounts the steps, and performs a sudden upward leap to ring the bell.

Ding, dong!

Suet, prone on Violet's eiderdown, lifts his head and yaps feebly at the doorbell. He has not been himself at all lately; his vegetarian diet has weakened him immeasurably.

'Oh, botheration!' mutters Violet Scrapie. She's still struggling with her corset, and wondering about whalebone.

Suet yaps.

The bell rings again. Ignoring its insistent jangle in the hope that her father will remember it is Mrs Jiggers' day off and answer it himself, Violet abandons her buttoning and lacing in order to fix her late mother's jet choker around her neck. Despite the jeweller's recent adjustments, it's still a fraction too tight, as though the Laudanum Empress is trying, by whatever means she can, to throttle her disappointing daughter from beyond the grave. Which indeed she is.

'Please, Mother,' croaks Violet, who has lately become increasingly aware of her ghostly presence in the house. 'A little less pressure!'

And the choker's grip is instantly relaxed.

'Chop, chop!' the phantom is bossing. 'Answer the bloody door, child! The future depends on it!'

'Did you say something, Mother?'

The doorbell rings again, wildly this time. Violet Scrapie shuffles over to the window, irritated by the noise, her white cotton bloomers swishing about her puckered thighs, and peers down on to the street, where a sulphurous yellow glow leaks from the gas lamps across the slush. A small figure directly below her, on the front doorstep, is hopping about in wide pantaloons. Taxidermy, like chess, attracts a strange breed of men, she reflects. Not artists, not scientists, neither fish nor fowl nor duck-billed platypus. Often, Violet has noticed, they have some kind of deficiency, physical or moral, which they must feel can be remedied by stuffing straw and sawdust into cured skin, and sipping Amontillado sherry at meetings of the Zoological Society.

Could the stranger be one such specimen?

No. He could not.

She realises this instantly, as the man looks up at her, and their eyes lock.

What round eyes he has, she notices. And what thin lips! Now where has she seen that face before? A peculiar and not unpleasant sensation – one Violet has seldom felt before, and certainly never with such exquisite intensity – insinuates its way into the most private interstices of her corset.

She knows this man.

She knows him!

'We have cause for celebration!' murmurs the Laudanum Empress, observing her daughter, and interpreting the delicate feelings playing across her face as only a dead mother can.

'A distressed spinster no longer, perhaps?' she shouts.

'Mother?' breathes Violet. 'Are you there? Did you speak?'

'A distressed spinster no longer, perhaps, I said!' yells the phantom. But Violet hears nothing but a buzz as she sinks heavily on her bed, suddenly aware that she is still in a state of undress. Her whalebone creaks, as the feeling she cannot identify creeps its way further into her –

Her loins, reader. Not to beat about the bush.

Should she go downstairs, and find out who he is? And why that face looks so familiar?

'Not yet,' Violet murmurs, putting her hand to her breast to calm the pounding of her heart. 'Clothes first.'

And she begins to rummage in her wardrobe, in search of her best red frock.

I have since asked myself: is love an instinct, or something learned? Is it part of Nature itself, or a reaction that comes from the way in which we are nurtured? What makes one man seek out the familiar, while another will travel the world in search of an exotic mate? What propels us? I do not have the answers. All I know is that I looked up at her, and our eyes locked.

That she was clad in nothing but a corset.

And that she was magnificent.

And that my heart shrieked within me, and that my tapeworm twisted my guts into a cruel knot of longing and delight and fear.

Yes, gentle reader: we met in the most particular of circumstances.

The cercumstancis woz most partikuler.

The nite of the storm, she wrote, *wen he took me in his arms, I did not no WOT he wos, or WHO. It woz the next day, or the next, that Higgins came and litte a candel, and I saw the Creetcha for the furst tyme.*

Meet a GENTLEMAN, sez Higgins. And larfs.

Remember, Parson PHELPS, I had no book lernin, and no understandin of SYENSE, and at that time I nowd nuthin of MISTER DARWIN'S BELEEFS.

All I nowd, woz that I had ikkstreemlie bad LUKKE in LUVVE.

CHAPTER 26

DARWIN'S PARADOX

I was still reeling from the sight of the magnificent corseted woman – reality or apparition of my crazed mental state, I knew not which – when the door of 14 Madagascar Street opened abruptly, and I found myself face to face with a thin, grey-bearded, grumpy-looking gent whose mouth appeared to be bristling with pins. In his right hand, he was wielding a hoof.

'Dr Scrapie?' I stammered.

'Yes?' With a gesture of disgust, he spat out his pins into his hand and settled his eyes on me, where they blazed uncomfortably. The shirt beneath his frock-coat was splattered with what might have been cochineal, or blood. A hole gaped in the sleeve of his jacket. 'Well, young man? What is it?'

'May I come in, sir?'

'What for?' he barked. 'I'm busy. State the nature of your business, sir, or bugger off.'

My heart began to thump crazily under my ribs. I must persevere, I thought. I have come this far. What I have started, I will finish. Betty Botter bought some butter. Peter Piper picked a peck. Axelhaunch. Fib's Wash. Blaggerfield.

'Well?'

'I would like to request you, sir –' I begin, trying to effect an entry. But he blocks my path.

'Yes?'

'– And as a matter of fact require you –' (Courage, Tobias!)

'Yes?' He was scowling at me now.

270

'– And furthermore demand you, sir –' (Yes!)

'What, dammit?'

'Humbly, sir, to –'

'To what? Get on with it, fellow!' His voice has growling thunder in it.

Three words left. Grasp those thistles, Tobias, and prove you are a man!

'Examine my body. Sir.'

Silence. He's looking at me as if I'm mad.

'I'm not a bloody physician,' he spits finally. 'I am a taxidermist. I stuff and mount animals. Whoever directed you here is an imbecile. Now bugger off.'

'Please, sir. Please!' I am wedging my way in now, and reaching in my pocket. 'There is something only you can answer.'

'I said NO!' he shouted. 'Now bugger off! I'm in the middle of stuffing –' He stops.

I'm pointing my revolver at him. My hand is shaking. Dr Scrapie freezes.

I can hear how thin and desperate my voice sounds. Like a tin whistle.

I say, 'You will do it, sir, or I shall blow your head off, and then my own!'

Yes: a man at last!

None of the plastic replicas of primates or the hologram exhibits resembled my towel-holder in any way. There was an interactive CD ROM, though. I scrolled through, beginning to feel that my visit here was already a waste of time. I'd been through all my old veterinary books, and even rung a friend who specialised in primates. He'd never heard of the Gentleman Monkey, and when I described my towel-holder, he drew a blank. The CD ROM display repeated a lot of the stuff I'd already come across in the virtual library that I'd accessed from Thunder Spit: how the monkey differs from the ape in crucial ways such as DNA structure, teeth, skull size, and skeletally, in particular with regard to the tail. There are only three living exceptions to this rule: Kitchener's Ape, which has a cingulum on its molar teeth, more in keeping with the monkey family, the Yeoman Baboon, whose skull is closer to the fossilised humanoid Neanderthal than an ape as such, and the extinct Ape of Mogador.

Mogador rang a bell. Wasn't Mogador mentioned in Scrapie's treatise?

'My God,' says Dr Scrapie, a minute later when Tobias Phelps has bashfully undressed. A brief glimpse of Tobias Phelps' anatomy would be enough to tell any zoologist that they had something remarkable on their hands. As Scrapie's expert eyes take in the sight of the creature before him, he stifles a gasp.

'Extraordinary,' he murmurs.

The hand-like feet.

The abundance of orange body hair, peppered with animal fleas.

The mutilated coccyx.

'And then there's that,' says Tobias Phelps, pointing to the jar.

Scrapie peers at its contents, and soon his pulse is racing furiously.

'Am I the first to –?' he asks Tobias Phelps in a haunted whisper.

'Apart from Dr Baldicoot, when I was a baby. And my mother, but she is dead.' Tobias Phelps is silent for a moment, and then confesses, 'I rarely have occasion to be entirely naked, sir. Even when alone.' Scrapie raises his eyebrows. 'My upbringing, you know,' Tobias Phelps whispers sadly. 'My parents – discouraged nakedness.'

Scrapie's heart does a complicated somersault.

'Yes,' he says, clearing his throat. 'I quite understand. Now lie down, please,' he instructs the young man. The phrase 'on a plate', keeps running through his head. Meanwhile Tobias

Phelps, for his part, cannot help noticing that the taxider-mist's manner has altogether altered, in the direction of sudden, extreme interest.

'Now,' announces Scrapie, forcing his mouth into a smile. 'My dear young man. I need to investigate you further.'

I keyed in 'Ape of Mogador', and waited for further details. As the computer was running the search, I looked about: the schoolkids were flowing up the stairs like an anti-gravitational pancake mix. Everything echoed. I didn't like this place. It gave me the creeps.

Just then there was a muted beep, and some text came up on the screen: in pink, on a yellow background, with an insistent techno-beat of music behind it. I began to read.

The Ape of Mogador: Also known – erroneously, because of its misleading tail – as the Gentleman Monkey.

Jesus Christ. And there was more.

As I read on, I began to feel sick with excitement.

Peter Piper picked a peck of pickled pepper, I said to myself as Dr Scrapie took out a small roll of measuring tape and encircled my skull with it. Miss Mosh mashes some mish-mash, I thought, as he shone a little torch into my eye. Minewort, lungwort, I thought, as he peered first into one ear, and then the other. Gudderwort. The arid Gudderwort. I can see his face. I can see his face and the distaste on it as he hands me the jar. And other faces, too: the Mulveys, the Cleggses and the Balls and the Tobashes. Tommy Boggs' wife was a Tobash. Jessie, who had called me Prune-Face. Jessie's belly, rounded with child.

The girl in my rooms, her hand down a student's trousers, fishing about for his –

The woman I had glimpsed in the upper window, beneath whose corset –

The jar that contained my –

'Now breathe in slowly,' Scrapie is saying; he has a cold stethoscope to my chest. Can he hear how fast my heart is pounding?

From this angle, with his flowing white hair, grizzled beard, and authoritarian expression, Dr Scrapie resembles God; the same God whose beard dissolved into the white storm-clouds of the Great Flood in the Noah's Ark picture on my bedroom wall at home. Have I not come to the expert of experts? The man who single-handedly peopled the Queen's ghastly Animal Kingdom Collection with its human-eyed bestiary?

His eyes are all fired up with a strange gleam, and it dawns on me that I will have no more need of my revolver. I have his attention.

'*Sir* Ivanhoe,' I hear him murmur.

'I beg your pardon?'

'Nothing,' he replies quickly. 'I am just trying to think how I can –' There is a long pause as he appears to search the recesses of his memory for the right word. 'Help you,' he says finally.

Now he is questioning me intensively, scribbling notes as he does so, and I am suddenly telling him everything. About being a foundling, discovered by the altar of St Nicholas's Church in Thunder Spit, the day after the Travelling Fair of Danger and Delight left Judlow, with a ghastly mutilation to my lower spine which had nearly killed me. About the way the animals of Thunder Spit growled at me, and how I was rejected by humans, too. About the Contortionist at the Travelling Fair, who had handed my father the jar containing the –

'The object in question,' I falter. Scrapie's eyebrows shoot up.

'Aha,' he says. 'Now we are getting somewhere.'

But he does not say where. Instead, he questions me in detail about what he calls my 'well-spokenness'. This prompts me to impress him further with a few tongue-twisters, and I recount how I used to read long passages from the Bible in church.

'Speech came to me late,' I tell him, 'prompted by the sight of a cake on my fifth birthday.' This seems to stir even more excitement in him.

'And before that? How did you communicate?'

'In squeaks and grunts, as far as I am aware,' I told him. 'They said it was a miracle.'

'A case of nurture overcoming nature, perhaps?' mutters Scrapie, almost to himself. And then, addressing me: 'In what manner were you raised?'

'In a Christian manner, sir,' I tell him. 'Cleanliness, reading, self-improvement and piety were encouraged. Indulgences of the flesh, nakedness and childish play were not. A traditional English upbringing, sir.'

He questions me further, and I find myself telling him more: about how I believed the jar to contain an umbilical cord, until it had smashed, and about how Kinnon had put me right. About how, when I had told Kinnon my fears, he had assured me I was mad. About how I had insisted on knowing the truth. About how he had advised me to come to London, and search out an expert.

'You could not have come to a better place, young man,' murmurs Scrapie reassuringly, as he begins to carry out a series of quick sketches of me in his notebook. 'You can trust me implicitly.'

This is a profound relief.

'And you say your foster-father will not see you?' Scrapie asked when I had finished telling him about Parson Phelps' removal to the Fishforth Sanatorium for the Spiritually Disturbed.

'That is so, sir.' I hung my head.

'I am – sorry to hear that,' he said thoughtfully. 'And nobody has any idea that you are here in this house? With me?'

'No, sir. Why should they?'

'No reason at all. Indeed not. My poor young man. No relatives? No friends? You are here completely – alone?'

It seemed important to him, though I could not see why.

'Completely alone,' I confirmed. Although I did not like

this lonely thought, Dr Scrapie seemed to find it particularly appealing; he started rubbing his hands as if I were a warm hearth.

Finally he blurted excitedly, 'You looked familiar to me, young man, as soon as I saw you.'

I was surprised.

'Are there others like me, then? I asked, filled with a sudden tremulous hope.

'In a manner of speaking, yes,' said Scrapie. 'Or at least there were. What I mean is, I have seen a creature that resembles you. Resembles you so closely, and according to my records so accurately, anatomically speaking –'

He went over to his desk and pulled out a notebook full of measurements and sketches. Then he said, 'Have you heard of a creature called the Gentleman Monkey? An extinct primate, from Morocco?'

'No.' I said. Why was my heart suddenly plummeting downwards like a leaden fishing weight?

'That is the creature you resemble, young man.'

I pressed the key to call the picture up from the CD ROM, and watched the 3-D image emerge. It was an artist's impression, and was accompanied by an etching of the creature, made in 1843 by a wildlife artist who had visited the last remaining specimen in the Jardin Zoologique in Mogador, Morocco. I gasped when I saw it. It showed the monkey standing with its hands on its hips, in a defiant and disconcertingly human posture, behind the bars of a large cage.

'It's him!' I shouted. 'It's bloody-well him!'

'*Lang*uage!' said the man in the mauve tracksuit. The pancake mixture had finished its progress up the stairs, and was now slurping Coke from cans and mock karate-kicking each other with feet clad in blocky trainers. 'There's kids about,' the teacher went on. 'If you can't keep your mouth clean you shouldn't be here in school hours.'

'Sorry,' I lied, desperate to get rid of him. He was glaring at me now like I was some kind of paedophile. When he finally shuffled off, trailing his charges behind him like a pedagogical jellyfish, I turned my attention to the text that accompanied the etching. The Gentleman Monkey was an unusual specimen, and had baffled naturalists at the time. Strikingly humanoid, with a larger brain than man's, and a fun-loving temperament.

Polygamous by nature.

That word 'polygamous' got me thinking. It was then that some phrases from Dr Ivanhoe Scrapie's eccentric treatise came floating back into my head, and my brain began to whirr.

'So this – Gentleman Monkey,' I croaked finally, gulping at air. 'What is it, exactly?'

'Was,' Dr Scrapie corrected me. 'It is no more. It was an interesting species of monkey; not so much a monkey, in fact, as a tailed ape. Anyway, highly intelligent, and strikingly human in appearance. Polygamous by nature, and a fructivore, but in other respects remarkably similar in many ways to the human. Child-like but courteous by nature; that's why they called him the Gentleman, I suppose. And probably also why he became extinct,' he added thoughtfully.

I was having trouble breathing by now. 'And what happened to it?'

'The last remaining member of its race is now housed in Buckingham Palace,' said Scrapie. 'I stuffed him and he became a towel-holder for the ladies' powder room in the banqueting suite. That's where he is now.'

If only I had heeded Kinnon's advice, accepted his diagnosis of madness, and remained in Hunchburgh! I would be ordained by now! I would be Parson Phelps the Second, preaching my anti-Darwinian sermon loud and clear from the pulpit!

I pictured the creature's skin being removed from its body,

and filled with sawdust, then dressed in human clothes, like the creatures I had seen at the Museum.

'And the – carcass?' I mustered finally, following the ghastly thought through to its conclusion.

'You'd rather not know about that, young man,' said Scrapie, looking suddenly tired and slightly throttled. 'Suffice it to say that it was highly toxic. It contained poison.'

'Poison?'

'So it would appear. Not something I discovered till – later,' said Scrapie. 'When I had cause to investigate the creature's remains.'

'You mean the monkey was poisonous by nature, or it had *been* poisoned?'

'It had been poisoned,' he said slowly. 'With praxin.'

'But why? Where? Who did it?' I felt my sanity slipping away as I spoke.

'Nobody knows,' sighed Scrapie. 'But I have my suspicions.'

The last of this species of ape, according to the interactive CD ROM display, had been purchased by the entrepreneur Horace Trapp from a Moroccan menagerie for Queen Victoria's collection and shipped over to Britain, but it had died in mysterious circumstances on the voyage back to London, following a mutiny on board Trapp's vessel, the *Ark*. The creature had later been stuffed by the Taxidermist Royal, Dr Ivanhoe Scrapie, as part of Queen Victoria's Animal Kingdom Collection, most of which was housed in the Museum. But the Queen had so taken a liking to the primates that she decreed they should grace the rooms of Buckingham Palace, which was where the ape was dispatched, once stuffed, sometime in the 1850s. But in 1864, to the dismay of later generations of evolutionary scientists specialising in primates, the stuffed creature was stolen from Buckingham Palace. And never traced.

It was there, as I flicked through the interactive zoology encyclopaedia, that I realised. The Gentleman Monkey in my bathroom was the only known specimen in the whole world of this breed of extinct primate. The only remaining evidence that such a creature had ever existed. There was no mention of its having been stolen in Scrapie's treatise. Could he perhaps have written it before the creature had disappeared from the Palace? And if he had not been lying about the rarity and the final extinction of the species – was it (I got all choked up at the thought), was it possible that the rest of his extraordinary document was also true?

That word 'polygamous' kept haunting me.

Yes: I'd definitely have to think about this.

'We found the Gentleman Monkey dead on the *Ark*,' said Scrapie, after he had finished telling me what he knew about Horace Trapp's career, first as a slave-trader, then as an animal-collector for the Queen. 'Along with all the other creatures. Over a thousand of them. Most of them half torn to bits. Nature's cruel, you know, young man,' he said, eyeing me in a strange way. 'But there wasn't a mark on the monkey. It was the praxin that killed him. It must have been injected.'

I winced.

'We found Trapp's head, too,' Scrapie continued, going slightly pale. He paused for a moment and re-filled his pen with ink. He did it slowly, applying great concentration to the task. 'Not a pretty sight,' he said finally.

'When was this?' I asked. 'When did Trapp's *Ark* arrive in London?'

'1845, the same year Violet was born,' said Scrapie. 'It was found floating on the Channel, and hauled in.'

'Violet?'

'My youngest daughter.' I remembered the face of a woman in the window. So this was Violet Scrapie. I felt my heart shift, and desolation sweep through me like a cold wind. 'It was a bloody nuisance,' Scrapie was saying. 'Had to ship an iceberg over to deal with it. Trapp's *Ark* kept me busy for fifteen years.'

279

I gulped.

'1845 was the year of my birth,' I told him. 'As far as it is known.'

Scrapie picked up his notebook again, and began to scribble furiously.

I had dismissed the assertions in Scrapie's treatise as nonsense; the ravings of a demented man.

But –

Hope gobbled at my innards, and my brain raced. I found myself actually having to grab hold of a fibreglass gibbon to keep my balance. The kids had moved off, but their voices wafted up from the hall below, a faint echo buzzing in my head.

What I was thinking was that, by a quirk of fate – that chance meeting in the pub with Norman Ball? Or was it even earlier, when the threatened litigation over Giselle catapulted me north? Or did it date back to my childhood wish to work with animals? In any case, by some quirk of fate, some kind of extraordinary missing link had fallen into my lap.

The de Savile Theory of Evolution, they would rename it. I would insist on it. I'd hold the Gentleman Monkey hostage, if necessary, until it was official. You try stopping me.

I'd be given a Euro Award.

Then I started thinking about the other stuff in the document, and my stomach heaved. There were implications. Phelps, the man was called. Tobias Phelps. I didn't recognise the name from the twins' family tree. But they hadn't finished it.

I was hallucinating now, surely. I had never seen their feet. They didn't have tails, that was for sure. But it was still possible – was it not? That –

No. I was going mad. It was impossible.

'Impossible!' I said.

Scrapie said, 'So you know, since you have become aware of

Mr Darwin's theories, that we are all descended from the humble primate?' He spoke slowly, as if I were suddenly a child, or a creature not too quick on the uptake. Perhaps he was right. '*All* of us,' he said. 'Even Her Majesty Queen Victoria.'

No, I thought. It wasn't like that. *The earth was without form and void, and darkness was upon the face of the deep.*

'Human beings stand at the top of Darwin's ladder of nature, you know, Mr Phelps. Of all the species of primate, we are the most evolved.'

Blasphemy!

'Have you ever seen a fossil, Mr Phelps?'

'I have. My father used to say that they were God's jokes,' I told him. My voice sounded weak and thin.

'Jokes?'

'God moves in a mysterious way,' I said, scraping about in my memory for the comfort of my fledgling sermon on God and the fossils. 'Fossils are clearly the Lord's doing, and evidence of His grand design.'

But my heart wouldn't stop pounding; I felt that I might explode and scatter, like a distraught firework.

'Well, according to Darwin and others,' said Scrapie, 'they are evidence of a distant past, of which we are the biological inheritors. Have you heard of natural selection, young man?'

'Yes,' I said. 'It is Darwin's theory. I have studied his book, and his profane ideas.'

'Natural selection,' said Scrapie, brushing my remarks aside, 'is Nature's way of making advancements. From simple to complex, from complex to even more complex, until you reach man. Darwin says that we must not, however, forget the principle of correlation, by which many strange deviations of structure are tied together, so that a change in one part often leads to other changes of a *quite unexpected nature.*'

Scrapie stopped in his tracks and steered me towards a *chaise-longue.*

'Sit down here,' he said. Obeying him, I found myself face

to face with the male object and related accountrements of a stuffed horse.

'A fine specimen, your horse,' I mustered politely. Miss Mosh mashes some mish-mash. The creature looked nothing like the horses back in Thunder Spit.

'Well, it would be an odd specimen, if it were a horse,' says Scrapie. 'Actually, it's a mule. An ass. A hybrid.'

'A hybrid? A sort of cross?'

Mildred doesn't like this idea one little bit, and wrenches violently at my long-suffering sphincter.

'Exactly. Father a stallion, mother a donkey. Or occasionally vice versa. They are always sterile,' continued Dr Scrapie slowly, keeping his eyes levelled on my face. 'They are sterile,' he said, 'because Nature doesn't like breeding across species. Yet – *paradoxically* – it has always happened. In the case of the mule, it has been virtually an institution. Most examples occur in the world of botany, but there are plenty of zoological examples as well. More than you'd think. Wallabies and kangaroos. Crocodiles and alligators. Lions and tigers, even. And then there are historical cases, or should I say mythological ones, though where mythology ends and history begins we can only guess at.'

'Cases such as, sir?' I falter faintly.

'Such as the Minotaur, the Centaur, the mermaid; Pegasus, the winged horse. Medusa, the snake-headed woman. The Devil is half goat, is he not? And then of course there's the Angel.'

Blasphemy and more blasphemy!

'I cannot agree with that, sir,' I retort, my cheeks burning. 'The Angel is a creature of Heaven.' But then I feel my face slacken, and I reach for my whelk. For I know, suddenly, and with a force that sets Mildred attacking my innards, that if a creature of Heaven is possible, then so is a beast from Hell.

'So how –? What –?' I stammered.

'Darwin,' said Scrapie, 'asked the following question: *"If the cross offspring of any two races of birds or animals be interbred, will the progeny keep as constant, as that of any established*

breed; or will it tend to return in appearance to either parent?"
I'll say this much for Darwin: he's asked some sensible questions.
But he doesn't have all the answers. Not by a long chalk.'

I am perched stiffly now on the edge of the *chaise-longue*.

'And – do you have answers, sir?'

'I think your existence upon this earth is beginning to provide
me with some,' he replied. He sat still for a while, lost in thought.
'A form of natural selection,' he finally murmured to himself.
'An evolutionary tangent. A new branch of the family. Or an
old one.' Then he jumped up and began to pace the room. I
could see his mind was tumbling in all directions. 'Yes; very
possibly an old one. Humans are evolved from other primates.
Apes. Monkeys, too, but further back. But what if –?' He paused,
then began to drum his fingers on a table.

'Hypothesis,' he said, his eyes dancing with excitement.
'Hypothesis. A human mates with another species of primate.
On board Trapp's *Ark*, let's say. Mates, let us speculate, for
the purposes of argument, with *the Gentleman Monkey*. And
creates a new breed of human-like primate. You, Mr Phelps!'

I was winded by the very absurdity of the suggestion, but
there was no stopping Scrapie by now. He was leaping up
and down.

'Yes, you!' he yelled, slapping me hard on the back. 'Raising
the intriguing scientific question: Can the unaccountable leaps
and bounds of our evolutionary path be explained by the
occasional injection of the blood of other species into the
veins of some creatures? Could the mouse have emerged from
the elephant, or vice versa, by an incredible act of sexual union?
Which occasionally bore fruit?'

I gulped.

Scrapie said that a man called Mendel had bred peas that told
such a story. The botanical examples were all about us. I thought
of the gourd plant on my mother's grave. Had it been trying to
tell me something, after all?

'Yes!' Scrapie was almost shouting. 'There's not enough time,
you see, for everything to have happened! To get from a fish to

an amphibian to a man takes longer than it should. It doesn't work on paper. So there have to be sudden changes, not just gradual ones. And you are the answer!'

My head was thudding, and the air about me seemed suddenly strangely dappled, as though my vision were disintegrating. 'I still don't understand.'

'Two different species, breeding, Mr Phelps! Imagine such a thing! Not possible now, to create a new species, out of two. But *was once*, maybe. Why on earth not? So imagine this, as the answer to Darwin's time-paradox: that man didn't evolve slowly from a gorilla or a chimpanzee. He appeared suddenly, like Adam and Eve in the Bible. Just one. A freak cross-breed. From two completely different – and perhaps incompatible – species. Two species that would perhaps otherwise not have *survived*! That would have *died out*! Two wrongs, therefore, Mr Phelps, making a right! You are living proof that it's possible.'

One of the briefest, but also the most potentially historic conversations on the theory of evolutionary science, had just taken place.

'*I'm all shook up!*' I sang. '*Oooh!*'
    Pedal to the metal. Go, cats, go.
    This was the biz.
    And I was the King.

So, I thought miserably, Genesis *was* a lie. And evolution *was* a fact. But its mechanics – its mechanics were not quite as Mr Darwin thought. It had progressed at times in great magical leaps. And I was proof of it. A mutant, an aberration, a misbegot. One year a green and stippled gourd. The next a yellow, blotchy one. The following year an orange fruit, with warts. The year after that, a mauve one with stripes. The year after that, a green one again, but with warts, or stripes, or mottled patches. A bit of this, a bit of that. Fling it in the primordial soup pot and await

God knows what! The world looked different, all of a sudden. It had transformed itself, before my eyes, from an ordered place, a hierarchy created by God, into a floating Darwinian whorehouse. There reigned a new, chaotic higgledy-piggledyness that defied belief and astonished the heavens. And I, Tobias Phelps, was part of this crazy hotchpotch of nature called evolution, a dangerous and wild and virtually unexplored new territory of understanding. But was I a victim or a pioneer?

Was I one of God's jokes, or the butt of it?

I hung my head in an unfathomable mixture of pride and shame.

Scrapie was fingering a syringe now, and giving me a strange look.

'Have you ever had laudanum?' he asked.

'Yes. Kinnon gave me some before I left Hunchburgh. To calm my nerves.'

'He did well. I would now like to give you some more. I shall administer it by injection; it'll act faster and more effectively that way. Now roll up your sleeve for me.'

Betty Botter bought some butter, I murmured to myself as the needle entered my vein and he squeezed. But, she said, this butter's bitter. Scrapie had been right; I began to feel both relaxed and dizzy immediately.

'How tall are you, Mr Phelps?' he is asking.

'Five feet two,' I reply, sinking back on to the *chaise-longue*.

'That's right. Make yourself comfortable. And your waist measures – approximately?'

'I have no idea, sir,' I murmured, feeling drowsy.

'Will you permit me then,' he asked, 'to measure you again?'

'With a view to what, Dr Scrapie?' I moaned.

But before I could hear his answer, I had succumbed to blackness.

I sped through the streets of Thunder Spit, went the wrong way round the one-way system, got flashed at by the speed-sensitive road-sign on the high street, and swerved to a halt at my front door. I thumped my way in; in the hallway I stumbled heavily and crashed over a double buggy; an ancient vehicle of steel and nylon, parked there like a tangle of dead crickets.

The twins were sitting in the kitchen knitting.

'Hi, gorgeous,' said Rose, not looking up.

'Been missing you,' lied Blanche.

Something was up. I could tell.

'How's tricks, girls?' I asked, trying to stay cool.

'We've finished the family tree, look,' said Rose, shoving a big chart at me with phoney-looking heraldic shields decorating the margins.

'We're descended from a parson,' boasted Blanche.

'Parson Phelps?' I asked. I could feel myself going white.

'Yeah, how did you know that?' But not waiting for my answer she went on, 'He used to live in Mum and Dad's house. The Old Parsonage.'

'According to the church records.'

'Quite a coincidence, eh?'

So they *were* descended from the man Scrapie mentioned in his treatise. The man who according to him, was –

'Mum said she could've told us that ages ago, but it would've been against Dr Bugrov's genealogy rules,' says Rose.

'It's cheating to get anything by oral history,' explains Blanche. 'You have to have the paperwork to back it up, or the Americans complain.'

I didn't have all day. 'Let me see that thing,' I said, grabbing it. I still felt uneasy, like there was something they weren't telling me. The huge sheet of card wobbled as I snatched it.

'Hey!'

'What are you doing?'

'Looking for Tobias Phelps,' I answered.

'He was our great-great-great-great-grandfather,' says Rose, pointing to a name near the very apex of the tree. 'See? Five generations back.'

Christ Almighty.

'Let me see your feet,' I demanded.

'No,' they said together firmly. 'No way.'

'Why not?'

'Because we think we're about to go into labour,' said Rose swiftly.

'Any minute now,' threatened Blanche.

'Along with twenty million other women,' I said impatiently, my mind still racing. 'Did you know they're slapping hundred-Euro fines on hoaxers?'

'We're not hoaxers!' shrieked Rose and Blanche after me, as I rushed upstairs towards the bathroom, two steps at a time. To hell with their feet, I thought. Let's get this monkey loaded in the car first. They were still yelling after me. Abuse, it sounded like.

But I wasn't listening. My mind was on the Gent.

In his workshop, the cage assembled and the padlock checked, Dr Scrapie sits in silence, drinking brandy, his brain racing faster than it has done in years. What he has seen is strange and not strange. Bizarre and yet obvious. Unthinkable, yet perfectly possible. Darwin did it. He made that leap of imagination. He made that crude and unwholesome and shocking yet brilliantly true connection. It is the connection a virgin bride makes on her wedding night. After the chintz and flowers and confetti-showers, after the dancing and the music and the merriment, after the well-wishing and the lace-handkerchief-waving and the cooing of doves, there is a moment when she comes face to face with a man's prick.

It is that sort of blunt information that Scrapie feels he has met in the case of Tobias Phelps.

But he cannot, should not, ought not, shall not and *will not* – God help him – make the same mistake twice, he thinks, his mind on the *Origin of Species*. Another opportunity will not pass him by. And this one has been handed him on a plate. As though by God himself!

Tobias Phelps will be the making of him!

It was then, as I sank into darkness, and all hope died within me, that my madness began. I let it happen. Where else could I flee?

I learned afterwards that my insanity involved neither ranting nor raving: just a terrible, introspective silence broken only by rasping groans and the occasional weak utterance of names such as Tommy, Father, Mrs Fooney, and Gudderwort.

All I knew at the time was the feel of her gentle hand on my brow. And the sound of her murmuring softly as she fed me the strangest food I had ever tasted.

Her. She.

In my miasmic half-sleep, I see the beach again, and I see myself as a young child, clambering among the rocks on all fours, and climbing the little gnarled trees of Thunder Spit, and my parents begging me to stop. I see Parson Phelps guiding my hand as he teaches me to write with a goose-feather quill, and I see me and Tommy Boggs playing in the sand-dunes, burying each other among the spiky sand-grass. I see myself at fifteen, watching with Tommy as the Contortionist argues with my father in the graveyard, and her handing him a jar, and him returning with thunder in his face and stuffing money into her hand. I see him in the church, the ripped pages of Darwin's book fluttering wildly down from his pulpit. I see the import of my holy vision, and then I see the smashing of the jar. I see my tail, and Kinnon picking it up for me with his handkerchief, and thrusting it back at me to keep. I recall my hasty visit to Fishforth for the purchase of Jared, the carrier pigeon, and then the train journey to London. The Museum with its dreadful knickerbockered creatures and their blue glass eyes. The boarding-house, the visit to Portobello Road and finally the trip to Madagascar Street. And in a ghastly caricature of consciousness that feels like half-dream, half-death, I pick along the shoreline of my past and I see my father, knitting in the Sanatorium. I see him knitting a scarf so long it could span the world. And I see Tommy in his forge, with his simple life and his bouncing babies, and the seashore, and the Thistle-Pulling Contest. How memory changes things: I see it now touched by my own nostalgia, transformed from a scene of ritual humiliation into an idyllic rural tableau, the cheering, yelling faces of the Balls and the Cleggses and the Peat-Hoves awakening in me a cruel longing for home. I see the Man-Eating Wart-hog.

I awake to find myself in a bed, with her warm hand again on my brow. I open my eyes. She is clad in a huge red dress, with small beads that glitter in the light of the chandelier.

'My name is Violet Scrapie,' she tells me.

She is magnificent. I find tears welling in my eyes. I do not know why. I would like to tell her how marvellous I think she is, but all that emerges is a hopeless groan.

She blushes a deep and fetching pink, and offers me a spoonful of something sweet-smelling, glutinous and green.

'Delicious,' I murmur, still half-choked with a feeling I cannot name. 'What is it?'

'Nettle preserve,' she murmurs, spooning more in. 'With caramelised beetroot. My own recipe.'

'Miss Mosh mashes some mish-mash,' I murmur.

Through my drugged haze, I feel the power of her.

Bom, bom, bom.

The sound of my heart. Its pounding suddenly fills the room.

What a woman! Her hand on my brow reminds me of home. Sometimes, floating far above me, I see her face. She doesn't speak, or if she does, I have gone deaf.

The days pass. I am a man, I am a man, I am a man, I say over and over again to myself.

I awoke screaming.

She held me in her arms. And I sobbed.

'Oh Miss Scrapie, help me, help me!'

She stroked my head, and pulled me closer to her chest. Made calming noises. Felt my forehead.

'All shall be well,' she murmured.

'No!' I groaned. 'It can never be!'

Nor could it. For I had realised in that moment, just as my manhood had been denied me, that this was the very moment that God had chosen to subject my soul to a torment more terrible, even, than the one to which I had just been subjected. I had fallen, madly and passionately, in love. The situation was utterly, utterly beyond hope.

Much later, I awoke again and heard her voice, a voice that made my heart veer about like a loose cannon, asking me sharply, 'Who is Mildred?'

'My tapeworm,' I confessed. 'Could I trouble you, my dear Miss Scrapie, for a banana?'

I pounded up the stairs two at a time. I'd thought it all through. This was a raid. I was bundling him in the car and taking him straight back to London pronto. I'd hold a press conference. That's what you do, isn't it, when you've made a discovery. I'd take the twins with me. Hold them hostage if need be. Force them to show their feet. Reveal the contents of Scrapie's treatise. Wheel out the family tree. And be declared the discoverer of a hitherto undreamed-of missing link.

A-be-bop-a-loo-bop, a-bop-bam-boo!

I burst into the bathroom, and there was Norman sitting on the toilet with his pants round his ankles, reading a DIY magazine called *An Englishman's Home.*

'Just performing a *mea culpa*,' he explained, folding his mag. 'Forgot to lock. Good article in here on all the child-proof gizmos on the market. Fancy a trip to B and Q next Saturday? We could get this place fixed up for you in two shakes of a lamb's whatsit, with the power screwdriver.'

I didn't say anything. I couldn't speak.

Norman reached for the toilet roll and measured out five sheets. He was staring at me, puzzled. My face must have shown something of my dismay, because he said, 'Sorry, mate.

But a man's gotta do what a man's gotta do, eh, Buck? I'll be through in a tick.'

'No,' I croaked. 'It's not that.'

It was the Gentleman Monkey. He had vanished.

CHAPTER 27

IN WHICH TOBIAS
PHELPS ATTEMPTS A
CONFESSION

They cald me the FROZEN WOMAN later, wen I came to the Workhous, run by that Fat BASTARD wot threw me out, but it wasn't in the SEA that I freezed, it was befor, wen I lernd wot TRAPP woz plannin for me and my Gentleman FREND. Wen I diskovers wot his Uther Biznis is. Its Higgins wot tells me. Sez it like a JOKE and LARFS and LARFS.

I dusn't beleev it at furst, and then I duz.

It's then I no it is TYME TO LEEV.

We must ESKAPE, I tells him, strokin His FUR. Wen I tels him about Trapp's Uther Biznis, wot hes plannin for our CHILD, he dusnt say nuthin, just givs me a LOOK. As tho hes sayin: so this is CIVILIZASHUN, eh?

We felt the STORM cumin, and that's wen we dus it. Higgins is REECHIN in for our plates of slop, and I distraks him, and my GENTLEMAN FREND filchis the KEES from his pockit, and it's dun in a flash.

We opens the CAGES, kwik as we can, bifor BOWKER and STEED and TRAPP cums down, and OUT they rushis, FRANTIK and PANIKING.

God! PANDYMONIUM, in ther. They attaks the slop-bin furst, the LYON and the ELIFANT gobbles neerly evrythin up, then the JAKALS and the RINOSSERUS chargis in, and the smorler BEESTS is grabbin wot they can from the floor, and FITIN over skraps. The doors of the CAGIS clangin and clangin.

The STORM is ragin now, and the creechers we has releesd

292

is yelpin and howlin and screemin, and wunce the SLOP is
gon, the FITING bitween them gets more and more vylent, and
thers NO stoppin it. Nacheral instinkts is takin over. HOWLS,
YELLS, SCREECHIN. Eetin eech other ALIVE, sum of them.
The ARKE is rockin, rockin on the WAVs, and then I heer a
clatter from ABUV, and it is the sound of TRAPP.

BLOOD everywer. Fur, fevvers, scales.

Then, clatter clatter, down the sters. Then I sees him. TRAPP.
Furie on his FACE. And feer.

He is sterin at me and my Gentleman FREND, and my
Gentleman frend is sterin bak.

In His hand, TRAPP has sumthin GLINTIN and SHARP.

In the days that followed my arrival in Madagascar Street, Dr
Scrapie took yet more detailed measurements of me, some of
a most intimate nature, and launched himself into a spate of
feverish scientific activity in his basement workshop, from which
the sound of his own laughter, his shouting or his impressively
loud farts would emanate at intervals. I felt almost flattered
that so much bustle and excitement on the part of the eminent
taxidermist was on account of me. Dr Scrapie informed me
that he was working on a treatise entitled *A New Theory of
Evolution*, about my 'unusual origins'. He swore me to secrecy
on this subject, and instructed me not to leave the house on any
account, unless accompanied either by himself or his daughter.

'You must speak to nobody about my hypothesis,' he warned,
'until I have finished my treatise, and have occasion to present
you to Mr Darwin himself.'

'Not even Miss Scrapie?' I asked him, feeling my spine tingle in
trepidation. Had he already told her the truth himself? Although
I had seen no hint of it in her behaviour towards me, which
remained both charming and courteous, I could not be sure.

'Most certainly not,' he replied. He cannot have guessed that
a huge warm wave of relief swept through me when he gave
me the blessed confirmation, that Miss Scrapie was ignorant

of my secret. Although I knew that it was only a matter of time before my lowly status on the evolutionary ladder was revealed, I wished to savour every moment of my new friend's most delightful company before she learned the truth. For what chance would I have then, of my growing interest in her ever being returned?

'How can I ever thank you for your kindness to me, Miss Scrapie?' I asked her one morning, as I sampled some more of the delicacies she referred to as *Cuisine Biologique*. Miss Scrapie looked surprised.

'The pleasure is all mine,' she assured me. 'Here, try this,' she offered, preparing to post a piece of pickled fungus into my mouth. I parted my lips, and she popped it in. 'I have taken great pleasure in nursing you, Mr Phelps, as you are a most useful guinea-pig for my recipes!'

I smiled. This was true; I ate everything she offered me with enormous relish, and was feeling healthier and in better spirits by the day as a result.

'But I hope it is not *only* my appetite that appeals to you, Miss Scrapie,' I ventured, and she blushed, and I blushed, too, causing her to blush even more, and her blushes in turn increasing my own still further, until soon we were both as fiery-faced as a couple of red-hot pokers.

Miss Scrapie and I had by now exchanged stories about our childhoods; she, too, had been lonely. All the more so, when she had parted company on ideological grounds with a man – a certain Monsieur Cabillaud – who had been more of a father to her than Dr Scrapie himself.

'All those years when he was stuffing the creatures from Trapp's *Ark*' (I winced at the mention of this vessel) 'I was in the kitchen with Cabillaud, cooking the carcasses,' she said wistfully. 'He taught me everything I know.'

I sympathised. 'I, too, am estranged from a loved one. When Mr Darwin published the *Origin of Species*, my father went insane.'

Miss Scrapie gasped. 'No! Did he really? Why so did *my* father!'

And she told me how Dr Scrapie had entered a monumental sulk and taken to his workshop with a bottle of rum, and stayed there for a week. In turn I recounted to her the story of Parson Phelps' public shredding of Darwin's tome, in full view of his congregation in the church, and his subsequent removal to the Sanatorium for the Spiritually Disturbed. Omitting, I must confess, the part about the jar and its contents.

'You must write to Parson Phelps,' she urged. 'He would surely not wish to be estranged from you for ever.'

'And you?' I asked. 'Will you be reconciled to your Monsieur Cabillaud?'

She shook her head slowly. 'I do not know,' she said, 'but I shall see him soon at a banquet.' All of a sudden she was looking anxious, and twisting away at the cloth of her voluminous skirt. I knew how she must feel.

'Fear not, Miss Scrapie,' I said softly. I put my hand upon hers. And she did not resist me, reader, or pull away. Was I right to draw hope from that?

I must tell her, I thought. But my cowardice stopped me.

The next day I begged Violet for writing paper on which to pen Parson Phelps a letter. For what had I to lose, that had not already been lost? What could I do, but appeal to his sense of justice? He was a fair man.

'*Should the sins of the mothers and the fathers be visited upon their children?*' I wrote. '*Surely not, dear Parson Phelps! If there is one thing you have taught me, sir, it is that God is just!*' Although I was personally beginning to question this. What was 'just' about the pickle He had landed me in? '*All I desire is that we shall be reconciled again,*' I ended my letter. '*If you cannot love me as your foster-child, then love me as one of God's creatures!*

'*Your loving son, Tobias Phelps.*'

Miss Scrapie, ignorant of the contents of my missive but pleased that I had followed her advice to attempt a reconciliation, accompanied me, with the ailing and now skeletal Suet, to St Pancras, where my carrier pigeon Jared was housed. I personally attached the tiny envelope containing the tightly folded letter to his ringed ankle. He fluttered out of his cage, disoriented for a moment by the cornices of the station, but he soon found a skylight, and as we watched him take wing northwards, I said a small and hopeful prayer.

With Dr Scrapie so preoccupied with his *New Theory of Evolution*, of which the Gentleman Monkey and my own self formed the unique basis, Miss Scrapie and I had been thrown together more and more. Thrown? Or dare I venture to say that it was by choice that we found ourselves in one another's company for the greater part of each day?

It was the following morning, emboldened by the fact that she had once again allowed my hand to rest upon hers, that I decided to summon the courage to confess to her the full truth. I trembled as I spoke.

'There is something I should like you to know,' I began. 'Concerning my origins.'

Did I imagine it, or did a ghostly figure appear briefly at my side as I said these words? Something in petticoats? I blinked. A trick of the light. She had gone. Violet looked up from her ledger, in which she was noting my comments about her latest recipe, swede regale ('Most delicious,' had been my verdict), and smiled.

'Your origins, Mr Phelps? You mean Thunder Spit, and Parson Phelps, and your late foster-mother? I thought we had told each other everything, Mr Phelps!' She smiled coquettishly. 'Or is there a shameful secret?'

My heart began pounding with slow and heavy thuds. But I could not stop now. I cleared my throat.

'Well, in a manner of speaking, there is, actually,' I began. Miss Scrapie's fine eyebrows arched questioningly. But then, observing my intense discomfort, her expression softened into pity and concern, and she held up a hand, gesturing me to halt my words.

'Please, Mr Phelps.' she begged. 'I would hate you to distress yourself over something that is after all a private matter.'

'No,' I blurted. 'I must tell you, Miss Scrapie. 'At the Travelling Fair of Danger and Delight, I saw a Contortionist, and she –'

Violet took my hand – so hairy it looked suddenly, next to her smooth padded flesh, as fine as uncooked pastry! – and held it tightly.

'Mr Phelps, you have turned quite pale!' she said. I swallowed, and breathed in deeply, willing myself to continue. My voice was cracked and thin.

'I have reason to suspect that this Contortionist was really my true mother.'

'A Contortionist?' Violet enquired, smiling. She did not withdraw her hand, but continued to clasp mine firmly. (So far, so promising!) 'A Contortionist! How – unusual!'

'There is more,' I said. 'More, that is even more unusual.'

I paused, then whispered, 'Concerning my true father. I have reason to believe, Miss Scrapie, unlikely though it may sound, and perhaps somewhat shocking to your delicate ears, that my true father was a –'

'Yes?'

I hung my head. 'Please, Miss Scrapie, will you be so good as to furnish me with a pen, ink and paper, that I may write it down for you? For I fear that I cannot bring myself to say it.'

'Why certainly, Mr Phelps,' she said, eyeing me in a puzzled fashion, then waddling over to the writing desk. She returned with the writing implements, and handed them to me in silence. She watched me with concern as I began to write my secret shame with a slow and trembling hand. But I had barely started when a violent clatter of shoes upon the stairway broke my flow and Dr Scrapie burst into the room. Instinctively, I crumpled up the half-completed confession and shoved it into Violet's hand, and she in turn stuffed it into a fold of her dress like a guilty child.

'I have an idea, Mr Phelps!' Scrapie was shouting excitedly. 'Would you do us all the honour of attending the Celebration of Evolution Banquet on Saturday?'

'The what?' I mumbled. 'Am I to understand –'

'You see,' he interrupted me, 'I would very much like to present you to Mr Darwin, before –' He paused for a moment, and shifted on his feet. 'Before you have to leave us,' he said finally. 'The Banquet will be the perfect opportunity!'

Before you have to leave us? I had not thought of leaving. Violet and I exchanged a glance of incomprehension. Dr Scrapie had been behaving rather strangely of late.

'I am in your hands, Dr Scrapie,' I replied courteously.

He seemed to like this idea.

'In my hands!' he beamed. 'Yes! Most excellent! Then I shall lend you one of my old dinner suits, and you will join us!'

Violet was smiling, and thrusting my piece of paper further into the folds of her dress.

'Us?' I asked, exchanging a glance with Miss Scrapie. 'Do I infer, therefore, Dr Scrapie, that your charming daughter will be among the guests?' I mustered, trying to hide my blushes.

'Who?' he asked. Then the penny dropped. 'Oh, you mean *Vile*. Yes, of course,' he replied, looking distracted. 'Violet always tags along to these things, don't you? Though she's not much of a dancer.' Violet, who had not missed the import of my question, was smothering a little embarrassed giggle.

'Then I will be even more delighted to attend,' I told him, attempting, but failing, to suppress the smile that was spreading across my face. I was to attend a banquet at the Palace, in the company of Miss Scrapie! I was so delighted at this prospect that for a moment I forgot that I had just handed her the beginnings of my hideous confession. My admiration of the taxidermist's daughter was surely by now as plain as the day, but Dr Scrapie seemed quite oblivious.

'Then come with me at once,' he commanded, striding out of the room. As I began to follow, I saw Violet smoothing out the piece of paper I had shoved at her, and reading it. Remembering what I had begun to write, my heart began to thud once more.

'Come on, Phelps!' Scrapie was calling me impatiently from the corridor. 'Let's get you fixed up with some clothes.'

I turned to Violet. She was looking at me with obvious consternation.

'Your revelation is indeed most unusual,' she whispered. 'What a singularly strange mixture you carry in your blood, Mr Phelps! Your mother a Contortionist, and your father a monk!'

A monk?

'No!' I blurted. 'Not a monk! I didn't finish writing it! Not a monk, a –'

'*Come on*, Phelps!' yelled Scrapie.

Fate had intervened. I shook my head and fled.

A firework suddenly went off in the sky above me, and I realised it was Bonfire Night.

'Where the fuck's the monkey?' I yelled at the twins, storming down the stairs.

'Gone,' said Rose, patting her huge belly. 'Ouch! I felt a twinge.'

'Me, too,' said Blanche. 'We're definitely going into labour.'

'Yeah, we felt a bit funny earlier,' said Rose.

'Like a dam about to burst,' explained Blanche.

'For Christ's sake,' I told them, wondering how many other blokes up and down the country were going through this very scenario. It was nine months to the day since the Government had announced the Fertility Reward. Coincidence, or what? 'You've probably just got flatulence or indigestion,' I told them. There are limits to a bloke's patience, I was thinking. 'Listen, I've just been up there, and there's no sign of the –'

'We've never been surer of anything,' warned Rose.

'Never,' agreed Blanche.

'Bollocks!' I said. 'Have you seen the news? The whole country's full of phoney emergencies. The ambulance service is going bananas. Just tell me where you put the monkey. It's urgent.'

I'd realised, of course, as I drove up the motorway, that

my discovery of the monkey carried the most extraordinary implications. I'd somehow always known that I deserved more in life than just being a vet. And here it was. Or here, all of a sudden, it was not.

'So? Where is it?'

'We sold it,' said Rose, smiling. 'At the car-boot sale.'

'The *what?*'

'Thought you'd be pleased,' offered Blanche.

'*Pleased?*' I yelled. 'Did you say *pleased?*' I felt so angry at their stupidity that I wanted to kick something to death. But I just groaned instead.

'Well, why not?' pouted Rose. 'You're always going on at us about paying our way. We made a list of ways to make some money. *Number three. Flog all our old junk at the car-boot sale.* Don't think we've just been sitting on our arses while you were in London.'

'We showed you our financial plan, Buck,' Blanche reproached me. 'So don't pretend you can't remember. We got quite a bit of money for it, in the end.'

'Twenty-five Euros,' boasted Blanche.

Keep calm, Buck. Just get the facts. I cleared my throat, and tied to sound mature. 'Who d'you sell it to?' Silence. Well, fuck that approach then. I'll start yelling. 'Come on! Where the fuck is it?'

'Slow down, Buck.'

'I said where the fuck is it? I've got to get it back!'

'Why?' they asked together.

'Because it's valuable,' I said. My hands kept making fists of themselves. The desire to kill and smash was almost over-whelming.

They looked chastened.

'What, worth more than twenty-five Euros?' questioned Rose.

'Worth millions, you fucking idiots.' My voice snagged on tears of rage.

There was a short silence. They hadn't seen me like this before.

300

Then Rose blurted: 'We sold it to Harry Gawvey.'

'He lives on Ladder Hill.'

'But he won't be there now.'

'He'll be over at the community centre. Dad's been helping him with the Heritage Firework Party.'

'Which is due to begin any minute,' said Norman. His weight made each stair creak as he descended, zipping up his fly. 'Fancy coming along, mate? You're a party animal. The Stoned Crow will be there *en masse* – hey! Whoah! No big hurry, mate!'

I'd snatched up the keys to my Nuance and rushed out.

CHAPTER 28

THE CELEBRATION OF
EVOLUTION BANQUET

If you are not familiar with Buckingham Palace, now is perhaps a good moment to contemplate its inner ballroom. It is situated in the West Wing, and occupies the same size, approximately, as Thunder Spit: four acres. How I would have loved to see the Barks and the Tobashes, the Peat-Hoves and the Mulveys and the Boggses watching me arrive at its grandiose portals in a hansom cab! And enter its arched galleries with Miss Violet Scrapie on my arm! But then, as the footman took our cloaks, and ushered us towards the centre of the Banquet, I wondered suddenly what Parson Phelps would make of it all. The thought of him sent a bleak shudder through me. Will Jared have arrived at Fishforth by now, I wondered, accepting a glass of chilled champagne and an unusual-looking sweetmeat which sent Mildred into instant convulsions. Will the Parson be reading my letter at this very moment, I mused, as Miss Scrapie, clad in a great meringue soufflé of a garment which suited her so well it looked as though it had grown out of her, like the wings from a butterfly, grabbed my hand (Oh joy!) and, catching me in the majestic tumble of her skirts (Oh further joy!), swept me along in the direction of the buffet.

Will I ever have the pleasure, I wondered, of addressing her as Violet?

I gasped at the scene that streaked past me as she dragged me in her wake, thinking: What a fabulous beast is man! Chandeliers probably do not come much more elaborate than this! Curtains probably do not come in much redder a velvet, or heavier, or more strangulated with gold silken cords than these! Ballgowns surely do not come so ponderous, or so fabulous, or so mesmerising!

'Look!' whispers Miss Scrapie in my ear. 'Over there! The Royal Hippo!'

And there she is, by the potted palm, Queen Victoria herself, a dumpy little madam, no taller than myself, in her widow's black garb, scowling a petulant fat-faced scowl, and surrounded by fawning courtiers and admirers – Dr Scrapie now suddenly among them, and barging his way to the fore.

'Old hypocrite,' murmurs my paramour, watching her father perform an elaborate and dangerously low bow, then unfold himself to kiss the Monarch's black-gloved hand.

'And look,' she says, pointing in the direction of the buffet table. 'Cabillaud has surpassed himself!' She says this with pride, but a hint of sadness.

A marvellous, glistening quilt of food is spread before us, on a white-clothed table which runs the whole length of the ballroom; guests, armed with china plates, are tucking in to pale jellied eels, glistening prawns, huge tureens of chilled turtle soup, tubs of pink paste, little pastry cases filled with odd-smelling chopped meats, mounds of Turkish Delight and other exotic *bonbons;* waiters are milling about bearing great platters of oysters with wedges of lemon and lime, huge blancmange desserts and nougat cake heaped with chocolate cream. On a small pedestal stands a great wobbling white jelly topped with a splash of fragrant strawberry sauce, surrounded by tiny dishes of liquorice and sherbet. Beneath it, upon the floor, stands an enamel bathtub containing a fruit salad; a waiter is ladling out raspberries, melon, blackberries and – my mouth waters as I spot the first slice – banana into little dishes, and adorning them with grated chocolate and swirls of cream.

Impressive.

So impressive, indeed, that suddenly Miss Scrapie is deserting me to congratulate the chef.

'Monsieur Cabillaud!' she cries, rushing headlong into the outspread arms of a small tubby man in a tall white hat.

303

'*Ma petite chérie! Ma petite Violette!*' he responds, pressing her to his bosom.

Oh, what it must be, to be reunited with a loved one! What would I not give to be so embraced by dear Parson Phelps!

Assaulted by my own sudden feelings of longing, I averted my eyes from the touching scene taking place before me. But it was an error to do so, for when I looked up again, having contemplated my shoes for the space of perhaps one minute, I saw that Miss Scrapie and the chef had vanished in the throng. The sudden loss of Miss Scrapie left me feeling horribly alone and ill-at-ease. I had been obliged to dress for tonight's occasion in a cast-off old dinner suit of Dr Scrapie's which was far too big, and which, thanks to the well-intentioned but ultimately unhelpful adjustments made by a certain Mrs Jiggers, hung off me in a way that Miss Scrapie could surely not find attractive.

'Stay where you are!' ordered Scrapie, suddenly re-appearing and grabbing my arm with force. 'Do not move. I'm going to find Mr Darwin, and bring him here, and we will tell him of your origins!' He was clasping *A New Theory of Evolution* to his breast, and his eyes were darting eagerly about the room in search of the great man. 'My dear, dear young specimen!' he choked, still clasping my arm tightly. I winced in pain. 'I must confess I was growing almost fond of you!'

Specimen? I felt foolish, and uneasy, as though an important fact hung just beyond my grasp.

'Stay right here by this pillar,' ordered Scrapie again, more bluntly this time. 'Don't move a bloody inch.'

So I stood there obediently, thinking of my sudden 'specimen-hood', and my imminent meeting with Mr Darwin, the man whom Parson Phelps blamed for the decline of Christianity itself. In short, the man responsible for a multiplicity of woes.

I very much hoped he would not expect my gratitude for the fine mess he had landed me in, I thought, as the band struck up a waltz.

*   *   *

304

The speakers in the community centre were blaring out some dated old techno rubbish. The place was teeming with people. The Cleggs, the Peat-Hoves, the Mulveys, the Tobashes. Harcourt, his grumpy Filipina swaying on his arm, grabbed me by the arm and thrust a foaming beer at me.

'Get that down you,' he said. There were plastic tables along each wall, with a mass of paper plates and decorated serviettes, bearing sausages on sticks, various dips, blobs of cheese, and an array of pizzas. Some meringue pavlovas were de-frosting at the back. I swigged my beer, my eyes still scanning the room for Gawvey. I'd had the foresight to stop off at the cashpoint in the high street on my way, and I had a hundred yos in my pocket to buy the monkey back. I'd offer him more, though, if he wanted it. I could get an overdraft, if the need arose. I reckoned it was worth going up to a thousand, without arousing his suspicions. After all, it was a family heirloom.

The music had changed to the Hokey Cokey, and a great human caterpillar was forming. I barged past.

'Where's Gawvey?' I shouted. 'I've got to find him!'

'Outside,' said Boggs. 'Easy does it, mate. He's doing the bonfire.'

Just then a tinkling burst of music cascaded down from a shiny orchestra perched on a balcony, and couples began to glide to the dance-floor. Soon the whole space was packed. As the dancers whizzed about me in a human hurricane of sequins and perfume and chinking medallions, my eyes scoured the ballroom once again for Miss Scrapie. But there was no sign of her in the crowd. Had I lost her for the whole evening? Perhaps for ever? Pondering this ghastly thought, a sadness and fear overwhelmed me. I thrust my hands deep into my pockets, and invoked Betty Botter, until a sudden instinct told me to ignore my promise to Dr Scrapie, and seek shelter from the crowd. To this end I found myself shuffling, half-tripping

305

on my over-long trousers, and with some difficulty arriving at a small table beside a huge marble fountain. And here I sat, fingering my crucifix, doing my best to become invisible, and attempting, with the help of a glass of port proffered me by a waiter, to pick up my flagging spirits, and to ignore the distinct feeling of unease emanating from my lower spine.

Then the quadrille came to a sudden halt and the clocks chimed eight. A hush fell, and a tail-coated Master of Royal Ceremonies struck a huge gong with a padded stick, signalling to the assembled ladies and gentlemen that it was time for the celebrations to begin in earnest.

'My Lords, Ladies and Gentlemen! Please raise your glasses to Her Majesty the Queen!'

The Monarch smooths her black skirts and purses her lips as we raise our glasses and ask God to bless her. The gong sounds again, and the Master of Royal Ceremonies gives further utterance.

'And to Mr Charles Darwin!'

The small bearded man next to Queen Victoria performs a neat little bow, as we salute him. 'To Mr Charles Darwin!' When he unbends himself, I notice that he has a twinkle in his eye.

'Now stand back, please, Ladies and Gentlemen, for the revelation of our gastronomic centrepiece this evening, the Evolutionary Time-Bomb, a masterpiece of cuisine designed and constructed by Her Majesty's head chef, Monsieur Jacques-Yves Cabillaud!'

There is a rustling of gowns and a clapping of hands as the crowd pulls back from a central area hitherto hidden from view by dancing bodies, hanging curtains and swathes of flowers. At first, the area is so huge and so grey it has the appearance of a wall – but suddenly, the eye adjusts and a new perspective is revealed: the thing we see before us, seated within an enormous clam shell, is nothing more and nothing less than an entire roast elephant!

'Good grief!' mutters a brigadier, an expression of surprise which is echoed, in various forms, throughout the hall, in a sudden windy rustle of words.

'Her name was Mona,' whispers a man who has appeared at my side out of the blue. 'She's from the Zoological Gardens. They slit her throat last Thursday, and it took a week for her to die. Have you heard the rumour that Monsieur Cabillaud used to be her keeper at the Zoo?'

A shudder goes through me as I stare across the room at Cabillaud, who has suddenly materialised next to his gruesome exhibit and is bowing deeply to the assembled throng. Now he takes a huge sword and places it, with an obsequious bow, in the hand of the dumpy little woman Miss Scrapie refers to as the Royal Hippo.

'If it please Your Majesty,' he says. He's all red in the face with pride. 'Would you graciously do us all ze great honour of making ze first incision into ze Time-Bomb?'

A murmur of appreciation rises from the ladies and gentlemen as the little monarch obliges by taking hold of the scimitar. I stand on tiptoe to watch her; as she takes a grip on the weapon, I see her mouth twisting into what might be a smile, or a pang of indigestion, I cannot be sure which. Then I spot Dr Scrapie stepping forward to help her.

'If I may be of assistance, Your Majesty,' he murmurs, standing behind her and encircling her with his arms. 'And if you will excuse the necessary intimacy . . .' Delicately, he places his own hands upon hers, and helps her to lift the heavy scimitar.

A burst of cheering and hand-clapping as Dr Scrapie helps the Queen make a deep cut into the huge creature's rubbery flesh.

'Raise your glasses again,' intones the Master of Royal Ceremonies, 'to Her Majesty the Queen!'

As we wish the Monarch a long life and good health, and the orchestra strikes up 'Rule Britannia', Scrapie and the Monarch are busy cutting a huge slit down the front of the elephant's chest. The grey flesh divides like a pair of thick felt curtains and –

Whispers. Genteel murmurings. Hushed gasps.

Out tumbles a lumpy waterfall of pungent mushrooms and garlic-ball stuffing. A gurgle of steaming liquid and more mushrooms follow, all captured in the huge natural tureen of the giant clam beneath.

Delighted screams. Whoops. Cat-calls.

For there, revealed inside the elephant's cavernous interior – Yes! It's true! – amid a mass of foliage that resembles parsley, there appears to be an entire zebra!

A massive cheer erupts spontaneously from the crowd.

'Bravo!' shrieks a woman next to me, whipping up a strongish wind with the excited flapping of her lace fan. And then a further and even more frenzied cheer emerges as seconds later, Queen Victoria, warming to her task, once again wields the scimitar, with Scrapie's help, and makes a deft incision in the zebra's exposed belly to reveal, among the baked apples and glazed onions, its skin criss-crossed with diamonds of cloves and apricots, a gigantic roast hog!

Astonishing!

We can hardly believe what we are seeing. But then – No! Surely not!

'Good Lord!' exclaims the fan-flapping woman next to me. 'I don't believe it!'

'Look!' yells a military gent, his medals crashing together as he jiggles with excitement. 'She's cutting again!

The Royal Hippo, who has warmed to her task enough to spurn Dr Scrapie's renewed offer of help, is indeed wielding the scimitar a third time. With a swift and expert lunge, impressive from a woman so small and stiffly padded, she stabs the hog, whose skin splits neatly along a stitched seam to reveal a cavity from which –

My God! From the heart of the Time-Bomb, a live woman is stepping out!

A dropped fan. Gasps and applause from the men. Excited screams from the ladies.

And a groan from me, followed swiftly by a ghastly surge of nausea.

For this is not just any woman.

It is a woman in a tutu and little ballet shoes.

It is the human herring gull, Contortionist Extraordinaire of the Travelling Fair of Danger and Delight –

My mother.

Ding, dong! chimes the Balls' doorbell.

The future is calling.

'Damn and blast!' says Abbie, under her breath. She's been rushed off her feet all day, and has only just finished her cookery rehearsal – a full ten minutes behind schedule.

'Hold on a second!' she calls, as she wipes the flour off her hands and glances at the Apfelkuchen. They're browning nicely in the oven. And the coffee's just on. She'd been planning to put her feet up.

'I'm sorry to trouble you,' says the young leather-jacketed stranger. He has a small gold earring in one ear, and is carrying a clip-board. He's waving a set of car keys at her apologetically. 'But my car's broken down, and my mobile phone's –'

'On the blink,' falters Abbie, suddenly feeling rather sick as a feeling of *déjà vu* engulfs her.

'Yes,' says the man, flashing her a handsome smile. 'How did you guess? Look, I'm sorry to ask you this, but –'

'Of course you can call the AA,' says Abbie. 'And perhaps while you're waiting, I might tempt you with some of my Apfelkuchen and a cup of nice fresh coffee?'

You could say that Abbie Ball has been blessed with a form of second sight, for is this not her dream coming true?

'May I ask you your name?' she falters, pouring a china cup of Colombian Special Blend.

'Of course,' says the stranger, whipping out a business card. 'Sorry, I should have – Anyway . . . Pleased to meet you.'

Abbie takes his business card with a trembling hand and reads.

OSCAR JACK.

ERA PRODUCTIONS.
At last!

The Apfelkuchen are going down a treat.

'Can I offer you a fifth?' Abbie asks, five minutes later, after she has completed her tour of the kitchen for Oscar, and he has settled himself on the settee in the living room with the air of a man who is no longer the slightest bit worried about his seized-up car or his broken mobile.

'Abbie,' he begins. He has a soft, cultured voice, but there's excitement in it. Genuine excitement. 'May I call you Abbie?' She swallows hard, and nods vigorously.

'I couldn't help noticing – well, your extraordinary poise. It struck me immediately – the minute I clapped eyes on you – that you have a certain *je-ne-sais-quoi*, and that – well.' He lowered his voice. 'This is rare, this is extremely rare, I don't want you to think that this is the kind of thing that happens every day, in fact, never before in my whole television career –'

'Yes?'

'Spit it out, then,' says the Laudanum Empress from Norman's armchair. She is darning one of her cobwebby old stockings.

'Well, Abbie,' says Oscar Jack, oblivious to the interruption, 'some people are simply what we call "television naturals," and –'

It always happens, doesn't it? Something. A crack of thunder. The ping of the microwave. An urgent call of nature.

Or the ring of the telephone.

'Excuse me, just one moment,' says Abbie. Her heart is pounding in a way it hasn't done since she met Norman for the first time twenty years ago, in the park. She'd been sitting by the sandpit babysitting her friend's little girl, and he'd rammed her in the bum with his nephew's remotely controlled racing car. 'It's probably your AA man.'

Abbie picks up the phone, and instantly turns as white as self-raising flour.

'Mum, it's us. You've got to come now. *Now.*'

310

'What's happening?' she whispers shakily.

'We've just gone into labour, Mum!' shrieks a twin. 'And Buck's buggered off!'

'Are you *sure*, Roseblanche?' asks Abbie nervously, cupping her hand over the receiver so that Oscar Jack can't hear. 'I mean there have been an awful lot of false alarms . . .' she whispers.

'Please, Mum!' shriek the voices in unison. '*You've got to believe us!*'

What mother can resist a cry of help from her baby?

The unfairness of it! Dilemma city. The recipe for disaster, thinks Abbie, drifting into a shocked reverie as Oscar Jack tucks into another Apfelkuchen. Cruel-world stew:

Take several ounces of extreme bad luck, and spike with a measure of ill-timing. Add a pinch of malevolence and stir up well with the base ingredient of injustice. Throw in some intolerance and bitterness. Pour on heavy dollops of meanness, spite and pessimism, and refrigerate until an uneasy chill is achieved. Dose in individual portions with a dash of bile and garnish with shite. Note: the result is addictive.

So much blood has drained from Abbie's face that Oscar Jack is thinking she'll need a lot of panstick when the time comes.

'Bugger,' she mutters finally.

'Language!' trills the Empress gleefully.

'Is there anything I –' begins Oscar Jack.

'Mum!' yells Roseblanche down the phone.

'Yes?' manages Abbie, faintly, her eyes on Oscar Jack's well-shaven, innocent face. He's already punched her name and address into his personal organiser. If only –

'I can't come now! My television producer's arrived! Just call an ambulance!' she hisses weakly into the receiver.

'We did!' shrieks Roseblanche. 'They don't believe us! They

think it's a hoax! They say they're getting three a night like this! We're nearly ready to push! Mum, help!'

Abbie groans. 'I'm on my way,' she sighs, and slams down the receiver.

The Contortionist, having made several curtsies to the crowd, is now scampering balletically atop the elephant's head and beginning, amid enthusiastic applause, to tie herself into a human knot.

Meanwhile below, at ground-level, a regiment of *sous-chefs* are busy attacking the Time-Bomb with carving-knives, cutting slices of elephant, zebra, and hog meat and placing it on the platters held by the *sous-sous-chefs*, who are in turn handing them to the *sous-sous-sous-chefs* for the addition of garnish. Minions further down in the kitchen hierarchy mill about, proffering plates of food to guests, who comment delightedly upon the unusual taste and texture of the meats.

The Time-Bomb, Cabillaud reflects, has certainly been the crowning triumph of his whole glittering career, the pinnacle of his own personal evolution. Even Violet, now a militant vegan, has mustered the *politesse* to congratulate him on it, despite her opposition to all forms of cruelty.

'May I present you with my book?' Cabillaud now enquires of Violet, thrusting a first-edition copy of *Cuisine Zoologique: une philosophie de la viande* into her hand. She is looking quite magnificent, he notes. Extraordinarily well, and happy. There is beauty in ugliness after all. The dress she is wearing suits her. She seems distracted, though. Her eyes keep scanning the room, as though she is looking for someone.

Which she is. And now, finally, Violet has spotted him. He's over at the buffet table, where he is serving himself to a generous portion of fruit salad. Tobias's gaze, she notices, is firmly resting upon the little ballerina-woman who recently emerged from Cabillaud's Time-Bomb. The woman, having untangled herself from her scorpion position atop the elephant's head, has now leaped off it and is pirouetting across the room at great speed in the direction of the ladies' powder room. Violet watches as, just as suddenly, Tobias abandons his fruit salad and strides across to follow the little ballerina.

'Violette?' Cabillaud is saying. 'You will accept a copy of my *oeuvre?*'

'Oh,' says Violet distractedly. She has lost sight of Tobias and the ballerina (surely he could not have followed her into the ladies' powder room?), and turns her attention reluctantly back to the chef. 'Thank you, Monsieur Cabillaud.' Despite the nature of its contents, she feels the need to accept the book with grace. Such is compromise.

'I am working on a plant version of my own,' she offers.

'Ze foliage?'

'Yes. I am planning to call it *The Fleshless Cook.*' Cabillaud raises an eyebrow.

'One day, my dear, you will learn that ze human being is not designed to eat plant life alone.'

Violet smiles. 'I survive very well,' she tells him.

'May I interrupt?' asks a small, bearded, twinkle-eyed man who has been hovering at the edge of their conversation.

Violet and Cabillaud exchange a glance.

'Please do, Mr Darwin,' says Violet. At last, an expert witness in their ideological dispute! 'We would be most grateful, Mr Darwin, for your opinion on the matter, wouldn't we, Monsieur Cabillaud?'

'Of course! And very honoured! Please allow me, Monsieur, to present to you Miss Scrapie.'

'Charmed to meet you, Miss Scrapie,' begins Mr Darwin. 'I am acquainted with your father. Now the human body originally evolved, as we know, from the primate. Primates are largely fructivorous, although there are exceptions. However, if we study the evolutionary path of man, we will discover hints that his descendence from several species of *ape*, descended in turn from a branch of the *monkey* family, involved an adaptation of the alimentary canal which –'

313

'Mr Darwin!' interrupts Dr Ivanhoe Scrapie, yelling from across the room, and fumbling his way through a mêlée of sparkling ballgowns. 'Mr Darwin! I have finally found you! You must come with me immediately, and see an extraordinary specimen. A walking, talking, human-monkey hybrid, here in this very room!'

Charles Darwin bursts out laughing. 'This is indeed an exceptionally entertaining banquet,' he smiles. And then, lowering his voice, to address Violet, 'And not at all what one would have expected from Her Majesty.'

'It is true!' yells Dr Scrapie, his faced flushed. 'And the creature's father is in the ladies' powder room to prove it! The Gentleman Monkey! I stuffed him myself!'

Violet, feeling something curdle violently within her, and recognising there is a strong risk that she will faint, collapses with a padded thud on a stiff little seat and begins flapping her fan furiously. A human-monkey hybrid? What is her father talking about? He couldn't possibly be referring to – her breath catches in her throat.

'My father was a monk.' Violet releases a quiet moan as Dr Scrapie and Mr Darwin continue their conversation. *'I didn't finish writing it,'* he had said.

'A monkey? Excellent!' Mr Darwin is exclaiming. 'I do approve of your sense of humour, my dear Scrapie! Lead me to this alleged specimen at once!'

As Violet fans herself with such force that she risks mimicking the un-aerodynamic bumble-bee and taking flight, Charles Darwin's laughter is overheard by a group of military gents and their wives, who, somewhat affected by champagne, repeat the joke and join in the laughter, which thereby becomes so amplified that the curiosity of others is aroused, and the joke is passed on, and more people are attracted to the steadily growing throng, until a huge gaggle of laughing banqueteers has encircled the two scientists. Violet, pale beneath her face-powder, and still seated near the heart of the kerfuffle, has the presence of mind to keep listening to her father's urgent and garbled speech to Mr Darwin, the content of which is causing her increasing unease.

'His name is Tobias Phelps,' continues Scrapie excitedly. As the import of her father's words dawns on Violet, she groans, then freezes, immobilised with shock. She has not felt such a churning confusion of emotions since the death of the Laudanum Empress. Her father is tugging at Darwin's sleeve.

'He is a creature aged some twenty years,' her father is telling Darwin. 'Nurtured as a man, and with quite remarkable – really *most astonishing* – success. What I am planning to do, Mr Darwin, once you have inspected him for yourself and verified my findings' – Violet leans forward, straining to listen – 'is to keep him captive for a few days, so that other zoologists may have a chance to view him while he is still alive' – Violet gasps, and clutches her hand over her mouth – 'then kill and stuff him myself, and present him thus to the Zoological Society.'

Keep him captive? Kill and stuff him?

Violet feels suddenly quite monstrously sick. She drops her fan to the floor with a clatter and clutches her chair, her knuckles whitening with the pressure of grasping on. It's as much as she can do to prevent herself from keeling over. So that is what Tobias was trying to tell her that day! That is why he was so upset, and why he had insisted on writing it down on that piece of paper. Not monk, but *monkey*! The Gentleman Monkey!

'Oh no!' she groans, remembering with sudden clarity the braising process, and the shrimp sauce that had accompanied the dish that killed the Laudanum Empress.

'I ate him!' she whispers to herself, appalled. 'I ate his father! I am a cannibal!'

'Come along, then, Mr Darwin!' Scrapie is saying. 'I left him standing over by that pillar. Let's go and meet him!' Another huge smile spreads across the face of Charles Darwin, and the naturalist once again throws back his head and laughs uproariously, shaking little fragments of food from his beard as he does so.

315

'I should have thought to come in fancy-dress myself,' he chortles good-humouredly. 'Dressed as a gorilla. I believe one can hire such a costume. Would that not have been more apt, for such an occasion, Dr Scrapie? Might the' – he lowers his voice conspiratorially – '*Royal Hippopotamus*, as you call her, have been amused?'

But Dr Scrapie is not laughing. He is looking strangulated instead. His face is almost blue. He is still clutching Mr Darwin's sleeve, and now starts tugging it again with urgency.

'There is no time to lose,' Violet murmurs to herself, gulping back her urge to vomit and smoothing the cream crêpe of her billowing skirts.

'But he is the answer to your paradox, sir!' Scrapie is insisting to Mr Darwin, who is by now laughing so heartily that he appears at serious risk of choking. 'I swear, sir, that this is not a joke!'

Darwin laughs some more. 'I do not possess a paradox,' he replies.

'Well, you do now!' explodes Scrapie, wrenching the man by the arm and frog-marching him across the ballroom. The bevy of interested spectators follows chattering and giggling in their wake. What an unexpectedly entertaining occasion this is turning out to be! As they move off, Violet bites her lip, her mind racing.

'Push!' Abbie is yelling at the twins.

'I warned you,' says the Laudanum Empress, hovering by the loo. She did no such thing, but Abbie is in no state to argue. When Abbie had made the call to the Baldicoot Medical Centre, she'd been referred to the Ambulance Service, which had refused point blank to send an emergency vehicle.

'But this is real!' Abbie had screamed.

'That's what they all say, love,' said the duty nurse wearily.

'We'll pay the fine – we don't care!' shrieked the twins.

'Sorry, love,' said the duty nurse, when Abbie relayed this. 'The fact is, all the ambulances are out. They're calling it the Day of Madness.'

'Well fuck you, then!' shrieked Abbie, distraught. What was happening to her? She'd never uttered a swear-word before in her life, until today. And now two (there was a 'bugger', earlier) in front of Oscar Jack! Could she be developing Tourette's syndrome? Good thing Oscar's here, though, she realises suddenly. Because there's no sign of Norman, or of that wastrel Buck. He's off on some wild monkey chase, apparently.

'Bless you!' she sobs at Oscar Jack. The television producer has grabbed the twins' camcorder, perched it on the kitchen table and left it running; no slouch he, when it comes to capturing a potential exclusive. In addition, he's rolled up the sleeves of his leather jacket and is now doing sterling work with towels and bottles of Perrier.

'AAAGH!' yell the twins again.

Wow. If this is another of those bogus ones, thinks Oscar Jack, then it's frighteningly realistic.

When I saw the Contortionist leap off the elephant's head and pirouette across the room, I knew I must confront her.

Following her with difficulty across the banqueting hall, tripping over the legs of my trousers and bumping into dinner guests with plates piled high with meat, I reached a corridor which led to a parlour which led to a door which swung shut in my face. LADIES' POWDER ROOM, it said.

I hesitated for a moment, and then entered.

And came face to face with my father, the Gentleman Monkey.

I stopped in my tracks and caught my breath. And stared. He was holding a towel of purple and yellow. His eyes were a bright and unnatural blue. His fur was a rusty orange-red – the same colour and the same coarse texture as my own hair. Like

317

me, he had a thick down on his arms. He was a little shorter than me. His expression was one of great nobility and poise. He had a short tail, which emerged from a slit in his red pantaloons and curled upwards behind him like a question mark.

The Contortionist was standing in front of him, gazing into his blue and strangely human eyes. She was oblivious to my presence; for a while, we both stood there staring at the monkey, each lost in his own thoughts. Finally I cleared my throat.

'Excuse me, madam?' I said.

She jumped, and turned to look at me. She seemed to be crying; the frills of her little ballet tutu were trembling.

'Madam, I believe you are my mother.'

She stared at me. She said nothing. She just stared.

'And this – gentleman – is my father,' I ventured. 'Am I right?'

'Lawks a mercy,' she said, sucking in her breath. 'Fancy meeting you here.'

She bit her lip. I held out my hand, and she took it. We shook hands formally.

'Madam, I think you owe me an explanation,' I mustered.

'S'pose I do, Tobias,' she said, sighing. 'S'pose I do.'

'You – know my name?'

'Yes.'

She told me everything. Horace Trapp had kidnapped her, and kept her in a cage on his *Ark*.

'It was an old slave-trader,' she said. 'Cos that's what he used to do. Travelled between London and Africa and Georgia, selling slaves. But then he had a shipload die on him, and there was a big scandal in London. So he switched to animals instead, got this caper going for Queen Victoria. The Animal Kingdom Collection.'

I nodded. This much tallied with what Dr Scrapie had told me.

'But I finds out he has some other business. And that's why

318

I'm in the cage with – this dear gentleman,' she said. Her voice softened, and she took the monkey's hand in hers as she spoke. It was an oddly moving sight.

'Other business?' I asked. 'What sort of other business?'

But she ignored me; she appeared to be speaking almost from a trance. 'It's Higgins tells me what Trapp's planning. Trapp never bothers to tell me himself, does he? There I was then, having this idea that I was just there to keep the gentleman company, like a playmate for him. But he's soon a lot more than that to me.'

I blushed, as the little woman continued the extraordinary tale of my genesis.

'I discovers I'm up the spout, around the same time as I discovers that this is what Trapp was wanting all along. *That* was his other business.'

'He *wanted* you and the – gentleman here – to . . . ?'

I was unable to find the words to complete my question.

'Yes. Higgins tells me he was hoping to breed from us.'

'*Hoping* to breed? *Hoping* to? Why?' I felt sick.

'Slaves,' she said. A chill ran through me. 'He had this theory. After the scandal over his dead slaves, and the campaign to have the trade abolished, he'd been hatching this plan to mate a human with a monkey, to get an offspring. To breed a new kind of slave, that's not completely human. "A race of natural inferiors", he calls it. If you're not strictly speaking a man, see,' she said, 'you haven't got no rights like men does.'

I gasped.

'But why?' I asked.

'Profit,' murmured my new-found mother. 'He was after making a profit. He'd seen the slave trade coming to an end. He reckoned the problem all along with the human slaves was that they'd end up with the same rights as other folk. The only way to ever get that kind of cheap labour again without a big hoo-ha was to create –'

'I see,' I said.

'Yes. But he hadn't bargained on my gentleman friend.'

319

We both looked at him, with a mixture of pity and awe.

'Anyway, when I finds this out, that that's what he's planning, that's when I know we has to escape, even if it means –'

She hung her head.

'They all died,' she said bluntly. 'It happened the night the storm was brewing. When Steed comes to give us our slop, I distract him with a few little favours while my gentleman friend sneaks the key to our cage from his pocket. When they've gone back up to their cabins, we opened all the animals' cages to take attention away from us, and they all shot out and started rioting, and ripping each other to pieces.' She paused, and squinted painfully at the memory. 'It was a nightmare. They was all killing each other and my gentleman friend, when he sees Trapp come towards us, he pounces on him, and grabs him by the throat, all ready to kill him, and I'm screaming at him to do it, to strangle him, but Trapp's got a syringe in his hand and as soon as the needle goes in, my gentleman friend just falls to the floor stone dead.' Her eyes fill suddenly with tears.

'So it was Trapp who killed him? With the syringe?'

'Yes.' She looks up at me, and the tears fall. She makes no attempt to wipe them away. 'He died trying to save my life, Tobias. And yours. I couldn't stop him.' She is sobbing now. 'I saw him die.'

Tentatively, I put my arm around her, and hand her my handkerchief. She grabs it and blows her nose furiously.

'He loved life so much,' she's whispering through her tears. 'He was so funny, so clever, so innocent. So good-hearted. He was all instinct. I realised as soon as I saw him in the light of day that he wasn't a man. I never pretended he was.' She strokes his arm. 'He was more than a man.' She pauses. 'And he was better than a man.' The tears begin again. 'He laid down his life for us, Tobias,' she wails. 'He wasn't called a gentleman for nothing.'

I swallow painfully. 'And then?' I whisper.

'When I sees he's dead,' she sniffs, 'that's when I jumps ship. I have no idea where we are. Could be in the Caribbean, for all I know. In fact it's the English Channel. We must've been on our way back. Anyway, I swims till I'm half-drowned. I'm just wearing my tutu. Bloody cold, it was. Near froze, but I'm a strong swimmer. Then I gets caught in a fishing net, and pulled along. Must've been dragged aboard with all the fish, cos when I wakes up, I'm on a fishing boat, stinking. The next thing I know, I'm in London bloody docks, of all places. Went straight to the workhouse. I got there, and gave birth to you.'

I felt myself swaying on my feet.

The Contortionist laughed suddenly. 'Silly of me, but when I saw your tail, I still got the shock of my life.'

'What is zis, Violette?' asks Cabillaud, reappearing before her with the fan she has dropped, and flapping it to cool her. 'You are not well, *ma chérie?*'

He has seen this look before. Years ago, on his own face, when he gazed in the mirror aboard the *Beagle*, and thought of his sweetheart Saskia.

'No. I am suddenly most terribly unwell!' croaks Violet, still clutching her chair. 'You must help me, Monsieur Cabillaud! My father is planning to kill and stuff the man I – the gentleman I –'

'Love,' finishes Cabillaud. He knows. It is written all over her face. 'You must escape wiz 'im, zen,' he suggests.

'How?' wails Violet, kneading her pudgy hands together in distress.

'I will open ze kitchen doors for you, *ma chérie*! Now go and get 'im! Quick!'

Violet, her heart beating like a war-drum in her heaving bosom, scans the room; the two scientists and their accompanying mob of laughing guests have finished their search of the northern corner of the ballroom, and are now heading west in the direction of another marble pillar.

'I told him to bloody-well stay put!' she hears her father

shrieking as he strides through the dancing throng, still frog-marching Darwin with him.

'This is a most amusing game of hide-and-seek, is it not?' laughs Mr Darwin good-naturedly. He had not wished, initially, to attend the Banquet, bad health and a hermit-like disposition combining to make him shun most public occasions – but he has been pleasantly surprised by this evening's turn of events.

'Hey! Has anyone seen a monkey-man?' yells Scrapie. And the mob takes up the cry.

Lifting up the billowing swathes of her skirts, Violet rises from her chair and hurtles off in the direction of the ladies' powder room like a human torpedo.

My mother had left me speechless.

'He's the only reason I come here to do this banquet job,' she said, still stroking the Gentleman Monkey's hairy arm. 'I heard he was here. Friend of mine, Nancy, I told her all about him and me. Her man Frank, he's a Palace footman. She says to me she's sure my gentleman's here, from what Frank's said. That settles it. When Hillber talks to me about the Time-Bomb, I says yes. I'd've done anything to see him again, one last time.'

The tears were running freely down her cheeks, leaving grey tracks. I, too, brushed away a tear as the Contortionist continued her story.

'So you were born in the workhouse. When they saw you, with your tail, and your monkey feet, they said I'd mated with the Devil, and they chucked me out. I came straight to the Fairground. I knew there was a way of making money, and we did – hand over fist. You were called the Devil-Child of Greenwich. It's the workhouse people in Greenwich, what gives me the idea to call you that.'

Devil-Child? I was far from keen on the sound of this, but I held my tongue. Instead I asked, 'And then what happened? How did I lose my tail?'

'Well, I kept you in a cage –'

'A cage?' I interrupted. 'You kept me in *a cage?*' I remembered my vision during the Flood: I had seen a cot with golden bars, guarded by a beast.

'I was working, wasn't I?' she said. 'I didn't have the choice. I had to do this contortionism thing: human knots and all that. Mr Hillber wasn't just going to pay me for existing, was he? But you wouldn't suckle from anyone else, so he had to keep me. Anyway, your cage is right next to the Man-Eating Wart-hog's.'

I had a sudden memory of the creature; its orange-ochre eyes, with their vertical slits; its vile carbuncles. I shivered.

'Well, it's thanks to him you lost it. He's a tricky customer. He's hungry one day, or playful. You tail is sticking through his bars. So he –'

She stops. Looks embarrassed. Ashamed. Then drops her voice.

'He bites it off.'

My God. Again I remembered my vision in the church during the Flood. Suddenly it all made sense. The Angel. The creature. The blood. The screaming, shrill and hoarse.

'I remember it,' I said. She had been the Angel.

'But he didn't like the taste,' she said, giving a little bitter laugh. 'He spat it out. We tried to sew it back on, but it was no use, so I stuck it in an old jar of pickle.'

She paused, and began to stroke my father's furry cheek wistfully. For my own part, I was having trouble taking all this in. All my life I had wondered about my origins. But now – it was as if a dam had burst, and the answers to all my questions were all gushing out at once. I was left reeling.

'After you'd lost your tail,' my mother continued, 'you were doing badly. You had a fever, and I knew that unless you saw a doctor, you was going to die. Mr Hillber said you'd have to go. You were no use to him without a tail, and to be honest, I knew that if you were to stand a chance, I'd have to –' She stopped again, clearly distressed.

'Abandon me,' I finished.

'Yes. That's about the size of it.' Her voice was a mere croak, lost in the increasingly wild noises coming from the banqueting hall. She wasn't looking at me when she spoke. She was looking at the creature. Staring into his blue glass eyes, as though she could read the past in them.

'The circumstances was most particular,' she murmured.

'I am sure they were,' I whispered. I felt a lump in my throat.

'So I left you in little church, in a village near Judlow. Thunder Spit, it was called. I kept your little tail as a sort of memento,' she said softly. 'To remind me of you, and of my gentleman friend, and what happened between us.'

'How did you know about Parson Phelps?'

'I didn't, when I left you. I had no idea. I just reckoned a church was as likely a place as – well, you know. Charity, and all that. And I wasn't wrong, was I?'

'No, I said, remembering Parson Phelps' story of finding me beneath the altar of St Nicholas's Church the day after the Fair left Judlow, and his piglet story.

Wrong animal, I thought.

'Parson Phelps saved my life, then,' I murmured.

'Yes. Parson Phelps,' she said. 'Though I doesn't find out his name till later. I asked about you every time the Fair came to Judlow. Asked a few questions, you know. Looked out for you. Didn't even know if you'd survived or not, but thought you would have. You were a tough little bugger. Then I meet a man who I service once a year at the Fair, a bit of money on the side, turns out he's a cobbler from Thunder Spit.'

'Mr Hewitt?'

'Dunno. I don't do names. Names is extra. They want me to use a name, they pay. Your Grace costs more. Any kids there with funny-shaped feet, I asked him. Great big fat man, smelt of leather. Just the Phelps boy, he says. The Parson's son. Tobias. I don't do names, but I remembered those two, Parson Phelps. And Tobias. Wrote them down, after. The cobbler docks me sixpence for jabbering while he was at it, and spoiling his peace and quiet, but after that I knew you were alive.'

She turned to look at me, and I saw that the tears were once more trickling down her face, leaving little painted rivulets on her cheeks. She looked suddenly old.

'I saw you,' I stammered. 'At the Travelling Fair of Danger and Delight. I saw you doing your act.'

'And I saw you, too,' she said slowly. She held out her arms to me, and we clasped each other tight. She was sobbing into my shoulder now. 'And I saw the fear on your face. It nearly killed me, that.' I fought back my own tears now.

'But then, the next year,' she's sobbing, 'some bloke in Hunchburgh attacks me when I'm doing my sherry-glass act, and I need some money bad. I tied myself in a knot, got all twisted up, couldn't work. Hillber refused to pay me. So when we goes on to Judlow, I goes to the Parson with the jar. And a letter, telling him the story.' She looked up at me then, and I saw that there was a small glimmer of pride on her face. 'I wrote it myself,' she said. 'I learned writing when I was a girl.'

But I pulled back from her. 'You blackmailed him with this jar, and your letter?' I asked, looking into her tear-stained face. Her eyes dropped, and would no longer meet mine.

'Call it what you like. He paid me all he had to get rid of me. He made me promise I'd never approach you, or tell you about the tail.'

'So he *knew all along* that my father was a –' I couldn't quite say it. 'Gentleman?' That sounded much better.

'From that day, yes. I told him. He wouldn't have believed me, he said, if it hadn't been for some book by a man called –'

'Darwin? *Origin of Species?*'

'Some such. He kept talking about it, said it was beginning to make sense. Anyway, after a while I think he sees I might be telling the truth. Either way, he curses me, and wants me gone for ever.'

No wonder her visit had put the seal on my poor father's madness: shortly after the *Origin of Species* had rocked the Christian world, Parson Phelps had had his own, personal

325

version of the crisis. I could imagine his distress on discovering that he had taken a half-monkey to his bosom all these years. He, who had so railed against the very idea of our origins being anything other than stated in the Bible! If you know of anything crueller than that, gentle reader, I would like to hear about it.

'And then?' I asked.

'I went to see a quack, and he fixed me up, so I could do my contortions again. Forgot you existed,' she said. She was still looking at the floor. 'Or tried to.'

'How do I know you're not lying?' I asked her, weakly, in a sudden, last-minute attempt to make myself believe the whole thing was falsehood. I was suddenly aware of a terrible commotion outside in the ballroom.

'You don't,' she was saying. 'I *might* be lying. Perhaps I wishes I was. But I bet you've got a scar at the base of your spine. And a couple of strangely shaped feet stuffed into those fancy shoes of yours.'

I could not deny it.

So here I was, at last, in the company of my two long-lost natural parents. Was that not something? I looked at my father. Despite being a towel-holder, he looked smart, I thought, in his ruffed shirt and his red pantaloons. There was nobility in the way he stood. And why not? He had after all died in an act of bravery, attempting to save the lives of a woman and her unborn child. His wife. That's what she was, though no priest had married them. Suddenly I was caught unawares by a great shudder of pride. It gave me a fierce urge to take the towel away from my father; it demeaned him, to stand there before us like a servant. Or a slave, I thought with a sudden chill, thinking of the fate Trapp had planned for me and my eventual siblings.

Then the Contortionist did a strange thing, which touched me deeply. She leaned forward, put her arms around him, and kissed the Gentleman Monkey on the lips.

'It was love,' she said, slowly. 'True love. Between me and

him.' She kissed him again. 'Can you understand that? Can you forgive me?'

At this, an extraordinary feeling of calm and of well-being and of Godliness swept over me. It came from nowhere, and filled my heart to bursting.

'There is nothing to forgive,' I said.

Just then a meringue-clad figure shot in from nowhere and grabbed me. She squashed me against her marvellous pastry bosom and squeezed me until I could hardly breathe.

I was choking in the beery fug of the community centre. I had to get some air. The heat of the bonfire blasted me in the face as I stepped out of the double doors.

'Welcome!' yelled a voice at me. It was Gawvey, his arms loaded with logs. Sparks were flying all around us, and I caught the unmistakable smell of burnt hair.

'Hey, that monkey you bought off the twins!' I yelled. 'I want to buy it back!' And I reached in my pocket and thrust the hundred yo-yos at him.

Gawvey straightened himself up and laughed. 'Tempting, mate,' he said.

The Hokey Cokey ended and a stream of people began to emerge from the community centre, their faces flushed with alcohol and merriment.

'Well?'

'Sure,' he said, jerking his head in the direction of the bonfire. 'If you can get him down from there, me old cock.'

I looked up. Through the smoke and the swirling fragments of ash, I could see the Guy standing on the pinnacle of the bonfire, his tail curled behind him like a jaunty question mark. His whole head was lapped by a halo of blue flames, and the towel he was holding in his crooked arm had transformed into a sheet of fire. I groaned. Then yelled at him.

'Christ! You can't do that!'

'Why not?' asked Gawvey, laughing. 'He's only an old

monkey, mate. Terrible old specimen, according to the Antiques Hotline. Hasn't even got a dick.'

'But you can't burn him!'

'Sure I can mate,' he said. 'Hey, who rattled your cage? Get yourself a beer and calm down, Bucko. Bloody original idea, if you ask me. Beats an old stuffed-clothes-and-a-mask job hands down.'

'But he's not a monkey,' I wailed, watching the halo of fire curl around the creature's head. I could feel water on my face. I brushed it with my hand, and realised I was crying. 'He's – he's a – a sub-human! He's almost a man!'

Gawvey laughed and laughed.

'That's why he's called a Guy, mate,' he said.

'Come on,' said Norman gently, taking my elbow and leading me away. 'Big boys don't cry.'

And he handed me a paper napkin decorated with Mickey Mice.

Violet and I kissed.

'Bless you both,' said the Contortionist, her arm around the Gentleman Monkey. 'You must take love where you can find it, and enjoy it while you can. I did, and I've no regrets.'

'May I present my mother?' I said to Violet. 'And' – I hesitated to call her this, but she had no other name that I knew of – 'Mother – Mother – this is Miss Scrapie.'

'Pleased, I'm sure,' said the Contortionist.

'Delighted to make your acquaintance, madam,' said Violet, curtseying prettily.

'I can see you're a fine young woman,' said my mother. 'My son's in good hands. You take good care of him, Miss Scrapie. I can see you love him, and that he loves you.' Violet and I glanced surreptitiously at one another and blushed deeply. 'But I must leave you now,' she continued, hitching up her tutu and adjusting her little stockings. 'I've got my scorpion act to do before they dance the polka.' And she was gone.

After a short silence, during which neither of us knew where to look, Violet cleared her throat. 'They're searching for you,' she whispered. 'We don't have much time. We must escape.'

I was puzzled. 'Who is searching? Why?'

She did not answer my question immediately. Instead she looked me in the face and said slowly and delicately, 'Mr Phelps, I am – *aware* – of your true origins.'

Oh God. My heart plummeted to the floor, and Mildred twisted within me.

'And?' I was quivering. 'Do you –?'

'Of course!' She cried. 'I love you all the more!'

I flung my arms about her marvellous bulk, and held her tight, and for a moment our two hearts seemed to beat as one. Then I noticed she was crying.

'I, too, have a confession to make, Tobias,' Violet sniffed. She looked into my face. 'I – ate your father's flesh.'

I felt myself going pale, and swallowed hard. Then I remembered. Something Scrapie had mentioned. 'Was that – *Cuisine Zoologique?*'

'Yes. I didn't know, Tobias!' she sobbed. 'I had no idea who he was!'

'Of course not,' I soothed her.

'It poisoned my mother,' she was saying. 'And Father and I were both nearly killed, too. His flesh contained –'

'Praxin,' I finished. 'Yes, I know. Trapp injected him when he and my mother attempted to escape from the *Ark*.'

'Can you forgive me?' she begged, clutching at my hands.

'Of course!' I assured her, clasping her hands in mine. 'You were an innocent!'

We kissed.

'Whatever I have learned here in London, Violet, in my heart, I am a man,' I whispered. 'I was born a half-breed, and I do not deny it. In fact I can say now, after all that I have learned tonight, that I am proud of my uniqueness. But monkey though I am, I was raised to be a man, Violet, and above all else, I should like one day to prove it to you.'

Violet blushed, and whispered, 'My monkey-man, Tobias! I love you no matter what!'

Outside, a single silver firework exploded.

A burst of music awakened us from the tender reverie that followed.

'We must go,' Violet said, glancing nervously about her.

'Why?'

'My father,' she said.

'What about him?'

She said bleakly, 'He plans to stuff you.'

A cold wave of nausea rushed through me. I also felt instantly foolish for not suspecting. But proud, too; Parson Phelps had always told me to think the best of people. Those measurements – of course!

Only men have rights.

'Quick!' said Violet, blowing her nose and getting creakingly to her feet. 'We must leave this place!'

Peering out from behind the door of the ladies' powder room, we saw a curious procession of ladies and gentlemen gyrating around the ballroom, in the wake of Charles Darwin and Dr Ivanhoe Scrapie.

'Find the Phelps creature!' Scrapie was yelling. 'Grab him, quick, and pin him to the floor!'

'AAAGH!' yell the twins in unison. The last bottle of Perrier slithers from Oscar Jack's hand and smashes. Abbie screams. Rose and Blanche lie prone on the emperor-sized bed, their four legs aloft.

It's real!

'Push!'

'I can see the crowns!' yells Abbie. 'Push again!'

'AAGH!' yells Rose.

'OUCH!' shrieks Blanche.

'YEEEEH!' they scream together. And one, two, out they come.

'My God!' breathes Oscar Jack. Although he has been moved to tears by the historic event he is witnessing – none other than the rebirth of *Homo Britannicus* – he has nevertheless maintained enough of his cool professionalism to check that the Camcorder is still running. For which footage he will surely clock up a Bafta nomination in days to come.

But what's going on now? Why are Rose and Blanche still screaming?

'AAAGH!'

Screams that are fierce enough to drown out the lusty cries of the two babies flailing about unheeded on the bed.

'Push again!' yells Abbie.

Three! No! My God! Four!

Two sets of twins!

'Hey!' murmurs a panting Rose, staring down at the writhing beasts. 'A whole litter!'

'We did it!' groans Blanche, choking and laughing at the same time.

Together, the four adults peer at the four babies.

'Look!' gasps Abbie. 'I can't believe it!'

They look. There are the family feet – more like hands, really. The deep, close-set eyes. The copious down of red hair.

But – down there – my GOD!

'Do you see what I see?' falters Abbie. They stare. Exchange glances. And stare again. Yes. They do.

'Throwbacks, surely,' murmurs Oscar Jack.

Violet lunged behind a pillar, and dragged me with her in the direction of the Contortionist, who had emerged from the ladies' powder room to resume her duties as artiste. As my mother scaled the carcass of the elephant and stood on its still-steaming skull juggling peaches, it was easy enough to gain a moment's anonymity in which to return to the ladies' powder room and steal the gentleman monkey. A ghostly petticoated

331

figure who had materialised at Violet's side ('My late mother,' she explained hurriedly) advised us to keep a cool head.

'Just brazen it out,' she advised, 'and they'll never notice. He just looks like a rather hirsute guest with bad dress sense who is a bit the worse for wear.' She had a point. 'Come on, Fatty,' commanded the phantom, giving Violet a shove. 'Get a move on.'

So Violet and I took one hairy arm apiece, and hauled my father, still attached to his wooden plinth, out of the ladies' powder room.

In the ballroom, the Contortionist was still giving the show her all. Letting out a high screech, she leaped around atop the head of the elephant, executed a sudden somersault in the air, and then proceeded to dance a wild and dangerous-looking jig in her little ballet shoes, pitter-patter, all the while maintaining her scream and hurling strawberries from a panier upon the heads of the throng below.

As far as distractions go, I had not seen better. With the room now raining strawberries, and the women beginning to scream as their ballgowns became increasingly spattered with red juice, as though a terrible bloodbath was occurring in their midst, we had enough cover to haul the Gentleman Monkey across the back of the crowd and through the door which Cabillaud held open for us, and to escape through the Palace kitchens.

'Zis way!' the chef yelled, indicating that we should follow him past the ranks of steaming pots and pans, and the flurries of chefs and the little clouds of icing sugar. Violet and I were both panting and dishevelled. I kept tripping on my over-long trousers, and Violet's hair had become unpinned and had tumbled across her face. Her meringue dress was clearly not designed as a garment in which to race, but somehow we managed to stagger to the back door of the kitchens, whence we escaped into the night.

'I wish you all ze best!' Cabillaud called after us, as we hailed a hansom cab and bundled the Gentleman Monkey inside with us. 'Do not forget zat you av ze blessing of Jacques-Yves Cabillaud!'

As the cab jerked into motion, I took Violet's hand in mine.

'If I am Adam,' I asked her, 'will you be my Eve?'

'Yes,' she breathed. 'Yes, my dearest Tobias! I will! I will! I will!'

Norman was still helping me blow my nose on the Mickey Mouse napkin when his mobile phone rang. He stuffed a finger in one ear and retreated to a corner.

'WHAT?' he shouted after listening for a minute. 'No! Say it again, clearly ... No. Abbie! You're kidding me! Abbie! Tell me you're bloody kidding me!' He began to jump about. Then he looked up in my direction, grinning his head off and signalling at the phone with his free hand. Finally he said, 'Right, I'm telling him now. Be over in a tic,' snapped the phone shut, and shoved it in his pocket.

'You'd better sit down a minute, mate,' he called across. His voice was breathless with emotional exertion. 'Cos you're about to receive the shock of your life.'

'I thought I just had,' I muttered. I didn't like the look of this. My priceless Gentleman Monkey had just gone up in smoke. Wasn't that enough for one evening? For a whole lifetime?

'What is it?' I asked, approaching him warily.

'Congratulations and celebrations!' yelled Norman. Then his face crumpled and he burst into tears. I handed him the Mickey Mouse napkin. Too much beer, I thought, as he grabbed me in a big bear-hug. That's his problem. 'I don't bloody believe it!' he whispered, and squeezed me tighter.

'Come on, Norman!' I muttered, trying to shake him off. But he was attached to me like a heavy rucksack. 'Are you going to tell me or not?'

'You're a father of four, mate! And I'm a bloody grandad! I kid you not!'

333

And with that he fell away from me, reeling with it.

I don't really know what I felt. Shock does the strangest things to a bloke. Look at me. I'm just standing there. Not moving. Covered in soot. My eyes are smarting. Must be from all the smoke. I'm rigid. Rooted to the spot, like I've been stuffed.

My head began to throb. The King was dead, I thought. Long live the –

The what?

'Come on!' I yelled at Norman. Swinging into action, I grabbed him by the scruff, dragged him out to the car-park, shoved him in the Nuance and drove home like a bat out of Hell.

'Bastard,' said the twins in unison, when they saw me. But their faces were flushed with joy.

'Come on, now, girls,' said Abbie. 'He is their father, after all. If it hadn't been for his, er – *input* –'

But I wasn't listening. I was looking at my babies. There they lay, on the bed, in four pillow-cases. I felt inexplicably humbled. And surprised. I hadn't seen a baby since the Millennium. But I didn't recall them looking anything like this.

'Strange but true,' murmured Norman.

And it was. Because the new *Homo Britannicus* did not take the form of four little Buck de Saviles, spiritual grand-children of Elvis Presley, as I might have wished. Nor, as one might have expected, did it take the form of four miniature Roseblanches.

I caught a sudden whiff of mothballs, and turned to see the sour-faced woman in petticoats I'd met once before. She smirked. 'Two miniature Violets, and two miniature Tobiases,' she pronounced. 'With more than a hint of towel-holder.'

'Champagne corks'll be popping tonight, eh, Buck?' said Norman, wiping away more tears and slapping Abbie trium-phantly on the bottom.

'Ouch!' she squealed, and looked nervously across at a man

with a leather jacket and an earring, who was inexplicably filming the scene with the Camcorder.

'Time for a feed,' said Rose, lifting a baby out of its pillowcase and nestling it against her left breast. It found the nipple and began to suck.

'Come on then, coochie-coochie coo,' murmured Blanche, doing the same.

'Pass us another one, Mum,' said Rose.

'And me,' said Blanche.

'Four boobs, four babies,' they said together, and giggled.

Abbie obliged, and there they were, Rose and Blanche, on the emperor-sized bed, with the babies clamped to their breasts. I felt tears of joy streaming down my face as I watched my offspring clinging tightly to their mothers with their perfect little hand-like feet. And as they suckled, their four little tails, curled like question marks, twitched in happiness.

'This is the future,' said the ghostly voice of the Laudanum Empress. 'Do your best to deserve it.'

EPILOGUE

Violet and I went to Fishforth by steam train. Nobb-on-Humber, Fib's Wash, Coleman's Haunch, Maggsdale, South Brill: as I gazed through the glass at the landscape I was returning to, my heart swelled with joy. In Fishforth, Violet and I climbed the hill to the Sanatorium. Seagulls and cormorants swung through the sky and a fresh wind, a sea wind, blew about our ears.

The fortress of the Sanatorium loomed above us; we craned our necks. And there he was at the window of a high, lonely tower, staring out like the Lady of Shalott. It was as though he had been waiting there, all this time, for our arrival.

We waved frantically. Then he seemed to see us. And instantly vanished.

'I'm going up!' I called after him.

'Wait! I am sure he's coming down!' said Violet, and we rushed through the gate and up the spiral stairway. In my desperation to reach him, I quickly removed my shoes, and scrambled up the stairs on all fours, two and three and four at a time, to greet him.

'I am Darwin's paradox,' I called up to him, as I saw him descending the stairs.

And he smiled down at me.

'Or God's joke,' he croaked.

We met halfway. And there, on the landing, we came face to face. We stood there for a long time. His moon-face had thinned, and what remained of his hair was straggled and white.

'I was wrong,' he said.

But I said nothing. I was too choked to speak. Instead, I flung myself into his arms, and he held me tight.

' "No man is an island," ' he said finally. ' "But a piece of the continent, a part of the main." '

He loved Violet instantly. Not least when I reported to him that it was thanks to her that I was free of Mildred.

'How?' he enquired, flabbergasted. 'Your mother did everything to rid you of that worm! Everything in her power!'

'Mildred never existed,' Violet announced. It was her discovery – one of which she was justly proud. When I had finally told her in detail of the bodily symptoms induced by my shameful inhabitant, her eyes had narrowed and she had looked at me assessingly.

'And how long is it since your tapeworm has bothered you?' she asked.

'Since I met you,' I told her, only realising it as I said it, 'she has left me, mercifully, in peace. Apart from at the Banquet, when I ate something that looked like –'

'Meat,' finished Violet. 'Or fish.' She laughed. 'Mildred will bother you no more,' she said with certainty. 'I have discovered that the Gentleman Monkey was a species that consumed nothing but fruit, vegetables and nuts. Anything else disagreed with him, and made his gut snarl up. You've inherited his alimentary system; that's my guess. You've been on the wrong diet all these years, Tobias.'

Could it really have been that simple?

Parson Phelps was much impressed by this news. 'If only dear Mrs Phelps could be alive to hear it!' he said, and wiped a tear from his eye, then put down the yellow jerkin he was knitting, and blessed us both on the spot.

We travelled home together, all three of us, by coach, with the bulky parcel that contained my natural father.

As we left the mainland shrubs of Judlow behind us and

caught our first glimpse of the herring-shaped peninsula that was my home, my heart soared.

'See, Violet, how it is in the shape of a fish?' I said. 'Its tail nailed to the mainland, and its head straining out to sea?'

'It is just as I imagined it,' she said, breathing in the salt air. And squeezed my hand.

The arid Gudderwort, hearing of our decision to return, had already left the Parsonage, grumpily, abandoning any show of Christian goodwill. I pushed open the oak door, still warped from the Flood, and stepped into our kitchen. The flag-stones still twinkled with salt. I was glad to see that some things did not change.

While Parson Phelps went to tend Mrs Phelps' grave, I unwrapped the Gentleman Monkey and dusted him down, while Violet ironed his shirt and pantaloons. Once we had stood him by the hearth, and I had polished his eyes, he looked well, I fancied, and in better spirits than before. Violet hung a tea-cloth in the crook of his arm. It gave him a homely look.

When Parson Phelps returned and saw him standing there, he was almost shy. He stood in the doorway with his hoe and trowel, blushing.

'Please, Father,' I said. 'Come and meet him. He will not bite you.'

Finally, tentatively, Parson Phelps stepped forward on the flag-stones, reached out, and took the Gentleman Monkey's hairy hand in his.

'I am pleased to meet you, sir,' he said formally. Then cleared his throat. 'I have spent many hours thinking about you, in the Sanatorium. And I can now declare that, although I maligned you in my heart, for which I beg your forgiveness, it is now a great honour to welcome you at last' – here he choked back tears – 'as a part of my family.'

Violet and I cheered.

As for Dr Ivanhoe Scrapie, he never recovered from the night of the Banquet. My disappearance, along with that of Violet

338

and the Gentleman Monkey – coupled with Scrapie's public humiliation at the hands of Mr Darwin – gave him an emotional shock so potent that he entered a brief phase of madness, followed swiftly by death. We read his obituary in the *Thunderer*. 'Scientist, craftsman, thinker, and immortaliser of beasts', the paper called him.

Three months later, some of his favourite works of taxidermy, accompanied by the petticoated ghost of the Laudanum Empress, arrived in a huge sealed wardrobe from London. Opening its creaking door, Violet and I found an ostrich in a nightdress; a kangaroo wearing pantaloons; a wombat in breeches, and various smaller mammals, in children's knickerbocker outfits. And the loyal corgi, Suet. He was the last animal Scrapie had stuffed, the Empress informed us as she dusted down her petticoats.

'How did he die?' wailed Violet.

'You killed him,' said the Laudanum Empress bluntly. 'With your silly vegetarian thing. He died on the night of the Banquet.'

Violet cried bitterly upon learning this. She needed no further prompting from her gruesome mother to blame herself for his death.

'Dog cannot live on veg alone,' she sobbed as she stroked Suet's stuffed and emaciated body, the husk of the dog that had been. A lesson had been learned.

'Rest in peace, dear Suet,' whispered Violet, kissing the corgi and returning him gently to the wardrobe.

The Empress snorted contemptuously, then began inspecting the kitchen. 'I recognise this house,' she said, peering into the gloom of the fireplace. 'It's the Old Parsonage in Thunder Spit, is it not? Look at the state of it!' she said, kicking a flag-stone with her lace-up boot, and dislodging a little puff of sea-salt. 'Believe me, in a hundred and fifty years you won't know it's the same place! There'll be a telephone over there, and these two walls will have been knocked through, and the TV room will be just –'

But Violet had taken hold of her mother's arm and was steering her firmly back in the direction of the wardrobe.

'And you can be laid to rest, too, now, Mother,' she declared, pushing her in and closing the doors firmly. 'Go and haunt someone else,' she said. And locked the door.

'All right, I will!' came the muffled voice of the phantom from within her mothbally prison. We never saw her again.

As Violet promised, the tapeworm Mildred has troubled me no more. While I have returned to the natural diet of my forefathers: fruit, vegetables, and the occasional insect, Violet's book, *The Fleshless Cook*, has been heralded by the Vegetarian Society and the *Times* newspaper as a masterpiece of its genre, and a worthy riposte to Cabillaud's *Cuisine Zoologique: une philosophie de la viande*, which proved to be a flash in the gastronomic pan.

'And I was so sure,' I told Violet, 'that my mother was trying to tell me something with those gourds on her grave!' I had told her about the foul purgative I had once made from them, to banish Mildred.

'Perhaps she *was* trying to tell you something,' murmured Violet. 'But not what you thought. Look.' She was pointing at a new fruit swelling at the base of a big yellow gourd flower. 'What colour did you say the first one was?'

'The one I planted when she was dying? Green. Green and sort of stippled.'

'Well, look at this.' I peered through the thick bristle-backed leaves and saw a small green fruit swelling.

'It's the same,' I said. Eight years and eight generations had passed.

'A throwback,' she murmured.

'Well, if it's a message, it's making no sense to me,' I confessed. 'Let us hope that the future may unravel its mystery.'

Parson Phelps went back to preaching, but it was a new message that he delivered from the pulpit.

'My son had a tapeworm called Mildred,' began his first sermon. 'We were convinced she existed, and did all we could to banish her. And then the day came when we discovered she was a mere chimera, and we were delighted, but there was sadness, too, because when you house a belief, a belief so real that it feels like a being, and you discover that it was a mere product of your own desires and thoughts, then there is loss.'

He looked about the congregation. They were hanging on his every word.

'God is like that tapeworm,' he said. Faces began to frown in puzzlement, and there was the sound of indrawn breath. 'An invisible presence, which we attribute to one thing. And then we discover He is the product of something else. Our hopes. Our fears. Our natural desire for order in the world. But I ask you this: Does the knowledge that He does not exist make Him any less necessary to our lives? Should we not be permitted to imagine Him? And for that figment of imagination to be so real that it becomes tantamount to fact? And then – simply – is?'

The congregation, intrigued by the parson's new-found understanding of the meaning of life, and relieved to be rid of the excruciating and po-faced Gudderwort, came flooding back, and in St Nicholas's Church, all the old familiar faces are there: the Morpitons, the Tobashes, the Peat-Hoves, the Barks, the Balls, the Harcourts. Parson Phelps' sermons are passionate in a way they never were before.

Now he visits the spiritually disturbed clergy of the Sanatorium in Fishforth once a week, and shares his new beliefs with them, bringing them succour in their distress. And every Sunday, St Nicholas's Church, which languished rudderless for so long, is full to bursting with worshippers who come from as far away as Hunchburgh just to hear him preach. In his sermons, Father doesn't mention God by name: just the wonder of things, and the glory. And as I sit in the front pew with Violet, her hand in mine, my mind wanders to the ocean, my old childhood toy-box full of miracles. The mackerel flashing

341

and jumping in the sunlight; the herring gulls wheeling in the sky. And there I see a Nature that is neither good nor bad, but its own pure self.

Reader, I married her.

After the ceremony in St Nicholas's Church, which still bore the watermark from the Great Flood, I took Violet to the beach, and to my favourite rockpool, and there we lay on the barnacled rock and stared into the water. We saw baby quillsnappers, and anemones, and shrimps, and whelks. 'God's doodlings,' Parson Phelps used to call them. To think, that such humble creatures are our origins. And that with every tide, and every lapping of time's wave, everything changes, and our world wakes afresh, and all is new again. New and brave, and peopled with miracles.

Miracles. We had never imagined that we could produce offspring of our own, after what Dr Scrapie had said about the nature of the hybrid, but in this, as in many things, he was wrong. I am delighted to report that a happy event is on the horizon. Violet is now in what is termed a delicate condition.

'I feel that it will be a girl,' she said smilingly, as she told me the news. 'We will have a daughter, Tobias.' And I thought of little Tillie and felt glad.

So in our attic bedroom, Violet and I lie together on the big wrought-iron bed, and await the evolution of events.

On the mantelpiece sit the eight generations of gourd, and my whelk shell, and my fossil, and my fish-knife, and the jar that still contains my amputated tail. Above us, on the wall, hangs the picture of Noah's Ark: God above, in a silver Heaven, with His great beard dissolving into the clouds of the flood-waters. Noah and his family on the deck. The beasts below, from mighty elephant down to humble ant.

And I think: We will call our daughter Tillie, and I will tell her the story of the *Ark*. But it will be a different story from the one Parson Phelps told me when I looked at this picture as a boy.

The story I will tell my daughter begins with the ocean. Huge. Ink-dark beneath a black sky. And a vessel, bobbing on the waters. A toy of wood and string.

But in this story, the *Ark* has no cages and no captain.

And there is land on the horizon. Look. A vast, bare continent, beneath a rainbow.

'That continent is the future, Tillie,' I will tell her. 'It is waiting for us. We are its creatures.'

And a boundless hope floods my heart.

ACKNOWLEDGEMENTS

While writing this novel, I drew great inspiration from Edmund Gosse's *Father and Son*, and Keith Thomas's *Man and the Natural World*. I am also grateful to Nick Baker, Viv Black, Chris Brandon-Jones, Valerie Jensen, Martin Lloyd-Elliott and Nick Royle for reading and commenting on the manuscript at different stages. But my deepest thanks go to my friend Polly Coles and my partner Michel Coleman, who have been supportive and generous beyond words.